DIANA
THE LONELY PRINCESS

Also by Nicholas Davies

Diana: The Princess and Her Troubled Marriage
Queen Elizabeth II: A Woman Who Is Not Amused

DIANA
THE LONELY PRINCESS

NICHOLAS DAVIES

A Birch Lane Press Book
Published by Carol Publishing Group

A Birch Lane Press Book
Published by Carol Publishing Group
Birch Lane Press is a registered trademark of Carol
Communications, Inc.
Editorial Offices: 600 Madison Avenue, New York, N.Y. 10022
Sales and Distribution Offices: 120 Enterprise Avenue,
Secaucus, N.J. 07094
In Canada: Canadian Manda Group, One Atlantic Avenue, Suite 105,
Toronto, Ontario M6K 3E7
Queries regarding rights and permissions should be addressed to Carol
Publishing Group, 600 Madison Avenue, New York, N.Y. 10022

Carol Publishing Group books are available at special discounts for
bulk purchases, sales promotion, fund-raising, or educational
purposes. Special editions can be created to specifications. For details
contact: Special Sales Department, Carol Publishing Group,
120 Enterprise Avenue, Secaucus, N.J. 07094

Manufactured in the United States of America
10 9 8 7 6 5 4 3 2 1

Library of Congress Cataloging-in-Publication Data

Davies, Nicholas.
Diana : the lonely princess / Nicholas Davies.
p. cm.
"A Birch Lane Press book."
ISBN 1–55972–360–2 (hardcover)
1. Princesses—Great Britain—Biography. I. Diana, Princess of
Wales, 1961– . II. Title.
DA591.A45D37 1996
941.085′092—dc20
[B]   95–26379
CIP

To Thomas

Contents

Author to Reader

———— ⚜ ————

For this unauthorized biography of Diana, the Princess of Wales, I have drawn on my sources and my friends over a period of seventeen years since I first met Diana on the polo grounds of Windsor in 1979.

Since that day Diana's name has barely been out of the headlines, and the friends and courtiers who have surrounded her in those years have changed time and again. But those who have left often remain in touch with their successors, for the courtiers and staff who advise and serve the Royal Family seem like members of an illustrious club, privileged to have been of service to the Royal House of Windsor.

Amongst those "club" members I have won a number of friends through the years, and it is to these men and women that I owe a debt of gratitude, without whose help this book could not have been written. When much speculation appeared in the national press, these people kindly provided me with their own accounts of circumstances as they actually happened.

Most of these people served both Prince Charles and Princess Diana at one time or another and witnessed the daily events: the triumphs and the tragedies, the arguments and the happiness, and their love for their sons Prince William and Prince Harry.

Other valuable sources volunteered to help, including a number of friends whom Princess Diana had become close to during the past three years, assisting her with advice, giving encouragement, and offering their services to someone who they felt needed their support.

The majority of the men and women who helped in researching this book talked to me on the understanding of absolute confidence and complete anonymity. None wished to endanger their relationships with members of the Royal Family or members of the respective royal households they served. So their names do not appear.

Diana's Last Battle

ONE COLD WINTER'S DAY toward the end of February 1996, Princess Diana drove purposefully out of Kensington Palace, threading her way through the busy afternoon traffic on the mile-long journey to Buckingham Palace. As she parked her car and hurried inside, a flurry of snow filled the air.

"Good afternoon, ma'am," came the quiet voice of the footman as he bowed his head to Diana.

"Good afternoon," she said. "I believe I'm expected."

"Yes, ma'am," came the reply. "This way."

Diana set off behind the palace footman on one of the most important journeys of her life. Later she would tell how her mind raced back sixteen years to the February day when she had been in Buckingham Palace, squeezing the arm of Prince Charles, blissfully happy after announcing their engagement to the world. That, too, had been a cold winter's day—but she remembered the sun had shone as they posed together on the palace lawns and the cameras clicked away.

Now she was desperately trying to save her marriage, to prevent divorce, a divorce that she never wanted and that she feared would mark the beginning of an estrangement from her beloved Wills and Harry.

Throughout January and February 1996 Diana gambled that she could ignore the demands her mother-in-law had sent in a letter, urging Diana to divorce Charles as soon as possible. Diana hoped that if she did so she could face down Prince Charles by simply refusing to attend to the matter, giving her solicitor, Anthony Julius, no instructions.

The Queen, however, had different ideas. She had no intention of permitting her daughter-in-law to manipulate the Royal Family and instructed the royal solicitors, Farrer & Co., to press the Princess of Wales to comply with her demands that there should be a speedy divorce settlement.

Anthony Julius had informed Diana that she would have to give him instructions, that she could no longer ignore the demands of the Queen herself. During her visit to Pakistan in February 1996 Diana decided to take one final gamble, to seek an interview with the Queen to try to dissuade her from pushing for a divorce, so that the family could remain together, though in name only.

On her ten-minute drive to the palace, Diana had rehearsed, as she had a dozen times already that day, precisely the argument she would put forward. Diana was ushered into the Queen's first-floor drawing room, and the doors were closed behind her.

Their conversation would last just ten minutes. Diana argued eloquently that her marriage to Charles should be allowed to continue for the sake of the two princes. She contended that it would be in their best interests if Charles and she remained married, though they would continue to live separate lives.

Diana then played her ace, telling the Queen in a quiet, dignified voice that neither Wills nor Harry wanted their parents to divorce and had come to terms with the life they now led, sharing time between their father and mother, understanding that their parents were living apart, separated but still married.

The Queen hardly said a word but simply sat and listened, which infuriated Diana. She had hoped to start a conversation in which she might have been able to involve the Queen, trying to persuade her that divorce could not be good for the boys.

After Diana had finished her argument and sat nervously on the edge of a large easy chair, her fingers twisting together, the Queen told Diana that she would promise nothing but would think over what she had said and would discuss her request with Prince Charles.

As Diana curtsied and left the room she felt that there could be some hope in that her mother-in-law had not denied her request outright. But Diana had also felt that coldness in that warm room, the Queen offering very little, simply sitting opposite her, listening to her pleas, and looking directly into her eyes.

Twenty-four hours later the Queen informed Diana that she should seek a meeting with Charles and discuss the matter with him. Before that meeting with Diana would take place, Charles was briefed about what had happened during the secret meeting at the palace and was informed that the Queen still believed that a formal divorce was best for the children, the monarchy, and the nation. Charles had been left in no doubt that his mother expected him to push for a divorce.

Charles immediately wrote a short, formal letter to Diana suggesting a meeting, informing her that the Queen and Prince Philip were urging him to reach a settlement with her as soon as possible.

At four-thirty on the afternoon of Wednesday, February 28, Diana and Charles met by arrangement in Charles's private rooms in St. James's Palace, two hundred yards from Buckingham Palace. Charles opened the discussion by telling Diana that there was no way back, that the Queen and Prince Philip had demanded that they move toward a divorce because of the effect the long-drawn-out affair was having on the image of the monarchy.

Diana made one final plea to Charles. She begged him to reconsider the decision to divorce. She pleaded with him "for the sake of William and Harry" not to divorce her. She urged him to stand up to his parents and do the right thing by their two sons—because *they* didn't want their parents to divorce.

With tears in her eyes, Diana told Charles in a voice barely more than a whisper, "You know that I loved you. Now I want you to know that I will always love you, because you are the father of William and Harry."

But Charles would not be swayed. He replied that the matter had gone too far, that there was no turning back; the divorce would have to go through.

Diana unfurled a piece of paper she had taken into the meeting, an offer in case her pleas fell on stony ground. She showed the paper to Charles; in it she agreed to yield her HRH (Her Royal Highness) status, effectively removing her from the official front rank of the Royal Family. Diana knew that the Queen would never permit her to keep the prefix HRH.

She accepted that after the divorce she would be officially titled Diana, Princess of Wales. But she demanded that she keep her royal apartments in Kensington Palace for the sake of the children, so that they would not feel they were being thrown out of the family home. And she suggested that she should keep her small suite of offices in St. James's, next to Charles's large office apartments.

However, she surprised Charles by suggesting that they should agree to a public divorce, covered by live television cameras, so that the entire nation could witness the formal end of their marriage, just as the entire nation had witnessed their wedding in July 1981. Charles was flabbergasted by the suggestion, and he told Diana that he thought the idea was "crass and stupid," that he was totally against it and wanted nothing to do with it. Diana argued that such a nationwide broadcast would offset their public image, that of a couple continually bickering.

Within minutes of the secret meeting, Diana decided to tell the world the details of what had happened. She told her new media adviser, Jane Atkinson, a woman who had held the job for only a matter of weeks, to issue a formal statement.

The statement read: "The Princess of Wales has agreed to Prince Charles's request for a divorce. The Princess will continue to be involved in all decisions relating to the children and will remain at Kensington Palace with offices at St. James's Palace. The Princess of Wales will retain the title and be known as Diana, Princess of Wales."

Prince Charles, the Queen, senior aides of both the Queen and Charles were taken completely by surprise at Diana's official announcement—for nothing had been agreed between Charles and Diana. They all believed the meeting had been in secret, the discussion absolutely private. They understood the princess had simply stated her demands for her solicitors to follow up, now that she had agreed to a divorce.

The whole affair became increasingly messy. After Diana gave a briefing to Anthony Julius, her solicitor, about her meeting with Charles, Buckingham Palace received a statement from Mr. Julius stating that divorce negotiations could be jeopardized if the Princess's version of events was not confirmed. He said, "If we cannot rely on agreements that have been made, it would be unsafe to continue our negotiations."

Wrong-footed once again, the palace instructed their solicitors, Farrer and Company, to put an end to the public wrangling and make sure that all future negotiations were conducted in absolute secrecy. In private the Queen was seething with anger that Diana had debased the divorce proceedings by the public statements, desperately trying to seize the initiative in matters which should have been kept entirely private.

No one knew the precise demands that Diana would make on the Royal Family. But some close to her suggested that she had demanded a one-time sum of $23 million, or annual payments of $2 million. These sums of course would be for her personal expenses. Charles, or the Queen, would also have to provide a home in London and another in the country, pay all staff salaries, run her cars, pay for the upkeep of her homes, and of course pay all the costs of the two princes.

Diana had thrown her last dice and lost. Now she would take everything she could for herself and for the boys. She already knew the measure of the loneliness which faced her but was determined to maintain the loving relationship she had with Wills and Harry. But in her heart she wondered how long it would be before her sons were seduced away from her by the ruthless power of the House of Windsor.

DIANA

THE LONELY PRINCESS

1

The Christmas That Made Diana Cry

———— ❦ ————

IN SILENCE, Princess Diana walked through the suite of rooms of her Kensington Palace apartment looking at the Christmas decorations. She entered the bedrooms of Wills and Harry and looked around, everything once again tidy, their Christmas decorations still in place, in the hallway the large Christmas tree a blaze of color, the tinsel and crackers reflecting the colored lights on the tree. But it was the deathly silence that unnerved her for she wasn't used to such peace and quiet in her palace home.

Only twenty-four hours before, the apartment had been a hive of activity, Wills and Harry rushing around, playing games, and talking nonstop of the presents to come, enjoying the time with the mother they adored, the staff going about their business though most had already left for the Christmas break.

Now Diana walked through the palace alone. Her sons would be at Sandringham with Charles, the Queen, and Prince Philip and one or two other members of the family who had decided to celebrate Christmas, 1995, at the family's Norfolk estate, one hundred miles north of London.

The tears began to flow as thoughts of despair and loneliness raced through her mind. It had only been a matter of days since she had received the news from her mother-in-law urging her to divorce "as soon as possible." She had eaten a cold salad for lunch, sitting alone in front of the television set, watching but not bothering to take in what was on the screen. She had decided to spend Christmas alone, to feel the trauma of loneliness, and had even told the duty staff to go off to their respective families and friends and enjoy themselves.

With some trepidation, she walked into the kitchen and opened the refrigerator door, the bright light momentarily dazzling her. It was half-full. Before she had taken in what food was there, Diana slammed shut the door and walked quickly away, back to the television set and the film she had been idly watching.

Later, Diana would say that she could not remember how many times that day she had gone to the fridge, intent on raiding it, wanting to eat everything she could see for the comfort she knew it would bring her. That Christmas day Diana fought many battles trying desperately not to slide back down to the depression that had controlled and wrecked her life for three long years when she had suffered from the awful effects of bulimia.

But only to one person, her trusted psychotherapist Susie Orbach, did Diana confess everything of what happened that Christmas day when she had never felt more lonely. She had revealed to a select few that Christmas had been "a difficult time," but she had tried to shrug it off, not wanting to reveal the extent of her misery and the daunting, shuddering specter of bulimia that had haunted her.

The Queen, her mother-in-law, had invited her to bring Wills and Harry to Sandringham on Christmas Eve, stay the night in a house on the estate, attend church with them the following morning, and stay for the turkey dinner. But Diana had declined the invitation, not wanting to spend that much time with the family she knew had turned against her, pretending to the nation that all was well despite the pending divorce she had not sought and did not want. She knew the whole episode would be a ghastly sham, the Queen and Prince Philip smiling for the cameras on Christmas morning as though the Royals were once again a happy family.

Nor did Diana want to see Prince Charles, the man whom

she had come to despise and sometimes hate, making an attempt to be a fun-loving father for Wills and Harry, merrily cracking jokes around the Christmas dinner table. From past years Diana knew the whole day would be a stilted, formal occasion bereft of real happiness and enjoyment, lacking spontaneity and fun, and with every member of the family sitting around that table pretending that she, Diana, was welcome.

During Christmas day Diana phoned numerous friends, wanting to share Christmas with someone, a telephone link being better than nothing. As she flipped through the pages of her personal phone book, Diana realized how few friends she now had. A number of her former close friends who had helped her through many crises during her marriage had faded from the scene. Kate Menzies, daughter of a wealthy Scottish family, Catherine Soames, the ex-wife of the Armed Forces Minister Nicholas Soames, and Julia Samuel, wife of banker Michael Samuel, were three of Diana's staunchest allies who had helped her through her marriage breakdown and separation. They would see Diana three or four times a week, take her to lunch, give parties for her, introduce her to friends. But during the past twelve months they had hardly been in evidence.

The three remained good friends, but Diana had moved away from them. Indeed, to the surprise of many, Diana was in Lahore, Pakistan, in February 1996 when Kate Menzies, once Diana's closest friend, married her longtime lover, restaurateur Simon Slater, who had also been counted among the Diana set of the early 1990s. A year earlier Diana would have been the principal guest at their wedding. But the relationships that had supported Diana in her hours of need had withered and died.

Diana knew the truth. A friend explained, "All Diana would ever talk about was her personal life, her problems, the misery of her marriage. It simply became too much for them. They had tried to help Diana in every way possible, but the Princess only had one topic conversation, herself."

However, she would make one important call that Christmas: to Susie Orbach, the woman who had in the past helped Diana battle her bulimia.

Almost in tears Diana asked whether it would be possible to see her the next day, Boxing Day, although she realized full well it would be a great imposition. Diana explained that Christmas had become a crisis that she could not cope with alone. But the person who had given Diana so much support and advice would never for a moment turn down such a cri de coeur. And the following day Diana drove over to Susie's house for an hour-long session.

Diana had needed Susie's expert help for some time. She had come to rely on Susie, to trust her, in a way that she had never been able to trust any other therapist. For Susie gave Diana the vital part of her character she had lost as a child and never regained, her self-confidence. In the eighteen months she had been treating Diana, Susie had succeeded in guiding her royal patient in her metamorphosis from victim to the almost mythical strongwoman she appeared to be in her famous hour-long television interview in November 1995.

Her Christmas crisis had, once again, been a question of confidence. The sense of elation she had felt following her sensational television interview had evaporated within weeks, leaving her demoralized, physically shaken, her confidence shattered as she realized all she had been striving to achieve had gone awry.

Only a month earlier Diana had given her extraordinary and moving interview to the BBC *Panorama* program in which she talked of her postnatal depression and bulimia, her miserable marriage, and her adultery with an Army officer. She pulled no punches in attacking the Royal Family and the Establishment while casting doubt on Charles's willingness to become king. She had also demanded that she be given a new wide-ranging ambassadorial role for Britain, arguing that she wanted to become "queen of people's hearts" rather than queen of England.

Princess Diana was determined to adopt that role whether or not she received permission from the Queen or the Foreign Office. She believes she has a unique ability to comfort the dying, the ill, the disadvantaged, and the homeless. In her interview, Diana had revealed an almost saintly image, amplifying the nation's concept of her as a generous and suffering young woman.

Within days of her interview twelve thousand people had written to her almost all supporting her decision to speak out about her life, her marriage, her adultery, and her bid to become a royal ambassador. Diana had thrown down the gauntlet in a way that surprised not only the courtiers, who never believed she would have the courage or the gall to challenge their authority, but also Prince Charles and other members of the Royal Family, who were quietly seething at Diana's obvious intention of causing as much trouble as possible.

"Now they know what I really want," she said after her BBC interview, a steely determination in her voice. "Now they know I mean business. And they know that I won't go quietly."

This was the Diana the world never sees. She all but spat out the words, and the look in her eyes told those to whom she was speaking that most of the nation and the Royal Family had totally misjudged the sweet, innocent virgin who had made such a shy impression on everyone sixteen years before. But that was the young Diana, before her miserable, loveless marriage and her years of incarceration, of isolation and loneliness in a royal palace.

Only Charles, some of her staff, and some close palace aides know the real Diana. The great majority of people believe the Princess of Wales to be the innocent victim of a broken home and a tragic marriage, her husband cheating on her, sleeping with his old mistress before the ink was dry on the marriage certificate. They understand Diana's cries for love and emotional security fell on the closed ears of the hard, unyielding Royal House of Windsor, committing her to the depths of despair, postnatal depression, and bulimia.

But Diana is no longer an innocent.

A few days after her BBC interview, when Diana spoke of her midnight visits to the sick and dying, she was on a high, convinced that by her interview she had outwitted Charles, the Queen, Philip, and their senior courtiers and would soon realize her ambition of becoming a royal ambassador, touring the world as "queen of people's hearts."

"I've got them on the run," she would jubilantly say. "I'm winning. They can't refuse me this time, they can't refuse me now."

So determined had Diana become to achieve her ambition that she began to make claims that did not bear scrutiny.

Shortly before midnight, on a cool, late November night in 1995, a dark blue BMW convertible drew up outside the Royal Brompton Hospital in West London. At the wheel sat Diana in jeans, a pink top, and a blue baseball hat with the numbers 492 emblazoned in white. She parked her car, clambered out, locked the vehicle, and walked toward the main entrance as two photographers approached from the darkness. She smiled happily as she stopped to talk to them.

Chatting to photographers was quite extraordinary behavior for the Princess of Wales for she usually walks on past them, often with her head down making it more difficult for them to get the shot they want. For years photographers have been the bane of her life, following her every step in public, and never ceasing to take pictures of her wherever and whenever possible. This November night, however, Diana not only stopped and posed for the photographers but waited while one of them answered a call on his mobile phone.

"Who is it?" she inquired.

"Our royal reporter," he replied.

"Could I have a word with him?"

The photographers were taken aback once more for the Princess of Wales never gives impromptu interviews to journalists on the streets.

"Yes, I'm sure he would be only too happy," the photographer replied, handing over the phone.

Diana at first asked the reporter from Rupert Murdoch's Sunday tabloid the *News of the World* not to mention the name of the hospital she was visiting, then happily chatted for a few minutes. It would be one of the most bizarre interviews Diana had ever given, for she will never even answer reporters' questions, let alone volunteer to talk.

She explained that she was in the habit of making midnight visits, on the spur of the moment, to several London hospitals two or three times each week, spending three or four hours a night chatting to sick and dying patients: "I hold their hands. I talk to them, tell them that everyone is on their side. Whatever helps."

The patients were total strangers. "They are not people that I know but they all need someone," Diana said. "I try to be there for them."

The tip-off to the *News of the World* that the Princess would visit one of two hospitals late that night came earlier in the day from a woman who said she was calling from Kensington Palace. When asked for name or more details, she hung up.

It seemed extraordinary that such information should have come from Kensington Palace unless Diana herself ordered the call to be made. The idea that the Princess of Wales would spend three or four hours a night, from 11 P.M. until 3 A.M., three times a week, walking around darkened hospital wards waking total strangers for a chat seemed most bizarre.

In Britain today, where there are usually between six and twenty-four patients in any single ward, hospitals only employ skeleton staff at night. Most patients are sound asleep around midnight, and even close relatives of the dying are not encouraged to spend those hours at their loved one's bedside chatting away for fear of disturbing other patients.

Diana had been photographed that November night outside the Royal Brompton Hospital at 11 P.M., saying she would be spending some hours inside. She was seen to return to her car parked in a side street outside the hospital four hours later, but she had not been visiting any patients in the hospital. In fact, she had not even been in the hospital but was visiting an old friend who lived nearby.

"We have no record whatsoever of the Princess of Wales visiting this hospital at that time," said a hospital spokesman.

"In fact we have no record of the Princess ever visiting this hospital late at night or during the early hours of the morning. It is not something that we would encourage."

Two other major hospitals in the immediate area, the Royal Marsden, where Diana is the president, and the Chelsea and Westminster, which handles 20 percent of the entire nation's HIV and AIDS cases, also had no record of the Princess of Wales visiting that or on any other night. Hospital authorities, doctors, and the Royal College of Nursing found the idea of Diana's midnight visits somewhat strange and hard to believe. Yet such was the mood of the country at that time, supporting Diana in her quest to bring comfort to the sick and disadvantaged, that her story of nocturnal hospital visits was taken as yet another example of her angelic character.

Some newspapers invited readers to phone with details of friends or relatives who had woken from surgery to find Diana at their bedside, helping and comforting them. None phoned.

This naive idea would be part of Diana's plan to seize and keep the initiative, to confuse the Royal Family's senior courtiers, forcing them to accommodate her demands, rather than finding ways to deflect her determination to become a roving ambassador. On this occasion, however, she was simply acting on the spur of the moment without thinking through what she said. Very ill patients do not need total strangers, not even the Princess of Wales, to comfort them, especially since many would be recovering in intensive care beds. Their great need would be expert nursing.

One week later Diana would continue pressing her claims to be taken seriously, speaking out stridently and emotionally in support of the homeless. This time, however, she would go too far upsetting cabinet ministers for what seemed to be her wholehearted support of a Labour attack on government policies. Some ministers were furious, accusing Diana of "meddling" in politics. She even warmly applauded the shadow home secretary, Jack Straw, who appeared on the same platform that day attacking the government's policy toward the homeless. There is a strict rule that members of the Royal Family stay totally clear of politics, on all occasions.

Diana gave her speech at the annual meeting of Centrepoint, the youth housing charity where two years before she had made her sensational announcement of her withdrawal from public life.

In her 1995 speech she said with much conviction in her voice, "Society must ensure young people are given the chance they deserve. I have listened to many young people whose lives have been blighted by their experiences. Teenagers are forced to resort to begging, or worse, prostitution, to get money in order to eat. . . . It is truly tragic to see the total waste of so many young lives, of so much potential. We, as part of society, must ensure that young people, who are our future, are given the chance they deserve."

Within hours of making her Centrepoint speech, Prime Minister John Major was forced to defend the government's housing policy during question time in the House of Commons.

Tory members of Parliament were angry that the Princess of Wales had become involved in political controversy, sharing a platform with someone clearly trying to score political points. Diana had not even cleared her speech with ministers, earning herself another bad mark. One outraged Tory MP, Sir Patrick Cormack, said, "We now have the Princess, who is a rather headstrong and willful young lady, on a platform in a preelection period on a highly contentious subject with a highly partisan politician. It is very, very unwise and it undermines the constitutional neutrality of the monarchy."

Most Tory newspapers used Diana's speech to point out her naïveté and lack of political skill, emphasizing that the Princess of Wales has no training in politics or diplomacy and should therefore not be permitted to carry out any ambassadorial role.

Diana would read the criticism with horror, realizing that she had made a serious mistake. She called her secretary, the much-maligned Patrick Jephson, into her room. "Why the hell didn't you warn me," she screamed at him. "You read the speech and you let me make it, you idiot. Now look what you've done."

The tirade would continue, off and on, through the day as Diana repeatedly reread the criticism and realized that one speech could have ruined everything she had worked for during the previous six months.

"Shit, shit, shit," Diana would be heard repeating as she stormed around her apartment. She would remain in a furious mood throughout the day.

Diana's mood swings are legendary in Kensington Palace. She will appear happy and relaxed one minute, joking and laughing with staff; the next moment Diana will change, a flash of anger will cross her face, and she will turn on whoever has upset her. Diana will yell at her personal dressers, at maids, at office staff; no one will be spared her venom.

Staff will know there is no point in arguing with the Princess of Wales when she is in that mood. Any reply will be met with a tirade of abuse from Diana, peppered with coarse words.

When Princess Diana had only been married a matter of months, she would ask one of her senior secretaries, half-laughingly, "Do you think I'm a bitch?"

"No, not at all," came the genuine and honest reply.

"Do you think I ever will be?"

"Yes."

"Why do you say that?" Diana asked, disappointed, yet she seemed eager for the answer.

"Because this is your life now. When you have had some years of having everything you want, whenever you want it, when you understand that if you want a car at midnight, one will arrive, when you know that you can give any order to anyone and that order will be instantly obeyed, you will not be able to stop yourself becoming a bitch."

"But I'm not a bitch yet?"

"Not yet."

"Thank you," Diana said. "I'll try to remember that."

Some who work close to Diana believe that she may now have earned that singularly brutal accolade. But she has never again questioned the man with whom she had that conversation back in the early 1980s.

She knows that Prince Charles thinks she is a bitch. During their warring days Charles would call Diana a "bitch" when the going became rough, and Diana hated the description. In return she would usually call him a "shit" or a "bastard," nearly always for the same reason—deserting her and the boys to run off to his mistress.

But the sledgehammer that felled Diana and crushed her self-assurance came in a personal letter from the Queen delivered to her by hand at Kensington Palace a week before Christmas. Though written elegantly, diplomatically, and sympathetically the letter in fact demanded an immediate divorce.

Diana's first reaction was fury that the Queen, the grandmother of Wills and Harry, would write such a letter to her hours before the boys' Christmas holidays. Throughout their most acrimonious battles, both Charles and Diana had tried to keep their marital rows away from their sons. At boarding school both boys were protected, to a certain extent, from the acres of column inches in the newspapers detailing the latest juicy revelations of both Charles and Diana.

Now the Queen had sent letters demanding a divorce that she knew would be splashed over every newspaper, would be read and reread on every television and radio news bulletin for days, exposing Wills and Harry to the publicity from which Diana had sought to shield them.

"How could she do such a thing?" Diana cried in anger in her office. "She knew the boys were breaking up this week. How could she? And what a Christmas present for them, their parents' divorce, on the orders of their own grandmother."

Contemptuously Diana added in anger, "Have they no feelings? Have they no blood in their veins? My God, they make me sick."

Before she read the news and the comments in the papers, Diana knew that her BBC interview had brought about the ruthless riposte from the Queen, the Establishment, and the senior courtiers, many of whom had wanted Diana sidetracked for some time, away from the spotlight where she could do little or no damage to the monarchy.

Diana knew in her heart that the Queen's intervention into her marriage was an act of vengeance. For in her interview Diana had challenged the Queen, describing those ranged against her as "the enemy" and even expressing doubts that Charles would ever be king, in what was seen as the most extraordinary and damaging royal statement since the abdication of Edward VIII in 1937.

She knew from her own aides that Buckingham Palace had been so shocked, and the Queen and Philip so angry, by the vitriol in her interview that they had decided the time had come to move against the Princess of Wales fearing what further damage she might inflict on the crown. Yet Diana was still surprised by both the speed and the timing of their actions.

Before deciding to give her interview Diana had thought long and hard about whether she should go through with her plan. She had also determined how tough she should be in the statements she would make. In the end she decided to gamble all, to reveal her true feelings and her ambitions for the future, for she realized that she had nothing to lose.

She realized that England's Establishment, including the Queen and Prince Philip, would never permit her to be crowned Queen, and that she would be moved aside.

Diana had been forced to tape her interview secretly because she knew, from bitter experience, that the Queen and the Establishment would have prevented such an interview from ever being broadcast. She would say, "Everyone was shocked that I did it secretly, but I had no option. I had to tell everyone what had happened in my life, to tell them the truth, as well as trying to seek a role for myself, as a charity worker. I had tried carrying out that role before, but nearly every invitation I was handed was withdrawn at a later date, after pressure from the palace."

Of course Diana had known divorce would one day occur,

yet neither she nor Charles had ever raised the matter. Diana knew pressure had been on Charles for him to divorce her so that the Establishment could begin to create the gulf they believed necessary, so that when Queen Elizabeth died, Charles's sole right to become king would not be challenged or even questioned. But Diana had hoped a divorce could be postponed for perhaps three or five years. That was why she stated, categorically, in her interview that she did not want a divorce.

Her eldest son and the heir to the throne, young William, now nearly fourteen, had begun to study constitutional history and the monarchy in September 1995. Courtiers believe within a few years William will fully understand the role he will be called on to play one day, and that role will not include his mother.

"I know the game they're playing," she said to one of her new, close male friends before her BBC interview, later shown on ABC in the United States. "I know they will freeze me out if they can. Well, they might have another think coming. It might not be that easy."

The nation perceives a rivalry between Diana and Charles as they campaign for the hearts of the people. But Diana knows she wins those battles with ease. The overwhelming majority of British people are not only convinced that Charles is responsible for the breakdown of their marriage, but that Diana is totally innocent of any wrongdoing.

Senior Tories and members of the Establishment believe the monarchy to be severely damaged by the continued warfare between the two. They perceive that Charles's office wages a subtle, dignified but rather sly campaign against Diana while she confronts them head-on, taking the war to the enemy, challenging Charles and the Queen publicly, on the streets, on TV, and in the media. Thus far, Diana has won the propaganda war with ease, a point that infuriates Buckingham Palace officials, who seem unable to dampen her ever-growing popularity.

While Diana took her eighteen-month sabbatical away from

the limelight to recharge her batteries, Charles was busy creating a new image for himself, increasing his staff and advisers, and completely filling his appointment diary. Quietly Charles set about rehabilitating himself and his tarnished relationship with the people who will one day be his subjects.

But the last few years of strain and emotional turmoil have taken their toll. At forty-seven he appears more careworn, the face thinner, the furrows deeper; the face has noticeably aged during the past two years. And he seems to smile far less, the laugh more forced. In December 1995, Prince Charles began visiting a well-known, highly respected psychiatrist, Dr. Alan McGlashan, in London's West End. But his aides would not confirm, deny, or comment on the visits, leaving the public to judge for themselves if they believed the heir to the throne now required the assistance of a psychiatrist, following in the footsteps of Diana, who had sought psychiatric help when her marriage was in turmoil.

And Charles has taken heed of Diana's remarkable success with ordinary people, those with whom Charles had never felt at ease and found great difficulty in establishing a natural rapport. His humor would appear forced, his demeanor awkward, his habit of constantly holding the cuff of his sleeve revealing how uncomfortable he felt. Now, Charles has lost his hesitancy and has become more friendly and understanding, particularly with the young people he meets. One of the reasons is the hugely successful Prince's Trust, a charity for the young, unemployed, and disadvantaged, including many teenagers, which he launched ten years ago and which has created twenty-five thousand small businesses across the nation.

Prince Charles spends at least one day every week with the Prince's Trust and the directors who run it, still personally involved with selecting many of the projects the Trust supports and funds. Those thousands who have received grants from the Trust—mostly funded by big business—all agree their involvement with Charles has brought pleasure, hope, and fulfillment. Yet, the world hears little about them and the national TV stations and newspapers virtually never mention them.

Diana, on the other hand, knows full well that she only has to step out of Kensington Palace, walk down a street, visit a hospital, pick up an ill child, and her photograph will be blazoned across the front page of every tabloid in the land.

Today, however, Diana has no sympathy for her husband. "He will get everything he deserves," Diana told a family friend whom she visits frequently. "He behaved like a shit and I will never forgive him nor will I ever forgive that bitch Camilla."

After Camilla and her husband, Brig. Andrew Parker Bowles, announced their divorce in January 1995, Diana commented, "Now wait and see what happens. In no time she will be seen in public on Charles's arm. She has been out to catch him for years and she thinks she has all but succeeded."

Every photograph of Camilla in the newspapers would be seen and commented on by Diana. Camilla dieted, changed her hairstyle, wore smarter outfits, appeared more in public, and began visiting Scotland for short breaks with Charles and stayed openly at Charles's country home, Highgrove. Diana would watch every move like a hawk, and her comments would emphasize the bitterness she feels toward the woman she believes stole her husband.

Despite her increasing number of public appearances where Diana, quite often, looks stunning, the charity work where she looks concerned and caring, the official engagements where Diana now appears serious and attentive, and her daily workouts at the gym where she looks fit and healthy, there is nevertheless an undercurrent of worry felt by those who know her well.

Diana will still burst into tears for no apparent reason, still purse her lips when her confidence wanes, and will look lost when in a gathering of people, many of whom will be her friends. With her boys away at boarding school, her sisters away from London with their families, her mother in Scotland, Diana seems only to become involved with people with whom she can hide, never wanting to be seen with them in public where she could exude some confidence and appear as a loving person in a wholesome, fulfilling relationship.

Ever since the public became fully aware of her life estranged from Charles, Diana has cut a lonely, unhappy figure. Her public persona now seems more forced, the smile less natural, her behavior and body language more deliberate and less spontaneous. It is not surprising. At home, in the privacy of the palace, she will frequently become distraught, crying in anger and frustration at her unhappiness, believing that no one really cares for her and loves her, save for the public at large.

For the past two years Diana has faced an unenviable dilemma to which only now she believes she may have found a partial answer. She may be unhappy with her present circumstances, but she has no clear sense of direction for her future. Her situation is exacerbated because she has no male or female role model or mentor to guide and advise her. Following her father's death, she seems to have grown apart from her mother, Mrs. Frances Shand Kydd, and also from her brother, Charles, the Earl of Spencer.

Perhaps this failure to chart a new direction is leading her to erratic behavior and swift changes of mood. On some days Diana will now speak with enthusiasm about her pending divorce or talk of seeking a new life outside Kensington Palace. On other occasions she will stridently refuse to take part in any divorce talks with her lawyers and tell them she has no intention of leaving Kensington Palace.

In the same vein she will request no public duties for a particular week and then, overcome by anxiety, change her mind, deciding to visit one or two of her charities. She often changes her mind because she suddenly feels lonely and knows that seeking out the public, feeling their respect and admiration, will give her back the self-confidence she still frequently finds slipping away.

At times she feels living in the country would give her a new perspective, away from the cameras and the bright lights. She will be happily discussing this idea with someone and then immediately change her mind, saying, "That's a stupid idea. I could never live outside London. I would be so terribly lonely and utterly bored."

Another example of her swift changes of plan occurred in December 1995. She had announced that, as in the previous two years, she would accept the Queen's invitation to spend twenty-four hours at Sandringham with the Royal Family. Everything had been arranged when, exactly one week before Christmas, Diana decided that she didn't want to spend any time at Sandringham and told the Queen she would simply arrive with her sons on Christmas Eve and drop them, returning immediately to London.

It was typical Diana. It is part of her nature to react instantly to events and situations. One of the bugbears of royal life, which caused her real problems, had been coming to terms with royal protocol, the necessity of keeping appointments, come what may, always arriving on the day, at the exact time, dressed correctly for the occasion, at the spot that had been decreed months before. And always smiling and looking happy and cheerful no matter how awful she felt.

Now Diana is living through what she refers to as "her twilight period," not absolutely sure what she wants to do with the rest of her life, not certain that she wants another man to marry because her first husband made her life so miserable.

Within minutes of receiving his letter from his mother urging a swift divorce, Charles had issued a statement agreeing with his mother's suggestion, relieved that she had taken the responsibility of urging a divorce. Charles's immediate acquiescence surprised Diana for her husband had never once mentioned to her that he was seeking a divorce, only a separation.

"He has never said no to his mother in his life," Diana said scathingly after reading the news in the press. "Typical that he has to get his mother to carry out his dirty work."

Diana had always known that her bid to keep the marriage intact, though in name only, would end one day. But she didn't believe even the Queen would be so ruthless as to demand an immediate divorce when Diana had explained to her on numerous occasions that she thought it better for Wills and Harry if they were a few years older and better able to cope with their parents' divorce.

She knew the "gray men," as she called them, had wanted her out of the way, removing her from the family and the monarchy so that her influence and popularity would slowly but inexorably diminish. Now she knows that they have got rid of her officially, but she is determined that her influence and her presence will be felt for many years to come.

2

A Furious Diana

———— ✺ ————

From the moment of her separation from Prince Charles in December 1992, Diana flew the royal nest, putting space between herself and Charles and the House of Windsor. During her first year of freedom she felt constricted by the requirements of the occasional royal duty, but continued her ever-increasing number of charity commitments. She wasn't quite sure what role she should play or how independent of the Royal Family she should become.

The separation had made Diana realize for the first time ever the burden of duty that she had had to accept as a Royal. Previously, she had never fully understood the strict code of duty that made Charles seem so distant and disciplined, but had believed, perhaps naively, that her life, as a wife to the heir to the throne and a mother to two young princes, would never be subject to the same strictures of royal life.

During those first blissful five months in 1981 as she prepared for her fairy-tale wedding to her beloved Charles, Diana had been too involved with her new royal life to realize just how much time Charles had to spend attending to his numerous royal duties. She had accepted that he would kiss her goodbye each morning and maybe return during the day, but more often than not, he would leave her again in the evening to attend some royal function.

She didn't realize that he had the Duchy of Cornwall to run, in itself a multimillion-dollar estate; speeches to write; the

Prince's Trust to organize as well as an ever-increasing work-load as he took over more official tasks from his mother's heavy schedule. Diana had been blind to the pressures on his time and his lifestyle because she had been swept off her feet, infatuated, some thought obsessed, by the man she believed could do no wrong.

However, only a matter of months later, after she discovered she was pregnant, Diana found that she needed Charles around her far more than before the wedding. She could not understand how a man who loved his wife could leave her to attend to some boring royal duty when she so obviously wanted him to be with her. During Diana's first pregnancy the principal issue that would destroy their marriage began to emerge. The second vital issue, the reemergence of his mistress Camilla, would occur some months after the birth of Prince Harry.

Charles's understanding of and commitment to duty had been drilled into him since birth. He knew that he had to live up to the motto of the Prince of Wales, *Ich Dien* (I serve), whatever else happened in his life. Duty would be paramount, above marriage, fatherhood, or family. Diana would never understand that Charles lived by that code of conduct, as later she, too, would be expected to do.

But Diana had not been brought up in such a strict regime. She had been allowed to run free, though not wild, during her childhood and teenage years with little discipline in her life and no duties. When Diana was only six years old, her mother, Frances, had fled the family home, meaning that Diana had grown up with no maternal influence, a severe handicap for someone who would be expected, without argument or dissen-sion, to put duty to the crown above all other considerations for the rest of her life.

Diana's understanding of life as a member of the Royal Family would be seen at close hand by Michael Colborne, who had served with Prince Charles in the Royal Navy for four years and then worked in his private office for six years. When Diana married, Charles asked Colborne to become her secretary to teach her the ways of royal life. He stayed in the job for three years.

"Throughout those years the Princess of Wales never seemed to understand that being a member of the Royal Family meant that duty came before everything else," Colborne said. "She did not understand that Charles had no option but to carry out his duties. It would never enter his mind that he ever had an option, but Diana could not understand how the Prince of Wales could not do whatever he wished. She could not grasp that Charles's life was far more disciplined and ordered than anyone else in the entire kingdom. He couldn't say no, he couldn't do what he wanted for duty came first.

"And that is what lead to the rows and arguments, the tears and the tantrums that eventually ended with the breakup of the marriage."

Colborne would witness their close, loving relationship fall apart when Diana realized that she, too, would have to put duty before all else. "Nearly all the rows that I witnessed were about the fact that Diana didn't see why she and Charles should carry out whatever was in the day's diary of events, come what may. That the only exception would be illness, but not simply a cold or cough, and never a diplomatic illness.

"Diana's objection to carrying out royal duties would escalate from discussion to argument to tantrums and, finally, to a total refusal to take part. No matter what I said or tried to explain, or what other senior courtiers suggested or Charles tried to explain, Diana would never accept that duty came before her wishes."

That basic failure to accept duty as paramount was also one of the reasons why Diana accepted Charles's request for a legal separation, though initially she felt panicked by it. They both knew their marriage had ended sometime in 1987 when they stopped sharing a bed. Diana was angry and mortified that Charles had left her to return to Camilla, a woman who she believed had behaved like a snake, deliberately ruining their marriage so that she could have Charles for herself. Diana's desperate unhappiness and her need for emotional security, someone to love her, had driven her into the arms and the bed of Capt. James Hewitt in that same year, 1987.

But when Charles finally suggested to her that they should separate, Diana didn't argue for she had been expecting that suggestion for two or three years, though she had never asked for a separation nor demanded one, not even in her wildest moments of anger. She believed that remaining the Princess of Wales would keep her closer to her sons and would mean she had more say in their schooling and upbringing. And she feared that without her around, the boys would lack the warmth of a mother's love, something she holds so dear because of her own horrid childhood when her mother left her husband and children. She only asked what would happen to her and the boys for she had no idea what the estranged wife of the Prince of Wales was supposed to do, how she was supposed to live or behave.

"Don't worry," Charles had told her, "you and the boys will not be thrown out of KP [Kensington Palace] to fend for yourselves."

He then explained that nothing would alter in her life nor in the lives of the boys. She would still live at Kensington, still have the same staff, the same privileges, and would retain her title. He assured her that she would continue to enjoy the same financial arrangements as before. Understandably, Diana felt relieved.

And there would be some positive benefits from a separation. She knew that by separating from Charles she would escape the awesome burden of royal duties, most of which she had come to hate. Diana hoped that being free of the Royal Family would permit her to live the life she wanted, enjoying as much time as possible with her growing sons, carrying out charitable duties whenever she desired.

She had not, however, considered the other pressures that would crowd her single life. Pressure from the media became almost unbearable as they eagerly sought to chronicle every waking moment of Diana's new life as a single mother. In Diana's eyes her decision to live a life apart from Charles had been taken by the media to mean she could be pursued and photographed, constantly asked for comments and sound bites, making her life miserable.

"Please, please leave me alone," Diana would plead as the paparazzi followed her down a street, off shopping, driving in her car, or out with her children, forever clicking away as she arrived or left any event, whether public or private. Sometimes they might oblige by leaving her alone for a day or more, but they would return with a vengeance.

"Oh, come on Di," they would call. "Just one picture, Di." "Smile, Di, for God's sake give us a smile." "Just one more, Di." The demands for her to pose for pictures never ended.

She understood that their primary interest was to photograph her chatting or meeting, dining or even walking, with a new man, a potential lover. Diana would occasionally meet old friends, both male and female, but she took the greatest care to ensure she was not caught in any compromising situations. Throughout her three-year affair with James Hewitt, the great might of Fleet Street and the cunning paparazzi had never caught her with him. She was equally determined that they would never catch her with any other lover.

Diana believed that Charles and the Royal Family as a whole had decided the monarchy would be better off without the woman they viewed as a potential "basket case," someone in whom they could never have faith or confidence. A separation had been agreed to in secret conversations among the Queen, Prince Charles, and senior courtiers. Of course, constitutional lawyers had been consulted and had offered their opinions. They were invited to suggest if the separation and possible future divorce would cause any problems for the crown. Diana had been totally unaware of these deliberations. She was never consulted and was only informed after agreement had been reached. To Diana, it seemed extraordinary, unfair, and hurtful that after twelve years of marriage she was not even entitled or permitted to be included in such discussions.

In the autumn of 1992, Sir Robert Fellowes, the Queen's private secretary, had talked to Diana, explaining the legal process and also informing her that she would still continue to be the Princess of Wales, still live at Kensington Palace, and still enjoy all the privileges that she had since the day she married.

Later, Diana would say to one of her older female friends, "I was not surprised but yet I was still taken aback by what I was being told. It's not very nice simply to be informed that you are to be separated from your husband, that you have no say, no rights, that your opinions are not sought on any matter. I just said thank you and walked out. In a matter of minutes my whole life had been shattered, but it was none of my doing. I had been cast aside, thrown out like an old coat. I felt sick, physically sick with fear and apprehension."

She stayed at home in Kensington Palace that night and the tears never ceased as she contemplated a life with no family. She wondered whether Charles and the Establishment would now try to have her removed from the palace and, worse still, whether they would try to restrict her access to the boys. The very thought brought more tears. That night she kept trying to reassure herself. "They can't do that," she would repeat in front of a group of people who had come to visit. "Charles wouldn't be that cruel."

And yet there was a nagging suspicion at the back of her mind that, though she doubted Charles would try to keep her sons, she knew others in Buckingham Palace might argue that it might be better for the boys if they were taken away from the influence of their mother because, as they would say, she is rather unstable. And she knew Charles did not have the backbone to fight such a move. Diana had on too many occasions witnessed Charles agreeing totally with something his mother had said, and yet she had known that, in his heart, he took a diametrically opposed view of the matter. Charles would never disobey his mother.

Diana would phone Charles to reassure herself that her worries were unfounded, and he did try to reassure her. In essence, he said, nothing would change. He also confirmed that he would never, under any circumstances, refuse her access to William and Harry and tried to reassure her that the suggestion had never even been discussed. Somehow Diana managed to push all these worries and fears to the back of her mind as she realized she had to get on with her life. That weekend she saw the boys, then aged ten and eight, and loved every moment she spent with them.

"I found myself wanting to hug and kiss them all the time," she confessed later. "But they have rather passed that stage. I kept reminding myself that they were nearly young men who didn't want to be kissed and hugged by their mother too much."

She had hoped the separation would give her a freedom she hadn't known since becoming engaged to Charles in 1981, twelve years before, free from the constant pressures on her life as a public figure. That brief illusion disappeared the first time she set foot outside Kensington Palace. From that moment the pressure intensified until she felt she had no life of her own and precious little privacy except when closeted inside the palace, her luxurious ivory tower, which had become a prison for Diana. Understandably, she became fed up, frustrated, and dejected with her restricted life and, a year later, in December 1993, made her famous announcement that she was reducing her time spent in public life.

Diana was trying to regain some privacy while removing herself from the strictures of royal life. One of her first actions would be to fire her ever-present armed police bodyguard. The Royal Protection Squad guards all members of the Royal Family, and these bodyguards had become Diana's shadows ever since her engagement to Charles in February 1981. She had never grown used to their presence and hated the fact she was never permitted to go anywhere alone. Their presence had quickly become another royal shackle she ended up hating with a passion. On occasions, Diana would plead with them, in her inimitable doleful manner, to let her go shopping, to walk down a country lane alone, or drive in her car. Every time the answer would be the same: "You know, ma'am, that we are not permitted to leave you alone, not for one moment."

Despite warning of the possible dangers from courtiers at

Buckingham Palace and senior police officers, Diana dismissed her bodyguards. The Princess of Wales felt like a new woman, freer and happier, able to do what she wanted whenever. She did, however, tell her girlfriends how awful it had been to always have a police officer at your side. And with a smile she added, "Whatever you do, don't even think of marrying a prince. It's not worth it. Take it from me. For if you do, your life will never again be your own."

From January 1, 1994—the date Diana decided to become truly independent—the Princess of Wales all but changed her official identity. When she booked seats on flights or at the theater she would give her name as "Ms. D. Spencer," her maiden name. She wanted to remove all reference to the fact that she was Diana, the Princess of Wales, or a member of the Royal House of Windsor or that she was a married woman with two growing sons. She knew that writing *Ms.* would make people realize how independent she had become.

She would say, "I much prefer people to know me as my father's daughter, a member of the Spencer family, rather than being seen as some sort of appendage to the House of Windsor. People tend to forget that by using the name Ms. D. Spencer I am simply using my maiden name. Anyway, I prefer it to Windsor because that sounds so dreadfully pretentious."

Diana wants to have as little contact as possible with Prince Charles because of the marriage scars that have still not healed, despite the fact they have been living apart since 1987. During the years that followed they would undertake official royal duties together as the Prince and Princess of Wales, but Diana hated every second that she was forced to live that lie, pretending all was well with the marriage.

Today, Diana still finds it extremely difficult even to be pleasant toward Prince Charles. She feels a bitterness bordering on revulsion for she believes that the man she adored never really loved her. She felt that he cheated her, not just sexually, by continuing his affair with his old flame Camilla, but in a far more insulting way by pretending to love and cherish her.

At home one night at Kensington Palace, in the early 1990s,

Diana told one of her lovers, "I don't despise Charles because he went off and had an affair. I despise him because he lied to me and the boys. I don't believe he ever loved me and yet he made me think that he did. He deceived us, making a mockery of our marriage, and I felt ridiculed, betrayed by his duplicity. Any woman treated like that will tell you the pain is so destructive to one's confidence, one's relationship, and one's whole inner being. I felt eaten away inside."

As one of Charles's private secretaries recalled, "At one stage in the 1980s virtually every weekend they stayed down at Highgrove, there would be violent arguments, often ending with two or more flower vases being smashed, hurled in anger by Diana at her husband."

Diana first began throwing things at Charles one night in November 1982 at Kensington Palace when she decided at the last moment she didn't wish to attend the solemn Annual Festival of Remembrance at the Royal Albert Hall in honor of those who died in the two world wars. Diana walked down the stairs to a waiting Charles and announced, "I'm not going."

"What do you mean you're not going?" Charles asked.

"I mean that I'm not going. I'm fed up of being at everyone's beck and call. I'm not going."

Charles would attend the Festival of Remembrance, come what may. Charles looked at Diana in astonishment, for not only did her insistence shock him but he realized that both the Queen and Prince Philip would be there.

At first Charles tried to humor Diana. "Oh, come on, we've got no option. We have to go."

"I'm not going," she replied.

Charles quickly lost his temper. "Don't be so bloody silly. There's no question of not going. We have to go. Now come and get in the bloody car this instant."

"Don't you dare talk to me like that," Diana shouted.

"I'll talk to you how I like, especially if you're going to behave in such a bloody silly, childish way."

"Don't patronize me. You're behaving like a shit. Just go and leave me here."

"Don't be so bloody stupid," Charles yelled. "And get in the bloody car, now."

That did it. "Don't you ever speak to me like that," Diana said, and, bending down, took off her shoe and hurled it at Charles. The shoe missed Charles, hitting the wall.

"Right. This is your last chance because I have to go. We're late."

"I have no intention of going," Diana said, turning and walking up the stairs, "and I'm certainly not going with you."

On that occasion Charles left on his own, but Diana thought twice about her actions and arrived ten minutes later, causing quite a stir because her chair in the royal box had been discreetly removed. It was quickly replaced, but the media soon learned the truth: the Waleses had had some sort of tiff.

From that time on Diana took to hurling anything she could lay her hands on during heated arguments with Charles. And the more the marriage disintegrated the more severe were her physical attacks. She would throw shoes, books, glasses, magazines, and table mats, but her favorite items were flower vases.

One of Charles's staff at that time recalled listening to one Highgrove incident in 1985: "Charles and Diana were in the drawing room and I happened to be next door. I could hear raised voices, and then they became louder and Diana seemed to be becoming hysterical. On that occasion Charles, too, lost his temper. I cannot recall the reason for the argument. They both seemed to be hurling insults at each other, the air blue with swear words.

"Suddenly I heard Charles shout, 'No, don't, for God's sake, Diana, put it down. . . . No . . . don't be so bloody stupid.' Then I heard an almighty crash of glass splintering and realized she had thrown another vase at him.

"For a moment there was silence. Then Charles said in a shaky voice I could hardly hear, 'You must stop throwing things. That very nearly hit me.'

"The door flew open and a red-faced, angry Diana stormed out, running up the stairs to her room. I waited a couple of minutes, then went into the room. Charles was on the floor gently picking up the pieces of what had been a beautiful cut-glass vase. He said nothing but looked at me with a look of resignation on his face.

"'Can I help, sir?' I asked.

"'If you wouldn't mind,' he replied. And together we picked up all the pieces, which had splintered across half the room."

On another occasion, Charles would not be so fortunate. Diana herself told the story to one of her girlfriends: "He had made me so furious. He had spent hours on his own in his fucking garden and then came in and said he wanted to listen to some music on the radio. I had been down there mooching around Highgrove all day on my own with no one to speak to and he didn't care a damn. I just saw red and went for him. He turned to walk away and I picked up a vase and threw it with all my might at his back. It hit him on the back of the head and he just went down in a heap.

"I began to shake as I ran towards him believing I had killed him. The vase had shattered. I thought, 'Thank God it wasn't a heavy cut-glass one but only a porcelain vase.' I turned him over and he began moaning and I felt a wonderful sense of relief. But I was still shaking because I realized how near I had been to killing him. Charles came round and realized I had thrown a vase at him. He looked at me as if he would throttle me. I stood watching, not knowing whether to help, but he got to his feet, then immediately sat down on a chair holding his head in his hands, still stunned. I knew I had gone too far, but for an instant I thought I had killed him. He just went down and lay there, not moving."

Diana confessed that the shock stopped her from throwing anything at Charles for some months, but she did return to her favorite form of attack sometime later. Nothing remotely as serious ever happened again because Diana believes she no longer tried to hit Charles with any heavy object, just throwing them near him to frighten him into understanding how angry he had made her.

And Diana will also recall how cold Charles would act

toward her and the effect that had on her: "After the wonderful few months we spent together before the marriage, it seemed that after I became pregnant, three months after the wedding, Charles rarely came near me. The warmth he had shown evaporated, and I don't think it ever came back. That hurt. On occasions, of course, things were good, but never great again as they had been before the wedding."

The colder Charles acted toward Diana the more she yearned for someone to love her, but her need for a lover, a companion, a man who would care for her, would lead Diana into a number of unfortunate and embarrassing relationships.

3

Bold and Wild

———— ❧ ————

Aᴛᴛᴇʀ Dɪᴀɴᴀ ᴅɪꜱᴄᴏᴠᴇʀᴇᴅ the truth about Camilla Parker
Bowles, sometime in 1986, the gulf between Charles and Diana
widened dramatically. Soon after, she fled into the arms of
Capt. James Hewitt, a man who had shown her respect and
kindness, who seemed to love her passionately and who offered
to marry her and give her a baby. Diana had believed every
word Hewitt had told her for she wanted to hear those sentiments. Above all, she needed love and someone to care for her.

When the affair with Hewitt ended three years later, Diana
immediately began the search for another all-embracing relationship in which she could love and be loved. When that didn't
occur, she would throw herself into some new sporting activity
or pamper herself with some new therapy. She would tell herself
that she could be happy on her own with no male companion.

But then, out of the blue, she would meet someone to
whom she felt some attraction, some *simpatica*, and a new
relationship would take off. The great majority fizzled after
nothing more than a couple of dinners, or an invitation for
drinks at Kensington Palace. She would suggest that she didn't
need a man or a lover in her life. Those comments were a little
white lie, for Diana has been keeping the proverbial eye open
for the right man ever since her disastrous three-year affair with
James Hewitt.

I have spoken to two men, both married, who admitted to
having affairs with Diana in the early 1990s. Because they are

31

still married, neither would talk unless I agreed to honor their anonymity. Both had remarkably similar stories to tell.

The first became Diana's lover in 1992. He was a former Cavalry officer, who worked in the City and had been married for some years. He first met Diana at a house party in the late 1980s. He recalled, "We were instantly attracted to each other. We flirted madly that first evening and we both agreed to see each other again. Of course I felt flattered that the Princess of Wales seemed to fancy me. Nothing happened and I thought it wrong to follow up such an involvement because she was married to the Prince of Wales. But we met by chance some years later, and with a glint in her eye, she invited me for drinks at KP. She knew I was married but it all seemed perfectly innocent.

"From the moment I walked into her drawing room it seemed obvious to me that Diana wanted a relationship. After a couple of drinks we went out to dinner to a little restaurant and kissed as soon as we returned to KP. We had more drinks, listened to romantic music, which Diana selected, and before midnight we were in each other's arms.

"She didn't want me to leave, but when I left, sometime after two A.M., I knew that we would become lovers. We arranged to meet early the following week. I arrived around ten P.M. and we had some wine and Diana rustled up a cold snack from the kitchen. We listened to music again, drank some more, and began kissing.

"Diana was unbelievable. I felt as though I had been hit by a hurricane. She left me absolutely breathless with her passion. We moved from the drawing room to the bedroom and we made love in her bed. I anticipated that she would want me to leave shortly afterwards, but she wanted me to stay. We must have made love four times in the next three hours, and she still didn't want me to leave her, as though frightened to be left alone. She kept pleading for me to stay with her, to make love to her again, and she seemed so fearful that I would leave her and she would be on her own. Finally, around five A.M. I did leave, exhausted, somewhat bewildered, and feeling rather guilty.

"Two weeks later we had another date, and I sensed from the first few moments that the evening would end up with the two of us making love again. We had a wonderful time fooling around in the drawing room, drinking and listening to music. She seemed on a wonderful high, laughing and giggling, looking shy and embarrassed and then becoming absolutely wild in her lovemaking, demanding more and more. But I didn't think it was me that she craved. It seemed that she had become desperate for company, and she wanted to share herself and her body with someone who would love her in return."

After several further visits to Kensington Palace, the man, three years older than Diana, felt the guilt of cheating on his wife and the Prince of Wales. He began to discuss his unease with Diana. "I don't want to know," she replied, "I don't want to know. All I want is you."

Two weeks later he decided the affair could not continue. He phoned Diana. "'I know what you're going to say,' she told me, 'I understand. Goodbye.' The phone went dead and I could not believe she could have become so dispassionate where she had been so romantic, so tender, and so demanding only a few days before."

In the summer of 1993, Diana met an older man, in his middle forties—about the same age as Charles—who attracted her greatly. They had seen each other on occasion during the past few years but had never really had the chance to talk. He was married with three children and worked as a banker in the City of London.

"We began to talk when we met at a cocktail party in 1993," he said, "and I found myself unbelievably attracted to her. I knew she was flirting with me, removing a hair from the shoulder of my jacket, asking me to find her a drink, offering me petit fours to eat, and one minute appearing shy, even coquettish, the next looking me straight in the eye as if daring me to kiss her.

"I wasn't sure how to react and whether this was the flirting Diana I had read about, the Princess who loves to tease, to toy, to play the vamp when talking to men she finds attractive. At the end of the evening Diana suggested that we should have lunch or dinner together to chat, and to get to know each other better.

"The encounter and her straightforward approach had surprised me, but I agreed. I wanted to find out more, to discover what made her tick and to see whether her apparent sexual interest was for real or simply a ruse to attract. I would soon discover that Diana's innocent appeal was no fantasy but the prelude to remarkable passion.

"Our affair lasted two months, during which time she proved a completely different person to the one I imagined. Diana would be both bold and wild and, at other times, gentle, loving, and sometimes tearful. What I found remarkable would be her passion, not just sexual, but in everyday matters that she felt important. I also noted an underlying bitterness towards Charles and the Royal Family in general, which surprised me. It seemed that she had been unable to forgive anything that had happened, continuing to feel cheated by Charles.

"At one point I wondered whether Diana was making love to me as a way of punishing Charles for his involvement with Camilla. It seemed that she wanted to make love to get her own back against Charles, and I began to feel that I was there to be used, as part of this macabre game she was playing in her mind. That feeling unnerved me, and although we had wonderful times together and Diana made me feel she wanted me emotionally as well as physically, I thought that whatever we had between us was not for real. I didn't like that.

"Diana must have sensed that, too, because the phone stopped ringing and my calls were no longer returned. We never actually ended the affair. We never said farewell or good luck. She just stopped phoning as though she knew the game was over and she wanted no further embarrassment. That is what I believed happened and I respected her wishes and never tried to contact her again. I just hope she manages to sort out her problems."

Diana had turned to sport, swimming, and playing tennis

so that she could burn away her excess energy while taking her mind off her search for the "ideal man."

Diana wondered whether she was searching for a father figure, who would replace the one person she had always loved and trusted, her father Viscount Johnny Althorp, who became Earl Spencer on the death of his father. Diana's father died in 1992, only months before her official separation. She knew she had always been attracted to older men, finding younger ones, such as her former lover James Hewitt, rather juvenile in their thinking.

Diana, however, bore no deep love for her mother. Diana had been too young to remember her really well for she had been only six years old when Frances Spencer had left her husband and their four children to live alone in London. From when she first understood what had happened, Diana would never wholly forgive her mother, even if she did try to understand why she had left her family for no apparent good reason.

Frances Spencer's second marriage in 1969 to Peter Shand Kydd, a paint millionaire, would also end in divorce some twenty years later. Frances would move to Scotland, open a gift shop, and settle down to a quiet, almost nunlike existence. She had a few friends and a few interests and a growing involvement with the Roman Catholic Church, which surprised Diana. In 1991, Frances sold the small Highland shop she had bought as an interest and an investment and, three years later, bought a larger house in the same area. The stone house had been a bed-and-breakfast residence, but Frances had no intention of taking in paying guests. She refurnished and redecorated the house and settled down to a quiet, rather lonely existence.

A year later Diana's mother announced her decision to embrace the Roman Catholic religion, having attended services at the Catholic cathedral in nearby Oban for six years. Diana wanted to find out more about the Roman Catholic faith to better understand her mother, whom she confesses she has never really understood. Some years earlier, Diana had met Dom Anthony Sutch, headmaster of Downside, Britain's premier Roman Catholic school, who had previously worked as a layman in the hard-nosed City of London, and she asked if they could meet in an effort to help her understand her mother's interest in Catholicism. They would meet and talk privately on a number of occasions.

Whatever had happened between her beloved, warmhearted father and her high-spirited mother, Diana could never imagine anything that could have been so terrible that her mother found it necessary to walk out, leaving her husband and four small children to fend for themselves. Diana never forgave her mother for what she perceived had been an act of desertion, leaving her elder sisters, Sarah and Jane, and her younger brother, Charles, who was only three at the time. Despite the dramatic traumas in her life, Diana has found it difficult to turn to her mother for help or advice.

Diana had often wondered why both of her mother's marriages had failed, and it worried her that her marriage to Charles might have failed because of some flaw in her and her mother's makeup, perhaps a weakness or a defect that made it all but impossible for them to have long-term relationships. She would try to put such thoughts to one side, dismissing them as unwarranted, yet a doubt would always remain. She wondered whether her mother's conversion from the Anglican religion to Catholicism might in some way help her, and it crossed Diana's mind that perhaps one day she, too, might convert.

Though Diana believes in God, she is not a religious person. She doesn't say her prayers at night or in the morning; she wouldn't go to church of her own volition, except to celebrate Christmas, a wedding, or as a duty. She has not, until now, thought too deeply about religion, but her mother's conversion did make Diana wonder whether she might find some solace, some peace of mind, in religion in her later years as she hopes her mother has done.

At the time of her conversion, in October 1995, Frances Shand Kydd said, "If Diana has inherited anything from me, I hope it's what I was given in childhood by my father. He was quite simply the most compassionate, caring, sensitive person I have ever met. He would hold our hands and teach us about caring, literally. I tried to do that in bringing up my children, and I think Diana has the gift of compassion, and she uses it."

Frances Shand Kydd, however, would not succumb to Diana's charms. Many women have suggested that Frances and her daughter could not become close because they were so alike, and their personalities would clash.

A friend of Frances Shand Kydd's, an older woman, commented, "When they meet, they are fine together for the first couple of hours, but then, invariably, an argument will develop. They know each other too well. They pretend to get on when there are other people around, but they both know they could not live under the same roof for one minute. Many so-called experts have asked why Diana had never rushed to her mother for advice to talk over the traumas in her marriage or her dreadful eating problems. The reason is that Diana would, more than likely, have received short shrift from Frances if she had done so. Frances would have been tough on her daughter and probably told her to return immediately to her family, concentrate on enjoying life as the Princess of Wales, and make sure she was a good wife.

"It didn't matter that Frances had never been able to do that herself, but she knew that Diana should have bitten her lip and learned to enjoy the privileged life she had been handed on a plate. She also believed Diana had a duty as the mother to the heirs to the throne to stick with her marriage, come what may. Diana knew her mother would react like that to her appeals, and that was the reason she kept her distance."

It seemed that Diana's mother had deliberately moved herself out of the limelight and away from her children, and there were no reports of her being visited by any of her four children or grandchildren. The fact that Diana never enjoyed a close relationship with her mother meant there was no older woman to whom the Princess of Wales felt she could unburden her troubles, whether they were marital, emotional, or the disturbing eating problems she experienced.

Diana's various problems continued and so did her numerous disastrous love affairs, only some of which the media discovered. Diana knew full well that she had to find a new interest in life other than searching in vain for a new man. She searched for other avenues of escape and discovered that one of life's pleasures was spending money.

As a teenage bachelor girl both in the country and in London, Diana semingly didn't care about fashion or clothes. She was happy wearing jeans and a shirt, a long skirt and a sweater, and all her clothes fitted comfortably in a single wardrobe and a small chest of drawers.

Her grooming after marrying Charles changed, and after Wills and Harry were born, she found that shopping for clothes was rather fun. She had an American Express card that would automatically be paid every month by the Duchy of Cornwall no matter how much she had charged. Whenever she felt miserable, she would pop off to Harvey Nichols or Harrods to buy a little something to cheer herself up.

Then she grew more adventurous and her advisers, including some friends at *Vogue,* introduced her to different and more exciting designers. At first, she was persuaded to support British designers to help British export sales, but this, too, would change as she became her own woman and she would fall in love with a variety of European and American designers.

With her photograph appearing on magazine covers around the world Diana became more confident and her clothes more adventurous. Diana was spurred on by those who hailed her as a fashion leader of the Western world. She loved that accolade. Today, wherever she travels, whether in Britain or abroad, the fashion experts as well as ordinary young women love to examine what the Princess of Wales is wearing and, if possible, to emulate her.

For some years now Diana recognizes that she has become a fashion icon. Originally, under the tutelage of *Vogue* fashion experts and Buckingham Palace, Diana played for safety with Catherine Walker, Tomasz Starzewski, and Amanda Wakeley, who dressed her in long jackets, short skirts, and overelaborate evening gowns.

But from the moment of her separation Diana felt like a new person, who could wear whatever she wanted with no one to raise an eyebrow if she appeared with or without stockings in the summer, with no husband to approve what she wore for royal duties, with no mother-in-law to look disapprovingly if she stepped out of line.

But she would go to the other extreme, flirting with very short skirts, acres of thigh, and rather glitzy German-style designs, as though trying to show how daring the real Diana could be. Some women pointed out that Diana's new dress code seemed to be a rather immature way of showing any available man what was on offer.

Throughout most of 1994 it appeared Diana wanted to show off her legs at every possible opportunity, even, for example, when collecting her sons from school. She began donning skirts that split to the upper thigh and arrived at church on Christmas day wearing a split skirt.

It seemed that Diana had completely lost her magic touch of never making a fashion error, for her split skirts had been the rage of the fashion runways two years earlier in 1992. During the following twelve months the split skirt electrified Main Street sales, irresistibly combining the demure appearance and security of the maxi with the freedom of movement and sheer sex appeal of the mini. Twelve months later fashion-conscious women banned them from their wardrobes and moved on, for they realized the split skirt would, on windy days, reveal far more thigh than intended, sometimes exposing the wearer's panties. The fashionable declared the split skirt cheap-looking, unladylike, and too risky.

But Diana persisted, wearing the revealing skirts and reaping the criticism, even the opprobrium, of the fashion world. Some fashion writers believed Diana's persistence could only be attributed to her determination to return to the public arena with dramatic effect, making the most of her physical assets like any showgirl returning to the limelight.

Journalists recalled Diana's penchant for using her body when she wanted to upstage Charles, or to show the world what a great body he had left behind when he quit Kensington Palace for the tranquillity of Highgrove and a woman with none of the physical beauty Diana possessed. As an example, they recalled the night Charles confessed on television to his adultery with Camilla Parker Bowles, when Diana appeared at an art gallery wearing a revealing thigh-skimming, figure-hugging black cocktail dress. Diana knew she was inviting the media to compare the sexy, gorgeous Princess in a stunning number with the older, ample-framed Camilla, who would never have been able to get away with wearing such an outfit. It was a perfect counterattack, which was not lost on the rest of the world.

In Kensington Palace the following morning a happy Diana spread out all the morning newspapers, examining them in detail. Every paper, from the broadsheets to the tabloids, had printed Charles's confession on its front page alongside a photograph of a radiant, sexily clad Princess. "Look at that!" she said ecstatically a dozen times to her staff whom she invited to see the front pages. "Fantastic, great. He's always hated me upstaging him. That'll show him."

Though few understood the true psychological battle going on inside Diana's head, some remonstrated with her to return to her more demure, less sexy, but more alluring dress sense that had won her so many plaudits from the fashion world. Diana ignored their advice. She saw that the newspapers continued to print large photographs of her dressed in split skirts, high heels, and figure-hugging outfits. She would continue to wear a black suit adorned with gold elephants (an ensemble from the up-market German fashion house of Escada, a safari collection costing $1,600). Or she would squeeze into ultratight black leather trousers, sport stilettos under tight jeans and apply her makeup too obviously. On occasion Diana would wear a black belt whose buckle depicted a pair of elephants mating!

She was thirty and for the first time was able to wear what she wanted, when she wanted. And Diana wanted to experiment, to wear not only her British designers when she felt like it but also to explore foreign designers. She chose to wear

Chanel, Saint Laurent, Armani, Valentino, Escada, and her all-time favorite, Versace.

When Diana finds a dress that she loves, she will sometimes buy two or three of the same design, but in different colors. Despite some criticism, Diana believed that her famous white, Versace, figure-hugging number, with thigh-high hem and plunging neckline, made her look twenty-five again, so she bought another in black. She also bought three lizard clutch bags in red, yellow, and black ($1,800 each) from Asprey, the Bond Street jewelers, to ring the changes with the dresses. Some critics wondered whether Diana should be seen wearing the same dresses in different colors. Diana didn't care. She was convinced the dress looked stunning on her.

On occasion Anne Beckwith-Smith, her secretary for eight years and now her chief lady-in-waiting, will ask Diana if she thinks her choice of a particular outfit is really wise.

"Why not?" is Diana's usual reply. "What's wrong?"

Anne will reply that perhaps the outfit is not "entirely suitable" for whatever function the Princess is attending.

"Is it that bad?" Diana will ask.

"No, not that bad. But we've seen better."

"If it's not that bad, then I'm going to wear it." And more often than not Diana will add, "Anyway, if it shocks them at the palace, all to the good. It's what they need."

The fashion writers urged Diana to return to tailored suits and silk blouses, suggesting the stylish and simple fashions of Ralph Lauren, DKNY, or Nicole Farhi rather than expensive, ostentatious styles. But Diana had given away scores of her tailored suits, which she had worn on official royal duties before she quit the public stage. She invited seven girlfriends to Kensington Palace and told them to take their pick while Diana entertained their children with tea and cakes.

The fashion writers, however, openly attacked Diana, describing her as an "Essex girl," a manifestly rude, even insulting description, for Essex girls (from the County of Essex, near London) are ridiculed as having the worst manners, appalling bad taste, an addiction to cheap, flashy clothes, and no morals.

Initially, Diana dealt with such criticism by telling her friends, "They're just jealous. I take no notice. They have always criticized me, no matter what I wear." And Diana would mischievously give the single-finger sign, with some feeling in the upward thrust of her hand.

The upper-crust *Tatler* magazine even took up the cudgel of criticism, showing Diana wearing outfits similar to those of TV soap stars. "It proves that if you dress five years out of date you look 'dead common.'" The article continued, "There are times when Diana gets it right, when she can be marvellous but we have endured terrifying taste blunders. Take the appliquéd jumpers, the court shoes with jeans, the almost permed marmalade hair and flesh-colored pop-socks."

And in a vicious summing up, *Tatler* added, "Will the real Diana please sit down and dress like a princess."

That attack, written in March 1994, stung Diana to the quick. Photographs, deliberately selected for their shock appeal by the tabloids, showed Diana wearing a number of unflattering outfits. They also liked to show a photograph of Diana sitting in a straight-backed chair, in front of an audience, sporting a short skirt that revealed a great expanse of inner thigh and all but revealed her panties. This, they noted, was the same Princess who took exception to snatched pictures showing her dressed in a leotard and exercising at a gymnasium, the LA Fitness Club. On that occasion, Diana had been photographed, by a camera secreted in the ceiling by the club's owner, with her legs wide apart pulling on a rowing exercise machine.

The photographs, published in the tabloid *Daily Mirror,* angered Diana and she sued the newspaper and the club owner, a New Zealander, Bryce Taylor, for breach of confidence and breach of contract. She also won an injunction ordering them to hand over the photographs, copies, and negatives and never to reproduce them again.

Diana was determined to win the case and told her lawyer,

Lord Mischon, that she was eager to take the witness stand to defend her honor since some people had suggested she had deliberately posed for the shots. Diana was strongly advised to settle out of court. Her lawyers knew that a topflight barrister would quite likely have caused the Princess severe embarrassment by the type of questions she would have been called on to answer. Her advisers worried that Diana had no idea of the intense pressure involved in answering tough questioning for a number of hours. At the last moment, just days before the case was to be tried in February 1995, Diana accepted the advice and settled. If Diana had taken the stand, she would have been the first Royal to have done so for more than a century.

4

A New Man to Love

———— ❧ ————

Pʀɪɴᴄᴇss Dɪᴀɴᴀ walked into the reception room at Windsor Castle during Ascot week in the summer of 1985 to meet the guests with whom she would be having lunch prior to that afternoon's racing at nearby Ascot. Every year Queen Elizabeth, a keen racing enthusiast, owner, and breeder, gives pre-race lunches at Windsor to which privileged guests are invited.

Standing in the light of a magnificent window overlooking the castle lawns, with the sun cascading into the room, Diana saw a young man, with rather long, dark, wavy hair, not very tall but dressed immaculately in a morning suit, the traditional Ascot dress. Diana looked again and noticed how handsome, relaxed, and friendly he seemed to be. Many in the room, most of them strangers to Diana, seemed nervous, not sure how to conduct themselves as they waited for the Queen to walk into the room.

But not this dark stranger. He smiled and laughed with the people who chatted with him. Diana noticed the laughter lines around his eyes and the twinkle in his eye and wondered who he was. By his side stood a young woman, perhaps a little older than Diana, who the Princess noted was most attractive and dressed in a beautiful silk, printed summer dress. She wondered whether they were married for they seemed eminently suited, both attractive, sophisticated, and at ease in the daunting surroundings of Windsor Castle. The man was Oliver Hoare, a millionaire art dealer, specializing in Iranian art and antiquities, then thirty-nine; the woman, his wife, Diane, then thirty-seven, the daughter of a French heiress, the Baroness Louise de Waldner, one of the Queen Mother's closest friends, who lived in a magnificent château in the heart of Provence in southern France.

Charles joined Diana, and accompanied by the Queen Mother, they went over to chat with Oliver Hoare and his wife. Diana remembers feeling rather shy when she shook Oliver's hand, not sure whether to look into his eyes, for they appeared so blue, attractive, and warm. She found herself looking into his eyes and smiled broadly, and he returned the smile.

Diana began talking to Diane and found they had much in common. Oliver and Diane had three children, two sons and a little girl, Olivia, then two. Prince Harry was then one year old. Diana recalls telling Diane that she would love one day to have a daughter, especially, like her, after two sons. The two women became quite close that day, neither terribly interested in the racing at Ascot, preferring to talk about other matters. Diane was of course well aware that Diana had a great interest in fashion, as she did, too.

The two men also chatted comfortably with each other. Charles would always attend the four days of racing at Ascot each year under some duress for he cannot abide the sport. However, he is under orders from the Queen to join her and chat with her guests. Charles would always leave before the last race so that he could prepare for the polo matches that are traditionally played at Windsor Great Park in the evening of Royal Ascot race days.

Charles, three years younger than Oliver, found him most interesting for when he discovered Oliver was an expert in Islamic art and antiques, the two had much to discuss. Charles was no great authority on Islamic art but had always been fascinated by the subject and was eager to learn more. Charles also rather appreciated Oliver's sophistication and air of confidence.

Oliver Hoare was born in July 1945, son of Reginald Hoare, a civil servant employed in the War Office in London. His mother, Irina, was a member of the Kroupensky family, who had come to Britain from Moravia, a onetime province of Czechoslovakia. In his family background Oliver Hoare could boast the Earl of Coventry, and distantly the famous Quaker Hoares, one of the families that had founded Barclays Bank, a major British bank. The Hoares, however, had little money and struggled to educate their children, though Oliver did finally attend Eton College, where Prince William now boards. When Hoare was only nineteen, and enjoying a student life at the Sorbonne in Paris, his father died suddenly, leaving exactly $2,500!

At that time many Iranians were living in Paris, and fortunately for Oliver, he came under the wing of a wealthy Iranian princess some years older than him, the famous Hamoush Azodi-Bowler, a woman who loved all forms of Islamic art. She would invite the handsome, dashing twenty-two-year-old student to study art in her Tehran mansion where she presided over and encouraged a circle of intelligent, artistic young men, many of them from England.

Those years in Tehran formed Oliver Hoare's life. There he learned everything about Iran and its art. He would tour the country, sometimes residing in palaces and mansions, at other times staying in peasant-style hotels in the far reaches of the mountainous country.

Through Hamoush, Oliver also met a host of young people with brilliant social connections, many from celebrated families, some of whom would become wealthy and famous in their own right. Some are still his close friends. In Tehran, Oliver met Prince Charles's lifelong friend, Nicholas Soames, now a minister of the British government; Victoria Waymouth, daughter of the Earl of Hardwicke; and David Sulzberger, the man who became Oliver Hoare's business partner, and whose family owns the *New York Times*. In the evenings the young people would gather for stimulating debate on art, music, and poetry while drinking wine and eating the wonderful Iranian dishes prepared by Hamoush's servants. It was here that Oliver found his spiritual home and his destiny.

The engagement that thrilled a nation. Charles and Diana at
Buckingham Palace, February 24, 1981 (Photo Buckingham Palace)

Diana on an official visit to a Royal
Navy base in 1988
(London News Service)

On parade at Royal Ascot
and looking stunningly
beautiful, June 1991
(London News Service)

The Princess of Wales on an official visit to the principality of Wales, 1994 (London News Service)

Diana visiting sick and disabled children with her hostess, Jemima Khan, during a visit to Lahore, Pakistan. They wore traditional Islamic dress, February 1996. (Express Newspapers)

Thousands turned out to greet Diana when she visited Tokyo, February 1995. (London News Service)

Surrounded by Italian security men, Diana steps aboard a gondola during her visit to Venice in 1995. (Express Newspapers)

Chatting with an AIDS patient in a London hospital, 1989
(London News Service)

Diana breaks down
in tears in Newcastle
while visiting residents
in a program for
housing the homeless,
April 1991.
(London News Service)

Leaving a charity event in the London rain, June 1993
(London News Service)

Diana is always happy to help other people fight their eating problems.
Here she arrives at a 1993 conference on eating disorders.
(Express Newspapers)

Diana opening the Mortimer Market Centre for Sexually Transmitted Diseases, HIV, and AIDS, December 1994 (London News Service)

Diana visits a cancer hospital for children during her visit to Pakistan in February 1996. (Express Newspapers)

Diana allegedly making midnight visits to hospital patients in December 1995. In fact, she never went to the hospitals. (London News Service)

Diana receives a kiss from a total stranger in Liverpool as she was strolling without a bodyguard or police protection. The young man was in fact a mentally disabled hospital patient who bet other patients he would kiss the Princess, July 1995. (Express Newspapers)

Hamoush recalled, "Oliver came to study and excavate and to read Arabic and Persian script. He was a brilliant scholar. In a matter of months he read them perfectly. Often I would find him in the house, late in the evening, studying while the others were out in the town enjoying themselves."

Oliver was a serious, rather studious young man, but he would later learn to relax and enjoy life to the hilt. His one relaxation at that time was playing the guitar, which he mostly taught himself. Late into the evenings a group of Hamoush's young protégés would sit around while Oliver would play, often to songs he had written himself.

Hamoush continued, "After a while people would invite him to the most sophisticated social parties and invite him to play and sing. His voice was stunning. Many suggested that he should become a pop singer, playing and writing his own music and words. He didn't want to. His style, his music, his voice, and his looks, however, meant that he rapidly became the object of many young women's attention. I can remember many young women, of different nationalities, openly admitting they wanted an affair with Oliver. He was so romantic, untouchable, wonderfully artistic, some would say gifted. And very, very good-looking. Many also wanted to marry him.

"They would tell me," Hamoush said, "'He is so, so sexy.' And I would smile and wish them luck."

Hamoush would say of her young protégé, "Oliver is half child and half old man. Like a child he is impressed by unimpressive things. He has something that probably God never gave him, a tranquillity of life."

I met Oliver Hoare sometime at the end of the 1970s when he came to my London apartment with the Russian ballet star Rudolf Nureyev. They became close friends and were part of the wild brigade of brilliant, artistic, world-renowned, wealthy young men and women who at that time were enjoying life to the full—infamous for sex, drugs, and rock 'n' roll—among them pop stars like Jimmy Page of Led Zeppelin and Mick Jagger and Laura Nelson, the talented Hollywood writer whom they all loved as a sister.

They all adopted pet names that they would use on phone calls and messages so that their identities would remain anonymous from anyone listening to the calls, taking their messages, or wanting to crash their circle. Oliver Hoare became part of that privileged in-crowd.

Nureyev asked Oliver to decorate his Paris apartment, No. 23, Quai Voltaire, on the banks of the Seine. Oliver Hoare found the task challenging and rewarding. Later, Nureyev could boast of one of the most magnificent apartments in the French capital, beautifully designed, the artifacts treasures from around the world, and the nearly one hundred paintings Nureyev purchased showed images of the male torso, some in exaggerated poses, others more erotic. There were also various tortured poses in bronzes.

Oliver took Nureyev, the actor Terence Stamp, and another dancer, Richard Collins, to visit Hamoush in Tehran. Hoare and Nureyev would enjoy wild times together, and years later Oliver would tell these stories to an enchanted Diana, who would ask him to recall his moments with the stars she had read about and admired from afar, but never met.

Hoare would later tell Diana how he had begun work, helping customers at the front desk at Christie's, the London art dealer. Later, his knowledge led him to specialize in Islamic art. But in 1976 he quit his full-time job to break out on his own, opening a small gallery in Kynance Mews in Chelsea with David Sulzberger.

Soon they moved to larger premises in Belgravia, London, launching the Ahuan Gallery, named after an Iranian caravanserai—a traditional Persian inn and watering hole—owned by Hamoush. She had planned to give her caravanserai to Hoare as a gift, but it was confiscated by the mullahs when the Ayatollah Khomeini came to power in 1979 following the revolution that overthrew the Shah.

In 1976, Hoare had married the beautiful Diane after a year-long romance. But their marriage, too, would have its share of problems. While Charles had rekindled his love affair with Camilla Parker Bowles, cheating on the beautiful Princess

Diana, Oliver Hoare was becoming seriously involved with another woman, Ayesha Nadir, another Islamic art expert, the estranged wife of the disgraced tycoon Asil Nadir.

But the relationship between the Waleses and the Hoares blossomed. Within a matter of a few weeks of that first meeting at Windsor Castle, Charles and Diana invited the Hoares to dinner at Kensington Palace. Again they got on remarkably well. Diana found both Oliver and his wife charming, with interests she, too, could relate to, a far cry from the usual guests Charles would invite to dinner, many of whom Diana would privately call "boring old farts."

Friendship between the four of them developed, and both Charles and Diana visited the Baroness's Provence château from time to time. Charles particularly loved to fly to the south of France to rest and paint in the peace and seclusion of the estate. As the Waleses marriage disintegrated in a blaze of arguments, verbal abuse, and tears, Charles would flee to the tranquillity of the Provence château for peace and quiet.

The Hoares knew that Charles and Diana were having major problems in their marriage for Diana began to confide in Diane, seeking advice. Diane would listen to what the Princess said and offer encouragement. She knew that simply by listening to the torrent of abuse Diana would describe she was helping in some small way to ease Diana's anguish. On occasions, Diana would phone her in tears, and Diane knew that the Princess, thin and hardly ever eating, was suffering from depression and a most unhappy marriage.

Oliver Hoare broached the matter with Charles and offered to act as a go-between if, or when, necessary, telling Charles that his marriage with the lovely Diane had also had its share of problems.

"Thank you," Charles said, "I think that might be useful."

During the protracted drama that went on behind the scenes as Charles and Diana edged toward a formal separation in 1990 and 1991, both Oliver and his wife tried to help them. Princess Diana knew that Charles had great confidence in the older Oliver, believing him to be a man of the world who had the self-confidence to advise Charles honestly and straight-forwardly.

When Charles and Diana stopped speaking to each other, she turned to Oliver Hoare. He would spend hours with her at Kensington Palace, much of the time listening to Diana's anger and frustration at what she saw as a most unfair situation.

She would talk for an hour or more pacing up and down the drawing room in Kensington Palace, sometimes calm, at other times wringing her hands, her eyes filled with tears of utter sadness.

On other occasions she would rail at Charles for walking out on her and their sons, living a life on his own in Highgrove with his mistress, Camilla Parker Bowles. She would become infuriated whenever she visualized Camilla in the double bed at Highgrove making love to Charles while Diana was meant to say and do nothing but care for Wills and Harry in London.

In part Diana favored Oliver Hoare as an intermediary because one of his great friends for many years had been Camilla. Hoare and Camilla had met earlier in the late 1970s, and she, too, had enjoyed his company, his sophistication, and his wit. Later, Charles and Camilla would dine with the Hoares at their London mansion, but Diana would not be told of that.

Diana wanted to know every tiny piece of information about the woman she believed had stolen her husband, the woman she would, more often than not, refer to as "that bitch." Diana would repeatedly probe Oliver, asking a hundred questions about her rival.

Hoare found himself in an impossible position. He was close to both Charles and Diana and did not wish to be seen taking sides in their wrangling. He told Diana what he thought he should about Camilla without going into any great detail. That of course was not enough for Diana for she wanted every possible tidbit of information, gossip, and speculation.

"But why," Diana would repeatedly ask, "why on earth would Charles want her? What's so special about her? What's her secret? She looks like a horse."

And Hoare would tell Diana that he had found Camilla to be a warm, intelligent companion who loved the country, horses, dogs, and the life of a country woman who had the money to enjoy the best of life.

Diana knew Camilla well herself. She and Charles had stayed at her home in Gloucestershire before they became engaged. Later, Diana would learn that it had been Camilla who had pushed Charles into marrying her after refusing Charles's offer of marriage years after she became Mrs. Parker Bowles. She knew the enormous, perhaps catastrophic implications to the monarchy that would follow if Charles married a divorced woman. Only forty years ago King Edward VIII had sacrificed the throne for his love of a divorced woman, the American Mrs. Wallis Simpson, who would become the Duchess of Windsor.

Charles had first proposed to a deliriously happy Diana in the cabbage patch at Camilla's home. But those were the days when Diana had been hopelessly in love with Charles, her true Prince who would take her away from her unhappy childhood, and together they would live happily ever after.

Diana found that she desperately needed the presence and the understanding of Oliver Hoare. She could not survive for twenty-four hours without seeing him or, at the very least, talking to him on the phone. She became dependent on him and would become agitated if she didn't stay in constant contact with him. She had no idea that during 1992 she had become a burden to Oliver Hoare. Nor did Diana realize for many months that her demands were putting a tremendous strain on Hoare's marriage. By this time Diane and Oliver Hoare had reconciled their differences and their marriage was once again on a fairly even keel. The demands of the Princess of Wales all but dashed their relationship.

Diane accused her husband of having an affair with the Princess for he would spend one or two evenings a week with Diana, either dining out, going for long drives in the country, accompanying her to dinner parties, or spending time alone with her at Kensington Palace, sometimes not returning home until the early hours. On weekends, Diana would spend thirty minutes or more on the phone talking to Oliver, much to the growing annoyance of his wife.

Sometime during 1992 Diana realized that she had fallen hopelessly and completely in love with someone who she felt had all the attributes of a real man—strength, honor, charm, wit, and sophistication. And she had never forgotten, could never forget, that she had been physically attracted to him from the moment she first set eyes on him seven years before. Diana came to the realization that Oliver Hoare was the man she wanted.

Diana, however, was not sure whether the attraction was reciprocated. She realized that Oliver found her attractive, but she wondered if the handsome art dealer, who was having financial problems with his business, needed the additional problem of escorting the Princess of Wales, the estranged wife of Prince Charles, the focus of every photographer and royal writer in Fleet Street and beyond.

Oliver Hoare had never enjoyed the limelight. A quiet man, he preferred to lead a more sheltered, less ostentatious life, shunning rather than seeking the glare of publicity. Even his car was ordinary, a standard Volvo. She knew that she would have to tread most carefully. Hoare enjoys the company of those in high society, whether in London, Paris, or New York, but prefers to be involved with people who share his passion for Eastern and Middle Eastern culture. He also enjoys his freedom.

But Diana believes she yearns for that lifestyle most of the time. She would love to go shopping, alone and unrecognized, to swim or play tennis, and be ignored. Sometimes she doesn't want to enter a room full of strangers, especially when she is on her own, for she feels vulnerable. Even today, she will on occasion shake with apprehension when she is about to make a speech. Her fear that she will misread or mispronounce a word only compounds her lack of confidence.

When asked directly whether she would not miss the excitement of being the center of attention, Diana will look shy and a wry smile will pass her lips, knowing that she does still feel thrilled by the cheers of ordinary people. The clapping, the call of her name, give Diana an inner strength, boosting her fragile self-confidence. More importantly, the warmth she feels from people delighted to see her makes her feel wanted and loved, which is what she has missed for most of her life and what she has always craved.

During the summer of 1993, Diane Hoare reached the end of her patience with the Princess of Wales. Diane had noted that whenever she did chat with Diana for a minute or so on the phone, the Princess, who had shown friendship and warmth during their earlier meetings, now seemed brusque, as though not wanting to talk to her at all. Diane became suspicious.

The constant stream of phone calls continued and her husband would continue to visit Diana two or three times a week. Diane became convinced that her husband and the princess were having a full-blown love affair. She knew from bitter experience that Oliver was capable of having an open affair with someone else. His relationship with Asil Nadir's wife, a former Turkish beauty queen, lasted four years until it ended in 1989.

Diane began to challenge her husband, demanding that he spend less time with Diana. She also told him in no uncertain terms that he must somehow stop Diana from constantly phoning their home, sometimes three or four times a day, sometimes late at night, demanding to speak to him.

Oliver would talk to Diana about the problem. She would respond, "Doesn't she understand what I'm going through? Doesn't she know that I need your help and advice with all the terrible problems I'm having?"

Diana would continue to pour out her most intimate fears, anguish, and concerns: the grief caused by Prince Charles and his affair with Camilla, the fact that Charles was now demanding a legal separation from her, the criticism she received from the Queen and Prince Philip, as well as senior courtiers. Their criticism would sometimes make her feel physically sick and exhausted. Usually, these sessions of rage and fear for the future would end in a stream of tears.

She would cry out to Oliver, "Doesn't Diane realize that I

have no one to whom I can turn? No one whom I can trust? You are my only friend. Doesn't she relaize that I am so bitterly alone?"

The phone calls and the demands on Oliver Hoare's time continued. But now Diana would invariably never speak to Diane Hoare if she answered the phone; she would either hang up or simply say nothing. On occasions, when Oliver answered the phone, Diana would sometimes remain silent, simply hanging on wanting to hear the voice of the man she loved.

Throughout 1993 the phone calls continued, though Diana would also see much of Oliver Hoare during most weeks of that year. For much of the time Diana smiled and seemed at ease. Her friends wondered whether there was a new man in her life. Some believed that Oliver Hoare had filled that role, and they were pleased that the Princess of Wales had found a soul mate with whom she seemed happy, relaxed, and on occasions excited. Some friends thought she had recaptured a spring in her step and exuded a certain je ne sais quoi that some women who are happy with their life display.

She had even managed to remain calm when she had been informed by Sir Robert Fellowes, the Queen's private secretary, that later that week, in December 1992, Prime Minister John Major would announce to the House of Commons the formal separation of the Prince and Princess of Wales.

She had felt a thrill when John Major had told the nation that despite the separation no constitutional implications were involved, meaning that when Charles became king, Diana could still be crowned queen. It had also been stated that both Diana and Charles would be involved in the education and upbringing of Wills and Harry.

The outcome could not have been better for Diana, though she would have preferred to remain married. Polls showed that the great bulk of the nation, and particularly women, wholeheartedly backed Diana, blaming Charles for the marriage collapse. When Diana resumed her official duties, the crowds greeting her were bigger, the reception more noisy and enthusiastic. And Diana's smile seemed more winning.

Despite her burden of official royal duties and charity functions, Diana worked out more, her tennis improved, and she swam more energetically and enthusiastically than she had for years. She seemed like a woman in love. The happiness, however, would not last.

5

The Mad Caller

———— ❧ ————

OLIVER HOARE BEGAN TO TIRE of his role. The demands on his time and his life were becoming unbearable and his wife, Diane, insisted that he should end the relationship with Diana. His business suffered a dramatic decline and in 1993 recorded a loss of nearly $1 million. His London gallery also lost money.

The phone calls to Oliver Hoare's $4-million four-story town house in Chelsea increased. They had now become pest calls, the caller saying nothing, waiting for a minute or so and then replacing the receiver. Most calls were taken by Oliver Hoare himself for he would usually answer the phone. There would be no heavy breathing and Oliver would try to persuade the caller to speak. On most occasions his requests were met by silence. Some calls, however, were positively malicious.

On one occasion, late at night in the autumn of 1993, Diane Hoare answered the phone and was startled to hear a woman's voice screaming, "You hard-hearted bitch... you're ruining my life.... Why don't you leave me alone.... Why don't you leave your husband alone.... Why do you behave like a jealous French bitch."

"Who is that? Who is that?" Diane demanded. But her questions were ignored and the phone slammed down. Diane didn't recognize the voice, but she suspected the Princess of Wales.

Diane demanded her husband phone British Telecom and report the malicious calls. Mr. and Mrs. Hoare estimated there had been about three hundred pest calls during a sixteen-month period.

Oliver Hoare wasn't absolutely convinced that all the malicious calls came from Diana. Not only had his business fortunes suffered during the 1990s, but several people in the world of Islamic art were casting doubts about some of Oliver Hoare's business deals. He had also wondered whether he or one of his family might be the target of a terrorist attack or a possible kidnap and ransom demand. Hoare decided that he could take no further chances in case he might be putting his family at risk.

In 1989, Hoare's business came under scrutiny during the trial of a man accused of handling goods stolen from Hoare's Ahuan Gallery during an exhibition. Under cross-examination Hoare admitted that he insured some individual artworks for more than ten times the price he had paid for them. Many in the art world accepted that practice as a sound way to deal with unique pieces of art.

In 1993, Dr. Nasser David Khalili, owner of one of the world's largest private collections of Islamic art, had to return items that he had bought from Hoare, among others, after it was discovered they had been stolen from a Dublin library. No suggestion, however, was ever made that Hoare had acted other than properly.

Oliver Hoare had no option but to accede to his wife's demand to contact British Telecom. In his heart he believed some of the calls could have been instigated by Diana, but he doubted that she had begun making violently abusive phone calls, especially to his wife.

British Telecom installed sophisticated tracker equipment, and the Hoares were given a code to tap into their handset as soon as the nuisance caller came on the line. For two months there was nothing. Early in 1994, however, the calls resumed in earnest.

The first call came at 8:45 A.M. on January 13, the second at 8:49 A.M., and another at 8:49 A.M. There would be three more that day. All were silent. More calls followed until, on January

19, Hoare was shown a list of the numbers from which the calls had been made. One he recognized instantly as Diana's personal number in Kensington Palace, the number he would use to phone her.

British Telecom gave all the information to the police as they do in all such matters. The calls were traced to two phones inside Kensington Palace, Diana's mobile phone, two phone boxes near the palace, and a line at the house of her sister Lady Sarah McCorquodale.

The information was passed to Comdr. Robert Marsh, head of the Royal Protection Squad, who discussed the matter with a senior civil servant at the Home Office, who discreetly informed Buckingham Palace. The matter was handled by Diana's brother-in-law, Sir Robert Fellowes, the Queen's personal secretary. He called Diana to the palace. Nothing is known of that conversation, but the calls ceased forthwith. The police elected not to prosecute. The extraordinary affair was allowed to drop after Oliver and Diane Hoare said they did not wish to take the matter any further.

Journalists who made inquiries to Scotland Yard and Buckingham Palace were told that absolutely no comment would be made about the incident. They were also informed that the matter was now closed and that no action would be taken.

In August 1994, Diana went to Martha's Vineyard in New England for a two-week holiday with friends. She stayed with Lucia Flecha de Lima, an older woman who has been one of Diana's staunchest and most trustworthy friends for many years. Some have suggested that Lucia has become so close to Diana she is her surrogate mother.

Diana and Lucia became friends when Lucia's husband, Paulo, had been his country's ambassador to London. Indeed, when Oliver was trying to persuade Charles and Diana to reconcile their differences, Lucia would allow Diana and Oliver to use her London home for their clandestine meetings. On occasion they would spend hours there together, in private. And Diana found herself depending more and more on the calm, gentle approach of the handsome Oliver.

That August, Diana had a wonderful holiday lazing on the beach, sunning herself, swimming in the ocean waters, and eating and relaxing with friends. Throughout the two weeks not a single paparazzi would be seen.

Dressed in a smart navy blazer and Bermuda shorts, the Princess of Wales returned to London off the British Airways flight from Boston at around five-thirty in the morning of Thursday, August 18, looking rested, suntanned, and happy. Two days later Diana went as usual to her health club for a swim and a workout.

As she emerged and walked to her car, a complete stranger approached.

"Excuse me, ma'am," he said, "I would like to speak to you about nuisance phone calls over a sixteen-month period made to Oliver Hoare, an art dealer."

Diana appeared thunderstruck. "I don't know what you're talking about," she stammered, and walked quickly toward her car, leaving the young man's question unanswered.

The young man was a reporter from Murdoch's sensation-seeking Sunday tabloid the *News of the World*. Fearing the newspaper would reveal her stream of phone calls to Oliver Hoare, she contacted a journalist friend, Richard Kay, the *Daily Mail*'s royal correspondent, and urgently asked to meet him.

They met on Saturday afternoon in leafy Talbot Square, in West London. Diana drove up in her Audi sports car, disguised in a baseball hat pulled well down over her face, and wearing a jacket and jeans. Kay, in jeans and open-necked shirt, waved to Diana, who parked her car opposite his Volvo. He ran over and for twenty minutes they talked in Diana's car. They then moved from her car across the road to his Volvo and drove off. Three hours later they returned, and Kay took Diana to her car and waved goodbye.

During that time Kay phoned the *News of the World* from a public call box to explain that he was speaking on behalf of the Princess of Wales and telling the newspaper there had been a mix-up, that Diana could not possibly have made the malicious phone calls at the times stated because she had been somewhere else.

The following day the *News of the World* reported the story of the malicious phone calls and the fact that suspicion had fallen squarely on Diana. The headline screamed, "Di's Cranky Phone Calls to Married Tycoon."

Her ruse had fooled no one.

That Sunday morning Diana was besieged by newsmen and photographers as she went to play tennis at Chelsea Harbour club. She smiled happily for the cameras. She wore her favorite American-flag sweatshirt, ultrashort light blue shorts, and trainers. Diana appeared not to have a care in the world. She was also wearing dark glasses. Questions were thrown at her by the waiting newsmen, but she said nothing. Every question she met with a confident smile. And as she reached her car, she gave the photographers a one-fingered salute with her middle finger, leaving her hand lingering in the air for a full five seconds.

A worried Oliver Hoare phoned Prince Charles that Sunday morning telling him about the exposé in the newspaper and explaining what had happened. He also reassured Charles that his relationship with Diana had been entirely proper.

Hoare himself said later, "All this speculation is nonsense. There really is nothing to it. I've known both the Prince and Princess of Wales for many years. They are friends and I get on with them both."

When asked if his wife had been concerned by the publicity, he replied, "Not particularly, because she knows the relationship is perfectly friendly."

The denials, however, would not stop the rumors of a romantic relationship between Diana and Oliver.

Diana herself tried desperately to head off the appalling embarrassment of the pest calls, which she knew would make her look irresponsible and childish. She also dreaded what Elizabeth and Prince Philip would think.

Britain's newspaper lonely hearts columnists wrote open letters to Diana, advising her to seek help, talk to a counselor or to call the Samaritans, a nationwide help line, to guide her through the difficulties of working out her life.

They reminded her that isolation and loneliness was the

price she would have to pay for the freedom she had demanded to live separated from her husband and members of the Royal Family.

One wrote, "No matter that you found the rigid, austere lifestyle stifling—or your in-laws cold and unapproachable—for ten years it was all you had and you're still trying to fill that gap."

Another's advice hit home when she wrote, "Naturally you're desperate to form new and close relationships with men and women. But most of all you want to share your life with a loving and supportive partner."

Psychiatrists suggested that Diana had made the calls to the Hoares' house because she was desperately lonely or had been rebuffed and simply wanted to hear the voice of a person she loved and trusted, perhaps someone who had in the recent past provided much warmth and support.

One of Britain's foremost psychiatrists, Dr. Dennis Friedman, commented, "Nuisance callers need to hear a friendly voice over and over again to comfort them in their loneliness. It's like taking a Valium tablet when you are in a panic. It's a comfort. But while a drug like Valium lasts up to five hours, the relief from a phone call may only last thirty minutes. That's why the caller has to repeat it, over and over again. These callers cannot control themselves. It's a compulsion. They often want to stop, and know they should, but they can't because they become addicted to the relief it provides."

Zelda West-Meades, one of Britain's foremost marriage guidance experts, said, "Constantly ringing someone but not being able to speak can be the sign of a very frightened and lonely person longing to make contact but not daring to do so. They are more likely to call someone they feel is loving and caring and who knows what they are going through, someone who has listened to them in the past or who they feel can help them. They may feel they need to talk—but are unable to acknowledge how great their own need is. And worse still, they fear if they do give voice to their emotions, the person they desperately want to talk to will be driven away. This only increases their sense of abandonment and loneliness.

Embarrassed and affronted that she should be labeled a phone pest, Diana believed that she could yet persuade the public to accept her claim that she was innocent of the allegation. She told Richard Kay she had been framed, saying, "What are they trying to do to me? I feel I am being destroyed. There is no truth in it."

And she produced her engagement diary to prove that she was elsewhere at times she was said to have made the calls. She said, "It is true that I have called Oliver Hoare, but not in the way alleged. It's not true that I've made three hundred calls, and I have never stayed silent on the phone."

Painstakingly, Diana then went through her diary to prove, as she put it, that the allegations against her were "a massive lie." She told Kay she was determined to clear herself of the slur.

On January 13, 1994, when it was alleged she made a call in the middle of the day, Diana's diary shows that between 1 P.M. and 3 P.M. she was lunching at Harry's Bar in London with Lady Stevens. The same day she is alleged to have made a call from Kensington Palace at 8:19 P.M. The diary indicates she was at the London home of a titled lady.

On January 15, 1994, she was said to have made a call at 4:55 P.M. Di's diary reports she was at the cinema watching a Clint Eastwood film with a close friend, Catherine Soames. Catherine Soames has said she could confirm the cinema date.

On January 17, Diana was alleged to have made a call at 5:33 P.M. The diary showed she was at Kensington Palace at the time having aromatherapy from Sue Beechey, who also said she could confirm the date.

On January 18, Diana was said to have made two calls from Kensington Palace at 10:41 A.M. and 11:36 A.M. But her diary says she was scheduled to be with hairstylist Paul Galvin between 9:30 A.M. and 11:30 A.M. at his West End salon.

Diana was able to quote many more examples from her diary showing she could not have made the calls that were alleged.

Despite her denials and the evidence she gave proving her

innocence, the great majority of the British public believed that Diana did indeed make those calls. But they forgave her. They thought that she had been driven to make the calls through misery and her fragile emotional state brought about by the collapse of her marriage.

The public accused Charles and other members of the Royal Family for their coldness toward her and a lack of concern for her lonely predicament. The public believed Diana needed help, and yet none appeared to be coming from Charles or the rest of the family. She had been cast adrift and left to care for herself. Women particularly demanded that Diana not be condemned for what she had done but given time and help from specialists to come to terms with her life alone.

Within days of the revelations Diana would read all the papers, particularly the tabloids, learning more about the Hoares than she had ever known. During her four-year affair, Ayesha Nadir would boast to her friends of the most intimate details of her lovemaking with Oliver Hoare. Their affair would become the talk of London, one of the worst-kept secret love affairs.

She would tell her society friends, "Oliver has the most amazing staying power. I call him Marathon Man. He is the most sensational lover. He can go on forever. He is wonderful."

But their affair would end when Ayesha became convinced that Oliver Hoare would never leave his wife, Diane, a strong practicing Roman Catholic. Ayesha would say, "I would sit at home and cry over him. In the end I couldn't take it anymore so I finished the affair."

That year, 1989, Ayesha was granted a second divorce from her multimillionaire husband, Asil Nadir, the boss of Polly Peck, which was then one of Britain's fastest-growing conglomerates. It was understood she received a $30-million settlement. The deal included an eighteenth century villa on the banks of the Bosporus near Istanbul, which had been lavishly restored. Ayesha returned to her native Turkey and reverted to her maiden name, Tecimer.

Diana and Oliver Hoare continued to see each other, but the

drama over the phone calls seemed to take the edge off their relationship.

Diana threw herself into keeping fit, playing tennis harder, swimming longer and stronger, and working out with more determination than ever. After such exertions she would feel better, believing the effort had somehow improved her mind and reinvigorated her body. But the anger remained.

6

Princess in Love: Diana and the Captain of the Guards

———— ✦ ————

SOME TWELVE MONTHS after Prince Harry's birth in 1984, Diana wondered how she would ever escape from the strait-jacket of her royal marriage. Her misery and loneliness only added to her desperate thoughts as she battled to recover from the awful postnatal blues that had left her feeling "absolutely bloody awful nearly all the time."

This time, however, the blues seemed much worse. She felt Charles had drawn away from her, not kissing or cuddling, paying less attention and spending weeks away at Highgrove, his country home one hundred miles from Kensington Palace.

Diana told some friends how she awoke in a cold sweat one night in the autumn of 1986 and suddenly realized that Charles was having an affair. "It was pure instinct, a woman's instinct," she said. "It was cold and dark and Charles hadn't shared a bed with me for weeks. He had barely touched me. I knew in that instant that he was having an affair, and I also knew the woman must be Camilla."

During the following weeks Diana would often cry herself to sleep at night and her bulimia escalated. Rarely a day would pass without her raiding the larder and the refrigerator before making herself ill, sometimes bingeing and vomiting four and five times a day. Almost with a feeling of righteousness, she would eliminate what had given her self-indulgent pleasure. She hated what she was doing but could not stop herself, for the eating disorder made her feel better. And when she realized the bulimia had taken a firm grip on her everyday life, she felt too ashamed, too frightened, to ask anyone for help.

At first, she would seek reassurance from Charles that he was not having an affair, and he would tell her not to be so silly. He would reassure her that he only stayed at Highgrove to escape the rigors of too much family pressure. Highgrove gave him a peace of mind that he couldn't find in London. Diana tried to believe him, but the more distant he remained the more she instinctively knew that he was lying. He was staying at Highgrove because of Camilla.

About this time a dashing cavalry officer, resplendent in the uniform of a captain in the Life Guards, that most royal of all the sovereign's regiments, rode into Diana's life. His name was Capt. James Hewitt.

They met in London in the summer of 1986 at a party where Hewitt was formally introduced. During their chat Hewitt offered to help Diana overcome her fear of horse riding, something that Charles had tried and failed to carry out years before.

After their first few riding lessons, Hewitt and Diana, who were about the same age, were having coffee one morning in the deserted officers' mess at Knightsbridge Barracks in central London, half a mile from Kensington Palace. Diana desperately needed someone to pay her attention. She wondered whether the smooth-talking polo player could be that man.

Realizing Diana's needs, Hewitt gave her the attention she craved. He would later provide the passion Diana realized she had never really enjoyed with any other man, not even Charles.

Their affair began shortly afterward. Diana loved Hewitt's kind and tender ways, and how he seemed to anticipate her every need. They would spend nights together at Kensington Palace, at Highgrove, at Althorp, her family's stately home, and at Hewitt's mother's cottage in Devon. There, they would push two single beds together and make love through the night while Diana's personal detective slept in the adjoining room.

For three years the passion, which Diana had missed all her life, continued, though the amount of time they could spend together would be limited by the demands on both their lives and the fact that Diana was still married to the Prince of Wales. Hewitt was a serving officer, and Diana not only had two growing boys to care for but was also taking on more royal duties. Her charity work had escalated at an extraordinary pace as the British public took her to their hearts and her popularity soared. Charities queued for her patronage.

Meanwhile, Hewitt's regiment would be posted to Germany and months would pass when they would not see each other. They would write and call, but Diana began to realize Hewitt would never become a permanent part of her life.

At first Diana had loved spoiling Hewitt, who she knew had no real wealth but survived on his Army pay. She would buy him Savile Row suits costing $2,500, Jermyn Street shirts priced at $125 each, shoes at $1,000 a pair. In return Hewitt gave the Princess of Wales one of his old cricket sweaters and a $50 Puffa jacket to keep her warm in winter.

Diana did find herself fretting when Hewitt was dispatched to Saudi Arabia to take an active role in Operation Desert Storm. The fact that her lover was fighting in a real war added a piquancy to her passion, instilling a feeling of intense nervousness, tinged with pleasure.

On his return, Hewitt realized that Diana had cooled and that their affair was about to end. He tried to resurrect the passion, but Diana had decided that Capt. James Hewitt would not be the man to rescue her from her marriage and become her lifelong companion.

She considered he hadn't the strength of character she needed to support her, nor intellect enough to keep her happy, nor the courage to woo and win the Prince of Wales's wife. She had never been sure whether Hewitt's protestations of love had been entirely genuine, whether he really loved Diana for herself or whether he took pleasure in the affair because it bolstered his vanity that he was bedding the Princess of Wales. In her heart Diana feared it was the latter.

She recalled that on one occasion a desperate Hewitt had asked a tabloid newsman reporting the Gulf War if he could borrow his mobile phone to call the Princess of Wales. And Hewitt then carried on a conversation with Diana for three minutes while newsmen around him listened. She read about it in one of the tabloids. She wondered at the time how the man she loved could be so stupid.

She remembered Hewitt cracking jokes about making love to the future Queen of England, which made him appear vain, shallow, and insensitive. Diana was anxious that perhaps the love she had felt for Hewitt had been one-sided, but she felt she could trust the word of an officer and a gentleman. She would take comfort in the Guard's motto, *Honi soit qui mal y pense* (Shame to him that thinks ill).

Throughout their affair Queen Elizabeth had been made aware of Diana's adultery with Hewitt. Senior officers of the Royal Protection Squad informed her private secretary, Sir Robert Fellowes about what was taking place. It seems extraordinary that Diana did not realize that such actions on her part would have to be reported to higher authority.

"I hope that girl knows what she is doing," Elizabeth said. "I hope she understands that she is the wife to the heir to the throne and that she is committing adultery."

And yet Elizabeth did not warn Diana or ask anyone, either her advisers or her bodyguards, to query the princess about her adulterous affair.

Years later, some would wonder why Elizabeth hadn't intervened, why she hadn't had a quiet word with Diana, advising her, as her mother-in-law, in her capacity as the Queen, head of the Royal Family, that she was playing a most dangerous game. But that is not Elizabeth's way. She has never intervened directly in any of the love affairs of her three sons or her daughter, Anne. She believes that their private lives are their own business to sort out for themselves. She also believes that they must take the consequences for their actions.

Naively, Diana believed she could trust her personal bodyguards, Insp. Ken Wharfe and Sgt. Alan Peters. She did not seem to realize that it would have been an offense punishable by instant dismissal if they had not kept senior officers informed of all Diana's movements including the people, both men and women, she met privately and in secret. She was not permitted to leave Kensington Palace without an armed bodyguard at her side. With an IRA action against the Royal Family always possible, members of the Royal Protection Squad were never permitted to forget that the IRA had assassinated Earl Mountbatten and half his family when they blew up his fishing smack in Northern Ireland in August 1979. They could strike at any time. There was also the constant fear of a terrorist attack against the world's most celebrated royal family.

And the possibility of blackmail could never be discounted. Diana would have been placed in an impossible situation if some blackmailer had seen her or taken photographs of her during her trysts with James Hewitt.

Diana discovered that ending the relationship with Hewitt would be far easier and less complicated than she believed possible. She had made up her mind after the war in the Gulf that the relationship should end, for she found herself losing respect for him. He was always nice to her, expecting presents in return, and would flatter her with his protestations of love. Diana suggested that perhaps they should see less of each other, explaining that she had "to sort out many of the problems" in her life. It seemed to Diana that Hewitt had expected the rejection and took it rather nonchalantly. She asked that he return the letters she had sent him during the Gulf War and on other occasions. He told her that he wanted to keep them as a memento of their love for each other. Reluctantly, Diana agreed. As she drove away that day, she wondered whether she had been sensible in leaving such incriminating evidence to Hewitt's safekeeping.

Hewitt would twice fail the exam to become a major in the Guards, exams that are not difficult and that he should have passed with ease. He knew that by failing those exams his future in the British Army was virtually at an end, for there was no need for officers incapable of passing them.

Three years after their affair ended, Diana heard rumors that James Hewitt was visiting tabloid offices trying to sell the story of his affair with Diana for $1 million. She heard that he boasted to editors that the story he could write would include explicit sexual details of his romance with Diana, including a claim they had made love in Diana's bedroom with a photo of Prince Charles by the bed, that he had given Princess Diana her first orgasm, and that Diana had said making love to Charles had been a duty but with Hewitt it was pleasure.

In September 1994, Diana learned that a book, *Princess in Love* was about to be published revealing intimate details of the affair. The thought that Hewitt might reveal all their private moments together sent shivers through her. She could not believe that the man she had loved and to whom she had given so much of herself could possibly have anything to do with such a book. Ten days before *Princess in Love* was published, Hewitt phoned Diana at Kensington Palace to tell her not to worry for there was nothing of substance in it. Unfortunately, Diana had misjudged Hewitt and he had deliberately lied to her.

She feared the letters she had written to him would make it impossible for her to deny the allegation and she would be branded an adulteress. Diana tried one last time to persuade Hewitt not to publish the book, which she was convinced would ruin her in the eyes of the British public. Toward the end of September she contacted him by telephone and asked to see him, but he refused to do so.

They did in fact meet and Diana tried again to persuade him not to publish his book. Later, Hewitt boasted how, in tears, Diana had begged him not to publish, telling him, "My God, if you go ahead with this book, it's going to kill me."

Hewitt confided that he had been so shocked by Diana's reaction that he had seriously considered scrapping the book because he didn't want to upset her. Allegedly, Hewitt told others that Diana knew all about *Princess in Love* and approved.

Diana read the newspapers over the days leading up to publication with growing anxiety and fear. There were hints that *Princess in Love* would shock the nation, suggestions that

Capt. James Hewitt, the man whom four years previously this author had revealed to be Diana's lover, in my book *Diana: A Princess and Her Troubled Marriage,* would tell the world that he and the Princess of Wales had enjoyed a long, passionate affair.

Pictures of Diana in those days immediately prior to publication show her distraught, her lips pursed, her face distorted in anguish, not waving to anyone or looking at the cameras that tracked every move she made whenever she left the protection of her home.

In the privacy of her palace apartment Diana wondered why the phone didn't ring. With all the speculation she expected a call from Prince Charles or the Queen or her brother-in-law Sir Robert Fellowes demanding to know the truth about an alleged affair that had started years before. But the phone stayed silent, driving Diana into bouts of tears and terror, for she realized *Princess in Love* would brand her an adulteress. Worse still, she worried what her sons would think and what possible harm her ex-lover's revelations might cause them. She also feared for herself and her future.

During those days and nights Diana cursed herself for having been so stupid, for having been involved in a love affair that she now understood would mean nothing to her. The more she examined her reasoning the more foolish she realized she had been in trusting such a man as James Hewitt. And yet she knew why, for Diana would later say, "I adored James. I loved him very much."

"Why? Why? Why?" she kept repeating over and over when discussing the matter with one of her closest girlfriends.

Days later, in October 1994, *Princess in Love* hit the bookstores throughout Britain. It caused a sensation and the public flocked to buy it, the first seventy-five thousand copies selling out within twenty-four hours. The book had been written by Anna Pasternak, twenty-seven, a freelance journalist and friend of Hewitt's and a great-niece of the Nobel Prize–winning Russian author Boris Pasternak.

Revelations in the book stopped short of the bedroom. *Princess in Love* includes much talk of love and passion but none of actual lovemaking. According to Anna Pasternak, the book was based on her conversations with Hewitt, who she said had shown her some letters from Princess Diana. It was written in the third person under Anna Pasternak's name.

Literary critics tore the book to shreds. Susannah Herbert, the arts correspondent of the conservative *Daily Telegraph* commented, "From the first thrill of the lovers' meeting to the last gasp of their final embrace *Princess in Love* is a squirm-inducing embarrassment."

Scathingly, she continued, "The author's fondness for slushy clichés...would be hilarious were it not for the humbug in which both Miss Pasternak and Captain Hewitt cloak their distinctly unromantic motives for producing this book."

In an editorial the *Daily Telegraph* noted bitingly, "Even in an age in which Mr. Rupert Murdoch and his imitators have reduced every moral property to sale goods, the spectacle of a former Guards officer selling for cash his claims to have enjoyed an intimate relationship with the Princess still commands revulsion."

In the book Hewitt claimed Diana told him, "I want to marry you and have your baby." He also claimed that Diana was about to leave Charles and settle down with him. Lurid scenes that took place in a bathroom, a summer house, on Dartmoor, and in a procession of beds were detailed. And the book was dotted with florid images when Hewitt recounted the most intimate occasions: "Di led me trembling to her bed"; "Diana fell into my arms in the bathroom and said, 'I need you; I want you now.'" Yet another passage read, "Diana whispered, 'Now no one will come.' The thrill was in being locked together so near five hundred party guests."

The furor that greeted *Princess in Love* had never before been witnessed for any other royal book and most of the vitriol was aimed squarely at James Hewitt. He was variously described as "a cad," "a bounder," and "vermin."

Members of Parliament, both Conservative and Labour, condemned the former Guards officer who had resigned from the regiment some months earlier with a $60,000 severance payment and a $9,000-a-year captain's pension. "Off with his bits [meaning testicles]," demanded one MP, while many accused Hewitt of treason.

One MP suggested that Hewitt should be executed in public, others that he should be flogged, and some thought he should be made to walk the plank. Diana was called on to sue Hewitt for libel. But she did not.

The debate over what quickly became known as "the Hewitt book" remained mostly one-sided with the former Guard officer taking flak from all quarters. Captain Hewitt was castigated because he had been a professional soldier, educated at Millfield, one of England's foremost public schools, and privileged to serve in the Life Guards, the sovereign's own troops. By his education, so the argument ran, he should have acquired a sense of honor, of decency, of what is done and not done by a gentleman who cares about his reputation and those of others. Many suggested scathingly that Hewitt was so dim that he probably didn't know how an officer and a gentleman should behave.

This slur was compounded by the author herself, Anna Pasternak, in ruling out any possibility of her having an affair with Hewitt. She commented bluntly, "He is far too thick. You insult me if you suggest I would have an affair with him."

Overnight, Hewitt became an outcast. Within hours Hewitt's name was "posted on the gate," the Life Guards' expression for banning someone from their midst. There was no public posting of his name, but from that moment Hewitt had been declared persona non grata not simply among the Guards regiments but in all military circles. The reason: he had broken his honor and that of his regiment, something that would never be forgotten by the Life Guards or the Household Cavalry. He was deemed to have gone beyond the pale.

There would be more. He was made "not welcome" (a polite euphemism for being banned) at the Cavalry and Guards Club in London's Piccadilly; he was officially banned from ever again attending the Cavalry Memorial Parade; he was advised never to return to the officers' mess at Knightsbridge Barracks, one of his favorite haunts; was banned from attending the Life Guards Officers' Club annual dinner at The Savoy; and advised not to visit the Turf Club tent at Cheltenham racing festivals.

All these actions were saber thrusts into Hewitt's personal life. For fifteen years he had been most welcome at all these events, accepted as a brother officer. One of his close friends in the Life Guards commented, "We understand that he made at least four hundred thousand dollars from that damn book. He should at the very least have gone into self-imposed exile for a year to indicate some remorse or regret at what he had done. That he did nothing of the sort has gone down badly among those of us who already consider he let the side down."

Residents of Hewitt's tiny country village, Topsham in Devon, rich in antique shops and "olde-worlde" tearooms two miles from his home, were flabbergasted by Hewitt's betrayal of the Princess of Wales, whom they all adored. Many described him as "a rat."

He was banned from his favorite restaurant and wine bar, Denleys in the High Street, banned from shopping in some of the local stores, and banned from the pubs. As one regular at the Tavistock Inn at Poundsgate put it, "If he dares show his face in here, I'll kick him straight out again with my boot up his arse."

And sensibly Hewitt stayed away from his local hunt, the South Devon, with whom he used to ride two or three times a week, after it was pointed out that two local landowners had said the hunt would be banned from their land if Hewitt rejoined it.

Others, however, had little or no sympathy for Diana. Richard Littlejohn, a columnist in Murdoch's *Sun* tabloid, wrote, "Diana is the scheming little shrew who had no qualms about betraying her husband in another project so she can hardly bleat when her ex-lover dishes the dirt.... At least the Hewitt revelations have exposed Diana's carefully-honed Mother Teresa act as a complete sham.... And if Diana thinks Hewitt shouldn't make money out of his relationship with her, then it's about time she stopped living off a man whom she quite clearly despises."

Three days later, on October 8, 1994, Diana awoke, pulled on her white toweling robe, and walked swiftly through to the drawing room in Kensington Palace where she knew the morning newspapers would be neatly arranged. She flicked quickly through them, glancing at the front pages, but saw nothing to alarm her. Then she began to scan them more carefully, for she had become desperate to know the nation's reaction to the book and to her adultery.

Suddenly, the air was rent with a great whoop of joy as Diana read the headline in the *Daily Mirror:* "We Don't Blame You, Diana," it proclaimed.

She then read the accompanying story eagerly, smiling throughout. The article read, "She may have been unfaithful to her husband. . . . But the verdict of *Mirror* readers is loud and clear: Diana, we still back you. . . . Most of our readers see Diana as a woman driven into the arms of another by a cold and unfeeling husband."

The *Mirror* poll revealed that 27 percent of its readers blamed Diana for having an affair with Hewitt while 73 percent did not. Only 15 percent thought less of Diana after her affair while 85 percent said it made no difference. However, only 39 percent thought Diana should have left Prince Charles for Hewitt but 61 percent did not.

Still, the majority of the nation seemed to blame Charles for the marriage breakdown. The poll revealed that 81 percent thought Charles had driven Diana into the arms of another man; 61 percent thought Charles and Diana should divorce immediately; and a remarkable 73 percent thought that Queen Elizabeth II should be the last British monarch.

Later that day Elizabeth's attention would be drawn to the same article. She was far from amused. She had given her entire life's work to the promise that she had made to her father, King George VI, before his death in 1952—to preserve the monarchy and secure the future of the Royal House of Windsor. Now it seemed that thanks to the stupidity of her daughter-in-law Diana, all her life's work had been put in jeopardy. Elizabeth could hardly contain her anger that day as she kept seeing the figures before her. The British public had turned its back on constitutional monarchy and wanted the House of Windsor to crumble on her deathbed. The idea filled her with sadness and remorse.

The report also meant that any residual affection or compassion that Elizabeth had felt toward Diana over the breakdown of her marriage to Charles had evaporated. "Stupid, stupid girl," Elizabeth would repeat time and again. "Stupid girl."

The revelations made Elizabeth believe that the final act in Charles's marriage to Diana could not be far off. They had officially separated in December 1992, which, according to British laws, meant they could divorce without any legal problems once they had been living apart for two years. To all intents and purposes, theirs had not been a proper marriage for many more years than that. Elizabeth understood that Charles and Diana had hardly shared a bed since 1985.

Perhaps, Elizabeth mused, the time was fast approaching when Charles should take steps legally to end the marriage. Until Hewitt's book, Diana had been able to occupy the moral high ground following Prince Charles's TV confession to author Jonathan Dimbleby that he had been guilty of adultery. Now the balance in the game played by Charles and Diana seemed to have shifted in favor of Charles. No longer would Diana be able to use the Prince's confession of adultery to put pressure on the Queen to secure favorable terms.

Officially, the only comment from Diana would be, "The Princess is extremely upset by the book's account of her friendship with Mr. Hewitt. It is simply not true that we ever had sex. He wanted to, but I never let it happen. He lives in a fantasy world."

A Buckingham Palace press officer commented with the full authority of the Queen, "This is nothing but a grubby and worthless little book." He added that Buckingham Palace would not take any legal action.

The palace also insisted the book would have no bearing on Diana's renewed round of public engagements. Diana read that announcement in the morning papers, relieved that she had at last received some support from the palace. For months the courtiers had ignored her, letting her carry on with her life without any intrusion, or even acknowledgment that she was part of the Royal Family and the mother of the two princes.

The tabloids, of course, enjoyed a field day. While panning the book on the one hand, they would run numerous articles about its contents, revealing many of the intimate details as well as throwing as much mud as possible at the "rat" Hewitt. They would also track down former girlfriends of Hewitt's and discover he had been a cad on more than one previous occasion. It seemed his appeal, besides his being an "officer and a gentleman," was his physical qualities. All agreed that Capt. James Hewitt was a very well endowed young man.

Anna Pasternak would later explain her motives in writing the controversial book that had so devastated Diana. She claimed that she had resolved to write a book about Hewitt's love affair with Diana on June 29, 1994, the night Prince Charles admitted in a television interview that he had been unfaithful with Camilla Parker Bowles. Ms. Pasternak said she had been appalled at the revelation. Earlier that year she had interviewed Mr. Hewitt about his friendship with the Princess for a slightly anodyne series of interviews for the *Daily Express*. Mr. Hewitt, whom she knew to be retiring from the Army, had been paid $60,000 for the series.

After Prince Charles's announcement, Ms. Pasternak said she persuaded Hewitt to cooperate with her on a book she would write. She told him, "At the end of the day the public will respect the truth. They condemn you because they don't know the truth about how you stood by this woman through the most traumatic time of her life and her marriage."

Ms. Pasternak commented, "My motives have only ever been to try and set the record straight for both of them. I am a great fan of the Princess of Wales. I think she has had a tremendously difficult time, and this is very much a book of a woman's journey to find herself, as it were, through adversity."

She went on, "Hewitt is a very lonely, very sad man who has lost everything. He has only ever wanted the best for her. I just feel that if the public could really see the true story; if they could try to understand that really he risked his life to be with this woman, who had such a tremendous need and put that need on him, and he was able to fulfill it, then perhaps they would not judge him with such a harsh tone."

Most critics were unconvinced by the reasoning, some describing her argument as "bunkum." Other critics con-. demned the book, written in the style of a romantic novel, as "clogging, nauseating and overblown."

Hewitt was hounded by Fleet Street tabloid journalists and photographers who trailed him across England and France. He was finally captured on film emerging from a French pigsty on a farm where he had stayed the night, fearful of being obliged to face the awesome pack of newspaper reporters scenting blood.

The Hewitt fiasco made Diana feel less secure than ever. She realized she had made a cardinal error of judgment, but she also understood that she had to take some of the blame herself. After all, she had encouraged their affair and had thoroughly enjoyed their time together, all of which helped her to forget Charles and her marriage, which had become a hell on earth.

After the weeklong uproar and newspaper headlines that detailed the most intimate and embarrassing moments of Diana's grand passion with Hewitt, Diana wanted nothing more than to go to bed and stay there, out of the limelight. And she did just that. She called close, trusted friends on her beloved telephone, but always from the safety of her sitting room or bedroom. With some of the younger ones, such as her friend of many years Kate Menzies, she managed to laugh at her embarrassment and some of the revelations in the book. Diana would say, "Please don't tease me. I feel so awful. I keep asking myself how I could have done such things with such an awful creep. Everything I've read makes me want to curl up and die. I am so embarrassed."

One of her girlfriends, determined that Diana see the funny side of the affair, asked her, "But did you enjoy yourself, you dirty stop out?" (An English phrase meaning that a girl stayed overnight at a man's apartment for sex.)

Diana would shriek and put her hand over her face to hide the blushes. Diana would say, "I couldn't have done all those things that were in the book, could I? It's just not me to behave like that, is it?"— all but demanding that the person she was talking to take her side.

"We never knew you had it in you," some teased her, and Diana would giggle and laugh and blush, but never reply.

Others told her bluntly, "God, after all you had been through with Charles, we don't blame you one bit going for whatever you could get. It must have been terrible. All we hope is that you bloody well enjoyed yourself. You deserved it."

Diana, however, would keep the secrets of what had occurred in bed, for the book had stopped at the bedroom door. Hewitt, however, would later tell friends of Diana's sexual secrets. He would relate how she would cling to him in bed, never wanting him to let go, demanding they make love time and again so they could stay together. He would describe how Diana would talk about her sex life with Charles; how awful and boring it had been; how she had never achieved the heights of passion with Charles that she experienced with Hewitt. And she would reveal all these intimate details while she was actually making love to Hewitt. It would seem to Hewitt that Diana achieved pleasure from revealing those marital secrets of her lovemaking with Charles while having sex with Hewitt, for it would drive her to ever greater and more intense pleasure.

There would be a more serious, far more concerned attitude to the issues provoked by Diana's fling. Once again the old chestnut of republicanism became the talk at society, political, and Establishment dinner tables, though some pointed out mischievously that if marital infidelity toppled English Royals, the institution would have disappeared years ago.

Historians recalled that before Queen Victoria came to the throne to clean up the Royal Family act, her Regency uncles had mistresses and bastards stretching to the horizon, and no one thought them any the worse for doing so. And a number of their wives took lovers to entertain them in their boredom. Such royal shenanigans were the talk of the coffeehouses and filled the papers of the time, revealing intimate details of royal lovers and mistresses and the games they played.

Most, however, argued that the notion of republicanism remains in Britain an eccentric diversion because all the country's leading politicians realize that tinkering with the monarchy would spell electoral catastrophe. While the nation argued, Diana calmed down and put her misdemeanor in perspective.

In late October 1994, when she finally summoned up the courage to make her first public appearance following the Hewitt scandal, Diana found the crowds cheering and shouting for her as if nothing had happened. When she returned home that evening, she told her butler, Harold Brown, thirty-seven, who had been with her for ten years, "Well, no one threw any rotten eggs."

"I didn't think they would, ma'am," he replied. Diana had survived another disastrous love affair with her reputation barely dented. But it had been close.

7

A Prince's Betrayal

———— ❧ ————

EVER SINCE CHARLES WALKED OUT on her and the two princes back in 1988, not a single day has passed without Diana feeling something of the pain, humiliation, and anger she felt at that moment. She can never forgive that Charles had lied to her throughout those years when he was virtually living with his mistress, Camilla Parker Bowles, at Highgrove in Gloucestershire, telling Diana that he resided alone in the country for the peace and tranquillity it gave him.

Diana had trusted Charles absolutely, given her heart and her soul to him, the only man in her life, other than her father, in whom she had put her faith. To this day she has never found anyone else whom she has been able to trust in the same way, and she fears that now she never will. In Charles, Diana found her prince who could do no wrong and who would always behave, so she believed, in the most correct, gentlemanly, and respectful manner.

Even today some minor occurrence will bring Diana's thoughts crashing back to the realization that Charles had left her and the boys to fend for themselves, alone. During the 1995 summer holidays, before Will went to Eton College, Diana, Will, and Harry were leaving Kensington Palace to go to the cinema. She realized, in a ghastly moment of fear, that she had ordered three seats to be reserved and yet she had wanted to ask for four.

"I went into a state of shock," Diana recalled. "I had to go back to my room, telling the boys I had left something there. I was shaking, physically shaking. They could tell something was wrong, but sensibly they said nothing. I pretended to search my bedroom for something I had left behind, but my legs became weak and I felt I would faint. It was awful, so awful."

Diana told all this to one of her older men friends who had been trying to help her come to terms with the separation and her life of loneliness. On that occasion Diana had managed to pull herself together, take a drink of cold water, and rejoin the boys, thankful they were going to a darkened theater where she could try to sort herself out before returning home.

Diana's friend explained to me, "That was typical of the way in which the breakup still affects Diana, and yet she has had more than seven years to accept what has happened. Today, she still finds it all but impossible to forget those dark hours when she realized she had lost Charles's love, when she didn't know whether she wanted to live or to die."

On another occasion on the M4 motorway in the summer of 1994, Diana was driving her Audi sports car with Wills and Harry in the backseat. She found herself following a Range Rover with a father, mother, and two boys in the vehicle. She followed the car for more than twenty miles watching the family and thinking that Charles should have been with her and the boys, rather than spending his time with his mistress.

After that occasion, Diana would tell her mentor, "I kept telling myself I must overtake the Range Rover and put such thoughts behind me. But I couldn't bring myself to overtake the car. I felt that if I overtook the car my problems would just be left behind, that I could forget about Charles and Camilla and the breakup, yet I continued to drive immediately behind them, thinking, fantasizing all the time of what life should have been with Charles, me, and the boys. I felt mesmerized, unable to concentrate on anything but Charles and the bitch, Camilla. I could see them in my mind's eye kissing, making love, having a meal together, going for walks together, riding out together, listening to music together, doing everything together while I was alone with the boys taking them to school. I drove along with the tears welling in my eyes. But my heart was full of anger and hatred."

Experiences like that cause Diana to feel she cannot forgive Charles for what he has done to her and the boys, leaving them to cope as best they can without him.

She has never forgiven Charles for announcing to the world in his TV interview that he had never loved her. That upset and hurt Diana deeply, far more than anything else in the two-hour program. She wasn't upset for herself but for Wills and Harry. She has commented, "How could he say something like that? Didn't he realize that was something terrible for the boys to hear about the relationship between their father and mother? Making that statement showed what a selfish prig Charles has become, as though nothing in the world matters, except his feelings—not his wife, his children, or any of their memories. I could gladly have scratched his eyes out for announcing that to the world, knowing the boys would read about it later. For that one statement I will never, never forgive him."

Diana always hated the fact that Wills, in particular, had learned of his father's goings-on by reading the occasional newspaper smuggled into school. The boys had been put through the mill far too often in their young lives having to read in newspapers of their parents' breakup, their father's goings-on, and later his confession of adultery.

The boys seem to have accepted that their parents have separated, that there is no going back to a full family life. Diana is fully aware that she is the one who has been unable to come to terms with her loneliness and life without a caring man. Diana readily accepts that she had been far too young and inexperienced to marry.

It was not surprising she would tell her elder confidant, "I had no role model. I could never remember my father and mother living together as man and wife. I had no memory of them kissing or showing any affection for each other. Mother had gone before I realized what was happening. When Charles proposed to me, I felt I was in a dream, that for the first time in my life I would learn what true love could be like. I think my father loved me, loved all of us, but he was not an affectionate or tactile man. He couldn't be. I wonder if he ever knew real affection. As far as Mother is concerned, I don't know. I've never known. She left me. That's all I can ever remember. Deep down I believe that I have probably never forgiven her for walking out on us all. With Charles I expected everything to change and life would be nothing but wonderful. I thought I knew what marriage was all about. In reality, I knew absolutely nothing."

And no one took Diana to one side and gave her a foretaste, or even any information of what to expect. She had been given no sexual advice, though she had made herself read a couple of books outlining the basics, of which she knew very little when she began dating Charles. Diana had only kissed and hugged a couple of boyfriends before she first dated Charles. She was a virgin, a girl who had never dated seriously and, at eighteen, still felt shy and embarrassed in the presence of young men.

She told her friend, "Sometimes, even today, after everything that has happened, I will laugh at my naivety at that time. I had no experience whatsoever, hardly any passionate kisses even, let alone anything else. I was eighteen years of age and very, very young for my age, an innocent. I would keep thinking that some girls had had a couple of babies by the time they were my age and knew far more about sex and life than I ever did."

Diana would read newspaper stories claiming that she and Charles had not enjoyed their honeymoon together because of his approach to sex. "Rubbish, all rubbish," she would say. "They simply didn't know that Charles and I had enjoyed the most wonderful time together during our six-month engagement when I spent nearly every night sharing his bed in Buckingham Palace. I was innocent but it didn't matter. I felt I was on cloud nine simply because I was in the arms of the man I adored and that I believed loved me. It was truly wonderful and I believed that feeling would continue forever."

Today, Diana sometimes blames herself for expecting far too

much of Charles and, also, of marriage. But then, in an instant, her mood will change, her eyes will flash, and she will find herself in a cold rage simply thinking of the deceitful way Charles behaved toward her when she needed him so much. She now accepts that she knew nothing of what to expect from a royal marriage, especially a marriage to the future king. She didn't really expect that he would have to spend so much time away, inspecting troops and factories, making speeches day and night, chairing meetings about a hundred different matters, and welcoming strange heads of state she had never heard of from foreign countries she never knew existed.

"I just couldn't cope," she would say. "I couldn't understand what was happening and didn't want to understand. I didn't trust anyone, except for Charles. I thought everyone was against me—all Charles's highly intelligent staff and his personal friends. I thought they didn't like me, that they didn't respect me because of my intelligence and my awful education. I felt so vulnerable, so lost."

Diana would be criticized by senior palace aides for seeking out the domestics, the cooks and the cleaners, the secretaries and the footmen, to chat to, people who she felt would want her to be their friend. From some she would even ask advice. At first, these were the only people she felt at ease with, whom she could talk to freely without being made to feel inferior and uneducated.

A few months after her wedding Diana received a rude shock. She had wandered into the kitchens at Balmoral to chat to the staff, smiling broadly and saying hello to everyone, happy to be among people she felt respected her as a friend. One of the senior butlers walked up to Diana, looking most serious.

He asked, "Can I have a word please, ma'am [pronounced "marm" as in *marmalade*]?

"Of course," Diana replied.

"I must warn you to stop coming into the kitchens. The staff do not like it, none of us do."

Diana was taken aback, startled, by the tone of his voice and the dressing-down he was giving her.

He continued, "You must understand, ma'am, that there are us and them. You are a Royal, one of them, and we should never mix. We don't want to mix with your lot, ever. We know our place and we expect you to know yours. I am afraid I must ban you from ever visiting the kitchens again."

Dumbfounded and forlorn, Diana turned on her heel and walked away, totally taken aback, tears in her eyes. She had believed they welcomed her friendly face in the kitchens, not dreaming for a moment she would not be welcome, for she had never understood the concept of being a Royal. But she had learned a lesson. And she vowed never to return to a royal kitchen until she had a house of her own.

Later she would say, "That was so painful. I had never looked at it like that. I thought they liked me popping into the kitchens for a chat. I felt desolate after being ticked off. Suddenly I felt even more lonely than before. But I understood they were right. That was their world and I had invaded it."

Diana told one of Charles's confidants with whom she had developed a good understanding in those early days, "No one talks to me. I stand around at every official gathering not knowing what to do, what to say, or where to look, worried that I might be doing something wrong. When people do speak to me, they seem to treat me like some schoolgirl, asking me how I am. I feel like a fish out of water all the time and can't wait for the whole thing to finish so I can go back to the apartment."

Charles's former Royal Navy colleague Michael Colborne would become Diana's secretary, but more importantly Diana would come to treat him as her "unofficial uncle," and they would become close friends. Twenty-five years older than Diana, he would become her principal adviser for the next three years, explaining the thousand and one different matters she would need to know about the Royal Family, the monarchy, and the way she would have to conduct herself.

Except for Colborne, there were few others Diana would ever trust. She believed that most of Charles's former aides didn't like the fact that their cozy little all-male world had been shattered by her arrival. They hoped everything would continue as before, with all-male meetings most mornings, polo or hunting in the afternoons, and quiet, reflective chats and drinks in the evening before dinner. And Lady Susan Hussey, one of the Queen's ladies-in-waiting, would phone offering help and advice, but Diana became suspicious of her and everyone else at the palace and found it impossible to seek their counsel. Eventually, the phone stopped ringing.

Later she would tell one of her girlfriends from her bachelor days of the problems she had had with Charles's staff: "They would never let me see Charles alone. They would keep him closeted in meetings as though I had no call on his time whatsoever, expecting me to stay in the background, the little woman whose duty was to be seen occasionally but certainly not heard. Most of them didn't like me around, and they hated it if I ever had the audacity to interrupt one of their cozy meetings. When I would pop into the room where they were chatting with Charles, all men together, they would look at me as though I was something the cat had brought in. They were really awfully rude to treat me like that. Unfortunately Charles never seemed to notice, though I did tell him how they treated me. He would just tell me that they all loved me, admired me, and that I was imagining things. That was why they had to go. If I hadn't made a fuss, I don't think I would have ever seen Charles."

Diana would have a particularly bitter experience with one of Charles's most experienced advisers, a man she knew to be gay. She said, "He told me when I first became pregnant with William that I could now be proud of myself, that I had done my duty by the crown and that I should be thrilled that I had been privileged to carry the child of the Prince of Wales. It seemed to me at the time that after giving birth he would have preferred for me to disappear into the nursery and only come out again if another child was required. "On that occasion I went to my room and wept, feeling that I wasn't wanted at all. I remember wondering whether Charles felt that way towards me. It frightened me."

Diana would later be accused of getting rid of all Charles's former aides and old friends. During the first four years of their marriage a remarkable number, forty or so of them, resigned, quit, or were fired. Diana always refused to accept that she deliberately went out of her way to have them dismissed or to make their lives so miserable and awkward that they had no recourse but to leave.

Challenged about that now, Diana will say, "I think that's a little far-fetched. Some simply left because the scene changed; Charles was no longer a bachelor."

However, with an impish twinkle in her eye and a wry smile she will admit, "I may have had something to do with some of the departures, but not all of them. Some of them were just hangers-on and others wanted to stifle both Charles and myself. I think Charles would admit that some had passed their sell-by date."

Diana had hoped that the arrival of William, a male heir to the throne, would win the hearts of Charles and the entire Royal Family, for many jokes had been made about the need for the marriage "to be blessed" with children as soon as possible.

Charles had decided to marry following the assassination of Earl Mountbatten, blown apart when an IRA bomb exploded in his fishing smack in Ireland in August 1979. Until that tragic moment Charles had no real intention of settling down, marrying, and producing an heir to the throne. That single act of terrorism made Charles realize how quickly death could strike. It also made him realize that it was his duty, first and foremost, to produce an heir for the future of the House of Windsor.

Whenever the name "Uncle Dickie" surfaces, or whenever she hears mention of Earl Mountbatten, Diana freezes. She has nothing against him; in fact, everything she ever heard of Mountbatten from Charles reinforced the idea that he would have been a wonderful man for her to know. He seemed so wise, so sensible. It's not his name she can't bear, it's the memories that flow from it, for Diana realized some years after her marriage that Charles would never have asked her to marry him if Uncle Dickie had not been assassinated. Thus she would not have had to go through years of misery and loneliness. And she would hardly have known Camilla Parker Bowles, the woman she still holds responsible for the breakdown of her marriage.

Diana, of course, knew nothing of the extraordinary, intense relationship that developed after Mountbatten's assassination. Diana did not realize how Camilla had saved Charles's sanity at that time when he was so full of hatred and anger, desolated by the fact that the Irish question, as he called it, would end in the murder of his beloved Uncle Dickie, the only man in the world whom he truly worshiped.

To Charles, Uncle Dickie would be the father he never had, the man he looked up to throughout his life, the man he turned to for advice and friendship, the man whom Charles wanted to emulate. His father, Prince Philip, never understood that, for Philip was far too cold, too severe, too offhand with his children, behaving more like a Victorian father with little time for his offspring. That was why Charles grew apart from his father from a young age and why the two men have hardly spoken to each other for the past fifteen years.

Now, Charles knows the principal reason. His father has always been absurdly jealous of him for Philip has never achieved anything in his life, could never do so, always made to walk two paces behind his wife, Elizabeth; with never a chance of being anyone of importance in the House of Windsor except a good father figure. And his character wouldn't permit that. The arrival of Charles, the male heir and someone instantly more important in royal terms than Philip could be, consumed him to such a degree he could never hide his deep-seated envy.

Charles turned to Camilla for comfort and reassurance after Mountbatten's murder. For the first few days Charles acted with remarkable sangfroid, for he had been trained as a Royal never to show emotion in public. In private, however, he would throw himself on his bed and weep for hours.

In his agony Charles phoned Camilla, someone he had always remembered with deep affection and with whom he had kept in touch by letter and the odd phone call during the years of her marriage to Andrew Parker Bowles, the Army officer she wed in 1974.

Charles had met Camilla in 1973 before going away to sea with the Royal Navy. They had been instantly attracted and Charles found Camilla wonderful, convivial company. They became lovers for a brief period and Charles would take Camilla for weekends to Broadlands, the country home of Earl Mountbatten. For Charles, then in his mid-twenties, marriage was a distant prospect. He had to go to sea to prove himself a competent naval officer. Within a year of his departure Camilla had married her Guards officer, Andrew, a thoroughly likable man some ten years older than Camilla and Charles, who were of a similar age. Charles, however, would become godfather to their eldest child, Tom.

After Mountbatten's murder Camilla recognized a cri de coeur in Charles's voice, and she immediately invited him to stay at her country home in Wiltshire for as long as he needed. During September 1979, Charles and Camilla would talk for hours, take long walks with her dogs through the woods and countryside, go for the occasional ride, and chat into the early hours of the morning in the drawing room of her home.

Her husband, Andrew, then a major, would be asked to go to Rhodesia for six months as a military aide to Lord Soames while the former British colony introduced black majority rule and the country became Zimbabwe.

Charles would spend most of that six months with Camilla, trying to come to terms with the trauma that had made him feel physically sick, angry, and desolate. Camilla offered him love and affection, and within a matter of weeks they became lovers again. In those months Charles discovered a sexual passion he had never found with any other woman. He found he needed Camilla completely and absolutely and would spend hours in her arms, sometimes in tears, at other times making love with a frenzy he never knew he possessed.

Charles pleaded with Camilla to divorce her husband and marry him. He told her that he didn't care if that meant he would have to give up the throne, as his great-uncle the Duke of Windsor had done, forced to abdicate in 1937 when he decided to marry the woman he loved, the American divorceé Mrs. Wallis Simpson. But the sensible Camilla would over the weeks persuade Charles that his first duty could not be to her or to his selfish needs, but to the nation, the crown, and the House of Windsor. Camilla offered to help find Charles a suitable young woman who would become the next queen of England, sitting on the throne beside Charles.

"I will never find anyone like you," he would tell her time and again.

Camilla would be adamant. "You must," she would say, brooking no argument.

During the early summer of 1980, Charles met Diana at a party and for the first time found himself attracted to someone other than Camilla. Eighteen months later they were married in a ceremony watched on television around the world. Charles had followed the advice of Uncle Dickie, who had told him, "What you must do is to go out and sow your wild oats for a while. Then find some suitable young virgin, marry her, educate her to be the next queen of England, and have some children."

Before marrying Diana, Charles needed the approval of Camilla, the only person he had ever trusted save for Uncle Dickie. Camilla and Diana met on a number of occasions before her engagement, and Camilla thought Diana would make Charles a good wife, a good mother to his children, and eventually a good queen. She persuaded him to go ahead. Diana had no idea that Charles asked Camilla for her seal of approval.

To Diana, Camilla had seemed the perfect older woman, a friend who had known Charles for many years and who was happy to advise and befriend Diana. She had no idea that Camilla and Charles had been lovers.

Even today Diana has been unable to forgive Charles for not telling her the truth of his relationship with Camilla at the very beginning. But she reserves her anger and hatred for "the bitch." She is convinced that when her marriage to Charles was going through a rough patch after the birth of Harry in 1984, Camilla happily provided Charles with not only advice and her shoulder to comfort him, but more importantly, her bed and her body.

On one occasion Diana went further and described Camilla as a rottweiler, suggesting that the woman she had come to loathe was more akin to a highly dangerous dog, capable of causing considerable injury to people. Diana had been greatly hurt by Camilla, and she would find other nasty, brutish words to describe Charles's mistress. On most occasions, whenever such phrases were splashed across the lurid tabloids, Camilla would simply shake her head, hoping that Diana would become more rational and understanding rather than blaming Camilla for everything that had happened to her marriage.

Diana would scour the newspapers for any reference about Camilla, reading whatever was written with the closest interest. In 1994 a book, *Camilla: The King's Mistress* by Caroline Graham, was published in London and serialized in two tabloids. As soon as Diana read of the book, she sent one of her staff to buy a copy. She would have gone herself but felt a bright shop assistant might have telephoned a newspaper with news of her purchase.

Diana devoured every word. The book included some colorful stories suggesting that Camilla and Charles regularly had sex outside on the grounds of Highgrove House; that when still married to Diana, Charles would spend four nights a week drinking wine and "romping" in Camilla's four-poster bed; and that Charles and Camilla would phone each other up to six or eight times a day.

Despite such evidence Diana had always, innocently, hoped that the relationship between Charles and Camilla had been platonic. She knew they had known each other for many years; she understood that Charles, Camilla, and Andrew Parker Bowles would frequently meet or have lunch or dinner. Diana remembered having had lunch at Middlewick, the beautiful

Parker Bowles home at Corsham in Wiltshire, not more than ten miles from Charles's country home, Highgrove.

On such occasions Diana had never noticed any particular intimacy between Camilla and Charles and never, for one moment, suspected anything untoward. When she did begin to suspect an affair, Diana challenged Charles repeatedly, but he would either deny the affair or simply not answer her questions directly.

Even this year Diana protested, "It was not until Charles told the world during that television interview in June 1994 that I knew for the first time, definitely, that Charles had been having an affair. I know it might sound extraordinary, but it hit me very hard."

8

Diana and Camilla

T HE NIGHT OF Wednesday, June 29, 1994, will forever be forged on Diana's mind. For that was the night at around ten-thirty that Diana for the first time in her life heard Charles confess that he had been unfaithful while married to her. He had never admitted that to her before, not even during their violent, and frequent arguments.

The whole of Britain knew that Charles would be interviewed on television that evening by the author and broadcaster Jonathan Dimbleby, who had been provided extraordinary access by Charles over an eighteen-month period to write a definitive biography of him. The Prince of Wales gave permission to his aides, friends, and staff to talk unreservedly to Dimbleby about Charles's life and his work.

An estimated 15 million people tuned in that night, but Diana would not be one of them. She had read leaked reports that Charles would confess to adultery at some point during the two-hour-long interview. Rather than stay at home alone to watch the spectacular, Diana accepted an invitation to a gala banquet at the Serpentine Gallery in Kensington Gardens, only a few hundred yards from her home. Dressed in a breathtaking off-the-shoulder, above-the-knee, black chiffon Valentino dress, she dazzled the assembled 250 guests, who had paid $250 a head toward the $2.5-million gallery renovation. In its twenty-five-year history the gallery had been a home for the sort of avant-garde art that Charles would find distinctly unpalatable. Diana's photograph, showing her smilng, relaxed, and confident, appeared in every newspaper the following morning, challenging Charles's TV confession for space.

The following morning Diana read every paper and felt a surge of pleasure that she had stolen much of the limelight. "You see," she quipped to her staff, smiling broadly, "I left Charles some space in the papers today."

She would not tell anyone until much later that she had secretly videotaped Charles's interview and watched every minute as soon as she returned to the palace that night. "I kicked off my shoes and sat down in front of the TV with a hot drink. I didn't want to miss a thing, I had to hear what he had to say. His confession of adultery surprised me, the fact that he admitted it publicly. But what hurt deeply was his statement that he had never loved me. I couldn't believe he said that, not when he knew the papers would be full of the story and Wills and Harry would read what he had said. That's what angered me so much. He had no reason to say that. It is awful for two boys to hear their father say that he never loved their mother. It's brutish, despicable behavior. I kept asking myself how could he do that to them."

Charles bared his soul that night in the most revealing documentary ever made about a member of the Royal Family. During the long and extraordinary candid interview Charles confirmed that he had not been unfaithful to the Princess of Wales until their marriage had "irretrievably" broken down after many attempts to save it.

Diana would later say, "At the moment he confessed, I was shaking with nerves, the palms of my hands sweating, not knowing exactly what Charles would say. I felt nauseous wanting him to tell the truth but not wanting to hear the truth. Part of me wanted him to say he had committed adultery, but the other half wanted him to deny it."

She went on, "If he had denied it, if he could have given me some hope, I would have probably cried with the sheer emotion of the moment, elated that there had been no one else despite everything my heart and mind had told me about Camilla."

Diana continued, "When Charles issued that word 'until' I had hope. Afterwards I felt so sad, so terribly sad, and so alone that he had been having an affair. I bit my lip but that didn't help. The tears came. There was nothing I could do to stop them. I knew I had been right to watch the TV interview on my own."

Later, Diana revealed that after the questions relating to Charles's adultery she had hardly listened to the rest of the interview for she had felt dead inside, as though a part of her had been opened up for the world to see that she had been cast aside like some piece of old clothing. That night she had hardly been able to sleep, her mind going over and over the words Charles had used to tell the world she meant nothing to him.

During the interview Charles would be shown at home and on royal tours abroad, chairing meetings, on public platforms, meeting dignitaries, making speeches, inspecting buildings and factories, and sharing intimate moments with his two children.

To the British people, however, those few seconds of his confession were all that mattered. His remarkable, unprecedented openness started a debate in political, church, and media circles over the wisdom of allowing the documentary to be made. The great majority of the media believed Charles had been foolish and reckless to agree to the interview and had made a blunder in confessing his adultery. One cartoon showed a scaffold with a huge ax resting against a TV set with the title of the program, *Charles: The Private Man, the Public Role,* on the screen. Overhead were black clouds, and a shocked crowd was watching. The cartoon was meant to resemble the execution of King Charles I in 1649.

Many debated that his extraordinary admission might well stop him from ever becoming king, asking whether Charles had embarked on constitutional suicide. Some wondered whether Charles had confessed all to test the water, to see whether his confession of adultery would so shock the nation that he might have to stand down in favor of his son William, leaving him free to leave public life and marry the woman he loved.

Many considered Charles may have found baring his soul in such a public manner a purifying experience, but others considered that his self-indulgence would inflict further damage on the monarchy and his relationship with it. Charles had gambled that laying bare his life would end the criticism that had surrounded him since his separation from Diana, for the nation had always blamed Charles for the marriage breakdown.

One or two media pundits suggested, with venom, that Charles had descended "into the gutter," along with pop singers and sports personalities, low-grade politicians, and TV soap stars, by trying to work on the public's affections through the television interview.

Within seven days, however, the pundits and politicians who had castigated Charles were made to eat their words. Charles had touched the heart of the nation. The people on whose behalf those papers claimed to speak so avidly had the temerity to disagree. In every form of phone-in, correspondence column, and opinion poll the people showed that they thought better of the Prince as a result of the TV interview. The constitutional crisis manufactured by Fleet Street and supported by some members of Parliament and the Established Church of England collapsed.

The nation had shown they were more fair-minded than their self-appointed tribunes. They recognized the film as a balanced portrait rather than a whitewash and were ready to accept the central theme, which was that Charles tries to live up to his motto that adorns his coat of arms: *Ich Dien*—I serve.

Many Brits feel Charles is odd, that some of his views are wrong or plain silly, his mannerisms maddening, his speech stilted, that he was the villain of his failed marriage. And yet the nation showed they could forget all those things because what shone through that night was that Charles devoutly wants the best for his country and works devotedly to achieve that aim. They felt sympathy for someone, however privileged, working relentlessly under permanent scrutiny.

Every poll taken immediately after his confession indicated

Charles's decision to bare his soul had gone down quite well. The nation still favored a monarchy and did not unduly worry about having an adulterer on the throne. One-third of voters in one poll believed Charles should be denied the crown, that he was not fit to reign. Two-thirds, however, said he should be king.

The TV interview stirred a host of related topics, some believing Charles's interview was but a sideshow to the need for a real agenda for change in Britain. Some argued that the prince's behavior was no problem; that, far more importantly, Britain faced a crisis that was not institutional but lay in the nation's failure to maintain consistent economic development. The monarchy in Britain used to be the authentic representative of a successful political, social, and economic order. Some argued that what remained of it was only a symbol of a decayed constitutional order.

Some pundits suggested that Charles's honesty, though admired by the nation, threatened in the long run to weaken him. For the rest of time he had risked his enemies speaking of "that self-confessed adulterer."

By the end of the interview Diana hoped that Dimbleby would have become more inquisitive. Like most of those watching, Diana found herself wanting to know the answers to numerous other questions that crowded her mind. He had admitted being unfaithful only after the marriage had "irretrievably broken down." When was that? Diana wanted to know. When did you see Camilla? How often did you see her? What did you do? How often did you make love? Where? And when? And why?

Charles had never realized Diana's abject feeling of personal failure when she finally realized that Charles had quit the marriage. All her life Diana had been a failure: at school, at music, at horse riding, at any exams she had ever taken. Charles had not understood how inadequate Diana had always felt, never comprehended that her feeling of inferiority had begun in her childhood when she tried to save her parents' marriage. She had constantly blamed herself for her parents' parting.

From her first meeting with Charles, Diana had always compared herself unfavorably to him and realized how unfit and mentally lacking she was to be the wife to the heir to the throne. Diana would try to understand the discussions with his intellectual friends, but would lose the thread of their arguments and give up, exacerbating her feeling of inferiority. She barely understood his work, his royal duties, or his responsibilities but would sit mesmerized by the brilliance of Charles's speeches, some of which she couldn't and, later, didn't bother to follow.

Diana wanted Dimbleby to ask questions about her so that she could understand where she had gone wrong, for in her heart Diana blamed herself and her lack of intelligence for the marriage collapse, just as much as she blamed Charles for turning his back on her and going off with his old mistress. She wanted to know why Charles no longer loved her. Was she a lousy wife? Was she hopeless in bed? Was she poor company? Was she boring? Was it the fact that she had no brains? Was she never fun?

She would recall the times she had spent hours alone agonizing over her marriage, and her approach to Charles. She would always wear the clothes he liked; always do her hair the way he liked it done; had lost weight to make herself more attractive; had been as seductive as possible, always showing her love in the way she thought he liked; tried to read intelligent books; tried to enjoy classical music and opera, but found them all boring and impossible. God how she had tried.

She would say to one of Charles's close confidants, "Doesn't he realize what he does to me when he leaves me on my own in this godforsaken hole? I tell him how terrible I feel when he leaves me, but he refuses to take any notice. I have told him that I cry on the bed waiting for him to come back, sometimes waiting three or more hours before he returns. "Then he walks in, sees I've been crying, and his voice heavy with sarcasm, says, 'What's the matter this time?'"

Diana would beg Charles's close advisers to explain to him the traumas she was going through every time he left her on her own. That message would be passed on to Charles, and he would nod in acknowledgment. But he had no idea how to placate Diana.

Those same advisers also knew that Diana would scream and plead with Charles when he had no choice but to attend meetings, consult staff, make speeches. For a while Charles had tried to placate his wife. He understood she was young and lonely, with few friends and fewer interests. He knew she would wander around Buckingham Palace listening to her Sony Walkman, spending afternoons and evenings lying on a sofa watching her favorite TV soaps. But the protests continued despite his attempts to calm his distressed young wife. He was at a loss at what to do.

He would ask Diana's adviser Michael Colborne, and her personal secretary, Oliver Everett, and others to make her understand that it was his duty to carry out royal functions and there could be no argument or debate about that. They tried, but it seemed Diana couldn't or wouldn't understand. Finally, he turned to the one person he believed might be able to help: an older woman, a friend of many years who knew Diana and who understood the pressures and the loneliness of the life she was leading with him. That woman was Camilla Parker Bowles.

At the time, Diana had no idea that Charles had turned to Camilla for help and advice. She accepted that they had been friends for many years, and on occasion, Charles and Diana would have dinner with the Parker Bowleses. She had never been aware of any frisson between Charles and Camilla. When they said goodbye, they would kiss each other on the cheek, but nothing more.

As she watched the interview, Diana wondered why Charles had ever married her, for she believed in her heart that he must always have been in love with Camilla. She also wondered whether Charles would apologize to her, to the boys, to the nation—for he would be their king—for his actions in marrying someone he didn't really love and then walking out on the marriage. She thought he wouldn't apologize because she believed him to be too arrogant, and as he often told her, she, too, was partly to blame for the breakdown because of her impossible behavior. She was right; there was no apology, to anyone.

And Dimbleby asked no more questions on that most private of matters, his adultery. Some viewers felt cheated; Diana certainly did. Many women viewers were sad and deeply sorry for Diana because she had to face such public humiliation, her husband confessing to adultery in front of the entire nation. But none of them knew of Diana's secret that Charles was not alone in his adultery. Diana's passionate affair with James Hewitt had started at about the time her marriage was falling apart around 1986.

Today Diana understands that Charles and Camilla are an item, that they live together most of the time, enjoying a quiet life, much like any other wealthy, upper-crust English couple fast approaching their fiftieth birthdays. She sees both Charles and Camilla as nearly middle-aged and believes they may be ideal for each other, listening to classical music and opera, reading serious books, and taking gentle exercise in long country walks and occasional days of riding to hounds.

At one time Diana wanted to show the world how stupid Charles had been when he dumped her for the rather frumpy-looking Camilla with the out-of-date hairstyle and the country-dress sense. The newspapers happily carried out that task for her by constantly printing pictures of Diana on one page and Camilla on the opposite page. The comparison may have been unfair, some would suggest cruel. Diana loved it.

Diana had often considered phoning Camilla's husband, Brig. Andrew Parker Bowles, thinking it might be sensible to chat and compare notes with the wronged husband, the fourth member of the quartet. She wondered how difficult, almost impossible, it must have been for him, having to make way for his former friend, his fellow officer, former polo-team player, and the heir to the throne.

Diana, however, never phoned because she felt it would be grossly unfair to embarrass him. "What would I say? What could I say?" she mused when discussing the idea with a friend.

She knew that Andrew had to call Charles "sir" on all occasions, even when having a drink together at a party. Since Camilla and Charles had begun their serious affair sometime in the late 1980s, Andrew had tried to avoid meeting Charles for fear of any paparazzi photograph that could cause Charles possible embarrassment.

Diana was surprised that Andrew never spoke a single word about his wife's adultery in public. I had known Andrew Parker Bowles during his tour of duty in Rhodesia in 1979–80, and we would sometimes chat, often about polo. In those days I remember Andrew to be a man who loved a party and a drink and who enjoyed the company of attractive, intelligent young women. He was also most conscientious, putting in long hours every week during that delicate transition from white government to black majority rule after a hard-fought, fifteen-year guerrilla war.

At that time he must have known that his wife was "taking care" of the traumatized Prince Charles, yet he did not show the least concern, proving most popular with a number of young ladies, and indeed, he struck up a strong relationship with a young woman photographer. By the end of his six-month tour of duty some people suggested the two had become an item, always attending parties together and seeing much of each other.

From the mid-1980s, Andrew Parker Bowles and Camilla were still man and wife but, according to friends, in name only. They remained friends, talked regularly on the phone, still enjoyed a good relationship with their two teenage children, but to all intents and purposes lived separate lives.

Andrew "understood" a "relationship" existed between Charles and Camilla, but he felt that since his marriage had in effect ended, it was no concern of his how close his wife was to the Prince of Wales. Most of the time he stayed in London while Camilla lived in their beautiful home at Corsham in Wiltshire, a short drive from Highgrove.

And yet Andrew had to show extraordinary restraint for more than seven years, dubbed the most selfless man in Britain, prepared to "lay down his wife for his kingdom!" Occasionally the odd rude comment would be made by someone in Andrew's presence. Most of the time Parker Bowles would simply ignore the remark. At other times he would fix the person with a hard stare and say nothing.

On one occasion a young toff, wearing a brown trilby, a green Harris-tweed suit, and brown brogues, appeared in the members bar at a race meeting at Newbury, Berkshire. In front of friends, he showed off by making a disparaging remark about Camilla. The comment was made only a few feet away from Andrew and in a deliberately loud voice. Andrew remained calm but flushed visibly. He turned, walked over to the young man, and looked him straight in the eye. "Is there anything you wish to say?" he inquired menacingly. "For if there is, then you had better say it to me outside."

For a moment the man, a little taller and heavier than Andrew but not nearly as fit, looked him in the eye. Andrew didn't move a muscle but continued to stare at him. He was determined the man should apologize or be humiliated in front of his friends.

One of the younger man's friends tried to intervene. "Who asked you to comment?" said Andrew harshly. "I'm talking to your rude friend."

The man looked at the ground, then back at Andrew, who stood stock-still. "I've got nothing to say," the man said.

"I think you have," Andrew said bitterly.

"What are you talking about?"

"I think you have an apology to make. To me."

"Oh, that," said the man, trying to laugh it off.

"Yes, that," Andrew said, unsmiling.

"I was only joking. Sorry if I offended."

"Yes," Andrew replied, relaxing, "you did offend. Thank you for the apology."

The man immediately offered to buy Andrew a drink, but Andrew told him, "No, thank you very much, I prefer to drink with my own friends." He turned and walked away.

The incident highlighted Andrew Parker Bowles's extraordinary predicament. To many, Andrew was the cuckold who should have protested about his wife's behavior. As it turned out, Camilla wasn't having an affair behind her husband's back for she had told him about herself and Charles. In private, Andrew was perfectly at ease with the situation despite the fact that Charles's emotional relationship with Camilla had started years before it became public knowledge. And Andrew enjoyed a discreet bachelor life of his own in London. Occasionally, like the incident at Newbury races, the odd remark would hurt, primarily because Andrew didn't want his wife's name dragged through the mud by people who received their information only through the tabloid press.

Only one point rankled with Andrew Parker Bowles. He believes that Charles, or most certainly Camilla, should have "done the decent thing" and warned him that Charles was to admit his adultery in the TV interview with Dimbleby. He had no idea that Charles would confess to such an indiscretion. Everyone knew the woman he referred to was his wife, Camilla.

Three months later Camilla and Andrew made it clear they were no longer together when they attended a memorial service for Camilla's mother, Rosalind Maud Shand. Camilla and Andrew arrived at and left St. Paul's Church, Knightsbridge, in separate cars. In that inimitable understated tradition of the English upper class, Camilla and Andrew had, without making any public statement about the matter, revealed their intention to live apart.

The signal inherent in the separate cars was timed to perfection. Three weeks later, in October 1994, Jonathan Dimbleby's biography of Prince Charles would appear revealing more of his relationship with Camilla. Their close friendship had developed from sharing a zany sense of humor, both laughing at jokes from the *Goon Show,* a highly popular cult radio show in Britain in the 1960s. They enjoyed a whirlwind romance around London in the summer of 1973, just weeks before Charles would leave for a nine-month tour of duty at sea with the Royal Navy. A year later Camilla had married Andrew.

In December 1994, Diana was told by one of her few

remaining friends within the senior ranks of the Queen's courtiers to prepare herself for a statement to be made about her marriage to Charles. She was informed one morning, privately by word of mouth, for her confidant believed the information to be too sensitive to risk telling in a phone call. They were drinking coffee at Kensington Palace at the time. Diana felt herself shaking, fearing the worst. She said later, "I tried to put the cup down quietly in the saucer but I found it rattling for I had suddenly suffered an attack of nerves."

She asked her confidant, "What statement? I don't know anything about any statement. Do you mean he's going to divorce me? I don't know anything about this, nothing. Charles and I have never even discussed divorce."

"No, no," said the confidant, "I don't know the details but apparently someone will be suggesting that divorce could take place at some future date."

Diana would not be so easily placated. Worried that she would be faced with the ultimatum of her own divorce without even being informed had been one of her worst fears since the separation. She knew only too well the power of the monarchy and the lengths to which the Buckingham Palace hierarchy would go if it suited their cause.

Before leaving, her confidant tried to reassure her, "If I learn anything definite, I'll let you know immediately."

Diana knew little of the divorce laws but suspected that Charles could, legally, file for divorce without informing her because they had been separated for two years. She decided to seek advice and contacted Lord Mischon, her lawyer. He reassured her that he was convinced nothing would occur. Diana was somewhat placated, but she didn't sleep peacefully that night.

Days later one of the Queen's most trusted and senior advisers, Lord Charteris of Amisfield, aged eighty-one, the man who had served Elizabeth for twenty years as her personal secretary from 1952, issued a statement making it plain that at some future date the "Prince and Princess of Wales would certainly divorce."

Diana would later say, "Those words hit me like hammer blows. I read and reread the statement to make sure I understood. I knew then that the Royal Family and their most senior advisers had decided my fate. I felt empty and defeated, as though my life's blood had drained from me. No one had said a word to me. No one had discussed anything. No warning had been given to me or my secretary."

Suddenly Diana exploded. A rage took hold of her. "Those fucking, fucking bastards," she screamed out loud. "Those shits," she screamed while her staff outside in the office pretended not to hear.

Diana would rage for about thirty seconds, yelling obscenities at the top of her voice, then be silent for a minute or more before another outburst took hold of her and the screams of anger swept through the apartment. Her staff heard her thump tables with her fists and wondered when the storm would subside. Those listening looked at each other, wondering whether to intervene. No one moved.

Her rage would end in tears of anger and frustration that she had been treated in such an offhand manner. Those who didn't understand the machinations of the palace would have thought little of Lord Charteris's statement. But Diana was nobody's fool. She knew what it meant. She understood the oblique statement by Lord Charteris only too well. Those few words from that man spoke volumes to her. A decision had been taken and this was the first shot to be fired in the crown's campaign to slowly educate and prepare the nation for the forthcoming divorce of Charles and Diana.

That night Diana felt lost and alone, not knowing what the future would hold for her. She had no man for whom she cared and no man who cared for her. It seemed that whomever she found attractive and warm, considerate and kind, was either married or found wanting.

Also, that night Diana thought of the only people in the world whom she genuinely loved, her boys. And they weren't with her either but away at boarding school, exiled for most of the year. That night she would feel more alone than ever, believing even her sons were growing apart from her, her influence becoming less as they became teenagers and more independent of her. Soon they would no longer need her. Then she would have nobody to care for, to worry about, to fuss over. She shivered at the thought.

Diana confessed all these thoughts to her newfound friend, a wealthy man in his fifties who worked in the City of London but whom she had met through her charity work. He would treat Diana more as a kid sister, but she believed that she had discovered someone whose advice she could trust. There was no sexual attraction between them, but Diana could tell him all her secrets with no feeling that he would betray her. She began turning to him more and more for advice. She felt at the end of her tether.

The next morning, after only a few hours' sleep, Diana would be at the Harbour Club by eight o'clock and would swim until physically exhausted. Yet, as she swam, she found new inner strength and greater determination.

Later she would say, "If they think I'm going to give in without a fight, then they have another think coming. I am going to tell Lord Mischon to fight them all the way until I get everything I want for myself and for the boys."

The New Year would be only a few days old when Diana would be surprised once more. Gossip columnists, and friends within the royal circle who had discussed the bizarre royal triangle over dinner and teatime for a number of years, finally learned of the outcome when solicitors representing Camilla and Andrew Parker Bowles issued a joint statement on behalf of the couple revealing that they had secretly been living apart for two years. It read: "Brigadier and Mrs. Parker Bowles have asked that it be known that they have instructed us to seek on their behalf a termination of their marriage, and that divorce papers have been filed. The divorce is by mutual consent, the ground being that they have lived apart for more than two years."

They also issued another, more illuminating statement, saying the real reason for the announcement was to ensure that their family and friends should be saved from harassment, especially their two children. In an effort to answer their critics and to overcome the general acceptance that Andrew had been a cuckold for many years, their statement went on, "Throughout our marriage we have always tended to follow rather different interests, but in recent years we have led completely separate lives. We have grown apart to such an extent that, with the exception of our children and a lasting friendship, there is little of common interest between us, and we have therefore decided to seek divorce."

Later that day Diana was brought a copy of the *London Evening Standard*. "Camilla Free to Remarry" was the headline. A subhead read, "Official: Divorce for Parker Bowles and Charles's Great Love."

Diana retired to her drawing room and read the five pages devoted to the sensational story. All that interested her, and most of the country, was the question of remarriage. Later she told her City friend that she burned with jealousy and anger at the thought that within perhaps a year or more the nation would accept both her divorce from Charles and, maybe, his marriage to the bitch.

Diana, however, had no idea that one of the primary reasons for the divorce announcement was that Andrew Parker Bowles had become involved with an old friend of the family, Mrs. Rosemary Pitman, whom Camilla also knew very well. Indeed, Camilla and Rosemary had in the past organized clothes sales together, and both were members of the elite West County social set, attending dinner parties at each other's homes over many years.

Mrs. Pitman, fifty-five, the mother of three grown children, comes from a wealthy family of solicitors. She divorced her husband, Col. Hugh Pitman, in 1991. Like Andrew, he was an ex-Army man who quit to establish a successful recruitment agency.

Both Camilla and Charles knew that Andrew Parker Bowles had become romantically involved with Mrs. Pitman. But the secret had not been shared with Diana. In February

1996, Andrew surprised all his friends, as well as Diana and Charles, by marrying Rosemary within twenty-four hours of anouncing their engagement. At Brigadier Parker Bowles's wedding to Camilla in 1973, several members of the Royal Family and a guard of honor were in attendance at the Guards Chapel. This time, Andrew married Rosemary in a quiet ten-minute civil ceremony at the Chelsea Register Office. The only people present were the five children from their first marriages.

Diana would discuss the surprise marriage with friends, wondering whether Camilla would ever remarry. Diana commented, "Camilla won't make the same mistake twice. She married the wrong person the first time round. There is still only one man in her life. And we know who he is."

9

A Princess Goes Cruising

———— ⚜ ————

AT THE FIRST OPPORTUNITY, Camilla and Charles opened a
bottle of Dom Pérignon pink champagne in the seclusion of
Highgrove, the country house that had been their sanctuary and
their home. "To *our* future," Charles said, proposing a toast.
They clinked glasses and Camilla felt that the trauma she had
been through over so many years was finally ending.

"To us," she replied in her husky voice, taking a sip of
champagne.

Charles would suggest to Camilla that nothing should now
stop them from leading a normal life like any other couple in the
same situation. Camilla, however, is understood to have proposed caution, reminding Charles that they had never been an
ordinary couple and never could be. As usual Charles would
agree that perhaps he was being a little hasty, that they might
have to wait a short while before appearing together in public.
Camilla was heartened by Charles's agreement because she
knew he tended to be impatient.

Charles and Camilla would continue to be invited to lunch
and dinner at friends' country houses where the hosts would
seek out only those close friends who could be trusted to
remain silent, and who would treat the Prince and Camilla as an
ordinary couple. They would dine and sometimes stay at
Anmer Hall, the Sandringham home of Hugh van Cutsem,
fifty-three, the millionaire farmer and pedigree stud breeder
and his wife, Dutch-born Emilie van Cutsem, forty-eight. Ever

since Charles had decided to live apart from Diana, he had frequently stayed with the van Cutsems with both Wills and Harry during school holidays. The young princes established a close friendship with the van Cutsems' sons, Edward and Hugh, both of whom are several years older than William.

So happy were Wills and Harry with the motherly Emilie that she became another surrogate mother to the boys. Emilie relished the idea of helping Charles in whatever way she could in bringing up his sons. The boys enjoyed the lively, happy, convivial atmosphere of Anmer Hall, which buzzed with noise and activity, so unlike the somber mood that prevailed at nearby Sandringham when the Queen and Prince Philip were in residence.

Diana discovered that when the boys were purported to be staying at Sandringham with Charles, she would sometimes telephone to find they were, in fact, all staying at the van Cutsems' home. Diana talked to the boys about their visits there and, on occasion, found that while Charles was absent, the boys would be left to enjoy life with the van Cutsems on their own.

Whenever Diana found that Charles had left Wills and Harry, she would immediately try to contact Charles to remonstrate with him, often in a string of four-letter words, telling him that if he was having the boys for a weekend or a few days, then he should be staying with them, not handing them over to strangers. She would also tell him that if he couldn't for any reason care for them personally over a weekend, then she would be only too happy to have them stay with her at Kensington Palace.

Diana would tell Charles he was being "beastly" and "unfair" for he knew that she longed to see her sons anytime, anywhere. "I am their mother for Christ sake," Diana would yell at Charles. "How dare you bundle them off to some fucking stranger without my permission."

In fact, both Emilie and Hugh van Cutsem were no strangers to Diana. Before her wedding, Diana would become very friendly with Emilie, whose son Edward, then eight, would serve as a page at Diana's wedding in St. Paul's Cathedral. Diana and Emilie would attend the Wimbledon tennis championships and sometimes dine together.

But Wills and Harry also informed Diana that Emilie had told them to treat her "like another mother," contacting her if they were ever in any trouble or wanted to come and stay or simply have a chat on the phone. Both Wills and Harry enjoyed playing with their new friends, Edward and Hugh, whom Emilie suggested they should treat like older brothers.

And there was more. Diana learned that both Camilla and Charles would stay at the van Cutsems, and so close was the friendship between Emilie and Camilla that, in 1993, the two of them went on holiday together to India, visiting historic palaces. They toured the Taj Mahal, on the banks of the sacred river in Agra, where Diana, by posing alone in front of the famous monument to love in 1992, deliberately gave credence to the rumors that her marriage to Charles was in serious trouble.

Diana believed that Emilie van Cutsem had betrayed her friendship. She felt that Emilie had gone out of her way to nurture a relationship during the early years of her marriage, always offering help and advice and, later, by offering her services as an independent go-between if there was any chance of a reconciliation with Charles. Emilie would phone asking whether she could help, and Diana would pour out her heart to the woman who seemed to have taken her side in the arguments and rows she had with Charles. Since that time Diana felt deceived by her actions, wondering how much of their conversations Emilie had passed on to Charles.

She would accuse Emilie van Cutsem of being a false friend, giving comfort to her while entertaining her husband's mistress under her own roof. Later Emilie would compound that betrayal by befriending Camilla. In Diana's eyes worse would follow in her attempt to usurp her role as the princes' mother.

"I will never speak another word to that woman as long as I live," Diana has said, and few believe she will ever do so.

There were other friends who Diana believed had betrayed her friendship and hospitality among them. Lord Charles Shelburne, fifty-four, and Lady Fiona, forty-five, who had been close friends with Camilla and Andrew Parker Bowles for a number of years. They lived at Bowood House, Calne, in Wiltshire, not far from the Parker Bowles country home, and through them they met both Charles and Diana. The Shelburnes were at the heart of what became known as "the Highgrove set," that group of wealthy country families who lived within a twenty-mile radius of Highgrove whom Charles and Diana came to know well, entertaining them on occasion and accepting invitations to visit some of their homes.

The atmosphere at those get-togethers would be far more relaxed and friendly than at similar get-togethers in London homes, where many would behave in such a formal manner simply because the Prince and Princess of Wales were in attendance. In the country, however, people were far less stuffy, and Diana would enjoy the relaxed atmosphere where their friends would happily chat about any number of subjects, whether it was babies or the local hunt, educating children or disciplining dogs. And people dressed in a far less formal fashion, which, to the surprise of many, Diana does thoroughly enjoy. Brought up on her father's Norfolk estate, Diana's wardrobe throughout her teenage years consisted mostly of jeans and sweaters with casual cotton skirts and shirts in the summer. Only since Diana became Princess of Wales and the fashion gurus of *Vogue* educated her had she become one of the foremost exponents of fashion and style.

Diana felt at home visiting the mansions of the Highgrove set. She was among trustworthy friends, many miles from the hard-nosed ladies of fashion and wealth who, she believed, more often than not, treated her with contempt, accepting her only because she was married to the Prince of Wales and not because they wanted her to be part of their snobby, elite set.

As Charles came to spend more time at Highgrove in the late eighties, Diana had noted a cooling off in her relationship with those friends she had felt had been genuine in their warmth and hospitality. Later she realized how much socializing Charles had done during those years with Camilla among the Highgrove set.

Ever since Charles had demanded a formal separation in the autumn of 1992, Diana had wondered when he would seek a divorce. And yet he had not raised the matter and she had never wanted to know what was in his mind for she was happy to remain the Princess of Wales, mother to the heirs to the throne.

Diana recognized that she owed her position totally to the fact she had married the Prince of Wales. She had said, "If I hadn't married Charles, I would probably never have had my picture in the newspapers throughout my entire life. No one would ever have heard of me and I would have led a quiet, unassuming life. I suppose I would have married, waited for someone to come along, because my sisters and most of my friends have married. But it would have been a quiet wedding with, at the most, a line or two in the *Times*."

Following the separation, Diana found herself trusting fewer and fewer people, whether girlfriends or men friends, her police bodyguards, members of her own staff, her chauffeur, or anyone with whom she came in close contact. She would go further, refusing to permit armed police bodyguards to accompany her as before they had shadowed the Princess of Wales's every move whether on an overseas tour, on a charity visit in Britain, to her gymnasium, or even to Harrods. Shortly after announcing her decision in December 1993 to retire from royal duties and lead a more private life, Diana informed the chief of the Royal Protection Squad that she would no longer be requiring the services of any of his officers.

Senior officers remonstrated with her, detailing the sort of attacks she could expect from terrorist squads or hard-line political activists capable of kidnapping or killing the Princess of Wales as worldwide publicity for their cause. There were also screwballs, "nutters," drunks, or hangers-on who might try to take advantage of her if she traveled around the country or around London unescorted.

Diana would patiently listen to all arguments. "Thank you very much, but I have made up my mind," she would say. "I don't want any escorts whatsoever. Nor do I want police tailing me in their vehicles either. Is that understood?"

"Yes, ma'am" would be the reply. The only response police could give.

But Diana's bid for freedom courted disaster, encouraging some to take advantage of her trust in the public. In November 1995, a twenty-seven-year-old mental patient cycled up to Diana while she was out enjoying a walkabout, pressing the flesh, chatting to housewives in Liverpool. The patient had made a bet with colleagues at the Broad Oak psychiatric unit that he could get a kiss from the Princess of Wales. He rode his bicycle along the street, where hundreds of people were standing behind barriers waving and calling to Diana, and stopped next to her.

The crew-cut young man, dressed in jeans, leather jacket, and trainers said, "Would you like a roll-up fag?" (a cigarette), which Diana refused with a laugh. "Can I have a kiss then?" he asked, and Diana leaned forward and the man kissed her on the cheek, before riding off to cheers.

Diana, of course, had no idea that the young man was a mental patient, named Paul Fahy, who once threatened to shoot the mother of his two children and who calls himself Damien—from the horror movie *The Omen*—claiming he is the son of the devil. The ex-con has more than twenty convictions, one for assaulting a cop.

After his kiss, Paul Fahy told reporters that, before dying, his father had told him that he was a distant relation to John F. Kennedy. "For some time after that I would get into a panic believing I might be the next president of the United States." But he also reassured Diana, saying, "No one need worry. The Princess was never in danger from me. I love her with all my heart. I think she's the most beautiful woman in the world."

Police chiefs of the Royal Protection Squad would use that example to try to persuade Diana to relent and agree to officers accompanying her whenever she leaves the security of Kensington Palace. She refused point-blank. However, unbeknown to Diana, armed officers do, on many occasions, follow the Princess from a distance, particularly when she is walking around London shopping. They will also try to follow her when she is driving recklessly around London and on the motorways. Though they will often lose her, they can always trace her. The police have concealed an automatic bleep signal under her car that pinpoints the precise position of the vehicle anywhere in Britain.

There had been a number of other scares since Diana had refused police protection. In September 1994, another mental patient, Ricky Cotlarz, a twenty-nine-year-old born-again Christian, pushed his way through a crowd and came face-to-face with Diana when she was walking to her car after attending a charity function in London. There was no police presence as Cotlarz, a married man with one child, shoved through the throng and raised his fist at her, shouting and gesticulating. Only quick action by a security guard saved her, for Diana was trapped, the man standing between her and her waiting car. The guard managed to open the car door and push Diana in as the man continued to shout at her. On that occasion members of Parliament demanded that Diana be given police protection whether she wanted it or not, angry that she should put herself in such danger.

Diana has also received two death threats, both delivered by phone to Buckingham Palace. Neither British Telecom or the police were able to trace the calls; as a result, Diana was persuaded that she should be accompanied by armed police when attending official functions where her presence would be well-publicized beforehand. Police armed with either a Smith and Wesson handgun or a semiautomatic Glock machine pistol accompany her but stay in the background. Even after the death threats Diana was far from keen on being escorted anywhere at any time by any officers.

Diana didn't tell the senior police officers the reason behind her decision. She believed she could not trust the men who, ironically, had been entrusted with her safety. She believed they were under orders to reveal everything about the Princess of Wales to their superiors: about her trips, her visits, her lunch dates, her private visits, and always the names and full information on the men she might meet at any time, day or night.

Diana knew that there would be a computer record of everyone she met and exactly what had gone on between them, whether they had just shaken hands or said "Good morning" after having spent the night.

Diana would tell friends of this author, "I had become fed up knowing that every aspect of my life was known not just to the police, but any senior palace courtier who decided, allegedly for security reasons, to spy on me and find out what I was doing twenty-four hours around the clock. I wanted once more to enjoy some privacy, and the only way I could achieve that would be to get rid of those bodyguards."

And Diana certainly had no faith whatsoever in those aides of the Queen, not even her brother-in-law Sir Robert Fellowes, who Diana felt had turned against her over the collapse of her marriage to Charles. She knew her brother-in-law's job was to preserve the authority of the crown, above all other considerations, even the future happiness of his sister-in-law.

Diana came to believe that her telephones and her magnificent royal apartment in Kensington Palace were constantly bugged. She would deliberately carry out searches in her bedroom and study, checking under the beds, tables, and other furniture to see if she could find a bug. She became convinced her conversations were taped, so that the authorities would know precisely her whereabouts, though ostensibly having no idea where she went or whom she visited.

No one could convince Diana the police were not spying on her. "I know they're bugging me," she would protest. "I just know they are. They want to know everything about me and I'm not prepared to let them. It's my life, for God's sake."

On occasion, Diana would test the Royal Protection Squad by leaving the palace around midnight, getting in her Audi sports coupe, and taking off around London, sometimes driving at 90 mph, always searching her rearview mirror to check whether she was being followed. She would stop in side streets, then turn her car around after a few minutes and race off in the direction from which she had come. Sometimes she would zoom off down the M4, a motorway she knows well, past

Heathrow Airport, and drive for maybe fifty miles before leaving the highway and returning to London.

Sometimes, she would deliberately tease other drivers who recognized her, especially if it was a young man driving alone. She would drive up close behind him, flash her lights, slowly overtake him, making sure the man had a chance to recognize her. Then she would pull over in front of the man's car and slow down, making the other driver slow down, too. He might then overtake and carry out the same maneuver and Diana would repeat it, laughing and waving to the man. It was a dangerous game but it gave her a buzz.

And she would take greater risks. On occasion she would leave the palace and drive into Soho, London's notorious red-light district, to cruise the streets around midnight watching the girls parading the streets, the drunks and the drug addicts looking for kicks, the late-night revelers enjoying themselves, and the young people out to enjoy a night in Soho clubs. The traffic at midnight can only crawl along. Diana would wear one of her favorite baseball caps but would wind down the window of her car, chat to people on the sidewalk, some of whom would recognize the Princess of Wales.

She would talk to these people as though she knew them when, in fact, she had no idea who they were. She would be extremely lucky for most would laugh and joke with her. If any of them had tried to get into the car or make a grab for her through the open window, Diana would have been in some trouble for the cars, nose to tail, were traveling at a snail's pace with no exit she could take.

Diana really enjoyed taking those risks. She loved proving she was no longer the prisoner in the palace but able to get out and enjoy herself, whether cruising the streets, swimming in a pool, or keeping fit in a gym. It would become one of her favorite ways of challenging the system, showing she could and would rebel whenever she wished. But Diana would go no further. As far as is known, she would never leave the security of her car, never park and walk to a bar or a club. She would get the thrill of momentarily living on the edge, passing through the hard street life of a red-light district.

Diana had also enjoyed the excitement of her three secret years with James Hewitt, dodging the paparazzi, telling white lies to her staff and the Royal Protection Squad, and feeling the thrill of an illict affair. She felt no guilt for the affair with Hewitt that began in 1987 when, to all intents and purposes, her marriage was over. By the end of 1986, Charles and Diana had stopped sharing the marital bed, but at that time there was no talk of separation or divorce.

When, later, the question of divorce arose, they both said divorce would be an unfair burden for Wills and Harry to endure. Apparently, the two boys had accepted the separation, which had taken place slowly over months, even years, with Charles telling them of his decision to move to Highgrove where he could work better. Later, he would move his office there and a number of his staff would move from London to the country.

The boys continued to see their parents at school functions, and they would still tour overseas together and sometimes attend royal duties together in Britain. Their dual appearance, however, would occur less often, mainly because Diana had decided to take on more charities of her own.

As events moved faster, Charles and Diana explained to their sons that they would be leading separate lives and living in different places, Diana remaining in London at the palace and Charles spending most of his time at Highgrove. Both Wills and Harry knew Camilla Parker Bowles for they had met her occasionally at Highgrove. But they didn't know her very well.

Occasionally, William would ask both his parents if they were planning to divorce and seemed greatly relieved when they told him that they had no plans to do so. Only later would the boys be made aware of their father's real relationship with Camilla Parker Bowles, but they would never learn of their mother's relationship with Hewitt, despite the tremendous furor that occurred following the revelations of the book Hewitt cooperated in writing.

Diana would tell her sons that Hewitt had been a dear friend, that he had taught her to ride in the same way that he had given the princes riding lessons, and that the revelations in the book *Princess in Love* had been grossly exaggerated. The boys were not surprised, for whenever they had seen tabloid newspaper stories about themselves or their parents, they knew much of what was written proved to be pure speculation or totally inaccurate.

Wills was only twelve, Harry barely ten, when the truly embarrassing revelations of their parents' affairs were splashed over the newspapers and the television news programs. Charles would confess on TV to adultery, and a year after *Princess in Love* appeared, Diana would reveal her three-year-long affair with Hewitt in her TV interview. Now there was no hiding place for the boys and they had to face the fact that both their parents had had lovers while they were married.

After the official announcement of Camilla and Andrew's divorce, Charles was happy with the arrangement. He had no wish to further upset his sons or risk alienating any lingering support that he still enjoyed with the public. He understood full well that the nation still loved Diana, far more than any other member of the Royal Family. They still wanted to hear nothing untoward said about her, nor see anything done to humiliate her or remove her from the forefront of the Royal Family.

When Charles publicly confessed to adultery, he felt a tremendous release from a burden he had been carrying far too long. And now since Camilla's separation he felt that he could begin to enjoy life with the woman he loved, without the appalling shame of resorting to the most embarrassing subterfuges. On occasion, both Charles and Camilla would hide in the trunks of cars to escape the paparazzi and be smuggled into each other's home. On other occasions Charles would change cars, pretend to drive in one direction, and then return via back lanes, and sometimes across ploughed fields, to be with Camilla. He deeply resented having to live that sort of life.

Charles and Camilla had telephoned each other constantly, often talking five times a day, always trying to say good night and wish each other a peaceful sleep as their last act of the day. Charles would come to rely more and more on Camilla, not simply for her love and strength but for her common sense and surprising sense of humor in the most trying circumstances. On occasion Charles wondered how he managed to stay sane when the papers were full of the bizarre triangle, which the public seemed to savor with every new prurient revelation.

From time to time, Charles discussed the question of divorce with his mother, though he never wanted to have such conversations with his father because he knew that Prince Philip would begin to hector him, as he had done all his life. The Queen would tell Charles that one day the question of divorce would have to be faced, but Charles would argue that neither he nor Diana wished to divorce yet, preferring to allow their children to slowly get used to the possibility. In conversations with his mother Charles put no time limit on their marriage. And his mother accepted that situation though she wished that Diana would melt into the background forever.

It wasn't that the Queen disliked Diana, for she hardly knew her. Whenever they spoke, Diana appeared shy and embarrassed and conversation was awkward and stilted. Elizabeth simply realized that Diana was a strong-willed young woman who demanded her freedom and was not prepared to accept the strict rules of being a member of the Royal Family. Elizabeth feared that Diana, with her sharp swings of mood, could cause severe embarrassment to the monarchy, and she wished to avoid such unwelcome occurrences at any cost.

Elizabeth would discuss Diana with her mother, the Queen Mother, who was in her nineties. Much loved and respected in Britain, the Queen Mother had led an exemplary life and had endeared herself to the British people during World War II, refusing to leave Buckingham Palace at the height of the blitz because she wanted to stay with her people. The Queen Mother simply did not trust Diana and gave her daughter and Charles, her favorite grandson, the same message. She would tell them, "You must be able to trust anyone who becomes a part of our family. But that is a young woman you cannot totally trust."

The Queen Mother would never give any reason for what seemed a totally unreasonable comment to make of a young woman destined to be the next queen of England. "I have my reasons" was the only comment she would make.

In conversations with her senior advisers Elizabeth was believed to have agreed with her son's interpretation of the mood of the nation. There was no need to rush the divorce for many reasons other than those stated by Charles. During the past few years the Royal Family and the institution of the monarchy had taken an awful battering in the press and, according to polls, by the nation. Newspapers and commentators were critical of the amount of money the monarchy spent each year for what they perceived were dubious rewards for the nation. The behavior of the younger Royals had revealed a growing public cynicism toward the monarchy. The fire that destroyed part of historic Windsor Castle in November 1992 also unleashed a pent-up resentment toward the Royal Family that had been simmering for some years.

The fire had destroyed the magnificent St. George's Hall, the adjacent Waterloo Chambers, and treasures that experts suggested were, literally, priceless; it also destroyed the unique relationship between the Queen and her people. The government immediately announced that the nation would happily pay for the full cost of repairs to the castle, estimated at about $75,000,000, since the castle was not insured. It had been accepted practice for decades that any such tragedy would be paid for by the nation, for the British taxpayer was responsible for sustaining their monarch in luxury and splendor. On this occasion the nation's taxpayers disagreed.

The British people demanded that the Queen herself pay for the repairs, complaining that the Queen, who paid no taxes, would make no contribution to the cost of the castle repairs while her people, who were heavily taxed, would pay the entire bill. The Royals were accused of meanness, greed, and blinkered disregard for the feelings of the people, a mark of a dying, not a lasting dynasty. Such a reaction of anger and hostility had never before occurred in this century.

Elizabeth was unable to comprehend such a dramatic sea change in the people's affection for the Royal Family and respect for the monarchy. The press turned its attention to the Queen's wealth, and a crescendo of criticism ended with renewed demands that she pay tax, like the rest of the nation. Intensive behind-the-scenes arguments took place at the political level and among senior Buckingham Palace aides because Elizabeth didn't want to pay any tax, arguing that as sovereign, she should be above such matters. However, common sense, and a strong case made by Prince Charles for paying taxes, finally prevailed. In February 1993, Prime Minister John Major gave details to the House of Commons about taxes the Queen would pay. Tax experts believed her main liability would be on dividends from the $100-million stock portfolio she is believed to own. The vast majority of the tax would be levied at 40 percent. She would also have to pay capital gains tax on any stock sales.

Taken aback by the strength of the feeling running against the monarchy, Elizabeth decided to cut back on crown expenditures, taking the minor royals out of the limelight. Throughout 1993 and 1994, the Royal Family faded into the background. She ordered Royals who were not members of Elizabeth's immediate family to stay away from the annual spectacular gatherings, such as Trooping the Colour, celebrating the Queen's official birthday.

The latest polls indicated the nation wanted a change from the distant, aloof, old-fashioned monarchy Elizabeth had epitomized throughout her forty-year reign. They preferred a slimline Scandanavian-style monarchy with fewer Royals involved, less ceremony, less grand living, and less ostentation. They also wanted all the lesser Royals to get proper, worthwhile jobs, rather than just opening the occasional hospital wing or fete, presiding over a charity meeting, or representing the Queen on official occasions. And they insisted on a significant cut in the cost of the Royals' upkeep.

Elizabeth feared the furor Diana's divorce might create. She and her advisers believed the nation would interpret the divorce as an act by the Royal Family to remove the people's favorite

Royal. However, powerful voices among the Establishment and the grandees of Buckingham Palace were advocating that the sooner a divorce took place, the better it would be for the future prestige of the Royal Family and, ultimately, of the monarchy itself.

Those pushing for a quick divorce would point to Diana's behavior and successive revelations about her life that still dominated the British press. Her three-year affair with James Hewitt had caused people to raise eyebrows; her relationships with a number of married men caused more serious disquiet; and her single-minded approach to her future, independent of the Royal Family, worried those responsible for advising the Queen. They could see Diana, young, attractive, royal, and a princess, creating untold problems for the dignity of the crown in her ambition to become the focus of attention, outshining all the other Royals, and in particular Elizabeth and Prince Charles.

Two years after their separation, the pressure mounted, for the divorce laws of Britain stated a couple could then automatically divorce on the grounds of an irretrievable breakdown of marriage. The nation waited for a statement from Buckingham Palace announcing the divorce. But none would be forthcoming. Commentators and newspapers demanded that they divorce "in the couple's best interests." In the autumn of 1995, after so many revelations of Diana's private life had been leaked, further demands for a divorce were made.

The conservative *Daily Telegraph* commented, "It is true that Diana has suffered a good deal, and that her situation, though privileged, is not enviable. But it is also true that what she is doing is not good for this country. The Princess melodramatically 'retired from public life' but now she seems to have returned to it, with equal melodrama. She remains royal, in title, in prestige, in her residence and paid for by royal money. Yet she is royal only when she chooses, not allowing her engagements to be run by Buckingham Palace and avoiding the full, irksome round of duties. She remains married, but to a man she is known to dislike, and with a rather too obvious interest in attracting his successor."

The highly critical article seemed to echo the views of the Establishment. It continued with even greater vitriol, "Even her undoubted brilliance as a public performer has more of a filmic quality about it than that of restrained, formal, self-effacing altruism which best suits British royalty. Her style is more Monaco than monarchy. She is damaging herself, and the public interest. Since she cannot be reconciled with her husband, she should divorce, and learn to hide her dazzling light under the bushel of motherhood."

Marital advisers sensed there was so much hostility between Charles and Diana it would be preferable for Wills and Harry for their parents to divorce. They argued a divorce would at least put an end to all the harmful stories of their parents' respective love lives. It might also help Wills and Harry heal the scars they must both carry and help them forget the awful scenes they had both witnessed. It would also end any lingering hopes the boys might still harbor of bringing their parents together again.

10

A Princely Dilemma:
A Kingdom for a Wife

———— ❧ ————

I T IS DOUBTFUL WHETHER Charles will ever marry Camilla, the woman he has loved all his life. When news of the impending divorce was announced from Buckingham Palace in December 1995, Charles declared that he had "no intention of remarrying."

Many took that remark as an unequivocal statement that he would never marry Camilla, but that is not necessarily the case. Charles has found himself in a most difficult situation, for when he becomes king he will also automatically become head of the Church of England. The regulations under which the Church currently operates were passed in 1938, partly in response to the abdication crisis. Those regulations state unequivocally that the marriage service should not be used a second time for anyone who has a former partner still living.

Individual clergy are free, as legal registrars, to marry divorced people in church, and an increasing number of them do so. But they act with what is called freelance compassion. The primary regulations of the Church, however, forbid such freelance compassion. Prince Charles, as heir to the throne, cannot act as a private individual and quietly visit a registry office, the places in Britain where marriages are conducted without religious ceremony. He can only marry with the sovereign's permission, and the Queen, as supreme governor of the Church of England, could not give permission for him to marry in England because Diana, his first marriage partner, is still living.

To marry, Charles requires a special license from the archbishop of Canterbury, and the archbishop will not issue his license to anyone who is divorced and has a former partner living. At the moment, therefore, Prince Charles could not marry anyone in the Church of England.

Even in the most unlikely event that Diana suffered a tragic and fatal accident, Charles could still not marry Camilla without jeopardizing his right to succeed to the throne, not even if the Church did change its rules. There is wide agreement in the Church of England that there is one circumstance in which divorced people cannot be married in church: that is, if the relationship of the two people wanting to get married was a significant factor in the breakup of the previous marriage. For the Church to marry divorced people in such circumstances would mean condoning adultery. So if Charles wanted to marry Camilla, the archbishop of Canterbury would have no alternative but to refuse permission.

If, however, Charles went ahead and married Camilla outside England, for example in Scotland, the archbishop would then have to raise serious questions about his coronation. With the monarchy in its present fragile state, no heir to the throne could afford to take that risk. And Charles has been drilled with one fact all his life: his principal objective must be to uphold the monarchy and the House of Windsor. Hence the categorical statement that Charles, under any circumstances, cannot marry Camilla and remain heir to the throne.

However, the prohibition against marrying Camilla will not alter their relationship. Charles and Camilla will continue to be a couple, Camilla caring for Charles and loving him but remaining forever in the background, even when he becomes king. That fact brings a wicked smile to Diana's lips.

Charles himself was never that keen on marriage. He loved the bachelor life of polo and shooting, stalking and skiing, opera and music and books, while satisfying his interests in architecture, ecology, and gardening. He thoroughly enjoyed having his crew about him, his band of former armed service personnel, loyal and keen; and he rather liked inviting his male friends to the palace for lunch or dinner for discussion and intelligent debates on any number of subjects. All that had come to an end shortly after he married Diana, and he hated those changes to his life.

As previously mentioned, Chief Petty Officer Michael Colborne met Prince Charles during his years with the Royal Navy and served with him on several ships during the 1970s. Such was the empathy between the two men that when Charles quit the Navy, he asked Colborne to become his secretary, and a firm friendship developed. After his marriage, Charles asked Colborne to become Diana's secretary to guide and advise her. After three years with Diana, Michael Colborne left royal service but has since remained friends with both Charles and Diana and still sees them.

Colborne understands Charles very well. He commented, "In many respects Charles was a born bachelor. He enjoyed a wonderful life as a single man and he never wanted it to change. He only married because he knew that it was his duty to provide an heir to the throne. It was the dramatic, sudden death of Uncle Dickie that persuaded him that he had to marry, and quickly. For suddenly, he had realized that his life, too, could be snuffed out like a candle at any moment.

"It was Camilla who persuaded Charles that he must find a suitable bride who would make him a good wife and have the aristocratic background to become a first-rate queen and consort. Camilla had refused his incessant pleas to divorce her husband and marry him because she realized only too well the enormous constitutional crisis that situation would create. Diana came along at exactly the right moment and Charles was hooked. She was young, beautiful, and vivacious. She was also from an impeccable aristocratic background and she absolutely worshiped Charles."

Colborne continued, "I also know that Charles did love Diana. Any suggestion that he never loved her is hogwash. I saw them together in the good times when they were wrapped in each other. They loved each other, pure and simple. It was a tragedy when it all went wrong. I now believe that having regained his independence, he is, once again, a happy man. I believe he will probably remain single even after his divorce from Diana, whenever that comes about. There is obviously a deep love and affection between Charles and Camilla, but they are both adults. They know they have the rest of their lives to be together, and the strength of their relationship won't be dimmed just because they don't live together as man and wife."

According to friends who have known Charles for some years, he is, once again, happy living a bachelor life with his mistress ensconced in a beautiful house not far from Highgrove. His sense of humor has returned and he has become more patient with his staff. And he no longer feels embarrassed because until 1995 he could only visit Camilla in her marital home or invite her over to Highgrove.

In the summer of 1995, Camilla bought Ray Mill House, a twenty-minute drive from Highgrove. A delightful Bath-stone, late-Regency villa, it is located near the picturesque National Trust village of Lacock, Wiltshire, and cost $1.2 million. She purchased it after selling the former marital home Middlewick House, her seven-bedroom, eighteenth century home in Corsham, to Pink Floyd drummer Nick Mason for $1.8 million.

Some work had to be done to make the six-bedroomed house into the home Camilla wanted, a bijou residence set in seventeen acres of beautiful Wiltshire countyside. The house is not too large, but comfortable enough for her children Tom, twenty-one, and Laura, eighteen, to stay in when they are down from university. And Ray Mill House makes a cozy home for a couple entering middle age.

Before buying the estate, which borders the banks of the river Avon, Charles went over the property with Camilla several times and both agreed it had great potential, with the a house well-hidden from prying eyes and long-range camera lenses. Charles went further and happily provided Camilla with a handsome check, estimated at more than $100,000, toward the renovations and interior decorations they both felt necessary to stamp their characters and personalities on the beautiful house they want to make their home.

Having spent two months refurnishing and decorating the main house, Camilla will now concentrate on converting the large stone barn into a luxurious four-bedroom retreat on the estate, two hundred yards from the main house, but first she must secure permission from the local planing authority. That might not be automatic because the authority has a reputation for not wanting the village spoiled or changed in any way. Camilla intends to invite her widowed father to move into the refurbished barn so he can be near his beloved daughter.

Charles and Camilla intend to make Ray Mill House their hideaway home where they can be totally on their own, whenever they want seclusion and intimacy. To Charles, Highgrove has few happy memories. They are mostly awful recollections of his disastrous marriage and the appalling battles that went on there between Diana and himself. After 1987, Charles carried on much of his work from Highgrove, moving his office from London to his country estate. Since the official separation in 1992, Charles has moved most of his business affairs and his staff back to London, taking a suite of offices in St. James's Palace, two hundred yards from Buckingham Palace. He also has a small apartment in St. James's Palace where he stays when remaining overnight in London.

Having recovered from the marriage he once described as "a life of absolute mayhem," Charles believes he is fortunate to have been reunited with the woman he loves and respects, and who makes him laugh and relax. Camilla is also in no hurry to urge Charles to marry her. She, too, believes Charles should remain a bachelor when he finally divorces Diana, for then there would be no constitutional problems for him to face when the time comes to ascend the throne.

Camilla believes the passage of time might alter his outlook on marriage. But that raises another consideration, which she has discussed with Charles, his all-important relationship with the two most important people in his life, Wills and Harry. For their sake Camilla feels it would be a major error if they thought, for one moment, that their father was eager to divorce their mother so that he could immediately marry the woman whom Diana, and much of the nation, blames for the marriage breakup. She also believes Charles should retain his independence for as long as he wants, perhaps as much as fifteen years. Charles would then be over sixty, Wills would be nearly thirty and Harry twenty-seven.

Camilla has great trust in her relationship with Charles, and she does not believe the passage of time will harm their deep feelings for each other. Ever since the dark days of 1979, following the assassination of Uncle Dickie, she has known that Charles needs her. She understands his strengths and his weaknesses. She is probably the only woman in the world who has held Charles in her arms while he openly sobbed, unable to control his tears after Mountbatten's senseless murder. She believes she knows his heart and his soul better than anyone else. She also understands that he needs time alone fishing and reading and listening to music. And she is all too happy to give him the freedom he must have.

In the unlikely event that Elizabeth, who turned seventy in 1996, should die in the near future, Charles would automatically become king. And, if still married, Diana would have been crowned queen. Charles, however, would not have been able to bear the sight of Diana sitting beside him in Westminster Abbey being crowned queen consort.

If Charles and Diana had not divorced before that time, Britain would have faced the unseemly prospect of King Charles III, supreme governor of the Church of England, divorcing his wife, the most popular member of the Royal Family, between the time of his mother's death and his coronation, a matter of perhaps six months. Such a quickie divorce would have proved a disastrous start to a new king's reign, and his advisers would never have permitted him to take such a step.

For these reasons the Establishment, the politicians, and

Church of England leaders advised Charles and Diana to
divorce sooner rather than later, despite the fact that neither
Charles nor Diana wanted to take such action until Wills and
Harry were some years older.

11

A Nanny Named Tiggy

———— ❦ ————

DIANA HAS ALWAYS BELIEVED that despite all his faults and lack of warmth toward her, Charles truly loves both William and Harry and throughout their lives has proved his love in his treatment of them. On many occasions during their early years together Charles had told her he would try his damnedest to be a good, natural, loving father to his boys, the exact opposite of the way he remembered only too starkly how his father, Prince Philip, had behaved toward him.

Prince Philip would treat his eldest son as though he were a junior naval rating rather than a beloved firstborn. Philip's attitudes toward child rearing verged on the Victorian: Charles was to remain quiet at all times, unless invited to speak; be sent to his room as a punishment for the least misdemeanor, even something accidental; and be threatened with a good thrashing for the faintest sign of naughtiness.

The German-born Philip frequently administered corporal punishment to his young son, usually his hand, giving four or six hard slaps on Charles's backside. Later, Philip would use a slipper or a tennis shoe to beat Charles. Philip once gave Charles a spanking for sticking out his tongue in public, another time for slipping an ice cube down a servant's neck, and in yet another instance for being rude to guests. And Charles would always be beaten for not immediately obeying his father. All these beatings took place before Charles was six.

Miss Catherine Peebles (nicknamed Mipsy), Charles's first

governess, believed that Prince Philip was partly responsible for the boy's nervous, oversensitive personality. Mipsy recalled, "If you raised your voice to him, he would draw back into his shell, and for a time you would be able to do nothing with him."

At first, Elizabeth tried to intervene to protect her firstborn from Philip's strict discipline, but he would say, "The child must learn to obey, and I intend to teach him."

Charles would tell Diana of all his childhood experiences at the hands of his father, but he would examine how his relationship had changed toward him over the years. Despite the beatings and the discipline, he loved his father, believing him to be brave, good, and invincible. He copied his every mannerism, the way he spoke, the way he walked, and above all, he absorbed his passion for sailing and polo. Charles desperately wanted his father's confidence, his love, and his acclaim. But they would not be forthcoming no matter how hard Charles tried. Years later Charles would realize that his father had resented the life Charles would lead as heir to the throne. Instead of encouraging him, Philip subjected his son to a regime of obedience, trials, and punishment. The man who should have been proud of Charles's achievements hardly ever praised him, and whenever he failed at anything, Philip was quick to condemn.

Philip's harsh approach to his son's development made Charles stand on his own two feet, but at a great price. Mistakenly, Philip would even refuse to help Charles when he needed it, nor give Charles advice when he sought it, and more important, turned his back when Charles yearned for affection and parental love. The adoration and love Charles bore his father gradually turned to estrangement and fear in the face of icy behavior. Charles had always respected his mother for her diligence and sense of duty and the way she had coped with her difficult, truculent husband for so many years.

Diana would tell her girlfriends who were mothers of young children, "Charles is wonderful with the boys. He may be a little naive about babies, not having any idea what to do, but he loves being with them, holding them, feeding them, playing with them, and enjoying their company. He gives them so much love because he realizes how little love he received from his parents. And thank goodness he realizes how important love is to a child's emotional development."

That simple but vital attachment between Charles and his sons is something that has always confused Diana. She would see the way he behaved with both Wills and Harry, observe the joy in his eyes when he picked them up, cuddled them, or later when he would take their hand while they walked beside him. She has not yet been able to understand how he found it possible to turn his back on them simply to spend more time with another woman.

When those thoughts flashed through Diana's mind, her mood would immediately change and anger would overcome her. "The stupid, fucking bastard," she would scream. "How could he leave us for that bloody woman? God, he infuriates me. How could he walk out on them if he really loved them? How could he?"

More often than not, her anger would end in a flood of tears, which she didn't want to shed but which simply welled up in her eyes.

Even ten years after the breakup Diana finds herself becoming overwrought whenever she thinks deeply about Charles and his relationship with their sons. She has to tell herself that Charles does still love them and he wants them to grow up with far fewer emotional hang-ups than he has.

In his famous 1994 TV interview Charles told Dimbleby that he wanted to mention his sons, and he did. He wanted to explain his relationship with them in an ordinary way so that everyone would understand the bond between them. "I have always mucked around with them a great deal. When William was tiny, I used to muck around with him as much as possible." The film footage showed Charles with Wills and Harry in the open air in Scotland, smiling, laughing, and joking together. The boys seemed happy and natural.

Diana has always disliked and has often violently objected to Wills and Harry being taught to shoot and to hunt, but she didn't mind their father teaching them to fish. She was concerned from the very beginning that simply being with the Royal Family in Scotland would influence them to such an extent that shooting and hunting would become natural sports to them. That was why she wanted to dissuade them from engaging in such sports from an early age.

She hated family holidays at Balmoral because Wills and Harry were so eager to accompany their father whenever he went out shooting, stalking, or riding. At first she tried to dissuade them by suggesting they stay inside with her, playing with their toy trains or cars, their board games, or reading or watching a children's video on TV. But the boys loved to emulate their father's sporting interests. They wanted to be like him, to be with him. And she had to confess they had that look of enchantment and excitement on their little faces whenever they put on their outdoor clothes to join their father in the cold and rain of the moors stalking, shooting, or simply walking the dogs.

Diana found she was losing the arguments over hunting and shooting, which continued for a number of years. By the time Wills was eight and Harry six, she knew there was no point in her objecting for they loved both those violent sports. Their decision upset Diana greatly for she felt powerless, unable to dissuade even her sons from indulging in what she believed to be "vile, disgusting sports" that she felt should be banned by law.

On one famous occasion at Balmoral, when the boys were very young, Diana had a ferocious argument over dinner with the whole family as she stridently explained in no uncertain terms that people who supported such cruel sports weren't fit to be parents.

"What?" interjected Philip. "What did you say?"

Diana would not be calmed. "I said," she repeated, blushing madly, "that parents who condone such cruelty aren't fit to be parents."

Elizabeth said nothing but looked angrily at Diana, then at Charles.

"I don't think Diana actually means that," Charles said, trying to diffuse the tension building up around the table.

"Yes, I did," Diana said, sticking to her guns. "I meant

every word. How can you call yourself responsible parents encouraging young boys like Wills and Harry to shoot birds and kill foxes. It's disgusting."

"I think you've said enough for one dinner," Philip commented, hoping to stop Diana from continuing her argument.

"Well, I don't think I have. I've only just started. I don't want my sons brought up enjoying such awful, cruel country activities. I don't want them to be taught to kill innocent animals and birds. They weren't brought into this world to kill."

Her voice rising higher, the tears began to well in her eyes as she looked at the family staring at her, unable to believe her blasphemy.

"I think that's enough," Elizabeth said quietly, and she began to eat again.

"Well, it isn't enough for me," yelled Diana, "not until I stop them practicing such cruelty. Only then will I have said enough. Good night."

With those words she picked up her napkin and all but threw it on the table before walking out of the room. No one is permitted to leave a royal table before the Queen departs without her express permission. And that applies to her own family in the confines of their own home.

Philip was about to leap to his feet to stop her, but Elizabeth raised her hand. The Queen wanted no more trouble, for Elizabeth cannot abide such scenes. The family, however, would never forget what they considered an extraordinary emotional outburst.

It was not surprising, with such scenes and with such an adverse view on the principal sporting pursuits everyone enjoyed at Balmoral, that Diana never liked visiting the castle and could never escape the place quickly enough. Charles loved Balmoral, situated in a desolate part of Scotland, devoid of paparazzi and journalists, a cold, windy place where the Royals could do whatever they liked with complete freedom.

"That godforsaken place" was Diana's description of Balmoral, where all she could remember was boredom, frustration, loneliness and unhappiness.

Diana would not admit this point to many, but she was annoyed that Charles had won the argument over blood sports, which made her feel useless and lonely. Often Diana would walk into a room to hear Charles and the boys deep in conversation about the events of that day, nearly always involving one or other of the field sports.

Though she knew her thoughts to be irrational, she would say, "Sometimes I feel the boys don't want me, don't need me, don't even love me."

Her dramatic mood swings would change everything. Wills and Harry would run into her bedroom and throw themselves on her bed, cuddle and kiss her, which happened after Charles had left London to move to the country. Thoughts of her unhappiness would dissolve in seconds, and she would hold the boys close. They would rush back to their bedrooms, dress, and go to breakfast, the noise of their laughter and shouts reverberating through the rooms as Diana, smiling broadly, pulled on a track suit to hurry to join them. At those times Diana was truly happy.

On many other occasions, however, when the children were away at boarding school or staying with Charles, Diana's moods turned black. Her thoughts would concentrate on Charles's "girl Friday," Tiggy Legge-Bourke, the thirty-year-old woman Charles employed in 1992, six months after the separation. Officially, Tiggy was hired as an assistant to Charles's private secretary, Comdr. Richard Aylard, but in reality she would become the boys' nanny whenever they stayed with their father or were with him in Scotland or on holiday abroad. She would be paid $30,000 a year.

Before employing her, Charles asked Diana to interview Tiggy to see whether she believed she would be suitable for the job. The interview took place in private at Kensington Palace with only the two women present. Diana posed all the pertinent questions, and although she had read her curriculum vitae, Diana asked her to recount her career so that Diana could interject an occasional question. They got on quite well.

One of the first questions Diana asked concerned Tiggy's unusual nickname. Her real name is Alexandra, but she so adored the character Mrs. Tiggiwinkle, Beatrix Potter's famous hedgehog, that her family called her Tiggy. The name stuck.

As Diana anticipated, Tiggy was the quintessential upper-class girl, raised in the Welsh countryside on her parents' family estate, Glanusk Park, which occupies six thousand acres around Crickhowell in Wales. She had first been educated at St. David's Convent in Brecon, south Wales, an independent Roman Catholic school of 150 pupils run by the Ursuline order of nuns. She then moved to the Manor House in Durnford, an elite preparatory school of only 50 girls owned by Lady Tryon, the mother-in-law of Charles's old friend Lady "Kanga" Tyron, with whom Charles once had a brief fling.

At age thirteen, Tiggy moved to Heathfield, in Ascot, Berkshire, one of Britain's top girls boarding schools, where she enjoyed herself immensely, excelling at tennis and netball.

Margaret Parry, then headmistress of Heathfield, remembers Tiggy as "one of the most agreeable people to have in the school; reliable, capable and very responsible, although not in the least academic." School records show Tiggy won her school colors at tennis, lacrosse, netball, and fencing, as well as being a member of the choir.

Academically, however, like Diana, Tiggy was below average, but she did manage to attain four O (ordinary) level examinations, four more than Diana achieved. Tiggy was then packed off to an exclusive finishing school, at Château d'Oex, near Gstaad, the Institut Alpin Videmanette, the same school where Diana had been sent to complete her education.

Diana, however, had only lasted six weeks, crying herself to sleep each night for the first week. At the end of six weeks Diana had returned home in tears. Tiggy was made of sterner stuff and lasted the course, brushing up her schoolgirl French, as well as her manners, deportment, and skiing technique.

At school, Tiggy earned a reputation for thoroughly enjoying life, keen to take part in all school activities, throwing herself into sport and social functions, remaining popular throughout her years there. After returning from Gstaad, she took a Montessori nursery-teaching course in London and in

1985 opened her own nursery, named Mrs. Tiggiwinkle's in the London suburb of Battersea. It would be hugely popular but she was forced to close the school three years later due to financial difficulties and staffing problems.

One problem had been that Tiggy was too kind, too generous, and too caring to the children, some of whose parents could ill afford the modest fees, so Tiggy would take them in for nothing. She had enjoyed the experience immensely and was sad for the children when forced to close.

When Charles was seeking a nanny, someone whom the growing boys could relate to and respect, Charles decided to search for a highly responsible young woman who could muck in with his sons, be almost an older sister, who could ride out with the boys, kick a soccerball, go swimming, and, if necessary, shoot rabbits! He was told that Tiggy would be ideal. Charles was told by his staff, "She likes the outdoors, she's not really bothered whether she's wearing up-to-the-minute fashions or jeans, Wellington boots, and an old sweater; most of the time she doesn't even wear makeup. Basically she seems straightforward and wonderfully uncomplicated. And there is another point: she has a reputation for being bighearted and generous."

Tiggy also had royal connections. Her aunt, Miss Victoria Legge-Bourke, had been an extra lady-in-waiting to Princess Anne for some years and happily talked about her niece, believing she would be most suitable for Charles and the boys. "Tiggy comes from a loving, happy family," she would say, "and you cannot help but warm to her. Charles couldn't have found a nicer person to take care of his children. And, what's more, she is absolutely discreet and loyal."

Charles was delighted with the young woman's no-nonsense approach to life, and her sense of fun and adventure. He believed she would get on well with the boys. Diana, too, approved, though in principle she hated the idea of another woman stepping into her shoes.

Tiggy was not a glamorous model. Overweight, with her long hair swept back with an Alice band to keep it in place, she would spend most of the time with Wills and Harry dressed in jeans and a shirt or sweater. She would, however, nearly always be seen with a smile on her face. There would be one drawback: Tiggy smoked cigarettes, something both Charles and Diana forbid in their homes. Tiggy agreed never to smoke indoors nor in the presence of the boys.

During the following few months a number of photographs would be seen of Wills and Harry, growing rapidly, enjoying a break from boarding school, and seemingly two happy youngsters. But now there would be no Diana in the picture. Instead, they would be seen walking along, linking arms or having fun with Tiggy, their new nanny, their big sister, favorite aunt, and stand-in mother, all rolled into one. All the photographs showed the boys to be happy and relaxed.

One day in October 1994 Diana saw a photograph of Wills and Harry with Tiggy in a newspaper. The caption read, "The royal princes enjoying life with their surrogate mother, Tiggy Legge-Bourke."

"No, no, no," screamed Diana, "They can't write that. It's not true." She jumped up and rushed into her bedroom in a flood of tears, crying out, "They're mine, they're mine, they're mine. How can they write that?"

On numerous other occasions during the following twelve months, Diana would become tearful and emotional, sometimes openly distraught, about her sons' relationship with Tiggy, fearful that they would become more fond of her than they were of their own mother.

When Diana collected them from school, knowing they would be spending a weekend or a number of weeks with her during school holidays, she would play one of her favorite tapes on the car radio and sing along to the music, so happy to be seeing and having them with her once again. When the boys are with her, Diana will unashamedly spoil them, permit them to choose what they want to do each day, and happily go along with their decision. She will give them whatever they want to eat at home, lashings of ice cream and lots of chips with home-made burgers.

"I know I shouldn't spoil them," she said, laughing, to

another young mother whose children attend Harry's school, "but they're mine and I love them and I don't see them nearly enough. In any case it will not be many years before they are leading their own lives. I don't think it harms to spoil them just a little bit." She adds, "In any case I can spoil them because I'm their mother."

Parting from the boys at the end of a weekend fills Diana's heart with gloom and makes her despondent. She would drive them back to school because it gave her more time with them, but for most of the journey Diana would find herself fighting back tears.

Diana found it almost unbearable if she was returning Wills and Harry to Tiggy's care. Diana and Tiggy would not meet frequently, but Diana would see occasional clips on television of Charles and the boys with Tiggy walking along together like a family. On those occasions Diana would need to bite her lip to stop the tears for she would feel despondent and lonely.

"They seem so happy with her around," she would complain to a close friend. "It's just not fair. I can't bear to see them being cared for by another woman. What hurts even more is when the boys tell me what they have been doing with Tiggy."

What irked Diana, and on occasion roused her to anger, would be Charles's habit of happily leaving the boys in the care of Tiggy when he could not for some reason be with them. In November 1994, both boys rode out with a special junior session of the Beaufort hunt near Highgrove. Charles could not be present so Tiggy rode along with them instead. Diana read about it in a newspaper, which showed the three of them together, without Charles. She read that they all had a marvelous time. That winter they would often go out riding with Tiggy from Highgrove while Charles stayed at home, working or reading.

After a matter of a few months Tiggy would accompany Charles and the children everywhere: to Balmoral for school holidays; to Sandringham for Christmas; to Klosters for skiing; to the Greek islands for sailing expeditions and Mediterranean beaches for summer sun. Charles would take all three of them

The fairy-tale wedding, July 29, 1981 (London News Service)

Off on their honeymoon through the streets of London. The world rejoiced.
(London News Service)

On honeymoon in Scotland. Love and tenderness.
(London News Service)

The Queen with Princess Diana in a state carriage drawn by six white horses down the Mall, summer 1992 (London News Service)

Diana attending a church service in summer 1994 dressed in a stunning but simple white dress and wide-brimmed hat. (Express Newspapers)

With the Italian opera star Luciano Pavarotti, attending a charity night in Modena, September 1995. Diana wore an eye-popping Versace dress. (Express Newspapers)

Chased by four paparazzi and wearing dark glasses to hide her eyes, a nervous, tearful Diana gets into her car after leaving the home of her psychotherapist, Susie Orbach. (London News Service)

Maj. James Hewitt pictured in Brigade of Guards mess kit, lying on the single bed in his mother's cottage where he used to make love to Diana (Express Newspapers)

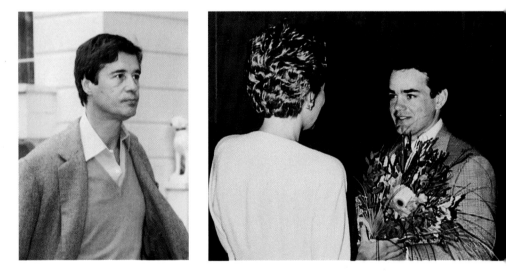

Left, above: Oliver Hoare, the handsome man who befriended both Charles and Diana as they battled to save their marriage. Later Diana would fall in love with the Islamic art dealer and bombard him and his wife, Diane, with annoying phone calls. (Express Newspapers)
Right, above: Diana with Will Carling, the England rugby captain, 1994 (London News Service)

Camilla Parker Bowles, Charles's mistress for the past ten years, pictured shopping, 1992 (London News Service)

The new, slim-line, fashionably dressed Tiggy Legge-Bourke leaving her London home in January 1996. Gossips inside royal palaces believed Tiggy and Charles were enjoying an affair. (London News Service)

Tiggy Legge-Bourke plays in the snow with Wills and Harry during a skiing holiday with Charles at Lech, Austria, in April 1992. (London News Service)

Diana pictured during her compelling hour-long interview for the BBC
in November 1995. Many praised the interview; others despaired.
Diana herself was thrilled with her performance. (London News Service)

A happy, smiling Diana
with a bounce in her
step as she walks across
the tiny airfield at the
end of a holiday on the
island of St. Barthelemy
in the French West
Indies, 1995
(Express Newspapers)

fishing, usually in Scotland, stalking in the highlands; and sometimes rabbit shooting. Brought up in the country, Tiggy proved to be a good shot, and she happily taught the boys the skills of shooting. They would go out rabbiting together and return with braces of dead rabbits killed on the estate.

Diana would see a photograph of the boys in Scotland with their father and Tiggy out shooting and explode, "How could he? What the hell does he think he's doing bringing up the boys to kill innocent wild animals? Can't he ever use his head? Doesn't Charles realize the world has changed since his childhood? Shooting rabbits for fun is no longer a sport, it's a barbaric bloody crime!"

Charles would be oblivious to such anger and criticism, but Diana would later phone him and say whatever was on her mind. On such occasions Charles would usually answer, neither agreeing or disagreeing with his wife, "I hear what you say," infuriating Diana even more.

"Why won't he ever give me a straight bloody answer," she complained. "He never did and I suppose he never will, the little shit."

Diana would note that Tiggy was given her own bedroom at Highgrove. She heard that Tiggy would happily play with the boys while Charles would be busily tending his beloved garden or working in his study. As the boys grew older, the four would have dinner together. When the boys had gone to bed, Charles would invariably kiss them good night, then watch TV or a video with Tiggy; sometimes he would listen to music alone in his study, but not often.

Charles found Tiggy easy and enjoyable company and would at night often discuss the day's events or plan excursions for the boys. He liked that she never argued with him, for it made his life so much more pleasant. And he would compare their weekends at Highgrove to the maelstrom of screaming and violent arguments on weekends he and Diana had spent together in the country. Charles also came to value Tiggy's down-to-earth approach to Wills and Harry.

12

The Duckling Becomes a Swan

———— ❦ ————

I N THE SPRING OF 1995, Charles noted that the well-built Tiggy, weighing somewhere over 140 pounds, began to lose weight somewhat dramatically. He feared that she might be suffering from anorexia, the eating disorder Diana had fought against for some years, but Tiggy reassured him. "You see how much I eat," she told Charles laughingly. "I'm a glutton."

After blood tests and examinations, which Charles arranged, Tiggy was found to be suffering from celiac disease, caused by an intolerance to gluten. It meant a complete change of diet and she was forbidden to eat many of her favorite foods such as bread, cakes, biscuits, pasta, and porridge because they were causing her severe stomach upsets. Her new diet would be restricted to vegetables and fruit. The pounds rolled off. By the summer of 1995, Tiggy needed a complete new wardrobe for she had shed more than twenty pounds. With the disease under control Tiggy began to feel better, to enjoy life more. That she had lost so much weight delighted her, the pain and the discomfort worthwhile.

Initially, Tiggy would be given a small apartment in St. James's Palace, two hundred yards from Buckingham Palace, where Charles moved his London base after the final split from Diana. Most of the time, however, Tiggy preferred to stay in her luxurious $600,000 apartment in Belgravia, a home she had inherited as part of a family trust. However, her family decided to put the apartment on the market and she moved into a home of a relative who lived in West Kensington. After discussions with the executives who manage his Duchy of Cornwall's properties in London, Charles found a suitable house for Tiggy. Her family trust fund happily paid the $250,000 for the terraced house in Kennington, South London, though neither the address nor the neighborhood could compare to the exclusive surroundings of Belgravia.

Staff at Kensington Palace noted the deteriorating relationship between Diana and Tiggy after only a few months, and by the end of 1994 there was a distinct antipathy. Understandably, Tiggy would need to visit Kensington Palace on numerous occasions to pick up or drop off the boys. Diana, noting that the boys really seemed to enjoy having Tiggy around, would become somewhat jealous. Palace staff understood this was a natural maternal reaction.

When Tiggy entered the room where Diana was having a meal or simply chatting to people, Diana would seem to freeze. She would rarely look Tiggy in the eye when they held a conversation. She began treating Tiggy in an offhand manner as though she were a junior member of staff, not the woman responsible for the care of her sons.

In all royal households the nanny is treated with respect, held to be enjoying a position of privilege and trust, and therefore accorded more dignity than all the other personal staff. When Diana spoke to Tiggy, however, a frost would be in the air, and Diana would answer any questions curtly, without any of the usual gentle, flattering chitchat that she enjoys with most of her personal staff whether maids, hairdressers, or those who simply care for the hundreds of items in Diana's prodigious wardrobe.

An old friend of Diana's, a man of mature years who had advised her during the early years of her marriage, was enjoying a quiet lunch at Kensington Palace with Diana in early 1995 when he was somewhat taken aback by her attitude. He recalled, "We were enjoying a snack lunch at the dining room table with a few other people when we heard a great commotion as the boys arrived home. They rushed into the dining room, kissed their mother on the cheek, and then politely said hello to everyone. That part was fine.

"A couple of minutes later Tiggy walked into the room and said good afternoon to everyone, politely and pleasantly. She added, 'Good afternoon, ma'am,' to Diana, who totally ignored her. Those of us at the table looked at each other feeling the uneasy tension that had suddenly descended on the room, ruining the pleasant atmosphere and the lunch. When Tiggy asked a direct question, whether she should take the boys out of the room, Diana suggested she was being rather rude interrupting her lunch party. Tiggy apologized and walked out of the room, ushering the boys with her.

"Within seconds of Tiggy's departure Diana said, 'That's better, perhaps we can enjoy our lunch now.' And yet we all realized that it was the interruption of two young, happy boys that had caused the hiatus, not the behavior of Tiggy. It illustrated to us all the bitterness Diana felt towards the nanny. And the fact that Diana seemed incapable of hiding her feelings showed how near breaking point Diana had reached in her relationship with the new nanny."

Diana would read everything she could find in the newspapers about Tiggy's life. She would chat to staff at Highgrove and St. James's Palace to find out all that was happening. In the early summer of 1995, Diana sensed something was very wrong. She heard from staff at Highgrove that Tiggy and Charles were becoming closer. They had been seen kissing—at first just pecks on the cheek—whenever Tiggy came down to stay at Charles's country house. And they would kiss farewell if either of them left, leaving the other behind. Diana knew full well that Charles would never kiss members of staff. He hadn't in the past and she doubted whether he now greeted his secretaries, grooms, housemaids, and cooks with kisses.

Diana heard that Tiggy would stay at Highgrove some weekends when the boys were with Diana in London. By June 1995, staff at Highgrove, who happily kept in touch with Diana, were convinced that Charles and Tiggy were having an affair. Diana was told, "Staff saw Charles and Tiggy all but making love. They were kissing and petting one Saturday night. Later they went up to bed."

Of course, Diana asked her sources for any concrete evidence that Charles and Tiggy had become lovers, but they could add nothing more. She was told that the relationship between the two had changed, that Charles was warm and more considerate to her and that Tiggy would do anything and everything for him, looking at him "with the eyes of an adoring spaniel."

Diana winced. She realized that was exactly the way she had looked at Charles in their early married life together when she, too, was mesmerized and had been made to feel she was the most wonderful girl in the world.

The thought that Charles and Tiggy were having an affair infuriated Diana. She was now convinced that Tiggy had not only taken over her job, as mother to the princes, but had moved into her husband's bed. She would tell her trusted adviser, "I am still receiving reports that they sleep together on occasions, but I am informed that the children have no idea whatsoever that their father is screwing their nanny. And I hope for his sake that he keeps it that way; otherwise there will be trouble."

She went on, "I asked them if Camilla was still around, and they said that she still stayed frequently, but usually during the week when neither the children nor Tiggy were about. My friends tell me nothing seems to have changed between Charles and Camilla, still acting like a happy, contented middle-aged couple going for walks with the dogs and enjoying music and dinners together at Highgrove. They are still very much together."

Later, Diana would say, "I wonder what on earth has got into him. He must be enjoying a new lease on life, running two women at once. It's certainly not the Charles that I remember."

Several months later Charles and Tiggy were caught by photographers kissing in public when they met at Balmoral. Charles clambered out of a Land Rover on the Scottish estate and walked around to the back of the vehicle as Tiggy came running across. She put her arms around his shoulders, looked him square in the eye, and kissed him on the cheek. Not simply a peck but a definite kiss. For seconds they held the embrace. Nearby were other members of the shooting party including the Queen and Philip, but apparently no one saw them embrace.

The gossips began talking only after that first public kiss, noticing that Tiggy Legge-Bourke had changed beyond recognition. The Alice bands, the pearls, the frumpy frocks, and big sweaters had gone; so had the double chin. Instead, Diana and others saw a degree of elegance, though nothing to compete with the Princess of Wales. Tiggy would be seen wearing short skirts, silk shirts, high heels, and discreet gold jewelry, her hair cut and styled in a sophisticated manner. And there was now a touch of makeup and lipstick!

In some respects, believing that Tiggy was having an affair with Charles rather amused Diana. She wondered whether Camilla knew of the affair and smiled when she thought of what Camilla's reaction might be to the news. Camilla had given up her marriage for Charles, and Diana felt sure Camilla would be absolutely furious if she believed Charles was now two-timing her. Diana also worried that Wills or Harry might twig what was going on between their father and Tiggy, and she certainly didn't want them to suspect such goings-on. Diana believes her sons have already experienced enough ghastly traumas in their young lives without more being piled onto their shoulders.

Both Wills and Harry enjoyed having Tiggy around; they liked that she could ride, fish, shoot, ski, swim, and enjoy all the country activities they, too, have learned to love. And they enjoyed teasing her about her total inability to stop smoking. On holiday at Klosters they pretended to copy her, smoking a cigarette while racing fast downhill. She would chase them and roll them in the snow and they would pelt her with snowballs, reveling in the fun of it.

Back home in London, Diana would chat with the boys, asking them about their weekends and various holidays with their father and Tiggy. She would say, "I know I should laugh and relish their happiness and their fond memories of holidays abroad with Charles and the nanny, but I find it very difficult to hide my true emotions on those occasions."

She would explain all these thoughts in some remarkable detail, and great honesty, with Fergie as well as her close adviser: "While the boys are talking to me about their exploits, sometimes both chattering away at once, I just keep thinking of them being with Tiggy, enjoying life with that woman who seems to be taking over my role, my place, and even supplanting my love. I try not to think like that but I can't help it. They seem so happy with her, happier than when they're with me at the palace. They seem to have more fun with her."

On occasion Diana admits that she finds herself actually hating Tiggy, unable to think rationally of her with her boys, holding them, kissing them goodbye, teasing them, having adventures with them, imagining Wills and Harry laughing and joking with Tiggy rather than with her. She tries to control her feelings, to think rationally about the whole sorry separation, but on many occasions she feels a rage within her that she can barely control.

"I feel that the boys have been torn from me," she said during one of her moments of despair in the summer of 1995. "I feel they have been taken away to enjoy a better life with someone else, someone whose interests may equip her to bring up the boys as young Royals better than I ever could. I can't bear country pursuits, and Tiggy loves them, all of them. Now the children love all those sports as well, and I feel useless, cut off from my own children, my own family. It makes me feel so lonely."

Diana tries to tell herself she is being silly and paranoid, and more often than not, she manages to shake off her feeling of desperation, of guilt and jealousy toward Tiggy. Far better, she persuades herself, that the boys are happy with someone they seem to genuinely like rather than be unhappy with some harridan who might ruin their lives, or someone who might be too kind, spoiling them instead. Diana understands that either of those possibilities would be disastrous for the boys.

But Diana's paranoia over Tiggy does sometimes erupt. Both Wills and Harry were proud of their nanny when she showed them she had become proficient on rollerblades, usually wearing a crash helmet and knee pads, considered essential by safety experts. When Diana heard from her sons of Tiggy's exploits, she bought herself a pair of rollerblades and practiced in private. Four weeks later, in November 1995, she had become sufficiently confident and capable to venture into Kensington Gardens, next door to her palace, joining with many others who enjoy the sport. She could manage speeds of 20 mph but appeared a little shaky on spins and turns. But Diana wore neither a crash helmet nor knee pads, considered a great risk for beginners. When pictures appeared in newspapers of the Princess on rollerblades, she showed them to her sons when they next spent a weekend with their mother.

Diana would also come under fire from safety experts in October 1995 for permitting William to drive around a go-cart racetrack in London's Chelsea without wearing a safety helmet or any form of protective clothing. The thirteen-year-old prince clocked 19.66 seconds, the fastest lap time on record since the track opened in 1993. His time was even faster than that of Formula One drivers including former world champion Damon Hill and British go-cart champion David Coulthard. Both William and Harry enjoy the thrill of motor racing and have attended Formula One world championship races with Diana.

Diana would be under further censure for permitting William to attend a Fiesta Ball at London's Hammersmith Palais in October 1995 where a thousand teenage boys and miniskirted girls danced, kissed, and cuddled until 2 A.M. William begged his mother to permit him to go with others of his class at Eton. In the end she agreed. Alcohol was banned, but some of the teenagers managed to become sick and a little the worse for wear. Virtually all the teenagers spent most of the night on the dance floor, enjoying a wild time, sweating, shaking, shouting, and petting. When the precocious teenage girls realized the blonde-haired William was present, a considerable number approached him, asking for a dance and a kiss. His Eton pals, however, came to his rescue, pushing the girls away. William had a great time.

Diana argued that she was determined to allow her sons to enjoy the normal activities of adolescents. But outside the ballroom that night were empty vodka bottles and beer cans, and inside a number of the teenagers were petting heavily and more. Reading the criticism in some newspapers, Diana shrugged and commented, "They're just overreacting. Why shouldn't he enjoy himself?"

Diana is determined William and Harry will experience as much as possible while growing up and not simply the field sports their father enjoys. She knows that Charles had little of an ordinary, normal life when he was a teenager and neither did Diana. She firmly believes that the more ordinary teenage experiences Wills and Harry enjoy, the better they will cope with their privileged life later.

As a result, Prince William has already enjoyed a wealth of opportunities, pursuits, sports, and pastimes far in excess of almost any other teenager in Britain. All due to Diana's determination. He has gone white-water rafting on Colorado's Roaring Fork River; raced quad bikes along an American mountain track; enjoyed in the pits the thrill of Grand Prix motor racing; surfed off the Caribbean island of Nevis; and been on Jet Skis off the coast of Sardinia. He has his own pony, hunts, rides, shoots, stalks, and fishes and plays tennis and swims at the Chelsea Harbour Club.

But it hasn't all been fun. Diana has also taken William to hostels for the homeless and to visit terminally ill AIDS patients in hospitals. In early January 1996, Diana decided that after all the festivities of Christmas, Wills and Harry should see the harsh realities of life. So one evening she took them to a hostel for the homeless run by the charity Centrepoint in the heart of London's red-light district. Only three days before the boys had returned from a skiing holiday in Klosters, Switzerland, with their father and Tiggy. It was the boys' first joint visit to a hostel for the homeless.

Wills and Harry sat down in the canteen with Diana and chatted to twenty-five residents, all teenagers who had nowhere else to live. One asked Diana, "Why do you bother to come here?"

Diana looked at her sons and said, "Because we care."

Afterward, Gareth Jones, one of the volunteer workers, said, "Both William and Harry appeared bemused at first. Harry seemed tired and stuck close to his mother's side. William seemed genuinely concerned by their plight."

It was supposed to be a private visit, but within minutes of their arrival reporters and photographers arrived on the scene, tipped off by a phone call from Kensington Palace.

But Diana's decision to take the two princes to a hostel for the homeless did not receive unmitigated acclaim from the media, some commentators arguing that Diana had arranged the visit as a photo opportunity to show her caring image. One outspoken commentator, Richard Littlejohn, wrote, "There seems no stunt she is not prepared to pull in her campaign to become a state-registered Queen of Hearts. This week she stooped to a new low, dragging her sons round a doss house... visiting a few tramps and winos."

Despite the criticism Diana plans to continue her education of both boys. "They're mine and I will bring them up to be rational, sensible young men," Diana will say when chatting to mothers of other teenage sons. "Later on, they risk being cut off from normal life, so the more they can enjoy and experience the real world while they're still young, the better for them."

She understands that her boys need a woman's touch around them when they are with Charles, but she never wants Camilla to be involved in any way in their upbringing. She hopes that when the boys stay for a weekend at Highgrove that Camilla isn't around. And Diana has warned Charles that he must act responsibly and never permit the boys to see their father sharing a bed with Camilla.

During rational moments Diana tries to be positive in her attitude toward Camilla, but she finds that harder than facing up to Tiggy's presence and influence on the boys. She still believes that Camilla should never, under any circumstances, have restarted her affair with Charles, which she and Charles agreed to end after the murder of Earl Mountbatten. Diana believes that Camilla should have made Charles return to his wife and his children and make a go of his marriage rather than giving him advice, comfort, and finally her love and her body.

Diana will still discuss the matter with friends and those close to her because she finds it all but impossible to get Camilla out of her mind for she believes Camilla deliberately cheated her and Wills and Harry. Diana will say, "I believe that she did refuse Charles's request that she divorce her husband and live with him after Uncle Dickie's murder. At that time she showed great determination and wisdom. She showed me nothing but kindness, but then I didn't realize that she had just been having a raging affair with Charles.

"She should have sent Charles back home. She could have done so because Charles has always been in awe of Camilla, always rushing to her for sympathy and advice, for she bolsters his confidence. Charles needs a strong woman like Camilla. But Camilla didn't do that. She saw her chance and took it and ruined my life and the lives of Wills and Harry. That is why I can never forgive her."

Camilla has behaved with remarkable equilibrium throughout the dramatic saga that has been going on for ten long years. As a child she was more of a tomboy, preferring climbing trees and riding horses to party dresses and doll-houses. As a young woman she loved London's social whirl, dances and parties every night during the season, with a host of young men eager to impress the daughter of one of Britain's wealthy families.

Broderick Munro-Wilson grew up with Camilla in Sussex, and they attended their first dance together when both were twelve years old. They have known each other ever since. "Camilla," he says, "was much more self-assured than other teenage girls. She stood out as a confident young woman and at school became quite a rebel. Even today she is a woman who catches your eye when you walk into a room, because she exudes fun and warmth. She also knows how to talk to men, how to flatter them, and how to get them on her side. She has a slightly wicked twinkle, which is definitely enticing. I don't mean that she's a terrible flirt, just that she's comfortable with men and enjoys their company.

"She looks you straight in the eye when she speaks to you and always has a smile on her face. She is witty and intelligent, too. And she has a mellow, husky voice. She is undoubtedly a most capable and strong character, and that's how she has withstood all the pressure."

He recalled that on one occasion when Camilla's name was first linked with Charles, some women in her local supermarket in Wiltshire threw bread rolls at her because they held her responsible for ruining the marriage of the fairy-tale princess. Camilla simply turned on her heel and walked out of the store with her head held high as if nothing had occurred.

Munro-Wilson went on, "She does make the most perfect hostess for Charles. With Andrew she would be used to running a large house and entertaining parties of a dozen or more for dinner. The food would always be superb, and the evening a great success, though you would hardly notice Camilla's presence."

Those few people invited to dinner parties at Highgrove with Charles and Camilla believe that they would have made an admirable couple for some describe Camilla as the quintessential upper-class English lady, sensible, confident, and very capable, a near-perfect match for Charles. Throughout the epic drama Camilla has never spoken out or reportedly thrown a tantrum. She has always been the perfect lady. For that alone she has won admiration and respect from her peers, mostly wealthy aristocratic women who find such attributes of the utmost importance.

Munro-Wilson spoke for them all when he said, "It is really tough luck on both the Prince and Camilla that they fell in love, but her background would never allow her to marry him because she would not want to rock the monarchy. I do believe, however, from everything that has happened in the last ten years, that Charles will never renounce Camilla."

Increasingly, Diana's animosity toward Camilla has turned toward Tiggy. The more that Diana sees her sons enjoying life when they are with Tiggy, the more hatred she feels for the nanny she now sees as her rival for their affections. So consumed with jealousy had Diana become that she found it all but impossible to speak about Tiggy with equanimity. Diana's feelings of rancor had almost become a phobia since she had been led to believe Tiggy and Charles had become lovers. Since that time Diana had tried to avoid meeting Tiggy, but understandably, they did have to see each other on occasion, for example when Tiggy collected or dropped off Wills and Harry at Kensington Palace.

In early December 1995, Diana was informed that Tiggy had been admitted to a hospital during the summer and, allegedly, undergone an abortion. Diana knew no other details. She asked friends if they could find out the date, the hospital, and the surgeon, but she could find no confirmation.

The allegation came to haunt Diana. She wanted to know whether the story was true and, more importantly, whether Charles was the father. Some weeks later Diana found the opportunity to ask Tiggy. And took it.

In December 1995, Charles and Diana, as they had done throughout their marriage, threw a Christmas party for their respective staffs at the Lanesborough Hotel, Hyde Park Corner, a few hundred yards from Buckingham Palace.

During the party Diana went over to Tiggy and quietly said to her, "So sorry to hear about the baby!"

Devastated by the remark, Tiggy stared at Diana, then turned and fled, fighting back tears. She all but collapsed into the arms of Charles's valet, the tears streaming down her face. Later that evening Tiggy told Prince Charles what Diana had said, but not until the following day did Charles discuss the matter fully with his personal assistant.

After further consultations with Prince Charles, Tiggy

instructed Peter Carter-Ruck, one of Britain's foremost libel lawyers, to write to the Princess of Wales's lawyers, Mischon De Reya, demanding a retraction of "false allegations" she was said to have made toward his client. Carter-Ruck also issued a statement to newspapers about unfounded allegations being circulated that were, he said, a "gross reflection" on Tiggy's "moral character."

Diana treated the demand for a retraction with complete contempt, not even bothering to ask her lawyers to reply to the demand. To friends, Diana would say, "I know where the truth lies."

Tiggy had also instructed Carter-Ruck not to invoke formal legal action against the Princess of Wales because of the embarrassment it might cause Prince Charles. Tiggy also realized that such an action would make her position with William and Harry untenable.

Diana's remark about the baby and Tiggy's legal rebuttal meant that the two women were now at war, and Diana was determined that the nanny whom she referred to "as that trumped-up little tart" would soon be sent packing. "I will do everything in my power to remove William and Harry from that woman's care and influence," Diana told her City friend. "It is absolutely disgraceful that Charles should continue to employ her to care for the boys now that he is bedding her."

In anger, Diana would add, "But once again I suppose the Royals will take absolutely no action against her. They knew all about Charles and Camilla and did nothing. Now they all know about Charles and that tart Tiggy, but I expect they will do nothing about that either."

13

Diana and the Rugby Hero

———— ❧ ————

D IANA LOVES TO TURN HEADS. And the more she captivates the attention of both men and women, the more she boosts her self-confidence and self-esteem. Even today she smiles at the way she would behave in the past before she found the confidence to lift her head in public or the pride to look people in the eye.

It has taken Diana a long time to achieve such self-assurance. Throughout her teenage years she would walk through the streets head down, too shy to show her face. Then no one knew her identity, or even cared. At the age of nineteen, when she first dated Prince Charles, Diana realized how diffident she behaved, particularly when meeting strangers. She loved caring for young children partly because she didn't have to face the agony of meeting strange adults with whom she would become self-conscious, unable to contain her blushes. She would wear little or no makeup, or lipstick and only colorless nail varnish for she didn't want to attract attention. She didn't bother with her figure, keeping fit, or exercising. She would have her hair cut and styled every so often, but nothing more. The rest she would leave to nature.

When Fleet Street discovered the identity of the pretty, but painfully shy nanny the Prince of Wales had taken a fancy to, she didn't care what people thought of her appearance, her looks, her makeup, or her dress sense. The fashion editors, however, would make the young Diana realize that she had to shape up. Stung by their criticism, she worked hard at her grooming, employing a team of talented experts from *Vogue* to advise and instruct her on how to change her image, become fashionable, make the most of herself, and overnight, transform the country girl into a sophisticated bride fit for a prince. The most difficult part of the metamorphosis Diana had to carry out on her own, losing more than fourteen pounds over a four-month period. On the day of her wedding in July 1981 she was proud of her achievements. She had every right to be. The world hailed a beautiful fairy princess.

The births of both William and Harry, in 1982 and 1984, caused Diana far more anguish and worry than she had ever before known in her life. She suffered from postnatal depression and her eating habits deteriorated so much she found she didn't want to eat at all. Her moods swung erratically and her relationship with Charles plummeted from a wonderful, all-embracing love to despising the man who was ill-equipped to cope with such behavior.

Diana lost twenty-eight pounds after the birth of Harry. The bones of her shoulders stuck out, her neck looked thin and scraggy, and her body and legs lost shape. She still remembers the Herculean task of rebuilding what she described as "my shapeless lump of a beanpole" after the years of battling alone with her eating disorders, suffering alternately from anorexia nervosa and bulimia.

Today Diana recalls, "I cannot think how awful I looked. I was ashamed of the way I looked, so thin, flat-chested, with no shape to my legs, and looking as miserable as sin. I couldn't even look at myself in the mirror without feeling dreadfully depressed."

Now, at the age of thirty-four and with no special man in her life, Diana finds that she needs to turn heads to lift her spirits and give herself the confidence to continue her lonely life. She will stand happily in front of her bathroom mirror totally naked to check how she is shaping up and whether she approves of what she sees. Two or three times a week she will make a detailed inspection of her body, but she also has the confidence to give herself a quick up-and-down check whenever she finishes drying after taking a shower. If she believes some muscle needs more tone or views the faintest hint of cellulite, she will discuss it the following day with her gymnastics teacher.

She told one girlfriend, "Sometimes I occasionally like what I see in the mirror, but not very often. I have to keep up the hard work otherwise I see cellulite at the top of my legs or on my bum. And I couldn't bear to see any flab at the top of my arms. That's really yuk. Lately, I have been finding the wrinkles mounting up around my eyes no matter what I put on to counteract them. To hide the wrinkles I just make sure I smile a lot or wear dark glasses, then no one's the wiser."

Laughing, she went on, "I wouldn't dare to let my hair return to its natural color because I'm sure it would be full of gray hairs after all I've been through."

Diana was determined to keep herself superbly fit during her break from royal duties and charity work that she announced to the world in December 1993. And yet the break would bring her a never-ending saga of dramas and public humiliations over her relationships with various men. During the first nine months of 1994, Diana relaxed, tried to enjoy herself, get fit, make more friends, and more importantly, sort herself out and decide her future. Her good intentions, however, would end in yet more tears.

She would train more often at the Chelsea Harbour Club, mostly playing tennis and swimming and doing minor workouts in the gymnasium. Afterward she would relax over a cup of coffee, usually a cappuccino, while she sat at the back of the cafe area at table number 8, which she all but commandeered as her own. From that vantage point she could see the arrivals and departures while remaining discreetly in the background.

Of course, Diana was being more than a little naive if she believed that she could ever again remain unnoticed in a cafe or a shop or anyplace else. At the Harbour Club every member present and the entire staff would always be aware that the most loved, talked about, notorious, and tantalizingly beautiful woman in Britain was in their midst. They all enjoyed basking in the reflected glory, for Diana's presence would cause a buzz of excitement, an undercurrent of tension that helped give the club a spark, as well as served as a never-ending subject of gossip.

She would have a coffee or a juice with her sports advisers and coaches and on occasion with other women who frequented the club that she had come to know well. She really enjoyed her time there. Occasionally she would have a chat with one or two of the young men who attended, but not too often. Most weeks she would visit the club three times, and on occasion more often.

In the early spring of 1994, Diana noticed a ruggedly built young man of about thirty. His face seemed familiar. She noted his broad back, his rippling muscles, and his stout legs and wondered where she had seen him before. He had a confident air, and she watched him, somewhat taken by him.

Some weeks later her elder son, William, wanted to watch the England Rugby Union International, televised live that Saturday afternoon. He persuaded his mother to sit with him. There on the screen, his face in full view, was the same man she had seen at the club. He was Will Carling, the celebrated captain of the England rugby team, probably the most famous rugby player in Britain.

She had met him before. On two occasions she had been the guest of honor at rugby internationals in which Carling had been the captain of the England team when she had been officially introduced to the teams as they lined up to be presented before the match.

The next time she saw Carling at the gym she said hello as she passed by, and Carling was rather taken aback at being spoken to by the Princess of Wales. A few days later she again approached his table and they began to chat. Later, on another visit Diana invited him to her table for an orange juice. They chatted about rugby, about the Harbour Club, and Diana told him that her sons hero-worshiped him. Carling liked that, smiled and blushed, appearing somewhat embarrassed as he sat eating his toast and talking to the Princess of Wales.

During the following few weeks the two would meet every so often, but Carling would wait for Diana to approach him, not wanting to impose himself on her. One day Diana simply walked up to Carling's table and asked, "Can I join you? I feel so conspicuous sitting on my own."

Carling was flattered and delighted. They would talk mostly about the club, keeping fit, working out, and their respective programs. No mention was made of their private lives. Carling, a former Army captain, did not tell Diana he was living with a beautiful, slim, blond girl, named Julia Smith, who had her own thriving public relations firm, Hands On PR, in London.

Will Carling had first met Julia at a dinner party in 1989 shortly after being appointed captain of the England rugby XV. Julia's love life had been high profile, for she had moved into guitarist Jeff Beck's home just after she left school. Following six years of enjoying "married" life in the quiet of the country, Julia then conducted a much-publicized affair with the guitarist Eric Clapton. From the first, Julia's effervescent personality and flirtatious nature, coupled with her serious side, appealed greatly to Carling. He would not forget her. Three years later they met again at a dinner party. At the time Carling had been dating a tall, beautiful, blonde, Victoria Taylor-Jackson, a real estate agent, and they were living together in Carling's basement apartment in London.

Victoria talked of their sensational two-year-long relationship, of Carling's likes and dislikes and his insatiable appetite for sex and women with firm bodies. "Will has always been a ladies' man who can't resist powerful women. He's mad about sex and has an obsession for blondes. He can't resist them. His previous girlfriend before me, a girl called Nicky, was a blonde. I'm a blonde, Julia's a blonde, and we all know the color of Diana's hair."

She went on, "What Will really liked about women was if they were into fitness and had strong personalities, like Diana. He would always tell me he loved women with good firm bodies. He would fantasize about having kinky and open-air sex with me, and he would sign his love letters to me with the words 'Big Willy.' He seemed to love writing me very sexy notes, detailing the sex we would have together when he returned from an overseas trip with the England rugby team."

Victoria and Carling were living together when Julia appeared on the scene. "During a party we threw in January 1993, I walked into our kitchen and found Carling whispering in Julia's ear. I thought nothing of it. Then I discovered that Julia, a close friend of mine, was sending him faxes every other day, calling him by the pet name she gave him, Bum Chin. "We were getting on brilliantly when the breakup happened. We were having fantastic sex and thoroughly enjoying life together. One Sunday he simply went cold on me, like an iceberg. It was as though he had flicked a switch and turned off the machine. His love had gone and he told me our affair was over, finished."

Victoria confessed to being upset and in a state of shock for several weeks while she sorted out her life without Carling. She recalled, "A few days later I picked up a newspaper to find Will pictured with Julia telling the world, 'This is my new girl friend.'"

She went on, "I was absolutely livid. I phoned him in a rage and told him he had behaved like a complete shit. He didn't have an answer and behaved very sheepishly. So that was it. In four weeks he had gone from telling me I was the only girl in the world for him to going out with somebody else."

Carling would be so captivated by the willowy, bubbly Julia that one month later he asked her to marry him. In June 1994, Carling and Julia were wed, three months after Diana and Carling had begun their regular, informal meetings at the Harbour Club.

When Carling met Diana a few weeks after returning from his honeymoon, Diana said, "I understand congratulations are in order."

"Yes, that's true," Carling replied. "Thank you very much."

"And who's the lucky girl? Have I met her?"

"No," replied Carling, adding with a smile, "she has to

work in the office while I'm working out at the gym. Someone has to bring home the bacon."

At that time, Carling was fast becoming one of Britain's top sports earners, driving a $150,000 Aston Martin while garnering endorsement deals that brought him more than $350,000 a year. He had also launched his own management consultancy company, Insight.

For several months the princess and the rugby captain continued to meet at the club. Slowly, Carling learned to relax in Diana's presence, and she would go out of her way to make him feel at ease. Their meetings began to take a more serious turn. They would arrange when they would meet, at what time and on what days. Always, the couple would laugh and joke together. The get-togethers seemed totally innocent. Carling began to tease Diana, telling her that she should become really fit rather than just playing at being fit. She rather liked that.

Principally, Carling would tease Diana about the shape of her body, telling her that her biceps were like sparrow's legs, thin with no muscle. He even began to call her "my little sparrow." She loved the nickname. On a more serious note Diana also asked him what she should do to give herself some real muscle, adding with a laugh, "But I have no wish to look like Arnie Schwarzenegger."

"I'll take you to my special gym," Carling told her. "They'll sort you out."

Carling took Diana to the BiMAL, a medical and sports rehabilitation clinic, a center Britain's top sportsmen attend for physical problems they have been unable to overcome with the help of their own physiotherapists. There, Diana was provided a training program designed to give her more upper-arm muscle, but no visible biceps. Diana would become a regular visitor, arriving at 8 A.M. most Fridays for a thirty-minute session.

Carling would also tease Diana about her wardrobe. Like everyone else in Britain who followed the fortunes of the Princess of Wales, Carling knew that Diana had the most amazing wardrobe, with literally hundreds of expensive, fashionable items costing thousands of dollars. However, on many occasions when going to the gym, Diana would arrive in a pink Martha's Vineyard sweatshirt, black cycle shorts, and white trainers. Carling would smile at her and crack a joke, suggesting that the poor princess was really a Cinderella with no other clothes to her name. Diana would blush and look shy, but loved being teased. It made her feel wanted.

As a joke, Will had a little two-inch china pig made with black shorts painted on it and a pink sweatshirt emblazoned with the words "Martha's Vineyard." The pig was lifting weights. Carling gave it to Diana's chauffeur, Steve Davis, to hand to the princess anonymously. Diana opened the present and roared with laughter. She knew precisely who had sent it.

Diana invited Carling to Kensington Palace during the summer of 1994, telling him that Prince William and Prince Harry were eager to meet their rugby hero. Carling went along. It would be the first of many visits to Diana's private apartments at the palace. She began inviting Carling for a drink and the occasional meal at the palace. The registration number of his car was logged into the police computer at the palace gates and Diana gave him her private direct phone numbers so his calls could bypass the switchboard.

During their meetings at the palace Carling would be introduced to several of Diana's assistants, including her butler, Harold Brown, her secretary, Patrick Jephson, as well as a number of others who kept her diary, helped with her clothes, and cared for the two princes. Caroline Wicker, an attractive, intelligent young woman, had joined Diana's staff in 1990, employed solely to open, sift, and catalog Diana's mail, which would arrive by the sackful most weeks. One day in September 1994, she told Carling, during idle chatter, that she needed another, more fulfilling job, and Carling offered her a position. But he had neglected to seek Diana's permission to approach her.

Diana was furious. Royal protocol dictates that Royals can fire staff whenever they wish, but no one, not even other Royals, are permitted to poach staff or ask whether they would be interested in another job before asking their royal employer for permission to do so. Carling, unaware of such royal protocol, had committed a cardinal error.

But there would be more. Caroline Wicker, in her twenties, is a bright, lovely-looking girl, and Carling had offered her a job in his own office working close to him. Carling would tell one of his pals later, "God, you would have thought I had nicked the crown jewels or something. She was furious with me. It became clear later that it was jealousy more than the breaking of protocol that annoyed Diana. I apologized and told her that I had no idea of the correct protocol, but it took some weeks before she totally forgave me for the gaffe."

Diana, however, would not forget. She would not present Caroline Wicker with the customary departing gift, a signed photograph of the royal household. And Diana ordered she be instantly struck off the Christmas card list.

One person who followed the escalating relationship between Carling and Diana was his former personal assistant, Hilary Ryan. She says, "For a while Diana and Will didn't even speak when they met at the Harbour Club, but Will would go at the same time as before just to see her. During those weeks he seemed awfully downcast." "But by February 1995 everything seemed to be back on track, and Will and Diana would meet three times a week for coffee and a light breakfast after working out. He would tell me that he would be out for several hours, and I understood that together they would be at Kensington Palace.

"Carling ordered a special 'hot' line telephone to be installed, which I was instructed must not be used or answered by anyone in the office, not even me, his PA [Personal Assistant]. I knew the phone had been installed for Diana so she never had to go through the switchboard. On occasions they would chat on the phone for an hour or more, laughing, giggling, cracking jokes, and, on occasions, deep in quiet, intimate conversation."

Carling had been captivated by the alluring, flirty Diana. Her attention flattered him; the very fact that they were having a relationship filled him with pride and self-importance. Already, as captain of the England rugby XV, Carling had considerable self-assurance. Now, less than a year after marrying Julia, Carling knew that the relationship with Diana had taken on an importance that never, for one minute, had he dreamed would be possible.

Diana began giving Carling pecks on the cheek when they met and a kiss on each cheek when they said goodbye. She would put a hand on his shoulder and offer her face to be kissed, gently, courteously, as one would kiss a close friend, but not a lover. In public when saying farewell, they would shake hands, but Diana's hand began to linger and she would give Carling a penetrating look that said more than any kiss.

Carling realized what was happening and loved it. He was becoming involved. Whenever he was with the Princess, Carling felt special, enjoying their time together whether they were snatched moments or hours of chat, tittle-tattle, having a drink, or discussing workouts. They gave each other pet names: Carling called Diana "The Boss" while she called him "Captain."

Carling decided to return to the mystic guru he had first consulted some years before when he was dating Julia and before he had even met Diana. By trade, Charlie Chan, thirty-seven, is an avant-garde society hairdresser with a salon in London's Piccadilly. But he also has a first-class reputation for reading astrological charts as a hobby, advising the rich and famous.

Chan said, "I told Will that he should never have married Julia. I still don't think the marriage will work. With their combined charts I don't think their marriage will ever work. They're just not matched."

During the early part of 1995, Carling returned to his guru friend to ask him what the stars were saying about his future and the future of a Cancerian friend of his with the birth date of July 1, 1961.

"I knew he was referring to the Princess of Wales. I just knew it," said Chan. "I told him that Diana was having a good year and he seemed happy with that. I also told him that he was having an extremely happy year but was ready to move on. Will is Sagittarian with Scorpio rising, so he's in a good position. I have told Will that there is no point in looking back. He has to go forward and I think he will."

Chan was adamant that he had never advised Carling to leave his wife. He said, "Julia is Pisces with Virgo rising and in a poor astrological position. She is fortunately very strong. The whole situation is very simple. If you love something, then you hold on tight and fight for it. If you don't love it, then push it away and move on. It's the only way."

In March 1995, two months before the Rugby Union World Cup finals were to be played in South Africa, Carling arranged for William and Harry to attend a get-together of the England rugby squad where they kicked a ball around and played with the squad members. The boys were in seventh heaven.

Diana began telling Will, as she would often phone him, of the problems that beset her. He would encourage her to get everything off her chest and was only too happy to be the man she wanted to help overcome the pressures and torments of her life. He would listen and advise and sympathize until Carling found himself wanting to throw his arms around her protectively, providing a shoulder to lean on, a collar to cry on.

On occasion the tears would erupt and Carling would feel sad and an affinity to someone who desperately seemed in need of friendship, support, and more importantly, warmth. Carling would happily provide tender, loving care for the lonely Diana. She warmed to that side of the man, though to many Carling had more often seemed a cold fish. Diana also appreciated his confidence and self-assurance, which seemed to give her strength.

And yet Diana would, on occasion, look at Carling and wonder why she had become so attracted to him. He was too stocky for her liking, too short, too muscular, and too young, being four years her junior. Sometimes he would also appear too arrogant. And yet she found him appealing, exciting, and she realized she found Will Carling sexually attractive. On occasion Diana and Carling would attend cocktail parties together, and people noted that Diana found it impossible to keep her hands off her hunky man, touching his arm, flicking a hair from his jacket, and just standing close to him, watching his every movement and listening intently to his conversation. She seemed smitten.

Sometimes when alone together at Kensington Palace, Diana would be so overcome with emotion that she wouldn't want Carling to leave her, lest she dissolve into floods of tears. She would beg him to stay, to hold her, comfort her, sometimes to cuddle her as one would a child. On those occasions Carling felt like her big brother. That made him feel good and he was happy, indeed felt privileged, to play such a role to the Princess of Wales.

Carling found himself becoming more involved, spending more time with her, more time on the phone, and less and less time with his wife. In the meantime Julia had become extraordinarily busy, running her PR consultancy and taking on more work, modeling clothes and discussing with producers the possibility of hosting radio and television shows. She had become a woman in demand and she luxuriated in the attention.

Before flying to South Africa to take part in the Rugby Union World Cup, Carling spent three hours alone with Diana at the palace saying farewell. During the tournament, Diana and Will Carling talked frequently on the telephone, sometimes three or four times a day. And, of course, he also called Julia. His wife, however, had no idea that Carling was calling the Princess of Wales.

Diana watched every game that England played during that series of matches, cheering whenever England scored and yelping with enthusiasm whenever Will Carling played particularly brilliantly. Staff would know what was happening during the games just by listening to the shrieks from the Princess of Wales. When things went badly for England, they would hear loud wails of "Oh, no, oh, no." That usually meant the opposition had scored, or Carling had been injured.

On his return from his six-week tour of South Africa, Carling and Diana spent more time together. The rugby season was over, and though Carling still kept in trim, he had more time to devote to his business, to the machinations of the rapidly changing rugby world, and to Diana. Everything was going well, particularly between Diana and Carling. The world at large had no idea the two had become lovers, but their secret affair, and their good fortune, would not last.

Hilary Ryan, who had been hired by Carling in 1994 at $35,000 a year as his personal assistant, was fired, allegedly for being too confrontational in the office, making waves where Carling wanted a quiet, smooth-running operation. Yet, on the day she was dismissed, Carling gave her a magnificent reference describing her as "highly efficient, very reliable and totally dedicated to the company."

A month after Will Carling's return from South Africa, Rupert Murdoch's sensational Sunday tabloid the *News of the World* splashed across its front page in big, bold letters, "Di's Secret Trysts With Carling." The accompanying story detailed in brief the couple's secret meetings and the relationship that had built up over an eighteenth-month period. The story created a furor and provided Britain's tabloid readers with weeks of speculation and prurient gossip. It would cause Carling's twelve-month-long marriage to break up and make Diana look more like a femme fatale than an innocent princess who was above suspicion.

A week later the strong-willed Julia Carling, thirty, pulled no punches in a vicious attack on Diana. She seethed, "This has happened to her before and you hope she won't do those things again, but she obviously does."

She added, "She picked the wrong couple to do it with this time because we can only get stronger from it. It's a horrible thing to go through. But it does make you stronger no matter how much someone is trying to destroy what you have. Our relationship is very strong anyway—and thank God for that."

Carling, too, seemed to want to end his relationship with Diana, stating publicly, "I have been incredibly naive, absolutely stupid. Diana is sad about it and says it's happened to her time and time again. But it hasn't happened to Julia and myself before, and I never want it to happen again."

He appeared to want to end the rift with his wife and do all in his power to continue his marriage. "My main feelings are about what it has done to people around me, the people I really care about and love," he said. "My wife, Julia, for example, look what's it done to her. That is unforgivable. I love my wife more than anything."

He insisted, however, that the relationship with Diana had been wholly innocent. "It was a perfectly harmless friendship with the Princess of Wales. Maybe I was just stupid."

Diana went to seek advice from her old friend and sister-in-law, Sarah Ferguson, the daughter of Charles's former polo manager Maj. Ronald Ferguson, the young woman with a past who married Prince Andrew in 1986 and separated from him five years later.

But Andrew and Fergie remained close and would spend time together with their daughters, Beatrice and Eugenie. The more Fergie saw of Andrew, the more Diana and Fergie discovered they had much in common. Once again they would come to rely on each other for friendship and shared interests, phoning each other for advice and long heart-to-hearts over their topsy-turvy lives. Much of the time discussions would revolve around their relationships with their husbands, other members of the Royal Family, lovers, and prospective lovers. It wouldn't always be deadly serious for sometimes they would be convulsed in laughter at one of their misdemeanors.

The relationship between Diana and Fergie has been far from steady. When Sarah Ferguson began dating Prince Andrew in the early 1980s, Diana and Fergie became a close couple, swapping stories, having fun together, teaming up to challenge the fuddy-duddy image of the Royal Family. They wanted to put some fizz into the House of Windsor and to show that life could be enjoyable even if one had become a part of the Royal Family. Fergie would help Diana overcome her bulimia, and they shared details of each other's escalating marital problems.

Diana, however, would be advised by Sir Robert Fellowes, her brother-in-law, to keep clear of Fergie. He explained that she seemed hell-bent on bringing the Royal Family into disrepute, determined to enjoy her life as she saw fit and not as a member of the Royal Family was expected to do, judiciously, correctly, her private life above reproach. Diana also frowned on Fergie's sexual encounters, first with the American Steve Wyatt, with whom she fell in love when pregnant with Eugenie, and secondly, and more importantly, when Fergie fell under the spell of Johnny Bryant—an American businessman she met through Wyatt—who boasted to the world of his sexual encounters with Sarah Ferguson.

Diana never liked Bryant, believing him to be an uncouth loudmouth. Fergie, however, was swept off her feet in an extraordinary four-year-long sexual affair with Bryant, unable to say no to his demands, which she found passionately exciting and wild. But Bryant would let her down, boasting in the most intimate detail to friends and strangers alike of their lovemaking, detailing Fergie's sexual proclivities. He would also speak of his lust for Princess Diana, saying, "I love Diana. I see her quite often and she's a wonderful girl. She's so sexy and attractive. I'm thinking bad thoughts whenever I see her!"

During 1995, Sarah would come to realize that her affair with Bryant had harmed her relationship with Andrew and, more particularly, with her daughters, Bea, seven, and Eugenie, five, who were fast growing up. She began to distance herself from her former lover, and Andrew and Fergie would spend more time together. Constantly, Andrew, Fergie, and their daughters would be seen together on some outing or attending school together as a family, and people noted how happy Fergie and Andrew appeared to be when together. There seemed nothing strained or awkward about their relationship, and the nation wondered whether a reconciliation would be possible.

Some cynics asked whether Fergie had finally realized that she would be much better off married to Andrew than living the life of an estranged, single mother with two daughters. Fergie herself commented to friends in the summer of 1995, "Andrew wants me back. I love him and we both love the girls. I don't know what's stopping us."

Encouraged by Diana, a new Fergie would take shape during 1995. In October 1994 at age thirty-four Fergie weighed nearly 170 pounds and would be seen wearing loose-fitting, shapeless dresses. By October 1995, after a year's programmed exercise and dieting, Fergie looked like a different woman, her weight down to 135 pounds and wearing size 10 (British size 10) dresses. "I've given up dairy products," she boasted, "even ice cream!"

Diana told Fergie about her relationship with Carling. And she insisted that despite all the hullabaloo, the innuendos, and the incessant gossip, the basis of their relationship had been fun and friendship. Diana would not tell Fergie whether they were lovers, but telltale comments made Fergie believe the relationship had become far more serious than straightforward fun. Diana also confided that Julia Carling's unprovoked attack on her had made her see red. Diana was furious that the "jumped-up little worm"—as she described Julia—could have the temerity to make such slanderous attacks when she knew nothing of Diana's relationship with Will Carling.

In the view of the general public and most of the newspaper columnists, Julia had won the first round in what was seen as the battle between two powerful women for the right to Will Carling's undivided attention. Never before had any wife whose husband had been attracted to the Princess of Wales openly attacked Diana or publicly accused her of trying to destroy their marriage.

The British public was agog at the comings and goings of the three participants in the extraordinary saga, fueled daily by fresh revelations pouring from the tabloid press. In no previous instance had Diana been involved in such a tug-of-love drama over a man. That Carling was one of the nation's best-known and most-respected sports idols only added to the interest. But few knew what was going on behind the scenes in Kensington Palace.

In fact, Carling had informed Diana that, like her, his marriage, too, had been going through a bad spell, even though he and Julia had been married for little more than a year. He told

Diana that he understood how ghastly her breakup with Charles must have been and commiserated with her.

Diana replied, "If I can be of any help, you must let me know. It's at times like that you find you desperately need friends, and somehow there are none around. I'm here whenever you need me."

Carling told Diana that he hoped that would never be the case, but he thanked her for her concern, adding, "If ever I need a comforting shoulder, I'll come running. I promise."

Julia continued her media blitz, telling newspapers that husband Will had decided to end his friendship with Princess Diana. "I didn't give him an ultimatum," she said, smiling broadly and looking remarkably confident. "The decision to end the friendship was Will's alone."

She added, "As far as we are concerned, it's over. It's a completely closed shop. That was an episode in our lives and you have to get on with things. Diana's business is her business. What is important is Will and myself."

Julia Carling seemed to enjoy her fifteen minutes of fame, her picture splashed over the newspapers, her name hogging the headlines day after day, rivaling Diana for the media's attention. Despite the fact her marriage was going through a crisis, Julia glowed in the spotlight of publicity.

For the talented, ambitious Julia Carling the timing could not have been better. London's Carlton Television announced that Julia would be taking over as host of their highly rated weekly daytime magazine show, *Capital Woman.* And her PR company launched a new beauty product for eye wrinkles, selling at a premium price, $300 a tube. Since she became Mrs. Carling, Julia's career had taken off, landing her lucrative modeling jobs, numerous TV and radio appearances, as well as bringing in business for her PR firm, including some topflight clients such as Mick Jagger, Paul McCartney, and Tina Turner.

She herself admitted with commendable honesty, "The fame thing has happened for me because I'm Will Carling's wife."

Throughout the drama, Julia would happily pose for photographs, and comments slipped daily from her lips. "If Diana tried to renew the relationship with Will, she would have a tough time," she boasted, adding, "Will would think it was a really stupid thing to do renewing the friendship with Diana. He's regretted it enough as it is."

In answer to journalists' questions the following day Julia Carling commented, "I have no sympathy for Diana. I don't know whether she has put this episode behind her. I don't really feel anything for her, that's her business. I wouldn't choose to have her as a friend, probably because of who she is. She seems to pick her friends badly, but that's not for me to dwell on—it's for her to sort out. You've got to learn to deal with your problems, and unfortunately she probably can't."

Diana had other ideas. She had decided that she wanted Will Carling for herself; that they had discovered they found each other exciting and both wanted the relationship to continue. At first, Diana refused to accept a cloak-and-dagger affair and would continue to meet her lover at the BiMAL Clinic and the posh Harbour Club. Within forty-eight hours of Carling's declaration that his relationship with the Princess of Wales was at an end, the two of them had breakfast together at the Harbour Club, giggling and laughing in full view of the other members, as if nothing whatsoever had been said.

The meeting was no accident. Diana arrived looking stunning in a tight-fitting white body T-shirt with jeans and went immediately to the cafe. Ten minutes later Carling walked in and went straight to the Princess, sat down, and ordered orange juice and toast. Neither had been working out or using any of the club's amenities; they just met for a late breakfast.

For the first few minutes Carling seemed tense, looking around the near-empty cafe, but Diana appeared in sparkling form, leaning her elbows on the table and looking directly into Carling's eyes as they chatted and laughed. They talked for about forty-five minutes, while other members did a double take when they saw the two of them sitting together. Somehow, this meeting would remain secret, Julia unaware the two were spending so much time together.

A couple of weeks later the wretched Julia Carling would be lost for words. Will Carling had phoned Diana to tell her that some presents he had promised her sons had arrived and asked whether he should deliver them to Kensington Palace.

"Of course you must come," she said. "It would be lovely to see you again and the boys so adore you."

Carling wondered whether he should bring the presents personally or have them sent round in case photographers were lying in wait. Diana pleaded with Carling to bring the presents—England rugby shirts—himself, and finally he agreed. He told her the time and the day he would arrive.

On Monday, September 4, 1995, Carling drove up to Kensington Palace, this time at the wheel of his wife's blue Range Rover, hoping the vehicle might fool any photographer, who would expect Carling to arrive in his Aston Martin. However, two newspapers had been telephoned by an anonymous caller telling them when Carling would be visiting Kensington Palace later that day. Carling was stunned when he drove up to the policemen on duty only to discover two photographers outside. Carling stayed only twenty minutes and Diana was not even there. Yet the visit would cause more trouble.

Later, Carling told reporters, "Julia knew I was popping round, although she didn't think it a very good idea. She knew I had a long-standing commitment to leave presents for the young Princes, and while in retrospect it was not such a good idea, she knew I was going. There was no question that this was something underhand or done without her knowledge. After all it was quite innocuous. I had made a promise and I didn't want to let people down."

Julia's only comment would be, "I am getting a little tired of all this."

Diana read the following day's papers with a smile on her face. "Will's at It Again," screamed the headlines. Diana grinned broadly when she noted Julia Carling's dusty comment. Diana had not forgiven "the worm" for trying to smear her name, making her appear as some femme fatale. Nor would she forgive her. Diana believed the upstart Julia Carling should be taught a lesson.

That day, her eyes blazing with anticipation and determination, Diana closed one of the tabloids, looked again at the front page, and commented, "The little worm hasn't seen anything yet. I haven't even started."

14

"Home Wrecker"

————— ❧ —————

AT EIGHT O'CLOCK ONE MORNING toward the end of September 1995, three weeks after Carling's visit to Kensington Palace, Diana arrived at the BiMAL Clinic for her weekly Friday workout, continuing her never-ending, self-imposed ritual of strengthening and toning her muscles. Diana worked out so ceaselessly and enthusiastically primarily because she feared that she would once again turn into the "lumpy beanpole" she felt she had become during the years following Harry's birth in 1984 when eating disorders dominated her life.

During the past twelve months a secondary reason had emerged that made the drudgery of workouts far more interesting and sometimes positively rewarding. By attending both the Harbour Club and the BiMAL center she could continue her relationship with Will Carling, the man who had become more important to her than she had ever envisaged during their early encounters. Now, the hunky Carling had become even more of a challenge. For much of the time, Diana rather enjoyed the headiness of the exciting, tantalizing duel.

She parked her Audi sports coupe, threw a towel over her shoulder, grabbed a small bottle of mineral water from the front seat, and almost bounded into the clinic, a spring in her step and a big smile on her face. As usual for such sessions Diana was casually dressed in a loose-fitting V-necked sweater, black cycle shorts, and trainers. Photographers were there to snap the Princess as she arrived and went inside. Fifty minutes later Will

Carling arrived at the wheel of a borrowed BMW and casually walked inside for a physiotherapy session to treat a trapped nerve in his hip.

Twenty-six minutes later Diana emerged alone looking angry, depressed, and red-eyed, so very different from the happy young woman who had walked into the clinic with a skip and a step. She climbed into her car, slammed the door, and drove off, accelerating hard as if wanting to escape from the scene as quickly as possible. Carling emerged a minute later, checked twice to see if any photographers were about, then walked to his car, his hands deep in his trouser pockets, his face like thunder.

During their brief encounter Carling told Diana that Julia wanted to make a fresh start, and he suggested that he and Diana spend some time apart, "to see what happened."

Forty-eight hours later Carling's wife would hear of the secret meeting, for the *News of the World* splashed the story on page one under the headline "Will and Di at It Again," giving minute-by-minute details of what the newspaper claimed had been another of their secret trysts. But they had no idea what had been discussed.

Carling protested, "I did not know the Princess was there. I did not see her. I was upstairs having treatment and someone told me that she was there working out in the gym below."

He went on, "I have discussed all this with Julia this morning. Any suggestion that the Princess and myself set up a meeting is crazy."

Later that day Carling would be seen to have spoken too hastily. He knew of Diana's schedule. It had been Carling who introduced Diana to the clinic, a no-nonsense sports organization run by highly qualified physiotherapists for sorting out the problems of Britain's high-profile sportsmen, athletes, and footballers. The gym has no swimming pool, no smart cafe area, no bar, and its reputation is based on high-tech equipment and the skill and advice of qualified physiotherapists experienced in rectifying stresses and strains of injured muscles.

Carling knew that Diana visited the clinic virtually every

Friday morning at 8 A.M., staying for more than an hour, before driving herself back to Kensington Palace. They had met there on a number of occasions during the previous six months. From time to time, they had left to breakfast together somewhere else.

When Julia arrived home later that Sunday she immediately contradicted her husband, insisting that her husband had not talked to her about the alleged meeting. "I've got a hangover," she told reporters, "and I've nothing to say."

Within hours of Carling's forthright denial, Princess Diana also contradicted his statement, confirming that she did have a meeting with Carling at the clinic. A senior palace spokesman said, "The Princess of Wales and Mr. Will Carling met at the fitness center on Friday, but it was by accident."

Diana spent most of that weekend with her younger son, Harry. On Friday afternoon she drove alone the forty miles to his boarding school in Wokingham, Berkshire, then brought him back to London, and they spent the remainder of the day together at the palace. On Saturday Diana took Harry go-carting in Chelsea, and later they drove to Windsor to see Harry's elder brother, William, play rugby at his new school, Eton College, England's premier private school. On Sunday, Diana and Harry, having spent the night at Kensington Palace, drove over to the home of the Duchess of York. Later, Diana took Harry back to school before returning to spend the evening alone at the palace.

Throughout the weekend Diana made sure she read all the newspapers, which were full of her secret trysts and the problems facing Julia and Will Carling. She would also spend hours on the phone, particularly when driving to and from Harry's school. Despite the problems she had experienced using mobile phones in the past, Diana would still drive along happily chatting.

Julia would comment the following day, "I am standing by my husband, despite everything. He's my husband and I am behind him all the way. I believe everything he has said. I don't believe there is anything going on at all."

Diana consulted friends of mine suggesting she should contact Julia Carling through an intermediary and that the two should meet to discuss the whole matter. On one occasion Diana said, "If I met Julia, I'm sure we would be able to thrash things out and then we could forget the whole affair."

She immediately giggled. "Oh! I shouldn't use that word *affair* should I? I meant *relationship*."

Friends made discreet inquiries and advised Diana that she should not even suggest a meeting for they believed Julia would refuse. They hinted that Julia could go further, telling the world that she had turned down a peace pact put forward by the Princess of Wales.

Diana was determined that everyone would see the Princess of Wales enjoying life, no matter the hulabaloo surrounding her private life. She would show that the fuss surrounding Will Carling and his wife were no concern of hers.

Diana telephoned a close friend, one of her special advisers, two days later. "I'm going to be a little naughty today," she said, giggling coquettishly. "I have written a poem about all the rubbish going on and I'm going to read it out today at the *Literary Review* lunch of the year."

The adviser asked if the poem was risqué or imprudent. "Oh, no," Diana replied, laughing, "nothing like that. It's about me and Will Carling and secret trysts, that's all."

At the annual lunch of the *Literary Review,* a magazine devoted to poetry and other literature, Diana, the guest of honor, looked stunning in a smart bright red suit. She smiled and waved to the cheering crowds who greeted her at London's Cafe Royal where she would make her speech.

She did not appear in the least apprehensive or nervous as she addressed the gathering of notable men of letters. "I feel privileged to be allowed to join a highly exclusive gathering of intellectuals," she said. "Apparently, some people are wondering what Diana, that notorious illiterate, is doing at a distinguished scholarly occasion such as this. So I've made time between therapy sessions and secret trysts to attempt a reply."

She cleared her throat and delivered her limerick:

The Princess was heard to declare,
Let gossips poke fun if they dare,
My real inspiration,
Is Bron's invitation,
Stick that in your tabloids,
So there.

The poem, read with gusto, was greeted with laughter and great applause, especially by Auberon "Bron" Waugh, the noted columnist and son of the late, celebrated author Evelyn Waugh. It was Bron who founded the *Literary Review,* which he now edits. Bron commented, "Today's prize is for poetry that rhymes and scans and makes sense, and so Diana's fitted in well. It was a limerick in the ancient tradition."

Diana was thrilled with the reception given to her poem. University professors, asked by the media to comment, praised her little limerick. But there was another reason for the smile on Diana's face when she read the tributes the following day.

During the previous few weeks much had been written about the brilliant Julia Carling, the girl who had the courage to tackle the "marriage wrecker" Diana head-on and show the world that she was the woman Will Carling loved and wanted, above anyone else, including the Princess. Julia Carling had been happy to tell the media that she, like Diana, was from a wealthy background; was brought up in the country, like Diana; had never taken drugs, like Diana; had lost her virginity at the mature age of eighteen, only a year earlier than Diana; and remarkably, had chosen to live with a much older man when she was still a teenager, just as Diana had decided to do with Prince Charles. There were other similarities Julia happily stressed. She, too, is an extraordinary mix of the naive and the knowing; she, too, can portray the shy little girl with the soft voice and engaging innocence.

Other people noticed more similarities. Both Diana and Julia are slim, attractive blondes who have the capacity to make themselves look like a million dollars. They both dress well and attractively and have a certain presence about them. They both

*Wrong~
Diana was
5' 10"*

love wearing expensive clothes and enjoy the power to turn heads. Julia, however, is smaller boned than Diana, just 5 feet 5 inches tall and weighing under 120 pounds, while Diana is 5 feet 7 inches tall and weighs around 130 pounds.

Their personal lives had also taken remarkably similar paths. Julia spent six years with the guitarist Jeff Beck, a star of the 1960s, who was thirty-nine when they began to live together. Julia had just turned eighteen. Jeff Beck had taken Julia to live in a lovely, big country house, but she, like Diana, had found herself growing more unhappy with her relationship, cut off from young people, from friends and from the hurly-burly of everyday life that both Diana and Julia had missed. It seemed extraordinary that Julia's relationship with Beck had lasted six years, about the same amount of time that Diana had managed to maintain her relationship with Charles.

There the similarities ended. For Julia had only to walk out of her relationship with Beck while Diana had become a lonely prisoner, more depressed with every passing year. Able to escape her relationship, Julia had never suffered from anorexia or bulimia as had Diana. Somewhat apologetically Julia would tell interviewers that she never goes to the gym to get fit or tone her muscles. "I hate the gym and I don't need it," she would say, leaving the interviewer to decide whether her remark included a deliberate gibe at the Princess of Wales. She would add, however, "But I do enjoy full body massages. They make me feel a new woman."

Julia would also proudly tell of her educational accomplishments, having passed eight O (ordinary) level examinations at school and three A (advanced) level exams, though she would drop out of university without taking her degree. She knew that Diana had an abysmally poor educational record, passing no exams, even failing those she sat again. It is a failure that has always embarrassed Diana.

Diana phoned friends the following day, eager to know what they thought of her poem, and received warm praise, even from those who normally doubted her mental ability. Teasingly, she asked one girlfriend, "Do you think Julia Carling would have enjoyed my poem? I hope so because she doesn't think I have any brains."

Diana had hoped that by poking fun at her secret trysts with Carling she would help to defuse the situation, which she believed was out of hand. Some columnists had cast Diana as a "home wrecker," accusing her of deliberately targeting married men with no thought for their wives. That tag hurt Diana. She maintained it was most unfair, as well as being untrue.

During the furor over the Carling affair, Diana had returned to her old habit of reading every newspaper and magazine piece written about herself, Julia, and Carling. Every mention of Diana as a "home breaker" or a "home wrecker" made her furious. She would storm around her apartment screaming obscenities and yelling, then erupt in tears of anger and frustration.

"How can they?" she would plead to Sarah Ferguson and other close girlfriends. "How can they say such things about me? It is so unfair and so untrue. Why do they pick on me? Why do the papers say on one day what a wonderful person I am and then the following day accuse me of being a home wrecker? Why are they being so beastly, so unfair?"

During the following few days, staff would know that Diana had become an unhappy woman. One minute she would be sweet and kind, the next angry and vitriolic about anyone and everyone who crossed her path. Her staff were well aware of Diana's violent swings of mood and would understand that during these phases it was advisable to keep their heads down and say nothing. Once again Diana was showing serious signs of paranoia, but none of her friends would tell her that.

Diana also let people know that she believed Julia Carling to be a "bitch on the make" who was trying to "use" Diana and the alleged affair with her husband to benefit her career. Privately Diana would say, "I've watched that woman on TV, and she's so wooden. She needs all the publicity she can get, and she is deliberately making the most of this rumpus to feather her own nest." To others Diana would be more outspoken: "Just because her marriage wasn't working, the little cow is trying to put all the blame on me. She's got a bloody cheek. She is some trumped-up PR woman who thinks that by using me she is going to become a celebrity."

Newspapers and magazines were thoroughly enjoying what they saw as a battle between two beautiful modern women, one the Princess of Wales, the other a bright, highly successful career woman with a bright future. The prize, the love of the England rugby hero. Others believed the three members of the triangle had their separate and different reasons. Diana wanted to demonstrate that she had the power and the sexual attraction to combat any rival, particularly Julia; many believed Carling thought he and Diana would become an item and that he would walk off into the sunset with a rugby ball under one arm and the Princess of Wales on the other; some thought Julia Carling was desperate to make the most of a marriage that had gone wrong and was happily milking the Diana link for all she was worth. They believed Diana had become caught up in the bad marriage and had enjoyed an affair with a man she found attractive and fun.

Diana's jokey limerick at the literary lunch, however, had singularly failed to ease the situation, for Julia Carling's bitterness would not be so simply assuaged. Six days after the controversial meeting-that-never-was at the fitness center Will and Julia Carling issued a joint statement that shocked their close friends and would begin TV news programs:

"Will Carling announced with regret tonight that he and his wife, Julia, have agreed to spend some time apart. They both believe that they need space and some peace for the time being. "They want to emphasize that nobody else is involved, and they hope that by allowing themselves time apart to reflect, they will be able to get back together as soon as possible."

Diana watched the TV news that night and confessed later that the news made her smile, giving her a feeling of triumph and satisfaction over the young woman who had dared to challenge her. Diana knew from Will Carling that Julia had been determined to show the Princess of Wales, and the British public, that she could not only compete with Diana but would prove more than capable of keeping her handsome hunk of a rugby hero as her husband despite any attempt by Diana to steal him away.

The love triangle had become a most public affair, and the world had witnessed Julia's contempt and bitterness toward her rival. Diana smiled because she believed Julia Carling had grossly exaggerated the relationship between Will and herself, and had made herself look foolish.

The statement, which made front-page news, appeared beside a photograph of Julia taken the previous day at the launch of an electronic beauty product her PR firm handled. She looked stunning, smiling, laughing, engaging in animated conversation, showing no sign of the turmoil in her private life. Later that evening, as the statement was making headline news on Britain's TV stations, Julia turned up unexpectedly at a party to celebrate the first anniversary of the cable-TV pop-music station VH-1 where she hosted a weekly show. She appeared in great form, chatting and drinking for two hours with everyone.

Julia was showing Will, Diana, and the media that she was a true professional PR consultant down to her well-manicured fingernails. "In the instant-broadcast age," she commented while the furor raged around her marriage, "it's not what's really going on that matters but how you make it look publicly."

Some thought that statement the height of cynicism, revealing that Julia equated her job on the same plane as her marriage. It made others wonder how serious Julia Carling's commitment could be to her marriage. Some suggested that the decision to separate, for however long, seemed remarkably hasty when only days before Julia had said, "We have even considered counseling, but there's not enough of a problem to sort out." She had paused and then added, "Look, if it ever came to that— well, it would have to be really severe. We wouldn't need someone to sort out any problem because Will and I are straight enough with each other."

Some of the in-depth interviews that Julia gave to the media would be avidly read by Diana. She would sometimes laugh out loud at Julia's remarks, for Will would have told her a different story to the one Julia was telling the media. Diana also loved reading what Julia had to say about Will.

On one occasion Julia commented, "I think it's a real advantage that Will and I are so different. We hardly share any of the same interests. I hardly ever go and watch him play rugby. I prefer to go home at night and listen to music, while Will prefers to go out with the lads. I like really up-to-date music, while I grimace at Will's taste, which is more the sort Princess Diana likes—Phil Collins and the like. "Will and I have always been straight with each other. We know what's going on in each other's lives. We may not live in each other's pockets, but we talk on the phone five or six times a day."

Julia admitted that Will had changed her. "Will has made me a better person. We were both pretty selfish people—I was spoiled by my father—and we have made each other less selfish. Well, you have to, when you have a relationship with someone else. Will's a calming person—he doesn't get neurotic about things, which has been very good for me."

Diana read that last sentence and wondered whether Carling's calm approach to matters was one of the reasons she had fallen in love with him. She respected him for never losing his temper, always staying cool and in command, the opposite to Diana's temperament, one moment in the blackest despair, the next happy and smiling.

The Carlings' decision to separate, however, cast a totally different light on the entire matter and worried Diana. From everything Will Carling had told her throughout their relationship, it seemed extraordinary that Julia would demand a separation to sort things out. Carling told Diana that he had been "flabbergasted" by his wife's demand to spend some time apart, suggesting to the world that his relationship with the Princess had been far more intimate and serious than had been the case.

Within twenty-four hours Julia would go out of her way to squarely blame Diana for the marriage breakup. She issued a statement saying, "I confirm that my husband and I have separated. It saddens me deeply that this has happened, but the recent pressures and tensions have produced this situation. I had always valued my marriage as the most important and sacred part of my life, and it hurts me very much to face losing my husband in a manner that has become outside my control. I have given total support to Will and this has unfortunately proved to no avail."

Understandably, most newspapers viewed her statement as a direct and open attack on the Princess of Wales. "I Blame Di" was the headline in some of the tabloids. Others went further, interpreting Julia's words to mean that she was branding Diana a "marriage wrecker."

"The little bitch" were Diana's words when she read the statement the following morning. "How dare she blame me for what's happened in her marriage? My God, what nerve. Who exactly does Julia Carling think she is?"

Carling warned Diana that they should not meet anymore for fear of the newspapers discovering their "secret trysts" and making their relationship front-page news again. He also told her that he didn't think it fair to Julia for the two of them to continue to meet, not at their sports clubs, not even for coffee or a snack, which might be interpreted wrongly by the public and certainly would be by the media. Diana disagreed, arguing that they should act as if nothing had happened, to show the world they enjoyed a friendship, and nothing more. Carling, however, would remain adamant.

Diana pressed Carling, telling him that if he had been kicked out of his house by Julia, then there could be nothing wrong with his occasionally seeing her, either publicly or in private. Quietly Carling told her it would be more diplomatic if they didn't see each other until the storm had settled and they could all resume their normal lives.

Julia would go home to her parents' house in an idyllic Northamptonshire village eighty miles from London. And yet the next day she would be snapped by a paparazzi taking her young niece for a walk in the country. The photographer had been tipped off when Julia would be there. Carling, meanwhile, stayed at the home of Colin Herridge, the media liaison for the Rugby Football Union, a close friend of Carling's for many years, who issued statements on his behalf.

After the separation statement, Herridge added, "Carling has promised that he will definitely not be seeing the Princess again. I don't think the relationship was an affair; it was a friendship. Will is determined to sort out his domestic affairs and is hoping for a speedy reconciliation. He is also determined to play his rugby."

Diana would be tempted to forget about Carling, to turn her back on him and let him sort out his life, with or without Julia. Despite all the thousands of words written about Diana and her relationship with Carling, only she knew the whole truth. She would tell it to only a tiny handful of people.

In essence, Diana told them that the relationship with Carling began in all innocence for she knew that her sons would love to meet Will Carling, their hero. She and Carling had met at the Harbour Club and he had agreed to visit Kensington Palace and meet the boys. He had also arranged for them to meet the England team prior to the World Cup. Her sons had idolized the England rugby captain, finding him wonderful.

But the relationship developed. She and Carling would meet three times a week at the club, and she found herself becoming attracted to the man she had not originally found sexy.

Friends of mine who saw Diana and Carling together at the club suggest that Diana is not being totally honest about the relationship. Diana would walk up to Will's table with a big smile on her face, openly flirting with him. She would invite herself to sit down, and at first, Carling would look rather sheepish. The more he gained in confidence, the more he enjoyed her approaches. Before long, club members noted a definite sexual attraction between the two—the way they chatted, looked at each other, and gave each other attention. Their body language screamed they wanted each other.

Carling would wait to see her at the club, wanting to join her for coffee and a snack, helping her with workouts and programs to develop her body. Diana loved the attention of the man she was becoming strongly attracted to. For Diana this affair would be far deeper and more meaningful than any she had enjoyed since James Hewitt. Diana had known that her relationship with Hewitt had blossomed, then gone out of control, because she had then desperately needed love, attention, some warmth, and emotional involvement, and Hewitt had been on hand, eager to oblige.

Diana admitted that on most days she and Carling would talk frequently on the phone, sometimes four times a day. At first their calls would be jovial and fun, but over time, their attitudes to each other changed. They gave each other pet names, joked and teased, but underneath the high spirits, a more serious relationship was developing.

They both realized they could not go on in that way. Without saying a word they both knew that, if they continued being so close and so intense, they would soon become lovers. Diana noted that throughout their relationship, even at the beginning, Carling had hardly ever mentioned Julia. And she had wondered why.

Diana told how she invited Carling to Kensington Palace. And the invitation both worried and flattered him. During most of his daytime visits Diana's staff would be working as they chatted over coffee or tea. Then Diana phoned inviting him to drinks one evening. Carling was flattered and was even more surprised when he discovered he was the only guest. Carling thoroughly enjoyed that first evening alone with the Princess of Wales, who flattered him and flirted and insisted on pouring the drinks. Diana, too, enjoyed that evening and realized she rather liked having Will Carling as a companion, with his sense of fun and humor.

More invitations followed. Sometimes they dined alone, and on occasion Carling would stay late into the night. They would drink a bottle of wine or champagne, listen to music they both enjoyed, and suddenly, naturally, find themselves in each other's arms. One thing would lead to another.

She believed Carling had fallen in love, and they agreed

spending more time together would be enjoyable. The more involved Carling became with Diana the less he appeared to pay attention to Julia and seemed to be living a more independent life. The ambitious Julia would spend more time concentrating on her career while Carling found life with Diana more frivolous, more relaxing. Carling would tell Diana all this saying that he did not know what to do about Julia. Diana told Carling that she didn't want to know about Carling's marital problems. She would tell him that he had to sort them out himself.

When their close relationship became known, Diana told Carling that he would have to make difficult decisions. She promised him nothing save the relationship they had, a friendship based on lots of fun, shared interests, enjoying time together whether in the gym or back at the palace. She also knew that Wills and Harry would not be too pleased if their hero no longer called round to the palace. The boys had no idea of the amount of time Carling was spending with their mother.

Later, Diana would explain that Carling could not decide what to do. He felt like a cork bobbing about on the ocean, thrown hither and yon by events and the two women in his life. He knew that both women were much stronger than he could ever be, but he couldn't make up his mind. He told of furious rows between himself and Julia over his association with the Princess, arguments that left him exhausted and unsure what to do. Julia, however, made up his mind for him by demanding a separation.

Diana felt that Carling had shown such weakness in the face of the trauma that it would probably be far better if they forgot everything and he returned to his true loves, playing rugby and spending evenings with his rugby mates. By the time of the Carlings' very public separation Diana had become less enamored of Carling, for he had proven not to be the man she had hoped for, lacking strength and determination, his gifts physical, never mental.

And yet Diana knew that she and Carling were ideally

suited, for they laughed and joked at the same things, liked the same music, and were undeniably sexually attracted to one another. Diana also realized that he provided something she desperately needed and had never found with Charles or James Hewitt, a strong shoulder on which to rest her head and a man on whom she could rely.

But the Carling affair would bring unwelcome repercussions for Diana.

One day in the summer of 1995 she walked into the ladies' locker room at the Chelsea Harbour Club and heard two women talking. Though not visible to them, Diana could hear everything they said.

The first asked her friend what she thought of the Julia Carling affair.

The second replied, "I think she is behaving like a perfect bitch."

"Why do you say that?"

"Will Carling and Julia had been married for less than a year and along comes Diana, who thinks she can have any man she wants. In my opinion Diana has behaved like a bitch."

"And Carling?"

"He didn't stand a chance. Diana took a fancy to him and that was it. Diana knew what she was doing."

The women's reaction to her affair with Carling made Diana angry and confused; angry that they should call her a "bitch" and confused because she believed she had done nothing wrong.

Meanwhile, Julia Carling seemed determined to milk every ounce of publicity she could from the love triangle. From the moment of the separation, on which she had insisted, Julia was seen in public, relentlessly photographed. She seemed to thrive on the media's intrusion into her marriage and its problems.

Despite the fact she had no professional singing career, Julia recorded her own version of "Stand by Your Man," which the record company hoped to produce for the Christmas market. She then posed for some quite extraordinary pictures of her with a DJ, Richard Allinson, her cohost on VH-1, showing Allinson with his head in Julia's lap, gazing up into her eyes as she strokes his hair.

Ten days after the separation, a paparazzi caught Julia taking a Sunday walk with her parents and her brother Adrian on Barnes Common, on the outskirts of London. The photographer was there purportedly by chance. The same would happen again a week or so later when Julia and a hunky friend, hairdresser Daniel Galvin, emerged from a late-night dinner at the trendy Julie's Restaurant in Holland Park. This time two photographers were on hand to snap Julia as she leaned forward, facing the cameras, to kiss her friend good night. *The Sun* tabloid had been phoned anonymously that morning tipping them off about Julia's secret date.

Julia Carling, however, didn't have only the publicity she wanted. Carl Pickford, the former assistant manager to one of Diana's old favorite pop groups, Duran Duran, had enjoyed a passionate ten-month relationship with Julia after meeting her at a party in 1990. He would kiss and tell in *The Sun,* a Murdoch tabloid, detailing their affair and advising Carling that he would be mad to let Julia go because she was so fantastic in bed. "Julia is as positive about what she wants in her love life as in her career. We would make love all night. It was great. The best sex I've ever had. During a two-week holiday at her parents' Spanish apartment Julia was insatiable. I couldn't believe her appetite. Sometimes she wanted sex twelve times a day."

He told the newspaper that Julia enjoyed making love in public places, especially on airplanes. "On almost all the flights we ended up making love in one of the tiny washrooms. She wanted it throughout the flight. We hardly even had time for the complimentary drink."

Diana would read the intimate details revealed by Julia's former lover, wondering whether her rival would be embarrassed by the accounts of her wild and "insatiable" sexual appetite. Diana believed that perhaps Julia welcomed such publicity, believing the old adage that any publicity is good publicity.

"I'm sure she hopes I read the article," Diana commented, adding, "the little tart."

Carling's fling with Diana appeared to have put an end to his marriage to Julia. The blond PR consultant would later comment that she felt "betrayed" and "hurt" by both her husband and Princess Diana. Some weeks later she confessed, "I can't compete with a princess. I feel so let down. Will is a changed person since he met Princess Diana, and I wonder if he'll ever be the same again. You can't change a person back, can you?"

For Diana, however, the time had come for decisive action. She did not want to be seen as a marriage wrecker but as the loving, caring princess the public still adored. She decided to continue her affair with Carling in the strictest secrecy until the storm had blown over.

She stopped frequenting the BiMAL Clinic, and Carling would not appear at the Harbour Club. They would not be seen together for several months, though Carling would continue to visit Diana at Kensington Palace, usually arriving and leaving under cover of darkness. To the public at large, and even the prying eyes of the paparazzi, Diana's affair with the rugged England rugby captain had apparently ended.

Many doubted that Carling and Diana had been lovers. But Sarah Ferguson and two or three of Diana's closest confidants knew the truth and realized that Diana had triumphed in her battle for Carling's affections, even though it had been necessary to face the anger and vitriol of a woman her own age, risking condemnation from the public, whom Diana was desperate to keep on her side. For Diana realized that she needed to retain the love and respect of the nation if her secret plans for her future were to succeed. And she was determined to push ahead with those plans to forge a new, independent career outside the jurisdiction of the Royal Family.

15

Angel of Hope

———— ❧ ————

Despite the criticism and the scandals that have swirled around Diana in the past few years, no one can deny that she has touched millions with her compassion for the sick and disadvantaged. And since the collapse of her marriage she has devoted herself tirelessly to helping and caring for others, bringing happiness and joy to thousands she has met.

Many who have judged Diana before ever meeting her testify that after spending some time talking to her they have been won over by her personality and warmth. One of Diana's earliest and scathing critics was the right-wing writer Auberon Waugh, the son of the novelist Evelyn Waugh, who would write caustic remarks about her in *Spectator* magazine. Since meeting her, Waugh admits to being stymied by her beautiful manners and sweetness, happy to retract his unkind and uncalled-for words.

Perhaps hitting the right note, he commented, "She has this genuine warmth, humor, and recklessness. That's what slays people. Men aren't complete fools, you know."

That is the essence of Diana's remarkable personality. For she does possess this extraordinary ability to win over people, for once having met her, many find their earlier criticism unjust. Most acknowledge that they have misread the strength of her character and her disarming charm and come away knowing that Diana is the epitome of womanhood.

Without doubt, many people grossly underestimate the Princess of Wales, including not only Prince Charles, the

Queen, and Prince Philip, but most of the senior courtiers, who believed Diana to be mentally unstable. But the time was fast approaching when the new, more confident Diana would make them all sit up and take note. A caring, loving person who looks down on meaningless royal duties and wants to help others, Diana brings hope and light to many sick people.

This author has attended lunches, dinners, cocktail parties, and informal get-togethers at polo clubs where Diana has been a guest. And I have also watched her closely during official royal visits to hospitals, children's homes, factories, armed services headquarters, as well as grimy towns and innocuous villages. On all these occasions she has exuded the most remarkable talent for attracting people and making them feel special in a single moment of attention. People smile when Diana smiles. They laugh when she does, and patients in hospitals and homes who speak to her say openly and honestly that Diana seems to care for them as no one has before.

Frequently, I have chatted with people who, a few minutes after speaking to Diana, would say, "She's special, she's something else." They would often add, "I don't know what it is; she said nothing different to me, nothing remarkable, yet she made me feel special."

With all the criticism, implicit and explicit, that has been made of Diana during the past few years, it is remarkable that she has retained the knack of making people, even those to whom she is not speaking directly, feel that she has an interest in them. During lunch and dinner gatherings Diana will sit at the top table, seemingly only interested in the few people seated around her to whom she can talk. At the same time, without its being apparent, she will scan the room, catching someone's eye and holding the look for little more than an instant, as if registering that person is someone special to her.

Friends of mine who have never met Diana face-to-face will say, "I saw the Princess across the room and, for little more than a couple of seconds, our eyes met. I have thought about her since and don't know whether she was flirting or simply registering me in her mind, yet knowing I would go away wondering if she did want to engage me in more than a fleeting look. It's uncanny, yet at the time, very real. If that same look had been given to me by another young woman, I would have considered the glance to be flirtatious, inviting me to approach her and perhaps start a conversation. Diana's look is that ambiguous, both disarming and devastating."

And it is not only in the United Kingdom that Diana wields her charms so successfully and so seductively. I was a guest at a dinner in Paris in 1989 celebrating the French bicentenary at which more than four hundred people were present. I watched Diana closely that night. She did in fact appear more nervous and shy than usual, but as the evening progressed, she became increasingly confident and began to use her eyes in her inimitable way, looking at people sitting at other tables, sometimes nodding gently to someone, throwing a quick smile at someone else, and giving that searching look, suggesting mild flirtation, to yet another person.

That particular night Diana appeared to be going out of her way to prove to the glamorous, sophisticated Parisians that she, too, could flirt as well as any of the beautiful young Frenchwomen. The following day the French newspapers were full of pictures of Diana, and the commentaries were all flattering. She had won her spurs in the most critical capital in the Western world.

On most occasions Diana is careful to show that her interest in someone, be it a hospital patient, a soldier, factory worker, or dinner host, is personal, not something that the two of them want the world to know about. That is of course part of Diana's attraction. On other occasions Diana loves to throw herself headlong into a relationship, in which she takes pleasure in the fact that the person who adores her is someone in whom she believes, as well as a person whom she knows others admire and respect.

Some of those people she admires include the brilliant dancer Wayne Sleep, with whom she loved to dance at every opportunity, or world-famous stars such as Luciano Pavarotti. In September 1995, Diana was invited by the world-renowned tenor to his hometown of Modena in northern Italy to make a guest appearance at a concert raising money for his personal charity, musical therapy for the children of Bosnia. Diana was only too happy to help Pavarotti, whom she adores, repaying him for flying to London on two previous occasions to raise funds for her charities.

Fifty thousand Italians watched on giant TV screens and millions watched on nationwide television as Diana arrived, looking more like a blond Italian vamp than a princess of royal blood. She was dressed in a $4,000 white Gianni Versace dress, the hem well above the knee. The wolf whistles echoed around the stadium as the glamorous Diana, with a deep-cut bodice and thin shoulder straps, kissed Pavarotti on both cheeks and hugged him closely.

Never before had one of Diana's dresses revealed so much cleavage, and the Fleet Street fashion writers were determined to discover for their readers the secrets of Diana's uplift. They revealed that Diana hadn't been wearing a Wonderbra but an old-fashioned, built-in corset! The fashion experts showed how the white silk crepe dress was cut to cling to all her curves and focus on the low neckline, which had been trimmed with diamanté buckles. The bodice had concealed boning in the lining and the shoulder straps acted as a lifting lever, creating, as they put it, a "cleavage to kill for."

And yet Diana has the ability to create that frisson of understated sexuality before a crowd of fifty thousand excited, ardent young Italians and, on other occasions, win over highly intelligent and high-brow diplomats and politicians. Britain's former foreign secretary Douglas Hurd is a most serious, well-respected, and mature politician who has been charmed by Diana's personality and presence. Hurd and Diana met on a number of occasions at the Foreign Office when he was the secretary of state and she was seeking his support to become a roving royal ambassador, traveling abroad to pursue her ambition of becoming more involved in international charities. She hoped that Douglas Hurd would become her wise counselor, and he in turn believed that Diana's magnetic personality and allure could be of great service for overseas charitable causes.

Hurd strongly supported Diana's plan against the advice of senior aides in Buckingham Palace, who felt her idea might detract from the role of both the Queen and Prince Charles and might even cheapen the monarchy in people's eyes. It was strongly suggested in palace circles that Douglas Hurd had become "besotted" with the young Diana. Not surprisingly, with such opposition the plan would be dropped.

Members of the House of Lords, clergymen, scholars, industrialists and business leaders, men of letters, and serving British officers have all in their turn found themselves captivated by Diana, who has held their attention and won their admiration. She appears to have a similar effect on people whom she meets around the world. Former U.S. presidents Ronald Reagan and George Bush found pleasure chatting with Diana during visits to Britain; President Jacques Chirac of France, Henry Kissinger, Gen. Colin Powell, have all come under her shy influence, which seemed magnetic and certainly enchanting and elusive. They all discovered they wanted to continue to converse with her, slightly taken aback by her disarming quality.

Diana wins so many hearts not only among the recipients of her charitable works but also among the administrators and managers of charity organizations, as well as the men and women who work within those organizations at every level. She will walk into a room of perhaps forty or more people, of whom only two or three will have disabilities of one type or another. Within minutes of meeting the officials and as though by instinct, she will have discovered the sufferers, who may be at the back of the room, and will spend some of the time talking to them. She will go out of her way to make them feel wanted and important, that they have as much to offer as anyone else in that room.

Every year Diana holds a reception at Kensington Palace for the charities of which she is either the president or royal patron. Perhaps the chief executive and senior manager of each charity attends with one or two of their disadvantaged people in attendance. Usually, more than two hundred people attend, and Diana makes sure, each year, that she spends more time talking with the disadvantaged than with the executives. She will tell them, "We talk at meetings, but this day is for them, so you will excuse me, won't you?"

Afterward, the patients will talk for days, weeks, and months about their few minutes' chat with the Princess. That meeting becomes one of the highlights of their lives. More importantly they will say that they found the Princess "warm and caring."

Mr. Barry Brooking became chief executive of the Parkinson's Disease Society in 1995 and has seen Diana at work during visits to patients of the charity, where she has been the patron for the past six years. He said, "When I took this job, I had no preconceived idea of how the Princess would be to deal with on a personal basis and how she would interact with patients. But within months I was totally won over by her knowledge, her expertise, her professionalism, and the warmth she exudes whenever she is talking to patients. And the effect she has on patients must be seen to be believed. And although cynics sometimes suggest the Princess is not being sincere when dealing with disadvantaged people, I can only say that I believe she is absolutely sincere. And I have witnessed her talking with them time and again. She is quite remarkable."

On a number of occasions Barry Brooking has held discussions with Diana both at Kensington Palace and at the society's London headquarters concerning problems as well as future projects of the charity. "She is tremendously keen to help in any way she can," Brooking said. "And she tells us openly that if there is anything that she can do, any way that she can help, then all we have to do is to ask her and she will do whatever is possible to help. One cannot ask more of a patron. And when one considers Diana is patron to more than one hundred and twenty separate charities, her offers are remarkably generous given the limited amount of time she can give to every charity."

Brooking has also been surprised at Diana's knowledge of Parkinson's. Wanting to learn more about the problems and the progress in research toward possible cures, Diana asked to meet Prof. Peter Jenner. Jenner is the head of pharmacology research at King's College, London, director of the Parkinson's Disease Society's research laboratories, and codirector of the Neurodegenerative Diseases research center. In 1995, Professor Jenner was awarded $500,000 by the National Parkinson Foundation of Miami for future research into the disease. Together, Diana and Brooking visited Peter Jenner at his research headquarters to see firsthand the progress being made. For more than an hour she talked to Professor Jenner and other research staff as well as a number of trustees and sufferers of Parkinson's disease.

Brooking said, "If people who doubt the Princess of Wales's intelligence had been present, they would have been forced to rapidly change their opinion. She showed not only great interest in the research going on but also a remarkable and genuine knowledge of the subject. The research team were surprised at the extent of her understanding of the disease and the research, showing that she must have studied Parkinson's quite thoroughly."

While at the laboratories Diana spent some time talking to Mrs. Janet McNelly, a trustee of the society and one of the youngest sufferers of the disease. Mrs. McNelly said, "I was only forty-three when I contracted the disease and that was five years ago. Diana wanted to know how I managed being a housewife, cooking meals, cleaning my house. She wanted to know how I coped with the drugs, and the drugs' side effects. She encouraged me to keep chatting to her and explaining everything, telling me to take my time and not to feel under any pressure. I found her surprisingly easy to talk to; so natural and relaxed, and she made me feel as though we had known each other for years. She was so understanding and warm, and I felt she really cared. I had never met anyone who seemed so genuine and kind since I contracted the disease. She is a remarkable young woman and people should understand that."

Diana will do whatever she can to assist one of her charities. The Parkinson's Disease Society plans to hold a charity lunch in

Wales this year, 1996, to raise $50,000 toward the cost of funding two specialist nurses to care for Parkinson's disease patients. Before Brooking had completed the sentence outlining the scheme, Diana said, "I know what you are about to say. If you want me to host the lunch, I will do so with the greatest of pleasure. I now understand that it is hugely beneficial for specialist nurses to be involved in the treatment of patients and is something which must be encouraged."

Ms. Ali Knowles is appeals manager of seeABILITY, a charity that helps those between nineteen and one hundred years of age with multiple disabilities, such as multiple sclerosis, ME (myalgic encephalomyelitis), cerebral palsy, and other diseases as well as blindness or visual impairment. Diana has always had a soft spot for seeABILITY. In 1983, when she decided to become a royal patron, she selected this particular charity to be her very first.

"The Princess of Wales comes to our residential-care home once or twice a year to see and talk to the residents," Ms. Knowles said, "and she is so warm and natural with them all. She makes their day, their week, almost their year, whenever she makes an appearance. Her warmth is so genuine and sincere. And the staff all love her for the manner in which she cares for people and always concentrates on the very ill patients, the ones who need support and encouragement."

Bethany, twenty-three, suffers from spina bifida, is blind and confined to a wheelchair. Bethany said, "She is wonderful. She touched me and held me and treated me as an equal. She made me feel so relaxed and confident."

Another resident, Ann, fifty-three, who also met Diana during one of her visits, said, "She seems so down-to-earth, so natural, and she seems to understand all our needs."

The comments are typical of sufferers, victims, and patients, as well as the staff who work for charities, in their praise of Diana, not simply for being a royal patron and giving of her time, but for the quality of her approach, her attitude, and the empathy she exudes when dealing with all of them.

Ms. Knowles added, "The younger residents appreciate

what Diana does and admire her for it, but the older residents really love her for the warmth, the care, and the individual attention she gives them. No other stranger ever gives them such a high. It's wonderful to see."

In the fall of 1986, some months after Diana had agreed to become the patron of Help the Aged, she went on her first visit to a small residential home, Moorhouse near Staines, Middlesex, about thirty miles west of London. The twenty elderly residents had been told that Diana was coming to visit, and they were all seated in one room when she arrived. Diana walked into the room with officials from the charity and went to a group of residents. She sat down on the floor, held the hands of two of the elderly people, and said, "Hello, I'm Diana. What are your names?"

John Mayo, director general of the charity, who was present, said later, "In an instant she had won their hearts and their admiration and put them all at ease. Most of the residents had been somewhat of a fluster waiting to see her, wondering what this young person, then not thirty, would be like meeting them. Diana was nothing short of brilliant. She met every one of them, shook them by the hands, and chatted to them individually. She smiled, made little jokes, held their hands, and comforted some of the very old. She was magic."

Mayo has also toured India and Africa with Diana in her capacity as a patron of Help the Aged. He recalled, "In 1992 she visited one of Help the Aged's residential homes in Hyderabad where about fifty very elderly and most infirm people lived. They knew who she was and she brought smiles to all of them. She went round the entire home shaking hands with every single person, comforting some, smiling with others, and encouraging others. She stayed for one and a half hours chatting to them all, asking about their families and their lives in the home. All I can say is that they loved her. She put them at their ease and they responded to her understanding and warmth."

John Mayo continued, "In Africa, in July 1993 we visited a Mozambican refugee camp in Zimbabwe where about fifty thousand refugees were living. We went to the area run by Help the Aged for the very elderly and infirm. Once again she was brilliant. She watched them making sandals out of old tires, tending their vegetable patches, weaving clothes, and cooking their food. She went into some of their tiny, darkened huts and chatted to those too ill or infirm to come out into the sun. She brought great smiles to their faces, she encouraged them in their work, asked questions, and became involved with them. They responded wonderfully to her. It was a joy to watch her with them."

Diana has become a world figure, not only through her overseas tours with or without Prince Charles but because of the magic of the fairy-tale wedding and the extraordinary numbers of magazines and newspapers that splash her photograph on their covers. John Mayo remembers being astonished to discover color photographs of the Prince and Princess of Wales stuck on the walls of straw and wooden huts in a tiny village at the upper reaches of the Amazon in Beni, Bolivia, in 1984. He said, "It simply emphasizes the extent of Diana's appeal throughout the entire world. It is truly remarkable."

John Mayo is also aware of the remarkable effect Diana's patronage has on the finances of Help the Aged: "I will give you one example. Each year we hold a Golden Awards lunch, usually at a large London hotel, and people pay to attend, swelling our coffers. Sometimes Diana will attend, but of course she cannot be there every year. In November 1995 she was able to attend the annual dinner held at the London Hilton. When it was learned Diana would be present, the six hundred and forty seats available were sold within hours."

Diana's name seems inexorably linked with one particular British hospital that tugs at the heart strings of the nation whenever its name is mentioned. The Great Ormond Street Hospital for Children cares for sick children under eleven years of age and is world renowned, not only for its quality of care, but also for its research unit and capacity for dealing with the most difficult cases. Diana is not only happy but proud and privileged to be the hospital's royal patron.

Robert Creighton, chief executive of the hospital, is full of praise for the work Diana does on behalf of the hospital and also for her encouragement and efforts to raise funds. He said, "Having the Princess of Wales as patron is hugely beneficial to the hospital, not only in public relations terms but also in helping us raise money for our many projects."

Once a year Diana will make a public visit to the hospital, trailing in her wake TV crews, newspaper photographers, and journalists, who are permitted to follow her for a short while as she tours one or two wards talking to staff and some of the sick children. The TV stations and the newspapers love the photo opportunity, and the nation sees her chatting and playing with one or two youngsters.

But the media and the nation do not realize that during the year Diana also visits the hospital on two or three other occasions in an entirely private capacity. She arrives alone, without even her secretary or a lady-in-waiting and with no camera in sight. On those visits she wants to spend time with the children, their parents, and the staff without the media circus.

Robert Creighton commented, "For eighteen months we cared for a poor little Bosnian girl, Irma, who was aged eight, who had been seriously wounded when a bomb exploded near her during the fighting in 1993. Irma was paralyzed from the head down and we tried to make her life easier. Diana came to visit her once or twice during the time she was alive. And then, sadly, on March thirty-first, 1995, Irma died. The following day Diana phoned asking whether she could come and meet the staff, all the staff, who had spent the previous eighteen months caring for Irma. There were probably a core of about a dozen doctors and nurses who had been closely involved with Irma, and she came and met each and every one of them. It was a sad, moving experience for everyone, including Diana. But the staff really appreciated that she wanted to come and say thank you to them for all their care and nursing of the poor little girl.

"That is typical of the Princess of Wales. She feels for people and understands them. She adores coming here in private without cameras and the press when she can sit and talk and encourage some of the sick children, most of whom know who she is because they have seen her on television. She also likes to visit when parents are with their children so that she can talk to them also."

Creighton continued, "I have witnessed Diana on a number of occasions now, meeting parents and sick children, and I must tell you that it is a remarkably moving experience. They seem to instinctively gravitate towards her and warm to her as though they have known her for ages. Usually, children take time to adapt to a stranger, but not Diana. She has a certain rapport with them that is warm and natural, and children respond to her. It's wonderful to see."

Diana also takes a close interest in the research carried out at Great Ormond Street into eating disorders among young children. In 1995 she made a private visit to the hospital's research unit to talk to the doctors and staff and also some of the young children who were suffering, encouraging them to eat, and telling them that she understood, more than anyone, the trauma and pain they were going through because she had experienced it herself.

In talking to sick children and other people who suffer, as well as the disadvantaged, Diana finds some of the happiest hours of her life. She hopes that her presence helps them and gives them encouragement to fight their battles and endure their pain and suffering. When pressed, all she will say on the matter is, "I understand them, I know how they feel, what they're going through. And they all need help."

Centrepoint, the London charity for young people at risk—the homeless and unemployed and those in danger of becoming drug addicts and prostitutes—appeals especially to Diana. It helps 2,500 young people under twenty-five every year. They are found places to live, whether they are seeking shelter for the night or more permanent accommodations. Many are also found places in educational and training centers; some are found jobs.

Ms. Mo Houlden, head of Centrepoint's fund-raising, has been with Diana on a number of her visits to see the charity at work. Some of the visits have been with media crews, but others have been private where Diana meets as many of the young people as possible.

Ms. Houlden says, "She gives them encouragement and hope for the future. Most of our youngsters have no homes, no jobs, and nowhere to live. Their futures appear to them to be very bleak, but they will open their hearts to Diana in a quite remarkable way.

"Usually we do not inform them that the Princess of Wales is visiting, just that a visitor is touring their accommodation or place of training. They are rather taken aback when Diana walks in, and at first most are shy. Within minutes, however, Diana has won their confidence and they open up to her, chatting happily and naturally. They confide in her, telling her things they would never tell the staff. Indeed, we nearly always tell Diana at the end of her visit that whenever she wants a full-time job with youngsters, she should come and work as a volunteer because she manages to persuade the young people to open up. She is very, very good."

Mo Houlden has seen Diana ring promises from teenage heroin addicts that they will try to give up their addiction. "And afterwards those kids have told us that they will try to do so because they made her a promise," she said. "We are not saying they succeed, but they try, and that is a start. "Most of them tell us the same story of how natural, how easy, how genuine Diana is, so very different from the person they imagined her to be. In every way she is a marvelous boost to the charity and the kids. They love her."

In October 1995, Diana visited King's Cross, London's most notorious red-light district, frequented by hookers and the homeless of all ages as well as vagrants, drunks, and junkies. She decided to see for herself the atrocious conditions in which they lived after a briefing from Centrepoint staff relating the problems facing many young people in London. This would be her first official visit into such down-and-out territory. The press were not informed and no media were present, but photographs were organized by the charity and later offered to newspapers.

Dressed in a warm red sweater and tight black jeans, Diana appeared in good spirits for her midnight tour, chatting to a number of people as she walked around King's Cross. To one, she quipped, "It's a good thing the press aren't here... they would think I had a new job walking the streets."

The young and the old were equally impressed. Diana happily shook hands with the homeless, the drunks, and the junkies. One junkie told her, "You've got some guts shaking hands with everyone around here. Half of these kids have got needles and lots have HIV."

Diana happily chatted with anyone she met and continued to shake their hands. She concentrated particularly on the young teenage girls, some of whom were pregnant, many being hookers, and told them that Centrepoint was trying to establish a new night shelter for the homeless in the area. A group of young teenage hookers asked Diana if she could do something to stop the pimps from taking most of their money, complaining that the pimps would give them a beating just for kicks. Diana looked pained and visibly winced, but she could hold out no such hope for them.

One drunk managed to spoil the occasion, shouting at Diana, "What do you know about the homeless, you live in a fucking palace. Why don't you give us some of your money?" Diana smiled and walked on. To a charity worker she commented quietly, "He does have a point."

The feedback Diana receives from talking to disadvantaged people, especially the young and those suffering acutely, gives her an inner strength to face the media onslaught that never ceases to bewilder her. Few people realize the time and effort she devotes to her 120-odd charities. She believes that she can do so much more for people by committing her life to charity work than she could every have done undertaking a never-ending round of royal duties that often bored her to death.

Diana would say, "I cannot understand why we have to visit the same places, the same institutions, meeting the same people year in, year out, when there is so much more vital and necessary work to be done caring for people who are the unfortunates of society. Nearly all the people I have to meet on royal duties are the privileged, the wealthy, and the successful ones, never the poor, the homeless, the sick, and those suffering from incurable diseases who cry out for help and support."

Perhaps her greatest talent is found in the remarkable relationship she establishes with children of all ages. Watching Diana with young children, whether she is talking, playing, hugging, or simply having eye contact with them, is to witness an immediate understanding between Diana and the child. She seems to bring a sense of joy and spontaneous happiness into their lives. Most of the children she meets have problems, caused by illness, accidents, of birth, or background.

Anne Houston, director of ChildLine Scotland, says, "We were all struck by her understanding of children's problems when she visited us in Glasgow. She has an amazing empathy with children and showed great interest in the training our volunteer counselors receive."

Stories of Diana's personal relationships with children are legion. Blond-haired Emma May, ten, suffers from a rare chromosome disorder called Turner's syndrome, which will necessitate difficult and painful stretching surgery. Already she has spent many months in hospital, but she now has a princess as a special friend. Emma met Diana in 1994 and they now write to each other. "She is wonderful," comments Emma. "She's my very own special friend. I don't call her princess. I just call her Diana now because we're friends. She calls me Emma."

Six-year-old Sian Marks has spent the last four years in hospital suffering from a virus that caused kidney failure. She has nearly died on a number of occasions. She asked to give Diana some flowers when she visited Great Ormond Street Hospital but became too nervous on that day. Diana bent down, talked to her, held her until Sian found the confidence. Then held her hand. Sian warmed to her almost instantly.

Her father, Peter Marks, commented, "Now she talks about Diana all the time. She seems to gain strength from that brief relationship. Diana just showed warmth and kindness that day and Sian understood. She is truly remarkable."

Shortly before twelve-year-old AIDS victim Bonnie Hendel died in hospital, she told her mother, "I don't need medication anymore, just lunch with Princess Diana every day." And Bonnie had never met Diana but had simply written to her, telling her she was in hospital and dying of AIDS. Diana sent her a short letter and a signed photograph of herself, which Bonnie kept by her bedside and would kiss good night.

Doctors at St. Mary's Hospital, Paddington, phoned Kensington Palace asking that Diana be informed that Bonnie was only hours away from death. Diana was out, but as soon as she returned she went immediately to the hospital, arriving two hours after Bonnie had died. Diana apologized to her parents, but they told her, "You were a heroine to Bonnie. She loved you."

Minutes later Diana was seen leaving the hopsital, unable to control the tears that ran down her cheeks.

During her self-imposed retirement from the limelight Diana decided to dedicate her life to charity work in all its forms. She knows she can help raise funds for any number of charities, and she hopes that her presence and personal approach to sufferers and the disadvantaged makes them feel better and brings a little cheer and encouragement to their wretched lives. She also wanted to do something worthwhile with her life rather than be categorized as nothing more than a fashion icon, married to the heir to the throne, whose life revolved around meeting important people, undertaking royal duties, and being seen for what she was rather than what she could do for others.

16

"They Made Me Feel Like a Leper"

———— ❧ ————

To MANY, PRINCESS DIANA lives a hectic life. It appears that her photograph is always in the daily newspapers, whether she's at some charity event, tending the sick and dying in hospital, or her name is in screaming headlines suggesting her involvement in yet another scandal. In reality nothing could be further from the truth.

Before she cut back on her charity work in 1994, Diana's life had become one mad whirl of activity in which she would be working perhaps four days of the week. But her life was no nine-to-five job. She would need to plan her expeditions in great detail with her team—with the police, local dignitaries, the charity involved. She had to make exact traveling arrangements so as to always arrive on time, no matter where she had to travel in the United Kingdom.

Diana might have to carry out three or four separate royal duties in one day, perhaps flying four hundred miles north to Glasgow for two events, the next in York, one hundred and fifty miles nearer home, and perhaps the final one of the day in Birmingham, another hundred miles nearer Kensington Palace. After that she would then travel another hundred and fifty miles by rail or car to London. Often, Diana would not arrive back at the palace before 9 P.M. That day had probably started at six in the morning, meaning fifteen hours when she had to appear immaculately dressed and alluring virtually every minute of every hour.

Diana also has to appear happy, relaxed, and smiling on all

her public occasions no matter what her mood. She finds dealing with people on a one-to-one basis invigorating and interesting and loves to feel she is helping ordinary people come to terms with an illness, a handicap, or a problem. But whenever she becomes the center of attention with great groups of people surging around her, trying to greet her, wanting to meet her, and to touch her, she becomes embarrassed and awkward. And though she tries to look as relaxed and comfortable as possible, she in fact hates being gawked at, on display for everyone to look and point at and to criticize.

And the cameras would never leave her alone from the moment she put her head outside Kensington Palace. They would follow her every waking hour wherever she went, sometimes thirty or more photographers, as well as a number of TV crews, catching her every move, her every glance, her every word.

In December 1993 she decided to withdraw from public life for several reasons. Diana felt exhausted and drained, physically and emotionally. She found it more difficult to maintain the pace and the pressure with the number of duties she was expected to carry out mushrooming almost monthly. Since her separation from Charles a year before in December 1992, her royal duties had contracted substantially yet her public life had become considerably more demanding. Now she had to make all the decisions, the arrangements, the speeches; she had to lead discussions, hold interesting and intelligent conversations with people she had just met, on subjects about which she seemed to know very little. People had come to expect so much of her that she found the work tougher and more exhausting than she had ever imagined. She needed to give herself a break, to retreat from the limelight, which, during the years leading to the separation, had become unbearably bright.

Overnight, or so it seemed, Diana disappeared from the front pages of the newspapers and the nation's television screens, and her name and her picture cropped up far less often in the glossy magazines.

Diana told one of her colleagues, "I can remember waking

the morning after announcing my decision and realizing that I didn't have to rush off somewhere or other to some charitable function or royal duty. I lay there feeling wonderful. I can remember soaking in a long, hot bath and realizing that I had simply stopped my madcap life, the life that used to give me nightmares. I could see myself on this treadmill, which was going faster and faster and which it was impossible for me to stop or get off. I would find myself exhausted but unable to stop. Then I would wake and find myself in a dreadful sweat as though I had been running flat out."

Diana had been nervous the day she made her historic announcement primarily because she was suffering from exhaustion. For months she had been on a knife edge, fearful that something awful would befall her now that Charles had demanded an official separation, casting her adrift from the family and leaving her to fight her own battles and lead her own life.

She didn't want Charles to see that she couldn't cope for he had always teased her, almost from the first months of their marriage, that she couldn't boil an egg or organize a tea party. And she could remember how the teasing became more vicious as their marriage disintegrated. A look of disdain would cross his face as he would interrupt another of her tearful sessions to tell her to "pull your socks up" and "sort yourself out."

And then there was the Queen, who Diana felt had always treated her as an interloper, someone to be tolerated because she had married the Queen's son and had done "jolly well" to produce two boys—an heir and a spare—as Diana was informed. She was determined to prove to her mother-in-law that she could manage perfectly well on her own without Charles.

More importantly, Diana didn't want Wills and Harry to see their mother unhappy and miserable, for they had observed the tears in her eyes on far too many occasions during their young lives. She was determined to show her happy, smiling, loving side, not the anguished mother who always seemed on the verge of tears. She wanted to show them that their mother was made of sterner stuff.

By retiring from the limelight and royal duties, Diana, at a stroke, cut herself off from the Royal Family and the palace courtiers, who seemed to take such a delight in running her life. At first she felt lonely, somehow missing the hectic life.

During those first few months of 1994, Diana became a new woman. But it had taken her longer and the task had been harder than she had envisaged. Despite the newspaper stories saying how stunning she looked, she could see in the mirror the wrinkles coming, the bags under her eyes, the acne on her chin, all brought about by her jangled nerves, lack of sleep, and constant, nagging worry about her life, her future, and more especially, what would become of her and the boys.

Yet she couldn't shake her fear of a life of permanent loneliness. She would lie awake at night and think of her sons in their beds at their respective boarding schools, cut off from their mother for most of the year. She was jealous of the life they shared with their father. Now it seemed, besides Charles, the rest of the family would turn their backs on her because she had dared to argue and not play the role of the little princess. In the end, she thought she would pack her bags, leave Kensington Palace, and live a quiet life in some mansion deep in the countryside, far away from the bright lights, the cameras, and her adoring fans and supporters.

And the Royal Family had cut her off completely. The phone never rang from any member of the family; no invitations came from the Queen for tea or dinner, none from Philip, Princess Anne or Andrew or Edward, and of course, none from Charles. She never heard from the Queen Mother or any of the other Royals. Diana began to feel that the Royal Family were treating her in the same way as the House of Windsor had dealt with an epileptic child, Prince John, born to King George V and Queen Mary in 1905. On orders of the German-born Queen Mary of Teck, young John was removed from the family and incarcerated in a small house on the royal estate at Sandringham, never to be seen in public, never to be accepted as part of the family, never included in any family gatherings, and never visited by his parents, brothers, or sisters. He died in

1919, aged fourteen, virtually unmourned except by a nurse who had devoted her life to him.

Diana would say, "Ever since the separation the Royal Family have made me feel like a leper."

She would tell the few friends she could trust, "I know they can't forgive me for what I've done. In their eyes I've committed the greatest sin imaginable, daring to challenge the Royal House of Windsor. They want to rub my face in the dirt, make me realize how stupid and wrong I have been demanding to lead my own life, organize my own charity events, rather than wanting to carry out their royal orders, attending the same boring events year in, year out. I know how the family works. Once someone has crossed them, they will never forgive and never forget. They want to see me suffer."

Later Diana became more courageous and she happily told people her thoughts of the treatment being handed out to her by the Royal Family. And she would say, "I can take everything they throw at me. They want me to crawl away from their lives and disappear somewhere, preferably thousands of miles away so I will be no further trouble. The Queen, Philip, and Anne, as well as some of the others, believe I have been stupid to behave as I have done. They believe I should have put up with whatever happened, kept my mouth shut, and carried out my royal duties. For the Queen and Philip believe it to be the highest privilege imaginable to be a member of the House of Windsor."

Wickedly, Diana would add, "But I can tell the world it isn't the greatest privilege. I've tried it."

At first the fact that no member of the Royal Family ever contacted her hurt. However, as the months rolled by, the isolation gave her an inner strength since they were all acting in concert to break her, and she was absolutely determined that they would not do so.

17

The Lonely Princess

DIANA AWOKE ON JANUARY 1, 1994, determined to fulfill a host of New Year's resolutions. For years she had read the magazines suggesting how to become a "new woman" by exercise, sensible dieting, various therapies, and leading a sensible, stable life. Now she would put into practice all she had read. Diana had told one of her men friends, "This year I am determined to sort myself out and get really fit. Do you realize that I'm going to be thirty-three this year, which means that in 1996, I'm going to be nearer forty than thirty?"

Mockingly, Diana exclaimed, "Oh my God! What will I do?"

First priority would be to get her body into shape once more. She knew that swimming, which she loved, helped her tone her muscles and keep fit. She would swim up and down the pool until exhausted, which gave her a feeling of satisfaction. She increased her regular exercise schedules in the gym, getting an adviser to program her workouts, concentrating on the muscles Diana wanted to tone. In particular she wanted to make sure no cellulite appeared on her thighs or buttocks or upper arms. "I can't bear that," she would tell her adviser. "One thing we must stop is that cellulite."

She continued to play tennis with her trainer and enjoyed matches with other friends. She enjoyed her coaching lessons enormously for it had always been one of her ambitions to be good at tennis. She loved to play singles against world-class players like Steffi Graf, not because she considered herself anywhere near their level but because she wanted the thrill of playing someone really good, a professional from whom she hoped she might be able to pick up some tips.

After her matches with topflight players Diana would seem embarrassed and become shy, saying, "Thank you very much. I hope it wasn't too awful for you. You've been very kind."

Afterward they would always chat and have a fruit juice together, and Diana would ask them to pinpoint the poor areas of her play that they believed she should work on. If any of the players didn't think it correct to criticize her play, Diana would insist, telling them, "I need the help, so please, pull no punches."

Most of the class players Diana encountered on court were in fact surprised by the quality of her play, particularly her service, which she had practiced and honed so that even her coach, Rex Seymour-Lyn, told her she was in danger of "becoming seriously competent." And he meant it.

More than anything, Diana reveled in her newfound freedom, knowing she could do whatever she wanted, day in, day out, spoiling herself in shopping sprees, talking clothes, discussing styles, hair, and makeup without having to rush. In a matter of a few weeks she began to feel better, more in control of her life than she could remember. She began to spend more time indulging herself. She had the money to do so, and now she had the time and the inclination. She would read of the latest fad, an interesting therapy, a new remedy, the attributes of an avant-garde treatment she had not known about, and more importantly, she found herself increasingly interested in feminist books.

Some newspapers and magazines suggested that Diana had become a "therapy freak," constantly indulging herself in a great variety of different therapies, repeating all of them once or more a week. She would alternate or drop some treatments for a while.

Aromatherapy is certainly one way Diana loves to indulge herself, and she receives regular treatments at the expert hands of Sue Beechey of Aromatherapy Associates in Fulham,

London. Diana always feels relaxed and happy with the world after a session and encourages Sue to vary her treatments with different oils.

On occasion Diana has experimented with acupuncture. An Irish specialist, Oonagh Toffolo, will visit Kensington Palace when Diana is feeling particularly nervous and stressed. In the 1980s, Oonagh helped Diana overcome her anorexia nervosa and bulimia. Diana once said, "I think Oonagh saved my life. She certainly saved my sanity."

One of Diana's favorite treatment and therapy centers is in Beauchamp Place, near Harrods, where Chrissie Fitzgerald carries out more exotic treatments for Diana. Under Chrissie's expert hands Diana undergoes the occasional colonic irrigation, the water treatment some people find difficult to understand and appreciate. The treatment is frowned upon by doctors, who say that people should not undergo it unless they have a specific bowel problem. Diana has no such health problem and yet she will, from time to time, indulge in the practice. She believes it clears out the "angst" and the "aggro" that builds up inside her, making her feel more relaxed and more at peace with the world.

Another of Diana's luxuries is reflexology, the treatment that involves massaging specific points of the feet to stimulate blood supply and nerves and, hopefully, relieve tension. This treatment is much favored by Japanese men and women, principally for relieving tension. Once again Diana relies on the expert hands of Chrissie Fitzgerald. Sometimes the treatment can be mildly painful, but those who enjoy reflexology say the relaxation and the draining of tension from the body make ample amends for the pain.

Diana occasionally enjoys osteopathy, which aims to correct supposed deformations of the skeleton that cause disease. This therapy is also gauged to help aches and pains caused by stress, including tension headaches. Her osteopath is Michael Skipworth, whom she will sometimes phone in near panic, asking for an immediate appointment, so severe are some of her headaches. Diana once believed she suffered from migraines, but she has been told her headaches are not migraines. As a result, she now has the confidence that her headaches will respond to treatment within thirty minutes in Michael Skipworth's soothing hands. She has known Skipworth for nearly ten years. She first began visiting his clinic for her recurrent backache, which has affected her, on and off, since her teens.

Two other treatments Diana will turn to occasionally, but certainly not weekly, are psychotherapy and hypnotherapy. During psychotherapy the patient transfers emotions connected with people from their lives onto the analyst in a bid to deal with the past, and eventually to forget those emotions that have caused the patient so much stress. Hypnotherapy can be used for many different aspects of someone's health. Diana undergoes sessions to treat her stress, and sometimes finds sessions useful to control her eating. Understandably, Diana is determined not to allow her eating to ever get out of control again. She wants no repeat of the pain, anguish, and feeling of desperation she had when suffering from anorexia and bulimia.

Anger therapy is another treatment Diana has tried, but she is not convinced that it works too well. She knows she loses her temper far too easily, shouts and swears when things go wrong for her. But she also believes those bouts of anger and rage are part of her personality. And although she hates to lose her temper, she does believe it sometimes gives her a feeling of wonderful release. In earlier efforts to contain her swings of temper Diana tried anger-release therapy and kick boxing. During anger-release therapy clients are encouraged to shout, scream, and punch inanimate objects, like beanbags. Kick boxing is a similar treatment, but here the client uses her feet to kick a punching bag.

When totally frustrated, Diana will usually go to her bed and thump the pillows, on occasion burying her head in the pillows and screaming at the top of her voice, the goose down drowning the noise so that no one can hear her rages.

During the past couple of years Diana has consulted one or more astrologers, rather than always relying on the same person for predictions. Nowadays, she puts less faith in their readings than she did in the 1980s. She fears that some astrologers, knowing her identity, treat her more gently, even putting a gloss on predictions they would not have for a stranger.

During many of her therapies Diana will peruse the latest magazines that are provided for clients. She will always read the articles concerning the latest health fad or therapy, which, she realizes, has become the religion of the nineties. Many people in Britain believe Diana to be the patron saint of therapy for as a result of all the publicity surrounding her various treatments, therapy has gripped the wealthy British, who have the money to indulge themselves.

In the past five years membership in the British Association of Counselling has risen by a remarkable 300 percent to ten thousand. In Britain in 1996, it is estimated that fifty thousand people work as therapists with a further half million people serving as volunteers, providing the backup for a new, thriving industry. Many therapists acknowledge that it is the publicity surrounding the Princess of Wales and her interest in so many varied therapies that has created the astonishing increase in business.

Diana will also try many beauty treatments that she has read about and thinks might help her. She is adventurous, believing these "new" therapies should be tried. She is determined to use whatever treatments she believes will help her stay and look young. "I am determined to fight age all the way," she has said with a smile, "and anything that I can do to help put off the aging process I will certainly try."

As a result of that determination Diana has undergone computer-aided cosmetology, otherwise known as the face-lift without surgery, at regular intervals at the hands of Chrissie Fitzgerald. Minute electrical impulses are sent through the skin to the roots of the muscles, recharging the tissue and purportedly easing fine lines. Diana knows that the lines of the middle thirties are starting to show around her eyes and hopes this treatment will help keep them at bay.

So successful were her workouts, swimming and tennis, her therapies and treatments, that Diana began to feel like a new woman. Only she couldn't conquer the feeling of loneliness.

Without making any announcement or even informing the senior courtiers at Buckingham Palace, Diana decided in the early summer of 1994 to end her self-imposed semiretirement and throw herself back into the limelight, but concentrating solely on her charitable responsibilities.

She would say with a certain glee in her voice, "The family will hate seeing me on the front pages again, particularly Charles. They will realize their campaign to silence and flatten me has failed and I'm alive and kicking. And they will note that I'm fit and healthy, ready to undertake many, many years of public duties for every charity that wants me."

There were, however, other reasons. Diana had become bored and frustrated. And rather annoyingly for Diana, her love life had not been going at all well. She had become involved with a couple of men, enjoyed one or two flings since splitting from James Hewitt, but only Will Carling had provided Diana with a serious relationship. She hoped that in Carling she had found the right man to stimulate her, to make her feel loved and wanted, and to provide the anchor to her life that, in her heart, she desperately pines for.

To only a few people Diana has confessed her feeling of loneliness and isolation. During the summer of 1995, Diana told one of her great close friends whom she has known for fifteen years how miserable she found living alone. "I try to pretend that I enjoy life on my own, but I don't. I hate being at home at night on my own when everyone has gone. And it seems I can't be seen out with anyone I fancy, so my relationships have to remain secret, which is very trying and not conducive to a lasting, fulfilling affair."

In the same tone, as tears welled in her eyes, she continued, "I drive through the streets and see couples everywhere and wonder what is wrong with me that I have no one. I see couples going shopping together to the supermarket and envy them; I see couples in their cars with the children in the back and wish it were me. I just want to enjoy those ordinary, everyday events, which I never enjoyed with Charles because we never lived like any ordinary couple. We never did anything together. Never went shopping. Never took out the children on our own. None of the things every other couple in the world does naturally, together, as a family. And now I wonder if I ever shall and it hurts. Life is flying by and I have no one to share it with."

She adds, "I wish I could just meet some man who would love me for what I am. Every time I look at a man nowadays I find they're married and their wives go berserk if I even talk to them. The women can be so hurtful towards me. I sometimes wonder if I'm destined to be an old maid, living my life alone."

After talking in such a vein Diana will usually snap out of her doleful demeanor, apologize, and say, "I'm sorry I'm being pathetic. I must stop feeling sorry for myself and get out there and find someone before it's too late." And a half smile will cross her lips as she fights back the tears.

It seemed to Diana that every new close relationship with any man was doomed to end in failure, unhappiness, bad publicity, and recriminations. She had begun to believe that she would be unable to form a stable relationship with a man for fear of the paparazzi, and the disastrous effect exposure would have on any meaningful affair.

A number of distinguished psychiatrists would question Diana's need for such a variety of therapies. Some considered that Diana's desire for constant grooming reflected an unease that bordered on self-indulgence, neuroticism, and narcissism, rather than a cry for a sound, loving relationship.

Dr. Raj Persaud is a lecturer in psychiatry at the prestigious Maudsley Hospital in London. Dr. Persaud worried that people with a narcissistic personality disorder, which some had suggested could be part of Diana's problem, mistake the attainment of perfect appearance with that of forging happy relationships. "It is really the extension of adolescent fantasy: 'If I can be perfect, I will marry the person of my dreams.' Often they cannot understand that, even though they are magnificently turned out, relationships founder. But the person they are trying to attract senses their self-absorption and fears there will be no time left over for them."

When Diana worried about her disastrous and near-empty

love life, she would become morose and would think back to the days when she could always pick up a phone and speak to the one man she had been able to trust, her beloved father. Even today, more than three years after her father's death, Diana still wishes he were there for her. She could always talk to him during those horrific years when she could see her marriage had failed and had no where to turn.

Sometimes, when in a reflective mood, Diana will say to a close friend, "I still miss him. When he was alive, I always knew he was there in the background, always supportive. I knew I could phone him at any time and we could chat about whatever was troubling me. He would always give sound advice and make me feel wanted and special. No one has been able to take his place since, and his death has made me feel more lonely than I ever did when he was alive."

When in one of her somber moods, Diana will still shed tears for her father, wishing she could bring him back, so that she could talk to him. And she has admitted that since his death she will, on occasion, particularly when feeling depressed, talk to her father as though he were still there. She knows he isn't and doesn't for one minute believe it is possible to speak to the dead, yet she finds comfort in the hope that he could be there. Diana knows that if her father were still alive, she would have greater confidence in her future.

18

Her Private World

──── ❧ ────

B UT OTHERS NEEDED DIANA. Senior executives of many of
the 120 charities that boasted Diana as their patron were
disappointed when she announced in the fall of 1993 her need to
escape from public life to seek some privacy. They knew that
Diana's presence, even if only once or twice a year, had become
the major event in their charity's life, eagerly anticipated and
always well attended. And most charities also recognized that
Diana's patronage meant healthier bank balances to help fund
their work.

Diana held a council of war at Kensington Palace, calling in
her private secretary, Patrick Jephson, the former Royal Navy
lieutenant commander; Anne Beckwith-Smith, her trusted
friend and chief lady-in-waiting; her "unofficial" press officer,
the Australian Geoff Crawford, who was based at Buckingham
Palace; and her equerry, Royal Marine captain Edward Musto.

Her right-hand man, Patrick Jephson, now thirty-nine, had
been Diana's equerry for some years before being promoted to
private secretary in 1990, succeeding Diana's great friend and
confidant Anne Beckwith-Smith. It is difficult to overemphas-
ize the importance of Anne Beckwith-Smith's role. She had met
Diana before her engagement to Prince Charles, and the two
had formed an understanding. Ten years older than Diana, the
mature, sensible Anne showed by her diplomacy and sound
advice that she would make the perfect lady-in-waiting for the
Princess of Wales.

Anne would be one of only three members of the staff of

forty-one employed by Charles and Diana at the time of their wedding in 1981 who would survive the dramas and traumas of those first seven years of the royal marriage. Indeed, the more Diana and Anne worked together, the closer they would become. At the end of Diana's first royal tour in 1983, Diana spontaneously threw her arms around Anne's shoulders and gave her a great hug before presenting her with a lovely brooch. "I couldn't have done it without you," Diana whispered to her. They were no empty words.

When Diana finally succeeded in getting rid of Oliver Everett, her first private secretary, she asked Anne to take the job. Anne accepted, and the two women forged a close bond that would last for more than ten years. During the dark days of the marriage Diana would frequently flee to Anne's Knightsbridge apartment and talk to her for hours, pouring out her heart. On occasion, Diana would even stay overnight rather than return to Charles at the palace. She would come to have absolute trust in Anne's friendship, loyalty, and sound common sense.

Anne is no yes-woman. She is known to have had a major influence on Diana and is happy to act on her behalf whenever necessary. She is also quite capable of making strong and honest arguments when she disagrees with the Princess and is not frightened to tell Diana when she believes Diana is going about things in the wrong way. On occasion they will argue, but if Diana cannot be persuaded that she should change her mind, then Anne will say, "Well, if you are determined, then that is your choice. But it is my job to warn you."

Those words would usually make Diana stop and think if the course of action she has decided on is the one she should carry out. Often Diana will reply, "I know, I know. But on this occasion I think I know what is best."

Diana values Anne's views, her advice, her integrity, and her diplomacy. In those first nervous days after the marriage Anne, too, found she was on a learning curve. She had to find out how to play the courtiers at Buckingham Palace, who tended to treat the young Diana and her ladies-in-waiting as immature, inexperienced young women who had to be taught the ways of the royal world. At first Anne and Diana's other friends whom she had appointed ladies-in-waiting did take advice from those who had been in senior positions with Charles.

Later, however, Anne became proficient at holding her own in arguments with senior Buckingham Palace aides, some of whom continue to look upon Diana's small team of friends and staff as amateurs playing on a sophisticated stage where only professionals should be tolerated. Since the separation, some senior courtiers patronize the Kensington Palace staff, but Anne has won a sound reputation as capable of putting in their place those she calls "the snobs at the palace," valiantly defending Diana.

During those first few years of the marriage Diana had been cared for by some of the most experienced palace staff. It is untrue, as Diana has repeatedly alleged, that she was given no training, no advice, no help, to settle down in her new role as the Princess of Wales. Prince Charles had asked Michael Colborne, one of his secretaries, a man with whom he had become close during his years with the Royal Navy, to teach her the ropes during those first few years. Colborne, then in his forties, agreed to help, and Diana looked to him during the first three years for advice on a wide range of matters. Colborne, who had been in Charles's private office since 1975, knew how the system worked, and he imparted as much advice as possible to the young Diana.

Prince Charles had also drafted another experienced royal hand to help the untutored Diana. Oliver Everett, a former polo-playing friend of Charles's and another of his secretaries, had quit royal service to resume his diplomatic career in the Foreign Office. He was working in Madrid, with the prospect of a great future in the service, when Charles urged him to return and become private secretary to the young Diana. He agreed, but his relationship with Diana would soon founder.

The Queen's principal lady-in-waiting is the vastly experienced and kindly Lady Susan Hussey, an intelligent woman who has been in royal service close to the Queen for twenty years. Almost daily during those first years Susan Hussey would telephone to ask Diana or Anne whether she could be of help in sorting out any problems. She bent over backward to aid and advise the young Diana. And yet Diana would later deny that all this help and advice had been offered.

Both Everett and Colborne also helped Anne Beckwith-Smith, who would become the most loyal and long-standing adviser to Diana. Some wondered whether Anne had deliberately sacrificed her chances of marriage and motherhood to remain by Diana's side. Ironically, Anne and Diana nearly fell out when Diana sacked Oliver Everett after eighteen months in the job. At first, Diana believed Everett to be her best friend and great at his job. But she would become suspicious of him, believing he was too close to Prince Charles. Diana also felt he patronized her. Anne argued forcefully for Diana to keep Everett, but Diana was adamant. Two days before Christmas 1983, Everett was forced to resign and Anne was rewarded with his job.

For ten years Anne worked tirelessly as Diana's personal and private secretary, her confidant and her friend, the one person, perhaps more than any other, who helped Diana combat her anorexia and bulimia and who tried to calm the Princess of Wales when she became overwrought and anxious. But Diana had come to rely more on her own judgment, and Anne felt her advice no longer carried the weight it had during their earlier years together. She would remain Diana's principal lady-in-waiting, though there was no special title and she would find employment in the celebrated Victoria and Albert Museum, half a mile from Kensington Palace.

Diana asked her war council if there was any reason why she should not quietly and without fuss resume her full load of charity work. She had never in fact ended all charity work, but to all intents and purposes the general public felt she had retreated behind the walls of Kensington Palace. They had most certainly noted her absence. Jephson thought it would be better if Diana asked Buckingham Palace to issue a statement, but

Diana had no intention of allowing such a move. She believed the senior palace staff would not want her to reenter the public domain.

She would say nothing of her inner thoughts to her team. She knew Charles would be annoyed, Philip angry, and the Queen quietly incensed at Diana's return, for they had encouraged her to center her life on her two sons. Indirectly it had been suggested to Diana that she take a lovely house near Windsor, in striking distance of Eton, where her sons would be educated during the next seven years. Diana had declined the invitation for she had no wish to be sidelined. She knew when her decision had been passed up to the senior aides and the Royal Family, they would be disappointed that another ruse to remove her from the spotlight had failed. The thought brought a wicked smile to her lips.

Patrick Jephson greeted Diana's decision to step up her charity work with some relief for he had seen the Princess becoming more frustrated and less focused, wallowing in self-indulgence. But he realized full well the consternation Diana's decision would cause at the palace, and he discussed the diplomacy of such a move with Diana.

"It's my life," Diana told Jephson. "And you know the charities want me back on the scene. The phone never stops."

Diana also had a secret yearning to throw herself back into the fray. Meeting people, seeing their faces light up, gave her a feeling of being wanted, and loved, which had sustained her during the dark years of the marriage. She now needed that comfort above all else.

There was, however, another personal reason for Diana's wish to return to work. In May 1994, Prince Charles had information leaked to the press detailing his wife's annual bill for her "grooming." In the year following their separation Diana had spent $5,000 a week, a total of $250,000 that year!

Apparently these accounts covered all her clothes, casual wear for the boys, her increasing interest in alternative therapies, makeup, hairdressing, and a few gifts. Charles drew Diana's attention to the high expenses, and Diana, too, had been shocked at the amount, believing she had cut down since ending her royal duties at the end of 1993. The press of course expressed surprise, with pictures of Diana in a range of her latest, expensive haute couture outfits, which the tabloids described as her "spend, spend lifestyle." They detailed her new therapies, her clothes, her clubs and restaurants, and her way of life, which some described as "outrageous." It was pointed out that the $250,000 did not cover any day-to-day living expenses, staff, cars, travel, or holidays. They were all extra.

Charles leaked the information because he was "absolutely furious" that Diana should spend so much money on herself for, what he perceived, was no good reason. When informed of the annual bill, Charles had flown into one of his infamous rages, shouting and swearing, kicking the furniture in his fury. Diana, too, would explode when she saw the details of her lifestyle splattered all over the newspapers, courtesy of her own husband.

"The spiteful little shit," she exclaimed. "How could he wash all my dirty linen in public?"

Diana of course knew that part of the huge expenditure had nothing to do with wanting to spend money, but was a natural reaction to the loneliness and the frustrations of her life, all of which had come about because of the disgraceful behavior of Charles himself and his demand that they separate. She always knew that Charles had little idea of how a woman's mind worked.

Shaking her head in disbelief, Diana said to Sarah Ferguson, "Doesn't he realize that any woman without a man in her life, with a failed marriage and no one to love her, would behave in the same way, trying to find some happiness in spoiling herself?"

Diana did, however, have her supporters. The "ladies who lunch," the euphemism for the wives of Britain's rich and famous, believed Diana's $250,000 annual bill was somewhat above average but certainly not in the superleague of spenders. None thought the amount outrageous because Diana had a certain standard to maintain as the Princess of Wales.

Diana recognized that the publicity would, more than likely, harm her image with her adoring public, who would not want to see her taking advantage of her situation, spending so much money on herself. She knew that most ordinary British house-wives, checkout girls, factory workers, and office drudges, who are her most adoring fans, wouldn't spend $2,500 a year on their clothes, let alone $250,000. They would also recognize that Diana had decided to take early retirement, living in a palace full of servants while still a young woman in her thirties. There she would indulge herself in some therapy while her sons were away at boarding school. The last thing Diana wanted was publicity that saw her as taking as much money as she could from Prince Charles but not doing anything, not even charity work, in return.

Even the straitlaced *Financial Times* found it necessary to comment, "The princess was reported to be embarrassed and contrite and to have set in train cost-cutting measures. Perhaps, given the political and economic climate, she was wise, even valorous, to opt for discretion. But if ever a woman was encouraged to become a spendthrift, it was Diana. She married into a family which elevated dowdiness to an art form."

Three days after the story of Diana's spending spree reached the media, as though to order a remarkable story appeared on the front page of the *Daily Mail*, by Richard Kay, a reporter who had become Diana's most trusted tabloid confidant. "Diana Rescues Drowning Man," ran the headline, and the story outlined how Princess Diana helped save the life of a drowning man in a dramatic rescue operation in London's Regent's Park. Allegedly, Diana rushed to the water's edge and helped pull out an unconscious tramp, hauling him onto the bank, where he was given mouth-to-mouth resuscitation.

Kay reported that Diana was "praying for the recovery of the man," Martin O'Donaghue, forty-two. She had since visited him twice in hospital where he was "fighting for his life." The experience of saving the man's life had "affected her deeply," and the man's welfare was "uppermost in Diana's mind."

The heroic story gripped the nation. As dusk was falling, the Princess was being driven through the park after having gone jogging. Her car was flagged by a group of tourists, who reported seeing a man fall into the lake. Having told her driver to make a 999 call on her mobile phone, Diana, still in shorts and trainers, ran back to the lake. She was standing by the parapet looking into the water when a Finnish student ran to the scene, climbed over the parapet, plunged into the water and dragged the man to safety. Having pulled the man from the water, the music student, Kari Kotila, twenty-nine, checked the man's mouth for blockages and gave him the kiss of life, pounding the man's heart between breaths. Later, police confirmed that Mr. Kotila had brought the man back from the dead.

Diana had not been the heroine of the moment but rather had simply joined a group of people looking over the parapet as the man struggled for his life in the icy waters of the lake. Mr. Kotila said later, "I was surprised that no one was trying to rescue the man. People were standing around looking, but doing nothing. I gave my backpack and wallet to this woman who was standing there because she looked honest. It was only later that I realized it was Princess Diana."

As the conservative *Daily Telegraph* pointed out in an editorial, "The first impression of the heroine plunging from her car into the icy deep had to be modified following further inquiries. The Princess's chief role, it emerged, was to hold the wallet of a Finnish student while he trawled for the waterlogged tramp. But the story may be added to a growing list of the Princess's neighbourly acts, many of which involve stopping her car to comfort victims of breakdowns, smashes and other mobile misfortunes.... The good deeds may enhance the Princess's reputation.... But the most impressive acts of charity are those undertaken without everyone knowing about them."

No newspaper mentioned that this revelation emerged within days after Diana's public image took quite a battering as she was exposed as the spendthrift princess. Nor did they know that during her second visit to the hospital to see the vagrant

Martin O'Donaghue, Diana left him a paltry £5 note ($7.50) as a present.

Diana enjoyed being back at work. She felt a new zest for life and determined to spend more of her time with the charities that particularly appealed to her. She had already decided to carry out fewer media-grabbing functions, such as appearing at glamorous film premieres or being pictured chatting to the disadvantaged. She had, it seemed, taken to heart the remarks of the *Daily Telegraph* editorial writer. She had always enjoyed the quiet, private visits she had made to many of her charities, for she felt it brought her closer to those she was seeking to encourage, to help, and to cherish. Now she would indulge in still more private charity work. It would become a vital part of her new life, giving her a feeling that she was undertaking worthwhile work, while hopefully bringing a little cheer to those who suffered.

In her new, more hectic existence, the Princess of Wales is usually out of bed and into her shower by seven o'clock each morning, listening to pop music on the radio. When swimming or going to the gym, she will leave the palace by eight o'clock, driving herself to her rendezvous. She may work-out or swim, or both, for an hour or ninety minutes, before taking another quick shower and having an orange juice and croissant before heading home to start work.

At ten o'clock she usually holds her first meeting of the day with Patrick Jephson, when together they go through all her correspondence as well as her diary for the next seven days, checking details, confirming dates, times, appointments, and discussing what she should wear. Diana has become a stickler for attending to her correspondence, making sure that people who write letters to her will, without fail, always receive a reply. And she hates formal letters being sent to anyone who has bothered to write to her. She always tries to make her replies personal, informal, and friendly. She understands letter writing is a wonderful contact with the public, those people who admire and support her. A small staff of three women attend to her correspondence, logging the letters and typing the replies on a computer.

In yet another break with royal tradition in June 1994 Diana dispensed with her equerry, wanting to become even more independent than all other senior Royals, who are always attended at official functions by an equerry. Diana decided she no longer needed someone to hold her umbrella, park her car, or wait in attendance, believing equerries to be outmoded.

On occasion one or other of her ladies-in-waiting will sit in on her early-morning meetings, as well as her dresser, who needs to know every minute of Diana's day so that her clothes can be pressed, prepared, and laid out in good time. After her meetings Diana will then have long discussions with her dresser, debating what she should wear for every outing.

Although she loves spending much of her spare time in casual wear, Diana still admits to the thrill of putting together an ensemble in which she feels confident. She knows that people want her to look special, even stunning, and she tries to oblige whatever the occasion. She plans each outfit with meticulous attention to detail and real deliberation, sometimes discussing possible variations and accessories with her team for ten or twenty minutes, wanting to make sure what she wears is absolutely appropriate. Some days Diana may change her clothes half a dozen times.

When asked about her clothes, Diana will nearly always say, "I love wearing casual clothes. For me it is a real pleasure because of the times I have to dress correctly to suit the occasion, the place, and the people I will be meeting."

After her working schedule has been decided, Diana usually conducts meetings arranged in Kensington Palace where she will sit with charity organizers to discuss plans. These meetings may last for two hours or more for she has become far more involved in the activities she supports. In those meetings Diana will stress two important points. First, she asks organizers to think of specific ways that she, personally, can help their charity, which, she realizes, is her primary task. She hates being just a figurehead and tells them so. She also urges the organizers to make sure that when she visits their headquarters, she meets the people for whom the charity is devised, not simply the charity workers. Diana wants to be sure she never loses touch with the people the charity is designed to help.

During the school holidays, when the boys are staying with her at Kensington Palace, Diana cuts down on her meetings, her charity work, and her workouts and concentrates on finding various things for the boys to do while making sure they ask friends to come round to the palace to play or for meals. Sometimes Diana will organize outings for Wills, Harry, and two or three of their friends.

Diana will usually invite the boys' friends' mother or father, or both, to the palace for a chat and a coffee or perhaps a snack lunch or evening drink so that she can keep in contact with her sons' school friends and their families. Diana tells the parents of her concern for Wills and Harry. "This is their home," she says, "and I want them to realize that they can invite whomever they want to share it with them. The last thing I want the boys to think is that they live in some palace, devoid of the realities of life and divorced from the real world. It's their home first and foremost."

When the boys are not at boarding school, Diana will try to arrange a lunch date with one or more of her friends, sometimes a man but more often a woman. Lunch is usually taken with a friend. She will usually select one of her favorite restaurants, Launceston Place, an intimate, quiet restaurant behind Kensington High Street, and Bibendum in Fulham, a slightly more trendy establishment, or perhaps an old haunt like San Lorenzo's in Beauchamp Place.

Since the separation Diana has tried to entertain at Kensington Palace, throwing an informal dinner party on alternate Saturday nights. Invitations asking her to house parties in the country or to lavish dinners or dances in London are now far fewer. The number of hostesses who want Diana at their gatherings has dropped remarkably from the days when Charles and Diana were invited to any number of events, the hosts falling over themselves to try to persuade the Prince and Princess of Wales to be their guests.

The Prince of Wales, and of course his wife, are by far the star attractions in British society. Hosts also realize the Queen and Philip much prefer to eat quietly at home on their own or with just one or two old friends.

Diana understands the new order. She knows that Charles and Camilla, accepted as an item by the Wiltshire set and others, have attended weekend house parties together ever since the late 1980s. The last person hosts could invite would be Diana. And understandably, Camilla's pals are only too eager to help encourage the relationship of their friend with the Prince of Wales, the heir to the throne.

Diana did not establish her own social circle. She had been too young before she met and married Charles, and understandably, his friends became her friends as well. She did not seek her own circle of friends, save for some younger wives, but they have mostly moved to the country. And since Charles left Diana to reside at Highgrove, nearly all his friends have remained close to him. Diana feels that loneliness and believes some of her erstwhile companions deserted her because she and Charles separated. To them it didn't matter that he had cheated on Diana and returned to his former mistress, for they all believed that Charles would one day be king and, more likely than not, Diana would not be queen. They preferred to stay where they predicted power would ultimately lie.

Those desertions hurt Diana. She would come to despise those women who had sought to be her friend but had discreetly moved away when they realized the marriage was over. Sometimes she would weep at their two-faced attitude, but on other occasions the thought of their treachery gave her added strength, so determined had she become to wage war on her husband and the rest of the Royals who wanted to disown her.

Faced with the necessity of building a new set of friends, Diana began her own Saturday soirees, when she would invite a number of people to Kensington Palace for a relatively informal dinner, music, drinks, and a chat. She will usually play the hostess on her own with no man as a support. She will invite those old friends who haven't gone to the country for the weekend, some enjoying a "girls' evening" without their husbands or men friends. Sometimes they are all-female parties, which Diana's contemporaries say they thoroughly enjoy away from their menfolk where they can dictate the topics of conversation.

One thirty-six-year-old married society lady commented, "I have been to four of Diana's Saturday-night dinners in the past six months. They are wonderful and relaxing. There were just eight women present, and because there were no men in attendance, we could all enjoy a wonderful bitch. I think the girls love those evenings, especially in such beautiful surroundings. And Diana is a wonderful, friendly hostess."

Most evenings of the week, however, are rather sad affairs for the Princess of Wales. When the boys are at boarding school, which is thirty-five weeks a year, Diana usually stays at home on her own for the entire evening. Sometimes she entertains the occasional visitor, and on occasion, one of the lovers with whom she has become involved since her break with James Hewitt in 1991. She also invites a girlfriend round for a snack and a chat. In these instances she will have her butler and a maid on hand for most of the evening. If she is alone, Diana usually sends them home around 7:30 P.M. and then has the vast Kensington Palace apartment entirely to herself. Diana finds it increasingly difficult to cope with this lonely existence.

When really bored at night, Diana will spend some time on the phone, but she soon discovered that most women do not have the time or the inclination to talk during the evenings for they were busy relaxing with their menfolk, entertaining, or simply having a quiet dinner at home. So, unable to find friends to talk to, Diana will be reduced to turning on the television, perhaps a television soap or a film. She will often watch the latest video release for she has become quite a film buff since living alone. Fed up with the "box," she will read magazines and listen to her type of music, the seventies hits, which she first enjoyed as a teenager.

Even today Diana is no great bookworm, preferring the instant, short editorial pieces found in magazines. During the past two years, however, under the guidance of her psychotherapist and friend Susie Orbach, Diana is reading more serious literature, much of it concerning women's interests and, in particular, feminism. She also enjoys the occasional special-interest book such as homeopathy, health food, or other such therapeutic interests. The novels she used to enjoy no longer hold the same interest.

Often, Diana will take a hot, scented bath as early as 9 P.M. and then spend an hour or more reading magazines in bed or propped up by pillows watching TV until she falls asleep. More often than not Diana wakes at around midnight or 1 A.M., turns off the TV, and puts down her magazine before falling asleep once again.

Quite frequently Diana resorts to sleeping pills because she finds sleep so elusive, but they make her feel drowsy the following morning, and she dislikes that feeling. She much prefers to be wide-awake and raring to go at first light rather than having to struggle awake, forcing herself to dress before driving half-dazed to the gym.

The one activity that Diana still adores is shopping. Throughout most of the year she will always find time to shop at least twice a week, perhaps a couple of hours one day and two or three hours later in the week. Much of her shopping entails chatting with representatives of the haute couture brand names, learning about their new designs for the following season and wondering if they will suit her. She still loves to browse, wandering through shops unrecognized, if possible, finding the odd knickknack or accessory that she feels may provide a highlight that, combined with one of her outfits, will attract the attention of the media, the public, and the fashion buyers.

She now enjoys buying casual gear for her sons when they are back home from boarding school. Ever since they have been toddlers, Diana has refused to go along with the royal tradition of putting secondhand clothes on the boys, hand-me-downs from older royal children. Charles, Andrew, and Edward were all dressed in clothes worn by other members of the family.

The thrifty Queen Mary and the Scottish Queen Mother, still going strong at age ninety-five, believed in the principle. Not Diana. She has ensured that both boys are always treated equally, and young Harry, two years younger than William, is never given his older brother's castoffs.

Even in small, insignificant ways Diana wants to distance herself from the Royal Family. She knows she must remain on terms with Charles for the sake of the children, though she still finds it extraordinarily difficult, for she openly despises him. But Diana has plans for the future, not just for her own life, not just for the boys, but for Prince Charles.

19

Diana's Perilous Gamble

———— ❧ ————

ROUND NINE O'CLOCK on the morning of Tuesday, November 14, 1995, Prince Charles's forty-seventh birthday, Diana lifted the telephone in her palace apartment and asked to be put through to Sir Robert Fellowes, the Queen's personal and private secretary, the most senior aide in the Royal Household.

"Hello, Robert, it's Diana here. I have something to tell you."

"Yes, what's that?" Sir Robert asked politely.

After a second's hesitation Diana took a deep breath and said, "I've done an interview for *Panorama* [a serious, high-profile BBC current-affairs program]. I'm phoning you to let you know that it's going out next Monday, November the twentieth."

For a moment there was silence. "You've what?" asked Sir Robert, his voice incredulous and questioning. "You've given an interview to *Panorama*? What about?"

"Me. It's an hour-long interview about me and my marriage. Just me, talking about everything."

"Does HM [the Queen] know of this?"

"No, she knows nothing. Nor does Charles."

"Do any of your staff know, Jephson [Diana's private secretary], Crawford [her press adviser]?"

"No. They know nothing. I have told no one. You are the first to know."

"Will you be around later? Because I will have to inform HM immediately. I might need to get back to you."

The man with whom Diana enjoyed a
passionate three-year affair, Maj. James Hewitt
(Express Newspapers)

A paparazzo caught Diana and
Major Hewitt kissing in 1990
(London News Service)

Will Carling with his wife, Julia, outside their London home in May 1995, just twelve months after their marriage
(London News Service)

The lovely Julia Carling, who fought a bitter tug-of-love battle with Diana over hunky Will Carling
(Express Newspapers)

Arriving at a gala night at the
London Coliseum, June 1993...
(London News Service)

...and at a cancer charity
event in London, December
1995 (London News Service)

Prince Charles with sons, William and Harry, in Klosters, Switzerland, 1994
(Express Newspapers)

Diana enjoying a skiing holiday with Wills and Harry in Lech, Austria, in
1995 (Express Newspapers)

On an early morning visit to
the Chelsea Harbour Club,
1994 (Express Newspapers)

Princess Diana in her bikini
enjoying the Caribbean surf
and sun, January 1993
(London News Service)

Learning to in-line skate in Kensington Gardens in November 1995. She would be castigated for not wearing a helmet or protective gear for knees and elbows. (London News Service)

Psychotherapist and feminist Susie Orbach, the woman who keeps all of Diana's secrets. (Express Newspapers)

Princess Diana with Prince Charles, Prince William, and Prince Harry at the official VE day celebrations in London, May 1995 (London News Service)

Princess Diana with Prince Harry during the official VJ day celebrations in London, August 1995 (London News Service)

"Not till much later because I am going to Broadmoor [a top-security jail for the criminally insane] on an official visit."

The contents of the conversation between Elizabeth and Sir Robert Fellowes is not known. Later, palace sources confirmed that Elizabeth had been shocked by the news. After questioning Sir Robert and other senior aides she would become absolutely furious that Diana had had the temerity and the impertinence to give such an interview without her express permission. Nothing like this had occurred before in Elizabeth's lifetime, for no other Royal would ever have had the audacity to undertake such a venture without the Queen's express permission. Without exception, all members of the Royal Family, through their private secretaries, would always clear any TV, radio, or press interview with senior aides at Buckingham Palace. They would only give permission after consulting the Queen.

Elizabeth immediately called Charles, who was on a five-day official royal visit to Germany, and asked him if he knew anything about the interview. He knew nothing.

What had enraged Elizabeth was not only that, in secret, Diana had given an interview without telling anyone, but that the BBC had agreed to Diana's express demand to keep the matter secret until she had informed the Queen. For the chairman of the BBC was Sir Marmaduke Hussey, whose wife, Susan, has been the Queen's chief lady-in-waiting and constant friend and adviser for more than twenty years.

The fact that Diana had chosen Charles's birthday to inform the Queen, and for the BBC to make a formal announcement later the same day, was not lost on anyone. Charles's staff with him on his royal tour, as well as those back home at St. James's Palace, were devastated. "The little bitch" and "the little vixen" were two of the polite comments made about Diana's remarkable coup.

Charles and his team, however, were in no position to complain for Charles had given his own two-hour television interview in June 1994 when he confessed to committing adultery with his longtime mistress, Camilla Parker Bowles.

Charles had been roundly condemned by the Queen, Prince Philip, and his sister, Princess Anne, for agreeing to the TV appearance, but he had first discussed the matter with his mother before agreeing to the television spectacular. They thought it was wrong, in principle, to permit the TV cameras into his life. And they told him so before the interview took place. It had been Charles's decision to go ahead. Afterward, they all chided him on how stupid he had been to confess to adultery.

Diana had taken the only course open to her. She had to adopt secret tactics to ensure the interview ever took place. She knew that the Royal Household, including the Queen herself, as well as Charles's office, would have moved heaven and earth to prevent such an interview from occurring if they had known about it in advance.

"I had to carry out this operation in secret," Diana confessed. "Otherwise they would have put a stop on it."

In such situations Sir Robert Fellowes would have had a private word with the BBC's director general, Sir John Birt, asking to be informed if the Princess of Wales had suggested an interview. The director general would then have been obliged to inform the palace of the deal brokered between Diana and the editors of *Panorama*. The palace would then have said they did not think such an interview would be appropriate "at this time," and the BBC, which operates under royal charter, would have felt obliged to drop the proposed program.

In her heart Diana believed that the palace had done all in its power since the official separation to keep her in the background, so that attention would focus on the dutiful, responsible, hardworking Prince Charles. Palace mandarins had rejoiced when Diana chose to retire from public life. Her reemergence into public life had been seen as a catastrophe, for the media's attention had once again focused almost exclusively on Diana. Her picture was back on the front pages; TV programs screened every photo opportunity. Once again, Charles would be relegated to virtual obscurity.

During those three years, Diana had come to believe that a

number of senior courtiers were actually plotting against her, trying to smear her image with the public and make her appear irrational. She talked openly to all her friends, as well as her staff, telling them how advisers to Charles and to the Queen were conducting a war against her to drive her out of the Royal Family. During many conversations, Diana would refer to them openly as "the enemy," and she would pull no punches describing their actions as deliberate machinations to destabilize her situation and make her feel alone and unwanted.

Diana knew one of those she described as "the enemy" very well indeed. Royal Navy commander Richard Aylard, forty-three, had been Diana's equerry between 1985 and 1988. He had been by her side throughout those three years whenever she ventured forth from Kensington Palace on both royal and charity occasions. And there had been hundreds of such functions to attend. And yet when an opportunity arose to become Charles's asistant private secretary, he leapt at the prospect. He proved himself so attentive and eager that when the top job— Charles's private secretary—fell vacant in 1991, he was promoted. He proved a worthy royal servant and struck up a good relationship with Charles, who came to rely more and more on his advice. He organized the Prince's life and was a prime mover in the Dimbleby TV documentary of June 1994 in which Charles admitted to adultery. Diana believes Commander Aylard to be primarily responsible for what she views as a concerted campaign to undermine and discredit her.

He has also changed the Prince of Wales's and the Royal Family's tradition of "never complain, never explain" into participation in the minefield of public relations with its sound bites, photo opportunities, and off-the-record briefings. He is viewed by the Queen and Prince Philip, and many of their senior courtiers, as a man who has tried to propel the Royal Family into the twenty-first century at too fast a pace and, as a consequence, brought discredit to the House of Windsor.

Diana heard that the fiercely ambitious, twice-married Aylard had apparently developed a nervous twitch and was in the habit of shutting himself away in his office, hardly speaking to his staff, who felt cut off. Aylard was also concerned about Charles's personal valet, Michael Fawcett, thirty-three, who Aylard believed wielded an ever-increasing influence on Prince Charles. Fawcett had become a junior valet to Charles in 1985 and won a reputation among staff for giving remarkably good impressions of Prince Charles. But since those days he has emerged as a considerable power, influencing Charles to a degree that worried not only Aylard but a number of other senior royal servants who have been with Charles for many years. Charles listens most attentively to Fawcett, a married man with two children.

From the moment Diana decided to retire from public life, she had been cut out of all royal programs. No longer would she be called upon to represent the Queen, as she had in the past. She was, of course, still the Princess of Wales, but now her work was restricted to her own interests, the 120-odd charities of which she had become a patron.

During 1994 the only royal event in which Diana was invited to take part, along with every other member of the Royal Family, was the fiftieth-anniversary celebrations of the D-day landing. And in 1995 she was asked to attend celebrations marking the fiftieth anniversaries of VE Day (Victory in Europe) and VJ Day (Victory in Japan). Diana was happy to have no further royal duties for it meant she had the time to concentrate on her many charitable engagements. She had so much more freedom now that she was no longer at the beck and call of the senior aides at Buckingham Palace.

The more Diana realized that Buckingham Palace and St. James's Palace were determined to keep her out of the newspapers and off the nation's TV screens, the more concerned she became about her future. Time and again Diana had received invitations from charities to visit their overseas projects. On numerous occasions she had asked permission to travel abroad to visit charities, but usually some excuse had been forthcoming from Buckingham Palace refusing the request.

The Red Cross had wanted Diana to take a high-profile position throughout their yearlong 125th-anniversary celebrations, participating in a number of Red Cross events around the world throughout 1995. Within days of the news being published, discreet intervention by Buckingham Palace put an end to the plan. Diana was upset and angry. Later, Diana would be asked to undertake work as an ambassador on behalf of the British Red Cross. That, too, was diplomatically turned down after the request had been passed to Buckingham Palace. Diana of course knew the reason. But she would still become furious at the thought that the Queen and Philip, along with their senior advisers, were doing their damnedest to bury the Princess of Wales.

Throughout 1995, Diana considered how best to counter such a deliberate policy, which she was convinced had the approval of both Charles and Elizabeth. It was enough that Diana was the darling of the British people, eclipsing every other member of the Royal Family. The last thing the Royals wanted would be for Diana to steal the royal limelight overseas as well.

Diana invited PR chiefs, former cabinet ministers and members of Parliament, newspaper and TV executives, captains of industry, and marketing experts to a series of power lunches. She would seek their advice, asking in what direction they felt her career should go. She would inform them of the problems she faced with senior aides blocking her ambitions.

The power brokers and influence makers would offer advice and come up with ideas for a new direction for Diana's talents. This author was invited, with two others, to put together a possible scenario for the Princess for launching a new career. We decided that a charity—perhaps to be named The Princess of Wales Foundation—could be one solution.

The foundation would have Diana as president with a director general, offices, and a small, full-time staff. The charity would be involved in whatever area Diana preferred— caring for the homeless, the disadvantaged, the unemployed, the deaf, blind, or mentally ill. The main point would be that Diana herself would become actively involved, perhaps spending two days a week at the foundation's headquarters, spearheading the charity, hosting lunches, and chairing meetings where she would persuade the leaders in all strata of British society to support her foundation. More importantly, we felt it would provide Diana with a real job on which to focus her life, direct her energies, and utilize her remarkable qualities. After the plan was put to her, Diana said she would study the project, which she found "most interesting."

At the following meeting Diana revealed that she had decided her future lay in working overseas and said that she had set her sights on becoming a royal ambassador, communicating directly with victims and the disadvantaged. She revealed that becoming a worldwide royal ambassador—jetting around the world visting charitable organizations, raising money for good causes, and helping the victims of society—had been her secret ambition for years. She had now decided to bring her dream to fruition as soon as possible.

As her plan developed in her mind, Diana began a new series of lunches and meetings, inviting a number of key people whose combined influence in the realms of psychotherapy, image grooming, self-esteem, and media know-how would provide the necessary expertise if she did decide to make her bid for her new career.

Close friends that she took into her confidence included Annabel Goldsmith, wife of the multimillionaire Sir James Goldsmith. Annabel, a mature woman, seems to have taken over as Diana's mother figure in place of Diana's close friend of many years, Lucia Flecha de Lima, the wife of the Brazilian ambassador who had moved from London to Washington with her husband. Angela Serota, the estranged wife of Tate Gallery director Nicholas Serota, has been an intimate friend of Diana's for five years, and they lunch together frequently. Diana would also discuss every detail of her plan with the woman who had become her closest confidante, her psychotherapist, Susie Orbach.

The wealthy, warmhearted, tousle-haired Susie Orbach, forty-nine, is the one person in the world who knows all Diana's secrets. Ever since a strong relationship developed between the two women in 1994, Susie Orbach has become the most dominant person in the life of the Princess of Wales, advising, guiding, and comforting her as no other therapist has before. The key to their closeness lies in Orbach's feminist stand, which she has advocated since writing her bestselling book *Fat Is a Feminist Issue*, which was published in 1978. In the book Orbach identifies the obsession with weight, shape, and food that haunts so many Western women and lays the blame squarely on men for controlling women within unequal partnerships.

She wrote, "Fat is not about lack of self-control or lack of willpower. Fat *is* about protection, sex, nurturance, strength.... it is a response to the inequality of the sexes."

Diana read and reread the book, which is punctuated with case histories of women suffering at the hands of men. For Diana, brought up in the patriarchal aristocracy to marry by arrangement, produce a couple of heirs, and withdraw quietly, relating to Orbach's writing came easily.

Much of Susie Orbach's evangelism stemmed from her experience of a course on compulsive eating. Having learned that women's needs are not contemptible, Susie was able to reject the rules society was hurling at her—and her body dutifully shrank. Her pattern of dieting and binge eating was broken.

Diana felt a sense of awakening after she met Susie and listened to her theory. To educated women Orbach's theory may now be commonplace, but to the innocent, uneducated Diana here was someone who understood her urge to control her body and who knew what it was like to gorge on chocolate and dry cereal.

Orbach suggests she had an uneasy relationship with her parents, who had an unhappy relationship. The daughter of a Labour member of Parliament and a mother who taught English as a foreign language, Orbach felt isolated as she was growing up, in the same way that Diana did. At fifteen, Susie had an abortion and was expelled from school. After failing to complete her degree at London University's School of Slavonic and East European Studies, at the age of twenty-one she escaped to America, "found herself," qualified as a therapist, and returned to London where she cofounded the Women's Therapy Center, renowned for teaching women to support each other. Having now written six books, Orbach is recognized as a highly reputable therapist who speaks with integrity. Diana became her willing pupil.

Orbach, too, had an unhappy marriage at a young age. In 1970, Susie married Manhattan architect Alan Feigenberg, but divorced him within eleven months following bouts of compulsive overeating. But she had always remained silent about that marriage. She has, however, enjoyed a twenty-three-year-long relationship with Joseph Schwartz, a physics and psychology professor turned psychoanalyst. They have never married. He is the father of her two children.

But Susie Orbach has her critics, who wonder if she is the best person to advise the Princess of Wales, responsible to a great degree for guiding Prince William, the heir to the throne. Orbach is a known left-winger who disdains the traditional family. In one of her books Orbach looks forward to an increasing narrowing of the gap between the sexes, a world where the conventional nuclear family may well disappear to be replaced by "an alternative way of living." She asserts that future generations will be the products of a completely different structure of parenting, that communal living will be accepted as conventional along with single parents and homosexual couples.

To these select few friends, Diana confided that if the Royal Family and the Establishment put a stop to her plan of becoming a royal ambassador, then she would seriously consider moving to the United States and setting up a permanent home there. She told of conversations she had held with prominent Americans in various walks of life who told her that she would be most welcome to live in the United States, suggesting she take an apartment in New York and a house in the country.

From New York she could then proceed with her plan of

becoming a royal ambassador, touring the world, working for any number of charities who would welcome her with open arms.

Diana told her friends, "I am deadly serious. This is no idle threat for I am determined to do the job for which I believe I am uniquely equipped. And if the Royals won't let me carry out that work, then I will go and live where I will be able to."

She told how she would plan her life if she did move to New York. She would spend school terms in the United States or working for charities in foreign countries, and holidays at home in England with her sons. She explained that both boys, at boarding school, often preferred to play games on Saturdays rather than be at home. As a consequence they were already seeing less of their parents. Diana would comment, "And if they need me, London is only a Concorde flight away. I could even buy a season ticket."

One of her principal advisers, a man on whom Diana has come to depend to a remarkable degree, is a highly intelligent, witty, irreverent, bald and overweight Australian TV chat show host by the name of Clive Vivian Leopold James, known universally as Clive James, the king of the put-down.

Clive James came to public attention as a spectacularly rude television reviewer for the *Observer* newspaper after studying at Cambridge University. But he desperately wanted to appear on the box himself. Eventually he became a highly successful host mainly by witty flourishes, clever put-downs, cynicism, and savaging those who appeared on television. Ironically, at the time of Diana's wedding he wrote a satire about it that did not receive rave reviews. Friends believe he would have "died" for an invitation to the wedding, but one would not be forthcoming. Clive James persevered, and finally, in the early 1990s, he met Diana, the woman he had admired from afar for more than a decade. His time had come.

When Charles and Diana separated, Clive James wrote a serious article in the *Spectator* urging the Prince and Princess of Wales to stay together—just like the Spitfires and Hurricanes of the war—to save British private life from the Nazis of the popular press. But he went further, many judging his wit had become obscene, for he compared the estrangement of Charles and Diana to the Holocaust, though he agreed the estrangement was "inherently more trivial."

He would assist in schooling Diana for her TV epic; he wrote some of the lines; he went over her replies to probable questions; and he advised her how to behave on camera, looking straight at the interviewer, speaking in short sentences. He advised on what she should wear and her general demeanor. He suggested she smile and laugh and crack the occasional joke to lighten the proceedings.

Since becoming a confidant, Clive James has also become fiercely loyal: "I would almost rather climb a ladder of swords than tell you about any little tête-à-têtes I have with Diana.... I would rather swim naked through a lake full of crocodiles than tell you about those."

At lunches with Diana and others he will be full of bonhomie and jokes, using his famous style of put-downs and mock savagery. Clive James is bright, some suggesting that he may be too bright for his own good. But he helps his lunch companions by laughing at his own jokes at the right spots, just to make sure the other guests haven't missed one of his witticisms. And he would give Diana great support.

Sometime during the summer of 1995, Diana decided the only way to achieve her ambition would be to make a direct appeal to the British people. She realized that such a cri de coeur would have to be made over the heads of the Queen and Charles and all their royal henchmen, otherwise she was convinced they would use their extraordinary, though subtle, powers of persuasion to squash her plan. Diana believed that the only way of achieving her objective would be via television, where she could gain so much popular support for her ambition that the Establishment would be unable to put a stop to it.

Unlike Charles, Diana could not just ask the BBC or any other TV channel to organize an interview, for that would be politely stopped by Buckingham Palace. Keeping the project secret would be vital, though difficult. She had never done anything like this before in her life and she had no idea whether it would be a success or a failure. But those attending her lunches agreed to do everything to help her, including writing most of the answers to questions that would be agreed to by the interviewer beforehand.

She never told those she invited to her innumerable lunches the real purpose for their visits, and they would leave Kensington Palace convinced that the Princess of Wales was being victimized by the Royal Family—her efforts to carve out a new career for herself blocked at every turn—with Diana trying to combat a totally unfair and unfounded smear campaign suggesting she was "unstable, mentally unbalanced, and suffering from paranoia."

The intimate lunches, usually one or two a week, took place throughout the summer and fall of 1995, usually held around a small circular table. Diana, relaxed, charming, and attentive, would entertain perhaps only two or four people on each occasion. She felt that small lunch parties would ensure that her message got through loud and clear, that she would be able to ensnare, seduce, charm, and persuade her guests to understand her terrible predicament, and, if possible, to advise her how best she could break out of such encirclement and lead a worthwhile life.

At the end of each lunch, Diana would seek advice, inviting her guests to phone or pop back for another chat if they felt they needed further information to reach a conclusion. She would impress on her visitors, "All I want to do is help people. I feel I have a role to play helping people, the disadvantaged, the homeless, the poor, the disabled. I would really appreciate it if you have any ideas how I could achieve this."

And she would refer quite openly to the senior courtiers and aides at Buckingham Palace and St. James's, where Charles had his official London headquarters, as "the enemy" who, she claimed, were determined to stop her from fulfilling her true potential as the Princess of Wales.

Nearly all would leave her presence believing that they had been given a mission to help the beleaguered Princess. Most would come under her spell, which they found remarkably arresting. Many thought they had been selected by her, privileged beyond reason to help this beautiful, misunderstood, lonely, aggrieved woman to find a role for herself. In the fullness of time, however, most would be disappointed; some would even feel cheated.

In the fall of 1995, Diana would invite others to Kensington Palace: her therapists, who had advised and helped her during the past twelve months to revitalize herself. They realized that Diana's problem was unique, for as a member of the Royal House of Windsor, she was enmeshed in what they all recognized to be one of the principal dysfunctional families in the land. And the most important of all her therapists was Susie Orbach. Another adviser who helped shape her thoughts was the American motivation guru Anthony Robbins.

Others invited to lunch, taken into Diana's confidence, and sworn to secrecy included Lord Attenborough, the director of *Gandhi* and *Chaplin*, who gave Diana extensive advice before her TV interview. Film producer Sir David Puttman would be another, along with Sir Gordon Reece, who helped to change and mold Prime Minister Margaret Thatcher's television technique.

But throughout those months her most important adviser would be Susie Orbach. Diana would drive to Ms. Orbach's $750,000 home in Swiss Cottage, North London, and Diana would be tutored in her approach to Prince Charles, the Queen, and the courtiers who run Buckingham Palace and advise the monarchy. More than anyone else, Orbach was responsible for preparing Diana for her forthcoming ordeal.

"Without Susie Orbach I would never have even considered doing a television interview. She gave me the strength I needed," Diana has said to many people since the remarkable TV epic.

By September 1995, Diana felt sufficiently prepared to face an interviewer. She had learned her lines well, rehearsed answers to possible questions with her therapists and advisers, and felt confident that she would give a good account of herself.

Diana had received a number of requests for an in-depth profile from TV interviewers, including Barbara Walters, Sir David Frost, and Oprah Winfrey. She felt they were all too high-powered and preferred someone less well-known. She had met Martin Bashir, a quiet, rather introspective, yet charming thirty-two-year-old *Panorama* reporter, a former sportswriter, and believed he would keep silent about the interview until the big day.

Bashir would spend three days with Diana going through the questions, one by one, line by line, taking one part of her life at a time until she was happy with the questions and she could concentrate on her answers. Her only demand was that no questions be asked about her relationship with Will Carling. She sought advice and stuck to it like glue. Her answers were always brief and to the point, exact and never rambling or hesitant. The interview was shot over five hours with many breaks so that Diana could check the next question and prepare her answer. She would leave nothing to chance.

News of the interview caused dismay, not only in Buckingham Palace, St. James's Palace, and Downing Street, but in every newspaper and TV office in Britain. It had come as a shock to everyone because no one thought Diana would have the courage, the intelligence, or the strength of character to carry through such a plan. Some newspapers described the secret filming as "deceitful and underhand." Others went further, the tabloid *Daily Mirror* asking on its front page, "Has She Gone Mad?" suggesting the Princess of Wales had committed an act of treason by undertaking the interview without seeking permission from the Queen.

The BBC played down the contents of the interview, but when it was shown during the evening of Monday, November 20, 1995, most people were taken aback by the content, Diana's remarkable performance, and the honesty of her replies. More than 23 million people in Britain watched the show, which many believed to be the most extraordinary and damaging royal statement since the abdication of King Edward VIII in 1937.

Diana's appearance in a dark suit with a simple white top was low-key and serious, so unlike the clothes in which most people see Diana. She wore dark makeup around the eyes, emphasizing the seriousness of the occasion. Within minutes in the hour-long interview Diana showed how much she had changed and matured. Her composure and fluency were remarkable. Pat, polished, and articulate, Diana showed no sign of her old self. Gone was the interviewer's flushed and flustered nightmare, with her flat voice, fiddly hands, and hesitant sentences.

No question took her by surprise and no answers were fluffed. Her honesty was compelling when she spoke of her eating disorders. She said, "It is true that I suffered from bulimia, bingeing and vomiting, for a number of years. It's like a secret disease. I was crying out for help. You inflict bulimia on yourself because your self-esteem is at a low ebb, and you don't think you're worthy or valuable. You fill your stomach up four or five times a day—some do it more—and it gives you a feeling of comfort. It's like having a pair of arms around you, but it's temporary. Then you're disgusted at the bloatedness of your stomach and then you bring it all up again."

She spoke of the postnatal depression after giving birth to William in 1982 and the effect it had on her marriage. "Well, it gave everybody a wonderful new label—Diana's unstable and Diana's mentally unbalanced. And unfortunately that seems to have stuck on and off over the years."

Bashir asked about her self-mutilation. Diana replied, "When no one listens to you, or you feel no one's listening to you, all sorts of things start to happen. For instance, you have so much pain inside yourself that you try and hurt yourself on the outside because you want help, but it's the wrong help you're asking for. People see it as crying wolf or attention seeking, and they think because you're in the media all the time, you've got enough attention. But I was actually crying out because I wanted to get better in order to go forward and continue my duty and my role as wife, mother, Princess of

Wales. So, yes, I did inflict upon myself. I didn't like myself, I was ashamed because I couldn't cope with the pressures."

Bashir: "What did you actually do?"

Diana: "Well, I just hurt my arms and my legs. And I work in environments now where I see women doing similar things and I'm able to understand completely where they're coming from."

She spoke of the devastating effect she felt after learning that Charles had renewed his relationship with Camilla Parker Bowles, in 1986. "I took refuge in rampant bulimia, if you can have rampant bulimia, and just a feeling of being no good at anything and being useless and hopeless and failed in every direction. For I knew that my husband loved someone else."

Diana explained that she knew of Charles's adultery and love for Camilla, not only through her own intuition but also through friends who cared about the marriage. And that made the marriage increasingly difficult.

She said, "Friends on my husband's side were indicating that I was again unstable, sick, and should be put in a home of some sort in order to get better. I was almost an embarrassment."

Bashir: "So you were isolated?"

Diana: "Very much so."

Bashir: "Do you think Mrs. Parker Bowles was a factor in the breakdown of your marriage?"

Diana: "Well, there were three of us in this marriage, so it was a bit crowded."

For most of the interview Diana appeared serious and concerned, though willing to answer all the questions openly and honestly, obviously wanting to clear the air. Sometimes she smiled, occasionally she laughed. She would keep eye contact with Bashir throughout, as if TV interviews were for her an everyday occurrence. She had been well schooled, and it showed.

Many people were shocked that Diana confessed to her three-year-long adulterous affair with Capt. James Hewitt.

Asked about the relationship, Diana said, "He was a great friend and he was always there to support me, and I was absolutely devastated when a book appeared, because I trusted him. . . ."

Bashir: "Were you unfaithful?"

Diana: "Yes, I adored him. Yes, I was in love with him."

Diana also praised Charles for admitting his own adultery during his TV interview in June 1994, saying, "I admired the honesty because it takes a lot to do that."

It was, however, Diana's remarks on the monarchy, on Prince Charles and "the enemy" ranged against her, that caused the most consternation in Buckingham Palace. In a bellicose reference to what she sees as the Establishment, Diana said that she was now motivated by the old adage, "'Always confuse the enemy'; the 'enemy' being Prince Charles's staff."

But Diana aimed her most deadly remarks so as to injure Charles, the husband she has come to detest and whom she is determined to ruin if at all possible. Her replies to questions about him revealed the bitterness within her, a malice bordering on hatred. With great subtlety Diana managed to impress on the viewers that her husband was not really fit to be king. And she achieved that ambition without saying one nasty word about him. Diana knew full well that to criticize another's ability to do his job, particularly one that has taken a lifetime of training, can be devastating. And she knew the savagery of that attack can be even more destructive if delivered in a small, quiet voice.

Bashir: "Do you think the Prince of Wales will ever be king?"

Diana: "I don't think any of us know the answer to that. Who knows what fate will produce, who knows what circumstances will provoke."

Bashir: "But you would know him better than most people. Do you think he would wish to be king?"

Diana: "There was always conflict on that subject with him when we discussed it, and I understood that conflict, because it's a very demanding role, being Prince of Wales, but it's an equally more demanding role being king. And being Prince of

Wales produces more freedom now, and being king would be a little bit more suffocating. And because I know the character, I would think that the top job, as I call it, would bring enormous limitations to him, and I don't know whether he could adapt to that."

Bashir asked whether it would make more sense if the position of monarch passed directly to Prince William once he becomes of age rather than Prince Charles. Diana replied, "My wish is that my husband finds peace of mind, and from that follows other things, yes."

And she hadn't finished. She would take an even greater risk during the interview, bringing herself in open conflict with her mother-in-law and her "enemies" within the palace, by daring to criticize both the Queen and the monarchy. Speaking quietly and sounding so sympathetic, Diana said, "I understand that change is frightening for people, especially if there's nothing to go to. It's best to stay where you are. I understand that. But I do think there are a few things that could change, that would alleviate this doubt, and sometimes complicated relationship between monarchy and public."

She continued, "I would like a monarchy that has more contact with its people—and I don't mean riding round on bicycles and things like that, but just having a more in-depth understanding. And I don't say that as a criticism to the present monarchy, I just say that as what I see and hear and feel on a daily basis in the role I have chosen for myself."

As they watched the program, senior aides at the palace were outraged that Diana had the audacity to feel herself sufficiently knowledgeable and competent to tell the Queen how the monarchy should operate. As one sixty-year-old palace veteran commented later, "Some were apoplectic at what they saw as an upstart's decision to go on TV and tell the Queen what to do. Others thought she must have lost her marbles. Others were resigned to the Princess of Wales's determination to destroy her husband and organize the future of the monarchy around her son William, guided, of course, by his mother, the Princess of Wales."

But cooler heads at the palace would prevail.

Yet Diana had managed to confuse some wise heads at the palace by confessing that she believed she would not become queen of England because sections of the Royal Household were determined that she should never sit on the throne beside Charles because she could not be trusted to behave with the quiet dignity expected of a king's consort. She continued, "The Establishment has decided they don't want me as queen because I do things differently, because I don't go by a rule book, because I lead from the heart, not the head."

Diana also stated, categorically, that she did not want a divorce from Charles. By stating that publicly Diana had set a trap for the monarchy and, more particularly, for Prince Charles. Most people had believed their separation in December 1992 had been instigated, even demanded, by Diana. She put that canard to rest by telling the nation that it had been her husband's decision to separate.

Diana knew that Charles would not want Wills and Harry to see their father demanding a divorce from their mother. She believed her remark would mean she could remain Princess of Wales for some years to come. But the Queen decided that Diana had been mischief making, trying to lead her own life at the same time as keeping her title and her royal privileges, but accepting no responsibilities and undertaking virtually no royal duties. So she stepped in, calling Diana's bluff, urging Charles and Diana to divorce as soon as possible.

More importantly for Diana's life, she proclaimed in quite strident language her ambition for the future, wanting to work as an ambassador for Britain, offering her unique talents to serve the victims of society across the world: "I see myself as an ambassador for this country. I would like to represent this country."

Diana explained, "I've been in a privileged position for fifteen years. I've got tremendous knowledge about people and how to communicate, and I want to use it. I think the British people need someone in public life to give affection, to make them feel important, to support them, to give them light in their dark tunnels. I see it as a possibly unique role. Let's use the knowledge I've gathered to help other people in distress."

She would go on to explain in more detail the type of ambassador she would become, saying, "I would like to be queen of people's hearts. Someone's got to go out there and love people and show it. . . . The perception that has been given of me for the last three years has been very confusing, turbulent, and in some areas, I'm sure, many, many people doubt me. I want to reassure all those people who have loved me throughout the last fifteen years that I'd never let them down. That is a priority to me. The man on the street matters more than anything else to me."

Such official overseas visits are the preserve of the Queen, Prince Philip, and Prince Charles and are always cleared by the Foreign Office, whose advice the Royal Family will always take whether to accept or refuse such invitations. Before the separation, Charles would be accompanied by Diana, thus ensuring the crowds turned out in the tens of thousands and the visits would prove public relations successes. Such overseas visits by Diana on her own would prove a considerable headache for the palace and the Foreign Office unless Diana only accepted invitations involving charities. Then the visits would be deemed personal rather than as her representing Britain. She would still need to consult the Foreign Office as well as Buckingham Palace, but at least there would be no protocol problems or official or diplomatic embarrassment.

Diana had watched her video three times before giving *Panorama* her permission to show it. She believed the interview had gone exactly as she had wished, if not better. "Brilliant," she repeated time and again. "Brilliant." She congratulated Bashir and his editor, Steve Hewlett, on "an excellent documentary."

The night the interview was screened Diana was not at home. She attended a gala dinner in London and smiled happily, some suggesting triumphantly, for the photographers who followed her every step. She looked ravishing, jubilant, dressed in a clinging, low-cut, full-length black dress with a choker of pearls. The sad, anguished woman in the interview seemed a different person than the confident woman going out to dinner that night.

Earlier that day Diana had arrived at her health club wearing clinging, sexy Lycra shorts and a sweatshirt, smiling broadly and striding toward the club confident and happy that hordes of photographers had arrived and waited in the cold November morning to get that final shot of her before the program.

Initially, the interview was hailed by the nation as a great success. Throughout, she made no vicious allegations, never overtly criticizing Charles or the Royal Family. She showed only sadness and humility despite her obvious underlying anger and bitterness. She made it clear she loves her country and her sons; the performance was compelling, undoubtedly the greatest of her life, asking the nation to judge a saintly, forgiving, understanding woman.

Within minutes of scanning the next morning's newspapers, Diana realized her life's gamble had been vindicated, indeed, accepted as a triumph. Diana read all the national newspapers, the four quality papers and the five tabloids, most of which highlighted Diana's confession of adultery with Hewitt, which she had managed to make sound both sad and pure. Most newspapers applauded "her gut-wrenching honesty," and some felt the nation had been "eavesdropping on a confessional, gate-crashing on the burial of a marriage." Others, more ominously, highlighted Diana's determination "not to go quietly."

She read the papers with growing satisfaction, bordering on jubilation. Repeatedly, she clenched her fist and punched the air in triumph as she read a piece that particularly praised her. "Done it. Done it. Done it," she said time and again.

The bouquets and the plaudits flooded into Kensington Palace during the days following the interview. "Magic," "Brilliant," "Magnificent," "Fantastic," "Congratulations to a star" were typical of the messages from friends and supporters. Her close friends were on the phone throughout the day congratulating her on a brave, fearless, and wonderful perform-ance. A Gallup poll taken the day following the program showed she had risen sharply in the public esteem. More than 46 percent thought more of Diana after the interview than they did before, and 74 percent believed she was right in giving the interview. Only 20 percent believed she should have remained silent.

Their reasons were even more interesting. Only 14 percent believed she gave the interview to exact revenge on Charles and the Royal Family; only 17 percent believed the interview was a cry for help. A remarkable 77 percent thought Diana simply set out to put her side of the story on record. Those consulted believed Diana to be strong, sincere, loving, and intelligent. They also think she is "a good mother."

Diana's performance, however, had not been entirely flawless, for 30 percent of the doubters believed Diana had revealed herself to be "self-centered, vengeful, and manipulative." Some critics immediately indicted Diana for using what they termed "psychobabble," to dismiss her performance. Certainly the influence of psychotherapy was evident throughout, from her unwavering discussion of self-mutilation and bulimia to comments on her strengths and ambitions.

Less than twenty-four hours after the interview Buckingham Palace made a peace offering, senior aides saying they wished to "see how we can help her define her future role and continue to support her as a member of the Royal Family." The offer was intended to be generous, constructive, and helpful and contained not a word of vexation. "Diana: Palace Peace Offer" was a typical headline.

With a one-hour television program Diana was convinced that she had achieved more than she had done since her fairy-tale wedding in July 1981. For the first time ever she had appealed to the British people, over the heads of her husband, the Royal Family, and the Establishment, and won their admiration and their support. She had also ruined the carefully laid plans of Buckingham Palace officials to sideline her, a policy that they had been implementing and nurturing for eighteen months. They had been confident that Diana, with her increasing number of unfortunate relationships going so wrong, would decide to avoid the limelight, concentrating solely on her charitable work, leaving the path clear for Charles to show the nation what a good king he would make.

To a few close friends Diana would talk openly, admitting that she had done much more than the man in the street realized. She had made her mother-in-law, the Queen, sit up and take note along with every senior aide who worked at the palace and in Charles's office. That realization warmed Diana's heart and made her feel more secure than she had been since her wedding day. For her message to the Establishment had been direct and to the point: "You never realised what a bright, tough woman I have become; ignore me at your peril."

Her interview caused two casualties. The first, Mr. Geoffrey Crawford, forty-four, an Australian diplomat who had joined the palace staff three years earlier as Diana's press officer, quit within twenty-four hours of her TV appearance. She had told him nothing whatsoever of the *Panorama* program. He felt humiliated at being kept completely in the dark. He had no alternative but to resign for Diana had shown she didn't trust him enough either to confide in him or to seek his advice.

Diplomatically, he commented, "I always enjoyed working with the Princess. I'll miss it. We've had some marvelous journeys together. She's brilliant at what she does. And completely natural. She's a great ambassador for Britain."

The second was Mr. Nicholas Soames, the minister of state for the armed forces and a close personal friend of Prince Charles since childhood. Within minutes of Diana's interview, the pompous Soames, a grandson of Winston Churchill, said on the following television program that the Princess "was showing the advanced stages of paranoia." He then rejected Diana's portrayal of herself as having been isolated by her husband's circle of friends and assistants and suggested that Diana's "most outrageous" contribution had been to question her husband's readiness to assume the role of king.

"I think that was the key to the whole interview," he said. "I think it has the potential to undermine very seriously the Prince of Wales's position, and I thought that it was a terrible thing to say because it is totally and utterly untrue."

The following morning Prime Minister John Major gagged his minister, telling him that he must not comment any further on the interview and suggesting his intervention had not been of help to anyone, including the Prince of Wales himself.

Diana was happy to read that her friend John Major had been so tough on the minister who had dared to criticize her. Having supported her decision to speak out on television, the prime minister would, she now hoped, support her ambition of becoming a royal ambassador. Diana knew that John Major's influence could be crucial in persuading the Queen and senior courtiers to agree to her new role.

20

A Triumphant Di

———— ❧ ————

TWO DAYS LATER DIANA FLEW OFF in triumph to Argentina on a charity visit that had been planned months before. To Diana, the visit would be of the utmost importance. Diana had planned her interview to take place a few days prior to her Argentina trip so that her adoring public could see her in the new role she hoped to carve out for herself. By timing the broadcast before the trip, she ensured the most massive TV and media coverage imaginable.

Quietly and politely, with that wicked smile on her face, Diana commented to a friendly businessman, "I thought I would arrange things like this so the Establishment will be able to judge for themselves how successful or otherwise the trip will have been. If it's successful, then maybe they will agree to let me carry out more such visits."

The visit would be a magnificent personal success for Diana. Ninety press photographers accompanied her on her four-day visit to Argentina, whereas only the week before, Prince Charles, on an official royal visit to Germany, was accompanied by only one photographer. No other newspaper or magazine wanted to know about the Prince's trip. It was a salutary experience for Charles, a memorable victory for Diana and her ambitions for the future. And she knew it.

She flew to Argentina with a skeleton retinue of only five people: her private secretary, Patrick Jephson, her lady-in-waiting, a detective, dresser, and hairdresser. Usually, for a four-day overseas visit, including lunch with the head of state, the Queen would be accompanied by a retinue of at least twenty people. Diana had kept numbers to a minimum to demonstrate her idea of a modern monarchy that was not "so distant" from the people.

Her first stop in Buenos Aires, at a center run by the Association for the Prevention of Infant Paralysis, brought the streets around the clinic to a standstill as the crowds stopped traffic to catch a glimpse of Diana, wearing a light, cream dress. The clinic's superviser, Susana Duranona de Vila, said afterward, "The children adored her. The children were very, very emotional with her. She is so charming and understanding."

Similar scenes followed at the Garrahan pediatric hospital and a Buenos Aires rehabilitation center for the disabled. Everyone seemed to love her, though most of the children she spoke to and stroked had no idea exactly who Princess Diana was or where she came from. At the Casa Cuna hospital, Diana spent an hour talking to battered wives, child victims of domestic violence, and teenagers suffering from drug and solvent abuse. The day had seen Diana at the top of her form, enjoying the best of both worlds, giving hope and comfort to victims and enjoying the adulation of cheering crowds.

In all, Diana visited seven hospitals and clinics in three hectic days, as she was whisked at speed through the capital. The media gave blanket coverage. From this visit—her first after proclaiming her desire for a new ambassadorial role—it seems Diana will have considerable difficulty in persuading people and politicians that she can ever be taken seriously as an ambassador for Britain. All the Argentine commentators viewed the Princess as a celebrity rather than a serious representative. Save for a lunch with beleaguered President Menem, she seemed determined not to become involved in any political matters whatsoever. The question of the Falkland Islands, over which Britain and Argentina waged a short, sharp war in 1982, never arose, and Diana did not venture near the capital's central Plaza de Mayo where the mothers of those who "disappeared" during the so-called Dirty War of the military regimes of the seventies were holding a meeting. She was invited but declined to attend. Indeed, Diana behaved so discreetly and diplomatically that the leading daily newspaper *La Nación* dubbed her "the mute princess."

Argentina was Diana's third major overseas working trip of 1995. In February she had traveled, again by scheduled flight, to Tokyo as the guest of several charities. The main reason for her trip was to visit the Japanese National Children's Hospital at Setagaya-Ku, which is affiliated with London's Great Ormond Street Hospital of which she is president. She would visit other hospitals and clinics, but once again, she would not be involved in any diplomatic or political matters. That visit was hailed as a great success, winning the hearts of Japanese therapists, doctors, and administrators who met and talked to her.

In June 1995 she visited Moscow, spending several hours at the Tushinskaya Children's Hospital. That trip followed an appeal from the hospital directly to Diana asking if she would like to visit the Russian capital, hoping she would spend some hours at the children's hospital. She leapt at the invitation for Diana had realized where her future could lie—as a royal ambassador.

In September 1995, Diana flew to Paris to raise $250,000 for the Great Ormond Street children's hospital and won rave reviews for her style and elegance. On that occasion she met President Chirac, who jumped at the photo opportunity of standing side by side with the beautiful Princess of Wales on the steps of the Elysée Palace. President Chirac needed all the good press he could get as his regime had been rocked by the worldwide condemnation of France's nuclear tests in the South Pacific.

Diana's determination to build on her new role, to become a major champion of good causes around the world, knows no bounds. She is not only confident that she has the full backing of the British people in her bid to challenge the Queen, Philip, and Prince Charles and bring the British monarchy into the twenty-first century, but also feels she has the charisma to win the hearts of the disadvantaged and the victims of modern society in cities around the world.

Another reason for the timing of her *Panorama* interview was that Diana had accepted an invitation to fly to New York in December 1995 to receive the Humanitarian of the Year award at a star-studded $1,000-a-head dinner attended by nine hundred guests. The dinner, in aid of the United Cerebral Palsy of New York Foundation, was also attended by Dr. Henry Kissinger, Gen. Colin Powell, Donald and Marla Trump, Randolph Hearst, Rupert Murdoch, and America's best known and most forthright sex therapist, the diminutive Dr. Ruth Westheimer. Diana won plaudits from the New York fashion conscious for her low-cut, sleeveless, and beaded black, full-length evening gown. More importantly for Diana she would be seen mingling with the rich and the powerful to illustrate that they accepted her as a royal ambassador.

Some queried whether Diana wanted to be accepted more as an ambassador of "swank," New York's favorite fashion word for winter 1995. Diana understood that postfeminism seemed to be gaining ground fast on the East Coast, that "glam" had returned, and even fur sales had increased 20 percent, so she decided to wear more mascara, more expensive jewelry, and daringly, show much more cleavage than usual. New York's finest seemed to appreciate the Jacques Azagury couture dress in double silk georgette as well as the stately curves she revealed, the embroidered sequin lace bodice specifically made to fit Diana's 36B figure.

To achieve the eye-popping décolletage, which she hoped would be admired in New York, the bodice was stitched from separate pieces of silk, lined with layers of cotton to keep it stiff and shape her figure. The secret lay in four plastic "bones," two at the front and two at the back, stitched behind the silk crêpe de chine lining. The front bones, bent manually into the required shape, act like a brassiere, pushing the breasts forward and upward.

Dr. Kissinger, the former U.S. secretary of state, greeted

her with a bow and then two kisses, not sure where to cast his eyes. He praised her "luminous personality" and said, "She is here as a member of the Royal Family. But we are honoring the Princess in her own right, having aligned herself with the ill, the suffering, and the downtrodden."

But the enthusiasm and heady sense of achievement that Diana felt in late 1995 would be sorely tested over the following months. As the days and weeks passed, the number of critics would increase and the doubts would come not only from staunch monarchists and friends of Prince Charles, but from the general public, once they had found the time to examine, discuss, and dissect the interview.

One of the first Establishment bibles to openly attack Diana would be *Country Life*, the landed gentry's favorite magazine, which condemned her TV appearance as "a deplorable broadcast." An astonishing editorial, read mainly by the hunting, fishing, and shooting set, described her suggestion that Charles might not be king as "ludicrous" and "tragic." The editorial dismissed as "impertinence" her claim that she would like to be "the queen of people's hearts" and compared her to Helen of Troy, another "beautiful but destructive woman."

Others pointed out that Diana's *Panorama* account of her many personal problems displayed distress, unhappiness, impulsiveness, and loneliness, coupled with an enormous desire to be loved. It had also revealed a remarkable degree of self-obsession, a lack of insight and of remorse, a determination to achieve her ends without regard to the consequences for others.

In particular, she would be condemned for inflicting damage on her sons by her ruthless interview. The revelations of slashing her arms and legs, her gorging and vomiting, and having sex with Hewitt in her own bed were considered abhorrent for William, thirteen, and Harry, eleven, in their vulnerable teenage years. As one writer put it, "She has given lethal ammunition to school bullies who will surely now taunt the two boys."

And in the case of William, some commentators asked whether Diana had been wise to support her son so openly by

seemingly trying to set him against his father as a future
contender for the throne. They feared that Diana's deliberate act
of spite against Charles could easily provide the makings of a
family vendetta that could continue for twenty years or
however long Queen Elizabeth reigns.

The interview raised a plethora of views and attitudes,
almost dividing the nation into two diametrically opposed
camps: for and against the Princess.

Those championing women's causes were adamant that the
most important thing about Diana's interview was that she had
given countless silent women a voice, claiming that her painful
eloquence had proffered hope to thousands of victims. Diana
has never seen herself as a revolutionary, but never before has a
woman in her position articulated personal pain so openly. The
immediate result was that she had mobilized an army of
supporters. She had spoken publicly about her isolation within
her marriage and within the Royal Family, explaining that her
bulimia had seemed like a friend in her traumatic state, just as
tens of thousands of other bulimia victims have felt in their
isolation.

Above all, feminists admired her strength in challenging the
Royal Family's determination to represent her mutiny as mad-
ness. Charles's friends had branded Diana "unstable" and a
"loose cannon," prone to alarming episodes of depression and
self-destructiveness. But in the aftermath of her interview that
argument was discarded by the vast majority of ordinary
women who understood her pain. They believed Diana's public
protest because they knew that thousands of women have been
sent to the asylum and to solitary confinement and recognized
that the Establishment had been locking up women unfairly for
centuries.

But Diana had decided not to go quietly. She broke the vow
of silence that is the Establishment's secret weapon. On this
occasion, Diana had not used her beauty to call the Establishment and more particularly the Royal Family to account, but
her stamina and strength of character.

Polls and much other evidence suggested the public lined up

overwhelmingly behind Diana, but the distinctions in the kind of support she received depended on class, income, sex, age, and temperament. Broadly speaking, the great bulk of the working class supported Diana. Class is still very much alive in Britain, though many think it is no longer a significant aspect of British society.

The officer class support Prince Charles to a man; the noncommissioned officers and privates are behind Diana. The middle class, now representing perhaps 65 percent of the British people, are divided, the older citizens backing royalty whatever happens, the younger ones understanding and supporting Diana and her demand for more space. Most in Britain take one side or the other, and the talk in the pubs and cafes, at dinner tables and the clubs, resounds with debate. The argument has occupied everybody's attention and seems unlikely to be resolved for a long time.

Within weeks of her interview the Establishment were sorrowfully shaking their heads and suggesting that any formal ambassadorial role for the Princess of Wales would have to be "limited" amid fears that she could find herself embroiled in political controversy overseas. Britain's infamous lobby system—whereby the views of the prime minister and other senior ministers are daily given on a nonattibutable basis to a coterie of political journalists—had churned into gear.

Prime Minister John Major, who has openly supported Diana, would discuss Diana's possible ambassadorial role with the Queen during his regular Tuesday-evening meetings. However, John Major would find himself agreeing with the Queen that it would be "unfair" to place Diana in a position where she was expected to speak for Britain on politically sensitive issues. One unnamed minister went so far as to say, behind the cloak of anonymity, "We could not trust her with a political brief."

And other "facts" began to emerge, seemingly by chance, in newspaper and magazine articles. If one simply glanced at the British media during the last ten years, it would appear that Princess Diana had been virtually the only Royal visiting

hospitals, opening care centers, chatting to the sick, the homeless, and the disadvantaged of society. Suddenly, establishment
newspapers and magazines began to draw attention, wherever
possible, to work carried out by other Royals, putting Diana's
work in some perspective.

In all the deliberations over Diana's future the public's
abiding impression has been of a determined, compassionate
woman fighting her way through a labyrinth of protocol while
battling against the Establishment to bring love to the needy,
while her estranged in-laws indulge themselves in selfish
isolation in Buckingham Palace.

Diana told the nation in her *Panorama* interview of the
British public's need for "someone in public life to give
affection, to make them feel important, to support them, to
give them light in their dark tunnels." The rest of the Royal
Family agrees, for that reasoning lies behind the thousands of
public engagements, many of them associated directly with
charities, that they carry out each year. The difference is that
Diana's glamor and natural touch mean that her appearances
will generate photographs and national headlines while an
identical engagement by the Duchess of Kent would be lucky to
make it beyond the local paper.

On the very day Diana held the world stage on *Panorama*,
the Queen, Prince Philip, and Prince Charles were playing host
to King Hussein and Queen Noor of Jordan; Princess Margaret
was opening a Scottish lighthouse museum; the Duke and
Duchess of Gloucester embarked on an official visit to Mexico;
the Duke of Kent visited the Devonshire and Dorset Regiment
in Germany; Princess Alexandra visited the Imperial Cancer
Research Fund. Princess Anne, whose age and charitable interests come closest to those of Diana, was in Scotland as president
of the Princess Royal Trust for Carers, which has projects
costing $15 million throughout Britain. Not one of those events
apparently merited more than a line in a national newspaper.

None of that worries Diana. She has set out her ambitions
and is determined, come what may, to become a royal ambassador, visiting charities throughout the world, caring for people

in her brilliant, inimitable manner. For her work she will rightly win a thousand plaudits and, more importantly, will finally have found a purpose to her life.

Within days of her TV spectacular, Diana boasted openly to a number of journalists traveling with her on the flight to Argentina, "I believe that through my TV interview I have finally won my independence."

Others would not be too sure. To achieve that the Princess of Wales may find she has to quit Britain and live elsewhere. Close friends wonder whether Diana would really want to live thousands of miles from the two most important people in her life, her sons. It would be a heartrending choice. But thirty years ago her mother faced the same dilemma—and left.

21

A Sad Ending

—————— ❧ ——————

PRINCESS DIANA IS FEARFUL of the future. And because she has
no confidence in what the future holds for her, she is confused
and uncertain of the path she should tread in her personal life.
She knows she needs a new challenge, a new job and she
believes that taking on the role of a royal ambassador would not
only give her the launching pad she needs to start a new life but
also a feeling of belonging, of being wanted. But today the grief
of her failed marriage still haunts her, and the hurt won't go
away though she has lived a separate life from Charles for nearly
ten years.

She had learned to cope with her isolation, for she still had
an identity as the Princess of Wales and the mother of the heirs
to the throne. She had successfully conquered bulimia and took
pride in becoming a really fit, healthy woman who could still
draw adoring crowds, demand the attention of most men and
the front covers of the world's glossy magazines.

The demand from Charles for a separation that she never
wanted hurt her more than she realized. But that demand could
not compare to the savage blow she felt when she opened the
letter from Elizabeth in December 1995, all but ordering her to
divorce "as soon as possible." Diana had not been prepared for
the Queen's urgent request and found life increasingly difficult
to cope with. She found herself breaking down, unable to stop
the tears that came for no apparent reason. Sometimes, to her
great embarrassment, even in public.

One night in early January 1996, Diana left the home of Susie Orbach after an hour-long therapy session and began walking toward her car. She had seen the paparazzi and wondered who had tipped them off that she was there. To the most photographed woman in the world, the sight of four photographers, their flashes lighting up the scene, usually caused her not the slightest concern. But this time she felt awkward, not wanting them to intrude on her every movement. She tried to smile but found she couldn't. All of a sudden Diana realized she was about to burst into tears and put up the book she was carrying to shield her face from the cameras.

To escape their attention, she ran toward her car, but the photographers ran after her, eager to capture the Princess of Wales crying, the tears streaming down her face. Suddenly she felt like a wild animal, trapped, with nowhere to hide, no way of escape.

As she reached her car, the tears really flowed, coursing down her cheeks. She couldn't find the strength to climb into the vehicle but stood leaning against it for a full minute, her shoulders shaking. She felt exhausted and forlorn and very, very lonely, hoping the photographers would stop their whirring cameras and leave her to cry in peace. But the torment would continue until she found the strength to open the car door, climb inside, and drive away into the night. It was one of Diana's most traumatic and public displays of emotion.

That night Diana felt betrayed by whoever had tipped off the paparazzi that she would be visiting Susie Orbach for the third time since Christmas, 1995. For some years Diana had felt that at least one or two of her staff were guilty of revealing her schedules to the media. At lunches during 1995 to which she would invite editors and senior journalists from Britain's national press and the media, Diana would ask them to tell her if they knew of the identity of the staff informants. She would say, "You have no idea how awful it is to have no private life whatsoever. And you must understand that it is terribly unfair on me and my sons. I can only appeal to you to put a stop to this sort of thing."

Most of the editors and senior journalists would nod in agreement and say they understood her predicament. But the phone calls did not cease and the paparazzi would continue to know nearly all of her movements every minute of the day. Forlornly, Diana would comment to her friend the London banker, "I hoped the editors might help but I suppose I was being naive. The trouble is that all they want to do is sell newspapers. But I do wish they would give me a break sometimes."

But in the first months of 1996, Diana had to face an even more vital problem—her divorce. At first, she decided not to take the slightest notice of the Queen's demand for an early divorce but to leave all the details to her lawyer, Anthony Julius of Mischon De Reya. She was in no hurry. She preferred to wait and see whether the Queen would grant her permission to become a royal ambassador. Diana suspected that the Queen had issued her statement so soon after Diana's public demand for the job of royal ambassador because she had seen an opportunity to force through a divorce in return for giving permission for Diana to become some sort of high-profile international charity worker.

"They might think I'm a fool," Diana would say, "but I know their game. It's as plain as a pike staff. Well, if they want me out of the way that much, they might have to pay for it."

But the going became tougher. She found herself becoming more prone to mood swings, which now seemed to affect her most days. For no apparent reason she would find herself in tears or screaming in anger at one of her staff. She also found that she was forever changing her mind. One day she would happily tell her loyal secretary, Patrick Jephson, that she intended to comply with all the demands for her divorce so the matter could be over and done with as soon as possible. The next day she would countermand her decision, telling him to have nothing whatsoever to do with the matter, even ordering him not to reply to her own solicitor's letters. And such changes of mind did not only occur with Jephson but with most of her staff, quite often over totally unimportant, irrelevant matters such as what to wear or eat for lunch.

Jephson found the situation so bizarre it was almost impossible for him to continue working at the palace. He wanted to
carry on as Diana's secretary because he realized that she would
need support and advice as details of the divorce settlement were
thrashed out. But he began to realize that his advice was not
being taken by Diana, that she seemed to be listening to other
voices, other advisers. By the end of January 1996 he could take
no more. He talked to Diana, telling her his job had become
impossible because she would not make up her mind and stick
to any decision she had previously made. Before he had
completed his argument, Diana interrupted, telling him that he
could be relieved of his duties forthwith. She simply turned and
left the room with no further remark, no pleasantries.

Always the gentleman, the former Royal Navy officer
issued a statement: "It has been a great honour to work for the
Princess of Wales, and I have very much enjoyed the challenges
of the last eight years. With a growing family [he has two
young children] however, I feel that I must now be free to
consider a new career path." He added that he had always
planned to step down sometime during 1996, but most royal
watchers noted that Jephson did not have another job.

Forty-eight hours later, Nicki Cockell, thirty-two, the most
senior of Diana's three secretaries—in palace terminology, lady
clerks—handed in her resignation. Nicki Cockell was responsible for the Princess of Wales's most important correspondence
and running the small office that is situated in the Court of St.
James's, two hundred yards from Buckingham Palace. Ironically, the office is next door to that occupied by Prince
Charles's office staff. But Charles's Duchy of Cornwall, which
makes profits from housing, real estate, land, and agriculture,
pays the wage bill for all Diana's employees. No statement was
issued, but Buckingham Palace press officers suggested that
Ms. Cockell had found her position "untenable" following the
resignation of Patrick Jephson.

Hours later, a third member of Diana's dwindling band of
employees quit. Steve Davis, thirty-two, her handsome chauf-

feur for just two years, announced that he would be leaving. Davis let it be known that he had been reviewing his position for some time and was understood to be negotiating a payoff. But Diana was not in the least unhappy that Davis had decided to quit, for the relationship between Davis and his employer had become somewhat strained during the past twelve months. Davis had found his job had become all but redundant during the past year as Diana would drive herself around London on most occasions, only requiring Davis to chauffeur her when out shopping or attending a charity function.

Before Diana announced her withdrawal from public life in December 1993, her team included a private secretary, an equerry, two detectives, three secretaries, a butler, a housekeeper, a cook, a chauffeur, a dresser, and a rota of ladies-inwaiting. By late January 1996, Diana employed just two secretaries, Angela Hordern and Victoria Mendham; Paul Burrell, who acts as butler and housekeeper; Darren "Shady" McGrady, her cook; and Helen Walsh, her dresser. With so few public engagements, a lady-in-waiting is asked to attend only occasional events.

"Just another changing of the guard," Diana quipped when asked why everyone was deserting her. But her flip reply concealed a worried woman, for she hated to think that she had been responsible for her staff leaving her. It made her feel yet more lonely and unloved.

After the Queen's demand for an early divorce, Diana had come to some conclusions as to what she would demand in her settlement. She was determined to keep the title "Princess," and though she recognized that she could not continue to be "Her Royal Highness, the Princess of Wales," she still wished to be known officially as "Her Royal Highness, Princess Diana," although she was certain the Queen would not allow her to keep the title.

She would demand either a substantial London mansion, costing perhaps $5 million or, as a permanent arrangement, the apartments she now uses at Kensington Palace. She also demanded another house in the country, a large country estate with land, costing perhaps another $5 million.

The Royal Protection Squad encouraged the Queen and her aides to permit Diana to remain in her Kensington Palace apartments because her security and that of the two princes could be more efficiently managed. With the IRA renewing their bombing campaign, and targeting members of the Royal Family, in February 1996 security had once again become all important. For the same reason senior police officers did not want Diana and the princes to be given another home in the country, fearing they could become an IRA target.

Diana told her solicitor Anthony Julius to demand a tax-free, personal annual income of $2 million a year after all expenses on the understanding that the upkeep of her homes, staff salaries, cars, and all ancillary expenses would be met by the Duchy of Cornwall, Prince's Charles's private estate. She also demanded that all costs relating to Wills and Harry, including their education, clothing, and holidays should be met by Charles.

Most important, she demanded the settlement be guaranteed for her lifetime, whether she remarries or not.

Diana recognized that the question of custody of Wills and Harry is quite different from that of any other British children caught up in their parents' divorce settlement because they are heirs to the throne. Diana accepted that as heirs to the throne they are the responsibility of the monarch who has jurisdiction over them.

Diana, for example, understands that she would not be permitted to take Wills and Harry out of the country except with the express permission of the Queen and, after her death, King Charles. She knows, and accepts, that she would never be permitted to live abroad with her sons.

However, Charles and Diana agreed that the arrangements for access to the children, which have been in force since the separation, will continue. They are both determined that their divorce should have as little effect as possible on the two boys and that Wills and Harry should see both parents as frequently as possible.

The Queen instructed her lawyers Farrer & Co. to include a clause in the divorce settlement that Diana must agree never to write, speak, or communicate any further information concerning the monarchy, the House of Windsor, Prince Charles, Wills and Harry, her marriage, or her divorce settlement. The Queen is determined to do everything possible to prevent another BCC *Panorma*-type debacle.

The Queen wanted Diana removed from the House of Windsor so that the full focus of attention could once again be trained on Prince Charles, as it was before Diana came on the scene in 1979. She knows that rebuilding the nation's respect and admiration for the monarchy will be a long, hard process, but she is a most patient woman, and a most determined one.

The Queen realized only too well that Diana will still be holding center stage, still grabbing the headlines, and will probably remain the most popular Royal for many years to come. She also understood the damage the Princess of Wales had inflicted on the monarchy during the past few years. Today, one-third of all voters believe the monarchy to be irrelevant, and more than half want to see less pomp, ceremony, and lavish lifestyles.

During her sixteen-year reign as Princess of Wales, Diana has caused the greatest upsurge of pride and passion in the British Royal Family. But in the latter years she has also inflicted severe wounds to the reputation of Prince Charles, to Queen Elizabeth, and to the monarchy itself. For that she will never be forgiven.

Diana was as eager to be rid of the House of Windsor as every member of that family wanted to be rid of her. But Diana never wanted to be forced out of the family, as she has surely been. She wanted no separation; she wanted no divorce; she wanted to remain a part of a family with her beloved Wills and Harry. Today she is a lonely woman, facing the future as an outcast with no family and very few friends.

Index

꧁꧂

279

NOV - - 2014

Understanding Parkinson's Disease

Understanding Parkinson's Disease

*An Introduction for Patients
and Caregivers*

Naheed Ali

ROWMAN & LITTLEFIELD PUBLISHERS, INC.
Lanham • Boulder • New York • Toronto • Plymouth, UK

Published by Rowman & Littlefield Publishers, Inc.
A wholly owned subsidiary of The Rowman & Littlefield Publishing Group, Inc.
4501 Forbes Boulevard, Suite 200, Lanham, Maryland 20706
www.rowman.com

10 Thornbury Road, Plymouth PL6 7PP, United Kingdom

British Library Cataloguing in Publication Information Available

Library of Congress Cataloging-in-Publication Data

Ali, Naheed, 1981- author.
Understanding Parkinson's disease : an introduction for patients and caregivers / Naheed Ali.
p. cm.
Includes bibliographical references and index.
ISBN 978-1-4422-2103-1 (cloth : alk. paper) -- ISBN 978-1-4422-2104-8 (electronic)
I. Title. [DNLM: 1. Parkinson Disease -- diagnosis. 2. Parkinson Disease -- therapy. WL 359]
RC382
616.8'33--dc23

2013021782

This book represents reference material only. It is not intended as a medical manual, and
the data presented here are meant to assist the reader in making informed choices regarding wellness. This book is not a replacement for treatment(s) that the reader's personal
physician may have suggested. If the reader believes he or she is experiencing a medical
issue, professional medical help is recommended. Mention of particular products, compa-
nies, or authorities in this book does not entail endorsement by the publisher or author.

The paper used in this publication meets the minimum requirements of American National
Standard for Information Sciences Permanence of Paper for Printed Library Materials,
ANSI/NISO Z39.48-1992.

Printed in the United States of America

Also by Naheed Ali

Arthritis and You: A Comprehensive Digest for Patients and Caregivers
Understanding Alzheimer's: An Introduction for Patients and Caregivers
The Obesity Reality: A Comprehensive Approach to a Growing Problem
Diabetes and You: A Comprehensive, Holistic Approach

Understanding Parkinson's Disease is dedicated to my readers, to Parkinson's disease patients, and to all who provided encouragement and support for my research.

Contents

Preface

The brain is in charge of a human's sensations, feelings, memory, personality, and movements. Brain cells, also called neurons, are able to send signals and communicate with one another through neurotransmitters such as dopamine, acetylcholine, serotonin, and norepinephrine, which are chemical messengers released by neurons and produced in different parts of the brain. Unlike the cells in other human organs, neurons are not replaced with new ones when they die.[1] Damage and death of neurons thus result in a progressive, irreversible malfunction of neurons, eventually leading to diseases of a neurodegenerative nature, which include the impairment of memory from Alzheimer's as well as brain-related movement disorders such as Parkinson's disease. Several movement disorders are linked to a part of the brain called the **basal ganglia**, a group of small masses of nervous tissue (a single mass is called a ganglion) located at the base of cerebrum, the "wrinkled" part of the brain. Basal ganglia are partly responsible for locomotive skills, with their neurons producing dopamine, the neurotransmitter used for communications that coordinate normal movement. The areas of the basal ganglia include the striatum and **substantia nigra**, or dark substance.[2]

The neurons in the substantia nigra produce the melanin-pigmented dopamine, which is the chemical messenger in control of transmitting signals between the substantia nigra and the **striatum**, the next relay station of the brain. This transmission of signals between the two components of the basal ganglia permits the smooth, coordinated function of the body's movement and muscles. Losing this type of neuron (1) decreases the amount of melanin-pigmented dopamine released and (2) impairs the smooth communication between the substantia nigra and striatum, resulting in Parkinson's disease. This deficiency is pathologically manifested by loss of dark coloration, also called depigmentation, in the substantia nigra. Round inclusions made up of

protein can be seen in the damaged or depigmented (lost dark pigments, or **neuromelanin**) substantia nigra, and they are called **Lewy bodies**. Lewy bodies are more than fifteen microns in diameter and have an organized structure—a dense core surrounded by a halo.[3] These inclusions, which are a hallmark of the disease, are visible only through a microscope, that is, their existence in the brain can be verified only during an autopsy.

UNCOVERING PARKINSON'S

Parkinson's disease is characterized as a common, chronic, neurodegenerative movement disorder, manifested by (1) **tremors** (shaking), (2) stiffness (rigidity), (3) slowness (bradykinesia), (4) balancing difficulty (posture instability), and (5) multitasking issues.[4] Males and females have almost an equal chance of acquiring the disease, with men slightly more susceptible. Most of the time, the initial symptoms become apparent only at the age of fifty and above, when 80 percent of the neurons in substantia nigra are already damaged or dead.[5] In about 5 to 10 percent of the reported Parkinson's disease cases, people younger than forty years old are diagnosed with the disease,[6] and although the disease is slowly progressive, the rate of neurodegeneration varies for each patient.

The disease is just one type from a wider group of movement disorders called Parkinsonism or Parkinsonian syndrome (a more generic term), a group of diseases that are all linked to inadequate dopamine in the basal ganglia, manifesting in impairments similar to those of Parkinson's disease.[7] Other forms of Parkinsonism differ from Parkinson's disease in terms of their clinical features. At present, the medical community is still grappling with the challenges of Parkinson's disease—there is no absolute diagnosis yet—based on only the patient's medical history and neurologist's clinical examination. As the reader may take note from chapter 4, the root cause of the disease remains obscure, although several theories exist. Consequently, there is no absolute cure,[8] and there will be none until the causes are determined in full. Treatments are available—medical, surgical, complementary—that are proven to alleviate the symptoms and improve the quality of lives of patients, with the help and support of caregivers around them.

THE GAIN FROM READING ABOUT PARKINSON'S

There are no cultural, geographical, or gender boundaries for who can be affected by Parkinson's—that is, anyone can be afflicted. Being aware of the disease, the symptoms, and the complexity of the brain and the disease itself, readers can help save someone they know and most especially someone close to them, such as family or friends, whom they might suspect to have Parkin-

son's disease. Diagnosis can be very difficult and uncertain. In some cases, someone diagnosed with Parkinson's disease does not actually have the disease, and in others, someone diagnosed with a different illness was actually manifesting Parkinson's. Many people assume that the early stages and symptoms of the disease are signs of natural aging or another illness since the disease is subtle at first. Friends and families may be the first to notice the symptoms, and early signs are difficult to detect.

Knowing that anyone can become a victim of Parkinson's disease, I sincerely hope that readers will be more observant of themselves and the people around them. Reading literature about the disease will equip them with the understanding of what it is and what it is not, its common symptoms, and the things one can do as concerned citizens (chapter 20) to contribute and to help other people's lives. Once diagnosed, it is important for both the patient as well as his or her family to cope in the process. Acceptance and adaptation are fundamental requirements in coping with a chronic progressive disease such as Parkinson's disease. Family as well as healthcare professionals are affected in the process. It is strongly recommended for the spouse or family caregiver to also take care of themselves in the process. [9]

Resources on Parkinson's disease such as *Understanding Parkinson's Disease* are accessible to inform them of all the possibilities they might encounter and thus avoid any fear of the uncertainties. These references provide them and their caregivers (1) the different approaches to managing and monitoring of Parkinson's, (2) types of treatments and medications available, (3) required changes in lifestyle, and (4) common problems and issues encountered by other Parkinson's disease patients and caregivers, from which they can learn. These texts also provide information on services and organizations that are accessible for further support, advice, and assistance to both the patient and the caregiver. Current progress and remaining challenges in Parkinson's disease research are also being disseminated. All these are done to continually reassure patients and caregivers about the availability of proven effective medications and treatments and encourage them that there is hope to help them cope with and end the clinical adversary they are facing. Their optimism is important as it indicates their willingness to adapt to changes imposed by the disease. Last, these pages are written and distributed to let them know and feel that they are not alone in the process.

IMPLICATIONS OF A COMPREHENSIVE APPROACH

Management of Parkinson's is as intricate as the disease itself. Briefly described previously are the motor symptoms that might impede the patient's daily activities, the difficulty of diagnosis because of the inexistence of absolute tests, and the unknown reason why dopamine-producing neurons die,

causing the inability to find a cure for the illness. All of these contribute to the complexity of this chronic and progressive disease. In addition to these challenges are uniqueness of the disease's progress, symptoms, and response to medications for each patient. Nonmotor symptoms such as depression and dementia[10] might arise during the process to worsen the disease and largely impact both the patient's and caregiver's quality of life.

It is therefore important to review and understand the disease in a comprehensive and multidisciplinary way, providing a holistic (both mind and body) interpretation of the disease.[11] A multidisciplinary approach to Parkinson's disease encompasses suitable and up-to-date medication and treatments tailored to a patient's performance, surgical options, nutrition, environment, and spiritual, physical, and emotional strengthening.[12] All these are required in improving the patient's quality of life.

Considering all the challenges mentioned, Parkinson's disease patients, caregivers, and physicians are all accountable to extensively study and grasp this still-incurable disease in order to successfully communicate with one another, leading to successful personal and professional relationships and, finally, coping successfully with the affliction. Dealing with Parkinson's includes periodic monitoring, support in all aspects, and multidisciplinary treatments, all geared toward improving quality of life, which is greatly affected by nonmotor symptoms. There are ways the disease progresses that are not recognized early, and thus patients can fail to get treated properly at the earliest possible time.

Understanding the disease comprehensively and the treatments both available and being studied will increase the success of the elderly patient's rehabilitation process. Being aware of recent developments in research, specialized tools, and treatments will enable the patient and care partner to wisely decide which to utilize. There are and will be many pieces of advice and solutions to the patient's problems, but patients themselves are greatly encouraged to be part of the decision making. With the chronic and progressive Parkinson's disease, adjustment is an ongoing process for the patient and any persons involved in order to live and sustain a normal and quality life. By learning as much as they can about the disease in a comprehensive way, patients and caregivers will increase their awareness, compassion, and hope in dealing with it. Hand in hand, keeping each other informed about Parkinson's may allow the medical research realm to finally put an end to it.

I

Groundwork

Chapter One

History of Parkinson's

Rapid progress has characterized the different areas of Parkinson's disease research—from symptoms, therapy, drugs, and diagnostic techniques to its biochemical basis. The results, according to most who undertake the difficult task of learning more about this disease, are very encouraging. Though much has been learned about Parkinson's, much of its history still remains a mystery. The pieces of the Parkinson's puzzle that researchers have yet to find are, ironically, the most important ones: what causes the disease, how it can be prevented, and what can cure it. Parkinson's disease continues to remain a truly idiopathic disease, and a cure to this very damaging disorder continues to elude medical science, even to this day. The costs of Parkinson's disease to society have been high throughout history and continue to rise, with billions of dollars a year spent for patient care, nursing homes, medication, and other indirect costs; its impact on the quality of life of patients and caregivers remains incalculable. However, as this short historical survey will show, much that is useful can be learned from history, and much can be hoped for from the advances that have been made to combat the disease. James Parkinson's rejoinder directed to "those who humanely employ anatomical examination in detecting the causes and nature of diseases" so that "by their benevolent labors" the "real nature . . . and . . . cure" of Parkinson's disease be revealed[1] remains relevant today.

COINING OF THE TERM *PARKINSON'S*

Parkinson's disease was named after the apothecary surgeon, geologist, political activist, and paleontologist James Parkinson (April 1755–December 1824), the author of the 1817 work *An Essay on the Shaking Palsy*; the disease itself has existed for as long as humans have had the potential for

3

insufficient formation of a simple organic chemical called dopamine.[2] James Parkinson referred to the disease named after him as *paralysis agitans*, or **shaking palsy**, the afflicted of which he described as having symptoms of involuntary tremors, lessened muscular power, and upper bodies bent in a forward manner, without sensory loss.[3] To achieve a better understanding of why the disease was named after Parkinson, a short survey of some of the most prominent references to this disease in history is in order.

Charcot: From Paralysis Agitans to Parkinson's Disease

The actual naming of Parkinson's disease is credited to the French neurologist and professor of anatomical pathology, the celebrated "father of modern neurology," Jean-Martin Charcot (1825–1893). Charcot's landmark neurological studies at the pinnacle of his career were instrumental to, among others, distinguishing Parkinson's disease from other disorders such as **multiple sclerosis**, and to naming the disorder after James Parkinson. Charcot rejected the term *paralysis agitans* on the grounds that patients suffering from this disease are not exceptionally weak and do not necessarily *have* to tremble. In recognition of James Parkinson as the first (to Charcot's knowledge; see the following section for an alternative view) to describe the four cardinal symptoms of the disease from six cases he observed, Charcot, while teaching in the Salpêtrière in the 1870s, was the first to suggest that the disorder be named after the eponymous writer of *An Essay on the Shaking Palsy*. The naming of the disease after James Parkinson was adopted universally by medical academia soon after Charcot's suggestion.

Among the researchers who contributed to society's present knowledge of the disease, it was Charcot, the neurologist from Salpêtrière Hospital in Paris, who first named it as *maladie de Parkinson*, which means "Parkinson's disease," to pay homage to the physician who first described the symptoms medically.[4] For scientific reasons, Charcot found the earlier term *shaking palsy* inappropriate.[5] He raised three important reasons: First, shaking was not always observed among all the patients. Second, muscular weakness is not characteristic of patients suffering from Parkinson's disease, and therefore "paralysis" was a misnomer. Third, he wanted to avoid the confusion with general paresis, which laypersons associated with dementia because of the French word *paresie*.[6] This appeared in his *Lectures on Disease of the Nervous System*.[7] Apart from distinguishing it from general paresis, Charcot defined multiple sclerosis as distinct from Parkinson's disease.[8]

Pax Corporis and the Issue of Historical Accuracy

It is worth noting that the historical references of real or assumed descriptions of Parkinson's disease that predate *An Essay on the Shaking Palsy* refer

to some aspects of the disease but almost never to all four cardinal symptoms that characterize it, with the exception of Ferenc Pápai Páriz in *Pax Corporis*. In addition to mentioning all four cardinal characteristics of Parkinson's disease, Ferenc Pápai Páriz also observed that the disease is progressive and affects the elderly more than those of younger age. Pápai also correctly suggested that the problems originate in the brain (via explicit mention that the disorder should be classed among the diseases of the head), in marked contrast to James Parkinson's suggestion that it originates in the *medulla spinalis*, or spinal cord. In view of the earlier and apparently more complete and accurate description of the disease, some neurologists and historians of medicine have suggested that Parkinson's disease (PD) be renamed Pápai-Parkinson's disease (PPD).[9] While the historical accuracy of a prior mention of all four cardinal symptoms of Parkinson's disease by Ferenc Pápai Páriz has been demonstrated, it does not in any way diminish the groundbreaking influence and enormous subsequent contribution to the study of the disorder of James Parkinson's *Essay*. This is admitted even by those who support a revision of the historiography of Parkinson's disease with a mention of Ferenc Pápai Páriz's *Pax Corporis*.[10]

James Parkinson wrote his monograph with the explicit intention of inviting further studies on the disorder in particular; he was the first to attach such a level of urgency to learning more about the disease, as he deemed it not warrantable to delay the publication of his essay. According to Parkinson, the disorder has historically "escaped particular notice," and the medical academia of his time seemed to be disinclined to "ascertaining the nature and cause" of it. In accordance with generally accepted current usage, this book will consistently refer to its subject simply as Parkinson's, PD, or Parkinson's disease.[11]

HISTORICAL OVERVIEW OF NEUROLOGICAL DISORDERS

A history of Parkinson's disease cannot be appreciated without an overview of the history of neurological disorders. However, it is important to remember that the factors that make a definitive history of Parkinson's disease a challenge also beset the history of neurological disorders in general. Among these factors are the differences in the understanding of the structure and function of the nervous system in history as compared with our understanding in the present; the methods used in the examination and the investigation of the nervous system; and the changing concepts of neurological disease. Historical accounts of cases now assumed to be Parkinson's disease may have referred to entirely different conditions with symptoms that may resemble PD. An excellent example of a disorder characterized by tremors that

may have been mistaken for what is now called Parkinson's disease is multiple sclerosis.

Pre-Twentieth-Century Classification of Neurological Diseases

The classification system, or nosology, of neurological disease was primitive prior to the nineteenth century. The evolution of medical classification can roughly be described to have progressed from Hippocrates's theory of the humors, to modern anatomical pathology heralded by Giovanni Batista Morgagni, and finally to Robert Koch's germ theory.[12] Neurological diseases were usually grouped by primary symptoms such as tremors or slowness of movement[13] and which area of the body was affected, based on Hippocrates's theory of the humors. Thus, headache and epilepsy were classified as afflictions of the hair and scalp. Though treatments for neurological disorders were performed successfully in the classical and medieval periods, Greek physicians of the classical age and Muslim physicians of the medieval age were particularly successful in this regard. As an example, Ammar bin Ali of Mosul, Iraq, was perhaps the first to successfully extract a cataract from the eye, circa 1000 CE.[14] The classification of diseases followed Hippocrates's symptomatic and topographical classification closely.

The first methodical classification of diseases was established by François Boissier de Sauvages de Lacroix's 1763 book *Nosologia Methodica*, following Thomas Sydenham's suggestion that all diseases could be classified in the same manner as botanists classify plants.[15] Particularly relevant to neurological disease similar to what is now known as Parkinson's is de Lacroix's mention of several movement disorders and convulsions in his book. De Lacroix's nosology was supplanted by William Cullen's more influential *Synopsis Nosologiae Methodicae*, first published in 1769. Other early texts important to the history of neurological disorders are *De Cerebri Morbis*, written in 1549 by Jason Pratensis; *De Anima Brutorum*, by Thomas Willis, written in 1672; and *A Treatise on Nervous Disease*, by John Cooke, completed in 1823.[16] One of the first authors to use an anatomical and physiological approach toward neurological diseases such as that which is now known to be Parkinson's was Moritz Heinrich Romberg in his *Lehrbuch der Nerven-Krankheiten des Menschen*, completed in 1846. Considered to be the initial systematic treatise on neurology, the *Lehrbuch* divides neurological disorders into "neuroses of sensibility" and "neuroses of motility," following William Cullen's classification.[17] Also worthy of mention is William Hammond's *A Treatise on the Diseases of the Nervous System*, published in 1871 and probably the first comprehensive textbook on neurology. In terms of conceptual organization, Jean Martin Charcot's *Leçons sur les Maladies du Système Nerveux faites à la Salpêtrière* has exercised the most significant influence, as it provided the first sound nosography for neurology based on

the clinical anatomical method. Included in his book are descriptions of Parkinson's disease, multiple sclerosis, amyotrophic lateral sclerosis, and tabes dorsalis, from cases spanning the 1860s and 1870s.[18]

Neurological Milestones of the Early Twentieth Century

Significant advances in the main framework of neurology, pathology of the nervous system, and other disciplines broadened the clinical spectrum of neurology in the early years of the twentieth century,[19] and with it, the understanding of the causes of neurological diseases. Armed with greater knowledge in the fields of immunology, metabolism, genetics, and, eventually, molecular biology and biochemistry, neurologists were able to devise approaches of greater complexity, and the theory of neurological diseases progressed from the theory of humors to the germ theory.[20] A very selective list of milestones of neurological importance during the first years of the twentieth century would include the following: descriptions of apraxia, progressive myoclonic epilepsy, **thalamic pain syndrome**, the lacunar state, distal myopathy, and pathological changes in **presenile dementia**; studies on the developmental patterns of cerebral myelinization, reflexes, aphasia, adrenalin, and the cervical sympathetic system; and the Nobel Prize–winning studies on neuronal staining and the neuron theory by C. Golgi and S. Ramon y Cajal.[21]

The second decade of the twentieth century provided neurologists with an unparalleled yet unwanted number of research opportunities with the outbreak of the First World War, in a similar way that the American Civil War had provided physicians with a rich source of nerve injury patients.[22] Many people were able to survive war wounds due to advances in the treatment of shock and infection prevention methods. Their survival notwithstanding, they usually did not escape their ordeals completely unscathed. Many survivors of the First World War sustained damage to the spinal cord, cerebellum, and other parts of the nervous system. There were also many sufferers of "**shell shock**," with symptoms of blindness, tremor, and paraplegia.[23] In 1917, many cases of **postencephalitic Parkinsonism** were seen due to the outbreak of encephalitis lethargica. Influenza killed twenty million people worldwide two years later.

More advances with neurological diseases such as Parkinson's in the decades following the 1920s were to come. The rapid introduction of myelogram, angiogram, electroencephalogram, and electromyogram techniques vastly improved the accuracy of neurological diagnoses. The outbreak of the Second World War in the 1940s led to millions of cases of war injuries, many of which were neurological or related. In 1955, Jonas Salk developed a vaccine to counter **poliomyelitis**, which eradicated the disease in the Western Hemisphere. **Phenytoin** and **phenobarbital**, and derivatives such as etho-

toin, were used to treat epilepsy. Neurological awareness increased during the 1960s, with neurology increasingly being recognized as a branch of medicine separate from psychiatry, something that began in the previous decade. Violent acts such as the assassinations of President John F. Kennedy, the Reverend Martin Luther King Jr., and Senator Robert F. Kennedy were also instrumental to this increasing awareness, as clinically their deaths were caused by brain death and neurotrauma. The widespread use of herbicides such as Agent Orange raised concerns about neurotoxicity. Psychedelic and hallucinogenic drugs were also increasingly used by several emerging countercultures; disorders due to the abuse of such substances were also pertinent to the neurological studies of the time.[24]

Neurological Disorders in the Latter Half of the Twentieth Century

In the 1970s, tremendous advancements occurred in the pharmacological, physiological, biological, and imaging fields of neurological studies. These advancements facilitated growth in patient care, education, and research related to neurology.[25] Combined carbidopa/levodopa was introduced in this decade[26] and greatly improved the treatment of Parkinson's disease by permitting high activation of dopamine for patients without peripheral side effects. This is addressed in more detail below. Mitochondrial disorders were delineated, and enzymes responsible for various lipid storage disorders were identified.

Neurology in the 1980s greatly improved on the imaging techniques made widely available during the previous decade. While computerized tomographic (CT) x-ray imaging was the primary advance of the 1970s, positron emission tomography (PET) revolutionized cerebral imaging in the 1980s.[27] PET was an improvement on the functional imaging techniques then available. Rapid advancements in nuclear magnetic resonance (NMR) spectroscopy made the high resolution, in vivo images of the human brain possible. Revolutionary new techniques in biology such as recombinant DNA and rapid DNA sequencing were used to evaluate patients with genetic and metabolic disorders, and this led to the discovery of the chromosomal location of the genetic defect in another neurological and movement disorder called Huntington's disease. New ethical problems were encountered by neurologists in issues such as establishing sound criteria for determining brain death and the persistent vegetative state, and using funds for fetal tissue transplant research. Such issues made the major neurological associations heighten their legislative activities and increase their funding. This resulted in a congressional resolution, signed by then president George H. W. Bush, declaring the years 1990–2000 as the "decade of the brain."[28]

Neurology involving debilitating diseases, including Parkinson's, also made rapid advancements in the 1990s. Demonstrably effective therapeutic

options were now available, and an important milestone in this regard was the first successful intervention of a stroke in progress in 1995. It was observed that **tissue plasminogen activator** administrated early in the course of a stroke increased the chances for a successful intervention. Thus, major public campaigns were launched to alert the public about the importance of prompt and immediate treatment of cerebrovascular attacks. Widespread occurrences of cerebrovascular accidents in that decade made these public campaigns particularly reassuring.

The 1990s also saw vast improvement in the application of human genetics to the treatment of neurological disorders. The previous decade's location of the chromosome instrumental in the development of Huntington's disease was followed in the 1990s by numerous observations of a similar nature touching every aspect of neurodegenerative conditions. Important genetic links in Alzheimer's disease, multiple disorders with trinucleotide repeats, motor neuron diseases, and—relevant to this book—Parkinson's disease were discovered in that decade. Though still far from obliterating these disorders, the vast amount of knowledge which can be used to combat them that neurologists gained in the 1990s looks promising. [29]

PARKINSON'S DISEASE IN HISTORY

The Ancient and Classical Periods

Descriptions of diseases suspected to be Parkinson's disease appear in several early documents such as the *Huang Di Nei Jing Su Wen* (the earliest known Chinese medical treatise),[30] ancient treatises of the traditional Indian medical system of Ayurveda (where the disease known in such texts as Kampa Vata, mentioned earlier than 1000 BCE, is possibly Parkinson's disease),[31] the *Iliad* (where old King Nestor says that his limbs are "no longer steady"), and both Old[32] and New Testaments[33] of the Bible (where aged people are depicted as trembling, bent, and incapable of standing erect). Ancient authors who mentioned conditions characteristic of Parkinson's disease include Erasistratus of Ceos (310 BCE–250 CE), Aulus Cornelius Celsus (ca. 25 BCE–ca. 50 CE), Pedanius Dioscorides (ca. 40 CE–ca. 90 CE), and the famous Greco-Roman physician Galen (129 CE–200 CE). Galen seems to be the one who coined the term "shaking palsy."[34] His descriptions of shaking palsy were referenced in James Parkinson's *Essay*.[35] Erasistratus of Ceos described a type of paralysis associated with slowness in the initiation of walking, which he called *paradoxos*. His description of paradoxos is reminiscent of Parkinsonian symptoms. Aulus Cornelius Celsus advised those who suffer from "tremor of the sinews" to resort to massage therapy, exercise, and abstention from sexual activity. He was also able to distinguish fine tremor from coarser shaking. Pedanius Dioscorides recommended a

mixture prepared from beaver testes, vinegar, and roses for tremblings, convulsions, and all "diseases of the nerves." Some of the symptoms he recommended his mixture for are decidedly Parkinsonian.[36]

Medieval and Renaissance Periods

The medieval and Renaissance periods also have their share of authors and books with references to what would appear to be Parkinson's disease. Paul of Aigina (ca. 625–ca. 690), from the Byzantine Empire, mentioned "senile paralysis agitans" in his *Medical Compendium in Seven Books*. He attributed these tremors to alcoholism. In the medieval Islamic world, the Persian polymath and leading physician of the time, Ibn Sina (known to the West as Avicenna), devoted space to the different forms of motor unrest in the chapter on nervous disorders in his *Canon of Medicine*. He recommended mineral baths and antispasm ointments common to the time for the treatment of the disorder. A medieval Syrian medical treatise also mentioned the ingredients of an ointment to be rubbed on limbs with Parkinson's-like rigidity.[37] The famous multitalented Italian artist of the Renaissance, Leonardo da Vinci (1452–1519), described people who suffered from Parkinson's-like tremors in his notebooks. England's most famous playwright, William Shakespeare (1564–1616), also had one of the characters of his play *Henry VI* respond to a query about his shaking that it was caused not by fear but by palsy. Another Englishman, the herbalist and botanist Nicholas Culpeper (1616–1654), recommended various substances as treatment for palsies, "the dead palsy," and "tremblings" in his book *Pharmacopeia Londinensis*. The ingredients of the cures he recommended were an unusual combination, to say the least—"the oil of winged ants," earthworms, mistletoe, and the like. The philosopher Thomas Hobbes (1588–1679) was described to have had a progressive case of shaking palsy in John Aubrey's (1626–1697) biography of him, titled *Life of Mr. Thomas Hobbes of Malmesbury*.[38] Ferenc Pápai Páriz (1649–1716), in his medical text *Pax Corporis* (1690), described all four major symptoms of what would be known as Parkinson's disease—**bradykinesia**, or slowness of movement, postural instability, rigidity, and tremors—well over a hundred years before James Parkinson's 1817 monograph.[39] *Pax Corporis* and its impact on the historical study of Parkinson's disease is discussed in more detail later.

Post-Renaissance Era

Another possible historical reference to Parkinson's disease is the mention of "palsy" in George Cheyne's *The English Malady*. In his book, Cheyne (1671–1743) defines palsy as a disease wherein the body or some parts of the body lose their ability to move; this is often accompanied by numbness of the

affected body parts. Cheyne also observes "tottering" and shaking in those who suffer from the disease, especially old people, for whom the condition is basically incurable.[40] Parkinson's disease also seems not to have escaped the notice of François Boissier de Sauvages de Lacroix (1706–1767), mentioned earlier in this chapter as the pioneer of the classification of diseases. He described a condition which he called *sclerotyrbe festinans*, or festination, the chief characteristic of which was difficulty in the initiation of walking (bradykinesia, or slowness of movement) due to decreased flexibility of the muscles (muscular rigidity).[41] The distinguished Scottish surgeon John Hunter (1728–1793) gave a description of the symptoms suffered by one "Lord L" in a lecture in 1776. The symptoms Lord L suffered from include the trembling characteristic of *paralysis agitans*. James Parkinson may have attended and been influenced by John Hunter's 1776 lecture. Others who mentioned aspects of Parkinson's disease include John Pratensis and Forensus, both from the sixteenth century, Sylvius de la Boë (who referred to "rest tremors") from the seventeenth century, and Johan Baptiste Sagar of Austria, from the eighteenth century.[42]

RESEARCH AND DEVELOPMENT THROUGHOUT THE HISTORY OF PARKINSON'S

Initial Problems

Parkinson's disease researchers have encountered and continue to encounter difficulties in their research, most prominently the accurate diagnosis of the disease and its symptoms; the development of demonstrably effective treatment and therapeutic methods to counter the disease or minimize its effects to those afflicted with it; the development of safe and effective drugs and medication; the proper assessment of risk factors that may lead to more accurate diagnoses; and, perhaps most importantly, the discovery of the real cause of the disorder in hopes of possibly preventing and curing it.

Historical Attempts in Search of Effective Medicine and Treatment

Developing effective treatments and medications that could pass the rigors of scientific examination was not an easy task. The treatment for Parkinson's disease in history has followed the medical conventions of whichever historical period one is referring to, a few examples of which were provided earlier. From unguents, ointments, ancient pills, and mineral baths, treatment and medication for this chronic disease have progressed tremendously since the discovery of its biochemical basis. A few historical examples of treatments not yet mentioned show how far people have come.

The English physician John Elliotson (1791–1868) was the first to claim a cure for Parkinson's disease since its first formal description in *An Essay on the Shaking Palsy*. He recommended, among other treatments, bloodletting, pus building, cauterization, and purging for Parkinson's disease.[43] James Parkinson had recommended bloodletting and pus building as well. Both Elliotson and Parkinson recommended these measures to decompress the *medulla spinalis*, which was believed by James Parkinson to be the seat of this dysfunction. John Elliotson's administration of iron as a kind of tonic and his suggestion that young patients could be cured using carbonate of iron are interesting in light of the fact that iron is essential for the formation of levodopa, the naturally occurring amino acid now used widely for Parkinson's disease treatment. A more detailed treatment of levodopa and dopamine are provided later in this book. Another pharmacological advance was Charcot's attempt to redress the cholinergic-dopaminergic balance to improve Parkinsonism. Charcot's intern, Leopold Ordenstein, suggested in his 1867 thesis that Parkinsonian tremors should be treated using **belladonna alkaloids**, due to belladonna's anticholinergic effects. Though the thesis advocating this pioneering use of anticholinergic drugs was published solely under Ordenstein's name, medical historians insist that the credit should still go to Charcot, as he strictly oversaw every aspect of the Salpêtrière's neurological program; it is nearly impossible that Ordenstein's thesis was published without Charcot's supervision, a view held even by their contemporaries. Charcot recommended the use of the plant-based anticholinergic hyoscyamine and rye-based ergot medicine. Modern-day dopamine agonists also have their chemical basis in the same ergot products that Charcot used. The function of these agonists is to stimulate the dopamine receptors in the striatum and simulate the activity and effects of dopamine. Note that much was still to be learned about dopamine and its immense significance to Parkinson's disease during Charcot's time.

Other treatments tried in an effort to find a lasting cure for the disease or to at least alleviate its symptoms include electrically powered shaking chairs, designed to replicate the effects of long horseback, carriage, and train rides, which were observed to relieve symptoms of Parkinson's disease; a portable, helmet version of the shaking chairs, made to vibrate the brain instead of the whole body; and even a suspension apparatus to stretch the patients' spinal cords. The last example was able to relieve rigidity and improve the sensory symptoms but was not effective against the tremors; the stress and other side effects patients experienced with this "macabre" treatment made Charcot abandon it immediately.[44]

Sir William Gowers (1845–1915), Britain's foremost authority in neurology and a contemporary of Charcot, advocated treatment strategies similar to those recommended by the latter. Like Charcot, Gowers was keen to stress that patients should be freed from mental stress and physical exhaustion. For

the treatment of tremor, Gowers recommended a more expansive version of Charcot's pharmacological inventory: hemlock, cannabis, **arsenic**, morphia, and other drugs were added to Charcot's hyoscyamine. **Cannabis**, in particular, has been discovered to have dopaminergic activation potential. The first half of the twentieth century witnessed a relative stagnation in terms of innovating new therapeutic strategies for the treatment of Parkinson's disease. Though many anticholinergic drugs were developed during this period, they were similar in both effects and side effects to those prescribed for Parkinson's disease treatment in the nineteenth century. Instead, supportive physical therapy was emphasized to help the patients cope with the disease. Neurosurgery was also frequently used for Parkinson's disease during this era. Surgery followed the conventions of this time period. Common procedures used include intentional lesions to evacuate the regions of the nervous system suspected to be the seat of the disease and its symptoms; cortectomy, **cordotomy**, and sectioning of the **pallidofugal fibers**, all with a mixed success rate and often with serious side effects and risks; and stereotactic surgery, often directed at the thalamus for more safety and greater impact on tremor symptoms. With the subsequent discovery of levodopa, there was a sharp decline in the frequency of surgical procedures performed. It would not be until near the end of the twentieth century that, with recent advances to surgical techniques, surgery to combat Parkinson's disease witnessed a modest revival.

Discovery of Levodopa and Its Effect on Symptoms

The stagnation of the early years of the 1900s helped to highlight the immense impact of levodopa and dopamine-based therapies, which were to be developed in the latter half of the twentieth century. G. Barger and J. Ewens first synthesized dopamine in 1910. It was first thought that dopamine is but an intermediate compound that helps in the synthesis of adrenaline and noradrenaline; however, its presence in various tissues suggested a more central role to bodily functions. It was the Swedish scientist, Arvid Carlsson, who demonstrated that **dopamine** is a neurotransmitter in the brain and that it is localized in the striatum; this led A. Bertler and E. Rosengred to posit that since dopamine is concerned with the function of the striatum, it is concerned with the control of movement. With the discovery of dopamine depletion in the striatal region of Parkinson's-afflicted patients and the knowledge that levodopa is the natural precursor to dopamine and can pass the blood-brain barrier, the testing of levodopa on human patients was initiated in the 1960s, to very encouraging results. The akinetic symptoms of patients administered with L-dopa were greatly ameliorated. Interestingly, some of the historical treatments mentioned above make use of ingredients that contain levodopa or iron, which is instrumental to its formation, or make use of dopaminergic

activation qualities. The use of mucuria pruriens, which contains levodopa, suggested in Ayurveda, the iron-rich "dark beer" of John Elliotson, Charcot's ergot-based medicine, even Gowers's advocacy of cannabis for treatment, all mentioned earlier, suggest a more prominent recognition in history of levodopa's ameliorative effects on Parkinsonian symptoms.

EVOLUTION OF PARKINSON'S DISEASE APPROACHES IN HISTORY

Since inpatient and outpatient diagnostics are organized into two separate chapters of this book, perhaps it is most fitting now to discuss the evolution of Parkinson's disease diagnostics throughout history. The first challenge for neurologists was defining Parkinson's disease in order to facilitate accurate diagnosis. This was not an easy task, given the primitive nosology of the previous eras. Physicians must exercise caution in diagnosing this disease because it can easily be confounded with the ordinary signs of mere old age or with other diseases that have similar symptoms; historical references to Parkinson's must be treated with similar caution. Progress occurred in the study of the disease as its known symptoms expanded. The philosopher and diplomat Wilhelm von Humboldt's (1767–1835) description of his own medical history was perhaps the first to associate Parkinson's disease with micrographia, or the smallness of letters in handwriting. In the years 1861 and 1862, Jean-Martin Charcot and Alfred Vulpian (1826–1887) added more symptoms to the clinical description provided by James Parkinson: the "mask face," rigidity, and joint contractions in the hands and feet. Charcot noted that sufferers of this disease were not necessarily weak but were slow in the execution of movements. William Gowers, in his study of Parkinson's disease demographics, *Manual of Diseases of the Nervous System*, correctly pointed out that there is a predominance of male sufferers of this disease. Gowers also conducted studies about the joint deformities associated with this syndrome, and he likened the movement of the fingers of those afflicted with the movement of the fingers of "Orientals" beating their small drums. Slowness of movement (bradykinesia), though described both by James Parkinson and Jean-Martin Charcot, was included as one of the four cardinal symptoms of Parkinson's disease by Lebert Claveleira.

Jean-Martin Charcot's contributions in this regard are particularly significant. He was able to establish different protocols for observing patients with tremors both in action and at rest. Patients with tremors in action displayed visual disturbance, spasms, and weakness, in marked contrast to patients with tremors at rest, who displayed the four cardinal symptoms of Parkinson's disease. With these archetypes, Jean Martin Charcot was able to distinguish Parkinson's disease proper from Parkinson-extended disorders, or diseases

known today as Parkinsonism-plus syndromes, which include diseases such as (1) corticobasal degeneration, (2) **supranuclear palsy**, and (3) multiple system atrophy. These distinctions, which did not escape the trained eyes of classical diagnosticians such as Charcot, would have a major significance in the treatment of these diseases; patients with Parkinsonism-plus syndromes react poorly to treatments and medication administered to patients of traditional Parkinson's disease.

Enormous negative consequences could have happened to the survivors of the massive outbreak of encephalitis lethargica in the early twentieth century had Parkinson's disease not been separated from disorders that resemble it. Many of these survivors developed postencephalitic Parkinsonism.[45] Postencephalitic Parkinsonism, with symptoms not to be found in traditional Parkinson's disease, points to a more diffuse neurological condition, of which treatment for traditional Parkinson's disease may prove inadequate.

Chemical differences in the brains of Parkinson's disease patients were identified in the 1960s, made possible by the rapid advances in neurological and other related sciences in this and the decades prior, as noted earlier. It was discovered that the brains of those suffering from Parkinson's disease were marked with a significantly low amount of dopamine, which causes the degeneration of nerve cells in the region of the brain known as the striatum, which consists of the **globus pallidus**, the **caudate nucleus**, the **putamen**, and the *substantia nigra*. The discovery of the relation of dopamine to Parkinson's disease provided a stable biochemical basis from where Parkinson's disease could be more confidently diagnosed and separated from diseases with similar symptoms. It also facilitated major improvements to the treatment of the disease; with the chemical deficiency identified, medicine and treatment could be more easily developed and more safely and effectively tested.

Historical Models of Pathology

The early models of Parkinson's disease pathology were the conflicting gene versus environment theories. Gowers theorized that heredity played a more crucial role in the development of Parkinson's disease.[46] His contribution to the body of demographic research provided early evidence that males were slightly more predisposed to be affected by Parkinson's,[47] although this has been disputed.[48]

The hereditary model was contested by the French neurologist Charcot, who was more inclined toward the potency of environmental factors in causing the disorder.[49] It was further challenged by the outbreak of Von Economo's encephalitis from 1918 to 1920, considered as the one of the more tragic flu contagions. Postencephalitic Parkinsonism was observed among

the patients who recovered from the flu, which strongly supported Charcot's and others' belief in the pathology of Parkinson's disease. [50]

One family became widely known in the research of Parkinson's disease not for their scientific or medical studies but for being the subject of many research studies as first investigated by Larry Golbe, a man very influential in the field, together with his colleagues. [51] In a town called Contursi in Salerno, southern Italy, several generations of the said family, who later came to be known as Contursi kindred, witnessed members developing progressing Parkinsonism at around the age of forty-five, earlier than the average onset for Parkinson's disease. [52]

Golbe's research implicated genetics again in the pathology of the disorder, [53] given that the Contursi clan shared characteristics common among other genetic disorders such as the intergenerational incidence of the disease with a 50 percent likelihood for the children of the patient to be affected as well, whether male or female. [54] It was finally concluded in 1997 that a mutation in a protein-encoding gene, now called "PARK1," was common among the affected family members. [55]

A Look at Treatment throughout History

After decades of attempts to illustrate, classify, and differentiate symptoms and to elucidate the pathology and progression at the turn of the twentieth century, significant advances in treatment finally emerged. Researchers and scientists have tried various options from neurochemical treatments to surgical measures, having witnessed some degree of success and failures in both types of treatment. One of the earliest treatments recommended was an alkaloid drug that inhibits **acetylcholine**, a neurotransmitter responsible in part for motor controls, principally in the autonomic functions of the basal ganglia. This was prescribed by Charcot and administered in the proceeding decades in different modifications until levodopa therapy emerged. [56]

Learning how the inadequacy of dopamine in the locomotive centers of the brain could lead to Parkinson's disease heralded a huge leap of progress in research. This suddenly put several dopamine researchers in an important place in the successful attempt to synthesize L-dopa in 1911. [57] Shortly afterward, Marcus Guggenheim made a name for himself in 1913 for being the first to isolate L-dopa from sprouts of the fava bean (*Vicia faba*). [58]

Arvid Carlsson, together with his colleagues in Sweden, subjected rabbits to a drug-induced stupor through a suspension of norepinephrine. They showed that these rabbits could be stimulated through L-dopa injection. Traces of dopamine, but not norepinephrine, were found, breaking the prevalent and conventional assumption of dopamine's being converted to norepinephrine. [59] Oleg Hornykiewicz, together with his colleagues in Austria, found that the striatum of patients with Parkinsonism had noticeably low

levels of dopamine.[60] From the end of the 1950s to the early 1960s, Isamu Sano's collaborations resulted in discovering four dopamine-rich areas of the brain, namely the lentiform, the caudate nuclei, the thalamus, and the hypo-thalamus.[61]

Such findings sparked more interest in dopamine, leading to the dopa-mine treatment of Parkinson's disease and schizophrenia. Carlsson found that L-dopa could heighten activity from the central nervous system.[62] A milestone was reached by the tandem team of Walter Birkmayer and Horny-kiewicz, when a significant improvement of symptoms two to three hours after administering levodopa was observed among patients for about twenty-four hours. Symptoms such as tremors, rigidity, and akinesia, or the difficul-ty or inability to start a movement, disappeared.[63] In 1967, dopa as a treat-ment to Parkinsonism was further supported by reports from Georges Cotzias indicating that symptoms abated with the intake of the said drug[64] at high oral dosages. Because of Bob Schwab's breakthrough findings on amanta-dine, development of dopamine agonists began.[65]

It was pointed out, however, that stable results were achievable only after enduring a couple of months of nausea, vomiting, and loss of conscious-ness.[66] Apart from the difficulty of achieving a stable level of responsiveness to levodopa, there has been growing evidence of the unfavorable effects of its long-term usage.[67] Hence, researchers have sought to treat Parkinson's dis-ease through surgical procedures. Prior to the era of administering L-dopa treatment, stereotactic neurosurgery was already taking root in the 1950s to 1960s with the clinical trials involving surgical lesions of different parts of the brain, such as the thalamus and subthalamus, the globus pallidus, and the ansa lenticularis.[68] It was debated at that time whether lesions on the corpus striatum and globus pallidus or ones on the substantia nigra were responsible for Parkinsonism. The debate was further complicated by the possibility that the normal lesions associated with senility were simply affecting some spe-cific nerve cells that led to symptoms of idiopathic Parkinson's.[69]

During an operation on an **aneurysm** in a Parkinsonian patient, Irving Cooper accidentally caused a lesion on the anterior choroidal artery. It brought unprecedented reversal of some symptoms. This discovery led to neurosurgical trials using stereotactic devices to lesion certain parts such as the globus pallidus and ventrolateral thalamic nucleus. With **pallidectomy**, as induced by chemical agents containing alcohol or via cryogenic and ther-mal procedures, symptoms such as rigidity and shaking were reversed. How-ever, other symptoms, such as those affecting speech, gait, posture, and balance either remained unchanged or were exacerbated.[70] Rolf Hassler then introduced thalamotomy as an alternative to pallidotomy.[71] Hassler's post-mortem examination supported Trétiakoff's pioneering correlational studies between Parkinson's disease and the substantia nigra.[72] His contribution led to more positive improvement of symptoms, especially of tremors, which

pallidotomy wasn't successful in lessening. However, pallidotomy was re-
vived after a paper was published evincing reversal of symptoms of those
who had complications from the long-term use of levopoda. Pallidotomy
became the first surgical treatment for Parkinson's disease recognized by the
scientific community, thus becoming globally widespread.[73]

In the past twenty years, the use of high electrical frequency in stimulating the subthalamic nucleus of the brain, called "deep brain stimulation"
(DBS), has garnered a lot of attention as a surgical alternative in the treatment of Parkinson's disease. Patricia Limousin, Alim-Louis Benabid, and
Pierre Pollak laid the groundwork in the research of DBS through which its
safety as a treatment has been demonstrated.[74] Hagai Bergman's group and
Tipu Aziz's with his collaborators independently supported the earlier works
of Limousin, Benabid, and Pollak through monkey models. Significantly
positive results were shown by both of two separate studies in the high-
frequency stimulation of the subthalamus nucleus.[75] Subthalamic DBS was
then favored over pallidotomy, given that its effects may be reversible. On
top of that, it has lesser side effects in comparison with bilateral pallidotomy.[76]

David Marsden's contributions are considered monumental toward advancement of contemporary research.[77] Early in his career, Marsden had
already authored two papers on the tremors of Parkinson's disease published
in *The Lancet*.[78] Over the years, Marsden focused on the functions of the
basal ganglia, and with this topic alone he produced more than eight hundred
reports, reviewed and widely acknowledged by the scientific community. He
was also responsible for pioneering, together with Stan Fahn, specialist journals when they initiated the journal *Movement Disorders*.[79] Together with
Andrew Lees, Marsden launched the first brain bank for Parkinson's disease
in the United Kingdom. David Parkes, David Chadwick, and Marsden also
pioneered the first British clinic specializing in Parkinson's disease. He also
collaborated with Peter Jenner to establish the MPTP (explained in chapter 3)
model of Parkinson's disease on marmosets.[80]

Chapter Two

Fame and Parkinson's

Parkinson's disease, as laypersons know it nowadays, underwent a long history of research before the world reached the current knowledge bank it now has regarding this malady. In Western medical history, the disease is named in honor of the first person to publish a detailed description of the disease chronicling its progressive stages. Nearly two hundred years after James Parkinson described the disease, a lot of notable names have suffered from it.

LIFE OF JAMES PARKINSON

James Parkinson is decidedly one of the most influential persons in science as his contributions really transcend the field of medicine. Parkinson's numerous contributions must have been driven primarily by his staunch desire to be instrumental toward social improvement.[1] He advocated social reforms and empowerment of the marginalized in many of his writings—from the impoverished to women and children.[2]

Personal Life

James Parkinson was born on April 11, 1755, into a family deeply rooted in the study of medicine. He was John Parkinson (1725–1784) and Mary Parkinson's firstborn.[3] He followed in the footsteps of his father, who was a home-based surgeon and pharmacist. James's father himself was known in his chosen profession, having been named anatomical warden or lecturer of the Company of Surgeons.[4] In 1800, the Royal College of Surgeons had supervened over this organization of medical professionals.[5] Two more generations of surgeon-apothecaries followed in the Parkinson family after

James.[6] Based on James's own remarks, it appeared that he had a solid education in the natural and life sciences and in Greek and Latin.[7]

Toward the end of his life, James dedicated himself as a churchwarden in the same church where he was baptized and married. On December 19, 1824, he was suddenly paralyzed on the right side of his body and he suffered from aphasia, a condition that disabled his articulation and language comprehension. Two days later, he passed away. His remains were then laid in an unmarked grave in the cemetery of St. Leonard's Church.[8] Posthumously, James's contributions to science endured. In 1833, transcriptions were published in *Hunterian Reminiscences* through his son John.[9]

Medical Career

James began a life in the medical field when he was only sixteen under his father's apprenticeship,[10] which continued for about six years. His father had an enduring influence on him as a mentor, as James greatly valued the knowledge on anatomy that his father emphasized.[11] The London Hospital eventually accepted James, where he interned for six months as a (wound) dresser.[12]

The Corporation of London assessed and verified James as a qualified surgeon. With his reviving of Brian Maxley, the Royal Humane Society recognized James with the highly distinguished silver medal in 1777. The significance of oxygen in the blood was one of the topics that James delved into in one of his first texts in the medical field, *Observations on Doctor Hugh Smith's Philosophy of the Physic*, published in 1780.[13]

James turned his writing efforts into producing some of the more widely read medical texts as he first had laypersons in mind as his target readers.[14] He published in 1799 two editions of a medical text titled *Medical Admonitions Addressed to Families Respecting the Practice of Domestic Medicine and the Prescription of Health*.[15] In this book, James had tabulated the symptoms of diseases and the extent of risk of each illness in order for laypersons to understand the distinction of one disease from another.[16] In 1800, James dedicated the entire book *The Hospital Pupil or an Essay Intended to Facilitate the Study of Medicine and Surgery* to relating his commentary on the curriculum of medicine.[17] In his time, a student wishing to pursue a career in a medical subject such as Parkinson's was faced with the fate of years of drudging apothecary duties, which were only remotely related to the skills needed as a modern physician. James intensely despised the system and could not have made a more stringent call for educational reform.[18] It was also in this book that he first proposed the system of certifying lunacy by at least two doctors.[19]

In 1802, James published two works with the titles *The Way to Health* and *Hints for the Improvement of Trusses*. The text *Mr. Whitbread's Plans*

for the Re-education of the Poor came out in 1804.[20] In 1805, James, having contracted gout himself at the age of thirty,[21] described the characteristics, etiology, diagnosis, and treatment possibilities of the malady.[22] He suggested that the etiology of gout can be traced in uric acid salts, which at that time was found to be too ridiculous of an idea.[23] It was in this work that James's interests in geology and his medical background merged as he demonstrated how gout dissection from the foot was similar to the retrieval of a fossil.[24] Also, in this medical text he expressed his motivations for putting into writing his observations—for the benefit of the people likewise suffering from it.[25]

In 1812, James—with his son as coauthor—featured the first scientifically documented case in English of appendicitis. The medical paper was entitled "Case of Diseased Appendix Vermiformis."[26] The patient was a five-year-old boy whose health was deteriorating but didn't report any complaint. He suffered from vomiting, intense fatigue, and agonizing abdominal pain for two days before death.[27]

The "Advent" of Parkinson's Disease

In 1817, James published his observations of six patients suffering from what was initially labeled as "shaking palsy." He remarked that many learned physicians had already taken note of the condition, such as Galen, Juncker, and Cullen,[28] though the initial descriptions were not sufficient. Other movement disorders were also ascribed to shaking palsy, such as a fright-induced tremor in the right arm comorbid with an intense stomachache as described by Thomas Kirkland. Another case also categorized as a shaking palsy was what appeared to be worm infestation of a twelve-year-old boy suffering from uncontrollable shaking.[29] However, James desired to specify the affliction as characterized by the resting tremor. To further distinguish this disease, which he termed *paralysis agitans*, he also described the gradual course of the disease and the tumultuous gait that accompanies it.[30] According to James's description, a first symptom that may be noted is weakness and shaking in one of the arms that may be initially negligible to the patient. But within a year or less, the initial symptom will radiate to other parts. More or less, in another quarter of a year, the patient's posture will also give in.[31] James speculated that the disease's pathology could be traced to stress.[32]

OTHER FAMOUS NAMES IN PARKINSON'S

Galen, De la Boe, Trousseau, and Charcot

Perhaps among the key features of Parkinson's disease, tremor must have aroused the interest of scientists and physicians the earliest, given its con-

spicuousness. If tremors were the topic, records show that as early as the Middle Ages, Galen had already described the involuntary motor movement and suggested that psychological distress, such as that originating from intense fear or clinical depression, and muscle failure were the causes.[33] In his essay, James Parkinson credited Sylvius de la Boe for the early recognition of tremors and for his successful treatment of them.[34] The same was done by Charcot, who observed tremors exhibited at rest and in motion.[35] With the help of his students, Charcot proposed two types of Parkinsonism, which he called "tremorous" and "**akinetic-rigid**"[36] as he believed the two to be distinct as a result of his observations.

Armand Trousseau highlighted rigidity in his *15th Lecture on Clinical Medicine*, which centered discussion on paralysis agitans and senile tremors. This characteristic was hardly touched by Parkinson, giving Trousseau the credit for acknowledging it.[37] While it was Charcot who identified bradykinesia, or markedly slow movement, as a main symptom of Parkinson's disease,[38] it was Trousseau who had first provided a clear clinical description of it.[39] He also contradicted Parkinson's claim that the intellect remains unaffected by the disease as he reported that memory is eventually lost.[40]

On the other hand, Charcot determined that bradykinesia was independent of the other cardinal characteristics.[41] He also added detailed descriptions of the other symptoms such as slow-paced, halting speech, unstoppable locomotion,[42] and the failure of the autonomic nervous system with accompanying pain.[43] One hallmark observation that Charcot contributed was the delay between the patient's intention and the intended act. Both Troussseau and Charcot noted the memory loss during the last years of the disease and the pneumonia that ends the life of the patients.[44]

Van Gehuchten, Hoehn, and Yahr

It was a Belgian neurologist whose works were seminal in the film documentation of Parkinson's disease and other neurological disorders and who was also a trailblazer in multimedia instruction. Arthur Van Gehuchten (1861–1914) began filming his patients from 1905 until his death in 1914. He took a hands-on approach, from the filming and developing of the footage to the postprocessing. His passion was strongly reflected in the volume of his film outputs. Parkinson's disease was discussed in thirteen pages, ten images, with twelve patients on film. Van Gehuchten demonstrated the symptoms of neurological disorders to his students using these videos, which were far more reinforcing in the study than illustrations or photographs.[45] Margaret Hoehn and Melvin Yahr became highly notable in research because of their discussion of the progression of the symptoms and mortality of Parkinson's disease patients, cementing their legacy through international recognition of the Hoehn-Yahr Scale.[46]

Gowers and Lewy

Given the effects of the disease on motor control, it was not surprising for many researchers such as William R. Gowers, a British neurologist, to attribute pathology in the motor cortex.[47] One of the parts of the brain with significant control on motion is the basal ganglia, the nuclei of which were of interest to Frederic Lewy, an American neurologist. He made a name in the study of Parkinson's disease when he reported abnormalities in the caudate and lenticular nuclei of basal ganglia.[48] This was among the first reports to implicate the basal ganglia in the pathology of Parkinson's disease.

Brissaud and Others

At the time that nothing was known about the anatomy of the substantia nigra, Edouard Brissaud, a student of Charcot, speculated that damage in that part of the brain may well be the cause of Parkinson's disease.[49] This hypothesis was actually a result of the collaboration of the Romanian neurologist Georges Marinesco and pathologist Paul Oscar Blocq. Marinesco, a student of Charcot, as Brissaud was, together with Blocq, examined a thirty-eight-year-old patient suffering from muscle rigidity and tremors. They found lesions on the subtantia nigra and attributed the patient's Parkinsonism symptoms to these lesions. Under Marinesco, Constantin Trétiakoff, a Russian neuropathologist, trained and studied the physiopathology of Parkinsonism. Trétiakoff's doctoral thesis was notable for the meticulous descriptions of the substantia nigra in nine brains with Parkinson's disease and three brains with postencephalitic Parkinsonism. He compared these brains with normal brains and found that there was less pigmentation among the neurons in the substantia nigra. He concluded that there is a significant correlation between Parkinson's disease and lesions in substantia nigra.[50] Brissaud took over Charcot's lectures at La Salpêtrière. In one of his lectures in 1895, Brissaud claimed that muscle tone is controlled by the substantia nigra.[51]

CELEBRITIES AND PARKINSON'S

Celebrities who have suffered from Parkinson's disease including the following:

- Terry Thomas, actor[52]
- Ulysses Kay, musician[53]
- Muhammad Ali, boxing great
- Abe Lemons, college basketball coach[54]
- Prince Claus of the Netherlands[55]
- Pope John Paul II[56]

- Donald Pederson, famed electrical engineer[57]
- Theodore Edison, son of inventor Thomas Edison[58]
- Michael J. Fox, actor
- Janet Reno, former US attorney general
- George Roy Hill, film director[59]
- Bud Greenspan, film producer[60]

That said, Parkinson's disease has had a very long history in which Nobel laureates to directors and actors to sportsmen have been affected. It shows that Parkinson's disease can affect any individual, whether famous or not.

Chapter Three

Anatomy and Physiology of Parkinson's

The first cohesive anatomical and physiological description of disease characterized by hand tremors and other problems was made by British doctor James Parkinson in 1817. Later, this disorder of neurological pathology was found to lead to the destruction of neurons and was caused by variable exogenous factors such as those discussed in the next chapter. Parkinson's is, in fact, the result of several anatomical and physiological processes, different in their roles in the disease. Some of these processes are still unknown and currently being investigated. One example is the strengthening of free radical oxidation in the elderly when the disease is usually detected (fifty- to sixty-year-olds). Death of these important brain cells causes a reduction in synthesis of the organic chemical called dopamine, which plays innumerable roles in the physiology of people. The initial physiological sign of Parkinson's disease is minor shaking of limbs occurring in stressful situations and disappearing after that. The clinical symptoms soon ascend, including a kind of posture that possibly reminds one of a mannequin. Speed of body movements is slowed, and sometimes, early immobility can occur.

ANATOMY OF PARKINSON'S

Cognitive and Anatomical Factors

Researching the possible methods of treatment for curing the disorders encompassed by Parkinson's disease requires a very deep knowledge of the brain's anatomy to understand the character of possible destructions and their influence on the patient's life and behavior. Moreover, the main anatomical

changes caused by Parkinson's disease first affect the different groups of the brain's neurons. Destruction of these important brain cells leads to the advent of well-known symptoms characterizing Parkinson's disease. Symptoms are dependent on a damaged part of the brain and its otherwise normal responsibility for specific movements or abilities. Generally, the human brain is an organized structure, which is divided into a number of components. Their responsibilities are to serve the most important functions of organisms, mainly so-called cognitive functions. Cognitive functions of the brain assist people's ability to learn, to process, and to perceive (to store, to use, to transfer) incoming information. They are the functions of the highest nervous activity projected by the central nervous system, and without these important abilities, a person's identity is lost.

Reduced cognitive and other neurological functions can present themselves during Parkinson's disease. Disruption of the processes of communication between cortex and subcortical structures plays a critical role in the mechanism leading to Parkinson's disease development. Disorder of the neurotransmitter systems can be described as the degeneration of dopaminergic neurons with a decreased amount of dopamine and related molecules, as well as decreased activity of other (such as noradrenergic) neurons. Exocytotoxic process (death of neurons) starts. Generally, the brain consists of the cerebral cortex, brainstem, and **cerebellum**. While the cerebral cortex forms both the left and right hemispheres, lesion of the left hemisphere of the PD patient may cause the following:

- **Aphasia** (inability to speak)
- **Dyscalculia** (inability to count)
- Inhibited mathematical ability
- Alexia (inability to read)
- Broken logic and analysis
- **Agraphia** (inability to write)
- Letter agnosia (nonrecognition of letters)
- **Apraxia** (disorder of purposeful movements)

Lesion of the right hemisphere can cause the following:

- Visual-spatial disorders
- Inability to fantasize or dream
- Disorientation of space
- Inability to perceive a situation as a whole

Cognitive disorders depend on a patient's age, the duration of the disease, motor damage severity, and related emotional and behavioral disease. Cognitive issues, regardless of the anatomical makeup of the patient, can happen

throughout the early stages of Parkinson's disease and could be temporary. However, with the development of the disease, the destruction of cognitive processes occurs, too, and in some cases, it can reach the level of **dementia** (feeblemindedness).

Anatomical Factors of the Brain Lobes

Undoubtedly, it is very important to know the various areas of the brain and the possible consequences of their destruction that can be traced to Parkinson's disease. The functional areas of the brain lobes are the speech and motor areas.[1] These regions also have dopaminergic properties and connect with basal ganglia and **dopaminergic neurons**. There are two related speech centers, which are mainly located in the left hemisphere. The lobe area situated on the lowest part of the left frontal brain cortex is responsible for producing speech. Its destruction leads to complete or partial loss of the ability to speak, but the Parkinson's sufferer with this type of damage understands words that others speak. In the upper part of the left temporal lobe is a center responsible for understanding speech. Damages in this part of the cortex make the ability to understand speech unavailable. The Parkinson's sufferer with this type of damage does not understand the interlocutor's words but can still speak fluently. The patient also does not understand the meaning of his or her own words and often produces completely meaningless speech. People with Parkinson's disease almost always suffer from problems with speech caused by destruction of these centers. The motor zones are situated on the back of the frontal lobes of both hemispheres. The left-hand motor area controls the movements of the right side of the body, and the right-hand motor area is responsible for the movement of the left side of the body. Destruction in the motor center leads to different motion problems, shaking palsy, tremor, and rigidity during Parkinson's disease. The motor dysfunction always manifests itself earlier than any other symptoms, and the disease usually begins with the smallest signs of movement complications such as the following:

- Bradykinesia (slow and hindered movements)
- Small tremors reminding one of counting coins
- Oligokinesia (rapid decreased amplitude and velocity of the repeated movements)
- Hypokinesia (reduced physical activity)
- **Plastic muscular hypertonicity** such as muscle stiffness

Moreover, the following symptoms can be observed as a result of problems in the Parkinson's patient's brain lobes: (1) nasal voice and blurred speech, (2) stiffness and awkwardness in movements, (3) stooped posture,

(4) changes in walking gait in the form of shuffling, small steps, with absence of other related movements such as hand wags, (5) poor facial expression in the form of infrequent blinking, and (6) changes in handwriting such as trembling when writing small letters.

Cognitive problems taking place in the lobes of brains with Parkinson's disease always aggravate clinical appearance and accelerate the onset of disability. Each lobe contains the structures controlling its own inherent limb's activity. All the brain's lobes play important anatomical and physiological roles in almost all cognitive processes, such as memory, attention, intent, expressive speech, abstract thinking, and planning. The frontal lobe is responsible for the most of functions, including motor skills, for example, voluntary movement, speech, intelligence, behavior, memory, concentration, temperament, and personality. Almost all people have the speech center located in the left frontal lobe, with only a small percentage having it in the right frontal lobe. Parkinson's disease sufferers are no exception. The motor area that is located in the back side of the frontal lobe controls the movement of the limbs on the opposite side of the body. The occipital lobe is situated on the back part of the brain, and its function allows people to receive and process visual material. It also helps in distinguishing colors and different shapes. The right part of the occipital lobe receives information obtained from the left visual area, while the left is responsible for the right visual area in both eyes.

The parietal lobe helps interpret and analyze the signals received from the other areas of the brain, such as vision, hearing, motor, sensor, memory signs. Orientation function and the ability to count depends on the right parietal lobe, whereas reading is regulated by the left parietal lobe. Perception of heat, cold, and pain is available in both parietal lobes. The temporal lobe sits almost at ear level and can be divided into two parts. One part is situated on the lower surface of each cerebral hemisphere, and the other part is on its side. The left region is involved in verbal memory and gives humans the ability to remember and to understand language. The central part of the temporal lobe helps one to interpret other people's emotions and reactions. Temporal lobes process auditory sensors and convert sounds into words understandable to people. A small area of the brain on the inner surface of the temporal lobes, called the *hippocampus*, controls long-term memory functions. Another main structure of the brain called the *brainstem* is found near the cerebellum and the spinal cord's border. The brainstem consists of three structures: midbrain, pons, and medulla oblongata.

The midbrain is an important center for the regulation of eye movements, while the pons is involved in the coordination of eye movements and rotations, facial movements, hearing, and balance. The substantia nigra is also located here, and its cells contain the black-colored pigment called *melanin*. This pigment exists only in human brains and starts being produced at three

to four years of age. The substantia nigra receives impulses from the cerebral cortex and striatum. In turn, the substantia nigra sends those impulses to the collicular neurons and nucleus of the brainstem, and after that, to the spinal cordial motor neurons, which are responsible for motion. Thus, the substantia nigra plays an important role in the integration of all movements and in the regulation of muscle tone. Axons of the nerve cells located in the substantia nigra make up the nigrostriatal pathway. Anatomical distortion of the cells of the substantia nigra, or any of its structures or functions, leads to Parkinson's disease.

Brain Parts Affected

All forms of Parkinson's disease start with a sudden reduction in the quantity of dopamine in the substantia nigra. The main reason for this is probably the activation of a genetically programmed mechanism. The structures surrounding the thalamus and containing the clusters of the brain's nerve cells called the basal ganglia are the most affected during Parkinson's disease.[2] This is scientifically confirmed for the majority of cases having clearly displayed clinical symptoms of Parkinson's, although those symptoms can be found in other neuropathological disorders such as supranuclear palsy, autonomic disturbances, or other cerebellar symptoms.[3]

Before the first symptoms of Parkinson's disease arrive, the pathological process will have already been progressing, on average, for five years. At the time that symptoms appear, the quantity of dopamine in the striatum modulating the activity of the thalamic pathway as well as the motor activity of patients reduces by up to 70 percent of the normal amount, as demonstrated by postmortem examination of the patient's brain.[4] Microscopic analysis of samples taken from this damaged substantia nigra demonstrates the reduction of melanin pigmentation, loss of the affected neurons, and surge of the Lewy bodies (harmful aggregates of alpha-synuclein protein) in most of the neuronal cells. Naturally, neuronal degeneration also presents with aging, but during Parkinson's disease, it progresses several times higher.

Dopaminergic Neurons and Their Anatomical Role

Dopaminergic neurons are situated not only in the substantia nigra but also in the midbrain structures, including the nucleus accumbens, which hinders the cognitive limbic-reticular complex. Dopamine released in the nucleus accumbens plays an important role in triggering the reactions of approximation, such as flexible nervous response and skills of avoidance. The dopaminergic neurons in the substantia nigra provide the synthesis of dopamine, and the axons of neurons in the nigrostriatal pathway produce a substantial amount of the brain's dopamine. In the peripheral nervous system, dopamine is a

precursor of norepinephrine, which is a major neurotransmitter in the sympathetic nervous system. In mammalian and especially human central nervous systems, dopamine has independent and very important mediator functions. Notwithstanding the production of norepinephrine, changes in the concentration of dopamine lead to the reduced metabolism of other neurotransmitters such as serotonin, acetylcholine, and glutamate. When there is too much glutamate, **excitotoxicity** can occur. Managing the psychomotor processes at the level of the striatum is closely connected to exchange of dopamine, a process highly affected in Parkinson's disease.

Decreased dopaminergic activities and increased activities of the glutamic and cholinergic systems in the striatum lead to disorders discernible by motor disabilities seen in Parkinson's disease. Destruction of dopamine neurons in the so-called dopaminergic pleasure pathway of the limbic system, particularly in the ventral tegmental area, leads to a gradual reduction of patient's motivation and energy, a reduced ability to feel positive emotions (**anhedonia**), and ultimately to the development of chronic depression.

Destruction of dopaminergic neurons in the frontal lobes of the cortex leads to developed intellectual disorders such as lost memory, reduced intellectual productivity, inability to learn, and possibly a future appearance of dementia. During the late stages of Parkinson's disease, organic psychosis with hallucinations, paranoia, or chronic delirium (disorientation in time and place, confusion, hallucinations, delusions) can happen. Most of these disorders can also be caused by medication. The primary dopaminergic pathways or centers of the brain are the limbic, oculomotor, associative, and orbitofrontal. Each and every one of these pathways is responsible for the separate systems of the organism connected with its name. Dopaminergic pathways have a somewhat limited anatomical distribution in the brain, and that is why the main treatment of Parkinson's disease lies in increasing the activity of these dopaminergic systems directly. The methods of such direct actions consist of (1) treatment by administering the dopamine's precursor levopoda (L-dopa) and medicines containing it, (2) using the **DOPA-decarboxylase inhibitors** that are reducing the lack of dopamine in the striatum, and (3) including the dopaminergic agonists in the overall treatment regimen. Nevertheless, increased dopaminergic invasion not only leads to controlling the **extrapyramidal system** but also compounds the different side effects of dopamine for the central nervous system, such as **gag reflex**, decreased **prolactin** secretion, and some psychotic symptoms. Prolonged approach by dopa-containing drugs also can cause various types of dyskinesia. However, the natural psychotic disorders, which are not provoked by dopaminergic medication, have a relatively subordinate role among the physiological aspects of Parkinson's disease.

More on the Anatomy of Parkinson's

Many scientists believe that notwithstanding nigrostriatal dopaminergic and mesolimbic pathways, there is a very special *peripheral* dopaminergic system. In everyone, including PD patients, dopamine causes the series of reactions which are unresponsive to classic adrenergic stimulation, for example, dilation of blood vessels in kidneys and organismal mesentery. Dopamine possibly manufactured by kidneys and gathering in high concentrations in urine may also participate in dopaminergic mediating effects in the urinary and other body systems. The nature of the peripheral dopaminergic system is not entirely clear, and there is no confirmed evidence of autonomic peripheral dopaminergic nerves, although their presence in the kidneys is likely possible.

PHYSIOLOGICAL APPROACHES AND THEIR IMPORTANCE

All forms of Parkinson's are divided into two main physiological groups: (1) idiopathic Parkinson's disease, or simply Parkinson's disease, and (2) secondary Parkinsonism, or a complex of symptoms characterizing Parkinson's: toxic, medical, posttraumatic, vascular, or a complication of encephalitis. A noteworthy pathological (when physiology is somehow corrupted) hallmark of Parkinson's disease detected during clinical tests is the availability of abnormal cellular inclusions called Lewy bodies.[5] Lewy bodies arise as the result of destruction in the neuron's skeleton and look similar to a system of microtubules. Quantity of Lewy bodies is variable from patient to patient and can be distinguished by using special medical dyes. Currently, successfully developed principles and methods of treating the disease can give gradual improvement of a patient's and (by extension) caregiver's health. These methods of treatment have to be based on different research, including the current understanding of the physiological aspects underlying the disease.

Understanding the Physiology of Parkinson's

It is important to know the pathophysiology of Parkinson's disease and to devise corresponding treatment. Many proven physiological disorders are the byproducts of symptoms, and every extrapyramidal disorder, including Parkinson's, serves as a model of subcortical lesions in brain structures. Physiological mechanisms of Parkinson's disease are not limited only by nigrostriatal complexes, and functional disorders are present at different levels of the nervous system when speaking from an anatomical standpoint.

One of the main approaches in the therapy of Parkinson's disease is through the physiology of body reflexes, which can be abnormal due to neurological disorders of the brain. The basis of the unconditioned response

in a Parkinson's patient is the physiological reflex arc, which includes pathways from the brain's memory center and to the center of interaction of the sympathetic and parasympathetic nervous systems. Normal physiological unconditioned reflex becomes *pathological* unconditioned reflex when the former starts to operate with some aberration induced by disorders or cell destruction.

In other words, a myriad of irritants leads to the genesis of reflexes. For example, touching any hot surface will cause the Parkinson's patient to immediately withdraw his or her hand. This is one of the innate, unconditioned physiological reflexes. If people were to react to all irritants, then every time there was an unconditioned reflex, there could be a variety of involuntary movements. A healthy brain's neurons provide the reaction only to sufficient irritants, not to minor ones. Neurons damaged by Parkinson's disease cannot provide the normal physiological unconditioned reflex, and things soon turn pathological. Consequently, the patient suffers from tremor, shaking, and other irregular responses from even the smallest irritants in ways that normal organisms never would. Prolonged prevalence of pathologic unconditioned reflex leads to the development of various aggravations and degrees of severity of Parkinson's disease.

Necessary Interaction between Physiological Approaches

Restoration of physiological unconditioned reflex interactions leads to the same restoration of sympathetic and parasympathetic nervous systems and their effects on the extrapyramidal nervous system. This restoration can be achieved after manual stimulation, including exposure to particular stimuli continuously arriving from the peripheral regions that have disorders. That is why a comprehensive physiological approach involves not only the general areas of the brain but also the cortical and subcortical levels, causing a number of positive **vasomotor** and hormonal changes. The goal of Parkinson's treatment from a physiological standpoint centers on (1) lesions and (2) the ability to develop compensatory mechanisms by activating the intact but previously inactive neural structures in damaged limbs as well as the brain. This whole process leads to improved spinal circulation and activity of motor neurons. Neuronal cells that are still mostly alive in the patient's brain and that belong to the extrapyramidal nervous system will be able to produce the compensating amount of mediators such as dopamine. Step by step, these dopamine mediators increase normal physiological unconditioned reflex and result in reducing the development of Parkinson's disease. Effectiveness of physiological treatment can be seen by sufficient improvement of the patient's motor and psychological conditions. For instance, Parkinson's disease sufferers begin to move better, they need less assistance, and they become more active. Treatments have to be initiated at the earliest stages and be

combined. Examples of stimulators that have an overall impact on the body via physical factors are varied and include baths, heliotherapy, climate therapy, massage, and different physiotherapeutic methods such as magnet therapy, microwave therapy, electrophoresis of the solutions containing levodopa, and hydrogen sulfide or radon baths.

Neurophysiologic approaches are very important because the clinical symptoms of Parkinson's disease are the reason for serious destruction in the brain, which can be slightly reduced by special medicines such as levodopa. The chief problem in controlling the disease by medicines is the eventual dopaminergic medication's failure, in which case the patient exhibits dyskinesia and different side effects, which happens in 75 percent of patients after five years of treatment.[6] Physiological medicines can also depress the ability of neurons still alive in the patient's brain to produce the compensative mediators.

Physiological Changes in the Parkinsonian Brain

Reasons behind the death of neurons that produce dopamine are: (1) the combinations of different degrees of genetic predisposition, (2) environmental factors, and (3) aging observed in each patient's case. William Gowers (see chapter 2) noted that heredity in Parkinsonism is a factor in no more than 15 percent of cases and is transmitted by an autosomal dominant pattern.[7] Experts attribute Parkinson's disease to pathophysiologic atrophy. Concerning environmental factors, first place currently goes to the intravenous consumption of surrogate drugs. Medications such as **meperidine** often contain the admixture of its byproduct's synthesis, which is abbreviated as MTP (1-methyl-4-phenyl-1,2,3,6-tetrahydropyridine). This is a chemical substance capable of destroying, selectively, only the dopaminergic neurons in the substantia nigra. As for infectious diseases causing transient and persistent symptoms of Parkinsonism, the leading culprits are influenza, measles, Coxsackie encephalitis, and Japanese encephalitis.

Primary age-related physiological factors of Parkinson's include (1) degeneration of neurons in the substantia nigra, (2) identification of Lewy bodies at autopsy in more than 45 percent of cases in the elderly, (3) reduction of the concentration of dopamine, **striatal tyrosine hydroxylase**, and the number of dopamine receptors, and (4) a higher rate of deterioration of the nigrostriatal function of Parkinson's patients in comparison with older but healthy people. According to the currently accepted point of view, mesocortical and mesolimbic systems are involved in the mechanisms of memory and learning. Extensive analysis of the physiological role of the nigrostriatal dopaminergic system shows that managing the processes of motor striatum is closely linked with the exchange of dopamine.[8]

There are two dopaminergic systems in the brain: the **nigrostriatal dopaminergic pathway** and the **mesolimbic pathway**. Both of them can be affected by Parkinson's. Degeneration ascended from the so-called nigrostriatal dopaminergic pathway is mostly responsible for the development and progression of Parkinson's disease. Concurrently, this degeneration can take place at different levels of anatomy and physiology. One way is when synthesis of dopamine in the dopaminergic neurons of the substantia nigra get disrupted. The disorder can also affect the dopaminergic pathway, starting from the place of dopaminergic synthesis. Recently produced dopamine is transported by cells moving to the caudate body, and there the dopamine concentrates in front of the presynaptic membranes. Normally, nervous impulses circulating in the neural system force the dopamine to go through the synaptic cleft. Part of this dopamine is involved in providing the postsynaptic membrane's depolarization, part absorbs back into the presynaptic space, and part is often destroyed by special enzymes (COMT—**catechol-O-methyltransferase**—or MAO-B—**monoamine oxidase type B**). Each of these stages can be affected during Parkinson's disease.

Neuronal complexes damaged in various areas of the brain during the development of Parkinson's disease can be conventionally divided into two physiological groups. The first one directly provides an immediate inhibitory effect on the brain's putamen (the internal segment of the globus pallidus). The second one is indirect, and it provides the "backdoor" activating effect of the subthalamic nucleus on the globus pallidus. The main types of dopamine receptors are D1 and D2 receptors, but there are also D3, D4, and D5 receptors. They are all positioned mostly on the postsynaptic membrane. Dopamine has a modulating effect on neurons of the neostriatum. With D1 receptors, modulation is more direct than with D2 receptors.

The mechanism of pathophysiological processes in the brain during Parkinson's disease is connected to oxidative stress for cells, surfacing alongside defects of dopaminergic metabolism due to the advent of different physiological byproducts such as hydroxyl radicals, hydrogen peroxide, and superoxide anions in cells and intercellular space. Lipid peroxidation of certain cells leads to destruction of their membranes and starts the process of cellular death, primarily through the mechanisms of **apoptosis** and **necrosis**. The processes of a cell's death can be attributed to toxins on the nervous system receptor's cells that "throw off" cell calcium regulators. In turn, amino acids, especially **glutamate**, (1) damage the nigrostriatal system and (2) their high activities and concentrations through so-called **NMDA receptors** launch the series of pathological courses causing the degeneration of the Parkinsonian patient's dopaminergic neurons.

II

Clinical Picture

Chapter Four

Causes of Parkinson's Disease

Throughout the years, Parkinson's disease has been one of those disorders with supposed etiologies (causes) that have been (1) talked about, (2) drawing the attention of medical practitioners, and (3) feared by those who are facing old age. Many contend that Parkinson's disease is experienced only by people fifty and above (old age).[1] Furthermore, the damage of brain neurons is actually normal with aging, but those neurons are supposed to be repaired naturally by the body to a certain degree. In the case of Parkinson's, cells degenerate or die faster and are not being mended or replaced. Amazingly, only those neurons in the substantia nigra are affected, while those neurons in other parts of the brain continue to survive even when a person has the disease. The death of the neurons has been known to science and medical practitioners for quite some time, but the answer to the question, "What causes the death of the neurons?" is still vague. Efforts to find the root cause of the death of the neurons are made in the hope that, if the cause of the disease can be pointed out, the cure for the disease can be made possible and individuals can finally be released from the anxiety of having the disease. Most importantly, deciphering the cause can cure those who already have the ailment and relieve them and their families from the sufferings that Parkinson's has brought them. Even though the exact cause of the damage or eventual death of neurons is not yet proved, there are factors that might explain the deterioration of brain neurons, including (1) genes, (2) environmental factors, and (3) free radicals.[2] Some also believe that age, gender, and ethnicity might be correlated to the occurrence of Parkinson's disease,[3] while others posit that one may also have Parkinson's disease due to prior head injuries and intake of drugs (medication) that lower the dopaminergic activity in the brain.[4] Viral infections can also somehow "cause" Parkinson's disease.[5]

GENETIC CONNECTION

If and when a family member is diagnosed, other members might possibly be anxious and worried that they might also have the disease. There are many disputes about the role of genes in the occurrence of Parkinson's disease since the possibility that the apparently causal genetic makeup of Parkinson's disease in the late 1990s was recognized due to the discovery of the specific genes of a particular family in Europe, with family members having been diagnosed as suffering from Parkinson's.[6] Together with the continual studies to find the cure for Parkinson's disease are the constant efforts to understand the underlying role of one's genes to Parkinson's. Family members have genes that somehow have some similarities. This led to the assumption that Parkinson's can run in the family or, in other words, be inherited. Many of these assumptions are not yet proved to be true; instead, medical science has found that Parkinson's disease does not necessarily run in the family. Rather, statistical data on the number of diagnosed patients with kin that also have the disease imply that it only places relatives at higher risk compared with other individuals in the population. In fact, 15 percent of the identified number of patients diagnosed with Parkinson's disease are found to have blood relatives suffering from the same disease.[7]

Inner Workings

Details matter, so at this point a closer look and deeper understanding of the part that genes play in Parkinson's is called for. What people know from biology and other areas of science is that genes make up the DNA "blueprint" of organisms such as humans and serve as the link between generations. They supply the coded instructions for the manufacture of protein, which is very important in order for the PD patient's body to take on its biological functions. An alteration or mutation of the genetic codes can contribute to the development of Parkinson's disease. Scientists have already identified a number of gene mutations that might put individuals and family members having similarities in their genetic makeup at higher risk of acquiring Parkinson's. These include the PARK1 through PARK10 genes, which affect the following chromosomal proteins, respectively: (1) alpha-synuclein, (2) parkin, (3) 2p13, (4) alpha-synuclein, (5) UCHL1, (6) PINK1, (7) DJ-1, (8) 12p11.2–q13.1, (9) HtrA2, and (10) 1p32.[8] A newly identified gene believed to cause Parkinson's disease is EIF4G1,[9] but compared with the genes listed above, which take part in the dopaminergic cell function, EIF4G1 help cells to cope with different forms of stress (biological stress) by controlling the levels of protein in the brain. A mutation of EIF4G1 will produce a defective EIF4G1 protein that serves as a "coping strategy" of the central nervous system against stress.

The alteration of the genes causes changes in the natural cell processes and hampers cells from implementing natural functions, such as when the PRKN or PRKN2 gene provides the instruction in the manufacture of a protein called **parkin**. Parkin helps in preventing protein buildup in the brain that could possibly lead to the impairment of dopamine-producing cells. A group of scientists has conducted simple experiments using mice in which the scientists altered the dopamine-producing cells of the rodents. The effect in mice was equal to that of the Parkinson's disease patient's impaired or involuntary movements, and, most significantly, the dopamine-producing neurons died abruptly.[10] It was found in the experiment that modifying such cells lessens the activity of mTOR enzymes[11] (proteins instigating biochemical reactions of the body) that regulate the intracellular signaling pathways, interrupting the function of the **mitochondria** (cell parts providing energy).[12] Furthermore, the reduction of the mTOR activity brings about oxidative stress in the cells of the Parkinson's patient.[13] Due to oxidative stress, highly sensitive oxygen compounds aggregate and damage many different molecules in the cell. Also, the researchers believe that this could be responsible for the nerve damage in Parkinson's disease because dopamine-producing neurons are found to be sensitive to oxidative stress.[14] Oxidative stress factors such as Lewy bodies, commonly observed in the impaired or dead neurons in the brain of Parkinson's patients, accumulate in the neurons and thereby attract other proteins that form harmful buildups in the brain.[15] This finding leads to another interesting hypothesis regarding the cause of neuron impairment and death, known as the *oxidation hypothesis*, or simply *oxidation*,[16] discussed later in this chapter. Free radicals also cause the alteration of human genes. Free radicals hit cells and their DNA thousands of times in a day, but the alteration or mutation of the genes is possible only when the DNA has been hit by free radicals and is not able to repair the damage immediately, before it is struck again by another free radical.[17]

Only 15–20 percent of diagnosed Parkinson's patients have a history of the disease in their family.[18] In the case of twins, some studies demonstrate that if either twin is diagnosed with Parkinson disease, the other twin has a greater chance of developing the disease if the twins are identical and not fraternal twins.[19] Going back to the question, "Can Parkinson's disease get passed down to or inherited by other family members?" it is important to note that genetic mutation is not seen as the sole reason for Parkinson's disease; it is also connected to environmental toxins unnaturally utilized by the body. Environmental toxins, whether internal or external, can lead to a modification of the genes and, as explained via scientific evaluation, Parkinson's disease could not be inherited per se, but altered genes responsible for the long-term progression of Parkinson's *can* be passed down to generations of a certain family affected by the disease.

THE CONTRIBUTION OF THE ENVIRONMENT TO PARKINSON'S

Environment is believed to nurture and mold people into what they are today and will be tomorrow. With this in mind, research shows that Parkinson's disease can be partially attributed to some environmental risk factors. Back when there were comparably fewer environmental toxins in the atmosphere, there were fewer cases of Parkinson's in comparison to today's figures. Scientists believe Parkinson's disease was not so common decades ago and that it began being observed as late as the early 1800s. This leads to the question, "What is in the environment today that makes the occurrence of Parkinson's disease rise to such a point?" The answer can be found in the increasing levels of environmental toxins that can be traced to the beginning of the Industrial Revolution, when manual labor was partially supplanted by machinery.[20] It is nonetheless very difficult to determine the number of Parkinson's patients before the Industrial Revolution due to the lack of records of the disease's incidence; consequently, it is difficult to prove a more *direct* relation of the Industrial Revolution to Parkinson's. Nevertheless, environmental toxin levels *have* increased tremendously as a result of the Industrial Revolution. Environmental toxins are chemicals that can cause harm to living organisms. These environmental toxins are commonly byproducts from machines and other technological advancements.

Environmental toxins have long been found to cause some known illnesses, but their uninterrupted role in causing Parkinson's disease is also under intensive study, exactly like the potentially similar role of defective genes. Exposure to toxins such as manganese, carbon monoxide, carbon disulfide, pesticides,[21] and herbicides, as well as wood pulp mills, may increase the risk for developing Parkinson's disease.[22] Rural living environments are also under scrutiny since many farming technologies and industries are found in these areas. Life in rural areas can also require ownership and longer use of certain technologies compared with life in urban places. Rural life also entails the consumption of more processed foods that contain possible toxins that could harm the body. In addition to the pollution present in the environment, radiation, smoke, other chemicals acquired from processed food, medicines, drugs, and other chemicals are absorbed by the body through many different means. As these toxins are taken in through the body, they tend to deteriorate healthy cells such as neurons (cells in the brain). The brain is constantly affected by thousands of toxins damaging the neurons, though they are quickly repaired through the help of antioxidants. The repairs ideally take place before toxins (1) damage the neurons and possibly (2) alter genetic constituents. Similar to the genetic "cause" of Parkinson's, environmental factors only increase the risk of acquiring the disease, and this possibility is very small because preliminary exposure to toxins is not enough to cause the disease in a deliberate way. *Prolonged* exposure to environmental

toxins augments the risk of having Parkinson's by some percentage.[23] For example, farmers are exposed on a prolonged basis to severe toxins such as strong pesticides. Such toxins also include internal toxins and not just those found in the surrounding environment (external toxins). Some toxins are readily available in the form of offshoots of biochemical processes that naturally occur in the body.

The Oxidation Hypothesis

The oxidation hypothesis has garnered the attention of researchers, scientists, and medical practitioners. It explains and answers many, but not all, questions pertaining to the development of Parkinson's disease. This hypothesis implies that **free radicals**, chemicals with unstable electron configurations, react with other chemicals to replace absent electrons to form a new compound so that they can be stable.[24] Since free radicals lack an electron in their normal state, they gain a positive charge and attract other chemicals to accumulate in the brain of the Parkinson's patient. This damages the cell lining and eventually leads to cell death through the destruction of the mitochondria, mentioned previously.[25] While oxidation is caused by unstable compounds that lack an electron (free radicals), where do these unstable compounds originate? Oxidation is, in fact, a byproduct of multifarious biochemical processes in the brain that use oxygen that we breathe in to produce ATP (an energy molecule), used for the survival of cells in the body.[26] The amount of unstable compounds is only small,[27] and an increase to these byproducts would lead to the creation of more free radicals.

Neurons involved in dopaminergic cell function are very susceptible to free radicals, but in the healthy human brain, free radicals are broken down to eliminate the possible harm that they might cause to the neurons. Simply put, dopamine gets destroyed when free radicals merge with oxygen. An example is the formation of **hydrogen peroxide** when dopamine is broken down by the enzyme *monoamine oxidase*.[28] Hydrogen peroxide leading to the formation of free radicals could cause harm to the brain cells, but in a healthy person, the radicals are being immediately removed to avoid further damage in the neurons through the help of **glutathione**. In the case of Parkinson's, this antioxidant (glutathione) is produced in a much lesser amount and sometimes at a much slower rate that can be traced back to the environmental and genetic makeup of the person. Antioxidants are proteins and therefore dictated by the genes. Environment-induced alteration of the genes can cause a difference in the protein that helps guard the neurons. In addition, iron level is increased in the dopamine-releasing region of the brain when antioxidants are decreased, and this should be of concern since it makes it easier for free radicals to penetrate and form in important neurons. When these antioxidants fail to disintegrate, **lipid peroxidation** occurs. Lipid is roughly synonymous

to fat, while peroxidation is the formation of peroxide molecules.[29] In lipid peroxidation, an interaction between hydrogen peroxide and lipids occurs. When it comes to free radical chain reactions, lipid peroxidation is one of the most studied, for some believe that it supports the oxidation hypothesis in totality. Calcium is also able to penetrate the cells as free radicals produce holes in the cellular membranes, deteriorating the health of cells in tissues in the body and, more importantly, in the brain of the Parkinson's disease sufferer.

Other Possible Causes

Genetics, environmental factors, and free radicals can all contribute to the risk for acquiring Parkinson's disease. Aside from those factors that are already common knowledge, others are still being evaluated. These factors do not directly cause Parkinson's, but rather they put an individual at higher risk of developing Parkinson's. The risk factors listed below are identified causes of Parkinsonism (also known as Parkinson's plus),[30] another condition involving Parkinson's-like symptoms. Due to very close similarities between the signs and symptoms of Parkinson's disease and Parkinsonism, it has been difficult to identify whether a patient has Parkinson's disease or the latter. Scientists also believed that Parkinsonism might eventually lead to Parkinson's disease, thus establishing yet another etiological correlation. Parkinsonism, however, is definitely brought about by Parkinson's disease, among other causes.[31]

RISK FACTORS AS "CAUSES" OF PARKINSON'S

Age

Many see Parkinson's disease in persons who are fifty or older. As a person ages, the risk of getting Parkinson's disease increases, and the fact is that a greater number of patients aged sixty and onward are diagnosed with Parkinson's disease than those who are fifty or younger.[32] Scientists theorize that neurons actively engaged in dopaminergic functions of the cells weaken as the body deteriorates with age,[33] and the production of defective antioxidants is also observed as a person ages,[34] leading to the acquisition of the disease. Some younger individuals are observed with the symptoms of Parkinson's disease, but these symptoms are not caused by full-blown Parkinson's but by standalone Parkinsonism.[35]

Gender

Data from surveys on the relation of gender to the possibility of acquiring Parkinson's suggest that more men acquire the disease than do women.[36] There is a 50 percent higher risk for males to get Parkinson's disease compared with females.[37] The reasons for this are not yet determined, although some studies suggest that X chromosomes in females are more capable of protection from such ailments than are the Y chromosomes in men.[38]

Ethnicity and Race

A few races are observed to have a higher prevalence of Parkinson's disease than others. Caucasians are among those documented to suffer from Parkinson's more predominantly than others.[39] People of diverse backgrounds and ethnicities can possess completely different lifestyles or living environments. The fact that some races are more prone to Parkinson's is attributable to genetic variations among populations.[40]

Head Trauma

Other case studies investigate the effects of having prior head trauma and injuries on the incidence of Parkinson's disease among people. Individuals with Parkinson's recall experiencing head trauma and head injuries years before they had been diagnosed with Parkinson's disease.[41] Such instances of head trauma and injury, such as traumas related to boxing, are still being studied and examined.[42]

Drugs and Medication

Ingesting certain identified drugs and medication has led some individuals to exhibit symptoms similar to Parkinson's disease, leading to a few new assumptions among experts on the disease.[43] Certain medications can cause an alteration of neurons known to have dopaminergic cellular functions,[44] including antipsychotics, antidepressants, and antiseizure medications.

Hyperactivity versus Immobility

The statement "What you do today will determine what you will be tomorrow" is all too real when it comes to Parkinson's and relates to how lifestyle influences the development of Parkinson's disease. It persuades researchers to compare people who have lived actively with those who have not: many patients with Parkinson's disease had active lifestyles that involved many instances of adrenaline "rush" years before they found out that they had Parkinson's. Body movements are carried out smoothly due to a proper bal-

ance between dopamine and acetylcholine, two neurotransmitters of the brain that act oppositely. Dopamine is responsible for smooth body movements, and acetylcholine is responsible for muscular contraction. A decrease in the amount of dopamine causes rigidity of movement because the excess acetylcholine that stiffens the muscles makes it almost impossible for the Parkinson's sufferer to move easily. This increase in the amount of acetylcholine is marked by the formation of **adrenaline**, the hormone produced when a person is in a situation of elevated stress.

OTHER POSSIBLE CAUSES OF PARKINSON'S

Thin Line between Cause and Mistaken Identity

Contrary to semipopular belief, there is only a minute possibility that viral infections cause Parkinson's disease.[45] Likewise, meningitis and **Shy-Drager syndrome** cause their sufferers to show symptoms that are in line with the symptoms of Parkinson's, further suggesting, but not confirming, that they cause Parkinson's.[46] There are also factors that bring about Parkinson's-like symptoms where the problems are not much noticed by most people, who are thinking that their symptoms are simply minor pains or ailments. Muscle strain and injury can cause muscle rigidity, shaking, and loss of or difficulty with muscle control. Even cold weather and temperature can cause symptoms similar to those of Parkinson's.[47] In cold temperatures, most people tend to have involuntary movements, or cold temperature tremor; Parkinson's disease sufferers also show greater tremor attacks during cold seasons.[48] Stress can produce symptoms that are quite similar to the symptoms of Parkinson's disease because acetylcholine is increased as one is under stress. Acetylcholine is increased because of the formation of adrenaline.

Due to the complex anatomy of the brain, it is not simple to point out the real cause of Parkinson's disease, but it has been partially possible through the use of animal models in which researchers simulate possible conditions (that might boost the development of Parkinson's) in the brains of the model animals. There could be a possibility that Parkinson's disease simply occurs in individuals with poor health. When a person is in poor health, he or she has decreased ability to produce chemicals with protective features such as antioxidants that are helpful in the elimination of (1) free radicals and (2) oxidative stressors, increasing the possibility of Parkinson's disease.

Past and Present Views

Documented Parkinson's disease was relatively very rare before the Industrial Revolution, which is why is there is no sufficient record of it prior to James Parkinson. Back then, "Parkinson's disease" was simply misconstrued

as a normal part of aging. Many misconceptions about the causes of Parkinson's disease were disseminated in the past due to the lack of facts and studies about the disease. Another remarkable difference between past and present views about Parkinson's disease is that in the past, many believed that Parkinson's disease was always a terminal illness.[49] Parkinson's disease can be mistaken for some other type of malady or misinterpreted as being caused by another illness. There was also no cure or even advanced treatment for Parkinson's back then,[50] partly because there were fewer studies and efforts to unravel the mystery behind this medical disorder. It was only after extensive research about the differences in the parts of the brain (chapter 3) of people suffering from Parkinson's disease versus those without the disease in the 1960s that experts correlated low levels of dopamine to Parkinson's. At present, there has been great advancement in the treatment of Parkinson's disease—especially considering that in the 1940s, medical practitioners implemented surgeries on the basal ganglia that in some measure improved the condition of Parkinson's sufferers but but also posed a high risk of death in patients.[51] Through the years, the search for a cure and the treatment for Parkinson's disease have been revolutionized so that it now carries a lesser risk of death, once again due to a better understanding of the causes.[52]

Many differences are evident between the past and present views of what causes Parkinson's disease, and this was made possible by the efforts of different parties and individuals who put their heart and mind to finding the reason and hopefully, someday, a cure for PD. These efforts have been fruitful so far, and there are many improvements in the treatment of Parkinson's disease. The perceptions of Parkinson's disease have also evolved quite a bit, such as the perception that it is an inevitable ailment of the very elderly. In summary, there is a greater amount of knowledge and awareness about potential causes of Parkinson's today compared with the past few decades.

Chapter Five

Symptoms in General

Parkinson's disease is a progressive neurological disorder which is, in a general sense, characterized by a large number of motor and also nonmotor features. These features can impact everyday functioning to a variable degree. Parkinson's disease affects movement, and that in turn results in production of motor symptoms, or a human's ability to process thoughts. When speaking in general terms, Parkinson's disease is commonly referred to as Parkinson's, idiopathic Parkinsonism, primary Parkinsonism, PD, or hypokinetic rigid syndrome (HRS). No matter how it is named, the disease is really a degenerative disorder of the central nervous system. Motor symptoms of PD are brought about by the death of dopamine-generating cells in the substantia nigra, a part of the midbrain. Preliminarily in the course of PD, the obvious *general* symptoms are movement related; they include shaking, rigidity, slow movement, and experiencing a difficult time with walking and gait. Later, as time goes by, cognitive and behavioral problems may start to show up. During the advanced stages of the disease, dementia may also occur. Other general symptoms include sensory, sleep, and emotional problems that are more common in the elderly or after reaching fifty. [1]

The general symptoms of Parkinson's are evaluated by following a detailed clinical examination. There are no laboratory tests or easily available imaging tests to help make the diagnosis. While single photon emission CT (SPECT) scanning may assist in making the diagnosis, it is available in only some centers. It is more likely to be used to exclude other conditions that may have similar symptoms. There are some conditions that have general symptoms similar to Parkinson's and are referred to as "parkinsonism." These include essential (familial) tremor, postencephalic Parkinsonism, cerebrovascular Parkinsonism, progressive supranuclear palsy (PSP), multiple system atrophy (MSA), corticobasal degeneration, and **Wilson's disease**.

GENERAL COGNITIVE SKILLS AFFECTED BY PARKINSON'S

The word *cognitive* refers to the process of obtaining knowledge through thought, experience, and the senses. The Latin term meaning "to consider," on which the word *cognitive* is based, really implies the act of thinking deeply or knowledge or apprehension of ideas by understanding something. Cognitive skills are in some ways affected by Parkinson's. People use cognitive skills whenever they try to understand anything fully or to get just the basic idea. The specific way it works goes something like this: a person is taught something, which could be any new information, by hearing it. He or she then thinks about it and then notices how this new information fits into other things the person knows. Cognitive skills are what separate the good learners from the struggling learners. Without developed cognitive skills, children fall behind because they are not able to integrate new information as it is taught to them.[2] When people think of cognitive skills affected by Parkinson's, they need to approach this in how and what general skills, such as attention, are directly affected by Parkinson's. A person's ability to attend to incoming information can be observed and broken down into a variety of subskills. These subskills can also be improved through properly coordinated training.

Attention Shortfalls as a General Cognitive Symptom

Sustained Attention

Sustained attention is the ability to remain focused and on task, and "testing" it involves measuring the amount of time a person can focus.

Selective Attention

Selective attention is the ability to remain focused and on task while being subjected to both related and unrelated sensory input (distractions). It is purposely focusing one's conscious awareness onto a specific stimulus. If the Parkinson's sufferer is in a noisy place with lots of people and purposely pays attention to the person with whom the patient is speaking, then the patient is engaging in selective attention. One general symptom of Parkinson's is that selective attention may be affected because a random stimulus comes when unprecedented or when attention is directed toward something else.

Divided Attention

Divided attention has to do with the ability to remember information while multitasking. It is affected by stimuli brought about by Parkinson's disease.

With divided attention, someone's ability to get more information from the things one is doing is interrupted by a third-party stimulus.[3]

GENERAL OR GROSS MOTOR SKILLS AFFECTED BY PARKINSON'S

The main motor symptoms of Parkinson's are as follows:

- Bradykinesia: slowness of movement.
- Rigidity: raised tone that is asymmetrical or limited to certain muscle groups.
- Tremor: involuntary shaking, trembling, or quivering movements of the muscles caused by muscles alternately contracting and relaxing at a rapid pace.
- Postural instability: this often presents as a later feature of "classic" (idiopathic) Parkinson's. It is important that there be an early diagnosis here. If the disease is suspected, a patient should be quickly referred—untreated—to a neurologist or a geriatrician with a special interest in Parkinson's.

Motor skills are broken up into two categories: general motor and fine motor. Motor use is the employment of the larger muscle groups in physical activities such as hopping and running. Motor skills are similar to detailed milestones in development, such as holding a cup. Motor *coordination*, however, involves combining all these skills together to control activities. For example, knitting involves holding the knitting needle and then manipulating the needles to make a scarf. Another example is playing a sport where one has to bounce a ball, use reflexes, think, plan, and so forth, coordinating the entire body. General motor skills as well as many other activities involve successful postural control.

Development of General Motor Skills in Relation to Parkinson's

Babies need to control their heads in order to stabilize their gaze and track any moving objects. They also must have strength and balance in their legs in order to walk. Newborn infants cannot voluntarily control their posture. Standing also develops gradually across the first year of life. Although very rare, infants affected by Parkinson's disease experience a slow or delayed development of posture. Others may not even develop posture as the disease ties down their confidence, and some lose interest in learning and focusing on the disease and its effects.[4]

Consider the childhood process of learning how to walk. Walking upright requires the ability to stand up and balance position from one foot to the

other. Although infants usually learn to walk around the time of their first birthday (when they are just about to become a toddler), the pathways that control the leg alternation component of walking are in place from a very early age, possibly even at birth. This is evidenced when one- to two-month-olds are given support with their feet in contact with a motorized treadmill and they show well-coordinated, alternating steps. This is exactly where Parkinson's disease hinders their capabilities of learning how to walk. If it were not for the problem of switching balance from one foot to the other, babies could walk earlier. Parkinson's disease may affect the child's practice in learning how to walk. Practice has a big part in a child's learning how to walk. Vision does not have an effect on muscle growth, but it could slow down the child's learning process for walking. According to a major non-profit organization,[5] if a visually impaired infant goes without special training, he or she may not be able to learn to walk at the anticipated age, and gross motor skills will fail to develop properly. It is also possible in many children that as a carrier of the disease, the child may lack motivation as the disease pulls the child's concentration away during play. When the child is not able to see an object, then there is no motivation for the child to use his or her general motor skills to even try to reach for it. Learning to walk is usually done by modeling others and watching them. Babies who do so will imitate others, picking up the necessary skills a lot faster.[6]

It has been observed by scientists that gross motor skills later lost through Parkinson's generally develop from the center to the body outward and from head to tail. Babies need to practice their skills and therefore be allowed plenty of recreation. This is sometimes affected by Parkinson's disease as it alters their normal life schedule compared with that of other children. They need space and time to explore in their environment and to use their muscles. At first, children are able only to lie on their belly on the floor, but by around two months of age, they start to gain muscle to raise their head and chest off the ground. Some are also able to maneuver themselves by their elbows. They will kick or bend their legs while lying there, as this helps to prepare for crawling. By four months of age, they are able to start to regulate the movement of their head and hold it steady while sitting in place. Rolling movements (from to belly to back) are started. At approximately five months, the baby wiggles the limbs to reinforce the crawling muscles. Infants can start to sit up by themselves and put a decent amount of weight on their legs as they hold onto something for support by six months. As they enter their first year, caregivers need to be more active. The babies will want to get into everything, so the house needs to become "baby-proofed." Babies are able to start to reach and play with their toys, too. Throughout their years of life, different motor skills are formed. Due to Parkinson's disease affecting movement, which in turn results in production of general motor symptoms, the disease can be a hindrance during learning all these processes. The ba-

bies' concentration on all this is undermined by production of motor symptoms. The child's confidence hence directly slows down, in some instances stopping the child from learning all these new things in his or her young life.

Caregivers should also consider the development of special-needs children, who, when as young as seven months, can learn to drive a power wheelchair. The chair may decrease the rate of development of the child's general motor skills, but there are ways to compensate for this. Such children usually work with a physical therapist to help with their leg movements. This can be a way to divert attention from Parkinson's disease to the children's special needs. Walkers and other devices help aid this process and help children avoid obstacles. The negative side to this is that the children are limited in their mobility. Research is currently being conducted to find a device that encourages children to explore their environment while gaining their general motor skills.[7] Hopefully, this will also help them with their exercise as they acquire new skills. At three years of age, children enjoy simple movements such as hopping, jumping, and running back and forth— simply for the sheer delight in performing these activities. This is affected when the children cannot experience a normal growth due to the effects of Parkinson's. At the preschool age, they also develop more goal-directed behaviors. This plays a substantial role at this age because children's learning focuses on play and physical exercise. With the disease present, they are unable to sustain focus on these activities.

The assessment of general motor skills in children who already suffer from or are at serious risk of Parkinson's can be challenging yet important. Different tests are given to these children to measure their skill level. During middle and late childhood, children's motor development becomes much smoother and more coordinated than it was in early childhood. As they age, children become able to gain control over their general motor skills and have an increased attention span. However, the contrary is the case when the child may be affected by Parkinson's disease. Having children participate in a sport can help them with their coordination as well as some social developmental aspects. Teachers may suggest that their students need occupational therapists in different situations. Students sometimes get frustrated at writing exercises when having problems with their school writing assignments. Because of the effects of Parkinson's disease, some children also complain of problems such as tiring hands. Occupational therapists in many places today offer students help for these particular general symptoms. Traditionally, therapists were used in times when something was seriously wrong with the child, but now they are used to help a child become the best he or she can be.[8]

Between the ages of seven and twelve, an increase occurs in the speed at which children run and skip. Jumping also improves, and throwing and kicking increase. At this stage, children are able to understand most things con-

cerning their health and physical conditions. As one approaches adulthood, movement becomes more clear and easier to control. Children are able to both bat and dribble a ball. General motor skills usually continue improving during adolescence. The peak of physical performance is before age thirty, between eighteen and twenty-six, when adults can manage their own conditions and take control of their general motor symptoms in some ways. Even though athletes keep getting better than their predecessors, running faster, jumping higher, and lifting more weight, the age at which they reach their peak performance has remained virtually the same. After age thirty, most functions begin to decline as older adults understandably move slower than their younger counterparts.

FINE MOTOR SKILLS AFFECTED BY PARKINSON'S

Fine motor skill is the coordination of small muscle movements that occur in body parts such as the fingers, usually in coordination with the eyes. In relation to motor skills of hands and fingers, the term *dexterity* is commonly used. When applied to the theory of human aptitude, this is called "manual dexterity." The high level of manual dexterity that humans exhibit can be attributed to the manner in which manual tasks are controlled by the nervous system.

Motor skills are categorized in two groups: general motor skills and fine motor skills. General motor skills, covered in the preceding sections, involve movement of the arms, legs, feet, or entire body and include actions such as running, crawling, walking, swimming, and other activities involving larger muscles. Fine motor skills are the small movements that occur in the hands, wrists, fingers, feet, toes, lips, and tongue. They are the smaller actions that occur, such as picking up objects between the thumb and finger, using a pencil to write carefully, holding a fork and using it to eat, and other small muscle tasks that occur on a daily basis. The two types of motor skills develop together and strongly involve coordination. Through each developmental stage of a child's life, toddlerhood, preschool, and school age, motor skills will gradually develop, and between six and twelve, children typically will have mastered the most critical fine motor skills. In general however, they will keep developing with (1) age, (2) practice, (3) increased use of muscles while using an instrument, (4) participating in sporting events, (5) using the computer, and (6) writing.

Common Problems

Fine motor skills can become impaired. Problems with the spinal cord, brain, joints, peripheral nerves, or muscles can also have an effect on fine motor skills and diminish control. If a child up to age five fails to develop his or her

fine motor skills, the child will show signs of difficulty controlling coordinated body actions with the fingers, face, and hands. In young children, the postponement of the ability to sit up or walk could be an early sign that there will be issues with fine motor skills. Children may also show signs of difficulty with tasks such as cutting with scissors, drawing lines, folding clothes, holding a pencil and writing, and zipping a zipper. These are tasks that involve fine motor skills, and a child who has difficulty with these might have poor hand-eye coordination and could need therapy to improve these skills.

Fine motor skills involve strength and dexterity. These skills are important in most school activities as well as in life in general. Weaknesses in fine motor skills early in life can affect a PD patient's ability to eat, write legibly, use a computer, turn pages in a book, and perform personal care tasks such as dressing and grooming. Bradykinesia (slowed movement) is another characteristic feature of Parkinson's. It is associated with difficulties along the whole course of the movement process, from planning to initiation and, finally, to execution of a particular movement. Performance of sequential and simultaneous movement is hindered. Bradykinesia is the most disabling symptom in the early stages of the disease. Initial manifestations are problems when performing daily tasks that require fine motor control, such as writing, sewing, or getting dressed. Clinical evaluation is based on similar tasks, such as alternating movements between either hand or both feet. Bradykinesia is not equal for all movements or times. It is modified by the activity or emotional state of the subject, to the point that some patients are barely able to walk yet can still ride a bicycle. Generally speaking, patients have less difficulty when some sort of external cue is provided.[9]

A Deeper Look

Studies of motor imagery and motor learning are usually concerned only with effects on healthy subjects. Therefore, in order to investigate the possible involvement of the basal ganglia as a general symptom of Parkinson's disease, a study was performed on the effectiveness of motor imagery in acquiring motor constants in a learning task. The study examined eleven nondemented, mildly affected Huntington's disease (HD) patients and twelve nondemented Parkinson's disease sufferers.[10] The patients received ten minutes of motor imagery training, followed by a motor practice phase. Additionally, a test battery for visual imagery abilities was administered in order to investigate possible relations between visual and motor imagery. The results showed that imagery training alone enabled the HD patients to achieve a significant approach to movement isochrony (when two or more movements occur at the same time), whereas the PD patients showed no marked improvements, either with motor imagery or with motor practice. Further-

more, the PD patients had more difficulties than the HD patients in solving the visual imagery tasks. Subsequent correlational analysis revealed significant relationships between the degree of caudate atrophy, or shrinking of the caudate regions of the brain, in the HD patients and their performance in the visual imagery tasks.[11]

There were no substantial correlations between the performance on the visual imagery tasks and the improvement of motor performance through motor imagery, which indicates that visual and motor imagery are totally independent processes. The study suggests that the dopaminergic input to the basal ganglia plays an important role in the translation of motor representations into motor performance, whereas the caudate nucleus atrophy in HD patients does not seem to affect motor imagery but only the visual imagery process. The deficits found in Parkinson's disease patients might also be related to their limited attention resources and difficulties in employing predictive motor strategies.[12]

General agreement about what exactly motor imagery is does not exist, and therefore neither is there agreement about how it can influence motor behavior. Nevertheless, one particular aspect of motor imagery that does not cause too much controversy is that it is a conscious process. That is, motor imagery refers to the imagining of performing a given motor action or motor skill. The debate is whether this conscious imagining is directly or indirectly related to the motor process. There is ample evidence that during the imagination of movements, neurophysiological activity such as that described in chapter 3 resembles strongly the activity seen during the actual execution of the movement. Given these similarities between imagining and *actually* executing movements, the next logical step would be to assume that the central fine motor changes occurring during motor imagery should also affect subsequent movement performance. People who suffer from Parkinson's are not able, through motor imagery, to adjust the spatiotemporal pattern of this particular movement toward isochrony. These observations suggest that the dopaminergic input to the basal ganglia, especially the striatum, plays an important role in translating motor imagery into motor performance.

Because of the highly complex, multifactorial spectrum of PD, a multidisciplinary team approach is considered to be beneficial to patients and caregivers in order to optimize quality of life and management of symptoms in general. Modern advances in the use of drug therapies, neurosurgical treatments, specialist nursing, Parkinson's-specific rehabilitation, and other interventions can all contribute toward optimizing the quality of life for people living with Parkinson's. Whether speaking of the symptoms in general or stage-based symptoms (chapter 6), drug treatments for Parkinson's aim to increase the level of dopamine that reaches the brain. Additionally, the treatments stimulate the parts of the brain where dopamine works and block the

action of other chemicals that affect dopamine, such as acetylcholine and certain enzymes that harmfully reduce dopamine's effects. [13]

Sexual Symptoms

Since there is no telling whether sexual outcomes of Parkinson's are *general symptoms* or whether they are in fact disorders distantly associated with Parkinson's, the topic has been split into two sections for the purpose of this book. The latter section is in chapter 9. In one of the first studies devoted entirely to sexuality in women suffering from Parkinson's disease, [14] definite differences were found when compared with an age-matched general population. These women reported greater anxiety or inhibition, vaginal tightness, and involuntary urination. All these are related to sexual activity. The study found a preoccupation with health problems as well as discontent with body appearance and sex, although these were not statistically distinguishable from the control group. Overall, the women with Parkinson's were less satisfied by sexual relationships. They were also less satisfied by their partners. There are other reports of difficulty with arousal, genital sensitivity (or decreased mucosal lubrication), orgasmic difficulty, and dyspareunia or vaginismus.

Women with Parkinson's may have their own specific concerns about sexuality that may not be recognized or anticipated by health-care professionals. The most commonly reported sexual problem for men with Parkinson's is erectile dysfunction. Causes include cardiovascular disease, diabetes, hypertension, hypercholesterolaemia, smoking, spinal cord injury, prostate cancer, surgery, psychiatric disorders, and the use of certain drugs. Treatment for generalized sexual outcomes of Parkinson's is discussed in chapter 11.

Chapter Six

Stage-Based Symptoms

Parkinson's is a degenerative, debilitating disease of the nervous system, and therefore it progresses through various stages as the neurons in the brain cells are destroyed or die off completely. The disease really has so many "symptoms" that are common to the aging process that it poses a challenge for early detection. These symptoms do not appear all at once but in stages as the disease progresses. One must be particularly observant of the physical capabilities and motor skills of the individual to notice these subtle changes at first. As the disease becomes more severe, symptoms become more visible, and detection is possible.[1] Individuals suffering from Parkinson's will exhibit more tremors in their limbs than persons whose muscles are merely weakened by age.

INTRODUCTION TO THE STAGING SYSTEM

At the onset of Parkinson's disease, there are no visible symptoms. Recent studies show that symptoms appear after the brain has lost 60 to 80 percent of the substance needed to transmit messages between the parts of the brain that control movement.[2] Dopamine is the chemical name of the substance responsible for relaying messages or signals between the two main components of the brain that control movement. As the level of dopamine in the brain decreases, the effects of Parkinson's disease become more visible, and the disease moves into another stage. The level of degeneration and the symptoms the degeneration produces are used to define the stages. Although several scales are used to categorize Parkinson's disease progression, the Hoehn and Yahr scale[3] is somewhat popular. This scale divides the disease into five stages and is widely used by Parkinson's disease caregivers and other individuals interested in studying the disease. The overall symptoms, effects, and

severity increase with each stage. Treatment is generally administered based on the stage at which the disease is categorized, and eventually, the limbs will stiffen and the torso becomes rigid. To provide an initial understanding of how the symptoms of Parkinson's disease are divided into stages, a bulleted summary is in order.

Stage 1

Individuals are suffering from the beginning stage of Parkinson's disease if the symptoms are as follows:

- Signs and symptoms are mild and are on only one side of the body.
- Tremors (if any) are usually present in only one limb.
- Symptoms are inconvenient but not incapacitating.
- There are noticeable changes in posture, locomotion, and facial expression.

At this stage, the disease is considered to be mild and does not significantly affect the individual's ability to perform regular duties.[4]

Stage 2

The disease has progressed to stage 2 if any or all of the following are observed:

- Symptoms occur on both sides of the body.
- Symptoms cause some disability.
- Posture and gait are affected.

During this stage, the person exhibits some discomfort while trying to complete tasks. Individuals suffering from Parkinson's exhibit more tremors in their limbs than persons whose muscles are merely weakened by age.[5]

Stage 3

A person is categorized as having moderate Parkinson's disease if the following symptoms are evident:

- Significant slowing of body movements;
- Having difficulty maintaining balance when walking or standing; and
- Generalized dysfunction of the nervous system that is moderately severe.

Although the disease is said to be moderate at this stage, many patients will have already experienced severe malfunctions of motor skills.[6]

Stage 4

An individual at stage 4 of the disease has the following:

* Ability to walk to a very limited extent;
* Rigidity and bradykinesia;
* More tremor than that of the initial stages; and
* Inability to live alone.

By this stage, the disease will have usurped at least 90 percent of the individual's neurosystem.[7]

Stage 5

Stage 5 is considered the most advanced stage of Parkinson's disease, and the symptoms are very severe. In this stage, the following occur:

* General reduction in strength of body;
* Some form of dementia;
* Invalidism (chronic illness); and
* A requirement for constant nursing care.

Paralysis may be complete, and other major complications develop.[8]

STAGE 1 SYMPTOMS[9]

Persons afflicted with Parkinson's disease generally experience mild symptoms at stage 1. At the beginning, they usually notice symptoms on only one side of their bodies. These symptoms include tremors, posture, and locomotion changes. Due to the fact that the symptoms are not dramatic, stage 1 sufferers are still very much capable of performing their regular day-to-day duties. This may cause the disease to be overlooked, as only very close acquaintances and people experienced with the mechanisms of the disease may notice these changes.

Tremors

The most common symptom at this stage may be mild tremors that are not always noticeable by outside parties. However, the tremor that accompanies Parkinson's disease has its own distinct characteristic. It involves mostly the thumb and forefinger, and they move rhythmically together, back and forth, in a steady number of beats per second. This rhythmic tremor is also referred to as *pill rolling* in some expert circles. Patients with tremor in this stage often notice the shaking in one of their hands, and it generally becomes more

obvious when the hand is not active but at rest. Additionally, the tremors can get worse when patients are in stressful situations. However, some persons experience tremors beginning in other parts of the body, including the jaw or one foot. There are no set criteria as to how the disease affects one at this early stage, as some individuals do not experience any tremor while others may show more symptoms. Tremors do not often prevent patients from moving about normally, and they often disappear or improve when the person is active or asleep.

Locomotion

Persons diagnosed with Parkinson's disease need not fear performing their daily tasks as their locomotion is not severely affected during this first stage. There is not much cause for concern that patients may hurt themselves, although the symptoms will sometimes become apparent. The main concern is keeping a firm hand while handling any form of liquids and maintaining balance of movement, particularly while walking. Patients may also experience mild cases of bradykinesia and rigidity.

Bradykinesia

Bradykinesia occurs in persons with Parkinson's disease when their movements become unpredictably slowed. This does not occur very often in stage 1 of the disease, but it can cause frustration due to its unpredictability. In essence, persons can move easily one minute, and in a few minutes the symptom may disable them to the extent that they need assistance. This may cause some distress to the affected person as it is probably the most disabling symptom at this stage. Activities that were once easily and quickly performed may start taking longer than usual. This slightly affects regular activities, even simple chores such as cooking, laundry, or doing the dishes. Although it may take more time to complete some tasks, bradykinesia will not prevent someone from accomplishing tasks that he or she could usually do before Parkinson's disease.

Rigidity

Individuals with Parkinson's disease experience a resistance in movement. The fact is that the body follows certain movement principles, one of which is the movement of opposing muscles. In essence, when a stage 1 Parkinson's patient moves, one muscle activates and the corresponding opposing muscle relaxes, allowing the active muscle to take over. In this stage, the muscles sometimes do not respond correctly to the brain's signals, and this disturbs the balance between the opposing muscles. This disturbance results in tensed muscles that contract, which in turn causes stiff and achy tissues.

The rigidity is not always obvious until an external party attempts to move the person's limb. Although not quite inflexible, this may cause some pain to patients as the joints are not very movement oriented once rigidity starts to set in.

Postural Instability

In stage 1 of Parkinson's disease, some persons may find that their posture has become affected. They may suffer from lack of coordination and impaired balance, which may result in a forward slump or a backward lean. This is often a cause for concern when detected, owing to the fact that individuals with postural instability tend to fall easily. Patients with a backward lean tend to take a step back just before they start walking. This reaction is referred to as *retropulsion*, and it helps patients maintain a certain amount of balance. In the early stages of Parkinson's, people may simply walk around with stooped shoulders and a bowed head, but as the stages progress, they may develop difficulty in walking. Persons with severe postural changes may walk briskly, but they are not necessarily hurrying, but rather trying to keep their balance as much as possible. They may also veer from side to side, depending on which side the muscles are more in control. Also, they may pause in the middle of a step and sometimes fall over. In scientific terms, this reaction is referred to as festinating gait or festination.

STAGE 2 SYMPTOMS[10]

Bilateral Effects

In the second stage of Parkinson's disease, the patient's symptoms are bilateral, affecting limbs on both sides of the body. Patients will begin to realize that something has gone wrong with their metabolism. Furthermore, the disease at this stage is classified as moderate, but patients will begin to experience some difficulties in their movements. Here, the symptoms are no longer benign, as some discomfort, particularly while walking, is evident. Parkinson's disease is a condition that affects the brain, and the brain is the main organ that controls the nervous system. As the neurotransmitter that relays information from one side of the brain to the other becomes affected, with signals being delayed in transmission or the wrong signals being sent, the patient becomes more affected by symptoms at this stage of the disease also.

People suffering from Parkinson's disease may become slower in their movements. Individuals at this stage will have difficulty sitting or rising without some form of support. They may adopt a stooped posture and walk with a shuffling gait. Due to the fact that the Parkinson's disease focal point

of attack is the part of the brain that controls movement, aside from hands and feet, other parts of the body will be affected as well.

Heightening Symptoms

Stage 2 Parkinson's disease patients may find it difficult to turn their heads from side to side and are apt to do full body turns instead. Their balance will also be affected, making them more likely to stumble or fall. Affected individuals have the propensity to bend the trunk forward and to accelerate from a walking to a running pace. Although this is caused by a lack of coordination or impaired balance of movements, the intellect and other senses are not impaired at this stage. Patients usually encounter problems walking or maintaining balance, and their inability to complete normal physical tasks becomes more apparent. Medication may be administered at this stage and typically involve one of the less-powerful Parkinson's disease medications.

The tremors displayed in the previous stage will increase in magnitude and spread from the hands to arms, face, jaw, and feet. Not only will the tremors spread to other limbs, they will also extend to include both sides of the body. The tremors are not continuous but attack sporadically. Parkinson's disease patients will find it difficult to use their hands to do common tasks without the assistance of another person because of these uncontrollable tremors. Patients affected by the disease at this stage will have some difficulty in striking a match, handling liquids, and completing other minuscule tasks that require a firm hand. These patients would have been affected by Parkinson's disease at least around fifteen years prior to the time of discovery.

Damages

The brain would have lost approximately 80 percent of the dopamine cells needed to effectively activate the neurotransmitter in the part of the brain that controls movement.[11] The result is an imbalance in movement not only of limbs but of other organs in the body. This stage is usually when masking of facial expressions or slight speech defects initiate or become noticeable in persons affected by Parkinson's disease. Patients may also experience slight difficulties in their control of bodily fluids. Medication is most likely to be administered at this stage, and patients are usually given one of the milder drugs used to treat the disease. Mild symptoms of bradykinesia or akinesia are apparent at this stage. Affected persons will have the tendency to hunch their shoulders and bow their heads while walking. Individuals afflicted with Parkinson's disease will experience a slight stiffening of the muscles, particularly in the torso, and this affects their posture. Although these symptoms

appear in stage 1, they are more pronounced at stage 2 as the disease intensifies. Progression of the disease can be slowed with medications or surgery.

STAGE 3 SYMPTOMS

Moderate Disease

At stage 3, an individual is considered to have moderate Parkinson's disease. The symptoms are unmistakable and can clearly be diagnosed and isolated from those of typical aging. By now, the person will have lost at least 80 percent or more of the dopamine needed to accurately activate the neurotransmitter that signals the act of purposeful movement between the substantia nigra and the corpus striatum.

As a result, patients will significantly exhibit the symptom of bradykinesia and slowness in body movements. This will be evident not only in their steps but also when they try to raise their bodies to a sitting or standing position. Owing to the increasing death counts of neurons and the lower production of dopamine cells, there will be some imbalance of the equilibrium. As the symptoms worsen through this stage, so will the individual's speed decrease and continually move at a much slower rate in order to try and maintain balance. The risks of injuries will increase as patients are more likely to stumble and fall. It takes some amount of concentration to walk along a straight line. Considering that the disease keeps eroding the part of the brain that controls movement, concentration may not be enough to help. As Parkinson's disease progresses, bradykinesia may be accompanied by akinesia. The limbs will begin to stiffen, and arms will swing less while walking. This contributes to movement imbalances in affected persons. Although total rigidity has not quite set in, postural changes will become more evident at this stage. Due to the effect of Parkinson's disease at this stage, individuals may have some difficulty executing a simple action such as the turning of the head. The muscles may "freeze" midway in their movements.

Writing and Speech

The limbs may begin to weaken, and this will impact patients' ability to perform certain basic tasks. Moderate changes in their handwriting will be visible. Although not totally illegible, written correspondence from a Parkinson's disease sufferer may pose a reading challenge to the receiver. Letters will be written smaller and will most likely run into one another. Certainly, marked changes will occur in the signatures of people affected by Parkinson's disease at this stage. Individuals who have deteriorated to this level will not only display physical symptoms but also mild signs of dementia. They will pause in the middle of a sentence, not because they are out of breath, but

because they have lost the thread or topic of the conversation. Items that are thought missing may be found in plain sight, but, although slowly, recollection will come to these patients eventually. Because of the impact on their powers of recall, persons affected at this stage may display mild irritability and frequent mood swings. This may be as a result of their inability to perform certain tasks. Apart from the physical effects of Parkinson's disease, affected persons will experience and exhibit some neurological disorders. Speech may become slurred, slow and soft, monotonous, or rapid as individuals struggle to keep abreast of conversational topics. The affected individuals may stop speaking in the middle of a sentence and stare blankly ahead. This is not intentional, but caused by the effects of the disease on the person's neurological system. The effects are also unpredictable, and so some people, with a little prompting, may recover the thread of the conversation and continue to have meaningful dialogue. Their faces may become expressionless, or their facial expressions may show moderate distortion, such as a slight deformation of the lips while speaking. Persons affected by Parkinson's disease at this stage gradually begin to blink less than normal.

At stage 3, moderate sleeping disorders will occur, along with some form of paranoia. Some individuals will have nightmares and constantly shake in their sleep while others will suffer from insomnia. The paranoia will be evident when persons affected begin referring to dreams as if they were facts. Depression is another symptom that persons at the third stage of Parkinson's disease may develop. This will result in the affected persons sitting silently for long periods of time with morose or blank facial expressions. They will display mood swings that will alternate between fear and irritability. The need of assistance in performing some basic, personal tasks such as washing oneself may be looked on as an invasion of privacy, and this may contribute to a feeling of insecurity. Other natural body functions may be interrupted, which may cause incontinence or some form of stress in the release of bodily wastes. This will cause some embarrassment, which may result in a deeper state of depression. Although medical treatment may begin at an early stage, stage 3 is generally where people affected by Parkinson's disease are given the drug levodopa to assist in slowing the effects on the neurological system. Not all individuals diagnosed as having Parkinson's disease experience these symptoms. Some individuals' symptoms remain dormant for a period of up to fifteen years, and then the patients rapidly decline.

STAGE 4 SYMPTOMS

Advanced Parkinson's

While stage 3 is categorized as a moderate stage of Parkinson's disease and persons affected may have been able to perform some basic chores, stage 4

has more impact on the individuals' intellectual and kinetic abilities. At this stage, Parkinson's disease sufferers are said to be in an advanced stage and require constant care. The symptoms are far more severe, and patients may show a rapid decline in both physical and mental stability. Along with the symptoms identified in the previous stages, more symptoms will evolve. Apart from the tremors, the symptoms shown in all the previous stages will be far more visually evident because of the level of degeneration.

Paralysis

Persons affected by Parkinson's disease at stage 4 will have limited to no mobility. Muscles may become *completely* frozen, therefore limiting or preventing the initiation of voluntary movement. Patients may not be able to move around. Those who can will not be able to do so without some form of balancing aid such as a mechanical walker or a wheelchair. Even then, they will be in need of personal assistance. Rigidity of the trunk will cause major discomfort when trying to perform simple physical movements. At stage 4, affected persons who are not totally immobile will exhibit serious paralytic symptoms. They will not be able to move their limbs in certain directions or raise themselves from a sitting position without help. This will prevent them from effectively seeing to their personal hygiene without assistance. However, patients who experience the symptoms listed in stage 4 are generally immobile.

Depression

The inability to perform the most basic personal tasks for oneself is in itself an embarrassment in some situations. This causes a lot of frustration in persons afflicted with Parkinson's disease, particularly those who were once very active and now have to depend on others to assist them in maintaining their personal hygiene. Patients become depressed over their their incapacity and act out their frustrations in various ways. The more dependent they become, the faster they recede into a depressive state. If friends and relatives are not there to give constant support, they sink into a deeper depressive state, as those who have periods of lucidity may consider themselves abandoned and sometimes resent the intimate care that is required to maintain personal hygiene.

Mood Swings

Depending on the level of depression patients of Parkinson's disease experience at this stage of their illness, mood swings may either increase or decrease. Mood swings are more likely to increase as these patients are not completely neurotic and can sometimes assess their own behavior. They may

be quite remorseful and apologetic one moment and then change into abusive, inconsiderate individuals in a few minutes. Bearing in mind that they have limited control of their nervous system because of the rapid loss and minimal production of dopamine at this stage, patients at stage 4 will depict some signs of mental instability. Owing to the effect of the disease on their neurosystems at this stage, they will deem dreams to be real, and they are prone to having constant nightmares, resulting in restlessness. They may even develop a fear of sleeping or of being left alone.

Imbalance

While the tremors visible in the first three stages may have decreased, at stage 4, patients suffering from Parkinson's disease are more susceptible to injuries due to locomotive disorder. As the effects of the disease increase, patients' muscles become more tense and inflexible. They lose control of certain muscular functions and are unable to maintain balance when standing or bending over. Due to the rigidity of the trunk, they are more likely to topple forward than to straighten themselves upward. Not only do the muscles turn rigid at this stage, but they also weaken. Those patients who are still able to move their limbs will not be able to grip objects firmly. Therefore, they may be able to push a soft button on a device, but they will not be able to propel a device such as a wheelchair.

Incontinence

Taking into consideration that bradykinesia and akinesia are severe at this stage, Parkinson's disease patients may become incontinent. The rigidity of their muscles will cause them to suffer from constipation, resulting in infrequent bowel action. Also, due to the damage done to their neurosystems, they may not be aware of passing bodily wastes. Those that do have limited control of how and when they pass waste matters may still not be able to do so because of the restriction of their movements.

Liabilities

At stage 4, individuals suffering from Parkinson's disease need constant care and should not be allowed to live alone. Those who are totally incapacitated need constant personal care along with medication. Patients who still have limited mobility need to be watched as they tend to forget easily and muscle "freezing" occurs more frequently. They are a danger to themselves as they may begin a task but are liable to either freeze or forget before the task is completed. They should not be allowed to prepare meals or go to the bathroom without attendance. They most certainly should not be allowed to self-

medicate as they may not remember to take their medications or may forget that they have already taken it and overdose themselves.

STAGE 5 SYMPTOMS

Stage 5 is the final and most severe symptomatic stage of Parkinson's disease. During this stage, the disease usually takes charge of the person's physical movements. At stage 5, individuals suffering from Parkinson's disease definitely need special care. As a result of the high percentage of death of the dopamine-generating cells in the substantia nigra or midbrain, the central nervous system has degenerated to a critical level. The cause of the death or degeneration of these cells is unknown, and therefore, there is no known remedy to prevent this catastrophic effect on the nervous system. However, there are some drugs that may be administered to slow the degeneration to a limited extent for a short period of time. This stage is also referred to as the cachectic stage because of its impact on the body and mind.

Invalidism

At this stage of Parkinson's disease, invalidism is complete. Sufferers will undergo a general reduction in strength of body and mind. Affected persons will not be able to stand or walk. They will not be able to change their positions even when lying down, and this will cause them to develop more complications. Constant care is needed, and people who are not admitted to a medical facility will need in-home health workers and maybe other assistants to take care of their daily needs.

Symptomatic Effect on Diet and Digestion

The digestive functions of the body will be severely disrupted at stage 5. Owing to the difficulty or inability of patients to chew, special supplementary diets will have to be planned. Although their digestive systems may not suffer a total collapse, patients will be affected to the point at which they will have major difficulty in swallowing and digesting food. Stage 5 PD sufferers will therefore need a more liquid diet. The rigidity or stiffening of the muscles causes the throat to contract, which results in patients' inability to consume solid foods. Owing to the impact on the digestive system, patients in stage 5 will become incontinent. The more common form of incontinence will be constipation, although this may not be completely related to Parkinson's disease. The patients' diet will have to be taken into consideration. Constipation will be mainly caused by the tightening or contraction of the muscles, depending on the state of rigidity. However, both bladder and bowel

incontinence are commonplace during this stage. As the nervous system deteriorates, so does the level of bladder control.

Complications

A number of both physical and mental disorders are present in this fifth stage of the disease. Apart from the tremors, those symptoms that were present in the previous four stages are more pronounced. Patients will develop various sleeping disorders such as nightmares and insomnia. Some forms of dementia also affect a fair number of those afflicted with Parkinson's disease at this stage. Vulnerability to infections such as pneumonia increases, and subsequent choking can cause death, although PD itself is not always fatal. In end-stage Parkinson's, patients experience a loss of appetite and lose weight, experience severe agitation, and have difficulty breathing and swallowing. Because PD progressively destroys balance and coordination, falls become more frequent, with many trips to the hospital for injuries. Anxiety disorders are common as PD progresses toward its end stage. Increased anxiety results from the underlying neurodegenerative process, and patients may develop phobias about such things as going out in public or being in confined spaces. Hallucinations, delusions, and personality changes also can occur. Psychosis may also become a factor at this stage.

Sleep Symptoms

Depending on the intensity of the disease at this late stage, PD-affected individuals may suffer from either insomnia or restlessness. Patients become restless and are prone to frequent nightmares. Their restlessness may be caused by either their level of discomfort with their immobility or their state of mind. However, the nightmares create a fear of sleeping, and this also contributes to their restlessness. Mobile patients are sometimes found walking around in the dark at night. Many persons at stage 5 of Parkinson's disease develop *chronic insomnia*. Insomnia is termed chronic when the individual has very little or short periods of sleep for at least three nights per week for four weeks or longer. Sleep issues in Parkinson's patients at this stage may be caused by discomfort at night or by stress. Incontinence and immobility together are secondary roots of insomnia in Parkinson's patients and result from patients' inability to express or indicate that they have had a bowel movement while having to remain in their immobile position until assistance is rendered. Depression and anxiety are also linked to the development of chronic insomnia in PD patients at this stage.

Dementia

Owing to the fact that Parkinson's disease is a degenerative disease of part of the central nervous system, the senses may also become affected. Dementia affects 30 to 40 percent of persons at stage 5 of Parkinson's disease. [12] They lose contact with reality as the disease continues to invade their intellectual functions. At this culminating point of Parkinson's, even those patients who are not totally cachectic may still lose their powers of reasoning and recall. Their auditory and visual senses become impaired to the extent that they may begin to hallucinate. They attribute sounds and images to those with which they are familiar. Health workers or personal assistants may be thought of as sons and daughters or other family members in stage 5 patients' minds. If patients deem someone is being good to them, then that person is associated with something or someone positive from their past. However, if a person resembles someone from the past with whom patients had a disagreement, then that individual takes the form of someone "bad." This will sometimes cause patients to "lash out" at caregivers.

Parkinson's disease patients suffering from dementia during stage 5 may become very uncooperative. Those who are still mobile will want to perform regular tasks for themselves, but owing to the dementia, they should not to be allowed to since they tend to forget the task they started, which may result in serious accidents. Patients who are mobile and suffering from dementia are more at risk than those who are immobile. Mobile patients may try to perform household chores such as cooking and cleaning. They may also wander away from home. Because of dementia, they may start a fire and be completely unaware that something is burning. With their propensity to fall, they should never be left alone.

Psychosis

Dementia may eventually lead to psychosis in persons affected at this stage. Psychosis is a symptom or feature of mental illness typically characterized by radical changes in personality, impaired functioning, and a distorted or nonexistent sense of objective reality. Due to the impairment of both the auditory and visual senses, Parkinson's disease patients who have deteriorated to stage 5 tend to hallucinate. They see and hear things that are not there. Therefore, they might be speaking quite rationally one minute and ranting and raving the next. Those patients who are still able to move their limbs, particularly their hands, should be closely watched as they may harm themselves. They are likely to aggressively remove any medicinal attachments to their persons, such as intravenous tubes and needles. The progressive deterioration of their intellectual faculties brought about by the degenerative effect of the disease will enhance these psychotic symptoms.

Other Stage 5 Complications

Because of the immobility of individuals, painful bed sores frequently affect patients of Parkinson's disease during stage 5. Chafing of pubic and anal body parts occurs often as patients are unable to indicate when they need to or have excreted bodily wastes. At this stage, some disposable clothing is best for both the patients and their assistants. Incontinence is a constant companion of PD patients at this level of the disease. Their skin may become oily or very dry, and some extra sweating may occur. Patients will need special ointments or powder to alleviate these conditions. Rigidity will be so acute that single-handedly moving patients from one position to another will pose a challenge to health workers and their assistants. This is because patients will be mostly inflexible due to the stiffness of the muscles. Afflicted persons at stage 5 will not be able to feed themselves, and this augments the overall responsibilities of caregivers.

Chapter Seven

Inpatient Diagnostics and Approaches

Neurodegenerative central and peripheral nervous system disorders suitable for inpatient diagnosis are characterized by gradual onset of signs and symptoms. Parkinson's disease is just one of the distinctive kinds of neurodegenerative disorders approached in an inpatient milieu. The sheer magnitude of the disease serves as a reason to learn its inpatient approaches, since PD affects about four million people globally and is expected to increase substantially.[1] Despite the unknown origin of the disease, its presence can still be diagnosed using different inpatient methods and procedures.

INTRODUCTION TO INPATIENT NEUROLOGY

An inpatient is a person receiving medical treatment within a hospital, perhaps because of needing extra attention by health-care attendants. Neurology is the medical field concerning the nervous system, its functions, and its disorders. So inpatient neurology can be defined as a patient being observed and treated from within the hospital regarding that patient's nervous system functions and disorders. The practice of neurology as it relates to Parkinson's is continually shifting from a descriptive and theoretical discipline to a more practical discipline that encompasses diagnostic and therapeutic approaches. And this practical approach is evident in inpatient neurology. Different cases involving the functions of and problems in the nervous system are more intensively observed if patients can be carefully monitored and any subtle changes recorded. This observation can then lead to more effectively applied curative solutions.

Parkinson's disease clinical symptoms do not manifest until 60 percent of the natural coloring of neurons is distorted and about an 80 percent decrease occurs in the dopamine level of the patient. When 75 percent or more brain

cells are lost, kidney malfunction begins to manifest, and the lost brain cells can no longer be recovered.[2] Through inpatient neurology, more elaborate descriptions of signs and symptoms of the disease at its various stages have become possible and are helping medical professionals efficiently and accurately diagnose the Parkinson's patient, which will allow a more appropriate approach and treatment for the disease. As part of inpatient neurological observation and diagnosis, the patient's history is also assessed and taken into consideration in order to find out the very nature of the patient's neurological functions and disorder. The studies in neurology continually grow and expand as new developments in the complex human brain are revealed through inpatient neurology.

ROLE OF THE HOSPITAL IN PARKINSON'S

Patients diagnosed with degenerative neurological disorder are dealt with at home for as long as possible. The regular daily activities of the patient are retained as much as possible through encouraging independence in the patient's movement. The patient can be admitted, particularly in cases of critical levels, for treatments and application of surgical operations if necessary. Premature diagnosis can be very difficult for the medical professional since there will be cases in which the patient is unable to distinguish differences in movements and *when* those changes began. Family members have important roles in diagnosing the patient with the disease. They are the usual company of the patient, and their observations can be truly helpful in stating the evident signs and symptoms, making early diagnosis in a hospital setting less difficult.

Parkinson's is not curable, but certain medical applications can aid the patient in coping with the disease while at the hospital. This is where the different medical groups and the hospital establishment can play a role of utmost significance. One of the roles of the hospital in managing the disease is to observe, monitor, record, and supervise the Parkinson's disease sufferer in terms of the changes and development in neurological activity and motor movements. Such observation and supervision can help establish guides and patterns that could give medical practitioners insights on how to address the disease, which in turn could give patients better quality of life despite experiencing the progressing symptoms of the disease. Another role of medical professionals in hospitals is to prescribe and manage dosage of medicines taken by the patients in order to properly manage and cope with their condition. In addition, scheduling of proper dosage can make the medication more effective and maximize the potency of the medicines. The patient can be allowed to consume certain medications outside the hospital, but there is a

risk that without close monitoring, those medications can be rendered ineffective.

Because there is no cure for the disease and no known medical procedure that can prevent its development, hospital-based approaches focus on managing the symptoms and maintaining the functional independence of the patient. Each inpatient Parkinson's disease admission must be treated with utmost care, and proper diagnostic procedures must be performed based on the sufferer's symptoms and emotional, occupational, and social needs. Pharmacological treatment is the main procedure to apply to patients diagnosed with Parkinson's disease. Patients are admitted to the hospital only in cases where several complications appear or where new medical procedures need to be applied.

INPATIENT PROCEDURES FOR DETECTING PARKINSON'S

Prior to treatment, properly diagnosing the patient regarding the presence of the disease involves observing several measures. Given that Parkinson's disease has many varied signs and symptoms, certain primary criteria are in place if one suspects that a person has Parkinson's.

Detecting the More Noticeable Symptoms

Tremor

Tremor is defined as involuntary and rhythmic muscle movement of certain body parts that basically disappears with voluntary movements and can become evident when other physical movements are static. Even with varying symptoms of the disease, 75 percent of the patients manifest unilateral resting tremors during diagnosis, whether inpatient or outpatient.[3] The medical professional diagnoses the patient by observing the rhythmic and slow turning motion of the forearm and the hand while at rest with its increased presence when the patient is walking, concentrating, or feeling anxious.

Rigidity

Rigidity is a condition characterized by abnormal stiffness of the muscle. This is diagnosed by checking the reaction of the arms, legs, face, and posture of the patient. Early manifestation of symptoms can be observed through shoulder pain caused by rigidity of movement.

Slowness

This is characterized by relatively slow movement of the patient and very slow movement as the disease progresses. This is diagnosed by simply ob-

serving the patient's movement and by performing tests to evaluate several basic tasks such as standing up or walking.

Balance Problems

Balance problem is a very common symptom of Parkinson's disease. In this case, the patient is diagnosed through observation of movement stability. Patients with Parkinson's disease pose a risk of falling due to poor motor coordination, and floors in the inpatient setting can be hard as many of the hallways of hospitals lack carpeting. Balance problems can be tested through a pull test, performed by pulling the patient toward a specific direction using relatively adequate force. An unafflicted person should be able to retain stability of posture.

Inpatient Detection of Secondary Symptoms

Here, the health professional focuses mainly on determining the presence of certain patterns, signs, and symptoms. During this part of the diagnosis, the Parkinson's patient will be observed for signs of disability and functional changes throughout the day. In order to obtain more reliable data about the patient, a hospital-based caregiver observes the inpatient for the following:

- Stiffness and/or irregular jerking of the leg or arm
- Cases of inability to move out of a position
- Excessive mouth watering
- Experiences of grimacing or chewing movement
- Specific activities the patient is experiencing difficulty in performing
- Quality of speech
- Facial expression
- Poor head control
- Body weakness
- Forward posture
- Mental slowness and confusion

MORE INPATIENT DIAGNOSTICS

From the secondary assessment data, the medical professional can proceed to a more in-depth analysis of the patient's current condition. This analysis includes observing the following:

- Impaired physical mobility
- Constipation and reduced activity
- Imbalanced nutrition

- Impaired verbal communication characterized by low speech volume, slowness of speech, and inability to move facial muscles
- Sleeping pattern disturbances
- Risk for activity intolerance
- Disturbed thought processes

Since hospitals tend to keep lengthy records of Parkinson's patients, the total diagnosis of the disease involves knowing and analyzing the patient's health history and manifestations of the above-mentioned symptoms and changes in the patient's posture. In some cases, the patient is not able to assess changes in physical movements or know when those changes occurred. Interview with the patient's family members in specially assigned hospital interview rooms is also a part of early detection of the disease. Since the family members are the usual company of the patient, they will be asked for some noticeable changes such as stooped posture, stiff arm, slight limp, tremor, and slow or small handwriting observed in the patient prior to or during the diagnosis.

Advanced Diagnostics

Although conducting several laboratory examinations may not be beneficial in diagnosing the disease, research with positron emission tomography (PET) and single photon emission computed tomography (SPECT) scanning are helpful in understanding the disease and determining proper treatment for patients. There is no *absolute* blood test to diagnose the disease. Moreover, the best way to diagnose is through proper neurological examination that is normally more powerful in the inpatient setting than in that of outpatient, due to better resources of the former.

Positron Emission Tomography

PET is a medical imaging technique found more in hospitals than at doctor's offices. It is used to produce three-dimensional images of different processes in the body.[4] A positron-emitting radionuclide or tracer is injected into the body in a form of biologically active molecules. The system detects gamma rays indirectly emitted by the tracers. From the signals emitted, the three-dimensional image is constructed by a computer.

Single Photon Emission Computed Tomography

SPECT is conducted in similar ways as PET, but the image produced is not as detailed. Through SPECT diagnostic procedures, the decline in dopaminergic neuron levels of the patient can be identified. Although diagnosis is

possible, such changes in dopaminergic neurons can also exist in diseases other than Parkinson's disease.[5]

Other Criteria for Inpatient Diagnostics

Inpatient diagnostics also take into account other possible causes of the disease. Through continual and intensive research, diagnosis can possibly be done through tracing manifestations genetically, although family history and genetics accounts for only a small number of PD cases.[6]

LIMITATIONS OF INPATIENT DIAGNOSTICS

Given all the specific signs and symptoms, accuracy of a diagnosis can be negatively affected by several factors. According to a reputable medical research center,[7] some of those factors that can lower the accuracy of a diagnosis are the following:

- Inadequate clinical and pathological observation
- Lack of operational definitions of the different criteria
- Age bracket inhibiting the symptoms of Parkinson's is undetermined since some cases are observed in younger age groups
- Studies involve people who have had the disease for years
- Lack of statistical data since these data are limited to certain number of cases

INTERVENTION FOR THE INPATIENT

Medical professionals working in a hospital have other functions than diagnosing Parkinson's disease. They also help patients cope with the disease by using a nonpharmacological and nonsurgical approach in dealing with physical and mental changes in the patient.

Improving Mobility

A progressive program of daily exercise will increase muscle strength and coordination, reduce rigidity, and prevent muscle contractures. Activities such as cycling, swimming, and gardening can help maintain joint mobility of the inpatient Parkinson's sufferer if the hospital permits. Because the disease also affects the flexibility of the body, stretching helps improve range of motion and joint flexibility. Postural exercise is also necessary in order to reduce the tendency of the head and neck to be drawn forward or downward. A personalized exercise program can also be prepared with the help of a physical therapist assigned by the hospital itself. A physical therapist offers

the patient further instructions and demonstrations of proper practices when performing the exercise. Therapists can also assure patients' proper positioning and help them observe safety measures that will maximize the effect of several physical movements. In addition, frequent exercise can delay the progression of the disease since the patient is trying to maintain certain physical attributes that are normally harmed as the disease progresses.

Warm baths and massage can increase the effectiveness of exercise because they relax the muscles and relieve muscle spasms caused by rigidity. Another effect of rigidity is the diminution of body balance. To counter the effect, a patient must perform special walking exercise, perhaps in the hospital hallways when permitted, and concentrate on walking erect. The patient is also advised to walk on the hospital grounds (if able) accompanied by music or by a ticking sound because this provides sensory reinforcement. Performing breathing exercise while walking can help move the rib cage and ventilate the lungs. Adequate resting periods are also necessary in order to prevent fatigue.

Enhancing Self-Care Activities

Encouraging and guiding the patient in performing daily activities can help promote self-care, as the patient can then be left unsupervised in his or her hospital room for hours or longer. Modifications to the patient's surroundings, depending on that patient's current condition, can greatly help him or her cope with the mental and physical changes. This is because as Parkinson's disease progresses, normal movement can become more and more impossible for the patient, who is perhaps already bound to stay in his or her hospital room for extended periods of time. Several devices or equipment, such as ropes and crutches, can assist the patient in performing daily activities. The goal of these activities is to make the patient perform daily routines independently as much as possible.

Encouraging Use of Devices Following Diagnosis

In the context of a mealtime, certain devices can be very helpful for patients. Electric warming trays provided by the hospital's food department can give a Parkinson's patient a rest during the prolonged time needed for eating each meal. Hospital caregivers must carefully choose the kind of utensils offered to the patient in order to avoid spills and be most convenient for the patient. In addition to assistive devices, appropriate positioning of items in the patient's surroundings can help the patient adjust well in the inpatient situation. For example, it is more appropriate to store items between the waist and eye level to avoid forcing the patient to bend and reach.

Improving Communication

Problems related to speech, caused by weakening of the muscles involved in voice and speech production, become more and more evident as the disease progresses, and staying in a hospital as an inpatient Parkinson's sufferer can create more communicative isolation than originally intended. To help patients coping with speech problems, hospital staff can advise the patient to always face the listener, exaggerate word pronunciation, shorten sentences, and perform some breathing exercise before speaking.

Supporting Coping Abilities

Depending on the respective inpatient setting, people with Parkinson's can also be supported by means of encouraging active participation and emphasizing that active participation can help maintain regular movements. A combination of physiotherapy, psychotherapy, medication therapy, and support group therapy is essential in helping the patient cope with the situation and reduce the depression accompanied by the disease. It is advised to always encourage the patient and further highlight the benefits of participation in physiotherapy. Planned daily activities must be carefully determined and carried out so that more time is allocated to active activities than to daytime sleeping. Continual effort must be exerted in helping the patient perform daily activities independently. *Always* helping the patient perform a task, especially just to save time, is discouraged as doing so defeats the very purpose of helping the patient cope with the situation.

Promoting Home and Community-Based Care

Once the critical diagnostics such as the SPECT and PET, mentioned earlier, are carried out, patient and family education plays a vital role in managing Parkinson's. The level and intensiveness of education the hospital provides really depends on the current condition of the patient. The goal of educating the patient and caregiver is not to overwhelm them with too much information but to educate them with proper knowledge of managing the patient according to his or her needs. This could make patients more adaptive to certain changes in the environmental setup as the disease progresses. The discussion must consist of explaining the nature and background of the disease, discussing the current condition of the patient, going over the necessary guidelines and precautions, and inculcating the goal of the assistance, which is to help the patient perform daily tasks independently. It is important that an explanation of the effects and side effects of different medications be included in the discussion. The patient and informal caregiver must also be informed about the importance of regular reporting of side effects to the physician who performs rounds at the hospital. If side effects occur or a

patient is not responsive to medication given by the hospital, the type of medication or its dosage may need adjustment.

Chapter Eight

Outpatient Diagnostics and Approaches

The earliest outpatient diagnostics and treatment of Parkinson's are reported to have been with the help of *Mucuna pruriens*, a tropical legume, as far back as in 5000 BCE in India. Unconventional approaches in outpatient settings can include gene therapy, GDNF therapy, stem cell therapy, and deep brain stimulation. Some medications used in outpatient settings reach the brain through the bloodstream and are then converted to dopamine. [1] Whether the diagnostics of Parkinson's are inpatient (chapter 7) or outpatient, both methods strive to provide an adequate care level, and the goal is to achieve a long-term recovery. The choice of the outpatient method depends on a number of factors, such as (1) the level the disease has reached, (2) the primary cause of the disease, (3) the patient's social life and responsibilities, (4) the extent to which the brain cells have been damaged, and (5) the age of the sufferer.

OUTPATIENT NEUROLOGY EXPLAINED

Basics

Outpatient is a term used for patients who are given medical treatment by a doctor or paramedic at a clinic or hospital facility without being admitted to the hospital. Thus, the Parkinson's disease outpatient does not have to go through an overnight stay to receive any medical care. Outpatient neurology can be defined as a study and practice rendered by hospitals and clinics to understand and treat CNS-related problems of patients without admitting them into hospital wards or after they recover adequately from hospital-based medical care. The facility takes the viewpoint of rendering services on a

regular basis but allowing the neurology patient to continue his or her daily life more easily. Outpatient neurology deals with medical conditions such as stroke, spinal cord injuries or disorders, physiotherapy, and counseling of patients and their families. Its full scope encompasses the fields of multiple sclerosis and movement disorders as well. Outpatient neurological services are also provided for **polyneuropathies** such as amyotrophic lateral sclerosis (ALS) and vestibular dysfunctions. These diagnostic services cater to (1) acquired brain injuries, (2) Guillain-Barré syndrome, (3) transverse myelitis, (4) cerebral palsy, (5) removal or partial removal of tumors either of neurological origin or having neurological impact, and (6) neuropathies. The physiotherapists working under the outpatient umbrella may also treat inclusion body myositis, ataxias, muscular dystrophy, polyneurophathies, motor neuron disease, and multisystem atrophy.

Significance of Neurological Outpatient Approaches

- In some cases, the treatment can be continual, requiring multiple sessions at the doctor's office. The patients are allowed to go home and visit the facilitation centers only for the required time.
- A Parkinson's disease sufferer who is cared for in the outpatient setting tends to have a more flexible schedule and can continue his or her normal life to certain extent. Thus, the patient does not require a leave of absence from work or studies.
- A team of consultants or a single specialist reviews the patient's case so as to minimize the waiting time. It also helps improve access and a speedy referral process.
- It is widely accepted that a patient feels more comfortable and recovers faster if given the proper treatment at home. Therefore, recovery is quicker in the comfortable and known atmosphere of the home.
- Outpatient diagnostics and treatment is less costly for Parkinson's patients compared with those found in inpatient settings. They are not billed for room occupation and other in-house facilities of the hospital.
- Outpatient diagnostic methods are convenient for hospital facilities. Such methods reduce the number of patients on campus, consequently reducing the number of caregivers needed, such as attendants and nurses, and enabling the use of fewer resources, such as beds and rooms occupied.

The scope of outpatient diagnostics of Parkinson's and other neurological disorders spreads over a large spectrum. Starting from a doctor's visit, lab tests, sonograms, and ultrasounds, it also covers some specific treatment procedures as well as rehab services.

Outpatient Services Centers

Outpatient neurological services can be provided at a number of places. Though hospitals can be used for the purpose, individuals with Parkinson's disease can also take advantage of smaller outpatient units or entities such as the following:

- Physical therapy centers
- Ultrasound centers
- Cardiac care centers
- Specimen laboratories
- Sports medicine centers
- Urgent care centers
- Ambulatory care centers and doctor's clinics

Occasionally, the outpatient treatment may also be provided at the patient's home, work, community, or any place relevant to their goal. Care of the neurological outpatient can pertain to any of the following:

- Patients undergoing physical therapies: the services would be rendered by experienced sports medicine hubs or in physical therapy centers.
- Patients undergoing rehabilitation for mental or psychological concerns: such facilities widely provide counseling, group work, and medication.
- Patients recovering from alcohol or drug abuse: the rehab programs for alcoholic patients are generally long-term, sometimes spreading from weeks to several months as needed.

Functionality of Outpatient Neurology

By and large, a physician assesses the patient and then refers him or her to a neurologist for treatment. The patient is usually older than fifteen; otherwise a pediatrician would take over the responsibility. The neurology patient is reviewed by either a single consultant or a team. Depending on the genre of the problem and its extent, the decision is made as to whether the patient should be treated by a general neurologist or a specialized neurologist. The doctor schedules therapy services for the sufferer, and a referral program is designed. Normally, each session has a duration of about two hours. The patient is responsible for consistently attending his or her sessions. Depending on the outpatient's progress, the doctor may encourage a home rehabilitation program. Motivating the patient (chapter 18) becomes of greater significance at this phase. The neurology outpatient facilities then become primarily a resource of information, explaining patient care procedures and offering information about professionals working with patients who have neurological disorders.

Team Members of Outpatient Neurology

Neurological outpatient treatment may group two or more of the following services.

Occupational Therapy

Occupational therapists assist neurology patients across their life span to perform better in their daily routine activities or occupations. This type of approach helps patients recover from injury and remaster their skills. Occupational therapy also helps neurologically disabled children cope with school activities and encourages them in having a positive role in society. The therapy also provides assistance for older patients who have physical and cognitive problems.

Social Work

Social workers hold a responsible position in making things easier for neurological patients. They strive to help the neurology patient develop a health plan addressing important issues affecting the patient's life. Social workers contribute to planning the patient's exercise program and schedule, planning medication, coordinating the patient's career with family and peers, and helping the patient plan his or her own nutrition and emotionally cope with chronic illness.

Psychology

The psychologist helps neurology outpatients and their caregivers cope with the changes brought about in the patient and in his or her relationship to the world. These experts approach the depression, anxiety, and tension the patient feels.

Speech-Language Pathology

Speech and language pathologists help not only evaluate but also assist in rendering treatment to movement disorder patients, helping patients whose communications have been affected. They render help in voice, language, and speech. In addition, they also address cough and swallowing problems patients might have. Speech and language approaches are discussed further in chapter 14.[2]

Therapeutic Recreation

Therapeutic recreation experts focus on reducing disability, helping neurological outpatients maintain their independence, and enhancing safety meas-

ures so that patients can continue a normal life with ease and even continue practicing their favorite hobbies.

OUTPATIENT SERVICES AND PARKINSON'S

Parkinson's patients may find the following services after being diagnosed with the disease.

A Multidimensional Approach

Group Programs

Parkinson's disease group programs encourage activities held in numbers rather than alone. A few of these types of groups are listed below.

- Group exercise
- Memory strategies group
- Fatigue management group
- Work skills group
- Therapeutic gardening group
- Upper limb therapy group
- Food preparation group
- Stroke self-management group

Movement Reeducation

Parkinson's disease patients suffer from movement disorders owing to the rigidity and trembling of their body. If this condition is not managed, it can lead to considerable disability. For this purpose, movement reeducation services are provided to the patient in an outpatient setting.

Vocational Rehabilitation

As Parkinson's disease affects almost all aspects of the patient's life, he or she is occasionally provided with vocational rehabilitation. Basically, the patient is helped to make adjustments at home and work to better cope with his or her newly acquired disability. Patients are counseled to come to terms with their reduced capacities in some areas and change their habits and routines to suit their abilities. Sometimes, the whole process also requires giving consultations to peers and caregivers. In some cases where the patient feels uncomfortable or has difficulty in identifying with the new disease, group therapy proves helpful.

Gait Training

In PD, the patient suffers from two main gait disturbances—speed and stride length. Specialists assist patients in improving their gait through a single intervention of structured, speed-dependent treadmill training (STT), or limited progressive treadmill training (LTT).

Assessment of Walking Aids

In Parkinson's, suffering and problems can differ among patients. This makes the task for occupational therapists and physiotherapists who work in outpatient settings more challenging. They have to structure individual strategies to assist with movement and tasks to help make the patient as independent as possible. For instance, if the patient finds that he or she is unable to eat or drink with normal speed, dinnerware can be replaced with insulated bowls, plates, and mugs that keep food warm for a longer period. Plates with a raised edge can help prevent food from slipping over the sides, and nonslip mats can be used to stabilize cutlery on the table.

Retraining for Everyday Tasks

As Parkinson's affects all spheres of life, the patient and caregiver must learn new ways to defeat the disease. The sufferer is aware that the disease cannot be cured 100 percent and then makes adjustments in the daily life pattern. The elderly patient may have to shift to living on the ground floor. He or she may have the bed moved next to a wall so as to get support from the wall when rising from the bed. Locks may have to be upgraded to easier-to-handle types.

Muscle Strengthening

Aerobic exercises and activities such as gardening, golf, pilates, tai chi, and yoga help strengthen the muscles of the outpatient. These activities have low or no cost and are highly effective, even more so if done in groups rather than alone.

Positioning and Posture

Physiotherapists who work in the outpatient setting teach the neurology patient exercises that he or she can do to maintain an erect posture. In most cases, family support is tremendously important for this activity.

OUTPATIENT ROLE OF NEUROLOGISTS AND OTHER
SPECIALISTS IN PARKINSON'S

Parkinson's patients are normally referred to a neurologist because the disease begins in the brain. However, as the disease progresses, its scope spreads into a number of scientific and medical fields. The following sections present an overview of the different fields of expertise and the roles of different specialists in the treatment of Parkinson's.

Geriatric Specialists

Geriatric specialists working in an outpatient setting deal with elderly Parkinson's patients. This type of specialist offers the diagnosis and treatment in both the emotional and mental domains of Parkinson's. Geriatrists render their expertise in the evaluation of the disease, monitor the improvements in their elderly patients, and advise on preventive measures against Parkinson's.

Neurosurgeons and Neurologists

A neurological surgeon specializes in providing operative treatment of CNS disorders and in disorders of the peripheral and autonomic nervous system, their supporting structures, and vascular supply. These surgeons are responsible for evaluation and treatment of pathological processes. The procedures that surgeons perform help modify the functionality of the nervous system. Specialists strive for managing the patient's pain through both operative and nonoperative procedures as required. They also provide treatment for (1) brain disorders, (2) problems with the meninges, (3) direct manifestations of skull fractures, and issues with blood supply to these vital body parts. They also treat the extracranial carotid and vertebral arteries, disorders of the pituitary gland, and disorders of the spinal cord. Neurosurgeons may prescribe allopathic medications as well as induce spinal fusion or instrumentation. Specialist neurological care can help minimize the time a person has to spend in the hospital if the person cannot be discharged directly from the emergency department to an outpatient status. Neurologists who have a special interest in neurogenesis approaches to Parkinson's also provide diagnostics for patients of the following:

- Fabray disease
- Gaucher disease
- Inherited and degenerative neurologic disorders
- Lateral sclerosis
- Neurofibromatosis
- Niemann-Pick disease

- Spastic paraplegia

OUTPATIENT PROCEDURES FOR DETECTING PARKINSON'S

Though blood tests can be useful, their results are not 100 percent absolute when it comes to outpatient diagnosis of Parkinson's. Therefore, some procedures are followed in order to categorize the disease. There are a great number of outpatient procedures that not only detect Parkinson's but that also assist in categorizing the type of the disease. Yet diagnosis is not an easy task, and all procedures hold a probability of error. Outpatient procedures, also referred to as walk-ins or ambulatory examinations, may take place in a doctor's office, a clinic, or an outpatient center. Outpatient procedures are less expensive than those performed on an inpatient basis, and technological advances have made outpatient procedures safer.

Procedure 1: Identifying the Symptoms

Parkinson's may be initially identified by diagnostics via a neurologist. Experience here matters significantly. The doctor will listen to the Parkinson's patient's complaints and may interview the patient's family as well. The aim is for the doctor to clearly understand all the descriptions of the symptoms. Parkinson's syndromes may be identified using a clinical approach. The physician asks the patient to form different gestures that the physician observes carefully for physical symptoms of Parkinson's. The patient may be asked to bend down, stand, walk, or pick up something from the floor. The degree of the symptoms the physician observes helps categorize the Parkinson's stage. In the initial stage of the disease, the symptoms usually are found on only one side of the body, but as the disease progresses, the symptoms start appearing on both sides. Two of the symptoms for which doctors are looking are discussed next.

Resting Tremors[3]

Resting tremors are the most easily detectable symptom in a Parkinson's disease outpatient. The hand of the patient, when in a resting position, shakes or trembles involuntarily. The patient feels no control over the hand and finds it difficult to hold the hand still. This slight shakiness goes away as the patient moves the hand. The doctor may ask the patient to pick up an object from his or her desk or to retrieve something from a pocket. To check the strength of the hand muscles, the doctor may observe the patient sipping from a cup of tea. The face might also be affected by tremor, making the patient lose control over the jaws and lips. Thus, the patient may have trembling lips even when not speaking. This facial symptom can be observed

during a quiet session in the doctor's office. Tremor may extend to the leg or foot, causing a jerky gait. The patient may also complain of an internal tremor, as if the body were trembling from inside.

Rigidity

The second most obvious symptom that the Parkinson's patient complains about is muscle rigidity. The patient experiences stiffness in the body muscles, especially while turning over in bed at night. Sometimes the muscle stiffness occurs only in the limbs, but in most cases, the patient suffers from full body rigidity. The patient may also suffer from cog-wheel rigidity, referring to a body motion (mostly in the arms) resembling the way cogs move in a gear. The arm of the patient suffers from a springlike, jerky action. The physician may ask the patient to button up a shirt or put some books on a shelf to observe this type of motion or other rigidity.

Procedure 2: Test Trials

When the symptoms of the disease are noteworthy, the doctor holds a trial test of drugs, which may be used to further diagnose the presence of PD. If a patient fails to benefit from levodopa, then a diagnosis of Parkinson's disease may be less certain to the doctor.[4]

Procedure 3: Imaging Procedures to Detect Parkinson's disease

Imaging procedures are called for once the neurologist sees adequate symptoms of Parkinson's in the patient. Neurological specialists will perform basic outpatient diagnostic procedures such as computed tomography, nuclear spin tomography, ultrasound, and other imaging procedures. The tomography helps categorize the various symptoms of Parkinson's that an outpatient may have.

Computed Tomography

This outpatient procedure is done after the patient has been diagnosed with Parkinson's. A computed tomography (CT) scan of the head is significant as it provides x-ray images of not only the soft tissues but also the bones and blood vessels of the brain.

Magnetic Resonance Tomography

Medical science presents yet another option for Parkinson's diagnosis in some outpatient facilities: magnetic resonance tomography, or MRT. This procedure is not primarily used for early Parkinson's detection but instead to differentiate Parkinson's-related syndromes from Parkinson's disease. The

scope of MRT includes other techniques, such as magnetic resonance imaging (MRI). MRT is useful in providing more exact images than standard computed tomography. The procedure renders tomograms from a strong magnetic field, enabling even the smallest changes to be detected.

Ultrasound Exams

One of the most important outpatient procedures for detecting Parkinson's is through the use of Doppler sonography. In this procedure, the blood vessels in the neck and head region, as well as the brain tissues, are examined through ultrasound. The radiologist determines whether and to what extent the blood vessels are blocked through arterial calcification. This outpatient procedure is most helpful in detecting a vascular category of Parkinson's syndrome, the treatment for which is different from that of other Parkinson's types. A heart ultrasound of the patient (echocardiography) shows changes to the heart that may occur while taking dopamine agonists—the most common drug prescribed to Parkinson's disease patients. Doctors recommend that Parkinson's patients on medication have an ultrasound examination of the heart once a year. As sometimes water accumulates in the heart or its surrounding regions, echocardiograms are helpful in discriminating between the side effects from Parkinson's medications and true heart disease.

Positron Emission Tomography (PET)[5]

PET is considered an efficient procedure for detecting Parkinson's in its early stage. The only drawback of this procedure is its high cost, which stops it from becoming an alternative popular procedure of choice. This procedure, found more often in the hospital than in the outpatient setting, involves radiochemists or nuclear chemists analyzing the images.

Single Photon Emission Computerized Tomography

As compared to its alternative method of PET, single photon emission computerized tomography (SPECT) is more common and widely used. The first reason is that it is much less expensive than PET. For this diagnostic procedure, the patient is required to discontinue medication for about two weeks prior to the examination. This essentially mars any discrepancies found in the results owing to the medications' effects on the body of the Parkinson's patient.

DaTSCAN

Relying on the presynaptic dopaminergic system, an important outpatient diagnostic procedure was developed in 2000, called DaTSCAN. This is a radiopharmaceutical process used for differential diagnosis of Parkinson's

disease as well as for Parkinson's plus. The limitation of this procedure is that although it diagnoses Parkinson's, it still cannot differentiate between the various symptoms of Parkinson's. This process has its advantage as it does not require the patient to discontinue previously prescribed medicines simply for the sake of examination.[6]

Procedure 4: Neurophysiological Examinations

This outpatient procedure evokes the nerves through stimulation. The nerve paths underneath the skull are examined using transcranial magnetic stimulation and evoked electrical potential. The pattern of nerve paths is different in a nonpatient versus an individual suffering from Parkinson's disease.

Procedure 5: Posturography

Posturography is a procedure that examines the balance of a standing person. The method acts as a balance measure and assists in gait analysis of a Parkinson's patient. The analyst identifies the **gait disorders** and any unsteady standing position. These procedures have been especially helpful for older patients in the differential diagnosis of "lower body Parkinsonism" (frontal gait disorder) and Parkinson's disease. The analyst also uses posturography for monitoring purposes during ongoing therapy.

Procedure 6: Electromyography

Electromyography is basically the measurement of electrical activity in muscles, abbreviated as EMG. This outpatient diagnostic procedure has proved helpful in differentiating tremors. In this procedure, the patient is spared from any injections, as the EMG is done only on the skin surface.

Procedure 7: Electroencephalography

This procedure is primarily used to verify the body's tolerance to medicine, as the majority of Parkinson's patients are aged. The electroencephalograph's, or EEG's, measurement of electrical activity in the brain evaluates the brain function, determines the extent of harm the disease has done, and analyzes the patient's condition regarding seizures.

Procedure 8: A Simple Phone Call[7]

Easy to perform in an outpatient setting, a recent development in the field of detecting Parkinson's is identifying the disease through voice pattern recognition. The technique works by experts listening to the voice of the Parkinson's sufferer and recognizing certain aspects of the latter's voice pattern.

Scientists are working on the next step of this method, to develop better soft- and hardware that will enable the patient to detect the disease by hearing his or her own voice and having the analysis personally available—to discover whether Parkinson's is present or not. The procedure was introduced by an applied mathematician working at the Massachusetts Institute of Technology. The Parkinson's Voice Initiative (the group developing this diagnostic procedure) has put together the mechanisms that analyze Parkinson's through voice patterns and are now detecting Parkinson's disease with an accuracy of 99 percent. Principally, the system evaluates the speech problems associated with Parkinson's disease, such as hypophonia, or reduced volume, reduced pitch range, monotone, and dysarthria, or difficulty with articulation of sounds or syllables. [8]

As the patient speaks over the phone, the analyst software not only looks for the sound pattern but also registers vocal trauma. The procedure, though new, is winning approval rapidly for being precise, being self-administered, and having an overall low cost to use. The mathematician responsible for the procedure has developed an algorithm identifying the unique characteristics present in the voice of a Parkinson's disease patient. He set up the Parkinson's Voice Initiative to facilitate and improve the machine's adaptive learning system and believes that by widening the user pool, the software will become a more accurate outpatient diagnosis tool. After some use, the software finds specific symptoms amid an array of speech variables. The new software has been tremendously important in recognizing vocal tremors, breathiness, and reduced speech volume.

III

Other Manifestations

Chapter Nine

Disorders Associated with Parkinson's

To better understand what effects PD can bring to the patient's health status, including related disorders, it is necessary to know how Parkinson's disease develops and how it affects other systems of the body. This disease is associated with decreased levels of dopamine due to destruction of neuronal cells in the substantia nigra fixed in the basal ganglia of the brain. Dopamine (an inhibitory neurotransmitter) and acetylcholine (an excitatory neurotransmitter) play a vital role in the physiological instruction of complex movements. When an imbalance in acetylcholine-dopamine levels surfaces due to the depletion of dopamine, secondary to several predisposing and precipitating elements such as genetics and head trauma, the impairment of extrapyramidal tracts occurs, thus affecting complex movements and voluntary movements as well as body coordination.[1] These factors can lead one to misinterpret Parkinson's as something else because they are present in such a wide array of other disorders.

Parkinson's is considered both as a *chronic* condition, which persists over a long period of time, and as *progressive*, which means that symptoms gradually worsen and overlap with other medical problems.[2] As Parkinson's disease progresses to a more advanced stage, different body systems may be affected, including the motor, nervous, cardiovascular, and genitourinary systems. While disorders associated with Parkinson's disease may be classified into three main categories, (1) motor, (2) nonmotor, and (3) neuropsychiatric,[3] the motor problems that affect physical movement typically appear at the early stage of PD, start insidiously, and develop slowly. The emergence of nonmotor and neuropsychiatric disorders can signal the worsening of the patient's condition and, unfortunately, poor prognosis.

PRESSURE ULCERS

Because of impaired mobility, PD patients are also predisposed to develop pressure ulcers, also known as pressure sores or bedsores.[4] A pressure ulcer is an alteration in skin integrity that develops when there is deficient blood supply in an area, especially in the bony prominences. The decreased blood supply is due to continuous applied pressure. Other predisposing factors in the development of pressure ulcers include old age and fragile skin.

Decreased nutritional status is one of the common problems of PD patients due to their diminished ability to swallow. If ideal levels of essential nutrients such as protein and vitamin C—both of which are responsible for wound healing and skin repair—are not met, PD patients may suffer from deep ulcerations that take longer to heal. On the other hand, PD patients may also develop urinary incontinence and **nocturia**, which can lead to bed-wetting. Increased moisture may lead to maceration (softening of the skin), which may irritate the skin. If the skin breaks, microorganisms can easily invade the tissues, and the wound that develops may possibly become deep and enlarged. Since bradykinesia may also develop as a result of Parkinson's disease, difficulty in initiating movement is also considered to be a cause of pressure ulcers. Aside from friction, shear force, which is the sliding over one another of tissue layers, may cause the stretching and twisting of blood vessels. This impedes the microcirculation in the skin and subcutaneous tissue.

Pressure ulcers are classified according to extent and depth. A stage 1 pressure ulcer is characterized by skin redness that does not blanch with pressure and that may progress to a dusky, blue-gray appearance, indicating an area of necrosis, warmth over the area, and discomfort. If not managed, it may lead to stage 2, characterized by tissue breakdown and presence of abrasion, blister, or crater, and edema in the person who suffers from Parkinson's or another disorder. The next stage (stage 3) of pressure ulcer is evidenced by ulceration affecting the subcutaneous tissue, while stage 4 affects the muscles and bones.

It is important to address this problem and for the family members and the health team to understand how important schedule adherence is. Moreover, proper positioning should also be observed to prevent prolonged pressure to bony prominences such as the sacral area and elbows. Other than proper positioning techniques, it may also be necessary to use lifting instead of sliding the patient and to use available resources in patient transfer. Aside from pressure ulcers, patients are also at risk for venous insufficiency secondary to immobility. Immobility impedes blood circulation to the lower extremities, which is a major factor in the development of venous stasis, or poor/stopped blood flow in the Parkinson's disease sufferer.

FREEZING

Secondary motor symptoms include "freezing" of the muscles, micrographia (cramped handwriting), and unwanted physical movement accelerations. Freezing can be differentiated from rigidity because it is characterized by a hesitancy to step forward, as if the patient's feet are glued to the floor. However, freezing is temporary. The patient is expected to overcome freezing once he or she is able to initiate the first step. Aside from walking, freezing may also be experienced by PD sufferers when they are pivoting. Freezing is manifested by the patient when he or she takes an exaggerated step as walking begins. Masklike expressions characterized by diminished facial expression or movement are also found in patients with Parkinson's disease. In contrast to bradykinesia, individuals with Parkinson's are sometimes observed to have unwanted vocal accelerations, which are evident as the patient speaks extremely quickly. This disorder is known as tachyphemia.[5]

ASSOCIATED AUTONOMIC NERVOUS SYSTEM DYSFUNCTION

Loss of Smell and Taste

Parkinson's disease may also affect other systems of the body. Most patients also experience a decline in olfactory function (sense of smell) preceding the emergence of motor signs of the disease.[6] Olfactory dysfunction is present in almost 90 percent of all PD patients.[7] Loss of sense of smell is said to be related to several neuroanatomical alterations such as a deficient number of neurons in certain parts of the brain. In connection to this, a decrease in cholinergic, serotonergic, and noradrenergic functions is a contributing factor that leads to olfactory function loss.[8] This loss is referred to as (1) anosmia if there is total lack of sense of smell, (2) hyposmia if there is decreased ability to recognize different odors, and (3) dysosmia if there is an inability to identify odor correctly. Aside from the marked decline in the patient's ability to recognize odor, the ability to identify the taste of food is also decreased. This may be classified as either ageusia (total lack of the sense of taste), hypogeusia (inability to distinguish between different tastes), or dysgeusia (inability to identify a taste correctly).

Cardiovascular Dysfunction

Many PD patients, ranging from 30 to 58 percent, suffer from orthostatic hypotension.[9] Orthostatic hypotension, also called postural hypotension, is characterized by low blood pressure when a person stands up from sitting or lying down. The American Autonomic Society defines orthostatic hypoten-

sion as a constant decrease of systolic blood pressure to ≥ 20 mmHg and the diastolic pressure to ≥ 10 mmHg within thirty minutes after a change in standing position. This condition is manifested by weakness, nausea, pain, unclear sight, and a feeling of dizziness or lightheadedness that may eventually cause the person to faint. Hence, orthostatic hypotension is also what predisposes a patient to falling. Orthostatic hypotension is known to be the result of sympathetic noradrenergic dysfunction of the cardiovascular target organs. Aside from this, orthostatic hypotension may also be related to inadequate fluid intake and the effects of medications for Parkinson's disease, including dopamine agonists and selegiline. In contrast to orthostatic hypotension, supine *hyper*tension, associated with low baroreflex-cardiovagal gain (when the body's internal pressure sensors do not work well) may also be experienced by PD patients. Thus, it is necessary to consider supine hypertension in treating orthostatic hypotension. [10]

ASSOCIATED GASTROINTESTINAL AND RESPIRATORY DISTURBANCES

Gastrointestinal disturbance is one of the disorders associated with PD that does not respond to levodopa treatment and other medications that alleviate the specific symptoms of PD. Patients with Parkinson's disease commonly complain of constipation, which accounts for approximately 60 percent of the cases. [11] Constipation is defined as fewer than three bowel movements per week. This problem is said to be the result of both decline in neurodegenerative process as well as the effects of dopaminergic medications that affect gastric motility. The primary intervention to manage constipation is to increase gastrointestinal motility by increasing fluid and fiber intake. If this intervention fails, administration of stool softeners may be considered. In connection to this, constipation is not the only gastrointestinal problem of patients with Parkinson's disease. Bowel function is also impaired in some PD patients, which can cause discomfort due to straining and incomplete emptying. This is secondary to the failure of the rectal sphincter to relax (also called anismus) because of spasms or dystonia in order to coordinate when the bowel movement is being attempted. However, straining during defecation (also referred to as Valsalva maneuver) can cause vagal stimulation but decreases cerebral blood flow and cardiac output.

Dysphagia (difficulty of swallowing) can also occur in the advanced stage of Parkinson's disease. It is associated with poor muscle control, tongue tremor, and difficulty shaping food into a form for swallowing, which also pose risks for aspiration pneumonia. In connection to this, rather than the overproduction of saliva, the patient's reduced ability to swallow, causing an accumulation of saliva in the mouth, is said to be the cause of hypersaliva-

tion, which results in drooling.[12] Patients with Parkinson's disease may also be at risk for bronchopneumonia because they are not aware that they are aspirating. In the case of Parkinson's disease, bronchopneumonia occurs as a result of aspiration of gastric contents, which is also referred to as aspiration pneumonitis or Mendelson's syndrome. Since PD patients are also at risk to develop gastroesophageal reflux disease (GERD) due to **gastroparesis** (discussed below), aspiration pneumonia is a great risk to their health. This type of aspiration pneumonia, known as chemical pneumonia, is due to the parenchymal inflammatory response secondary to chemical burns of the tracheobronchial tree brought on by the acidity of the gastric contents. This is all followed by an inflammatory reaction.

Bruxism may also be one of the disorders associated with PD patients. Bruxism is the grinding or clenching of teeth, which may eventually lead to dental damage and jaw dysfunction. Bruxism can be classified as bruxism when the patient is awake or bruxism when the patient is asleep. Sleep bruxism may be related to sleep disturbances such as arousals secondary to certain medical conditions such as obstructive sleep apnea. Unfortunately, there is no medication to treat this condition. Different devices to suppress teeth grinding have been effective for bruxism. These include (1) mandibular advancement devices to hold the lower jaw, and (2) occlusal splints, or mouth guards, to keep the upper and lower teeth apart.[13]

Another gastrointestinal disturbance experienced by PD patients is delay in gastric emptying secondary to PD treatment, which occurs in 70 percent of the cases.[14] This condition is called gastroparesis. Patients with gastroparesis may complain of a bloated sensation and nausea, even if they consumed only a small amount of food. Discomfort is not the only negative effect of gastroparesis. Another negative effect is the decreased therapeutic effect of levodopa, a PD medication that is well absorbed in the intestines. Because of delayed gastric emptying, the medication could possibly stay in the stomach much longer instead of going into the intestines within a shorter period.[15]

Complications

Gastroparesis can cause the food to stay in the stomach for a longer period of time and may permit the growth of bacteria due to the fermentation of food. In addition, food can harden into solid masses, referred to as benzoars. These can cause nausea, vomiting, and obstruction in the digestive tract as they move from the stomach to the small intestines.[16] Gastroparesis is also associated with gastroesophageal reflux disease (GERD). GERD is described as the backflow of gastric and duodenal contents into the esophagus, which is manifested by **pyrosis** (burning sensation in the esophagus), dyspepsia (indigestion), regurgitation, dysphagia or odynophagia (difficulty or pain in swallowing), hypersalivation, and esophagitis. Gastroparesis is a disorder linked

to Parkinson's disease,[17] so to prevent further aggravation of gastroparesis, it is necessary to use techniques and implement interventions to control symptoms of GERD in PD patients. These include restricting intake of fatty foods, which are slow to digest, alcohol, and caffeine. Smoking cessation may also be necessary, and avoiding supine positions after meals and during sleeping may also be beneficial. One way to avoid the supine position (as much as possible) is to place a hard object at the patient's upper back. The main disadvantage of using hard objects is that they may cause the patient discomfort, including back pain, so specially designed pillows can be used to achieve the same objective.

URINARY DYSFUNCTION

Parkinson's disease is also associated with changes in genitourinary function because of an altered dopamine-basal ganglia circuit that affects the reflex responsible for normal urination and continence. Consequently, bladder dysfunction related to detrusor muscle hyperactivity ensues, leading to urinary urgency and frequency as well as nocturia (waking up at night to urinate).[18] In contrast, a *hypo*active detrusor muscle may result in delaying bladder emptying and difficulty initiating urination, thereby leading to urinary tract infections.

Emptying of the Bladder

Urinary tract infection (UTI) is defined as an infection affecting any part of the urinary tract, including the kidneys, bladder, and urethra. Delay in bladder emptying resulting indirectly from Parkinson's may cause urinary stasis, which is considered to be one of the factors predisposing patients to UTI. This is because urinary stasis permits the proliferation of the bacteria present in the urine. Urinary tract infection may be put into two classifications, based on which part of the urinary system it affects: lower urinary tract infection (LUTI) and upper urinary tract infection (UUTI). LUTI affects the bladder (cystitis), prostate (prostitis), and urethra (urethritis) while UUTI affects the kidneys (pyelonephritis). The most common manifestations of UTI are dysuria (pain in urination), a burning sensation in the urethra upon voiding, difficulty in initiating urination, frequency in urination but in small quantity, and hematuria (presence of blood in the urine), which suggests UUTI. Aside from these symptoms, the Parkinson's patient may also feel pain in the lower abdomen, fever accompanied by chills (if it already affects the kidneys), or pain in the lumbar area. The patient may also experience nausea and vomiting. These symptoms are indicative of LUTI. Aside from urinary stasis, poor hygiene may also be one of the causes of UTI among PD sufferers, especially the elderly, due to self-care deficit and decline in functional capacity.

ASSOCIATED SEXUAL DISORDERS

Sexuality is one of the most complex aspects of being human, and many people experience sexual difficulties in their lives. There are many reasons, physical, psychological, and social, that people with Parkinson's might experience problems related to intimate relationships. For some, the recognition that life with a diagnosis of Parkinson's will never be the same again can cause a total disruption to what those individuals perceive as normal. Diminishing communication skills, fluctuating mood, a negative self-image, and social isolation can cause distress not only for the person with Parkinson's but also for the person's sexual partner. It has been accepted for some time now that neurological disease and trauma cause sexual dysfunction, and in people with Parkinson's, sexual dysfunction is not uncommon. While 50 percent of men and women suffering from the disease may have a sexual problem, it is important to remember that having Parkinson's does not mean that sexual dysfunction is inevitable.[19] Both men and women with Parkinson's may undergo a decrease in sexual interest, desire, arousal, or orgasm. Not all problems can be explained by Parkinson's or a drug's side effects. The management of sexual dysfunction in a person with Parkinson's must include an initial screening for other underlying causes. Things such as diabetes, excessive alcohol intake, antihypertensive drugs, depression, and anxiety can also be the cause of impotence and sexual dysfunction. Therefore, listening skills in both the patient and caregiver are very important to help with anxieties about sex and relationships.[20]

Male erectile dysfunction (also known as impotence) is also reported by more than 60 percent of PD patients.[21] This is related to different contributory factors such as depression, physical disability, and autonomic dysfunction.[22] Erectile dysfunction associated with Parkinson's disease is due to the impact of PD on the central nervous system, specifically the brain, which in this case has diminished ability to send impulses to sustain erection. Aside from erectile dysfunction, one study[23] with more than thirty women and about forty men affected with PD also indicated other problems in sexual functioning. For women, these problems include difficulties with arousal (almost 90 percent), with reaching orgasm (75 percent). with low sexual desire (around 45 percent), and with sexual dissatisfaction (almost 40 percent). The group of male patients with PD reported erectile dysfunction (approximately 70 percent), sexual dissatisfaction (65 percent), and difficulty attaining orgasm (40 percent).[24]

ASSOCIATED NEUROPSYCHIATRIC AND SLEEP DISORDERS

Cognitive impairment and changes in mental function may also be observed in Parkinson's disease patients, including depression, dementia (progressive mental deterioration), which occurs at the late stage, sleep disturbances, and hallucinations. Depression is considered as a first manifestation of PD, which appears before the onset of motor symptoms.[25] Its prevalence rate ranges from 7 to 76 percent in PD cases.[26] Depression is thought to be related to several complex and interrelated factors that include depletion of dopamine and other chemicals in the brain. This whole process affects the mood and the stress of living with Parkinson's and its possible impact on the patient's relationship with others. Symptoms that signal the presence of depression are a feeling of hopelessness and having little interest in the things a person enjoyed doing before developing Parkinson's. At the early stage of PD, an individual may also manifest mild cognitive impairment, evidenced by disrupted patterns of thinking and an inability to perform activities that require planning and organization. This disorder is found in 36 percent of PD cases, according to a clinical report,[27] and it may be attributed to disturbance of fronto-subcortical circuits. Processing of information may also be affected, causing *bradyphrenia* (slow thought process). As the symptoms of PD worsen, this mild cognitive impairment may result in a more serious condition known as dementia. This condition shows a marked change in the patient's level of learning, considering both spoken and written language, and the patient's memory, which makes the person unable to realize previously familiar places and people, including family members. Some PD patients are also observed to have unexpected outbursts of emotions such as anger, excitement, and frustration; poor concentration and decreased attention span; and delusions and visual hallucinations, believing and claiming that they see things that are actually not real. When the patient experiences hallucinations, he or she may see, hear, smell, or taste something that does not exist. Visual hallucinations typically involve seeing and feeling small animals or other people in the room that are really not there.[28]

Anxiety is a normal feeling at the time the patient is diagnosed with PD. However, it is expected to subside in time. Anxiety may not be a mere result of thinking about what PD may bring to the family, including the financial burden associated with the medical treatment. Anxiety secondary to PD may also appear as an intrinsic form that can make PD patients (1) irrational, (2) worrisome, as if something dangerous and detrimental will happen to them, or even (3) powerless.[29] If the caregiver does not manage the anxiety and support systems are not used, anxiety disorders such as panic attacks during off periods, generalized anxiety, and simple and social phobias can possibly occur as an effect of Parkinson's disease. PD patients may avoid socializing

with other people or refuse to participate in the treatment because they are preoccupied with their worries about the disease.

Sleep disorders related to Parkinson's disease include insomnia, excessive daytime sleepiness, rapid eye movement (REM) behavior disorder, and sleep apnea. Insomnia, when described as difficulty falling and staying asleep, is experienced by two-thirds of PD patients.[30] Insomnia can be caused by muscle cramps, immobility, nocturia, anxiety, and possible side effects of prescribed medications. In contrast to this, PD patients also experience excessive daytime sleepiness or sudden dozing during the day that may be dangerous if they engage in activities that require alertness, such as driving. This problem can be caused by several factors, such as lack of sleep at night secondary to insomnia, depression, and drug therapy, particularly dopamine agonists, which can cause sleepiness as a side effect.[31]

In connection to the above-mentioned sleep disturbances, **sleep apnea**, defined as difficulty or cessation of breathing while the person is asleep, is also one of the factors that can cause insomnia and excessive daytime sleepiness. This condition can also cause a reduction in oxygen flow to the brain, causing impaired thinking and concentration. Sleep apnea may be manifested by snoring, which may affect the patient's significant others. REM behavior disorder is another sleep disturbance that PD patients experience. Normally, muscles are suppressed during REM sleep, rendering movement virtually impossible. Thus, during this stage of sleep, the Parkinson's disease sufferer normally does not have control over the body and cannot "act out" what he or she is dreaming. In REM behavior disorder, muscle suppression is inhibited; hence, if a person dreams vividly, that person tends to act out violently while asleep.

Aside from anxiety, depression, and sleep disturbances, PD patients are also noted to have behavioral disorders such as **impulse control disorder** (ICD), characterized by the inability to resist a desire, drive, or temptation to perform an act that can harm other members of the family or even those around the patients, such as a caregiver. Patients who develop ICD are usually males, are at a younger age at PD onset, have a longer duration and early disease onset, and have a personal or immediate family history of alcohol-use disorders or a prior history of ICDs. Pathological gambling is one of the ICDs noted among patients with Parkinson's disease. This means that the patient fails to resist the desire to gamble despite the possible consequences it may bring to the patient, his or her family, or his or her entire career. Pathological gambling may occur anytime during the onset of PD. Another common impulse-control disorder is hypersexuality, appearing in approximately 7 percent of PD cases.[32] Hypersexuality is manifested as increase in libido, which could also involve exhibitionism, excessive use of phone-in lines, use of prostitution services, and frequenting of sex shops. Other than the aforementioned ICDs, Parkinson's disease is also associated with compulsive sex-

ual behavior disorders, compulsive buying, and binge-eating disorders. It was found that PD patients may present up to two impulse control disorders at any given moment.[33]

Chapter Ten

Pain and Parkinson's

Pain is broadly defined as an unpleasant feeling transmitted to the brain by sensory neurons. The senses give people physical awareness and perception to interpret the discomfort. Acute pain goes away after an injury heals or the cause of pain is removed. Chronic pain persists after an injury heals or if the pain is related to a persistent or degenerative disease. PD patients do not always tell their doctors about their pain or physical discomfort, and so it often goes untreated. Very little research has been done to study how sensory signals are disordered (when speaking in more physiological detail than that of chapter 3) in Parkinson's, but research is progressing in helping caregivers understand the types of pain associated with the disease. Pain is a disabling symptom and a major complaint of patients even prior to confirmation of PD. Pain complaints range from muscle stiffness and rigidity, to dystonic spasms, to a rare pain arising from the abnormalities in the central nervous system. Further investigation about the origin of pain in PD, common areas of pain in the body, and traditional and alternative treatments for pain are discussed in this chapter.

ROOTS OF PAIN IN PARKINSON'S

Pain in Parkinson's disease usually stems from one or more of the following causes: (1) muscular and skeletal pain, or the aching of muscles and joints, (2) pain that occurs close to a nerve or nerve root, (3) painful dystonia, the forceful and sustained twisting movement of a muscle group, (4) pain associated with akathisia or restlessness, and (5) primary or central pain syndrome caused by changes in the central nervous system.

Muscular and Skeletal Pain

Musculoskeletal pain is the most common type of pain that PD patients experience. Muscle stiffness, rigidity, and problems with movement and posture all contribute to musculoskeletal pain. The constant motion of the tremors or spasms represents a considerable amount of work done by the muscles, so it is natural that symptoms of muscle fatigue are occasionally experienced. One common complaints from patients is shoulder stiffness, which is also termed *frozen shoulder*. It is said that the frozen shoulder is known to be an early symptom of PD. Patients may also experience aches in the neck, hip, and back. The pain is constant and may affect the whole limb. Muscular pain also has a tendency to precede the onset of motor symptoms by one to two years.[1] Some people experience a sense of aching soreness before the first occurrence of the tremor by even a year or more.

Muscle cramps are also associated with Parkinson's and may happen at night or during the day. At night, it usually causes pain in the legs and calf muscles, which leads to disrupted sleep. Normal painkillers may not always work, so exercises and physiotherapy is recommended for patients. Skeletal pain, on the other hand, is related to the effects of aging, pressure and thinning of the bones, and arthritis. In patients with PD, a common disorder that causes skeletal pain is spinal stenosis. Spinal stenosis is the narrowing of the spinal canal that can cause compression of the spinal cord or the nerve roots. It typically occurs in the lower back or in the neck area, along the cervical spine. The frequent cause of this condition is degenerative arthritis of the spine. A Parkinson's disease sufferer with spinal stenosis usually needs to take frequent breaks when walking over long distances and may adapt a bent-over posture because it lessens stenosis from a mechanical standpoint. PD and spinal stenosis commonly exist together in patients.[2]

Radiculopathy

Parkinson's is essentially a degenerative disorder of the central nervous system; hence it is commonly associated with neurological disorders and radicular pain.[3] Radicular pain occurs close to a nerve or a nerve root. Patients often describe the pain as a sharp sensation that extends to the end of a limb. A classic example of radicular pain in PD is *sciatica*. Sciatica refers to pain, weakness, numbness, or tingling in the leg or lower back area. It is usually caused by an injury or pressure on the sciatic nerve. Sciatica is a symptom of another medical problem and not a medical condition on its own. It may be caused by a pinched nerve in a disk or irritation of the nerve from an adjacent bone, tumor, or muscle. A patient with sciatica usually experiences pain down one leg to below the knee, and the pain can be exacerbated by coughing, sneezing, bending down, and prolonged standing or sitting.[4]

Neuropathy

Neuropathy or neuropathic pain occurs because nerve fibers themselves could be damaged or dysfunctional. These damaged nerve fibers send signals to the brain's pain center. Some of the symptoms of this type of pain also include numbness, tingling, and painful *paresthesia* in the hand or feet. Paresthesia refers to an abnormal tactile sensation with no apparent physical cause, a feature of Parkinson's proved by clinical survey.[5] Paresthesia is usually described as a burning, pricking, tickling, or "pins and needles" feeling. Most people have experienced temporary paresthesia at some point, when they have sat with legs crossed or have fallen asleep in a crooked position. It goes away once the pressure is relieved. Chronic paresthesia, on the other hand, is often a symptom of an underlying neurological disease or traumatic nerve damage.

Painful Dystonia

Dystonia refers to the prolonged or sustained involuntary muscle contractions or twisting movements that usually result in the abnormal posturing of the involved body part. Dystonia is caused by a variety of diseases involving the central nervous system and is classified in two ways. Primary dystonia is caused by a genetic abnormality; it appears without known cause and is more likely due to the physiology of the person's nerve cells. Secondary dystonia is a result of an injury to the brain, or it can be due to degenerative disorders such as Huntington's disease and Parkinson's disease.[6] In PD, this pain usually affects the limbs, neck, face, jaw, swallowing muscles, and vocal cords. It may affect a single muscle or a group of muscles. PD patients with dystonia may report varying degrees of pain from minimal to severe.

A frequent form of dystonia in PD patients involves the feet and toes, which may curl painfully in a clawlike position due to spasms in the calf muscles. The foot may also turn in at the ankle, and the big toe may extend. This can be very uncomfortable, especially when wearing shoes. A similar cramp may develop in the hand, which is usually aggravated by tasks that require fine control. This condition has been termed *writer's cramp* or *mogigraphia*. The condition is a task-specific focal dystonia, which means that the symptom is limited to one location and is triggered when an individual engages in a particular activity such as writing.

A cramp that occurs in the neck may cause wryneck. Also called *torticollis*, this refers to the sustained posturing of the head turned to one side. If the head bends forward, it is called *anterocollis*, and a backward bend is called *retrocollis*.[7] There is also a condition where the eyelid muscles are affected. The eyelid muscles may contract to close the eyes every now and then for a prolonged period of time. This condition is called *blepharospasm*. It usually

starts with one eye and eventually spreads to the other. Aside from the involuntary contraction of the eyelid muscles, patients may also experience other symptoms such as excessive blinking, irritation, a burning sensation in the eyes, and sensitivity to light. It is said that activities such as reading, looking up or down, and driving and conditions such as bright lights and even stress can worsen the symptoms.

When dystonia affects the side of the face or the jaw, it is called *hemimasticatory* or hemifacial spasm. It normally affects just one side of the face. The condition initially starts to affect the muscles around the eye and then spreads to the other muscles on the same side of the face, particularly around the jaw and mouth. In addition, dystonia may also affect the vocal cords and is referred to as *laryngeal dystonia* or *spasmodic dystonia*.[8] The spasms make it difficult for the vocal folds to vibrate and produce words. Patients often find it hard to start speaking, and words get cut, making speech sound choppy but not necessarily stuttering. Some would describe the voice of an individual with spasmodic dystonia as sounding strained, strangled, or full of effort. These types of cramps and the resulting abnormal postures are collectively referred to by neurologists as dystonia or dystonic cramps.

Dystonia is considered to be a part of the disease process; however, it can also be caused by the medication used to treat PD. It also occurs more often in people with young-onset Parkinson's disease.[9] A few patients experience dystonic spasms as a complication of PD medication such as levodopa. These patients may experience a dystonic facial grimacing or uncomfortable limb posturing. For this reason, doctors take into consideration the timing of the dystonic spasms so that they can establish its relationship to dopaminergic medication. Treatment also varies and may consist of oral medications, injections of medication into the muscles, and brain surgery. More details about the medication and treatment are discussed in the succeeding topics.

Pain Due to Akathisia

Akathisia may simply be defined as restlessness. It usually manifests with an inability of a person to sit still or remain motionless. This condition involves an increased level of the neurotransmitter **norepinephrine**, which is essentially related to mechanisms that regulate alertness, aggression, and arousal. Akathisia in PD patients may range in intensity from anxiety to severe discomfort. Common symptoms include increasing discomfort, insomnia, poor concentration or attention, impatience, fatigue, neuropathic pain, muscle stiffness, hypertension, pacing in the knees, and a rhythmic leg movement at night, a condition known as periodic limb movement disorder (PLMD).

Central Pain Syndrome

Central pain syndrome is caused by the abnormal functioning of the central nervous system (CNS), which includes the brain, brain stem, and spinal cord. Central pain is rare and is usually characterized by sensations of stabbing, burning, or scalding. It can be a mixture of sensations, but the most prominent is burning. The pain may be chronic and can be moderate to severe in intensity. Central pain may affect a specific part of the PD patient's body or affect the person as a whole. This unusual pain can involve the face, head, stomach, pelvis, and genitalia. It has also been observed that pain increases with changes in temperature, most often in cold temperatures. It may also worsen by touch, movement, and emotional changes.

Other Roots of Pain in Parkinson's

Headaches

Pain caused by headaches can occur at any time during the course of the disease. It may occasionally be caused by the medication used to treat Parkinson's. Severe headaches are rare, and regular over-the-counter painkillers are usually enough to alleviate the pain.

Restless Legs Syndrome

Restless legs syndrome is a disorder characterized by an urge or need to move the legs to stop unpleasant sensations. Most patients claim that the sensations are mainly unpleasant but not painful. For some patients, however, the syndrome contributes to chronic pain. In instances where patients may experience pain with restless legs syndrome (RLS), pain may first be considered as a part of the urge-to-move sensory component. Second, Parkinson's disease patients may have pain and an urge to move that are two separate conditions. RLS may also be related to neuropathy since patients experience a burning pain in their feet. A third cause may be due to learned helplessness (awareness and anticipation of the pain) and sleep deprivation, which lessens the pain threshold. Finally, pain may also be an effect of PD medication such as *dopaminergics*.[10]

Pain in the Mouth and Jaw

Some patients report having experienced a burning sensation or pain in their mouth or jaw area. It is a problem that can happen at any stage of Parkinson's. Dryness of the mouth is said to be caused by some PD medication, specifically the **anticholinergic agents**. These are substances that inhibit or block nerve impulses that help to control the muscles of the arms, legs, and body. Pain caused by mouth dryness can be attributed to the increased rates

of tooth decay and gum disease. "Burning mouth" syndrome has also been reported as more common in PD patients than in the general population. A study[11] determined that burning mouth syndrome occurred in approximately 25 percent of PD sufferers, which is about five times higher than that of the general population. The study hypothesized that the decreased dopamine levels and dopamine deregulation play a role in the occurrence of the symptom in PD patients.

Akinetic Crisis and Pain

Akinetic crisis usually occurs in the advanced stages of Parkinson's. Akinetic crisis is an ill-defined complication occurring during the course of PD with infectious diseases, bone fractures and the gastrointestinal tract disorders described in chapter 9. It is characterized by an acute worsening of Parkinson's symptoms and transient unresponsiveness to current treatments or to increments of dopaminomimetic treatments. It can also be brought about by an abrupt withdrawal of PD medication. Some of the symptoms include severe stiffness, fever, pain in the muscles and joints, headache and whole body pain.[12]

RECOGNITION OF PARKINSON'S-RELATED PAIN

Pain is listed in many of the early descriptions of PD, although it is not considered as a major feature of the disease. For a number of patients, the painful symptoms fluctuate in parallel with the motor symptoms and are designated as nonmotor sensory fluctuations. For some, the pain may be so severe that it overshadows the motor symptoms of the disease. The challenge for clinicians is to recognize when a patient's complaint of pain requires further evaluation and to categorize the painful symptoms of PD into a framework for diagnosis and treatment. A few useful pointers can be used as a guide to determine whether pain is related to Parkinson's:

- The pain is concentrated on the side most affected by Parkinson's or the side where the motor symptoms are more severe.
- The pain is relieved by Parkinson's medication.
- In the presence of motor fluctuation, the pain is usually present during the "wearing off" phenomenon and "off" periods and is relieved during the "on" periods.[13] The "on-off" effect is essentially the rapid change between (1) the "on" state, or the period of symptom relief and acceptable mobility, and (2) the "off" state, or a return of the Parkinson's disease symptoms with decreased mobility.

Chronic pain that is left underdiagnosed and untreated can affect a patient's daily activities and overall quality of life. The PD patient should take the first step by reporting the pain to his or her doctor. The patient should provide a specific and detailed description of the pain. The doctor will then assess the pain through a clinical interview and neurological examination.

Pain Assessment

Only patients are capable of describing the intensity of pain they experience. A careful pain evaluation should be performed on PD sufferers when taking patient history. A number of factors are considered in the patient's medical history, which include (1) the time of onset of the pain, (2) location, (3) an accurate description of the intensity of the pain, (4) any specific triggers, (5) activities that relieve the pain, and (5) relationship of the pain to Parkinson's symptoms and to PD medication. The doctor may ask some of the following questions, which are helpful in identifying the location and intensity of the patient's pain.

Location

- Where is the pain located?
- Where does it hurt most? The back? The shoulder? The hip?
- Does the pain stay in one place?
- Does the pain radiate anywhere?
- If so, where? From the shoulder down the arm?

Intensity

- How bad is it?
- Describe it on a scale from zero to ten, where zero signifies a lack of pain and ten feels as if a body part is being yanked off or the skin is being torn off.

Duration

- How long have you had the pain? Hours? Days? Weeks? Years?
- Do you continuously have pain, or is it only at certain times?
- During a typical day, how long does it last? All day?

Association

- Do your anti-Parkinson's medications relieve your pain?
- Do you have arthritis?

- Is the pain associated with discoloration, inflammation, redness, swelling, or warmth of the overlying skin? The pain in PD should not be associated with those conditions.

Position

- Is there any position or posture that lessens the pain?
- Does the pain occur when doing a particular activity?
- What are—if any—the positions that make it better? Which positions make it worse?

Description or Quality

Parkinson's patients use many ways to describe pain. Examples of some of the commonly used words include aching, biting, stabbing, cramping, gripping, burning, throbbing, and pinching.

Pain Diagnosis

Multiple locations of muscular pain in PD patients are often associated with the sustained contraction of muscles. Rigidity, characterized as the stiffness or inflexibility that appears during the course of Parkinson's disease, can be considered a muscle spasm of supraspinal (above the spine) origin. Muscle contraction can be clinically measured with the electromyography (EMG) of the muscle fibers. Electromyography (EMG) is a technique used for evaluating and recording the electrical activity from the skeletal muscles. A muscle can be stimulated voluntarily via anterior horn cell activity or by electrical stimulation. The anterior horn cell is essentially a nerve that conveys impulses to muscles or glands.

For a skeletal pain diagnosis, EMG can be performed together with other physical examinations and methods such as an x-ray or magnetic resonance imaging. An x-ray of the spine may be performed to look for a fracture or narrowing of the spinal canal to find out whether a patient has spinal stenosis and to see other degenerative changes. An electromyography (EMG) examination is done to show signs of a nerve-root injury or neuropathy and at times can help sort out whether there are active or chronic changes. Spinal MRI or computerized tomography scan (CT scan) may be done to find disease of the spine, disks, spinal cord, and nerve roots.

There are also a couple of diagnostic tests that can be performed to diagnose neuropathic pain symptoms such as paresthesia, which causes the numbness and tingling sensations in PD patients. Blood tests, including complete blood count (CBC), electrolytes, thyroid function tests, and vitamin B-12 levels, can be used to identify the underlying cause of peripheral neuropathy. Imaging studies such as CT scan or MRI of the head and spine may be

done. EMG, x-ray, and a lumbar puncture (spinal tap) can also be used to look for inflammation or infections.

For dystonia, the assessment involves a careful medical history and physical examination to determine the cause and type of dystonia. Dystonia is a disease entity itself and has many subtypes, as mentioned previously. Details such as the location of the dystonia, time and day of the onset, degree of pain, and relation to PD medication are carefully considered in arriving at the proper treatment or management.

PD patients may also be routinely screened for anxiety. Akathisia in PD ranges from mild anxiety to extreme discomfort. Similarly, a careful medical history and physical examination is performed to rule out other causes of anxiety and to differentiate it from PD symptoms such as internal tremors or restless legs syndrome. Pulse, blood pressure, and respiratory rate often increase with anxiety. Blood tests and electrocardiogram (ECG) can also be used. There is also a self-administered screening tool called the Beck Anxiety Inventory (BAI) that can help discriminate anxiety from depression.[14]

The diagnosis of central pain, in contrast, is a rather straightforward process when a patient complains of pain or other abnormal sensations. It is normally caused by a CNS abnormality or injury. A neurological examination reveals areas of hypnoanesthesia (a technique used for pain management) to thermal stimuli and pinch. The areas are then assessed clinically with cold and warm stimuli and pinprick. Evoked pain is measured using pain scales. An MRI may also be done to check or confirm damage in the central nervous system.

ALTERNATIVE TREATMENTS FOR PAIN

Pain treatment in Parkinson's depends on numerous factors, including the type of pain, location, duration, intensity, and relation to Parkinson's symptoms. Pain management in PD usually consists of pharmacological treatment and nonpharmacological treatment. Alternative treatments for muscular pain include physiotherapy, bodywork therapy, chiropractic treatment, acupuncture, hydrotherapy, aromatherapy, nutritional therapy, and herbal medicine for muscle pain.[15] A physiotherapist assesses the PD patient's muscles and movements that are affected. A set of exercises and activities are then given to help ease the pain, stiffness, and soreness of the muscles and perhaps also improve posture. Bodywork therapy can ease muscle pain and restore body function. Massage is particularly recommended to relieve muscle pain and tension and to boost blood circulation. Chiropractic treatment is based on the concept that the nervous system coordinates all the body's functions and that disease results from a lack of normal nerve function. *Chiropractic* was derived from the Greek term *chir-*, which means "hand," plus the word *prasse-*

in, which means "to do" (to manipulate). This treatment primarily employs manipulation and adjustment of body structures.

For patients with spinal stenosis, nonsurgical treatment includes medication to relieve pain and inflammation such as acetaminophen and nonsteroidal anti-inflammatory drugs. Physical therapy may also be done; it involves (1) educating the patient about the course of the condition, (2) giving instructions on how to relieve the symptoms, and (3) giving advice on self-care. Weight loss is encouraged in order to slow the progression of stenosis, and exercise is also recommended to relieve symptoms. Cold packs and heat therapy may also help lessen the pain during flare-ups. If the pain does not go away with traditional treatments, surgery may be performed to release pressure on the nerves or spinal cord.

Muscular and Skeletal Pain Treatment

The most common treatment for mild muscle pain is the use of over-the-counter analgesics such as acetaminophen and ibuprofen. To address moderate to severe pain, prescription analgesics may be given to PD patients. These may include codeine, hydrocodone, fentanyl patch, and so forth.[16] It is important to note that with these analgesics, PD patients are at an increased risk for constipation and confusion. Some physicians may inject medication directly into the affected area as a supplement to medication therapy. Such injections usually consist of a combination of a numbing agent (local anesthetic, which provides immediate relief) and a corticosteroid for reducing inflammation. Nonpharmacological management for a Parkinson's disease sufferer who has painful or nonpainful dystonia includes physical therapy, speech therapy, and a technique call "sensory trick."[17] Physical measures such as massages, application of heat, and stretching of the affected body part are often used. For patients who experience toe curling and foot dystonia, proper shoe fitting is advised. Speech therapy is done for patients with laryngeal dystonia. With sensory trick, stimulation is applied to the affected or nearby body part to reduce the muscular contractions. By simply touching this area, PD patients can control their own contractions. Some of the sensory tricks done by individuals include the following:

- Touching the chin, back of the head, neck, or cheek gently can help with neck dystonia (torticollis).
- Pressing the fingers against the side of the face can help with eye dystonia (blepharospasm).
- Tapping the foot slowly in a rhythmic way.
- Squeezing the thumb and finger together rhythmically.
- Squeezing the earlobe.

- Using a toothpick, chewing gum, or boiled sweets can help people with jaw dystonia.
- Concentrating (cognitive thought) very hard on something can help.
- Using cold water to help in improving performance when writing (for people with writer's cramp).
- Holding the wrist to prevent tremors in the hand and writer's cramp.
- Holding the chin, earlobe, and neck for a person who has dystonia in the abdomen/trunk area.

Deep Brain Stimulation

A surgical procedure called deep brain stimulation (DBS) may also be done on patients who experience painful dystonia. Here, surgeons implant electrodes into a specific part of the patient's brain. The electrodes are connected to a generator that is usually implanted in the patient's chest. The generator then sends electrical pulses to the brain, which helps control or regulate painful muscle contractions. The invasiveness involves risks, including infections, stroke-like problems, and speech difficulties. DBS as it relates to nonpainful manifestations of Parkinson's is covered in more detail in chapter 14.

Acupuncture

Acupuncture is an alternative methodology to treat pain. It originated in China, and patients are treated by manipulating and inserting thin, solid needles into acupuncture points in the skin. Although researchers are still working on establishing a full understanding of how acupuncture works, it is said that acupuncture is an effective treatment for chronic pain. Hydrotherapy, formerly called *hydropathy*, uses the physical properties of water for pain relief and treatment. Some techniques include alternating hot and cold compresses to ease the pain, underwater massage, water jets, whirlpool bath, hot or cold plunge baths, and mineral baths. Another alternative therapy to treat pain is aromatherapy. It makes use of essential oils from certain plants and herbs to relieve pain and any accompanying spasms or inflammation. The essential oils can be applied with gentle massages or compresses. Some oils can also be added to bathwater. Commonly used oils for muscle pain include ginger, helichrysum (Italian everlasting), marjoram, peppermint, and thyme (linalol and red).

Nutritional and Herbal Therapy

Nutritional therapy for pain—whether speaking of Parkinson's or not—is usually tailored to the type of muscle pain involved. Muscles usually respond positively to proper nutrition. For instance, calcium and magnesium supple-

ments may help treat nighttime leg cramps. Enzyme therapy with bromelain can also treat certain types of pain. Other enzymes and nutrients that help ease muscle aches include oral doses of astaxanthin, bromelain, creatine, MSM (methylsulfonylmethane) and protease enzymes.[18] Herbal medication uses medicinal herbs to prevent or treat a disease and to promote health. Common herbs such as arnica, comfrey, and ginger can be applied externally to painful body parts. Nutritional therapy and herbal medicine are options, but it is always important to consult the doctor. Some over-the-counter herbal medicines are not regulated as prescription drugs are. In addition, some herbal medicine may interact with other PD medicine or may have harmful side effects. Nutritional therapy may include B-complex vitamin supplements, particularly vitamin B12. Vitamin supplementation is something that should be pursued with caution, since research[19] has determined that an overdose of vitamin B is one of the causes of paresthesia.

TRADITIONAL APPROACHES FOR NERVE PAIN

Radiculopathy

The standard treatments for pain due to sciatica are over-the-counter and prescription narcotic and non-narcotic medication as well as anti-inflammatory medication. Rest and physical therapy or chiropractic treatment may also be helpful. Patients with radiculopathy are also advised to avoid activities that strain the neck and back. These are conservative forms of treatment, and patients' symptoms gradually improve within six weeks to three months. For patients who do not improve after the standard treatments, an epidural steroid injection may be done. The physician providing care for the Parkinson's disease sufferer injects steroid medication between the bones of the spine adjacent to the involved nerves. This helps reduce the irritation and inflammation of the nerve. For more severe symptoms, surgery may also be an option. The purpose of the surgery is to remove the compression from the affected nerve. Depending on the cause, a laminectomy or discectomy may be performed. Laminectomy is done to remove a small portion of the bone covering the nerve, which allows it to have additional space. A discectomy is done to remove the portion of the disk that has herniated out and is compressing a nerve.

Neuropathy

To treat pain caused by neuropathy, steroid injections can be used to reduce the inflammation around a nerve. Phenytoin, carbamezipine, or tricyclic antidepressants such as amitriptyline may also be used to reduce nerve pain. An implantable medication pump may also be used to supply pain medication

directly into the spinal fluid. To replenish the pump, drugs are injected through the skin into a small port at the center of the pump. Paresthesia treatment—whether speaking of Parkinson's or other neurological disease—depends on the accurate diagnosis of the underlying cause. Mild pain can be treated with anti-inflammatory medication such as ibuprofen and aspirin. People with more difficult paresthesia (such as late-stage Parkinson's patients) may also be administered antidepressant medication that alters a person's perception of pain. For severe cases, opium derivatives such as codeine may be prescribed. Another alternative treatment available to assist in relieving paresthesia symptoms is nutritional therapy. People who experience paresthesia are also advised to avoid alcohol consumption. Acupuncture and massage are also believed to provide a level of relief from the symptoms of paresthesia. A massage with aromatic oils is sometimes helpful as well. The application of topical ointments that contain capsaicin, the substance that makes peppers "hot," might provide relief from paresthesia. [20]

Akathisia

Akathisia is often attributed (as a side effect) to antipsychotic drugs. The occurrence of akathisia in Parkinson's disease and its association with dopamine antagonist drugs suggest that dopaminergic drugs are involved in the pathophysiology of akathisia. Pain management in akathisia mainly involves altering or regulating the medication that is causing the akathisia and is considered the most reliable treatment for akathisia.

Painful Dystonia

For dystonia, the pharmacological treatment usually involves an optimization of PD medication in an attempt to decrease or minimize dystonia. This is a trial-and-error sequence that depends on whether the dystonia is related to too much dopamine, too little, or not at all. Botulinum toxin injections are also used for certain types and locations of dystonia. The toxin blocks the release of acetylcholine at the neuromuscular junction. It is administered by a direct injection into the affected muscle. Electromyography guidance is also used when the muscles involved are close to a body organ such as a lung. Botulinum toxin treatment is expensive; however, it has significantly improved the functional status and quality of life for many patients. The duration of action is three to four months, with patients receiving injections three to four times per year.

Aside from using botulinum toxin, tetrabenazine is another drug that can be used to block dopamine. The patient, however, may experience side effects such as sedation, nervousness, depression, or insomnia. Other medications such as trihexyphenidyl and benztropine may lessen dystonic symptoms

by working on neurotransmitters. Some of the side effects of these medications include constipation, memory loss, blurred vision, drowsiness, and dry mouth. The following medications can also act on neurotransmitters—diazepam, clonazepam, lorazepam, and baclofen. These medications can cause drowsiness.[21]

Non-opioid Analgesics

Pain in patients with Parkinson's is often associated with the other problems the disease brings. These aches and pains are usually headaches, stiff joints, and joint pains caused by rigid muscles, poor posture, and immobility. Examples of over-the-counter (OTC) medications that a person with Parkinson's can take to treat these aches and pains are non-opioid analgesics or painkillers that include nonsteroidal anti-inflammatory drugs (NSAIDs) such as acetaminophen, mefenamic acid, ibuprofen, naproxen, and even salicylates such as aspirin to help with the mild to moderate pain or discomforts associated with the disease.[22] These medicines are generally considered safe to use. However, before starting on this therapy, the patient must consult the physician treating the Parkinson's disease because some OTC medications may react with other medications being taken and could lead to lower absorption of the medications, increased risk for drug toxicity, and other side effects. For example, analgesics in general should be taken with or after meals because of their tendency to irritate the stomach lining, which could lead to gastric ulcers when taken over a prolonged period of time. If the patient has comorbid illnesses, such as cirrhosis or another existing liver problem, analgesics should be used with caution. The patient or caregiver must always read the label carefully and remember to check the expiration date and read the warning labels. Also, the patient should take only the suggested dose within the recommended time interval, especially if later-stage Parkinson's is present. If pain symptoms are not relieved by OTC medications or if symptoms get worse, the individual should seek medical attention; these symptoms may indicate an underlying illness or other problem.

MORE ON PAIN AND PARKINSON'S

Central Pain

Pain medications often deliver some reduction of—but not ample relief of—pain for Parkinson's disease patients affected by central pain syndrome. Tricyclic antidepressants such as nortriptyline or anticonvulsants such as gabapentin can be useful. Lowering stress levels appears to reduce pain as well. The last resort is neurosurgery.

Other Venues

Restless legs syndrome (RLS) in patients with Parkinson's is usually treated by PD medication. PD medication is aimed at reducing the amount of motion in the legs by changing the level of dopamine in the patient's brain. For the treatment of moderate to severe RLS, two drugs are commonly used—ropinirole and pramipexole. Other PD drugs may also be used, such as a combination of carbidopa and levodopa. The known short-term side effects of these drugs include mild nausea, lightheadedness, and fatigue. Opioids (narcotics) may also be used to relieve pain from RLS.[23] A study[24] has shown that clozapine (an antipsychotic drug) in low doses is effective in treating drug-induced delusions or hallucinations in Parkinson's.

IV

Team-Oriented Resolutions

Chapter Eleven

Allopathic Treatment

Individualized treatment is required in Parkinson's disease as patients usually manifest distinct symptoms that may be unique in their condition. An allopathic doctor (one who holds an MD degree) is someone who applies allopathic medical science. The practice of allopathic medicine is founded on evidence-based practice and hence is also known as modern or conventional medicine. This is the form of medical practice most people are used to—the standard approach that addresses the disease itself. Moreover, allopathic treatment is directed toward addressing the *direct* effects of Parkinson's disease symptoms. It is the treatment of choice when the objective is to provide straightforward management and reduction of the debilitating symptoms. Parkinson's disease can cause a significant disability that could affect the quality of life of the patient and indirectly affect the victim's family members and caregivers. [1] Allopathic treatment, then, has the objective of reducing the debilitating symptoms in Parkinson's disease both through surgical approach and through administering therapeutic medications. Allopathic doctors play a crucial role in evaluating the specific symptoms of PD that the patient manifests and in determining which allopathic treatment is best to correct the abnormalities in the brain that produce the symptoms.

Significant attention is given to allopathic medicine as one of several alternatives in treating Parkinson's disease today. This approach is gaining popularity as the concept of treatment in allopathic medicine is one directed at suppressing the symptoms of Parkinson's by means of specific methods of treatment. Various medical researches were undertaken primarily to determine the main cause of Parkinson's disease. Their outcomes always point to the abnormal function of the neurotransmitter dopamine in the brain. While other causes are attributable to different factors, the culprit in the occurrence of symptoms in Parkinson's disease is the abnormal function of dopamine.

Allopathic medicine is designed to reduce the symptoms of Parkinson's disease through variable methods and approaches that minimize and prevent the abnormal functions of dopamine that trigger the different symptoms. There are limitations in the treatment of Parkinson's disease with allopathic medicine, and the allopathic doctor usually needs to take precautions and give consideration to the PD patient's condition before deciding on the treatment approach to use that will be of the best benefit.

ROLE OF ALLOPATHIC MEDICINE

Treatment using an allopathic context as a form of medical intervention was coined in the nineteenth century to refer to a mainstream of medical approaches. These approaches consist of the use and application of certain pharmacological agents and other forms of physical interventions that are designed to treat and suppress symptoms.[2] Allopathic medicine is widely used across Europe and the United States today,[3] and allopathic doctors are trained professionals with expertise in using counteractive measures in treating diseases. A licensed allopathic doctor has the ability to obtain a patient's medical history, evaluate the patient through physical and laboratory tests and examinations, diagnose a disease, and prescribe medications to the individual who has Parkinson's.

Clinical Principles

The fundamental basis of allopathic medicine involves the way that diagnosis and treatment of diseases are characterized. Diseases are regarded as entities that can be identified, and allopathic treatment is designed to address specifically the entities that cause the disease.[4] Allopathic medicine centers on the treatment of the disease as an entity instead of directing the treatment at the patient himself. Thus, allopathic approach is engaged, for example, in treating diabetes instead of the diabetic patient. The form of treatment used in allopathic medicine comprises evidence-based application of drugs, radiation, and surgery. Allopathic treatment was viewed by many health practitioners, including those who treat Parkinson's, as a form of Western medicine that had its origin two hundred years ago and was developed along with modern science. The fundamental principle that is observed in allopathic medicine is that the body and mind are separate entities independent of each other.[5] Moreover, allopathic treatment considers the human body as being composed of separate body parts. Clinicians who apply allopathic medicine treat the symptoms as a manner of aggressively fixing the underlying problem a patient exhibits as those symptoms.

The application of allopathic medicine is most appropriate in emergency cases that require immediate treatment. With the allopathic system, the treat-

ment provided is straightforward and immediate, and the treatment is directed toward relief of symptoms. Surgical techniques used in allopathic medicine are becoming more highly innovative with advanced technology and provide a reliable and life-saving approach when aggressive treatment is required for certain medical disorders such as PD. While allopathic treatment is effective in acute conditions—such as when immediate treatment is required to reduce symptoms—some believe that allopathy is not the most effective in treating chronic conditions.

Other principles of treatment used in allopathic medicine include the belief that healing is dependent on outside agents in order to cure a malady such as Parkinson's. The treatment usually delivers a quick result; thus allopathic treatment is regarded as an aggressive form of treating conditions. These days, allopathic medicine is gaining popularity because of its organizational edge over other forms of medical treatment. While doctors of the ancient world relied mostly on what is today regarded as naturopathy and homeopathy, there are growing numbers of clinical practitioners using allopathic medicine in treating medical conditions.

Discovery

Allopathic medicine was in use as early as the twentieth century, when doctors experimented with implanting electrodes into the brain area specifically affected with Parkinson's disease. The effect was markedly positive when it produced improvements in the neurological functions of the brain and improved the movement deficits seen in Parkinson's disease patients.[6] This new discovery by scientists in probing through the brain marked the advent of allopathic medicine in treating Parkinson's disease. The application of electricity into the brain using the electrode inspired allopathic doctors to make the result of their experiment a formal study until improved allopathic surgical treatments were discovered and introduced as a Western medical treatment for Parkinson's disease.

Allopathic Approach

The practice of allopathic medicine considers mental ailment and emotional disorders not as diseases, but as character flaws. While physicians would address mental illnesses and other disorders of the mind by pharmaceutical intervention, behavioral modification, and counseling, the allopathic concept does not put emphasis on the role of the mind in health and healing. The allopathic approach in treating diseases consists of viewing the body parts as separate components and defining the physical causes of the illness. When it comes to Parkinson's, this could mean evaluating the various lobes of the brain (chapter 3) and devising a special approach based on the brain's struc-

tures. Spiritual healing is also beyond the scope of allopathic treatment. The scientific progression of allopathic medicine has gained dominance over other traditional systems of medicine. Owing to the successful production of certain vaccines and medical drugs that can treat various diseases, allopathic treatment becomes a frequent choice of treatment in many medical disorders, including Parkinson's disease.

The objective of the treatment approach in allopathy as it relates to Parkinson's is one of alleviating the sufferer from the symptoms of disease. The direct cause of the sufferer's symptoms is uncovered using modern diagnostic tools such as x-ray, CT scan, and other forms of laboratory tests on urine and blood. With the aid of modern medical science and technology, the diagnosis is more accurate. The treatment process becomes more efficient owing to the advanced technology used in the management of symptoms and through the aid of a surgical approach, pharmaceutical intervention, physiotherapy, and psychotherapy. Lifestyle reform (especially in the earlier stages of Parkinson's) is often integrated in the allopathic approach for a better recovery.

Approaching Sexual Symptoms

Sexual dysfunction, in the context of Parkinson's disease and as outlined in chapter 9, could be something the allopathic doctor has to treat in his or her career. Just as in female sexual dysfunction, the treatment approach for erectile dysfunction needs to be multidisciplinary due to its complex nature. There are several therapeutic options to enhance erectile function that enable intercourse, resulting in an improved quality of sex life. This can include the use of psychosexual counseling, external vacuum devices, surgically implanted penile prostheses, or drug treatments.[7] Drugs can be given locally (intracavernosal or urethral) or orally. Oral medications such as sildenafil (Viagra), which increase blood flow to the penis, are well tolerated in Parkinson's patients. However, as the drug causes vasodilation, it can lower blood pressure substantially. This can be a danger in patients with orthostatic hypotension, as in **multiple system atrophy** (MSA), where the hypotension can be severe, causing collapse. MSA can be difficult to distinguish from Parkinson's, especially in the early stages. It is important, therefore, to monitor lying and standing blood pressure before prescribing sildenafil to men with Parkinson's and to make them aware of the symptoms of orthostatic hypotension. Symptoms include feeling dizzy, vague, or light-headed, having blurred vision, experiencing angina-type pain, and generally feeling fatigued or unwell.

ALLOPATHIC DOCTORS AND PARKINSON'S-RELATED SURGERY

Stereotactic Surgery

Surgery is one of the treatment approaches used in Parkinson's disease that an allopathic doctor can perform (when a surgeon). This approach is chosen for Parkinson's disease patients in the event of long-term complications from levodopa therapy. One of the considerations when choosing this type of treatment for Parkinson's is the presence of dyskinesia and motor fluctuation symptoms that cannot be effectively managed by medication.

Deep Brain Stimulation Surgery

Allopathic doctors can apply the deep brain stimulation approach that uses an electrode to deliver a surge of current into the brain in order to inhibit the actions of the nerves that produce Parkinson's symptoms. The electrode delivers a current of 100–130 Hz while connected to the specific area of the brain that is responsible for movement control. The current has an inhibitory effect on the brain function that helps retard the abnormal function of the brain that is causing the Parkinson's disease symptoms.[8] An allopathic doctor usually implants one or two electrodes in the brain and can effectively reduce neurological symptoms and other symptoms of Parkinson's disease. There are, however, potential risks involved with the surgical approach in allopathic medicine. Parkinson's disease patients report experiencing mood changes, suicidal thoughts and depression. Possible causes for these side effects are usually attributed to the placement of the electrode that must be positioned accurately on the affected brain.[9]

An allopathic doctor who is not a surgeon usually evaluates the Parkinson's patient before prescribing surgery, but the process can involve a multidisciplinary team composed of a neuropsychologist, neurophysiologist, and psychiatrist, plus a rehabilitation team for postoperative care.[10] Coordinated efforts of this team of medical doctors are needed for better decision making on which treatment approach would best benefit the Parkinson's disease patient.

Thalamotomy

An allopathic specialist physician can perform a thalamotomy, another surgical approach to treating Parkinson's disease. The doctor orders a detailed brain analysis for the Parkinson's disease patient through a CT scan or magnetic resonance imaging (MRI) in order to find the specific target area of the brain where the surgery will be performed. The thalamus is a part of the brain responsible in controlling involuntary movements. The allopathic surgeon

uses a surgical drill to create a small hole in the skull where a hollow probe containing liquid nitrogen is inserted. The probe is capable of destroying the target brain tissues in the thalamus liable for causing tremors in Parkinson's disease. For example, if tremor occurs in the right hand, then the left brain hemisphere will be the site of treatment.

Tremors taking place in both hands usually require repeating the procedure in the other side of the brain. Allopathic doctors, however, are usually very careful in performing bilateral thalamotomy in both sides of the brain as doing so increases the risk of speech and cognitive impairment after surgery. Some possible risks and complications that might arise from performing a thalamotomy and that an allopathic doctor will discuss with the patient and the immediate family include the following:[11]

- Hemiparesis
- Dysarthria
- Gait deformity
- Confusion
- Dystonia
- Infection

- Dysphasia
- Hand ataxia
- Hyperkinesia
- Numbness
- Seizure

The recovery period from the thalamotomy procedure usually takes up to six weeks. This form of allopathic procedure is a treatment option only for Parkinson's disease patients who are below the age of sixty-five. It is also reserved as a choice of treatment only in the presence of severe tremors in one side of the body.[12] These days, thalamotomy is rarely used because the effectiveness of the less-invasive mode of surgical treatment, deep brain stimulation, is the preferred approach among allopathic doctors.

Neural Tissue Transplantation

This kind of surgical management involves transplantation of porcine neuronal cells, human fetal cells, and stem cells.[13] Neural tissue transplantation is a method of treatment used for neurodegenerative diseases, most especially in Parkinson's and Huntington's disease.[14] The procedure is performed in order to replace the neurons lost in the brain. It has limited implementation due to legal, ethical, and political issues surrounding the use of fetal brain cells and stem cells. The greatest progress of neural tissue transportation is seen in Huntington's and Parkinson's, and more clinical trials are under way to improve its effectiveness in other diseases such as Alzheimer's disease, multiple sclerosis, and epilepsy. The neural tissues that are used for the transplantation are from embryonic or neonatal tissues. The allopathic doctor will essentially select the ideal area for the graft placement to ensure the

survival of the tissues being transplanted. There are limited areas in the Parkinson's patient's brain where the graft may be transplanted, and this is one of the challenges that the allopathic doctor has to resolve prior to surgery.

Cell transplantation is usually preferred for younger patients, where better results are realized. One of the roles that an allopathic doctor performs is to evaluate whether the patient is a good candidate for neural tissue transplantation. Age is a consideration for improved recovery after the procedure, and patients with less severe Parkinson's disease are more likely to receive the best benefit from it.[15] The allopathic doctor also considers the important factor of the patient's immune response. The brain is known to be immunologically privileged because it has a blood-brain barrier that prevents immune cells and antibodies from infiltrating the brain, thereby preventing any immunologic adverse reaction to the graft.[16] However, there is still the risk of intracerebral transplants undergoing immune rejection in certain cases.[17] The role of an allopathic doctor when prescribing this procedure is to ensure that the PD sufferer is a good candidate for the neuronal tissue transplant with lesser risks for an immunologic rejection of the graft.

Pallidotomy

Abnormal motor movements such as tremor, stiffness, and rigidity are very common among Parkinson's disease patients. These are caused due to the hyperactivity of the globus pallidus in the brain. The main objective of an allopathic doctor using pallidotomy is to destroy small areas of the globus pallidus with hopes of inhibiting its abnormal activity. In determining whether a person is a good candidate for pallidotomy, the allopathic surgeon considers several factors, such as the age of the patient, the manifestations of symptoms, and nature of the disease.

Patients (1) with predominant unilateral Parkinson's disease, (2) those with motor fluctuations such as dyskinesias, (3) individuals unresponsive to prescription, and (4) those suffering from pain and with unpredictable symptoms are considered to be good candidates for pallidotomy.[18] Surgery is performed using a local anesthetic, with the patient wide awake throughout the procedure. The procedure produces an effective relief from the abnormal motor movement, most especially in reducing contralateral dyskinesia.[19]

Other Allopathic Surgery

Variations of allopathic surgical procedures for Parkinson's disease are currently undergoing clinical tests, such as the infusion of a growth chemical into the basal ganglia. The procedure can prevent the death of the cells and also enhance their regeneration. Also in research is the use of a gamma knife

surgery, which is a type of "lesioning" in the form of a radiotherapy that an allopathic doctor can perform by applying a dose of gamma radiation in the skin and skull. This treatment is currently unacceptable due to the lack of sufficient monitoring, but it does offer a promising possibility for a future form of allopathic treatment for Parkinson's disease.

LIMITATIONS OF THE MD IN TREATING PARKINSON'S

The role of allopathic doctors in the treatment and management of Parkinson's disease is limited to only reducing the symptoms. Through the use of a straightforward medical treatment such as the administration of pharmaceutical agents and surgery, the most the allopathic doctor can attain is reducing the debilitating effects of the symptoms and their manifestation. Because Parkinson's disease has no cure, the allopathic doctor's role is constrained to ensuring that the patient gets the most ideal treatment to alleviate his or her symptoms; the doctor cannot provide any cure for the condition itself. An allopathic doctor's major responsibility when caring for Parkinson's disease patients is to evaluate the extent of the disability and how it interferes with the patient's activities of daily living. By targeting the reduction of symptoms through the use of different allopathic treatment options, the allopathic doctor can give patients with Parkinson's disease the ability to have a higher-quality life even in the presence of their medical condition.

It is also important to point out that there is and can be no perfect drug for Parkinson's disease. No allopathic remedy has been discovered that can provide complete relief and cure for the disease. The decision of the allopathic doctor is based on the symptoms that each patient uniquely manifests. Each patient has distinct, unique manifestations of symptoms and a different tolerance level for medications. The type of drugs, dose, timing, and type of symptoms are all important considerations in determining the appropriate treatment for Parkinson's disease.

ALLOPATHIC PRESCRIPTION PARKINSON'S MEDICATIONS

The first line of treatment and management that an allopathic doctor considers for Parkinson's disease is pharmaceutical intervention. Because Parkinson's disease is incurable, medications are prescribed as a form of supportive management for the condition. The symptoms of Parkinson's disease can interfere in the ability of patients to live a quality life. The objective of pharmaceutical intervention is to manage, reduce, and alleviate symptoms of the disease. The role of the allopathic doctor is to identify the symptoms of Parkinson's disease that the patient manifests and to select which pharmaceutical agent will help manage the cause of the symptoms. Parkinson's disease

is a progressive neurological disease, and suppressing its progression through allopathic means is crucial. Most medications that an allopathic doctor will prescribe are designed to provide a sufficient amount of dopamine in the brain in order to produce smoother and more coordinated movement in the body.

The broad spectrum of medication categories that an allopathic doctor can prescribe for Parkinson's disease includes dopamine agonists, levodopa, COMT inhibitors, anticholinergics, MAO-B inihibitors, and amantadine.[20] The decision of which drug would be best for a Parkinson's disease patient primarily depends on the symptoms that the patient manifests. Medicines are the best supportive and preventive measure that can be given in managing Parkinson's disease. The symptomatic drug treatment for Parkinson's is directed toward providing compensatory support and enhancement of dopamine action in the brain.[21]

Anticholinergics

The anticholinergic drug is capable of reducing the hyperactivity of acetylcholine in the brain that causes movement disorders seen among Parkinson's disease patients. In this context, the principle of treatment in Parkinson's is to regulate the action of the brain's neurotransmitter acetylcholine, which is mainly responsible for activating movement. Acetylcholine activity is regulated by the neurotransmitter dopamine in order to prevent abnormal movements of the body. In either the absence of or poor dopamine action in the brain of Parkinson's disease patients, there is no control over the action of the acetylcholine in stimulating motor movements, thereby resulting in tremors and rigidity. Anticholinergic agents are capable of inhibiting the acetylcholine reaction and hence in reducing their hyperactivity.[22]

Combining anticholinergic drugs with levodopa can result in the long-term side effects of dyskinesia or slowness in physical effort. Other side effects that an allopathic doctor might watch for in PD patients include constipation, blurred vision, hallucinations, urinary retention, dry mouth, confusion, and memory loss.

Levodopa

Without doubt, the gold standard of present allopathic therapy for Parkinson's is the drug **levodopa** (also called L-dopa). This drug is considered to be the most important medication prescribed for Parkinson's disease.[23] L-dopa (from the full name L-3,4-dihydroxyphenylalanine) is a simple chemical found naturally in plants and animals. Levodopa is the generic name used for this chemical when it is employed in medicating patients. Levodopa is also known as dopamine replacement therapy among allopathic physicians. Levo-

dopa is a synthetic drug that is converted into dopamine when administered into the body. Levodopa is usually used as a combination drug with other medications for Parkinson's disease.

Nerve cells can use levodopa to make dopamine and supplement the brain's declining supply. Dopamine itself cannot be given because it does not cross the blood-barrier, the elaborate web of fine blood vessels and cells that filters blood reaching the brain. Normally, patients are prescribed levodopa in combination with carbidopa. When added to levodopa, carbidopa delays the conversion of levodopa into dopamine and prepares it to reach the brain, diminishing some of the side effects that often accompany levodopa therapy and also reducing the amount needed.

The success of levodopa in the allopathic treatment of diminishing the major symptoms of Parkinson's disease is a triumph of modern medicine. First introduced in the 1960s, the drug delays the onset of debilitating symptoms and allows the majority of Parkinson's patients—who would otherwise be very disabled—to extend the period of time in which they can lead relatively normal, productive lives.

Although levodopa helps at least three quarters of Parkinsonian cases, not all symptoms respond equally to the drug. In the course of the illness, symptoms of Parkinson's disease, especially the hyperactivity (tremor), must be watched carefully. Bradykinesia and rigidity respond best, while tremor may be only marginally reduced. Problems with balance and other symptoms may not be alleviated at all. People who have taken other medications before starting levodopa therapy may have to cut back or eliminate these drugs in order to feel the full benefit of levodopa. Once levodopa therapy starts, people often respond dramatically, but they may need to increase the dose gradually for maximum benefit. Because a high-protein diet can interfere with the absorption of levodopa, some physicians recommend that patients taking the drug restrict protein consumption to the evening meal.

Levodopa is so effective that some people may forget they have Parkinson's disease, yet it is still not a cure. The drug can diminish the symptoms, but it fails to replace lost nerve cells and does not stop the progression of the disease. Although beneficial to a countless number of patients, levodopa is not without its physiological confines and side effects. The most common side effects are low blood pressure, nausea, vomiting, involuntary movements, and restlessness. A lower dose can be effective and the side effects reduced if levodopa is used with carbidopa. The latter product is also available in a slow-release formula, which helps patients to benefit from a longer-lasting effect.

Dyskinesias or involuntary movements such as twitching, nodding, and jerking are common in people consuming large doses of levodopa over a lengthy period. These movements may be either mild or severe and either very rapid or very slow. The only effective way to control these drug-induced

movements is to lower the dose of levodopa or to use drugs that block dopamine, but these remedies usually cause the disease symptoms to reappear. Doctors and patients must work together closely to find a tolerable balance between the drug's benefits and side effects.

Other more troubling and distressing problems may occur with long-term levodopa use. Patients may begin to notice more pronounced symptoms before their first dose of medication in the morning, and they can feel when each dose begins to wear off (muscle spasms are a common effect). Symptoms gradually begin to return. The period of effectiveness from each dose may begin to shorten, called the wearing-off effect. Another potential problem is referred to as the on-off effect—sudden, unpredictable changes in movement from normal to Parkinsonian movement and back again, possibly occurring several times during the day. These effects indicate that the patient's response to the drug is adjusting or that the disease is advancing.

One way to ease these side effects is to use levodopa in smaller amounts and more often. In order to improve the response and to manage the consequences of long-term levodopa therapy, physicians sometimes advise patients to stop taking the drug for several days. This controversial technique is known as a "drug holiday" and should be attempted only under a physician's direct supervision, because the extent of the complications is unknown. Moreover, it is best to take the "drug holiday" while the patient is hospitalized. Parkinson's disease patients should never stop taking levodopa without their physician's knowledge or consent because of the potentially serious side effects of rapidly withdrawing from the drug.

One study[24] compared two drugs—levodopa and pramipexole—that are generally employed as the first line of treatment for Parkinson's disease. The two drugs use different mechanisms to counteract the decline in the production of dopamine in the brain that is a result of a progressive loss of cells that secrete the neurochemical. Pramipexole is a dopamine agonist that binds with dopamine receptors on cells in the brain and mimics the chemical's molecular function.

While levodopa is considered to be better at addressing the motor control symptoms of the disease, pramipexole is less effective with respect to motor control symptoms and more often causes sleepiness, but it is less commonly associated with dyskinesias and wearing off. Pramipexole is often prescribed because clinicians believe it essentially extends the window in which the patient can benefit from levodopa by delaying the initial use of the drug— and its eventual wearing off. Most Parkinson's patients end up taking levodopa at some point regardless of their initial treatment because it is more effective at improving the symptoms of the disease. The study confirmed that patients who are initially treated with levodopa are more likely to develop motor complications such as dyskinesias and wearing off even six years after

treatment. However, it also shows that these complications did not have a significant impact on the quality of life or disability of the patients.

The most common symptoms experienced with excessive levodopa intake include vomiting, nausea, restlessness, reduced blood pressure, drowsiness, psychosis, lack of sleep, and hallucination. Painful dystonia, intensified tremors, and dyskinesis are often seen among Parkinson's disease patients. Dyskinesia usually occurs when a large dose of levodopa is taken for a longer term.[25] This drug-induced movement can produce either a very fast or very slow movement. It is necessary to find the tolerable dose for the patient because the symptom may still occur even with lower doses of levodopa.

MAO-B Inhibitors

There are drugs whose action is capable of inhibiting the enzymes that break down dopamine in the brain. Monoamine oxidase B (MAO-B) inhibitors help retain a sufficient amount of dopamine in the brain to accumulate in the nerve cells in order to reduce the symptoms of Parkinson's disease. It is a form of antidepressant, suppressing the neurotransmitters that could cause hyperactivity (tremors and such) seen in Parkinson's disease. One of the MAO-B inhibitors is selegiline, a drug administered in combination with levodopa therapy. Initial take of selegiline could delay the need for a levodopa therapy among Parkinson's disease patients for at least a year. When used in combination with levodopa, selegiline can enhance the action of the levodopa, thereby reducing its fluctuating effectiveness.

Selegiline is also prescribed as an antidepressive drug that helps reduce the symptoms of Parkinson's disease while also improving the symptoms of depression seen in some patients.[26] The drug is well tolerated, although reported side effects may include insomnia, orthostatic hypotension, nausea, and stomatitis. Taking the drug in combination with mepiridine and fluoxetine could produce harmful side effects.

Dopamine Agonists

Dopamine agonist is a treatment of choice in the early stage of Parkinson's disease. It stimulates the nerve receptors in the brain that dopamine normally would. Its action mimics that of dopamine, and there is no need for its conversion into dopamine when administered into the brain. The drug is most effective among younger patients and may delay the motor fluctuations such as stiffness and slowness in movement that occur as side effects during long-term levodopa therapy. A dopamine agonist is well tolerated by patients with Parkinson's disease, with mild side effects consisting of insomnia, somnolence, and edema. Others might experience hallucinations and dyskinesia, which can occur during the early period of taking the medicine and may go

away later on. It is necessary to immediately call the doctor when experiencing more serious symptoms such as difficulty in breathing, chest pain, or swelling of the face, mouth, and tongue. Compulsive behavior was reported in rare cases, and the dopamine agonist could also cause the development of fibrosis in the heart valves that goes away when the patient stops taking the medication. An allopathic doctor should provide close monitoring of Parkinson's disease patients and note whether they are receiving benefits from the drugs and how the patients tolerate the drugs.

COMT Inhibitors

Catechol-O-methyltransferase (COMT) inhibitor is an enzyme that assists in the action of dopamine in the brain by enhancing the therapeutic effect of levodopa. Tolcapone and entacapone are the two forms of COMT inhibitors approved in the United States for allopathically treating Parkinson's disease.[27] Among the valuable actions of these drugs is their ability to maximize the therapeutic effect of levodopa and effectively reduce in varying degrees the wearing-off symptoms seen among Parkinson's disease patients. COMT inhibitors primarily prolong the actions of levodopa by preventing or inhibiting the breaking down process of dopamine in the brain. The most commonly reported side effect from the medication is diarrhea. Others will experience dizziness, nausea, disturbance in sleep, discoloration of urine, hallucinations, or low blood pressure. The most severe side effect with COMT inhibitors is the development of severe liver disease, which is seen among patients taking tolcapone.[28]

Amantadine

Generally used as an antiviral drug, **amantadine** is prescribed primarily to reduce the symptoms of Parkinson's disease. It can also help reduce the levodopa-induced dyskinesia often seen with long-term levodopa therapy. It has an anticholinergic property and acts to enhance the transmission of dopamine in the brain. It can be used as a combination drug with levodopa and other anticholinergic drugs. Common side effects of amantadine that are commonly seen as well in anticholinergic drugs include constipation, blurred vision, mental confusion, and dryness of mouth. Amantadine is prescribed with very rare serious side effects since anticholinergic drugs seldom produce adverse reactions except isolated cases of allergic skin rash and liver inflammation.[29]

ALLOPATHIC BENEFITS AND DRAWBACKS

Benefits

Allopathic medications prescribed for Parkinson's disease primarily act directly to influence the dopamine action in the brain. Levodopa is a mainstay therapeutic drug that increases the dopamine levels in the brain to control movement. The most common COMT inhibitors that hinder dopamine breakdown are entacapone and tolcapone. Dopamine agonists that are commonly prescribed for Parkinson's disease are apomorphine, ropinirole, bromocriptine, and pramipexole. They all can mimic dopamine actions in the brain. Anticholinergic drugs can decrease the action of acetylcholine in the brain that could trigger hyperactivity in motor movement, and the most commonly prescribed anticholinergic drugs for Parkinson's disease are trihexyphenidyl, benztropine, and ethopropazine. Selegiline is an MAO-B inhibitor whose main action is to impede the breakdown of dopamine. Amantadine is considered to be a beneficial drug combination with levodopa as it enhances its therapeutic effects.

Drawbacks

The use of therapeutic drugs as an allopathic treatment for Parkinson's disease is not without limitation. Parkinson's is a progressive condition, and the aim of treatment is to control symptoms and delay the progression of the disease. However, it is important for both patients and caregivers to note that although allopathic medication helps alleviate the symptoms of Parkinson's disease, it does not provide a cure for the condition. It can delay but not retard the progression of the symptoms entirely. Often, an allopathic doctor will modify prescriptions as symptom magnitude changes. Patients will be reevaluated and may be prescribed a changing medication regimen as needed.

It is crucial for Parkinson's disease patients to constantly consult their allopathic doctor if that is the treatment approach the patient chooses. An evaluation of patients' tolerance to the medications prescribed for them is important, especially in the management of side effects. An allopathic doctor will likely gauge any potential difficulty experienced by patients with respect to their tolerance level.

Allopathic medications sold over the counter can also become potentially risky and dangerous to consume. Drugs taken for Parkinson's disease should be combined safely and with precaution as they could produce adverse side effects and interact with other medications. With insufficient scientific studies to support the effectiveness and safety of taking natural supplements and over-the-counter medications for Parkinson's disease, it is prudent to observe

high caution when choosing such an option. It is highly recommended to consult an allopathic doctor who can evaluate the symptoms, assess needs, and prescribe a safe, therapeutic, and appropriate drug.

RESEARCH OUTLOOK

Because of the promising results and positive response of Parkinson's disease patients to allopathic treatment, more research is undertaken in order to improve the quality and advancement of treatment in the allopathic field for Parkinson's disease. Many experiments are under way to discover better treatment options for Parkinson's disease. One of these objects of research is the neurotrophic protein called the conserved dopamine neurotrophic factor (CDNF), which significantly prevented the degeneration of dopamine in the brain of rats. It is believed to have a significant value with a neuroprotective and neurorestorative effects to dopamine in the brain.[30]

Research is also focused on the potential of neuroprotective agents, primarily curcumin as a good agent to treat the neurological symptoms in Parkinson's disease. Its therapeutic potential is currently explored by clinical researchers because of its antioxidant, anticancer, and anti-inflammatory properties and as an agent that easily crosses the blood-brain barrier.[31] More potential research that could help improve treatment of Parkinson's disease involves neural tissue transplants from fetal pigs into the brain to restore the degenerative area of the brain. The tissue transplant produces a significant improvement in the neurological symptoms seen in Parkinson's disease. Genetic engineering is also explored in the field of allopathic medicine to modify the genetic code of other cells in the body in order to create new cells capable of producing dopamine.

Chapter Twelve

Osteopathic Treatment

The effectiveness of osteopathic manipulative treatment/medicine (OMT/OMM) on symptoms of Parkinson's disease is a subject continuously under investigation, but some patients significantly increase their gait parameters after only a few osteopathic sessions. Using this method, patients are expected to move freely with improved arm swings, longer strides, and quicker steps. The results are consistent with positive results in motor function as observed with physical therapy and other studies because this type of treatment can minimize various symptoms that are associated with the tight muscles and stiffness of the body. Its ultimate goal is to reduce pain, improve function, and maximize health. Furthermore, several factors are essential to interpreting the changes seen in Parkinson's patients in current studies. Among these is the introduction of osteopathic medicine to further assist the improvement and development of each patient.

OSTEOPATHY OVERVIEW

Osteopathy is a medical philosophy and an alternative medical practice that emphasizes the interrelationship between function and the body's structure and that recognizes the body's ability to heal itself; it is the role of the osteopathic practitioner to assist the progress of that process, principally by the practice of manual and manipulative therapy. [1] In Parkinson's, osteopathy is a process of diagnosis and medical treatment that focuses primarily on the mechanical issues of body framework. Osteopathic physicians or doctors of osteopathy are licensed to practice medicine and surgery in all states and are recognized in fifty-five additional nations, including the Canadian provinces. [2] It was founded in the late 1800s in Kirksville, Missouri, by a medical doctor (Andrew Taylor Still) who conceded that the medical prac-

tices of the day often administered more harm than good. Still focused on developing a system of medical care that would promote the body's innate ability to heal itself and called this system of medicine osteopathy, now known as osteopathic medicine.[3]

Osteopathic medicine is a total system of medical health care with a philosophy that combines the needs of the patient with current practices of medicine, surgery, and obstetrics as a whole. Treating the body as a unit, it emphasizes the interrelationships between structure and function with a particular appreciation for the body's ability to heal itself. In the United States, osteopathic medicine is currently practiced by nearly sixty thousand DOs (doctors of osteopathic medicine).[4] Osteopathic medicine is being used in diagnosing and treating the body's structural issues associated with many conditions. Parkinson's disease is one example, since OMM can minimize various symptoms related to and associated with the body's tightening or stiffness of muscles and therefore helping mobility and overall body function. Most of the osteopathic schools are at the forefront of providing comprehensive osteopathic care with the goal of reducing pain, improving function, and maximizing health.

Some patients with initial or prior diagnosis of idiopathic Parkinson's disease who are capable of moving around freely without assistance or off medication (such as those in the initial Hoehn and Yahr stages introduced in chapter 6) and with normal psychomotor controls received a few weeks' course of a specific osteopathic manipulation treatment regimen. Quantitative gait parameters were monitored using three-dimensional gait analysis systems before the start of treatment, at the end of treatment, and a few weeks after treatment was discontinued.[5] Most of the test results from recent studies such as this one indicate that gait parameters, including movement velocity, range of motion of joints per axis, and angular velocity, are improved in treated Parkinson's patients and, to some extent, in treated normal psychomotor control group participants. Some patients, however, might respond differently regarding the diminished beneficial effects of treatment, but those effects will still be noticeable a few months after treatment. Most of the results suggest a clear functional benefit of osteopathic manipulation in Parkinson's patients who are treated for a period of a few weeks to a few months. Beneficial effects of treatment appear to persist even after treatment is discontinued.

Osteopathic manipulative treatment (or *osteopathic treatment* in other countries) is the therapeutic manipulation and application of manually guided forces by an osteopathic physician, or osteopath, to improve physiologic functions and support the body's homeostasis that has been altered by such somatic (body) dysfunction. Somatic dysfunction is an altered or impaired function of all related components of the somatic body framework system, such as skeletal, myofascial, and arthrodial structures and their related lym-

phatic, vascular, and neural elements.[6] One form of somatic dysfunction is *acute somatic* dysfunction. This is a short-term or immediate impairment and altered mechanical and physical function of interrelated components of a somatic framework of the Parkinson's patient. It is characterized and described in early stages by edema, vasodilation, tenderness, pain, and tissue contraction. It is included in the patient's history and physical assessment of motion asymmetry, muscle tenderness and relative position, restriction of motion, and tissue texture change. Another dysfunction is the *chronic somatic* dysfunction, which is defined as the impairment or altered function of related components of the somatic or body framework system. It may be characterized by itching, tenderness, fibrosis, **paresthesias**, and tissue contraction.[7]

While many treatment techniques can be used, OMT methods are grouped as active or passive and direct or indirect in nature.

- Active: This is a technique in which the person voluntarily performs a manipulative or an osteopathic practitioner-directed motion.
- Passive: This is based on techniques in which the patient holds or refrains from voluntary muscle contraction.
- Direct (D/DIR): This is a manipulative method in which the normal physiologic barrier is engaged and a final triggering force is applied to correct the somatic dysfunction.
- Indirect (I/IND): This is a manipulative method where the normal physiologic barrier is disengaged and the dysfunctional somatic body part is moved away from the barrier until the tissue tension ratio is equal in one or all axes and directions.

Opinions differ on the significance of osteopathic principles. Osteopathic philosophy is closely and significantly related to the tenets of holistic medicine. It is believed that osteopathic philosophy is a type of social movement within the medical community that encourages a more patient-centered and holistic approach to medical practice and that emphasizes the role of the preliminary care physicians in the health-care industry. Others favor the American Osteopathic Association's focus on the main principles and core values of professional indoctrination, a process that promotes osteopathic practices and policies while downplaying those of the allopathic medical community. Some might believe that there is nothing in the principles of osteopathy that would distinguish DO (doctor of osteopathy) from MD training in any basic way.

The osteopathic medical practice has evolved into two general divisions: (1) the nonphysician manual medicine osteopathic practitioners and (2) osteopathic practitioners that offer the full scope of medical practice. These two branches are so distinct that in the field, they function as separate profes-

sions. In modern years, the osteopathic profession has actively engaged to enhance communication and intercorrelation between the two branches. The policy for nonphysician manual medicine osteopathic practice varies greatly from one jurisdiction to another. In countries such as Australia, the United Kingdom, and New Zealand, this type of medical practice is overseen by a regulatory board that requires registration with the relevant regulatory authority. The Osteopathic International Alliance has a nationwide guide per country with details of practice rights and professional registration.[8] In some countries such as Canada and the United States, nonphysician osteopath practitioners cannot provide diagnosis as this is a federally regulated act.[9]

Osteopathy can sometimes be viewed not as a set of techniques, but rather, a philosophy. This philosophy is simple and very sensible. When applied in practice, osteopathy can cause profound changes in a Parkinson's disease sufferer's health. The osteopathic medical philosophy is defined as the approach to health care that embraces the concept of the unity of the living organism's structure (anatomy) and function (physiology). The four major principles of osteopathic medicine are: (1) structure rules functions, and vice versa, wherein the body is an integrated unit of mind, body, and spirit; (2) the unity of being, where structure and function are reciprocally interrelated; (3) "the body heals itself," wherein the body possesses self-regulatory mechanisms and has the inherent capacity to defend, repair, and remodel itself; and (4) "the rule of the artery is supreme," based on the belief that circulatory health is key. These principles are not held by doctors of osteopathic medicine to be empirical laws; they serve as the underpinnings of the osteopathic philosophy on health and disease. The above mentioned principles are explained next.[10]

Structure Directs Function

From the smallest cell to the largest bone, all of anatomy is alive and in constant, dynamic, rhythmic, pulsing motion. Blood flows, lymph drains, and cerebral spinal fluid fluctuates. The heart beats; the ribcage expands and contracts with each respiration. Each and every structure has its own inherent rhythmic activity. Disease or dysfunction such as that seen in Parkinson's is the effect of a change in the parts of the physical body. Osteopathic dysfunction in an abnormal body is just as natural as is good health, when all parts are in place and all system forces are balanced. When even a single chemical compound is not balanced and is distorted, it cannot fit into its appropriate molecular site to accomplish its designated mechanism and function. If the system parts do not fit well with one another in any machine, the parts at best wear abnormally or fail as a whole. The same happens inside the Parkinson's disease sufferer's body. The architecture of the human somatic system and its entire natural environment exists the way it does because it fulfills a specific

function. Form is the one thing that determines the body's functions, while function determines form. Satisfactory health emerges when form and function are perfectly balanced and expressed.

Unity of Being

Organ systems exist throughout the Parkinson's disease sufferer's entire body. The circulatory system supplies blood flow throughout. The nervous system connects and integrates all functions. A third unifying system is made up of a connective tissue called *fascia*. It surrounds every muscle, organ, nerve, and blood vessel. Its function is to support and lubricate. It is composed of collagen, which is organized microscopically in little "tubes." The somatic lymph runs smoothly through the fascia because fascia is all over the body. Fascia has other names and is termed differently, depending on which part of the somatic area it resides in, but it is all one piece that folds over and mixes into itself. It becomes stressed, compressed, and twisted by trauma. The nervous system, circulatory system, and connective tissue matrix all organize the total body functions into an intercorrelated and unified somatic mechanism according to the unity of being principle. Another system to consider is the interdependently regulated functions of the endocrine system. No single body part exists independently of the whole—which means that if even a small somatic dysfunction occurs, the entire organism or totality of mechanism is affected.

Body Heals Itself

The human body is constantly working to preserve a state of balanced function. Physical examinations and lab tests are designed to measure those physiologic activities the body keeps constant: even in Parkinson's disease, blood pressure, blood sugar, heart rate, and other critical features are supposed to stay within a normal range. In terms of posture, the body remains balanced in three-dimensional spaces. A single healthy person can stand on one foot, hold a book in one hand, read, and at the same time bring a cup to the lips without even looking and without falling over.[11] This is a complex task requiring a constant self-correcting mechanism. When a patient suffers a laceration, a medical practitioner can assist by cleaning the laceration and bringing its edges together, but healing occurs automatically on its own. This principle recognizes the body's ability to heal and seeks its clearest and most flexible expression.

The Artery Is Supreme

When blood and lymphatic fluid flow freely, the body systems can perform their physiologic functions without obstruction; with the occurrence of any

somatic trauma (physical or emotional), the tissues may be contracted, twisted, and compressed, and the liquid flow becomes obstructed. Microclimates of underperfusion result and are considered to be an important contributor to the first onset of dysfunction. Osteopathic medical treatment applies its processes and principles with a complete and thorough knowledge of human anatomy and physiology. An osteopathic medical approach to psychophysical dysfunction (such as in Parkinson's) typically combines osteopathic manipulation to restore functional and mechanical freedom in the overall body system, enhance fluid flow throughout, and create the maximum setting for healing to occur as a whole.

ROLE OF THE OSTEOPATHIC DOCTOR IN TREATING PARKINSON'S

There are many ongoing disputes concerning the difference between MDs and DOs. It is perhaps better to start by comparing the two. Osteopathic physicians believe in the principle that a patient's history of somatic dysfunction and physical trauma can be diagnosed by in-depth study of the body's structure. The osteopathic practitioner's highly developed sense of touch allows the doctor to feel or palpate the patient's "living anatomy" such as the flow of fluids, motion axes and texture of tissues, and structural makeup. Like MDs, osteopathic physicians or practitioners who treat Parkinson's disease patients are licensed at the state level. Osteopathic physicians who wish to specialize may become "board certified" in much the same manner as with those MDs, by completing a two- to six-year residency within the specialty area and passing the board certification exams.[12] In short, both DOs and MDs are fully qualified physicians who, when licensed accordingly, can prescribe medication as well as perform surgery. Confusion arises because DOs practice in all specialties of medicine, ranging from emergency medicine and cardiovascular surgery to psychiatry and geriatrics. A majority of osteopathic doctors use many of the medical and surgical treatments employed by other (allopathic) medical doctors.

One of the major differences between DOs and MDs is that DOs receive additional education in the science and practice of medical diagnosis and treatment using osteopathic manual medicine (OMM) skills. DOs are trained to perform a structural diagnosis and integrate it into the entire study and physical examination process and to use OMT techniques when appropriate. As caregivers, they work in partnership with their Parkinson's disease patients and consider the impact that lifestyle and community have on the health of each patient, and they work to break down barriers to good health.[13] Osteopathic doctors are licensed to practice the major scope of medicine in all states in the United States. They practice in full scope and in all types of

medical environments, which includes the military, and in all types of specialties, from family and general medicine to obstetrics, surgery, and aerospace medicine. They are trained from their first days of medical school to look at the whole person's total body mechanism and behavior. This means that they see each person as a whole and more than just a collection of organ systems and body parts that may be affected by PD. This holistic approach to medical practice means that osteopathic medical practitioners learn how to integrate and intercorrelate the patient into the health and patient care process in partnership.[14] They are well trained to communicate with people with diverse backgrounds, and they get the chance to practice these skills in their regular daily classes and application laboratories, frequently with standardized and simulated persons as patients. In addition to a strong history of providing high-quality patient care like any other medical practitioners, DOs conduct clinical and basic scientific research to help advance the future of Parkinson's-related medicine and to well demonstrate the osteopathic approach's effectiveness to health and patient care. In coordination with a major osteopathic center,[15] several organizations nowadays are involved in osteopathic clinical research. The center's staff develops, facilitates, and conducts multicenter, collaborative clinical research studies on Parkinson's.

Throughout history, osteopathic treatment has consistently shown a great improvement in the gait function of many patients with Parkinson's disease. It is not absolutely clear yet, however, if the acute effects of treatment will be improved or maintained with continued or discontinued treatment.[16] Treatment appears to produce functional improvements in the gait of patients with Parkinson's disease if applied over a period of two months, but continued research and study is still ongoing. There is a wide range of literature developing on osteopathic manipulation of Parkinson's patients. The benefits of osteopathic manipulation do warrant further exploration as to specific manipulative protocols. An osteopathic physician will often use OMT, which is a hands-on approach to an array of manipulative techniques that may be combined with other treatments or advice, for example, on diet, physical activity and posture, or counseling. This is simply a free-motion technique that ensures all of the body's natural healing systems are able to work unhindered.[17]

Limitations of the Osteopathic Doctor in Treating Parkinson's

One of the challenges is ensuring that an adequate number of primary care physicians include osteopathic medicine where the majority of most osteopathic medical school graduates choose careers in primary care. Osteopathic medicine is not concentrated in treating one ailment or therapeutic dysfunction, and PD is just one case in point. The osteopathic approach has a special focus on providing care in rural and urban underserved areas, allowing DOs to have a greater impact on the US population's health and well-being than

their numbers would suggest. While DOs constitute 7 percent of all US physicians, they are responsible for 16 percent of patient visits in communities with populations of less than 2,500.[18] Osteopathic medical practice is also growing rapidly, and a high percentage of medical students in the United States are enrolling and studying in an osteopathic medical school. When speaking of limitations from an educational standpoint, it is said that osteopathic medical students take more than one hundred additional hours of training in the art of osteopathic manipulative medicine. This system of hands-on techniques is proved to help alleviate pain, restore motion, support the body's natural functions, and influence the PD patient's body's structure to make it function more efficiently.

Various criticisms circulate about DOs. Traditional osteopathic medicine, specifically OMM, has been under scrutiny for many of its methods, such as cranial and craniosacral techniques of manipulation. The current debate within the osteopathic community is over the feasibility of maintaining osteopathic medicine as a distinct entity of US health care, of maintaining a difference between MD- and DO-qualified physicians. Osteopathy is really not intended to treat potentially life-threatening illness or injury. DOs still need to refer patients to emergency rooms if they feeling a sudden chest pain, have a severe headache, or suffer an immediate loss of speech.

SAFETY AND EFFICACY OF OSTEOPATHIC TECHNIQUES

Osteopathy has one of the safest records of any medically related profession, but no medical treatment is deemed completely safe. Due to the gentle nature of osteopathic treatment, it is extremely rare for osteopathy to make the Parkinson's disease symptoms (or pain) worse. However, if a patient suffers from osteoporosis or osteopenia, then the DO must be aware of such a condition as well as any particularly delicate areas that the patient has. While some osteopathic patients may not experience anything negative, there are some *possible* aftereffects:[19]

- Common: general ache or soreness for twenty-four to forty-eight hours following a positive response to osteopathic treatment
- Infrequent: exacerbation of symptoms due to reaction to osteopathic treatment
- Extremely rare: serious complications requiring medical intervention

In some cases, if a DO uses essential oils, medical creams, or powders to help patients move their hands over the body or affected areas, then the DO must be aware of any allergic reaction it may cause to the patient at the start of osteopathic session, especially if the Parkinson's sufferer has any of the

skin disorders described in chapter 9. It is highly unlikely that a patient will be allergic to any of the ingredients (as osteopaths use highly sensitive oils and creams made with only natural ingredients) except in some cases of very sensitive skin in those suffering from dermatographism. Another rare reaction is that a patient might experience feelings of extreme weakness and tiredness right after the treatment. If this is the patient's reaction to osteopathy, then the individual should be accompanied by someone when leaving the hospital or might be asked to stay overnight to take a complete rest before being discharged.

In the case of OMT, patients with conditions such as bone cancer, bone or joint infection, osteoporosis, and spinal fusion should avoid this therapy, which might cause harm rather than cure. For any complaints, the patient should inform the respective DO about the nature of the complaint. Osteopaths are regulated by law, and some countries such as the United Kingdom have a statutory register to oversee the conduct of all registered osteopaths. Osteopaths work with their hands, and treatment may consist of soft-tissue massage, gentle passive mobilization techniques, and specific joint manipulation. Very gentle cranial techniques may also be used, and these may be applied to all areas of the body, not only the head. Many people think that osteopaths are simply physical manipulators, but this may only be part of the actual treatment, especially in the case of OMT for Parkinson's patients. Manipulation techniques used in OMT are beneficial and can help to free up spinal joints. Most people experience little or no pain but may hear an audible click during spinal manipulation.

A first consultation and visit with a DO is similar to that with an allopathic physician. Although DOs take a holistic approach to the Parkinson's patient's health and well-being and will ask questions based on the diagnosis, it is still the patient's responsibility to make the DO aware of other health concerns that might be induced during the treatment. Osteopaths also consider the PD patient's medical history, including previous surgery and illnesses, heart conditions, family history, and hospitalization background. Some DOs use the information they gather from the patient to better facilitate the treatment on a per-patient basis. Next, they conduct a detailed examination of the affected area and then assess it in the context of the rest of the body. The osteopath examines by touch to pick up details of hot and swollen areas that could be a sign of inflammation, or cool dry areas that may mean a more chronic condition. In addition, DOs assess how freely the body moves; this may include leaning to one side and then the other to assess the patient's spinal movements. The osteopath may perform other tests such as blood pressure, neurological assessment, or checking the blood supply to the affected areas. Once the examination is complete, the osteopath has developed a good idea about what has happened and will discuss this with the patient.

Like any other medical practitioner, DOs are required to always have the Parkinson patient's best interests at heart.'

In general, osteopathy is safe for people of all ages. Parkinson's disease patients, with the exception of those in rare cases of having contraindications and limitations, have found relief from pain and dysfunction as well as improved mobility through OMT. Many DOs incorporate OMT into their treatment plans for top athletes, workers with on-the-job injuries, and people with illnesses and injuries such as Parkinson's disease, asthma, and low back pain. This treatment is being used to diagnose and treat injuries and illnesses and utilizes passive thrusting techniques but also includes a variety of nonthrusting methods designed to affect muscles and soft tissues. It also optimizes blood circulation to the Parkinson's-affected brain to maintain and restore health while other forms of manipulation tend to focus more on spinal misalignments interfering with nerve transmissions.

Chapter Thirteen

Naturopathic Treatment

Naturopathic medicine is the natural curative system of treatment and prevention of diseases—nature's way of healing life.[1] The field of naturopathic medicine constitutes an increasing importance in Parkinson's disease treatment and a challenge to the modern understanding of medicine, as well as a key issue in the management of healing strategies. Naturopathic approaches include the identification and use of neuroprotective agents to slow down a disease's evolution. The principle role in naturopathic curative strategies is held by the doctor, who in the prescriptive world is referred to as the naturopathic physician. The doctor must be skilled in combining nature's wisdom with scientific empiricism. Parkinson's disease has been recognized in all cultures since ancient times, and many ancient treatments have become popular and increasingly accepted and validated by modern medicine. Naturopathic remedies such as coenzyme Q10, botulinum toxin, broad beans, St. John's wort, and extracts of *Mucuna* have certain effects on PD but cannot completely reverse the symptoms of the disease. Other alternative strategies that can supplement medication are diet, exercise, meditation, massage, herbs (Ayurveda medicine), and acupuncture.

INTRODUCTION TO NATUROPATHIC MEDICINE

Naturopathy is not considered to be a recent trend, as it holds a set of principles of Ayurveda inherited from antiquity. Ayurveda is native to India and practiced today by various practitioners. Naturopathy, even when speaking in relation to Parkinson's, uses the means and the language of nature, and this "language" is available only to nature itself. This alternative branch of the medical sciences can be illustrated in Hippocrates's words *natura sanat,*

medicus curat, which basically translates into "the medicine cures, [while] nature heals."[2]

A renowned naturopathic book[3] stresses the direct opposition between a healthy state and an unhealthy state considering the naturopathic point of view. Much as in the osteopathic dogma described in chapter 12, a healthy body is the expression of a naturopathic stable, balanced condition of all its parts (including the brain and peripheral nervous system) and encompasses a state of being that allows the person to perform work naturally, delightedly, without anxiety, and thus exist in a "jolly mood."[4] Such a state of being is possible only when a person keeps the body pure and the blood clean. The opposite of this state of body and mind is the disease, the morbid waste, caused by wrong actions, errors, and unnatural modes of living, the inability to keep a healthy state in proper conditions, or, in other words, a disturbance of the vital force.

Concerning the principles of this curative method, theories are based on various forms of the mind-brain connection as well as on functionalist views. The sources of naturopathy can be considered as two philosophical concepts: vitalism and holism, as well as a historical background that includes (1) herbal medicine, (2) nature's cure, (3) Hippocratic health, (3) homoeopathy, (4) hydrotherapy, (5) dietetics, and (6) physiologically manipulative theories. There are also a series of elements borrowed from certain social movements that emphasized a holistic approach to the environment and ecology and from the counterculture movements such as "new age," transpersonal and humanistic psychology, spirituality, and metaphysics.

Principles in Relation to Parkinson's

The underlying principles in basic naturopathic practice include the following:

- To limit side effects and to avoid symptoms;
- To teach patients and encourage them to be responsible for their own health;
- To consider the person regarding all factors: emotional, spiritual, genetic, physical, mental, social, and environmental, when establishing a treatment;
- To analyze risk factors and make appropriate recommendations to prevent illness;
- To identify and remove roadblocks from the body's natural development in maintaining health; and
- To use a causative approach in which focusing on the cause is far more important than overworrying about the symptoms.

In this sense, a naturopathic textbook[5] highlights the main principles of the naturopathic curative system. The first is the healing power of nature, *vis medicatrix naturae*, and refers to both appreciation and acceptance of the power of nature. Naturopathy recognizes nature's capacity, as an intelligent and balanced system, to maintain and to create matter. The Parkinson's disease patient's body is a complex "machine" that has its own mechanism of healing but can still operate according to these laws of nature. Following the process of regeneration currently present in nature, the body itself can redevelop without artificial intervention. While absolute regeneration of nerves destroyed by Parkinson's disease is currently impossible, it is interesting to note that nature's healing agents, such as water, sun, earth, and air, can be used in a combination with good sleep, relaxation, meditation, diet, and exercise based on naturopathic philosophies that cater to the health of the nervous system. All of these are external factors that can support and influence the human body's innate ability to cure. In retrospect, the naturopath's role is to encourage and facilitate the natural ability of Parkinson's patient's body to heal.

The second principle (1) consists of identifying and treating the cause (see chapter 4), (2) encompasses the understanding that all illness has some "cause," and (3) agrees with the notion that for restoring health, the underlying factors must be attentively analyzed and removed. Naturopathy is employed to cure the disease and to prevent its return and the development of new states.

The third principle recommends treating the whole person. Health and disease such as PD are states of being that respond to an intricate interplay of mental, spiritual, physical, social, familial, and professional factors. If conventional medicine fails to understand this holistic interplay, it is because it does not address all these aspects. In contrast, naturopathic treatment systems are fully aware of all relevant aspects of the patient's pattern of disease and health and does not ignore the complexity of the human being. The concept of prevention is difficult to promote in conventional medicine because it is a sickness-focused system of healing. This preventative attitude can be easily applied once the person follows the indications of a naturopath. The process of healing begins once risk factors, genetic tendencies, and constitutional susceptibility are analyzed.

The last principle focuses on the naturopathic approach as a celebration of simplicity with the promotion of living a natural life. The concept of simplicity expresses the intelligence of this system of treatment. The conventional approach to Parkinson's usually addresses symptoms and suppresses disease states, but naturopathy is not limited to identifying and treating the interrelation of symptoms. Integral healing process and optimal patient care represents naturopaths' understanding of their role. This is how naturopathy can be exploited to the benefit of the Parkinson's disease patient.

In assessing the efficacy and the safety of naturopathic care, there are some principles to consider. Naturopathy is not a substitute for conventional care, and relying on this curative system, avoiding conventional medication, may fall short in treating a disease or in some circumstances may have considerable health consequences. Some principles and approaches of naturopathic physicians do not make use of conventional medicine and their safety is not tested and supported by scientific evidence. When it comes to Parkinson's disease, this is obviously a significant concern. Certain therapies used in naturopathy are potentially harmful if not used under the direction of an experienced naturopathic physician or practitioner.

Notable Pioneers in Naturopathy

In thinking about the long history of naturopathy, one can mention Charaka, the founder of the Ayurvedic medical system, Hippocrates, the founder of allopathic medical science, Pantajali, the founder of the yoga system of philosophy, and the Greek physicians Herodicus and Democritus. Another important contributor is Samuel Hahnemann, the founder of homeopathy, who (1) pointed out errors and wrong practices in the medicine that prevailed in his time and (2) promoted a simpler and humane mode of treatment. Vincent Priessnitz founded hydropathical treatment (also called hydrotherapy) after he cured himself using a hydropathic treatment for broken ribs. Hydrotherapy treatment has been scientifically proved to help relieve the symptoms of Parkinson's.[6] Edwin D. Babbitt was a great pioneer of chromopathy and heliotherapy and showed that even incurable diseases can be treated using light and colors.

THE ROLE OF THE NATUROPATHIC DOCTOR IN PARKINSON'S

Neurological disorders, such as Parkinson's, multiple sclerosis, and Huntington's disease, leave patients searching for an alternative medical practitioner because there is no treatment or procedure that entirely solves such neurological conditions. Naturopathic professionals try to respond to two major questions: "What might other types of doctors be missing in their approaches?" and "Why is a certain process happening?"—questions that are invaluable when it comes to finding the right approach to Parkinson's.

Naturopathy, as a natural curative system of treatment, requires, generally speaking, an experienced professional who can manipulate natural curative strategies and combine nature's means with modern science's rigors in order to obtain considerable effects. In naturopathic philosophy, this combination of skills and strategies responds to the opposition between naive realism and scientific empiricism. This opposition tends to treat medical qualities as nonphysical, regarding them as independent objects distinct from brains and

even individuals and therefore implying a disembodied mind. Another general principle consists of minimizing the risk of general harm and to facilitate the Parkinson's patient's ability to maintain and restore general health.[7]

An important concept in naturopathy concerns the attributes and status of the doctor. The Latin origin of the word *doctor* means "teacher." The idea of the doctor as a teacher reiterates the maxim that, as part of the whole of nature, a body can achieve healing without any special treatments and human intervention. The capacity to eliminate the PD to a certain degree and optimize health is in the body itself and does not lie solely in the action of the naturopath or the physician. The naturopath simply assumes the role of a teacher so that the process of healing becomes a natural healing mechanism. Taking on this coaching role, the naturopath must be capable of motivating and inspiring an individual suffering from a degenerative disease such as Parkinson's.

Clinical Relationship

The clinical relationship throughout the entire naturopathic process of treating Parkinson's—which encompasses empathy and authenticity as vital parts of the healing process—is patient centered. The holistic consultation supposes, according to the Nelson-Jones model,[8] five phases:[9]

* Exploring the range of problems
* Understanding each problem
* Determining the goals
* Providing treatments
* Consolidating the patient's independence

Parkinson's disease represents a challenge for both conventional medicine and naturopathic medical care because it is a multifactorial condition. Dopamine loss can be somewhat determined by the free radical damage in the neural tissue. In this sense, antioxidants can neutralize free radicals, preventing them from provoking brain damage. One of the most important antioxidants in the body is glutathione, and studies[10] have demonstrated that Parkinson's disease patients have lower levels of it. From a naturopathic viewpoint, glutathione levels can be increased by the administration of vitamin A, selenium, N-acetyl cysteine, and vitamins C and E supplements. Vitamins B and coenzyme Q10 can also neutralize free radical groups. A proper diet (see chapter 16) is extremely important in Parkinson's disease naturopathic treatment, and a Mediterranean diet is recommended since it reduces the risk of developing Parkinson's disease by 13 to 30 percent.[11] This diet contains fruits, vegetables, whole grains, lean meats, fish, and olive oil and is considered a diet low in saturated fat and cholesterol. It is also important to analyze

protein consumption because scientists have demonstrated that limiting protein intake improves symptoms in Parkinson's disease patients.

Traditional Chinese medicine shows profound benefits for Parkinson's disease patients. Concerning herbal medicine, plants that show protective effects are ginseng and licorice root. Insomnia, a common symptom of Parkinson's disease, can be reduced with nutritional supplements such as 5-HTP and melatonin. 5-HTP, or 5-hyroxytryptophan, has been proved effective for Parkinson's patients.[12] In counterpart, melatonin is a hormone naturally produced in the brain tissue and is responsible for regulating sleep. Total sleep time as well as sleep-wake cycles are significantly helped by supplementation with melatonin before going to sleep.

LIMITATIONS OF THE NATUROPATHIC DOCTOR IN TREATING PARKINSON'S

A key article[13] contends that naturopathic medicine, as a recent manifestation in the field of medicine, is a nineteenth-century *movement* that disagrees with combining natural and conventional medicine.[14] Despite their intensive training, naturopathic physicians learn only a small fraction of what a medical doctor learns, considering both academic and clinical training. In this sense, the naturopathic doctor unfortunately might be looked on by allopathic circles as a magician, a shaman, and not a proper scientist. The limitations of the naturopathic doctor in treating Parkinson's are represented by the conflict of interests between conventional medicine and naturopathic cure systems. These two options in healing should be complementary, but there are cases when naturopathic doctors reject drugs recommended by a conventional doctor. The conclusion is that naturopathy offers only complementary alternative strategies that simply cannot replace the standard treatment of Parkinson's disease.

PRESCRIPTION NATUROPATHIC MEDICATIONS

History of the Naturopathic Prescription

According to an academic journal article,[15] both naturopathic medication and traditional medicine limit dopamine's decline, but aspects of traditional treatment of Parkinson's disease have existed in different parts of the world since ancient times. The oldest description was found in the ancient system of Ayurveda, the Indian medical system, under the name of *kampavata*, the Ayurvedic name for Parkinson's disease. This treatment is a prescription naturopathic therapy encompassing herbal preparations that contain anticholinergics, levodopa, and monoamine oxidase inhibitors used in the treatment

of Parkinson's disease in China, India, and the Amazon basin. Nagashayana mentions that ancient naturopathic science was being practiced in India from 1500–1000 BC, and Parkinson's disease has a low prevalence in India (except in a certain part of the Parsi community). The otherwise naturopathic treatment of *kampavata* is also mentioned in *Caraka Samhita* and *Madhavanidhani*. Clinical features include tremor, head tremor, tremors of hands and feet, rigidity, drooling of saliva, depression, reptilian stare, somnolence, difficulty in body movements, and disturbed sleep.

Parkinson's disease was well known in India, and traditional doctors used the powder of *Mucuna pruriens* for its treatment. The naturopathic and holistic approach of Ayurveda takes advantage of the active biochemical compounds of the plant tissue. The treatment does have some disadvantages, such as bulkiness of the preparation as well as the difficulty in its administration.

Naturopathy and Levodopa

Naturopathic methodology considers major causes of the development and progression of Parkinson's disease: living in a polluted environment, exposure to pesticides, drinking well water, and constipation, among others. Modern medicine is not able to put a finger what exactly triggers the loss of neuronal tissue, and conventional medications are useful only in a short-term alleviation of the symptoms of PD. In the 1960s, the introduction of levadopa, the first choice of treatment for most patients, reformed the treatment of Parkinson's disease, and it is still considered, in modern medicine, an effective therapy.[16] L-dopa, as a neuroprotective, has considerable side effects as the disease progresses, such as dysarthria, hallucinations, cognitive decline, and impaired balance. The treatment of advanced PD is also complicated by the emergence of motor fluctuations and dyskinesias related to pulsatile and continuous administration of L-dopa.[17] In these cases, naturopathic Parkinson's patients are informed of therapeutic options other than standard treatment with L-dopa.

Coenzyme Q10

Prescriptive naturopathic strategies of treatment, such as those based on coenzyme Q10 (ubiquinone-10) administration, speculate pathogenesis and mechanisms of cell death by limiting the loss of dopaminergic function.[18] The mechanisms responsible for cell death in Parkinson's disease are unknown, but it is known that the molecular characteristics of Parkinson's disease involve free radical dysfunctions as a major component in the damage process of neuronal tissue. In such a context, the naturopathic administration of the mitochondrial factor coenzyme Q10 has major benefits in limiting

the disease's progression.[19] Coenzyme Q10 also serves as an important anti-oxidant in lipid membranes and mitochondria. Research with animal models using high doses[20] are relevant for establishing neuroprotective properties.

Extracts of *Mucuna*

Drug-induced dyskinesia caused by levodopa, a dopaminergic anti-Parkinson's medication, can be reversed by *Mucuna pruriens*, a legume mentioned and used in Ayurveda for treating Parkinson's disease. Commonly known as cowitch or velvet bean, *Mucuna* is a naturopathic legume originating in southern China and eastern India. Currently, it is available in most tropical regions of South and Central America, Asia, and Africa. Researchers[21] proved that the seed and the powder of *Mucuna pruriens* containing water-soluble ingredients either have a *dopa-decarboxylase* inhibiting action or mitigate the demand for an *add-on* type of dopa-decarboxylase inhibitor to ameliorate Parkinson's disease symptoms. These are considered to be unique long-term anti-Parkinsonian effects that provide a platform for future naturopathic drug discoveries and treatment strategies. The *Mucuna* plant contains between 2 and 9 percent L-dopa.[22] It is a natural source of L-dopa, which might posses advantages over conventional drug treatment with L-dopa in long-term management of PD.[23]

Botulinum Toxin

Botulinum toxin type A reduces sialorrhea (drooling) in Parkinson's disease by controlling drooling frequency and saliva production.[24] Botulinum toxin type B also provides long-lasting benefits by administrating it via injections into the parotid glands to reduce drooling. A placebo-controlled study enrolling thirty-six Parkinson's disease subjects showed botulinum toxin type B as an effective and safe tool in Parkinson's disease therapy related to drooling, ensuring a long-term effect on this symptom.[25]

Broad Bean

In Australia, research shows that broad beans are an efficacious natural source of levodopa, and the highest concentration is centralized in the pod, so the recommendation is to consume it whole. Broad bean (also known as *Vicia faba*, or fava bean) seeds contain 2 percent levodopa.[26] In Turkey, doctors received reports from their Parkinson's disease patients that they were consuming favas on a regular basis in addition to their medicine and they observed improvements. This kind of bean contains tyrosine and phenylalanine, the precursors of levodopa, and tyrosine hydroxylase is the enzyme responsible for converting tyrosine into levodopa.

Chapter Fourteen

Nonprescription Treatment

A multidisciplinary approach to Parkinson's should involve all the traditional therapists in conjunction with alternative modalities. This includes the dietician, the occupational therapist, the physiotherapist, and the speech and language therapist. Alternative or complementary therapies may accompany conventional medicine. Alternative therapies, a category that includes nonprescription treatment, may benefit people with Parkinson's and can include acupuncture, art therapy, conductive education, homeopathy, hydrotherapy, music therapy, pilates, reflexology, and tai chi.[1] While the scope of nonprescription treatment is too large to cover in a single volume, this chapter explores some of the options available to soon-to-be patients and sufferers of Parkinson's.

OVER-THE-COUNTER MEDICATIONS

Over-the-counter (OTC) medications are those medicines available at local pharmacies and that can be bought without a prescription from a physician. These medicines are usually considered safe to use and are nonaddictive; they range anywhere from a bottle of vitamins to a bottle of acetaminophen. Usually, people with Parkinson's take OTC medications to treat individual symptoms either related to the disease process, such as joint pain or runny nose, or for other maladies that afflict someone who already has Parkinson's. These may include influenza, headaches, or stomachaches. Taking over-the-counter (OTC) medications is one method of treatment for Parkinson's disease that generally helps manage and lessen the severity of symptoms of the disease.[2]

Decongestants

Idiopathic rhinorrhea, or a runny nose that is not due to allergies or infections, is a common manifestation in patients with Parkinson's disease, affecting approximately 35 to 70 percent of a studied population.[3] There is no exact cause as to why it occurs, but researchers and doctors have hypothesized that it is due to the sympathetic degeneration of nerves in the nasal mucosa. Rhinorrhea affects the quality of life of a person with Parkinson's in a negative manner because it is both embarrassing and bothersome to the patient; it could also worsen and cause coughing and postnasal drip. To help manage rhinorrhea, over-the-counter decongestants can be used. Decongestants work by decreasing the secretions and mucus production of goblet cells in the linings of the nasal passages. These nonprescription medications may come in an oral form, such as pseudoephedrine and phenylephedrine, or as nasal sprays, such as oxymetazoline. However, prolonged and continued use of these medications may lead to a rebound effect and result instead in an increase in nasal secretions. It is best to consult the health-care provider or physician about the medications being taken to manage the rhinorrhea in order to evaluate the need to continue or discontinue the treatment after the recommended period of therapy.

Alternative methods for managing idiopathic rhinorrhea in people with Parkinson's are also available, the most common and cost-effective of them all involving regular blowing of the nose to clear the air passages. Blowing overforcefully, however, could lead to inflammation of the nasal mucus linings and lead to even more secretion of mucus. When caring for a Parkinson's patient with this problem, it is best to encourage increased fluid intake as well as to wash hands frequently after blowing the nose. If the patient is in the advanced stage of the disease and cannot blow his or her own nose, the physician may advise having a trained caregiver who can vacuum out the secretions by using a suction machine as needed.

Laxatives and Stool Softeners

In individuals afflicted with Parkinson's disease, the development of constipation is a major possibility, as discussed in earlier chapters, mainly because there is a loss of autonomic nerves in the gastrointestinal system with advancing age and progression of the disease.[4] People become constipated when they have inadequate fiber and water intake as well as when not moving the body frequently. Parkinson's drugs such as dopaminergic agents and anticholinergics can also slow peristalsis and lead to constipation. Chronic constipation can lead to fecal impaction and even bowel obstruction.[5] Nonprescription laxatives and stool softeners may be used to help relieve constipation, but this method is not advisable for long-term use. Daily use can lead

to dependence on laxatives or even rebound constipation. These laxatives are usually used during the acute stage of constipation. It is best to take them at night before going to bed in order to follow the time for elimination as close to the usual time as possible and to stimulate bowel movement in the morning.

Coenzyme Q10

Coenzyme Q10, more commonly referred to as coQ10, is a substance required for the chemical processes that occur within the mitochondrion of a cell. This substance is necessary for the normal functioning of cells and, in general, the entire group of body systems in a human being. It is also a potent antioxidant protecting the body from both environmental and cellular toxins and free radicals. In a study conducted by the University of California in San Diego, trial results have suggested that the use of coenzyme Q10 supplements in patients with Parkinson's disease actually slows down the rate of functional decline in their bodies.[6]

NUTRITIONAL SUPPLEMENTS

Parkinson's disease is a debilitating illness that weakens not only the mind but also the body. Nutritional supplements are substances made to provide additional vitamins and minerals that are needed to meet the daily required amount in a person's body. Vitamins and minerals are essential in the optimum functioning and general health of a person's body because insufficient levels of these vitamins and minerals are detrimental to health and may lead to complications and other illnesses. Weekly monitoring of the patient's weight is important in determining whether the caloric intake of the patient is sufficient. It can help determine how the patient can be supplemented to maintain adequate nutrition. This countermeasure can be best applied at the time the patient is starting to experience slowness in food intake and difficulty chewing and/or swallowing. It is important to keep track of the patient's nutritional needs and intake with the aim of sustaining the patient's current condition and increasing responsiveness to medication.

Multivitamins

One of the most common nonprescription elements for Parkinson's disease is a daily dose of multivitamins. As the disease progresses, the individual's movements become slower and more difficult to perform. Day-to-day tasks such as eating or drinking may become too difficult and tiring. Because of this, the individual's nutritional status and daily caloric intake is compromised, which may lead to other potential complications of the disease such as

malnutrition and an increased risk for acquiring an infection. Multivitamins help supplement the daily requirement of vitamins and minerals such as vitamins A, B complex, C, iron, zinc, and calcium, among others. These vitamins are essential for the optimum functioning of the body. Vitamin A, or retinol, improves the immune function as well as eye function. Vitamin B complex (vitamins B1, B2, B3, B6 and B12) is needed for improved brain processes such as thinking and mental alertness; these B vitamins also help in the quick regeneration of muscles and tissues, aid in healthy red blood cell production, and prevent degeneration of nerve and brain cells. Vitamins are categorized and explained in much greater detail in chapter 16.

Zinc and Calcium Supplements

As a person ages, bone density lessens due to inactivity, poor diet, and the aging process. Immobility also promotes osteoclast production, decreasing the calcium content in the bone and making it more prone to osteoporosis and fractures. Aside from vitamin D, the body needs minerals such as zinc and calcium in order to increase bone density as well as prevent osteoporosis from occurring. Zinc, although not as commonly heard of as other minerals, plays a role equally as important as the other vitamins and minerals. Zinc has many functions, such as boosting the immune system, promoting faster wound healing, and preventing osteoporosis. Calcium, on the other hand, is one of the most important minerals involved in bone formation and structure. It also helps in the cardiac activity of the heart; too little calcium can cause cardiac arrhythmias, or irregular beating of the heart, which can be dangerous and even fatal if not treated.

Iron Supplements

Parkinson's sufferers face iron deficiency throughout their ordeal with the disease.[7] Iron is a mineral vital to the production of healthy red blood cells. It is needed in the creation of hemoglobin, which acts as the oxygen-carrying mechanism of a red blood cell. Foods high in iron include horseradish, organ meat, green, leafy vegetables, and fish products. Iron supplements may be suggested to prevent the development of iron deficiency anemia (IDA) in a person, especially the elderly and those with problems in nutrition. Iron supplements may also be advised by the physician to a person suffering from Parkinson's who has inadequate nutritional intake of iron in his or her diet. Considering that circulation is a very important health factor in osteopathic medicine (chapter 12), nonprescription iron supplementation could be ordered by a DO treating Parkinson's.

Fish Oil

Other nutritional supplements may include fish oil, a widely used supplement among people living in Asian countries such as Japan and China. This oil is rich in vitamins A, D, and E as well as omega-3 fatty acids and eicosapentae-noic acid (EPA) and docosahexaenoic acid (DHA), which are both antioxi-dants and cholesterol-lowering agents. An experimental study[8] conducted by scientists showed that omega-3 actually had a neuroprotective effect on mice exposed to toxins. Scientists are hopeful that this neuroprotective action could help protect the brain cells of humans from damage and prevent the development of Parkinson's in the future. Fish oil supplements come in either a liquid form or softgel capsules and are sold in most health shops and even some pharmacies.

Herbal Supplements

Fava beans are plants that contain some amount of levodopa. These can actually be beneficial or dangerous to humans, depending on the intake. Having enough levodopa in a person's system is beneficial as it improves cognitive and physiologic functioning; however, too much dopamine in the system can lead to changes in orientation and even hallucination in some cases. It is best to eat this with caution and consult a physician before ingest-ing this plant with other Parkinson's drugs, especially dopaminergic agents, to avoid accidental overdose and harm to the patient.

Gingko biloba is a relatively common herbal supplement sold in various health shops. It is believed to improve blood circulation in the body, most especially to the brain. Also, this herb may be related to an improvement in the delivery of dopamine within the human brain.

Ginko biloba is an extremely popular herbal supplement, made from ex-tracts of the ginko biloba tree. Although the manner in which extract of ginko biloba works is not clear, it contains several active compounds that work as antioxidants in protecting neuronal cell tissue from free radical damage that plays a large part in Parkinson's disease.

It is important to note that although these nutritional supplements, oils, and capsules help meet the daily vitamin requirements, they should not be used as the main source of calories and nutrients. Judicious and recom-mended daily intake should be observed; ingesting too many supplements or too much of one supplement may be detrimental to health with or without Parkinson's and can overwork the kidneys and liver upon metabolism and excretion of the substances, especially in the cases of comorbid conditions such as diabetes, cirrhosis, or kidney failure.

NONPHARMACOLOGIC TREATMENT OF PARKINSON'S

Diet

The physician may advise a patient suffering from Parkinson's to consume a low-protein diet to maximize the effect of dopaminergic agents such as levodopa or carbidopa in the body. A nutritionist may be required to create a diet specially tailored to this individual in order to attain an acceptable amount of protein in the body that will not interfere with the absorption and efficacy of his or her medicines while at the same time suit and meet daily dietary needs.

Fiber

Adequate intake of food rich in nutrients and fiber is essential to the general well-being of the person with Parkinson's, especially since the disease slows down the peristaltic movement in the intestines as well as makes the person move slower, even leading to physical immobility and being bedridden. Fruits and vegetables are a great source of fiber in the diet, as well as whole wheat products, oats, wheatgrass, and nuts. Snacks and meals should be soft, easy to chew and swallow, and easily digestible. Food supplements with fiber are also available at most health shops to supplement the daily recommended intake of fiber in the diet.

Fluids

Adequate fluid intake is also an important part of a Parkinson's disease sufferer's diet. The recommended daily fluid intake is around six to eight glasses of water, fruit juices, and other beverages, depending on the weather, activity, body build, and individual needs of the patient.[9] Fluids such as water, fruit juices, and vegetable juices are recommended as they cleanse the colon and provide additional calories and fiber in the diet. Some fruits and vegetables also have antioxidant properties that help decrease the toxins in the body. The timing and frequency of feeding the patient helps decrease fatigue, indigestion, and feelings of bloating. Provide small, frequent, nutritional snacks spaced evenly throughout the day because heavy meals may tire the individual even before he or she finishes a meal. If the patient has difficulty swallowing, a nasogastric tube (NGT) may be inserted on doctor's orders for parenteral nutrition and other purposes such as medicine intake.

For Drooling

Sialorrhea, commonly known as drooling, is also a common effect of having Parkinson's disease, affecting up to 70 percent of people diagnosed.[10] As the disease progresses, the person may start to lose the function of the throat and mouth muscles, making swallowing increasingly more difficult to do. As a

result of infrequent and ineffective swallowing, saliva pools in the mouth and causes episodes of drooling, especially when the neck is in a flexed position. This is a cause of concern as pooling of saliva in the mouth and throat increases the risk of aspirating, or choking, on it; furthermore, drooling also affects the individual's psychological well-being and social life. Constant drooling may cause the patient embarrassment and feelings of shame or frustration, lowering self-esteem and the sense of dignity and pride. Other patients are hesitant to go out of their homes because of their drooling issues. However, drooling can be managed through proper posture and positioning and by avoiding sweet or sugary food as this may increase the production of saliva. Studies show that sucking on solid, sugarless candy, ice chips, or even chewing gum improves the frequency of swallowing in Parkinson's patients. [11]

Juicing

"Juicing" is one healthful habit that can have many benefits. Juicing proponents state that valuable and sensitive micronutrients become damaged when foods are heated. While cooking and processing foods, their shape and chemical composition are altered because the micronutrients are destroyed. While following this dietary plan, a person reaches an advanced nutritional level where they avoid all processed foods and eat only natural vegetables and fruits. Through juicing, the daily target of vegetables is reached, providing a quick way to ensure all the necessary vitamins and nutrients. The majority of juicing is of fruits, but if the individual with Parkinson's is overweight or has high blood pressure, diabetes, or high cholesterol, it is best to limit using fruits until the person succeeds in normalizing these conditions. Since lemons and limes do not contain sugar and fructose that can cause most of the metabolic complications, they can be consumed on a daily basis. Moreover, they eliminate the bitter taste of the dark, deep green leafy vegetables that offer the best advantages of juicing.

Vegetables

One of the reasons to start a juicing diet is that juicing helps the body absorb all the necessary nutrients from the vegetables. This is important because Parkinson's patients have impaired digestion, [12] perhaps as a result of making less-than-optimal food choices over many years, which puts a limit on the body's capacity to take in all helpful nutrients from the vegetables. Juicing acts to "predigest" them so that the body will receive most of the nutrition rather than eliminating it. Another reason for juicing is that it allows one to consume a proper amount of vegetables in a correct manner. People who prefer plenty of carbohydrates should consider eating one pound of unprocessed vegetables per fifty pounds of body weight per day. [13] Some people

might consider this difficult, but it can be easily attained with a quick glass of vegetable juice.

Further arguments suggest that consumers add a wider variety of vegetables to their diet.[14] A Parkinson's patient might be used to eating the same type of vegetables every day. The principle of regular food rotation is not practiced, and the chance of developing an allergy to a certain food is increased. With juicing, one.can juice a wide variety of vegetables that one may not normally enjoy eating whole. It is vital for Parkinson's disease patients and caregivers to understand that the juice made from vegetables contains small amounts of protein and scarcely any fat, so it cannot be considered a complete food. It is not recommended to replace regular meals but rather to accompany them. The juices can be consumed with meals or between snacks, and if (and only if) a person is undergoing special fasting or a detoxification program, they can become a replacement.

When talking about protein type, juicing needs to be done cautiously. Celery, spinach, asparagus, string beans, and cauliflower would be the best vegetables to juice. Dark leafy greens such as collards, kale, and dandelion greens can be added, but cautiously and by paying careful attention to the body and its needs. At the beginning, the serving size of juice should be limited to no more than six ounces, and the juice should be stored properly, with the patient consuming small amounts during the day. Again, it seems likely that diet could wield a notable influence on one's risk of suffering from Parkinson's. For example, a study[15] conducted by Harvard University showed that adamant coffee drinkers (one to three cups per day) had their risk of developing PD cut in half. This protective effect is also observed for green tea consumers: a daily intake of two cups or more of green tea can reduce the Parkinson's risk by 25 percent.

Recent results suggest that vegetables rich in polyphenols could also contribute to preventing Parkinson's.[16] By studying the eating habits of 130,000 people over a twenty-year period, scientists found that individuals who consumed an abundance of foods rich in flavonoids (berries, apples, tea, orange juice, and red wine) saw their risk of developing Parkinson's reduced by 35 percent over those who consumed only small quantities of these foods and drinks. Overall, these observations suggest that in addition to participating in the prevention of chronic illnesses such as heart disease and many types of cancer, certain foods rich in polyphenols, such as berries and green tea, could also reduce the neurodegeneration that leads to Parkinson's.

Vegetarian meals that include whole grains, beans, lentils, and vegetables should be eaten, and fish should be consumed at least twice a week (tuna, lake trout, herring, mackerel, salmon, or sardines). Moderate amounts of low-fat dairy products are indicated each day or weekly, such as milk, cheese, or yogurt, moderate amounts of poultry and eggs are indicated every two days or weekly, red meat is limited to only a few times a month in very

small amounts. For example, a suitable serving of meat is three ounces. This is about the size of a deck of cards. Sweets and desserts, including sugar-sweetened drinks (soda) can be consumed only a few times a week.

Mediterranean Diet

Apart from these nutrition tips, experts recommend the Mediterranean diet, which is really a way of eating rather than a formal diet plan. It contains foods from Greece, Spain, southern Italy, France, and other countries in the proximity of the Mediterranean Sea. The Mediterranean diet emphasizes eating foods such as fish, fruits, vegetables, beans, high-fiber breads and whole grains, and olive oil. Meat, cheese, and sweets are limited. The prescribed foods have high levels of monounsaturated fats, fiber, and omega-3 fatty acids. The Mediterranean diet is similar to other heart-healthy diets in that it recommends eating plenty of fruits, vegetables, and high-fiber grains. This type of diet may help lower the risk for certain diseases, improve mood, and boost energy levels. It may also help keep the heart and brain healthy. The diet reinforces the benefits of eating products such as fruits, vegetables, fish, high-fiber breads, whole grains, and healthy fats. For the heart and body, a Mediterranean-style diet may prevent heart disease, lowers the risk of a subsequent heart attack, lowers cholesterol, and helps prevent type 2 diabetes and metabolic syndrome. When thinking about the brain, this diet is helpful in preventing Alzheimer's disease and other dementia, depression, and Parkinson's disease. Anyone can do a few simple things to include more foods from the Mediterranean diet. The traditional diet calls for eating a variety of fruits and vegetables each day, such as grapes, blueberries, tomatoes, broccoli, peppers, figs, olives, spinach, eggplant, beans, lentils, and chickpeas.

When There Is Too Much Iron

Eating a diet too high in iron puts people at an increased risk of developing Parkinson's disease.[17] While iron is a necessary part of staying healthy, too much iron can be devastating. Aside from the excess iron that can result from taking iron supplements, iron overload, or hemochromatosis, is actually the most common inherited disease. When the Parkinson's patient tries to optimize his or her health, it is important to balance and constantly estimate iron levels, especially for men and postmenopausal women, since high levels of iron are usually common among these groups. However, simply evaluating serum iron is a not a good method for determining one iron level because almost all the time, the serum iron will be normal. The most useful of the indirect measures of iron status in the body is through a measure of the serum ferritin level in conjunction with a total iron binding level.

Fatigue Management

Fatigue is a disabling and unpleasant symptom common in Parkinson's patient. It mars the patient's daily activities and motor rehabilitation programs. It feeds on the patient's emotional reactions to PD symptoms and makes them all the harder to bear. Fatigue management becomes highly important as fatigue undermines the patient's capacity to cope with the challenges the disease presents. Thus, fatigue makes it even more difficult for the individual with Parkinson's to connect with others, sometimes isolating the patient further in his or her own cocoon. In order to manage fatigue without medical prescription, the doctor either recommends a trial of stimulants or plant-based antidepressants.[18]

Enhancing Swallowing

As noted from other chapters, difficulty in swallowing is common among both inpatients and outpatients who suffer from Parkinson's. This is caused by the irregular contraction and weakness of facial muscles. A solution to this is to assist the patient in sitting in an upright position during mealtime. This can help the patient cope with swallowing difficulties while exerting less effort since the food movement is downward. Determining the kind of food to eat is important in view of the fact that patients need the right kind of food and adequate nutritional contents. Guiding a patient to a more convenient way to swallow food can also be beneficial. It is advisable that the Parkinson's patient be taught to place the food on the tongue, close the lips and teeth, lift the tongue up and then back, and then swallow. In addition, the patient is encouraged to chew food on one side of the mouth at a time. This can also serve as the patient's exercise for the chewing muscles.

Education

Once a client is diagnosed as having Parkinson's disease, both the client and caregiver should be educated about the important facts and instructions regarding the disease and its processes. Knowledge about these topics, as well as a list of possible treatments and therapies to manage symptoms and changes in lifestyle, enables the patient and the family to prepare themselves both emotionally, psychologically, and even financially. This will also help them gain a sense of control over a situation that is life changing and difficult. Getting briefed about significant information related to the illness also lessens anxiety and is in accordance with the "patient's bill of rights," the right to education and information. Pamphlets, lists, journals, books, magazines, even educational videos are good sources of information for both the patient and the family members. Using simple, direct, and easily understandable words and approaches are best for teaching the patient and family;

encouraging them to ask questions is also considered to be a good communication skill to develop between the health-care provider and the Parkinson's disease patient.

Support

The diagnosis of Parkinson's could create a feeling of hopelessness, anger, or depression, and could even lead to psychological problems. A very important part in adjusting to a life with Parkinson's is to have a support group to help the individual cope with the perceived loss of control with his body and self. A support group, or even supportive people such as family, friends, or significant others addresses the psychological effects on an indivudual with Parkinson's. Support groups allow people suffering from a similar illness to talk about their experiences, their feelings, and how they cope with problems and complications, and they permit an individual to feel less alone and to be comforted in the fact that they are not the only ones going through the whole process. Also, support groups are a great way to explore and share other treatment methods and effects among people who all have Parkinson's.

Support groups are not only for the person suffering from Parkinson's disease but also for his or her caregivers and family members. Caregiver role strain (see chapter 20) is a common but often overlooked problem among caregivers and family members, especially since the focus of attention of most people involves the patient, not the ones giving care. Significant others often have feelings of pity, frustration, and sadness from seeing their loved ones slowly grow worse despite their best efforts at caregiving. These support groups for family members and friends allow them to express their emotions and thoughts to others who can understand, sympathize, and empathize with them. In this manner, caregivers can learn how to cope with the stress and other difficulties with the help of the support group members. They can also interact and share new information pertinent to the subject as well as provide insight and advice to others.

COMPLEMENTARY THERAPIES

Alternative therapies can also be used to treat people with Parkinson's disease. They are called alternative or complementary therapies because they are often used along with taking the prescribed medications and other treatment regimens to help the individual cope better with the disease. Although there are no proven scientific effects as of yet, many people have sworn that they have felt better and believe that there is a great improvement in their quality of life after trying alternative therapies. A survey showed that around 40 percent of Parkinson's patients use one or more complementary therapies to manage their disease.[19] These therapies could range from acupuncture and

acupressure to tai chi and yoga and vary, depending on an individual's preferences and capabilities. Also, these therapies should be chosen depending on the area and physical, social, or mental aspects that need work.

Music Therapy

Music therapy is one method of diverting the attention of the person from problems such as stress, anxiety, and even pain. This kind of alternative therapy uses music to stimulate the brain, specifically the different sensory pathways, eliciting both emotional and motor responses. Music therapy commonly uses soft, soothing music and songs; sometimes it uses the sounds of nature, such as the sound of water flowing, a bird chirping, or even the sound of crickets. Some people prefer listening to classical music to help soothe the nerves and promote relaxation. In a study[20] conducted on Parkinson's patients, results showed that music therapy significantly improved movement in patients with bradykinesia as well as improving their moods and happiness levels.

Physical Therapy

Physical therapy is one of the most common adjunct therapies for treating people suffering from Parkinson's disease. This may or may not be prescribed by the physician; if it is, however, the physician refers the patient to a licensed physical therapist for daily or weekly sessions. Physical therapy involves various exercises and forms that are designed to target specific groups of muscles in the body. For example, the physical therapist may flex and extend the patient's knees or legs in order to exercise the leg muscles and promote optimum range of movement. It is through this type of therapy that multiple, if not all, muscles in the body are used, thereby preventing contractures and atrophy while improving motion and blood circulation. Physical therapy also improves a person's balance and gait, making it easier for him or her to move about while at the same time minimizing the risk for falls and accidents.

Speech Therapy

Speech therapy can be suggested for patients who have dysarthria, those who are having difficulty with speech, and those who have dysphagia, or difficulty swallowing This type of therapy helps exercise the throat muscles as well as the tongue and enables these muscles to become stronger, making swallowing and speaking easier and making drooling episodes occur less frequently, thereby improving the quality of life as well as preserving the functions of the Parkinson's disease patient's body for as long as possible. A speech therapist may be hired to work with the client around twice or three

times a week or so, depending on the suggestion of the doctor and the preference of both the client and the family.

Occupational Therapy

Occupational therapy is aimed at helping patients with Parkinson's perform the activities of daily living and at providing support and assistance to those who are experiencing cognitive and physical alterations and disabilities. One of the main goals of this kind of therapy is to help the individual cope with and adapt to changes in his or her body functions, lifestyle, and capacity to do previously easy tasks. Occupational therapists assist these people in doing simple tasks on their own using many different methods. They may enable the person to sew, cook, paint, draw, do grooming and hygiene, and even dress themselves. However, as the disease progresses to the later stages, doing activities that require fine motor skills should be minimized. Activities should be simple and within the person's scope of capabilities in order to increase a sense of control and achievement; doing difficult and complex tasks will only frustrate the individual and may even lead to depression and feelings of worthlessness.

Exercise

Exercise is a great way of keeping the blood circulating and the muscles working. It also helps prevent a person from acquiring negative effects of being inactive such as bedsores, blood clots, and even osteoporosis. Moderate exercises such as swimming or biking are great for people in the early stages of Parkinson's. Mild exercises such as walking or stretching and simple actions such as flexing the arms and bending the knees are recommended for patients with advanced stages of Parkinson's to keep the body as functional as possible for as long as possible. When maintaining balance is a problem, or if bedridden, one can exercise on a bed by moving body parts and flexing limbs. Periodically exercise the facial muscles, since Parkinson's disease can cause a masklike expression with little facial movement. Facial exercises include, raising the eyebrows, blinking, smiling, chewing, moving the lips, and reading aloud. These facial exercises are done multiple times for ten to thirty minutes daily to maintain the optimum tone and function of the facial muscles.

Therapies that involve body movement such as yoga, tai chi, and even dance therapy help maintain motor function in patients with Parkinson's by exercising and using numerous muscles in the body during workouts or sessions. Moreover, dance therapy has been shown to improve balance, gait, and posture, as well as improving the sense of control and feeling of general well-being of a person with Parkinson's.[21] These therapies are best used during

the early stages of the disease to maintain a maximum level of motor functioning for as long as the person is able.

It's not enough to exercise only the body; one must also exercise the mind. Cognitive and mental activities include reading newspapers or books, watching television, and playing mind games. For elderly Parkinson's disease patients, reminiscence therapy is encouraged. This works by letting the client talk about life, sing songs popular during the patient's youth, and even naming sons, daughters, and grandchildren. Other activities that exercise the mind such as playing chess or backgammon or even solving simple math problems are also recommended.

Acupuncture

Acupuncture has long been a traditional Asian treatment for relieving stress, body aches, and other symptoms. It involves inserting needles or pins at specific points in the body where the "energy," or *qi*, flows. Recent studies have shown that acupuncture produces a systematic stimulation of the skin and acts as a stimulus to increase activity in special areas in the brain. These areas are the motor cortex and the putamen, which are impaired or not functioning in Parkinson's disease patients. By using acupuncture, researchers have found a significant improvement in simple motor tasks of patients, such as tapping the fingers. They have theorized that acupuncture is actually some form of deep brain stimulation, which improves movement and motor functions of patients with Parkinson's.[22]

Deep Brain Stimulation

This procedure, described here in slightly less detail than the allopathic standpoint described in chapter 11, involves an electrode placed in the thalamus and connected to a battery-operated pulse generator implanted in the patient's abdominal pouch. The pulse generator sends high-frequency electrical impulses through a wire placed under the skin leading to the skull. The electrode blocks the targeted nerve pathways in the brain that cause tremors. This procedure is used to relieve tremors but can cause complications in the case of problems in the connections of the devices or the device itself. Further complications can occur if a leak occurs in the device attached on both the thalamus area and the abdominal pouch. The role of the hospital in Parkinson's is crucial not only in terms of diagnosing a patient for prevalence of signs and symptoms but also in applying appropriate medical treatments to accurately and safely address the patient's need.[23]

Psychological Therapy

One major and common effect of Parkinson's disease is a feeling of helplessness and depression in patients. They may feel useless or afraid of what is happening to their bodies. Psychological therapy aims at addressing these thoughts and finding ways to make an individual feel in control over his or her life again. It involves helping the person assess perspective and views on having the disease and assisting him or her to accept the condition and to guide the person to becoming productive and happy despite the gradually declining functions of the body. A psychologist also evaluates the person for signs of depression, anger, and other emotions that may be harmful and provides suggestions on ways to channel these emotions into productive tasks that are at the same time beneficial to the overall health and wellness of the patient. Psychological therapy helps the Parkinson's patient cope with the perceived loss of status, freedom, independence, and control.

DIVERSION ACTIVITIES

People with Parkinson's, especially after being diagnosed, tend to become stressed because of the diagnosis and prognosis of the disease. Diversion activities help refocus the attention of the individual with Parkinson's to other aspects. These activities have both physical and emotional benefits to the patient, the most notable being able to minimize stress and anxiety; also, patients report increases in their levels of happiness, freedom, independence, and their sense of peace and calm.

Imagery

A good example of a diversion activity is imagery, whether guided or not. Imagery involves letting the person close both eyes and think good thoughts or thoughts of peaceful places. These thought vary, depending on what makes the Parkinson's disease patient feel well and relaxed. Some may think of beaches, cool springs, or even happy memories from their past. Guided imagery, on the other hand, works by having a guide, usually a psychologist or a close friend, lead the flow of the person's thoughts. For example, the caregiver may instruct the person to close his or her eyes and try to relax, after which the guide will start describing some things in detail and ask the client to imagine those descriptions until a complete image has been formed in the mind. Many people have tried guided imagery as a means of reducing stress and inducing relaxation.[24]

Recreational Activities

Recreational activities help individuals release stress, tension, and negative feelings through safe and artistic means. In this type of therapy, Parkinson's disease clients are encouraged to transform their emotions and release them through various mediums such as drawing, painting, singing, dancing, and even poem writing. They are able to feel relaxed and creative and to express themselves freely and fully as well as enjoy the process.

Aromatherapy

For centuries, aromatherapy has been used by people in many European and Asian countries to relax and unwind and even remove stress and anxiety from their minds. This type of complementary therapy helps individuals affected with Parkinson's to decrease their stress levels and feel more relaxed; it does not treat or address the underlying cause of the disease but rather the effects of the disease on the person's mental and psychosocial status.

Whether referring to over-the-counter pills and syrups, vitamins, yoga, and even dancing, nonprescription and alternative therapies are used by millions of people diagnosed with Parkinson's all over the world. Individuals afflicted with the disease use these therapies to improve their motor, cognitive, and psychosocial functions as well as to summon a greater sense of well-being. However, as in all adjunct and complementary therapies, a person must first consult a licensed physician about the intended regimen before taking it on. This is to be certain that such therapies are not only beneficial to the patient but that they ensure the individual's general safety and integrity.

PARKINSON'S AND THE PLACEBO EFFECT

Regardless of the origins of the term, the word *placebo* had a different meaning in medieval English. A placebo represented a flatterer, someone capable of pleasing others with superficialities, artifice rather than substance. When it comes to nonprescription treatment of Parkinson's, a placebo is an inert substance that is believed to have healing effects through the actions of the human body's natural healing capacities. It represents any procedure that a patient believes has effects on a disease or symptom. The placebo effect is a controversial notion and has been the subject of many clinical trials and caused clinical and ethical debates. The treatment of pain (chapter 10) and insomnia has demonstrated the power of placebo, and researchers have found that the placebo can increase immunity, cure depression, improve angina, and prevent asthma. Researchers have also concluded that several types of placebos are more efficient than others: for example, two placebo pills are

more efficient than a single one, larger pills that are purple or brown seem to be more powerful than smaller pills, and small yellow-red pills demonstrate an increased healing action. The concept of *nocebo* is similar to the placebo effect but is much less reported. It is based on a substance containing inert properties that increases pain and unfortunately contributes to health deterioration. Estimations show that 20 to 30 percent of patients receiving placebos experience different side effects. [25]

One noteworthy book[26] explains the response considered to be the physiological and psychological effects of "meaning" in the treatment of a disease. When the mentioned effects are positive, they are the expression of what people usually call placebo effect, but when the effects are negative, they include what has been called the nacebo effect. The interaction between behavior, neural endocrine function, and immune processes is the object of study of psychoneuroimmunology, a relatively new field introduced in the 1980s by Robert Ader, who was a professor of psychology and psychiatry. Ader revealed that immunoregulatory processes were determined by brain function and that neural activity, endocrine processes, and behavior are in turn determined by the immune system.

V

Personal Resolutions

Chapter Fifteen

Prevention of Parkinson's

Overusing medications to control Parkinson's can be an ill-advised solution, and now those who use this "cure" have something new to worry about: they risk losing their life savings in a rare but very real effect—gambling.[1] Parkinson's disease affects near one million Americans,[2] and the symptoms worsen over time. That said, prevention is the best option when fighting Parkinson's disease. This chapter explores several preventive tactics that one can use to avoid or lessen the development of the disease.

PREVENTING PARKINSON'S

A guidebook on Parkinson's disease for patients and caregivers would probably be incomplete without a few notes on prevention. Research scientists are still trying to discover a way to completely prevent Parkinson's disease. One hypothesis claims that the cause of Parkinson's disease is free radicals that may contribute to nerve cell death, thereby leading to Parkinson's disease. Free radicals are unstable and potentially destructive molecules brought about by normal chemical reactions in the body. Normally, free radical damage is held under control by antioxidants, chemicals that protect cells from this damage. Many naturally occurring substances are thought to have antioxidant features. Some of these include vitamin E, vitamin C, coenzyme Q10 (coQ10), nicotinamide adenine dinucleotide (NADH), and ginkgo biloba. Because of their antioxidant properties, scientists have speculated that supplementation with these products may provide some protection against developing Parkinson's disease. To date, there has been little research supporting that these products are helpful in the prevention of PD. Nonetheless, recent research demonstrates a possible connection between increased coffee consumption and a lower risk of Parkinson's disease. The answer to how to

prevent Parkinson's disease is still uncertain, although there is support for the hypothesis that coffee and tea can provide a certain level of protection against the development of Parkinson's.[3]

Caffeine and the Prevention of Parkinson's

Important studies have shown that caffeine absorption is associated with a reduced risk of establishing Parkinson's disease in men. For example, a study[4] found an annual incidence rate of 10.5 cases of Parkinson's disease per ten thousand person-years (one year of life for one person) among non-coffee drinkers. The occurrence rate lowered to 5.5 for those drinking four to eight ounces of coffee per day, 4.7 for those drinking twelve to sixteen ounces, 3.6 for those drinking twenty to twenty-four ounces, and 1.7 for those drinking more than twenty-eight ounces. Adapting for other factors, the scientists estimated that non-coffee drinkers were two to three times as likely to develop Parkinson's disease as coffee drinkers consuming four to twenty-four ounces per day. When compared to men who drank the highest amount of coffee (twenty-eight ounces or more per day), non-coffee drinkers were five times as likely to develop Parkinson's disease. These results include an improvement by the researchers to account for cigarette smoking, a previously identified protective agent for Parkinson's disease.[5]

The researchers studied survey data from more than 77,000 nurses who participated in the Nurses' Health Study, a comprehensive twenty-year endeavor designed to take a closer look at women's health.[6] In this group, more than 150 women were diagnosed with Parkinson's disease during the study. Overall, there was no difference in disease incidence between women who were and weren't using hormone replacement therapy (HRT). When caffeine consumption was factored in, HRT made a big difference in the person's risk of developing Parkinson's disease.

Among women taking HRT, an increased risk of Parkinson's disease was confined to women who drank more than five cups of coffee per day. Drinking small amounts of coffee per day did not appear to affect the risk of Parkinson's disease in these women. The type of hormones and the duration of use did not seem to affect outcomes. The researchers noted that they controlled for possible effects of cigarette smoking, which has repeatedly been shown to be associated with a decreased risk of Parkinson's disease.

Diet and Prevention of Parkinson's

Diet may play a role in preventing neurodegenerative diseases. A diet filled with antioxidants helps prevent Parkinson's. Antioxidants are molecules within the body that assist with protecting healthy cells and destroy damaging molecules. In Parkinson's disease, the neurotransmitter dopamine loses

its ability to function well. A study[7] published in the *Journal of the American College of Nutrition* assessed the effect of antioxidants on dopaminergic neurons in rats. The researchers gave the rats extracts of cocoa, tangerine peel, grape seed, and red clover, since these contain antioxidants, for four days. No protection was seen with cocoa and grape seed, but there was an improvement from the red clover and tangerine peel extracts. Researchers think the amount was too small to see benefit, but further experimentation needs to be done in this area.

Moreover, urate or uric acid may lower the risk of (and thus prevent to a certain degree) Parkinson's disease. Urate is a strong antioxidant that scavenges free radicals associated with dopamine. Experimental results published in the *American Journal of Epidemiology*[8] assessed the effects of a high-urate diet on risk for Parkinson's. The researchers found that a high-urate diet had a protective effect on developing the disease by dampening oxidative stress. Research in this area is new, and attempts to increase uric acid may also increase the risk for kidney stones. Therefore, a high-urate diet should be tried only with a physician's supervision in a clinical environment.

Vitamin B6 controls and coordinates the homocysteine metabolism. Homocysteine, which is an amino acid in the blood, if elevated, may speed damage to dopaminergic cells in the brain, thus contributing to the progression of Parkinson's. However, if B6 levels are raised, then homocysteine does not succeed in rising to damaging levels. An experiment in the *British Journal of Nutrition*[9] explored the risk of Parkinson's with consumption of various B vitamins. Low intakes of B6 were linked with an elevated risk of the disease, but low folate, riboflavin, or B12 were not. Foods that have an increased level of B6 include asparagus, broccoli, bananas, spinach, crimini mushrooms, cod, turnips, garlic, tuna, and brussels sprouts.

Coenzyme Q10, or coQ10, is a molecule found in nearly every cell of the body, and it has several roles. Primarily, it assists with energy production and acts as an antioxidant in mitochondrial and lipid membranes. CoQ10 has shown somewhat beneficial in preventing Parkinson's. A study[10] in the *Journal of Neurochemistry* explains that coQ10 is neuroprotective by preventing mitochondrial disorder and oxidative damage. CoQ10 food sources include whole grains, tuna, salmon, and organ meats. As provided in the sections above, research has shown that people who eat more fruits and vegetables, high-fiber foods, fish, and omega-3-rich oils (sometimes called the Mediterranean diet) and who eat less red meat and dairy may have some protection against Parkinson's disease. But the reason for this is still being examined.

More on Preventive Diets

While the next chapter is based on diet and Parkinson's, much research is still being done on Parkinson's with emphasis on the topic of diet as it relates

to the *prevention* of the disease. A few foods have the power (to some extent) to prevent or at least delay the onset of Parkinson's.[11] The disease can have a devastating effect on the brains of those affected. People can fairly well come to terms with physical ailments, but they find it difficult to cope with an ailment that has the ability to ravage their mental and cognitive abilities and thus lead to brain atrophy such as that observed in Parkinson's. Prevention is always better than cure. The maximum possible care should be taken to ensure that the onset of Parkinson's is either prevented or its progression at least slowed. Monounsaturated fats such as the ones found in olive oil are very good at preventing cognitive decline in older people. Parkinson's disease mostly targets people over the age of fifty. This is, incidentally, the time when care should be taken regarding cognitive skills and memory. So including monounsaturated fats in the diet can help in this respect because even a small amount of negligence, as well as ignoring the subtle symptoms, might lead to more serious issues, keeping in mind the ability of Parkinson's disease to ravage cognitive capacities.

People with Parkinson's can benefit by being liberal in using turmeric in their diet as it is composed of a compound called curcumin, which, when used in abundance, is highly effective in inhibiting Parkinson's. Cranberries, blueberries, and strawberries are full of nutrients essential to keep the brain cells from getting damaged, which in turn save the mental and cognitive abilities from getting rusty. Apples are a leading source of quercetin, an antioxidant plant chemical that permits the free flow of mental juices in the person, thus allowing the brain to function at full capacity. Quercetin also defends the brain cells from free radical attacks, which can lead to the damage of the delicate neurons, thereby adversely affecting cognitive abilities.

Eggs are usually seen as a food that only increases the harmful cholesterol, but they are actually rich in choline, which ranks high in the prevention of mental decline. Then there are the whole grains, which are great for preventing brain disorders such as Parkinson's. Whole wheat, wheat germ, and bran have high contents of folate, as do barley, brown rice, whole-grain breads, and oatmeal. All of these foods work to increase blood flow to the brain, which means pumping of a higher quantity and higher-quality blood. These whole-grain foods also contain a lot of vitamin B6, which is good for improving memory. Foods such as spinach and nuts contain nutrients that may help reduce the loss of dopamine-producing neurons. Carrots are heavily loaded with a potent antioxidant called beta-carotene, and it is a widely known fact that antioxidants have the ability to fight the neuron-destroying free radicals, thus donning the role of a "preventer" that is engaged in shielding the cognitive skills and mental abilities from degeneration.[12]

High Flavonoid Intake

Not only are scientists and researchers interested in finding a cure for Parkinson's, but they are also much more enthusiastic about finding a way to prevent it or, at the very least, reduce the risk for acquiring it. It has been reported that dietary flavonoids may lower the risk of having Parkinson's, especially in men. Flavonoids are plant pigments found in fruits and food such as berries, apples, and tea. Men who eat plenty of flavonoids may lower their risk of Parkinson's disease, according to a study published in the journal *Neurology*.[13] Researchers of the study from Harvard Medical School analyzed the diets and medical histories of more than ninety thousand female registered nurses and almost fifty thousand male health professionals enrolled in two long-term studies, the Nurses' Health Study and the Health Professionals Follow-Up Study, which began in 1976 and 1986, respectively.[14] This long-term study required patients to complete questionnaires about their lifestyles, diet, and health status every four years. The researchers calculated the total flavonoid intake based on the participants' responses and then examined each individual's medical history in order to determine which of the participants developed Parkinson's.

The results showed that 850 participants out of the thousands who joined developed Parkinson's disease during their twenty to twenty-two years of follow-up checkups. Based on each participant's flavonoid intake, researchers have found that men who consumed the highest total levels of flavonoids had a 40 percent lower risk of Parkinson's disease (in terms of prevention) than those who consumed less. However, researchers found no significant relationship between total flavonoid consumption and Parkinson's disease risk in women. One possible reason for this discrepancy is that bodies of men and women break down flavonoids differently. This study suggests that, indeed, an individual's diet, particularly his or her flavonoid intake, may influence Parkinson's disease risk. Those who consume plenty of berries rich in anthocyanins may be able to slightly lower their risk of having Parkinson's. Although a diet rich in fruits and vegetables is advisable for all individuals, confirmation from additional studies is needed to determine whether berries and apples can indeed lower Parkinson's risk.

Chapter Sixteen

Diet and Parkinson's

Many tactics are available for a person to adopt to preserve health and assure well-being. Diet is one of those crucial and critical elements that either makes or mars a person's fitness. This very critical element gains even more significance and prominence when the person shows symptoms of Parkinson's disease (chapters 5 and 6). There is no diet specifically prescribed for a Parkinson's patient, and there is no such thing as a single diet chart applicable to all the people affected by the disease. It is a known fact that the symptoms of Parkinson's disease vary from person to person and—not only that—the intensity of the symptoms also vary. Parkinson's patients are in fact encouraged to embrace wholesome and balanced diets, which of course should be monitored, assessed, and modified from time to time by a medical practitioner with expertise in diagnosis and prognosis of the symptoms. There is no denying that the people affected by this disease should exercise more caution than others regarding their diet, and they are also expected to keep tabs on what they eat, how they eat, and when they eat. There are foods that either inhibit or encourage the symptoms of Parkinson's.[1] Yet responses to food vary from person to person, so each patient needs to decide whether a certain food helps or hurts his or her symptoms.

DIET AND BRAIN HEALTH

It is usually said that "you are what you eat." In fact, it is true that certain foods have a vital role to play in the health and functioning of the brain. Many foods have been shown to enhance memory or to prevent certain types of cognitive decline. Because Parkinson's is a class of disease that results from issues within the brain, eating a diet high in the foods that ward off cognitive decline is one way of preventing Parkinson's as well as other brain

diseases. Just as effective wiring ensures proper electricity supply, the right food ensures ample flow of blood in the right channels, which in turn establishes communication between the brain cells. The green leafy vegetables such as spinach and cabbage are considered to be excellent food for the brain. These foods enhance the activities of the brain by providing thorough nourishment to it. Spinach and cabbage are enriched in nutrients such as vitamin B6, vitamin B12, and folate, which are highly equipped in breaking down the homocysteine levels, which are the ones responsible for the outbreak of forgetfulness and eventually diseases such as Parkinson's and Alzheimer's in a person.[2] Spinach and cabbage are also great sources of iron, without which cognitive activity slows down.[3]

DIET AND PARKINSON'S

Overview

It is not an exaggeration to say that a person suffering from Parkinson's disease can lead a life that is uncompromising in all aspects—from personal activities to social life. Control and rigidity is not the norm for persons suffering from Parkinson's. It is true that they do not have to lead a controlled and rigid life, but they have to lead a disciplined life when it comes to their diet. For that matter, all people ought to be disciplined with respect to the diet they follow. Diet takes a person a long way, as both health and success have their origins in diet. When a Parkinson's disease sufferer follows a good diet regimen, health follows, and when health is under the person's control, he or she will have already covered half the distance toward success.

Each nutrient is special and unique in some way or another. A diet is called wholesome when all the nutrients are present in appropriate quantities. The maximum benefits of a particular food and nutrient are derived only when the food or nutrient is taken in moderation, nothing more and nothing less. Nature has tuned and tamed the human body in such a manner that it functions effectively and optimally only when it is taken complete and thorough care of in terms of diet. The importance and significance attached to diet increases manifoldly when the person has Parkinson's. It is highly important that the right amount of medicines be absorbed in the body of a person with the disease to have a desired impact. The right diet, in the right amount, taken at the right time plays a vital role in keeping symptoms from aggravating and in enabling the PD patient to lead a life that is independent and fulfilling. People suffering from Parkinson's are always encouraged to give the disease a tough fight and never to give up, and for them, the battle starts with their diet.

When the patient includes varied foods in the diet, the body is introduced to a medley of nutrients, namely proteins, carbohydrates, vitamins, minerals, and antioxidants. All these are dubbed as nutrients because they provide the body the fuel necessary to operate smoothly and effectively. Each nutrient has multiple benefits, and when multiple nutrients come together, the benefits are innumerable; that is the beginning of great nutrition. The best thing a person with Parkinson's can do for his or her body is to feed it a great diet that is full of vital and indispensable nutrients. A diet might have a specific nutrient that acts as an elixir, but if the other parts of the diet are made up of unhealthful items, there is no point in including the one good nutrient in the diet as it cannot counteract all the harm caused by the bad. A person diagnosed with Parkinson's should strive to maximize the intake of a nutrition-enriched diet rather than fillers with fewer nutrients.

Protein

A person suffering from Parkinson's disease is bound to suffer injuries more frequently compared with others owing to poor motor skills and declining abilities to maintain balance and stability. Protein is one very essential nutrient, especially for Parkinson's, as it serves an important function in repairing the damaged and injured tissues in the body and assists the body in gaining normal form. The protein that a person consumes is usually broken down into individual amino acids, which perform the task of revamping damaged tissues. The protein also has extensive and intensive influence over other activities and functions such as the nervous system, the hormonal system, and the immune system. It also helps in the rapid buildup of new tissues in the body. Animal meat is not the only source of proteins, as is believed. Proteins are found in abundance in almost all unrefined foods apart from meat, such as rice, potatoes, soy products, oranges, legumes, nuts, and milk and dairy products apart from meat. Utmost care should be taken while consuming high-protein food as it can interfere with the effectiveness of levodopa, a drug normally prescribed for the disease. Interference with the drug should not be a reason for excluding protein from the diet of a Parkinson's patient, however, as doing so could lead to further damage and aggravation of the disease. Instead, earnest effort should be put into redistributing the protein rich foods appropriately throughout the day.

Carbohydrates

Carbohydrates are essential and vital nutrients that can easily be obtained in good amounts from almost any fruit and vegetable. The healthiest complex carbohydrates can be found in the following:

- Potatoes
- Lima beans

- Brown rice
- Corn
- Yogurt
- Lentils
- Bananas
- Peaches
- Oranges
- Whole grain cereals
- Brown rice

- Bread
- Peas
- Kidney beans
- Apricots
- Apples
- Berries
- Raisins
- Whole grain breads
- Whole wheat pasta

The best way to get rejuvenated is to eat something that is high in complex carbohydrates as they are responsible for providing energy and also aid digestion. This nutrient becomes essential for persons suffering from Parkinson's disease as they are easily overcome by fatigue and exhaustion. Carbohydrates should be made an indispensable ingredient in the diet of a person with Parkinson's since this is the best possible nutrient for supplying ample energy. People with Parkinson's disease tend to lose more weight than is ideal for various reasons.[4] A diet rich in complex carbohydrates can also serve an additional purpose of helping the person maintain an ideal weight by supplying the necessary calorie count. There are "bad" carbohydrates, and the right choice should be made in order to derive significant benefits. Sugar is also a source of carbohydrates but supplies "empty" calories. A complex carbohydrate is laden with benefits for the brain and is seen as the "good" carbohydrate while a simple carbohydrate such as sugar is simple, as the name suggests, and carries empty calories, thus providing zero value. A deficiency in carbohydrates can disturb the tender balance of minerals such as potassium, sodium, and other important minerals.

Antioxidants

Antioxidants are substances controlling the process of oxidation; they put an end to the damage caused by free radicals. The cause behind Parkinson's partially points to the generation and accumulation of free radicals, which have the capacity to damage the brain cells or neurons producing dopamine. As a result of the damage caused to the dopamine-producing neurons in the brain, communication between neurons almost comes to a standstill, which prevents the brain from absorbing, processing, and disseminating the information necessary to establish communication between the neurons, ultimately resulting in the collapse of entire nerve communication. Nature makes potent antioxidants available in the form of fruits and vegetables such as the following:[5]

- Blackberries
- Blueberries
- Tomatoes
- Broccoli
- Carrots
- Cranberries
- Green tea

- Strawberries
- Pomegranate
- Garlic
- Red kidney beans
- Blueberries
- Plums
- Green leafy vegetables

A special mention of apples needs to be made here as apples have a very high content of an antioxidant plant chemical, quercetin. This chemical is responsible for protecting the brain from being attacked and damaged by neurodegenerative diseases including Parkinson's. Antioxidants are known to have the components that can delay the progression of PD. The best dietary sources loaded with potent antioxidants are carrots, nuts, and whole grains. The dark-colored fruits and vegetables, namely green leafy vegetables such as spinach and broccoli, garlic, strawberries, blueberries, red kidney beans, green tea, apples, and plums, are among the most effective weapons to fight Parkinson's. Salmon, which is an excellent source of omega-3 fat and vitamin D, is believed to fight against cognitive decline.[6] When it comes to diet, there are other key nutrients that also should find a prominent place in the diet of persons affected by Parkinson's. They are described next.

Vitamin B3

B vitamins are capable of converting the carbohydrates into glucose, which is one of the primary sources of energy. Vitamin B3, or niacin, is one of the eight B vitamins. All B vitamins assist the body in producing energy by converting carbohydrates available in the food into fuel called glucose. The benefits associated with the inclusion of foods containing B3 are plenty, but they provide their best benefit in the form of ensuring the effective and efficient functioning of the nervous system. Nature provides plenty of foods that enable us to derive the benefits of vitamin B3 to the maximum extent possible. People who include appropriate amounts of niacin in their diet can lower their chances of developing Parkinson's. The best sources of niacin or vitamin B3 are fish, salmon, tuna, sunflower seeds, peanuts, cereals, poultry, eggs, and dairy products.

Vitamin B12

Vitamin B12 is a nutrient that helps keep the nerve and blood cells in the body healthy, and it also helps in making the genetic material in the cells, the

DNA. Vitamin B12 also prevents Parkinson's patients from becoming unnaturally exhausted by preventing the anemia responsible for making the human body tired. Vitamin B12 helps ward off the effects of stress by providing nourishment to the nervous system. The best sources of B12 are whole-grain foods, fish, meat, eggs, yogurt, and milk.[7] This nutrient is hardly found in plant foods but can be supplied through fortifying a particular food with vitamin B12, as done in breakfast cereals.

Vitamin B1

This nutrient is also known as *thiamine*. Almost all the organs in the human body have high chances of being affected by the lack of vitamin B1 in appropriate quantities, but the worst affected are the nervous system and the heart, owing to their very high oxidative metabolism. Vitamin B1 deficiency can lead to impairment and inconsistent performance of motor, sensory, and reflex functions in the form of muscular atrophy, memory loss, and confusion, which are exactly the symptoms experienced by a person with Parkinson's. Oatmeal, cauliflower, brown rice, whole grains, asparagus, potatoes, rye, chicken, flax seeds, and sunflower seeds are some of the foods rich in this nutrient.

Vitamin C

Vitamin C predominantly plays the role of "protector." It does this by duplicating the role of antioxidants. It is one of the most widely used nutrients from the vitamin family that works to strengthen the bones, skin, tendons, and tissues. This nutrient is equipped to protect dopamine-producing cells from being damaged by free radicals. It enhances iron absorption and also assists in the regeneration of vitamin E. People suffering from Parkinson's disease are highly prone to infections as the functioning of their immune system declines. When the immune system is functioning at a low level, chances are high that one infection will lead to another. A situation such as this can bring down the quality of life of a person with Parkinson's. To avoid such a situation, a person affected by Parkinson's should take precautionary steps in the form of including foods rich in vitamin C in his or her daily diet. Vitamin C is found in abundance in tomatoes, strawberries, broccoli, papayas, parsley, cauliflower, lemons, and oranges.[8]

Vitamin C, or ascorbic acid, is a water-soluble vitamin that is essential for the normal growth and development of body organs. It has many functions, such as boosting the immune system of a person, making the body less likely to acquire an infection and skin breakdown, and helping wounds heal faster. Vitamin C is also an antioxidant that blocks the harmful effects of free radicals that otherwise harm the Parkinson's disease patient. The human

body is incapable of producing vitamin C or storing it; because of this, a daily intake of foods rich in vitamin C is required. Such sources include citrus fruits, peppers, and berries, which all have high concentrations of vitamin C. Synthetic sources in the form of supplements and tablets are also available commercially and are safe to take. High doses of vitamin C have been shown to slow down or even stop the destruction of dopamine cells in the brain.[9] However, this vitamin must be paired with vitamin E in order to get the maximum desired effect.

Vitamin E

This nutrient is quite high in antioxidant properties and thus carries out the task of protecting cells and tissues in the human body. As it prevents damage to cells in the body, it enables flow of effective communication between neurons. A person suffering from Parkinson's disease develops problems relating to digestion and the digestive system, which result in improper absorption of nutrients from the digestive tract. This can lead to excessive and drastic weight loss. Vitamin E is a nutrient that supports the body of a person with Parkinson's by enabling the appropriate amount of absorption of nutrients from the digestive tract.[10] The uniqueness of this vitamin lies in the fact that it provides a great deal of assistance to the body by playing the role of a catalyst when it comes to accepting the nourishment from the food. A person with Parkinson's can also suffer from reduced sensation in the arms, hands, legs, and feet, which is an indication of problems in and with the nervous system. Vitamin E can help a person with Parkinson's get relief from the above symptoms. The principal dietary sources of vitamin E include almonds, spinach, asparagus, bell peppers, and turnips.[11] A daily dose of vitamin E is also recommended as a nutritional supplement for people diagnosed with Parkinson's, since it has long been considered as an antioxidant that helps protect the body from the effects of environmental toxins and free radicals. Vitamin E helps with the production of red blood cells, the cells that deliver oxygen to different parts of the body, including the brain; it also promotes regeneration of tissues and improved functioning in the body. Food sources rich in vitamin E include organ meats, green leafy vegetables, eggs, fish, soybeans, nuts, and whole grain products. Vitamin E capsules are also available at most pharmacies and health stores.

Vitamin B6

B6 is also called pyridoxine and is one of the eight B vitamins. It assists the body in metabolizing fats and protein. Vitamin B6 ensures that all the nerve cells communicate with one another, which is of utmost importance for the normal development and effective functioning of the brain, one of the prime

targets of Parkinson's disease. Also, this vitamin performs another very important function of helping the body manufacture the hormone serotonin, which plays a major role in influencing a person's mood. Animal foods rich in vitamin B6 are meat, liver, turkey, shrimp, and kidney. Vegetables and fruits high in vitamin B6 are sweet potatoes, pumpkin, spinach, dark green leafy vegetables, carrots, broccoli, and fruits such as apricots and grapefruit. Other foods rich in this nutrient are whole-grain foods, brown rice, milk, cheese, eggs, and lentils.

Vitamin D

Contrary to popular belief, vitamin D is not produced by sunlight. Vitamin D is contained within the skin in an inactive form, and the sunlight only activates it. This vitamin is crucial for the absorption of calcium as well as maintaining the hardness of the bones. People with Parkinson's usually have lower levels of vitamin D in their body [12] and may need to take supplements to meet the minimum daily requirement. Vitamin D is available in foods such as fish, eggs, and fortified dairy products. A person with Parkinson's is highly prone to falls, which can result in fractures and broken bones. This problem can become even more serious as the bones in the body of a person with Parkinson's tend to become brittle, which could result in decline in the functioning of motor skills in the person. Vitamin D contributes to the strengthening of bones by assisting the body in extracting the maximum possible calcium from the diet. [13] A good diet contains minerals, too, found in foods, which contribute to the nutrients beneficial for a person affected by Parkinson's. Some essential minerals are listed next.

Calcium

This is the most abundant mineral in the body. Calcium is important in maintaining healthy and strong bones, in helping the blood clot, and in providing support for effective functioning of nerves and muscles. [14] By including foods rich in this mineral in the diet, a person with Parkinson's can gain a lot as this mineral can prevent bone fractures and muscle atrophy. Excellent sources of calcium include spinach, turnip greens, mustard greens, collard greens, tofu, yogurt, sesame seed, milk, and cheese.

Iron

Proper amounts of iron in the diet can ensure that the person suffering from Parkinson's is not exposed to fatigue and weakness, as this mineral is responsible for enhancing oxygen throughout the body as well as producing energy. [15] When oxygen is being pumped in many possible directions, the person feels energized and is therefore able to concentrate and focus better, which

helps in warding off depression. With a lack of iron, a lesser amount of hemoglobin is generated, which results in an inadequate supply of oxygen to the tissues. The following are excellent sources of iron:

- Spinach
- Lean meat
- Whole grains
- Soybeans
- Turmeric
- Lentils
- Cumin
- Thyme
- Lima beans
- Sesame
- Olives
- Legumes

Phosphorus

Phosphorus is the second most abundant mineral in the body after calcium. This mineral is present in the teeth, bones, and other structures in the form of cells and tissues. It plays a prominent role in the way the body stores and expends energy. This mineral is central for the growth, development, maintenance, and repair of all tissues and cells. It has distinction in the diet of a person with Parkinson's, keeping in mind the role it plays in protecting the cells, tissues, bones, and mental well-being of the Parkinson's sufferer. Phosphorus can be obtained through foods such as fish, milk, nuts, grains, cheese, potatoes, legumes, and other protein-rich items.

Potassium

Potassium is responsible for restoring cells and tissues in the body and also ensures proper nerve functioning, a critical topic when it comes to PD. The body requires this mineral in order to break down and utilize the carbohydrates for building muscles and proteins. Potassium is available in abundance in citrus fruits, bananas, milk, yogurt, nuts, apricots, kiwi, prunes, lima beans, potatoes, sweet potatoes, broccoli, tomatoes, peas, fish, and soybeans.

Magnesium

Magnesium is a great source of nutrition for the Parkinson's patient. This vital nutrient has many applications in metabolism. It plays a critical role in the production as well as transport of the energy that it produces. It is also a great source of relaxation for the muscles. Magnesium even contributes to the synthesis of protein, another primary source of nourishment.

Fatty Acids

Omega-3 and omega-6 fatty acids are those nutrients that help a person have more clarity of thought and also help a person to think positively. These fatty acids act as natural antidepressants. They accomplish these tasks by contributing to the flushing out of toxins from the body, which can endanger the mental well-being of the person with Parkinson's.[16] The best dietary sources of this essential nutrient are olive oil and fish.

Water

Water is vital in the transport of nutrients and in certain metabolic reactions. When the Parkinson's disease patient is not supplied with an adequate amount of water, symptoms of dehydration will surface, which include decreased levels of concentration, reduced mental abilities (already present in Parkinson's), and mood swings. Drinking the right amount of water can help the person have regular bowel movements, too.

Fiber

Fiber, also known as roughage, is a carbohydrate found in plant foods. If there is something in a plant that a human body cannot digest, then this is it. Fiber performs a very important function of keeping the digestive system healthy and in proper shape to function effectively. Fiber assists in the disposal of waste and toxins from the body in a smooth manner, thus preventing constipation. Fiber is found in abundance in potatoes, edible peels of fruits, nuts and seeds, oatmeal, beans, lentils, soya products, peas, brown rice, and whole grain cereals.

Parkinson's Symptoms and Diet

It is very important to ensure that the neurons do not stop communicating with one another at any point in time, which ensures the preservation of a person's memory. But this is exactly what a person affected by Parkinson's experiences. The notoriety of the disease lies in the fact that it can leave a person stripped of his or her cognitive skills, motor skills, appetite, bone health, and mental well-being. Parkinson's disease can also deprive the person of his or her energy and also leave the patient enervated and exhausted. Depending on the stage and the symptoms, it can sometimes be extremely difficult for the person to discharge his or her common duties. This gets even more tangled when the person's body is devoid of proper nutrition. It is also true that the symptoms, to a good extent, can be managed by gaining a fair understanding of the diet a person should have in order for the body to be

nourished with the blend of right foods, in right amounts, and at the right time.

SYMPTOM-SPECIFIC DIETS FOR PARKINSON'S

Diet for Motor Skills

Walnuts are an excellent addition to the diet for enhancing motor skills. In fact, the performance of impaired motor skills in a person with Parkinson's can be improved by including moderate amount of walnuts in his or her diet.[17] A person with Parkinson's also experiences muscle weakness. To add to this, he or she also has to bear with numbness in the hands and feet. These to a very large extent can be controlled by including vitamin B6, vitamin B12, and phosphorus in the diet.

Diet for Cognitive Skills

Saturated fats, termed as "bad fats," which are found mostly in animal products such as red meat and pork, are associated with contributing to the decline in cognitive function and memory. Monounsaturated fats such as the ones found in olive oil work toward improving and sharpening the cognitive functions. Nuts and seeds such as hazelnuts, walnuts, cashews, peanuts, sunflower seeds, almonds, and pumpkin seeds are rich in omega-3 and omega-6 fatty acids along with folate, vitamin E, and vitamin B6, which can do wonders for the brain and cognitive abilities.[18] Some of the nuts and seeds are also rich in thiamine and magnesium, which are excellent for memory and brain nourishment.

Diet for Easing Constipation

Constipation can be prevented or controlled to a very large extent by (1) including in the diet foods rich in vitamin B12 that have high fiber content and (2) increasing fluid intake. Plant foods are rich in fiber content, whereas animal foods have no fiber content. Fiber is the only part of the plant that cannot be digested by the human body. Fiber enables the body to have regular bowel movements. Constipation is quite common in Parkinson's, be it the nature of the disease itself or a result of medication. Constipation, if left untreated, can be painful, bothersome, and sometimes life threatening owing to the blocked passage.

Diet for Maintaining Bone Health

Bone health can be maintained by ensuring that the diet of the person with Parkinson's is rich in calcium, magnesium, and vitamin D. Plenty of vitamin D can also be obtained by exposing oneself to the sun, which activates this nutrient. Bone health to a very large extent determines the quality of life of the person affected by Parkinson's as frequent falls, fractures, and injuries are not only painful but can also limit and restrict movement, which can be quite frustrating.

Diets to Facilitate Swallowing

The difficulty a person affected by Parkinson's faces in chewing and swallowing can sometimes be so vexing that the person finds it difficult to even *enjoy* the meal, let alone complete it. This can lead to further consequences such as losing interest in food and losing appetite, which can take an even worse turn in the form of drastic weight loss. This can prove detrimental to health as the body is deprived of the nutrition, which affects the body's ability to absorb medication, further aggravating the symptoms. The act of chewing and swallowing can be simplified by opting to prepare softer but high-flavor foods such as soups, well-cooked vegetables, rice, milk, yogurt, and pureed fruit. Plant foods are always easier to chew and swallow, unlike animal foods. They also retain their nutritive values even after cooking.

Suggested Diet to Prevent Fatigue

Persons affected by Parkinson's are easily overcome by fatigue and exhaustion. The conditions caused by the disease, such as the tremors patients experience, also add to their already physically taxing condition. The tremors they experience result in loss of calories, which makes them feel sapped of their energy. This can lead to their feelings of fatigue and tiredness. Fatigue, though it cannot be completely eliminated, can to a great extent be reduced and controlled by including foods rich in phosphorus and catechins in the diet. Catechins are available in abundance in green tea. They relax the brain and keep the mind fresh.

Suggested Diet to Prevent Depression and Mood Swings

Foods containing thiamine, folate, omega-3, and omega-6 are excellent for improving the mood and also for lowering chances of the mental depression seen in Parkinson's. These nutrients are abundant in nuts and seeds such as walnuts, almonds, cashews, peanuts, and sunflower seeds. Intake of nuts and seeds improves generation of the amino acid tryptophan, which regulates the mood, feelings, and behavior in a person. Sugary foods are better avoided as

they can cause a surge of energy for a brief period followed by a feeling of tiredness and exhaustion. Alcohol is best avoided or at least minimized, for it has the ability to trigger depression. Apart from the psychological effect that alcohol can have on the brain, the body is forced to deplete its reserves of the minerals thiamine, zinc, and other important nutrients in order to detoxify the body.

The symptoms arising in a person diagnosed with Parkinson's vary from person to person and also depend on the stage and critical level of the stage. As the disease progresses, new symptoms emerge that can pose even tougher challenges to the person with Parkinson's. Regardless of the stage and symptoms, the person with Parkinson's should continue to strive to eat well and maintain a healthy weight. This not only helps the person to ease the symptoms but also to battle the disease and lead a resourceful life. It is known that a lot of patience and effort goes into dealing with the symptoms of Parkinson's, but a lot of thought should also go into the planning and preparation of a diet for a person with Parkinson's. This can go a long way in helping the affected parties deal with the disease effectively.

Chapter Seventeen

Parkinson's and Exercise

Exercise can be any specific bodily movement for developing strength and agility.[1] Many use exercise in one form or another to achieve their desired weight, physique, and overall well-being. Getting physically fit gives one confidence and higher self-esteem. On the other hand, exercise is also a vital means that physical therapists use in rehabilitating accident victims and other patients who suffer from impaired mobility or motor skills. Patients with Parkinson's disease are one such group that benefits from exercise. Constant exercise may not slow the progression of the disease, but it helps alleviate muscle stiffness and rigidity. As long as the patient continues the exercise program, the benefits can persist and may even prevent further complications. These complications may be caused by, or are the effects of, rigidity, flexed or bent posture, and shoulder, hip, or back pain.[2] For individuals with PD, exercise is a vital component so that they can maintain balance, mobility, and normalcy in their daily lives.

OVERVIEW OF EXERCISE BENEFITS

Exercise is very important and necessary for remaining healthy. It tones one's muscles, helps respiration and movement, and improves a person's outlook. Regular exercise can also protect a person from diseases such as stroke, high blood pressure, diabetes, obesity, back pains, and certain heart diseases, among others. Exercising regularly can also help manage stress and put one in a better mood.[3] Different exercise regimens are available for patients suffering from one type of disease or another, to augment bodily functions that might have been impaired. Exercise helps patients feel better physically and mentally as well as regain motor and cognitive functions affected by the ailment they suffer and live normally as much as possible. For

197

individuals suffering from Parkinson's disease, regular exercise offers (1) improved control of motor movements such as walking, (2) increased muscle strength and flexibility, (3) reduced stress level, (4) improvement in the mobility of joints, (5) improvement and maintenance of good posture, and (6) improved coordination and balance.[4] Fifteen minutes of exercise per day is the minimum recommendation, starting with stretching and targeting each joint and muscle group. Warm-up and cool-down procedures are a must, such as marching in place or stretching.[5] Following are some of the major benefits of exercise to the PD patient.

For Both Physical and Psychological Health

Exercise, as a form of therapy, can provide people with a better perception of themselves. It gives one a sense of completeness and boosts confidence. "Looking good" by having well-toned muscles and a healthy physique makes one feel positive about everything. This sense of positivity also helps one to be psychologically balanced and lessen stress and other factors that could cause depression or anxiety. For individuals suffering from Parkinson's and other diseases that severely hinder motor function, exercise helps maintain physical coordination despite the disability. Only certain and specific types of exercise are recommended. Overly strenuous exercises such as running could worsen the condition of a patient rather than improve it.

Premature Death from Heart Disease

An exercise regimen recommended by an expert helps improve not only blood circulation but also how the heart pumps blood. A properly functioning heart evenly distributes blood where it is needed, thus avoiding untimely deaths from heart problems, high blood pressure, and other heart-related health impediments. Persons suffering from a long-term disease such as Parkinson's may not have a cure for their ailments, but a constant exercise program and related therapy can extend their lives compared with those who do otherwise. Heart disease and high blood pressure may result in stroke and subsequent death if not treated early. A routine exercise regimen can lower these threats and even help a patient maintain physical and mental balance. It is always best to practice preventive exercise early on than to look for a cure at the advanced stages of a disease. As far as blood pressure is concerned, having a regular set of exercise greatly helps in controlling blood pressure and the function of one's heart. As the Parkinson's disease sufferer grows older and older, high blood pressure and other heart-related issues may not be avoided in entirety, but regular exercise reduces these threats greatly.

Anxiety and Depression

Every person may have his or her own set of standards, but when it comes to stress, everyone shares the same effects—depression, anxiety, and compulsive behavior, to list a few. This means health is jeopardized in the long run, which leads to poor physical and mental condition. If a person constantly exercises, stress levels are reduced, and physical functions are normalized. Patients suffering from diseases such as Parkinson's also greatly benefit from exercise by improving and regaining motor skills that may have begun to decline and reduce depression caused by physical impediment brought about by the disease.

Stiffness and Rigidity

For patients with mobility impairment, such as Parkinson's disease, exercise helps to maintain balance and reduces the threat of falling or becoming rigid. Stiffness and rigidity brought about by Parkinson's disease can be alleviated by proper exercise that targets parts of the body needing work. For example, fingers that are difficult to flex may be massaged slowly to help alleviate the pain caused by stiffness, or patients can wiggle their fingers slowly, one at a time. In short, physical activities, including regular exercise, help an individual with Parkinson's feel better, whether that person is suffering from the most severe stage of the disease (chapter 6) or has a minor infirmity.[6] Always consult a physician before starting any regimen or program to know which type of exercise is recommended, depending on the patient's condition or how often the patient needs to exercise per week.

EXERCISES TO IMPROVE COGNITIVE SKILLS

An individual suffering from Parkinson's disease loses control of cognitive skills faster as he or she grows older, mainly because of the constant decline in brain cells that help a person think, plan, and organize. This may result in an early onslaught of senility for Parkinson's patients compared with their contemporaries who are not suffering from this ailment. Although a patient does not always lose memory, he or she may have difficulty in thought organization and emotional control, which can lead to a change in personality. Factors such as these would hinder the patient's ability to fully participate in activities and integrate with peers. There are forms of exercise that may help in retaining one's cognitive skills, even if one suffers from this progressive neurological disease. Following are some of those exercises.

Toe Wiggling

This form of exercise provides stimulation to the brain and helps improve motor control and cognitive skills. This simple exercise can be done any time of the day, anywhere; however, it is best recommended to do when one wakes up in the morning by slowly moving the toes one by one and continuing for a few minutes. This exercise is said to help the brain become more alert and thereby improve cognitive function over the years. This also "awakens" the muscles and helps in improving how one walks, as well as one's hand-eye coordination. This basic exercise is very suitable for Parkinson's disease patients, especially those who are suffering from major rigidity and stiffness, since it is recommended for them to move slowly, even tentatively, to avoid possible accidents that can worsen their condition.[7]

Visual Memory Games

According to a major news article,[8] memory games allow people to exercise concentration, memory improvement, attention to detail, and recall speed. Parkinson's disease sufferers are no exception to these benefits. One game to try works like this: the patient has a family member show him a few pictures for five to ten seconds each before putting them away. After a few minutes, the patient must go to another room or go outside, where he or she writes down or says, in as much detail as possible, what each picture was about.[9] Writing or speaking about what is remembered is a way to help keep the brain alert and recollect data from a visual image. This simple exercise can help a patient suffering from Parkinson's disease cope with memory loss caused by the disease and old age.

Creation of Nerve Pathways by Learning

Learning to do things in a different way may also help the Parkinson's patient; for instance, if she is right-handed, performing tasks with her left hand can help enhance brain function by using a different neural pathway than the brain is accustomed to. If the patient is asked to (1) try and dress with eyes closed, (2) use the less dominant hand in clicking the computer mouse, or (3) perform other daily tasks such as holding a glass of water with the less dominant hand, cognitive function is exercised. These very simple and effortless practices allow the brain to learn something new each day.[10]

For the caregiver of a Parkinson's disease patient or an elderly person suffering from senility brought about by old age, one might guide the patient to get up on the other side of the bed, opposite the side he or she uses often. This creates a new sensation for the person and stimulates the brain. Effects or reactions may vary from person to person, but the goal of teaching something new to somebody and creating new nerve pathways is achieved.

Sleeping

When a person lacks sleep, the brain cannot fully function as intended.[11] This means that a person's creativity, cognitive, and problem-solving skills are impaired. The sleep-deficient person will be grumpy, less proactive, and less productive. The individual with Parkinson's disease should be sure to get enough sleep every day. A well-rested mind and body beats all forms of medications and mind-enhancing drugs.

Aerobics

Aerobics is a type of exercise that involves a workout for the lungs and heart.[12] The Duke University Medical Center conducted a research experiment demonstrating that aerobics is effective in treating middle-aged and elderly individuals suffering from depression.[13] Recently, the same team reported that aerobics also helps improve the cognitive abilities of those patients. A significant improvement was found in terms of the higher mental processes of a person's memory, including, but not limited to, planning, organization, and multiple other mental tasks. Attention to detail, concentration, and psychomotor skills were also improved, thus showing that exercise indeed slows down mental decline while improving cognitive function.

EXERCISES FOR MOTOR SKILLS

Motor skill is a sequence of movements learned to produce smooth and efficient action. In layman's terms, motor skills are movements in their most basic form. The term *motor skill* includes the act of walking, winking, holding a spoon, smiling, and frowning, to name only a few. These are simple movements that a person does without thought every single day. However, certain diseases affect these skills and prevent a person from moving efficiently and normally. Individuals suffering from Parkinson's disease generally have difficulty using most body parts needed to move around effortlessly. Joints are the most commonly affected areas when rigidity sets in, and hands and other involuntary muscles twitch uncontrollably when tremors start. This section offers a review of exercises that are beneficial to counter and—to some extent—prevent motor skill decline. The exercises aim for the patient to retain mobility and counter the effects of Parkinson's, allowing the patient to live normally among family and friends.

Cycling

Cycling on stationary bicycles may prove to be an effective way for Parkinson's patients to control mobility issues brought about by the disease. A

study[14] conducted at the Cleveland Clinic Lerner Research Institute found that cycling at a forced rate proved beneficial to more than twenty-five study participants ranging from age thirty to seventy-five with mild to moderate Parkinson's disease. The research group found changes in upper extremity functions and blood oxygen in the brains of the patients. Fast cycling proved to be a low-cost, effective therapy regimen for people with Parkinson's.

Researchers have also studied and concluded that individuals with Parkinson's may still be able to ride bicycles since their ability to do so may not be affected by the freezing of gait in Parkinson's. This new research could provide an alternative and realistic exercise option for Parkinson's patients who have difficulty in performing other physical therapies or activities.[15] The sudden inability to move while walking, or freezing of the gait, often affects a patient's ability to perform day-to-day tasks. Researchers in this study interviewed forty-five patients and observed them during their activity hours. Out of the forty-five, twenty-five were counted to have regular freezing of gait. Out of these twenty-five, nineteen were still able to use a bike. Fourteen out of the nineteen able to ride and use bicycles reported that they had no difficulties in cycling. An important study such as this reinforces the idea of many that once freeze affects gait, all forms of movement are then disabled. It proves that many individuals with Parkinson's may retain the ability to cycle despite freezing of gait. No treatments are yet available to help freezing of gait for people who experience it, in spite of drug treatment with levodopa. It is encouraging, however, to know that bicycling may be an alternative means of exercise and transportation for patients with Parkinson's. The authors of the study recommend that patients with Parkinson's must be cautious when cycling outdoors and must do so only if they can mount and dismount safely; those who cannot may use stationary bicycles instead. Like any other form of outdoor exercise, individuals with Parkinson's should consult their doctors first before beginning this exercise program.

Walking

From a scientific angle, walking is defined as an action that entails moving one foot forward after the other.[16] This form of physical activity may not mean much for a healthy young person, but for an elderly patient suffering from Parkinson's disease, the simplest of movements such as walking may prove to be difficult, especially when joints become stiff. Just the act of lifting one's foot to move forward can take too much effort, which may result in loss of balance. According to the *Journal of the American Medical Association*, walking does not exert the body to more strenuous physical workouts, thus cutting down the use of more oxygen and glucose.[17] This makes walking one of the highly recommended exercises for Parkinson's disease pa-

tients. Walking allows a patient to regain mobility and reintegrate into society, socialize with neighbors and friends, and participate in activities with the rest of the family.

Flexing Facial Muscles

Muscles that are not used become stagnant. For individuals with Parkinson's disease, this can mean locked jaws or involuntary twitching of facial muscles and eyelids, which creates a "frozen" expression. It is recommended to exercise the facial muscles as much as possible. Patients are advised to make defined chewing motions when eating or to massage the face vigorously when bathing or washing. Massaging one's face not only helps facial muscles; it also exercises the hands and fingers.[18]

Tai Chi

T'ai chi ch'uan, or *taijiquan*, is a form of Chinese martial art practiced for its health benefits. Many practice tai chi because of its slow, relaxed, and flowing movements, and it is highly recommended for Parkinson's disease patients. This form of exercise helps the patient maintain stability and balance-related effects of the disease. This form of exercise demands slow, controlled movements that focus mainly to maximize arm and leg motions as well as gradual shifts of body weight without losing balance. Research[19] performed to show the effects of tai chi on a patient with Parkinson's disease demonstrated that participants had visibly fewer falls in the six-month observation time frame, compared with patients who participated in stretching exercises.

Pilates

Pilates was developed by Joseph Pilates. It is a form of exercise that highlights the balance of bodily development through core strength, flexibility, and awareness for efficient, graceful movement.[20] Pilates focuses on six core principles, namely concentration, control, centering, flows or efficiency of movement, precision, and breathing. These principles coincide with the purpose of helping a Parkinson's patient cope with the effects of the disease as it progresses. Parkinson's disease patients suffer a significant decrease in mobility as the ailment progresses. However, simple forms of exercise can help alleviate "frozen" muscles and minimize a patient's chance of falling. Some of these exercises are so simple that one could do them anywhere.[21]

Head and Shoulder Rotation

The idea here would be to (1) turn the head slowly as though about to glance over one's shoulder, (2) hold the position for a few seconds, and then (3)

repeat on the other side. One should roll the shoulders forward and backward gently to ease any tension in the neck or upper back. This simple routine can be performed anytime and paired with facial muscle flexing exercises for better results. [22]

Stretching

Stretching is highly recommended, as this allows muscles all over the body to stretch and flex. This simple form of exercise can help revive the cramped muscles of an individual with Parkinson's, especially when waking up. Before getting out of bed, one should gently stretch arms and legs to their full extent to awaken the muscles. Stretching is also recommended before performing other more complicated exercises such as aerobics or tai chi. [23]

Hand and Wrist Exercises

This simple exercise requires the most minimal of movements and can be done whether a patient is sitting, standing, or walking. The Parkinson's patient can start by touching the tips of each finger with the thumbs and rotating the hands so that the palms face upward, and then rotate until the palms face down. An alternative position is to bend the hands up and down from the wrist. Clenching and unclenching one's fists would also work wonders on the finger joints. [24]

Feet, Leg, and Knee Exercise

This exercise is best performed inside a bedroom or in the gym. A Parkinson's sufferer can begin with a simple inhale-exhale warm-up and then lie flat on his or her back. The patient then lifts a knee and hugs it close to the chest, holding it for a second or two before repeating with the other leg. While sitting down, the patient can rock the feet from side to side, then forward and backward, ensuring full ankle rotation. [25]

Marching in Place

Parkinson's disease patients are prone to falling every now and then, so running is not a highly recommended exercise. An alternative way to move the entire body without running is by marching in place. Stationary marching strengthens leg and thigh muscles, thereby creating more balance. The person performs the exercise in place, lifting the leg as high as possible while moving the arms in congruence to an actual marching action. This form of exercise not only mobilizes the legs, it also moves one's arms, waist, hips, and back. [26]

Trunk Bending and Twisting

Here, the person should place both hands on the waist and bend the upper body forward and backward, then side to side. The patient may also lift the hands at chest level, palms down. Then the patient "laces" the fingers and twists side to side from the waist up, while both feet are planted about a foot apart.[27]

OTHER BASIC EXERCISES

Following are a few additional exercises that a patient can perform alone. These exercises can help improve mobility and balance.[28]

- Bring the toes up every time a step is taken. When stepping back down, be sure to bend toes fully before lifting the foot.
- Spread the legs wide when walking or turning, about ten inches. A wider base provides a better stance and prevents falling.
- People with Parkinson's disease are prone to falling. Constant movement of the body helps improve balance, as this helps the patient familiarize how his or her body functions as the disease progresses. Do simple forward, backward, and side-to-side movements or exercise for at least four minutes per day.
- Use small steps when turning, making sure that feet are widely separated. Do not cross one leg over the other when turning. This could potentially cause legs to entangle and cause a fall. Practice this exercise about fifteen minutes a day by walking for a few yards before turning.
- If getting out of a chair is difficult, practice it several times a day. Sit down on the chair slowly, with the body bent forward in a sharp angle, until the backside touches the seat. Rise as fast as possible to overcome the pull of gravity.
- Falling is one of the major hazards of Parkinson's disease. Once the legs feel frozen or "glued" to the floor, lifting the toes eliminates these cramps and spasms, enabling the patient to walk again and subverting the fear of falling down.
- When walking, swing both arms freely as this helps take the weight off the legs. This lessens fatigue and bunching of muscles on arms and shoulders.
- When the body lists to one side, try carrying a bag filled with weights or carry heavy books using the opposite hand to create balance.
- Use hands and fingers constantly. Use a rubber "squeeze ball" to flex hands and fingers. Wear clothes with buttons to practice precise finger movements.
- Sing or read aloud with forceful movement of lips and facial muscles. Practice exaggerated facial expressions in front of a mirror.

SAFETY MEASURES FOR EXERCISE

Exercise is highly recommended for individuals suffering from Parkinson's disease. It is a healthier and more wholesome option than relying solely on drugs for remedy. Following are some basic tips and safety measures when exercising.

Talking to a Doctor

A physician's analysis and recommendation is a must before starting any exercise program. This helps the Parkinson's patient understand what exercises are "doable" and how the body can cope with the activity based on medical condition.

Physical Activity Readiness Questionnaire (PAR-Q)

This is a sheet with a series of questions to help trainers assess a patient's readiness to start working out. The patient or participant is required to fill out this form before starting any exercise program. Questions may include information about (1) one's health history, (2) bone or joint problems that could be made worse by exercise, (3) dizziness or other forms of vertigo, and (4) whether the patient is fit to undergo programs offered in that gym, or if a set routine is required.

No Rush

A Parkinson's disease sufferer may not be ready to take on strenuous exercises in the first session. It is recommended that the patient work with a trainer for recommendations of exercises that allow for basic methods before progressing to more complex regimens. Exercise can become a health hazard if overdone. If the patient intends to work out for half an hour, it might be a good idea to start with ten- or fifteen-minute sessions before proceeding to longer and more complex sessions. This reduces the possibility of getting overly strained muscles and joints.

Before and After Exercise

It is advisable not to simply jump into an exercise program without proper warm-up procedures, since that can lead to a sudden and excessive strain to the muscles and might cause injury. Warming up loosens the muscles and stimulates better blood flow, thus preparing the body for more intense activities. The Parkinson's patient should work with a trainer to come up with warm-up methods that cater to the patient's needs. After completing an exercise regimen, a cool-down method is also a must. Following a vigorous set of

exercises, the body needs to transition from the rigid movements of one's regimen, thus proper relaxation exercises are also recommended. Inhaling and exhaling lightly for five minutes or so after the exercise program allows the heart rate to gradually decrease, while stretching exercises help in loosening sets of muscles that were overcontracted during exercise. Correct execution of an exercise is very important. The individual with Parkinson's should have a fitness trainer walk through the proper technique in performing various exercises to maximize results and reduce possible injuries that can worsen the signs and symptoms of the disease. [29]

Safety

When it comes to Parkinson's and exercise, safety not only pertains to how a patient handles his or her body, but also to *where* the patient performs the exercise. It is important to check the area of execution first and avoid (1) slippery or uneven floors, (2) inadequate lighting, and (3) nonstationary items such as rugs that are not weighted down in place by an object or furniture, even if the venue of the exercise is inside one's own bedroom.

Maintaining Balance at All Times

The caregiver of the Parkinson's disease patient should have the patient use grab bars or rails if the patient has difficulty maintaining balance. If the patient has difficulty in standing up or experiences back problems, the exercise can be performed on a bed or exercise mat. An exercise that puts pressure on a patient's back is not exactly an effective method considering the pros and cons in the long term.

Knowing When to Stop

A fitness trainer might come up with a "perfect" exercise program for a Parkinson's patient, but one needs to consider one's bodily limits as the procedure progresses. It is advisable to take a break or stop immediately if one starts to feel discomfort or pain.

Selecting Suitable Physical Activities

If a patient is not into exercise, he or she can indulge in other activities that maintain constant movement. The PD patient may join an arts and crafts club or join friends in gardening activities, knitting, or even cooking. As long as the patient moves around a lot, there is lesser chance of becoming rigid or still. [30]

Chapter Eighteen

Motivation in Parkinson's

Parkinson's not only affects the way the body operates but can also have repercussions for the patient's psychological, emotional, and motivational health. Clinical features of Parkinson's disease confirm that the main motor symptoms should be considered *psycho*motor—not just motor. For example, increased tremor and rigidity can be observed in situations when a patient suffers from emotional stress; however, tremor and rigidity are reduced or disappear after relaxation and suggestion. Even a very difficult aggravation of the disease, called akinesia, or immobility, can be temporarily relieved as the result of a certain mental condition of the patient, for example, affection that occurred during a life-threatening situation or, alternatively, during confidential and warm emotional contact with others, or under conditions of a sleepwalking episode or during sleep.

Thus, addressing the psychological needs of Parkinson's patients can have tremendous results on their perspective and even, perhaps, on their symptoms. After getting a positive psychological interpretation, a patient's underestimated sense of self-worth can be enhanced and his or her motivation thereby boosted. Parkinson's disease sufferers can feel like normal human beings again and can continue to enjoy and engage in life in similar ways. Correction of mental conditions resulting from Parkinson's via special psychological exercises leads to (1) growth of optimism, (2) reduction of emotional stress, and (3) increased desire to resist the disease. Obviously, psychological approaches such as motivation contribute to minimizing the clinical impact of emotional distress and symptoms of Parkinson's disease. Consequently, motor and daily living activities demonstrate improvement, confirmed by tests conducted in the dynamics of various diagnostic scales, and finally the patient's quality of life is optimized. Complex and lengthy therapy requires including the specific anti-Parkinson's medications, seda-

tives, physical therapy, exercise therapy, and psychotherapy and—plenty of motivation. In essence, motivation is needed according to pathological etiology, patient's age, and clinical forms and stages of disease.

ROLE OF MOTIVATION

Consider a young male student who is aware that he is a poor learner. He goes to school with his homework undone, cuts classes, and consistently fails exams and is hence unable to graduate from high school or college. No one ever convinced or advised the student to do something to improve his status. The individual ended up in an undesirable state not because of what he has or what he cannot do. The undesirable state happened because of something that anyone can achieve but that the student never tried to give himself—motivation. This is an example of what could happen if a person has no motivation and no one pushes or encourages him. The same applies to an individual diagnosed with Parkinson's or in various spectrums of life, such as when CEOs, executives, and managers need excellent skills in motivating their employees and team members. In the education field, the faculty and parent's associations are encouraging students in different ways to push themselves to study, to focus and strive to be successful in their future. People make use of motivation exploitatively as it is legal, free, and has countless benefits. Motivational therapy can also be applied in nonpharmacologic management of different chronic maladies such as Parkinson's. For instance, a male patient with self-determination and motivation has the advantage of dealing with the chronic illness in a more beneficial manner. He can determine how to be proactive and can cooperate with his doctor(s) and other caregivers regarding such things as therapy responses. These patients are more likely to seek out further specialty consultation, new clinical opportunities, and other medical and surgical intervention strategies. With motivation, Parkinson's-diagnosed patients will have enough drive and long-lasting endurance to fight the ailment. Built-in motivation shows a relationship with fulfillment, control, less depression, and more satisfaction with life.[1]

The purpose of finding motivation is to minimize the pain and suffering of a patient and help that person endure the everyday burden that Parkinson's disease brings. It is essential in order to provide the patient and family with control over the disease. It will also aid them toward a more comfortable living despite the infirmity they have. Motivation is always the best tool that can be used in any circumstances by any of us. It may not be a permanent solution to Parkinson's, but it can serve as a temporary relief. In summary, it can be the start of a better life for a patient and his or her loved ones.

Motivation as a Cure

Anyone could be a Parkinson's disease victim. It could be a friend's relative or parents, someone in the neighborhood, a former teacher, a celebrity, a politician, a public servant, or the worst case, a family member. Once a person is shown to have the symptoms of this disease, not only the person who has the illness is affected. The trauma can easily be passed on to the family, relatives, friends, co-workers, and other people who know the patient. An everyday life of (1) physical inability, (2) difficulty with fine movements, (3) neuropsychiatric disturbances with a possible chance of apathy, or (4) dementia can put a halt to people's ability to do a lot of the things they once could do. It surely has an impact on the patient's life, starting from the person's job and social activities to everyday household chores, physical exercises, and even small hobbies that meant a lot. Even though it can slow down a person's life, Parkinson's cannot entirely stop anyone from living a happy and contented life. The problem is that most of the patients and their families who act as caregivers are not aware of this or lose hope instantly after they learn of the illness. Once the patient feels handicapped by this ailment, he or she might realize how serious it is, be frightened, or totally give in to the idea that he or she can no longer live a happy life.[2] The same goes for the family members, who may be optimistic at the start but eventually become discouraged once they feel that the sickness is getting worse or their loved one is slowly being tormented by the disease. What these people should know is that there is always hope, and it is never too late for the patient to be comfortable and happy in spite of having Parkinson's disease. Motivational push, understanding, knowledge, and attention from caregivers are the main things the person inflicted with the disease needs. The most important element in empowering patients to continue to live a whole, satisfied life is free of charge and can be found within themselves—it encompasses the full breadth of what is called motivation.

QUEST FOR MOTIVATION

Motivation can come from within the person who needs it. It can also be found in other people such as family, friends, public figures, and motivational speakers. Many tools and methods for motivating people have recently become available, such as audios, videos, online tutorials and conferences, healing missions, and online group therapies. As a Parkinson's patient, knowing where to find motivation can be a start, but it might not be enough to keep someone fully motivated. Motivation is always free and obtainable, but learning how to stay motivated requires time and patience. Knowing the steps and the important elements is very important in order to effectively move a Parkinson's patient to the brighter side of life in spite of all the

problems that come with the disease. It is a serious and continuous process that, if a patient practices faithfully, can endow that person with the power to survive life's hardships even under the condition of Parkinson's.

Keeping up with Morale

Morale is the capacity of an individual or group to maintain their belief in a certain goal, particularly in times of hardship. It is often referenced as a generic value judgment of the willpower, enthusiasm, obedience, confidence, loyalty, and self-discipline regarding the function, task, or goal at hand. Patients of Parkinson's disease often experience symptoms that can make them feel as if they have been handicapped. These symptoms include tremor, rigidity, bradykinesia, and others mentioned throughout this book. Individuals also experience nonmotor symptoms that can diminish morale, including cognitive dysfunction with dementia, psychosis and hallucination, mood disorders such as anxiety and apathy, sleep disorders, fatigue, pain, and other dysfunctions which badly affect their autonomic capacity. All of this could lead to depression and may pull down the patient's morale. Morale affects many factors that contribute to an effective process for motivation. Since this is the case, it is important to keep up the patient's morale in order to maintain a smooth progression and development of motivation in a patient who has Parkinson's disease.

Important ways to keep up morale even with this disease include (1) staying content, (2) feeling wanted in the family setting in spite of having Parkinson's, (3) participating in as many activities around the house as possible, such as playing cards, puzzles, and other games, (4) being read to, or (5) having a quick chat with a friend or with someone who visits the house. This may require a certain amount of supervision by a caregiver to ensure a comfortable adaptation to any activities that a Parkinson's disease sufferer might want to participate in. For example, if a man with Parkinson's disease is involved in a card game, shuffling cards could be a challenge. He can ask for someone to shuffle the cards for him. This can save the patient from being embarrassed if he spills the cards on the floor. The same precautions should be considered with other activities that could entail potential embarrassment from a spill, mess, or destruction of the patient's or someone else's belongings. Another way to keep up morale is by giving the patient the same amount of respect he or she was receiving before acquiring the infirmity. As part of the overall quest for motivation, high morale in a Parkinson's patient can be achieved by consulting the patient often about family affairs and encouraging attendance at parties, reunions, ceremonies, and other important occasions. Because of difficulties in movement as well as slowness, Parkinson's patients should be given more time to do some activities such as dressing up or taking a bath. Rushing them to do things faster could lead to

disaster and may only offend them as it will seem as if their inabilities and weaknesses are being rubbed in. Family members should also consider spaces, as respect also entails giving space. A seat at the dining table or in the living room or office suite should be saved or be exclusively for the patient's use. To summarize, Parkinson's patients must be made aware and feel that they are still a priceless source of esteem to the family and that they are loved, wanted, and important.[3] Morale plays an important role in building up motivation, and family members, caregivers, and other friends are the best support that a Parkinson's disease patient can get. It is necessary for all (sufferers and their caregivers alike) to know what help and assistance is available.

Positive Thinking during the Quest for Motivation

Treasure boxes are locked, and every lock has a key. The key for motivation is positive thinking. This means that people can motivate themselves only after they start to think positively.[4] If a patient begins to think constructive thoughts, he or she can build on it and progress, and eventually, the constructive thinking will help boost self-confidence and self-esteem, reduce depression or stress, create control and balance, and help the patient achieve happiness. If one wants to adjust easily and live a happy life in spite of Parkinson's, he or she must believe that there are ways to do exactly that. A simple thought that the person yearns to be somehow better is a great start and an example of positive thinking. Another way to enforce positive thinking is to try to be happy at all times. Emotion plays a big role in a Parkinson's patient's quest for motivation, and this is why it is an important factor to consider.[5]

Emotion affects the patient's thoughts, vital activities, and defenses. If a person is happy, positive thoughts are most likely in the patient's mind. Another important aspect is support. The patient needs to know what kind of support he or she needs and should be aware of where (or from whom) he or she can motivational backup. This will increase confidence as the patient will feel that he or she is not alone and that someone is always there for support and encouragement. (1) Reading this book, (2) diligently researching other treatments and therapies, (3) consulting the doctor, (4) seeking out specialty consultation, (5) adhering to medication schedules, (6) keeping in mind the "do's and don'ts" and (7) simply trying to live normally serve as additional examples of how to think positively.

Acknowledging the Motivational Needs of the Parkinson's Sufferer

Individuals with Parkinson's obviously have different reasons for doing different things. These reasons can be related to their needs or desires in life as a

person. People motivate themselves for a reason—it could be social necessity, biological, cognitive, affective, or spiritual. Knowing their own motivational need (by reviewing the symptoms and other problems patients are going through) is analogous to being well aware of the goals patients have set for their own success. Patients' needs and goals may not be for a permanent relief or cure, but it is still important for them to recognize their needs so that they will be aware of the benefits that they can receive by following a certain course. Keeping themselves attentive to their own wants and wishes will give Parkinson's disease patients a higher chance of succeeding in their objectives.[6]

Acquiring and Reinforcing Motivation

Motivation can be acquired in different ways and in different places. PD patients can obtain it within themselves or can find it from a doctor, spouse, caregiver, family member, friend, therapist, quotation, or group therapy. The process of acquiring motivation starts with positivity, awareness, and interest. If patients use positive psychology and are aware of what they need, it should be easier for them to motivate themselves. One important item that can assist them with this is by thinking of all the advantages of staying home, such as devoting more time to family or having enough time for lengthy chats with a friend. Thinking that exercise can be carried out by walking outdoors with a young grandson and granddaughter, partner, or pet is another good example. Patients can also start thinking about being free from the stress of a previous job, grumpy inconsiderate bosses, or heavy workloads, and now perhaps enjoying retirement pay. By simply trying to stay happy every day, enjoying new activities, spending time with family, knowing the importance of positive thinking, and maintaining a focus on their goals, Parkinson's disease patients can motivate themselves in spite of the pain and symptoms that the disease throws them.

Even if patients can find motivation easily within themselves and in their environment, staying motivated is not as straightforward or quick. For a patient to have truly obtained motivation, that newfound motivation must be maintained in the long term.[7] Acquiring motivation could be as easy as one-two-three, but staying motivated is definitely a struggle—even harder for a person with a disorder such as Parkinson's. It is like having the feet chained and struggling to reach for a key or a lock pick to get freed every time the person enters the room. Once a patient has motivation, it remains purposeful if it is *kept* active. Motivation can only help a patient get better if it is reinforced on a regular or continual basis. Consider, for example, a patient who goes to see a motivational speaker. The encounter could be a private consultation or a full-blown seminar. The speaker is excellent and can really expound on the importance of being motivated and what the power of posi-

tive thinking can do for everyone. The speaker can boost the patient's confidence, self-esteem, and, more importantly, motivation level. The expert lectures about what motivation and positive thinking can do in the patient's life and after this, the patient leaves, ready to fight every negative thing that will come his way and start thinking positive thoughts. After a few days, these feelings start to diminish until the patient is back to where he was prior to listening to the motivational speaker. Once the patient has motivation, it needs to be conserved as much as possible. The key to maintaining or reinforcing affirmative behaviors is a *reminder*. Patients need to remind themselves at every turn to keep the motivation of positive thinking in the front of their thoughts. Following are some examples of the steps that the Parkinson's patient could put into practice to properly acquire and reinforce the motivation that a caregiver may have provided.

Keeping Things Small and Simple

The patient can surround herself with the small, detailed motivators mentioned above that can offer an initial spark to keep going.

Keeping Good Company

The patient can meet people who are positive or well-motivated. He can ask these people to visit him at his place for a small chat twice a week or so. Or he can simply have a quick discussion with a friend who likes to share ideas and experiences. Some institutes conduct group therapies or discussions for people with Parkinson's disease in which they talk about how they cope and stay motivated. The patient can acquire more information and new ideas to try.

Staying Informed or Updated

Having a lot of knowledge is always an advantage, even for a patient with Parkinson's. Even though she may have some challenges, she can still learn by attempting to fill her mind with everything useful that she can. The more a patient gains information and updates, the more she will be motivated about her health as a whole.

Staying Positive

Patients have a tendency to be positive for a while but lose the motivation as time passes. From the psychological and emotional standpoint, positivity must be maintained, and patients should always try to look on the bright side and find good reasons why things happen. It is a simple statement of seeing both the good and bad. For example, when having problems such as body

aches, patients should practice a habit of finding ways to relieve themselves of the pain.

Weaning from Too Much Thinking

Strategizing is prudent if it is in moderation. For a patient with Parkinson's disease, it is not a good idea to keep doing nothing but *thinking* about a better life; one must *take action*. After a quick plan of what they need to do or what they want to achieve, patients simply need to take the initiative to make their plans a reality.

Progress Tracking

It is important for Parkinson's patients to be aware of their own progress and note it to themselves. In doing this, they will realize the importance of staying motivated and optimistic that they will achieve their goals in spite of Parkinson's.

Reward

A reward, whether tangible or intangible, can be provided with the intent of causing a wanted behavior to be repeated. If the person suffering from Parkinson's receives the reward immediately, the effect is heightened as time passes. And when the behavior becomes repetitive in anticipation of a reward, an action becomes a *habit*. Patients can come up with simple rewards they can give themselves. They can also ask their family, spouse, or caregiver to surprise them with a reward once they have accomplished a task or achieved a target, such as consistently exercising for a week or adhering to their schedule of taking medicines. Reward must be given on a regular basis and can be withdrawn little by little as the desired behavior turns into a habit.

Setting Up Reminders

Getting a positive reminder should also be a daily occurrence. One example is an everyday quote about positive thinking posted on a wall. Another option is for patients to carry a notebook so that when they need a boost or have some spare time to relax, they can reinforce their positive thoughts.

More on the Quest for Motivation

Caregivers should note that every step of staying motivated meeds to be practiced on a daily basis in order to be fully effective. Patients should also keep in mind that their perception and expectations will be the ultimate guide toward achieving their goals. Once they get to the stage where they are setting up a reminder for themselves—be it a wall poster, a sticky note, or a

mark on a calendar—they will find the sequence easier to repeat, and each aspect of staying motivated will be improved. Parkinson's disease sufferers need to keep the impetus going throughout the day and take short breaks when needed. There are unique methods of staying motivated, including a myriad of tips and useful information that people can secure, but individuals can also make a list of personal steps on remaining determined that work for them. The list can include their favorite indoor or outdoor activities such as a short exercise, setting goals, and watching football or other sports that can "pump them up." Sometimes, people display nudges of determination, hope, enthusiasm, and motivation. They start doing things with gusto but lose the momentum after a while only because they find it hard to sustain. People with Parkinson's need to absorb and digest the whole process and the importance of motivation wholeheartedly to remember how much they could gain and what they could lose without it.

DIFFICULTIES AND ROADBLOCKS IN FINDING MOTIVATION

Not every goal can be achieved without encountering challenges. No matter how simple and fixed the target a person is setting, he will certainly encounter some obstacles that will test his patience and determination to be triumphant. Everyone knows how difficult it is to battle the challenges that Parkinson's disease bestows. Despite every ailment it gives to the body and every instance of confusion or chaos that it brings to the mind of a patient, a rebuttal in the form of motivation can be used as a defense. A patient can encounter and identify some hindrance that might interrupt or totally distract her while in the process of motivating herself. Difficulties can dishearten and strip patients of their inner will, determination, and motivation. Following are some of the roadblocks that Parkinson's disease patients might encounter while on their journey to find and reinforce motivation, along with the actions they can perform to counteract these challenges.

Negative Thinking

Positive thinking obviously has its counterpart. If positivity is always present, so is its archenemy, negativity. A Parkinson's disease patient can always come across negative thoughts such as "I am too fat," "I am too old for this," or "I am just a poor guy." Such thoughts have more impact on patients with Parkinson's disease as they may have a longer list of lines they can think of and will put themselves down emotionally. Furthermore, issues with autonomy make them feel handicapped. The above are examples of one form of negative thinking, or pessimism. Negative thinking may comprise shame-inducing thoughts, catastrophic thoughts, critical thoughts of remorse, and uncontrollable regrets that are very difficult to let go. Parkinson's disease

sufferers may become obsessed about their failures and limitations, and this can lead to severe depression. These negative thoughts defeat any efforts to reinforce motivation. For example, if the PD patient thinks that he looks worthless because of his disease, he might not give his attention to any productive activities and assume (in the long run) that his efforts are (1) going unappreciated, (2) perceived as failures, or (3) rejected by others of the same social circle. Negative thinking can also instill fear of what others might say, low self-esteem, or a simple lack of faith.

Fire can defeat water when there is not enough of the latter, but a lot of water can obviously put out fire. Negative thoughts can always be neutralized by their counterpart: positive thoughts. The key on initiating the reversal is by the emotion. Since emotion plays such a big role in thought, the patient needs to keep or make himself happy to fight all the negative ideas in his mind. Patients can do this by reading jokes in magazines or doing anything else that they know will produce smiles. Another way is by using motivation to replace the negative thoughts with positive ones. Every negative word that PD patients are subject to can be replaced with a positive one to avoid letting the negativity boil inside their minds.

Symptoms Are Motivation Roadblocks

Apathy as a symptom of Parkinson's or any other medical ailment suppresses emotions such as passion, concern, excitement, and motivation.[8] This is one of the heaviest roadblocks that Parkinson's disease can place in front of a patient. With apathy, patients may lack a sense of purpose or meaning in their life, which directly affects the elements needed for motivation. Apathy can also make Parkinson's patients feel as if they don't possess the level or skill required to confront a challenge. Apathy, in ways similar to that of negativity, is often caused by frustration and causes patients to withdraw (to an extent) from a happy life. Some patients are positive enough and use psychological tactics in order to muster the willpower to fight the illness, but this is not always the case. Since people afflicted with the disease might find it increasingly difficult to motivate themselves on their own due to apathy, they may need support from their spouses and caregivers.

Patients need to follow instructions from knowledgeable doctors regarding eliminating or slowly weaning themselves from medicines used for removing psychological roadblocks. There are nonpharmacological methods that a patient can use to minimize the effects of apathy and thereby regain motivation. Patients can exercise to boost levels of serotonin, the substance responsible for making a person "feel good." Another method is positive thinking, more specifically, thinking of good things in the patient's past and present. It can be childhood experiences or other events that make them smile at just that single thought. Patients can also move away from apathy by

reaching out to other people, exploring their interests, asking for some help if needed, and being more open about their feelings.[9]

LAZINESS, PROCRASTINATION, AND LOSS OF INTEREST

Laziness, procrastination, and loss of interest are all related to one another. When combined, they results in a complete halt of the motivational process, almost guaranteeing a complete failure for the patient in achieving a goal. It is natural for Parkinson's patients to be "lazy" sometimes, especially when they are not feeling right or are exhausted. All people have come across this scenario where they "chilled out" and took a long rest but still did not feel like doing anything at all. As far as Parkinson's disease is concerned, there will be times when patients will not be interested in doing anything productive. The remedy is to make use of a jolt: a jolt of desire, motivation, or realization of losing something important may be able to excite patients out of an idle mood.

Home-Based Support and Motivated Caregiving

Before a family member, spouse, sibling, friend, doctor, nurse, caregiver, or anyone can give motivational advice or support to a Parkinson's-diagnosed patient, that person must be motivated and a positive thinker as well. As the environment or surroundings of a patient can affect his or her way of thinking or emotions, it is important that the people around have a positive outlook so that the patient can absorb it. An onlooker who is not in a good mood should not be encouraged to come near the patient and pass on any negativity. For example, a man in his eighties is living with his son's family and at some point is diagnosed with Parkinson's disease. His son and daughter-in-law often argue a lot about money, and the man can hear their arguments. Soon the couple is not only arguing about money but is contemplating sending the man to a "home." In this case, the man, instead of being motivated, gets the idea that he is unwanted, and this eventually progresses into a deeper level of depression. In the end, it is a Parkinson's disease caregiver's duty to keep the patient away from stress and other things that might badly affect the patient's morale, esteem, and progress in finding motivation.

Chapter Nineteen

Parkinson's Disease at Home

One very disheartening facet of Parkinson's disease is how thoroughly and adversely this ailment transforms the patient's existence after onset, diagnosis, and progression of the disease. For the patient, diagnosis and treatment of the disease may be at the hospital (chapter 7), doctors' offices (chapter 8), nursing homes, the patient's residence, or a combination of these locations. However, in the United States approximately a decade ago, more than 90 percent of persons suffering from Parkinson's disease were living with their families at home.[1] With continual advances in the medical sciences and the concomitant improvements in health care at *home*, one may safely estimate that this statistic still exceeds 90 percent today. Afflicted with Parkinson's disease and living at home with family members, the patient needs all the support the family can provide. Optimal treatment of the patient is directly related to the accommodating adjustments made by the patient and household members. The treatment of the disease is not the sole responsibility of the doctor or any other health professional because treatment does not end at the doctor's office: it extends to the household.

FACING PARKINSON'S AT HOME

At home, optimal health care is attainable for a Parkinson's disease patient if there is synergy between the patient, the doctor, and the patient's household. This type of cooperation will make it possible for the patient to be resolute in facing the difficulties arising from the illness.

Doctor's Role in Home-Based Approaches

At the doctor's office, the groundwork is laid for treating the person diagnosed with Parkinson's disease. The doctor must inform the patient and corresponding household members about the character of the ailment. This communication, if done effectively and compassionately, will help ensure the most effective treatment for the patient. Away from the offices of doctors and other health professionals, the Parkinson's disease sufferer living at home is still under the supervision of his or her doctor because the doctor will have prescribed the regimen for the patient's care at home. In this case, the doctor's supervision is indirect but pervasive because the patient and the family members are motivated to try to comply with the health professional's instructions. At no time does the doctor exclusively manage and treat the patient. The management is jointly constructed by the physician, the patient, the patient's household members, the patient's primary caregiver, and even the general community. In the medical field, however, one doctrine is that the treatment of Parkinson's disease can be subdivided into nonpharmacologic, pharmacologic, and surgical therapy.[2]

The Patient's Role at Home

While living at home, a patient with Parkinson's disease can contribute significantly to the optimal treatment of the disorder. The patient's contribution can include maintaining a healthy diet, engaging in regular exercise, membership in a support group, and participating in clinical trials relating to Parkinson's disease. Specifically, in relation to manifestations of PD, the patient's contribution may include responding effectively to trembling, muscular rigidity, drooling related to eating, sexual dysfunction, speech problems, memory loss, dementia, and depression. These symptoms and effects of Parkinson's disease can be mitigated by the patient's effectual responses to them and other similar occurrences.

Jointly with family members, the patient may simplify his or her daily routine to utilize energy economically. Furniture and other commonly used items can be arranged so that the patient's mobility in the home can be facilitated. This will help the patient to operate more independently in his or her domestic milieu. With the assistance of home health-care professionals, the Parkinson's patient can cope adequately with a complex approach to the disease.[3]

Home and the Patient-Doctor Relationship

Successfully treating Parkinson's disease in a patient who lives at home requires a good relationship between the patient and the respective doctor. Vital attributes of this relationship must be the patient's honesty, candor, and

inquisitiveness concerning his or her health matters. Similarly, the doctor must relate honestly, candidly, and interestedly with the patient. In advising the patient who lives at home, the doctor can provide plenty of information and suggestions that will improve the patient's quality of life when with friends and family. A neurologist is best able to treat the Parkinson's disease patient—and assist in managing the disease—if the said physician and the patient have a good working relationship.

Treatment at Home

In its early stage, Parkinson's disease may not significantly interfere with the afflicted person's routine activities, but with the passage of time, the condition increasingly disables the patient. During the progression of the disease, home treatment will enable the patient to adjust to his or her changing circumstances and remain independent for extended periods. Quality of life may depend partly on the patient's ability to continue gainful employment, perform household responsibilities, or care for family. As the disease progresses and takes its toll on the individual's body, the patient may need adaptive devices such as a cane or a walker.

Caring for Children as a Parkinson's Patient

A widely held perception is that Parkinson's disease is an ailment that occurs during old age; consequently, the condition is often described as an "old person's disease."[4] The disease is directly related to advanced aging because the average age for its onset is sixty years and it worsens as the patient's age increases. Notwithstanding these observations, there have been exceptional cases of persons between the ages of thirty and forty being diagnosed with the disease. Muhammad Ali, a former professional boxer, was forty-two years old when he was diagnosed with Parkinson's disease in 1984. In 2009, 5 percent of Parkinson's disease patients in the United States were less than fifty years old; many of these younger Parkinson's patients were parents of children who were under eighteen.[5]

Parkinson's disease drastically alters the existence of the patient afflicted by it. Consequently, the patient's interpersonal relationships are also similarly affected. Altered circumstances often result in formerly healthy caregivers ironically changing into Parkinson's patients who need care by others. The disease causes radical and adverse changes in the patient's most basic activities, such as socializing with friends, enjoying family relationships, earning a living, and taking care of a home. These unplanned and seismic changes affect the patient's ability to care for his or her own dependent children and also have negative repercussions for the patient's independent, adult children. To a certain degree, even these children's future offpring and grand-

children are adversely affected by the altered circumstances of the Parkinson's disease patient.

The dependent children and wards of Parkinson's disease patients start out as the primary beneficiaries of the patients themselves while patients (hopefully) remain competent caregivers whose duties are unaffected by the disease. But with the onset and progression of the disease, the patients and their dependents most likely will be mutually concerned about their individual and collective welfare.

The Patient's Concerns

In caring for their dependent children and wards, Parkinson's disease patients should include preparing the minors to cope with the effects of the disease on their lives and the life of the patient. Afflicted patients, directly or with the assistance of other adults, should also hire household help to take care of the minors as soon as the patients know they cannot care adequately for children. With the other adults, who may be relatives or other unrelated but empathetic persons, the patients must also make provision for their own care—particularly as the disease advances.

The Parkinson's disease patients' care for dependent minors should include briefing the minors appropriately about the disease and the diagnosis. Individuals suffering from Parkinson's and living at home must help minors understand how the disease starts and progresses, eliciting from the minors their feelings about the patients' sickness and reassuring the minors that their feelings are appropriate in the existing circumstances. In doing so, patients may seek assistance from capable and compassionate professionals who can provide the patients' dependents with accurate information about Parkinson's disease and related coping mechanisms. The patients, accompanied by all or most of their elder and dependent children, might attend meetings of Parkinson's disease support groups. At these meetings, other children with similar needs may be present, and all such children can benefit from sharing their needs and applicable solutions. If patients have difficulty finding support groups for their children, they could even take the initiative and start their own support groups. These groups will enable the children to realize that they are not alone in their concerns and that other families have similar concerns.

Children's Concerns

The children of Parkinson's disease patients, whether adults or minors, usually find it traumatic to adjust to the drastic changes the disease causes in and for the patients. The resulting concerns include fear, a sense of stigmatization, and the inability to answer questions about the patient's disease. Some children wonder whether they also may become afflicted by the disease, and

families carry the burden of wondering whether the condition is hereditary. This worry is justified because the disease has genetic elements and the Parkinson's gene is considered a factor in the cases of persons who get the disease while still young. According to one estimate, 7 to 9 percent of Parkinson's patients get the disease genetically.[6]

The children may wonder about the prospect of their ailing parents or guardians suffering indefinitely and getting worse, since the parents and guardians previously were in good health and were the principal caregivers in the home. The minors very likely will have doubts about being able to request and garner necessary help from their ailing parents and guardians; they may also be concerned that, as minors, they may not be able to assist their own ailing caregivers in any significant way. Insecurity, anger, and frustration may beset some minors as they observe their well parents devoting nearly all their time to caring for the other parents who are Parkinson's disease patients. In these situations, the ailing caregivers should try to allay the concerns of minors by addressing their anxiety, anger, depression, guilt, sadness, or sense of loss.

Rasheda Ali-Walsh was fourteen years old when her boxer father, Muhammad Ali, was diagnosed with Parkinson's disease. Ali-Walsh has said that although her father initially shook a little and spoke more softly, he did not have pronounced symptoms of the disease and, therefore, she was unafraid when she learned of the diagnosis. Despite the diagnosis, Ali-Walsh reported, Ali continued taking his children on outings, and she had no concerns about his health. Additionally, she stated that her parents had no explanations about the disease. As she matured and Ali's disease progressed however, Ali-Walsh was unable to answer her children's questions about their grandfather's condition. She wrote a book,[7] partly to answer these questions and partly to assist other parents and their children,

As a Parkinson's disease patient, Mr. Ali contributed the foreword to his daughter's book and, in this and numerous other ways, has responded to the concerns that his grandchildren and other children have about Parkinson's disease. The book describes and gives the reasons for the common symptoms of the disease. It also addresses children's fears that they may inherit the disease genetically. From writing and helping her children understand Ali's ailment, Ali-Walsh observes that her children often can identify other people who have Parkinson's disease. According to Ali-Walsh, her young children were able to understand that the patients had no control over the condition and probably needed medical assistance.

There do not seem to be many scholarly and systematic studies of the needs, coping mechanisms, and common concerns of children of Parkinson's disease patients. The University College of London Medical School released two studies about the effect of parental Parkinson's disease on children whose ages ranged from twelve to forty years.[8] The researchers observed that

parental Parkinson's disease had a profoundly grave impact on the children and that all the children wanted more facts about the disease and the prognosis for their parent.

FAMILY MEMBERS AND PARKINSON'S AT HOME

The Patient's Support System

When based at home, a Parkinson's disease patient has a support system that includes family members, at least one primary caregiver, neighbors, and members of the wider community. In some cases, the primary caregiver is a member of the family; in other instances, the primary caregiver is a paid employee hired by members of the family. Whatever the composition of the patient's support group, the support system is vital to the patient, the family, and the caregiver. The families and friends of Parkinson's disease patients need to know about the disease so that they may help the patients in the best manner possible; they must continually learn about the patients' condition and adapt to the patients' status at home as it is influenced by the disease. Supporters should also take an interest in necessary changes to the surroundings and lifestyles of patients. The family of the Parkinson's disease patient usually has primary responsibility for the patient, particularly as the disease progresses and causes the deterioration of the patient's health. In this case, the onus is on the family to manage every aspect of the patient's life. On account of the patient's declining health, family members usually are involved in the minutest details of the patient's life. Consequently, family members make decisions concerning the Parkinson's disease sufferer's finances, medical attention, home conditions, and any occupational therapy that will enhance the patient's ability regarding self-care, domestic chores, and other activities.

In some instances, it may require much skill for the responsible family members of the Parkinson's patient to tell other persons about the patient's medical condition. Neighbors, visitors, servants, other relatives, and friends will want to know why the patient's health seems to be declining in spite of so much attention. The family members must truthfully and candidly tell these people that the patient has Parkinson's. This type of communication will prevent interested parties from conjecturing about the patient's health.

Family members caring for a Parkinson's disease patient need to operate as if they are managing a family enterprise, particularly when everyone is home. Accordingly, they must devise systems and mechanisms that will facilitate their caring for the patient. In doing this, they need to be mindful that their primary objective is to provide optimal health care for the patient in a familial environment. Usually, one adult family member has overall responsibility for the patient's welfare, and other family members have indi-

vidual supporting roles in the effort to deliver care to the patient. In striving to provide the best health care possible for a relative who has Parkinson's disease, family members will devote themselves to ministering principally to needs that relate to the patient's person, activities, and surroundings. Services that minister to the patient's person pertain to diet, body weight, medication, attire, personal hygiene, exercise, self-esteem, and sleep. The family's services that will aid the patient's activities relate to time management and recreation; services that will benefit the patient's surroundings relate to housing and furnishings.

Dining at Home with Family

Family members will observe that with the passage of time, the patient will take longer than the customary periods to have his or her meals. This happens because the patient's timescale for any activity increases as the disease advances. Relatives need to be mindful of this fact when the patient undertakes any activity. In this context, family members need to be patient with their ailing relative whenever he or she eats. Instead of leaving the patient to finish a meal because of the longer time he or she takes to do so, minors and other family members should keep the patient company and engage everyone in meaningful conversation. The patient's period at the table can be more pleasant if loved ones anticipate and facilitate tasks that may be difficult for the patient to do.

To make dining tasks easier for the Parkinson's patient, relatives may cut the patient's meat into bite-sized pieces before the meal begins. This will eliminate the usual difficulties that patients experience while using knives during the later stages of their illness. For the patients, an electric warming tray would be an advantage since it would maintain the food's warmth and palatability during the longer period required for patients to finish eating their meals. If Parkinson's disease patients have difficulty eating some foods, they should be given foods and cutlery that they can manipulate better. Patients should be allowed to eat some of their foods with spoons instead of the customary forks. If they use dentures or find it difficult to chew hard meats and vegetables, their food should be ground and served as meat loaves, stews, or thick soups; otherwise, they will eat minimally, and this will produce the undesirable consequence of losing critical weight that they simply cannot afford to lose.

On Body Weight

In caring for a Parkinson's disease patient at home, family members must make the maintenance of the patient's body weight a priority. Many patients often exhibit varying levels of noticeable weight loss during the course of

their illness. This results from the their inability to ingest adequate calories for their daily requirements, especially if other household members are designing incorrect meal plans for them. Other reasons for weight loss include (1) failure to finish eating in a reasonable amount of time and (2) the difficulty patients experience while chewing and handling foods on their own. The diet of a Parkinson's disease patient must be meticulously monitored and supervised in order to ensure that the patient's daily calorie intake ranges from 1,500 to 2,000 calories.[9] A duo of renowned doctors[10] opine that each patient may be better off having six meals per day: a light breakfast, a midmorning snack, a light lunch, a midafternoon meal, a moderate supper, and a light meal before bedtime. These doctors recommend weighing patients weekly to monitor their weights; they also advocate implementing strict mechanisms to increase the number of calories patients consume if they have had an undesired weight loss of. Patients' doctors should implement the means of increasing the number of calories patients ingest at home and, as deemed necessary, prescribe vitamins and other supplements.

Family Members and Medication at Home

Having prescribed the regimen for the patient's care at home, the respective doctors will issue the patient and family individual schedules detailing drugs the patient must take for tremulousness and muscular rigidity; the doctors also will prepare and issue the appropriate timetables for taking those drugs. With family members present and supportive in the home, people with Parkinson's disease should have help in adhering to the doctor's schedules for medication. The assistance of the patient's spouse or other family members could include measuring and pouring liquid or fluid medicine into containers from which the patient can consume the measured doses at the appropriate times indicated on the timetables. Similarly, family members can count capsules and tablets and leave them in small containers so that the patient can take appropriate doses at the designated times.

Some medications cause adverse reactions in some patients; if this happens to a Parkinson's patient, family members should discontinue administering the medication and consult the patient's doctor personally or by phone for advice on how to proceed. Some medicines prescribed for Parkinson's patients are laxatives for the constipation that typically besets these patients; other medicines are for sleep disorders that affect patients, who tend to be sedentary, particularly during the daytime.

The Family's Role with Home Attire

Many recommendations have been made concerning the types of attire best suited for Parkinson's patients. Some businesses specialize in making

clothes, shoes, and other garments that make dressing easier for Parkinson's and other patients with motor and muscle limitations. With or without the patients accompanying them, family members can visit some of these businesses when seeking appropriate clothing for their relatives. In the absence of special garments, family members may seek the help of a dressmaker or tailor to make or adjust clothes that homebound patients can easily maneuver—without assistance from anyone.

One widely held view is that buttons are always problematic for patients and that smaller buttons are particularly problematic. For Parkinson's disease patients, zippers should be used—in lieu of buttons—on dresses, coats, shirts, and trousers. Shoelaces are also considered as problematic for Parkinsonian patients since these items, if not fastened properly, can cause accidents and injuries to the patients. Elastic shoelaces have been proposed as the best for Parkinson's patients because such cords (unlike the regular ones) can be permanently tied to the shoes. Shoes with elastic laces can be removed without the patient untying the laces. Zippers and snaps are alternatives to shoelaces. Bowling shoes are considered suitable for Parkinson's patients because such shoes' upturned toes lower the incidence of scuffing and stumbling. For male Parkinson's patients, clip-on ties, not regular neckties, are relatively easy to maneuver and simply slip under shirt collars.

Home Hygeine and Family

Maintaining high standards of personal hygiene at home is an onerous duty for Parkinson's disease patients, particularly those who need to coordinate the bilateral involvement of lethargic *and* inflexible muscles. Coordinating the actions of these muscles is arduous for the patients and presents frightening difficulties for those who attempt to perform two motor acts simultaneously. These difficulties often result in Parkinson's disease patients needing help with dressing, bathing, and toileting. For these activities, patients may be helped if family members install support bars and frames on or near baths, toilets, furniture, and other objects. One solution to patients' difficulties with using the toilet is to get a plumber to heighten the toilet seat a few inches above the bowl,by installing metal or wooden supporting legs. If family members prefer, they can procure special elevated toilet seats from surgical supply stores.

Family and Self-Esteem

Parkinson's disease can make patients ashamed and self-conscious because of the tremulousness they endure with the ailment. Members of their family, with necessary assistance from doctors, must help patients accept this symptom of Parkinson's disease without being embarrassed. The patients must

learn that the shaking alone does not weaken them or cause significant decline in their motor skills; only the finest finger movements are adversely
affected by the shaking. Family members should encourage the patients to
discuss the shaking openly and freely with anyone. The patients' relatives
should also closely supervise the handling of objects that may spill or cause
spillage, giving only the minimum assistance necessary since excessive help
might undermine the patients' confidence. Families can enhance patients'
self-esteem by involving them in family meetings and decisions. The family
members should treat the patients such that they know their relatives love
them and consider them to be important and highly valuable contributors to
the family. Patients should be invited and taken to parties, outings, ceremonies, and other events that promote their positive socialization. In this regard,
patients should be introduced to new acquaintances and friends.

Family and Sleep

Parkinson's disease patients usually sleep well, although (as briefly noted in
an earlier chapter) sleep disorders can occur. The patients often fall asleep
while seated and reading or watching audiovisual equipment such as a television. The patient's family members should accommodate this propensity to
doze or nap, particularly during daytime hours, since it usually does not
prevent the patient from getting adequate nighttime sleep. Some Parkinson's
patients may have difficulty sleeping at night if their living conditions give
them a feeling of sensory deprivation. The sleeping difficulty may cause
confusion and hallucination. To prevent these frightful occurrences, family
members might use their own resourcefulness to make the situation more
pleasant for themselves and the patients. To minimize or eliminate a patient's
fears, family members might leave a light on at night in the patient's room or
leave radios on but at low volume. Patients can also benefit from reassuring
visits from their relatives throughout each night.

Time Management at Home

Invariably, Parkinson's disease makes its victims slow in executing any activity. The slowness makes each patient perform only one motor task at any
time. The patient cannot do two or more tasks simultaneously but can do
them individually and consecutively. Therefore, each patient will always take
longer than normal to do ordinary tasks. The respective families need to
understand the patients' slowness and inability to multitask even on a simple
scale. Having this understanding, families will be motivated to help their
Parkinson's-afflicted relatives manage their time efficiently and effectively.
The family members and the patients should cooperate in devising appropriate timetables for activities. With these timetables in effect, patients will

never be hurried or under duress to accomplish their tasks, even though they will take full responsibility for their tasks and execute them. The patients need to do the tasks themselves so that their muscles and minds will be kept active and will not atrophy. By accomplishing their own tasks, patients maintain their independence. If they maintain their independence, they will be motivated (chapter 18) and content. Depending on each patient's energy level at any particular time, the individual with Parkinson's disease is to be allowed to forgo or curtail some activities so that he or she will not become exhausted. In this regard, patients and their relatives can cooperate for their family's collective good.

Recreation

Travel is a wholesome leisure or business activity for patients in the early stages of Parkinson's disease. This is true because the patient's spirits can be buoyed by new experiences and changes in the landscape. Depending on the status of their ailment, Parkinson's patients may travel alone or with companions who will assist when necessary. Patients may travel by air, rail, sea, or road. Some health-care professionals have posited the view that traveling by car is especially beneficial for Parkinson's patients since the movement of the vehicle usually relieves some of the muscular rigidity that often besets the patient. Relatives may allow their Parkinson's relatives to drive cars, for business or pleasure, in light traffic, or in places where a relatively slow speed will not create a hazard for anyone. Should family members consider it prudent, they should take the precautionary measure of having someone accompany the Parkinson's patients who do the driving.

Parkinson's disease patients may use some of their leisure time to indulge in hobbies they may have fostered during earlier periods of their lives. These hobbies are always beneficial for the patients' health, pleasure, morale, and desire to be industrious; this is even more so in the patients' later years, when illnesses such as Parkinson's disease set in. The patients' hobbies may range from those that can be done at home to hobbies pursued outside the home. Patients engage in some hobbies individually or as members of groups. Craft, watching television, using computers, reading, and games are a few of the hobbies that Parkinson's disease patients may undertake. However the patients use their leisure time, they should be kept occupied and interested in life during their waking hours, particularly during their periods of recreation.

SURROUNDINGS AT HOME

Housing

In defining the housing requirements of Parkinson's patients, relatives need to consider the risks of the patients having accidents because of their illness and because of the layout of their surroundings at home. Parkinson's disease predisposes patients to sudden and recurring immobility, tardy muscles, stumbling, and even falling. Consequently, the patients' residences should be laid out to minimize the risks that patients might fall or collide with objects. When Parkinson's patients walk within their residences, doorsills frequently cause stumbling. As far as possible, caregivers should have the doorsills modified to minimize risks to the patients. Modifications might include leveling the floor surfaces or converting doorsills to ramps. Relatives should also ensure that sharp, angular furniture and other perilous objects are ideally placed so that the patients will not harm themselves because of accidental contact with them. To protect some of the families' assets, costly and fragile objects should also be kept out of patients' ways.

Relatives should spare Parkinson's patients the difficulty of using stairs at home. If staircases exist in the residence, they must be made secure, particularly for the patient. For the patient's sake, rails and other types of supporting fixtures should be on both sides of the stairways. In residences with interior stairs, the street-level floor is the most desirable location for the living quarters of Parkinson's patients. Rails, bars, handles, and other supporting objects should be strategically placed throughout the residence for the patient's benefit. Also for the patient's benefit, the residence should be adequately ventilated and should always be maintained at temperatures in which the patient is comfortable. These conditions will enable a patient to wear only the minimum number of layers of clothes, which will minimize any difficulty a patient might have while changing clothes.

Furnishings

Owing to the abrupt immobility that usually troubles patients with Parkinson's disease, the patients often have difficulty using chairs. They sit and get up from seats with much discomfort and awkwardness. One solution to this difficulty is to assign special chairs for patients' use. Each special chair should have rear legs that are so heightened that the chair, instead of being upright, tips forward more easily whenever the patient so desires. This simple convenience makes life more comfortable for each person living at home while afflicted with Parkinson's disease. The sudden immobility characteristic of Parkinson's also presents problems when sufferers of the disease use their beds. Parkinson's patients will have easier access to and from their beds

if family members ensure that the beds have bars or other features and accessories that aid patients as they rise from or go to bed.

Chapter Twenty

Conclusion

In the end, it should be clear that Parkinson's disease is the most common form of Parkinsonism and is a degenerative disorder of the central nervous system.[1] It belongs to a group of conditions called motor system disorders. The primary symptoms are: (1) tremor or trembling in hands, arms, legs, jaw, and face, (2) rigidity or stiffness of the limbs and trunk, (3) bradykinesia, or slowness of movement, and (4) postural instability or impaired balance and coordination.[2] As these symptoms become more pronounced, patients may have difficulty in using their motor skills (walking), talking, or even carrying out a very simple task.[3]

HOPE AND PARKINSON'S

Currently, there is no single defined drug or treatment that can cure Parkinson's disease, which is one reason why hope is necessary. Surgery or medications, however, have sometimes been useful in providing dramatic relief for those suffering from Parkinson's.

Various Support Therapies

Aside from surgery and drug treatment, a wide variety of complementary and support therapies are serving very hopeful purposes when it comes to confronting the disease.[4] Most common of these therapies are physical, occupational, and speech therapy, which all help in rehabilitation of the known symptoms of Parkinson's mentioned above. These therapies prove beneficial not only for the physical wellness of those with Parkinson's, but for patients' mental toughness as well. Some other supportive therapies include maintaining a balanced diet and a good exercise regime.

Research

Modern research has generated much anticipation, enthusiasm, and hope in the Parkinson's disease community. Dedicated scientists and researchers are now garnering enormous support from multisector organizations worldwide with hopes of finding a cure to this perplexing disease. The developments currently demonstrated and under way by some of the renowned research institutions in the world plus the unending drive of health scientists and researchers truly show how hope is still alive for those who have Parkinson's disease. There is hope in and through research and social support from all over the globe. True enough, there is a bright and shining hope for patients with Parkinson's despite its degenerative nature.

CONTRIBUTIONS OF ORGANIZATIONS

Numerous health organizations in the United States and around the world help Parkinson's disease victims live better lives. These organizations come from a wide range of specializations as they cater to the various needs of sufferers of the disease.

Research-Focused Organizations

One of the more important neurological organizations that focus on finding and developing a cure and treatment for Parkinson's disease is the National Institute of Neurological Disorders and Stroke (NINDS), a national organization under the National Institutes of Health (NIH), which is also the nation's medical research agency. The NINDS and some parts of the NIH work together in conducting and furthering research on coenzyme Q10 as a supplement said to be beneficial in slowing down the progression of the early stages of Parkinson's. Apart from this current research, the NINDS in conjunction with the NIH also funds studies and gives medical grants to widen the research arena in finding whether or not caffeine, antioxidants, and other dietary supplements can be beneficial in preventing or treating Parkinson's disease.[5] Another health organization is the Parkinson's Disease Foundation, which aids in the funding of research, patient care, and public advocacy for PD.[6] Many other organizations focus on finding a cure for Parkinson's disease, such as The Michael J. Fox Foundation for Parkinson's Research and the Muhammad Ali Parkinson Center. Their special interests include (1) looking for the right doctor, (2) managing Parkinson's disease, (3) treatment procedures, and (4) how to donate to the cause.

Caregiving and Treatment-Focused Organizations

Research is not the only facet that organizations fund and advocate. Like most others when ill, people who have Parkinson's disease also have to be given care and attention, especially when it comes to managing their symptoms. One of the most active organizations involved in the care and physical treatment of patients with Parkinson's disease is the National Parkinson Foundation (NPF). From the caregiving standpoint, the NPF has raised funds for more than $150 million in care, research, and support services.[7] Its services range from global support groups to medical centers and care centers, all welcoming patients suffering from Parkinson's. All the aforementioned organizations also cater to and focus on improving the quality of care, the treatment facilities, and treatment programs of patients with Parkinson's disease. Similar to the caregiving organization NPF is the American Parkinson's Disease Association (APDA), which was established to provide information to the public about the various services available to all patients with Parkinson's. The association has more than sixty information and referral centers all over the United States.[8] Other organizations focus on the treatment of movement disorders. The Bachmann-Strauss Dystonia and Parkinson Foundation is one of the organizations that specialize in providing medical and patient information as well as funding innovative studies and research with the goal of finding better treatments and cures for movement disorders.

To answer to the growing needs of caregivers to have someone to talk to and share their burdens with, a number of caregiver organizations have been established. One of the caregiving organizations is the Family Caregiving Alliance, or FCA. The FCA stresses the importance of caregiving in any given society and promotes the well-being of caregivers, who are equally as important as those they care for.[9] The FCA's website expounds on many ways and techniques caregivers can use to help manage and deal with the stress of their work. These techniques include (1) identifying one's personal barriers, (2) taking steps to reduce and manage stress, (3) setting goals, (4) seeking solutions for both the PD patient and the caregiver, (5) communicating well with the physician, and, finally, (6) asking for and accepting help.

Another organization that aims to help caregivers of disorders such as Parkinson's is Caring for the Caregivers. This organization has developed different types of support groups and group therapies exclusive to caregivers only. This exclusivity makes the group participants feel at home and at ease, and they are much more likely to share their feelings, concerns, and grievances with the group they join or belong to. The Caring for Caregivers support groups and healing circles also maintain a close monitoring of their participants to know which participants are improving and making progress in dealing with their own personal stress and health management. Caregivers from all over the country are encouraged and welcome to join any of the

support groups at any time of the year. Groups, organizations, and associations such as these are essential to the Parkinson's and healthcare professions community as a testimony that caregivers are not alone and that many others share the same experiences as they do.

Public Advocacy, Policy, and Fundraising Organizations

Some organizations contribute their efforts in raising funds and increasing awareness of the general public about Parkinson's disease. The Parkinson Alliance is one of the many organizations who stand up for this cause. The main objective of the Parkinson Alliance is to foster philanthropic activities to raise funds for conducting the Parkinson's research that will eventually and hopefully find a cure. This organization brings together the community and encourages everyone to join and become proactive in contributing to the research, development, and treatment improvement of patients with the disease. The Parkinson's community does not limit its concern to matters of research and therapy or treatment development. The Parkinson's Action Network is actively involved in voicing the opinions, needs, and responses of the Parkinson's disease community regarding public policy issues that affect it. Some of those issues include those of health care, insurance, local health institution agendas, along with many others. There are numerous organizations and foundations from all over the world that help in catering to the different needs of patients with Parkinson's. From medical and scientific research and physical, speech, and occupational therapy, to caregiving, fundraising, and public policy—the wide range of organizations that provide for the different needs of Parkinson's disease victims only goes to show how immersed the community is in taking action toward the betterment of the overall lives of those with Parkinson's. The multifaceted involvement of society at large plays a great role in the development of research and, more importantly, the improvement of quality of life of those individuals with Parkinson's.

A SOCIETAL, COLLECTIVE EFFORT

Social Support

Social support plays a significant role in the quality of life of people suffering from Parkinson's. Just as it is for everyone else, so being cared for and given time and understanding really provides Parkinson's sufferers a sense of hope, importance, and belonging. To individuals suffering from the disease, this makes a big difference in their emotional well-being. Social support has been shown to be an important factor in the life of healthy people as well as those with illnesses.[10] Not all patients with Parkinson's disease have the

same symptoms, which is why it is important to acknowledge that different patients may have different concerns and feelings as they go through their life's journey knowing that they have an incurable disease. This is exactly where social support comes into play. While some may require less support, most patients will greatly benefit from a social support network, starting with their very own families and continuing into the community in which they live. Conditions of the patient may vary from day to day, and tasks for caregiving may range from extensive therapeutic conversations and encouragement to aiding the patient in simple, everyday activities such as walking or opening a bag of chips. Proper physical and emotional care and commitment must come from the social circle if immediate family (chapter 19) is unavailable. The circle's support in any magnitude may cause significant changes in the patient's mood, perspective, or even hope for his or her life in the future.

Society and Overall Patient Well-Being

Social support in the context of patients with Parkinson's disease is as "official" and important as finding a cure for the disease. Researchers in psychology have found this topic to be of grave importance in the overall well-being of patients with Parkinson's.[11] These experts discovered that when individuals with Parkinson's disease procured greater social support, their self-perceived motor and psychological problems were fewer in number, which suggests that relationships with the people around the patient as well as their awareness of a supportive community may impact their mental well-being.

Social Responsibility of the Global Community

Of note is the role social support plays in a Parkinson's disease patient's life. This type of support is not the kind that can be treated by drug therapy, surgery, or other treatment. To determine appropriate intervention strategies, a person who has Parkinson's disease must be carefully observed, treated, and encouraged to live as active a life as possible by the global community (not just the Parkinson's community) so as to keep the patient from falling into depression. This is why there are many organizations that call on the public to help out and donate to their cause in finding the cure to the perplexing disease. Public advocacy is one of the many causes health organizations are active in to inform the public of the realities of the disease and encourage others to realize their potentials as donors not only in the financial sense but in the communal sense as well. As a global community, the awareness of Parkinson's may still be needed in some developing countries around the world, but the World Health Organization has pledged to the worldwide community its goal of spreading the word about Parkinson's and how one

can help battle this disease. A simple donation, a word of encouragement, or a little conversation can give a spark of hope to any Parkinson's patient. One may not know its impact right away, but a monetary contribution's value will be most apparent in the long run. With this in mind, a collective effort must certainly be made when dealing with Parkinson's. Whether one may be a scientist, a researcher, a doctor, a caregiver, a patient, a family member, or a friend, being aware and concerned about the challenges of Parkinson's and helping to champion its cause is a significant step in achieving the common goal that the global community should be working responsibly to attain.

CARING FOR THE CAREGIVERS

Caring for patients with Parkinson's is a great responsibility. It definitely involves a lot of work, a length of patience, and, of course, a great deal of emotional stress. Often, those who take care of patients with Parkinson's forget to take care of themselves.

Risk of Being a Caregiver

Research[12] has shown that caregivers are at risk of having a higher mortality rate due to the strain and inability to deal with the stresses that come with the job. Caregivers of long-term patients such as Parkinson's disease sufferers are faced with problems in attending to their own health since they do not have enough time to balance it with their occupational duties. Some of the more common problems caregivers encounter is sleeplessness, poor eating habits, failure to stay in bed when ill, and failure to get to their own medical appointments.

In an aircraft, the flight attendant always reminds passengers to put on their oxygen mask first before attending to a minor if a change in cabin pressure happens. This simple example sheds light on the importance of helping oneself and being fit in order to help others become fit as well. It is important for caregivers of Parkinson's patients to know that they are entitled to their own days off if need be. Some caregivers who are deeply immersed in their hectic work schedule do not notice that their moods, eating patterns, sleeping patterns, stress, and all other anxieties in the job may be detrimental to their own health. Other caregivers even develop depression when dealing with patients every single day without anyone to share their burdens with or even just someone to talk to. Caregivers must keep in check their emotions and maintain a healthy and balanced social life so as not to become personally entrapped in their job.

Stress in Caregiving

Coping with everyday stress is one of the many challenges a caregiver faces. Family member or not, caregivers need to stay fit and emotionally prepared in dealing with their job. By understanding how patients deal with their own disease, caregivers and family members as well may be enlightened as to why certain behavioral or physical changes occur in the lives of their Parkinson's-afflicted patients. The role of the Parkinson's disease caregiver in the life of a patient is crucial. Having a good caregiver—one who will not only attend to physical needs, but emotional needs as well—can drastically improve the patient's outlook in life. When faced with the reality of having a degenerative disease, patients are the most likely to succumb to the downside of the illness and lose hope. But caregivers are similarly affected by these sentiments, and most of the time, it is the caregiver who usually takes in all the emotional stress so as to continue with his or her job. It is impressive to see how caregivers manage the personal and emotional stress they get from work yet still be able to balance it with their caregiving responsibilities.

Importance of Caring for the Caregivers

Putting a premium on the overall health and well-being of caregivers is equally as important as taking good, proper care of patients with Parkinson's. Those who give care to a patient ultimately make a difference in the lives of not only themselves and their patients but others. This is why it is important for caregivers to equally be responsible for their own health. Patients cannot make it on their own, and caregivers are one of the many important contributing factors in improving the lives of people affected by the disease.

FAREWELL

Seeking Medical Attention

The symptoms for Parkinson's start subtly; some may not even think or consider small tremors or muscle stiffness to be early stages of the disease. This is why it is important for an individual to see a physician or a specialist when experiencing symptoms such as those related to the disease. It may seem paranoid to think right away that what one is experiencing are early signs of PD, but it is much more constructive to become aggressive and protective about this disease by keeping in check one's health and having routine medical checkups. It is important to see a neurologist or Parkinson's specialist to get an accurate diagnosis. Dealing with the diagnosis is always difficult for an individual who has just heard the news. But having a structured Parkinson's program and following it, along with following nutritional

advice, is just one of the benefits a patient gets when he or she goes to a physician to ask medical questions. When a person with Parkinson's seeks medical attention as soon as early signs (of what could be the disease) surface, proper medical, physical, and mental measures can enable the patient to start fighting and managing the symptoms.

Structured Treatment Program

As a final thought, Parkinson's disease patients and caregivers should realize by now that the diagnosis is only one part of the whole clinical and personal experience. The proper treatment and medical attention given to the patient is the more crucial part of dealing with the disease. Without the advice, diagnosis, and referrals of physicians or specialists, those with Parkinson's would be left to take matters into their own hands, using inaccurate self-medications and treatments that might lead to worsening of the disease rather than improvement. Close communication and cooperation with one's physicians or other caregivers is crucial in the course of treatment. A doctor can provide a streamlined medication plan as well as give referrals to movement disorder specialists who can help in the physical, speech, and occupational therapies of patients. As much as patients might want to treatment themselves or seek alternative procedures and medications, the fact still remains: getting treatment from a qualified specialist is still the best way to deal with and fight the progression of Parkinson's disease.

Appendix A

Parkinson's Disease-Related Links

www.aans.org
www.apdaparkinson.org
www.edition.cnn.com/HEALTH/library/parkinsons-disease
www.epda.eu.com/en
www.europarkinson.net
www.journalofparkinsonsdisease.com/JPD/Home.html
www.mayoclinic.com/health/parkinsons-disease/DS00295
www.michaeljfox.org
www.mwpf.org
www.ncbi.nlm.nih.gov/pubmedhealth/PMH0001762
www.neura.edu.au/health/parkinsons-disease
www.nice.org.uk/CG035
www.nihseniorhealth.gov/parkinsonsdisease
www.ninds.nih.gov/disorders/parkinsons_disease/parkin-
    sons_disease.htm
www.nlm.nih.gov/medlineplus/parkinsonsdisease.html
www.parkinson.ca
www.parkinson.org
www.parkinsonalliance.org
www.parkinsonassociation.org
www.parkinsonfoundation.org
www.parkinsons.ie
www.parkinsons.org.au
www.parkinsons.org.nz
www.parkinsons.org.uk

www.parkinsonsassociation.org
www.parkinsonsdisease.com
www.parkinsonsdiseaseindia.com
www.parkinsonsingapore.com
www.parkinsonsmi.org
www.parkinsonsnsw.org.au
www.parkinson-study-group.org
www.pdf.org
www.thepi.org
www.umm.edu/altmed/articles/parkinsons-disease-000123.htm
www.wemove.org/par
www.wpda.org

Appendix B

Research and Training

American Parkinson Disease Association
    135 Parkinson Ave.
    Staten Island, NY 10305
    (800) 223-2732
    www.apdaparkinson.org

American Society for Neurorehabilitation
    5841 Cedar Lake Rd., Suite 204
    Minneapolis, MN 55416
    (952) 545-6324
    Fax: (952) 545-6073
    www.asnr.com

APDA National Young Onset Center
    Central DuPage Hospital
    25 N. Winfield Rd.
    Winfield, IL 60190
    (877) 223-3801
    Fax: (630) 933-4380
    www.youngparkinsons.org

Association of Parkinson Groups
    3 Chemin du Grand Fosse
    St. Nazaire 44600 France
    (33) 4022 00 84

Bachmann-Strauss Dystonia & Parkinson Foundation
Fred French Building, 551 Fifth Ave. (at 45th St.), Suite 520
New York, NY 10176
(212) 682-9900
www.dystonia-parkinsons.org

Chilean League against Parkinson's Disease
Arturo Prat 1341 Barrio Av.
Matta, Santiago, Chile
(55) 2555 7716
Fax: (55) 2555 7716
www.parkinson.cl

Cure Parkinson's Trust
St Botolph's, Aldgate High Street
London, EC3N 1AB England
020 7929 7656
www.cureparkinsons.org.uk

Cyprus Parkinson's Disease Association
PO Box 27653
Nicosia 2431 Cyprus
(357) 99678445
Fax: (357) 22371425
www.cyprusparkinson.org

Czech Parkinson's Disease Society
Volynska 20
Prague 10 100 00 Czech Republic
(42) 02-7273-9222
Fax: (42) 02-7273-9222

Danish Parkinson Association
Hornemansgade 36
Koebenhavn, OE DK2100 Denmark
(45) 3927 1555
Fax: (45) 3918 2075

Davis Phinney Foundation
1722 14th St., Suite 150
Boulder, CO 80302
(303) 733-3340

Fax: (303) 733-3350
www.davisphinneyfoundation.org

European Cooperative Network for Research, Diagnosis and Therapy of Parkinson's Disease (EuroPa)
  Philips University Marburg
  Medical Center, Department of Neurology
  Rudolf-Bultmann-Str. 8, D-35033 Marburg, Germany
  049-(0)64 21-586 5272
  Fax: 049-(0)64 21-586 53 08
  www.europarkinson.net

European Parkinson's Disease Association (EPDA)
  1 Northumberland Ave.
  Trafalgar Square
  London, WC2N 5BW England
  (440) 207 8725510
  www.epda.eu.com/en

Finnish Parkinson Association
  Suomen Parkinson-litto, PB 905
  Turku 20101 Finland
  (358) 2 2740 400
  Fax: (358) 2 2740 444
  www.parkinson.fi

Georgian Society for Parkinsonism and Movement Disorders
  71 Gorgasali St.
  Tbilisi 0114 Georgia (Caucasus)
  (99532) 226807
  Fax: (99532) 226807

German Parkinson Association
  Moselstrasse 31
  Neuss 41464 Germany
  (49) 213 141 016/7
  Fax: (49) 213 145 445

Italian Parkinson's Association
  Piazza IV Novembre, 6
  Milano 20124 Italy
  (39) 02 669 79 85
  Fax: (39) 02 67 07 00 73

www.parkinson-italia.it

Japan Parkinson Disease Association
1-9-13-812, Akasaka, Minato-ku
Tokyo, Japan
(3) 3560 3355
Fax: (3) 3560 3356

L'association France Parkinson
37 Bis rue la Fontaine
Paris 75016 France
(33) 145 202 220
Fax: (33) 140 501 644

Luxembourg Parkinson's Disease Association
169 Avenue de la Liberation
Schifflange 3850 Luxembourg
(352) 546 221

Maryland Parkinson's Disease and Movement Disorders Center
University of Maryland Medical Center
Department of Neurology
110 S. Paca St., 3rd Floor
Baltimore, Maryland 21201
(410) 328-6483
www.umm.edu/parkinsons

Melvin Weinstein Parkinson's Foundation
1340-1272 N. Great Neck Rd., #193
Virginia Beach, VA 23454
(757) 313-9729
Fax: (757) 496-7946
www.mwpf.org

Mexican Parkinson Disease Association
AMPAC, Apdo. Postal 27003
Col. Roma Sur D.F. 06761 Mexico
www.ampacparkinson.org.mx

Michael J. Fox Foundation for Parkinson's Research
Grand Central Station
PO Box 4777
New York, NY 10163-4777

(800) 708-7644
www.michaeljfox.org

Michael Stern Parkinson's Research Foundation
1115 Broadway, Suite1200
New York, NY 10010
(800) 470-0499
Fax: (212) 710-2601
www.parkinsoninfo.org

Michigan Parkinson Foundation
30400 Telegraph Rd., Suite 150
Bingham Farms, MI 48025
(248) 433-1011
Fax: (248) 433-1150
www.parkinsonsmi.org

The Movement Disorder Society International Secretariat
555 East Wells St., Suite 1100
Milwaukee, WI 53202-3823
(414) 276-2145
Fax: (414) 276-3349
www.movementdisorders.org

Movers & Shakers
880 Grand Rapids Blvd.
Naples, FL 34120
(239) 919-8287
www.pdoutreach.org

Muhammad Ali Parkinson's Center & Movement Disorders Clinic
St. Joseph's Hospital and Medical Center
240 West Thomas Rd,, Suite 301
Phoenix, AZ 85013

National Parkinson Foundation, Inc.
1501 N.W. 9th Ave./Bob Hope Rd.
Miami, FL 33136-1494
(305) 243-6666
www.parkinson.org

Neurological Institute of New York
710 West 168th St.

New York, NY 10032
www.cumc.columbia.edu/dept/neurology

New York University Langone Parkinson's and Movement Disorders Center
145 East 32nd St., 2nd Floor
New York, NY 10016
(212) 263-4838
parkinson.med.nyu.edu

NINDS—Neuroscience Center
Division of Extramural Research
6001 Executive Blvd., Suite 3309
Bethesda, MD 20892
www.ninds.nih.gov

Norwegian Parkinson's Disease Association
Schweigaardsgt. 34, Bygg F, Oppg. 2
Oslo 0191 Norway
(47) 22 175 861
Fax: (47) 22 175 862
www.parkinson.no

Oxford Parkinson's Disease Centre (OPDC)
John Radcliffe Hospital
Oxford, OX3 9DU England
Fax: (0186) 5750750
www.opdc.medsci.ox.ac.uk

Pakistan Parkinson's Society
67-1 3rd St. KH Badban phase 5 DHA
Karachi, Sindh 75500 Pakistan
(9221) 5841669
Fax: (9221) 5841669
www.parkinsons.org.pk

Parkinson Alliance
PO Box 308
Kingston, NJ 08528
(800) 579-8440
Fax: (609) 688-0875
www.parkinsonalliance.org

Parkinson Association of Iceland

Hatun 10b, 9th Floor
Reykjavik IS-105 Iceland
(354) 5524440
www.parkinson.is

Parkinson Association of the Carolinas
5970 Fairview Rd., Suite 725
Charlotte, NC 28210
(704) 248-3722
Fax: (704) 375-7497
www.parkinsonassociation.org

Parkinson Association of the Rockies
1325 S. Colorado Blvd., Suite 204B
Denver, CO 80222
(866) 718-2996
Fax: (303) 830-2577
www.parkinsoncolorado.org

Parkinson Federation of Spain
235 Padilla
Barcelona 08013 Spain
(34) 93 232 91 94
Fax: (34) 93 232 91 94

Parkinson Foundation of the Heartland
8900 State Line Rd., Suite 320
Leawood, KS 66206
(913) 341-8828
Fax: (913) 341-8885
www.parkinsonheartland.org

Parkinson Foundation of the National Capital Area
7700 Leesburg Pike, Suite 208, South Lobby
Falls Church, VA 22043
(703) 734-1017
Fax: (703) 734-1241
www.parkinsonfoundation.org

Parkinson Research Foundation
8586 Potter Park Dr.
Sarasota, FL 34238
(941) 870-4438

Fax: (866) 317-0593
www.parkinsonresearchfoundation.org

Parkinson's Action Network
1025 Vermont Ave. NW, Suite 1120
Washington, DC 20005
(202) 638-4101
Fax: (202) 638-7257
www.parkinsonsaction.org

Parkinson's Association Chile
Av. Belisario Prats 1597-B
Santiago, RM 6532509 Chile
(562) 7321927
Fax: (562) 3572319

Parkinson's Association of Ireland
Carmichael Centre, North Brunswick Street
Dublin 7, Ireland
(01) 8722234
www.parkinsons.ie

Parkinson's Association of San Diego
8555 Aero Dr., Suite 308
San Diego, CA 92123
(877) 737-7576
Fax: (858) 273-6764
www.parkinsonsassociation.org

Parkinson's Australia
PO Box 717
Mawson ACT 2607 Australia
(0407) 703 328
www.parkinsons.org.au

Parkinson's Disease Association of Slovenia
Institute of Clinical Neurophysiology
University Medical Centre
Ljubljana 1525 Slovenia
(38) 661 316 152
Fax: (38) 661 302 771

Parkinson's Disease Clinic & Research Center

University of California, San Francisco
505 Parnassus Ave., Room 798-M, Box 0114
San Francisco, CA 94143
(415) 502-1672
Fax: (415) 476-3289
www.pdcenter.neurology.ucsf.edu

Parkinson's Disease Foundation
1359 Broadway, Suite 1509
New York, NY 10018
(212) 923-4700
www.pdf.org

Parkinson's Disease Foundation and Research Association
214-A, Talwandi
Kota, Rajasthan, India
(92) 744 421 966
Fax: (92) 744 427 759

Parkinson's Disease Foundation of India
302 Jaltarang, Kishore Kumar Lane
Juhu Tara Road, Mumbai
400 049
www.parkinsonsdiseaseindia.com

Parkinson's Disease Society of Karnataka
No. 633, 3rd Cross, HMT Layout, RT Nagar
Bangalore 50032 India
(91) 80 3439038

Parkinson's Disease Society of Singapore
c/o SNSA
26 Dunearn Road
Singapore 309423
www.parkinsonsingapore.com

Parkinson's Disease Society of Turkey
Department of Neurology, Cerrahpasa School of Medicine, Ýstanbul University
Aksaray, Istanbul 34303 Turkey
90 212 5883770
Fax: 90 212 5883770

Parkinson's Foundation of Bombay
Jaslok Hospital & Research Center, 12th Floor, Pedder Road, Bulbhai
Bombay (Mumbai)
Maharashtra 400 026 India
(91) 22 56573230
Fax: (91) 22 23521458
www.parkinsonsdiseaseindia.com

Parkinson's Institute and Clinical Center
675 Almanor Ave.
Sunnyvale, CA 94085
(408) 734-2800
www.thepi.org

Parkinson's New South Wales Inc.
Building 21, Macquarie Hospital
120 Coxs Road (corner of Norton Rd)
North Ryde NSW 2113 Australia
(02) 8875 8900
www.parkinsonsnsw.org.au

Parkinson's New Zealand National Office
Level 3, James Smith Building
55 Cuba Street
Wellington 6142 New Zealand
or
PO Box 11 067
Wellington 6142 New Zealand
(04) 4722796
Fax: (04) 4722162
www.parkinsons.org.nz

Parkinson Society Canada
4211 Yonge Street, Suite 316
Toronto, ON M2P 2A9 Canada
(416) 227-9700
www.parkinson.ca

Parkinson's Society of Jamaica
7 Glendon Circle, Hope Pastures
Kingston 6 Jamaica
(809) 972-2236

Parkinson Study Group
   265 Crittenden Blvd. CU-420694
   Rochester, NY 14642
   (585) 273-2862
   www.parkinson-study-group.org

Parkinson's UK
   215 Vauxhall Bridge Road
   London SW1V 1EJ England
   (020) 7931 8080
   www.parkinsons.org.uk

Puerto Rican Parkinson Association
   PO Box 66
   Carolina 00986 Puerto Rico
   246-5000

Rehabilitation Institute of Chicago
   345 East Superior St.
   Chicago, IL 60611
   (312) 238-4410
   www.ric.org

Southeast Parkinson Disease Association
   6530 Metrowest Blvd. #606
   Orlando, FL 32835
   (407) 489-4124
   www.sepda.org

Swedish Parkinson's Disease Association
   Skeppargatan 52 NB
   Stockholm 114 58 Sweden
   (46) 8 666 20 70

Swiss Parkinson Association
   Gewerbestrasse 12A, Postfach 123
   Zurich, CH-8132 Egg Switzerland
   (41) 1984 01 69
   Fax: (41) 1984 03 93
   www.parkinson.ch

Thai Parkinson's Disease Society
   Pramongkutklao Army Hospital

315 Rajvithee Rd.
Phyathai, Bangkok 10400 Thailand
(662) 245-5526
Fax: (662) 245 5526

We Move
5731 Mosholu Ave.
Bronx, NY 10471
www.wemove.org

World Federation of Neurology
Hill House, Heron Square
Richmond, Surrey TW9 1EP England
+44 208 439 9556
Fax: +44 208439 9499
www.wfneurology.org

World Parkinson Coalition
1359 Broadway, Suite 1509
New York, NY 10018
www.worldpdcongress.org

Appendix C

Parkinson's Disease Organizations

PARKINSON'S ORGANIZATIONS IN THE UNITED STATES

American Parkinson Disease Association
135 Parkinson Ave.
Staten Island, NY 10305
(800) 223-2732
Fax: (718) 981-4399
apda@apdaparkinson.org
www.apdaparkinson.org

National Parkinson Foundation
1501 NW 9th Ave./Bob Hope Road
Miami, FL 33136-1494
(305) 243-6666/(800) 327-4545
Fax: (305) 243-5595
contact@parkinson.org
www.parkinson.org

Parkinson Alliance
PO Box 308
Kingston, NJ 08528
(609) 688-0870
Fax: (609) 688-0875
www.parkinsonalliance.org

Michael J. Fox Foundation for Parkinson's Research
    Grand Central Station
    PO Box 4777
    New York, NY 10163
    (212) 509-0995
    www.michaeljfox.org

Parkinson's Action Network (PAN)
    1025 Vermont Ave. NW
    Suite 1120
    Washington, DC 20005
    (800) 850-4726/(202) 638-4101
    Fax: (202) 638-7257
    info@parkinsonsaction.org
    www.parkinsonsaction.org

Parkinson's Disease Foundation (PDF)
    1359 Broadway
    Suite 1509
    New York, NY 10018
    (212) 923-4700
    Fax: (212) 923-4778
    info@pdf.org
    www.pdf.org

Parkinson's Institute and Clinical Center
    675 Almanor Ave.
    Sunnyvale, CA 94085
    (408) 734-2800
    Fax: (408) 734-8522
    info@thepi.org
    www.thepi.org

Parkinson's Resource Organization
    74-478 Hwy. 111
    No. 102
    Palm Desert, CA 92260
    (877) 775-4111
    Fax: (760) 773-9803
    info@parkinsonsresource.org
    www.parkinsonsresource.org

Worldwide Education & Awareness for Movement Disorders (WE MOVE)

5731 Mosholu Ave.
Bronx, NY 10024
(347) 843-6132
Fax: (718) 601-5112
wemove@wemove.org
www.wemove.org

Bachmann-Strauss Dystonia & Parkinson Foundation
Fred French Building, 551 Fifth Ave. at 45th St.
Suite 520
New York, NY 10176
(212) 682-9900
Fax: (212) 987-0662
info@bsdpf.org
www.dystonia-parkinsons.org

Davis Phinney Foundation
4676 Broadway
Boulder, CO 80304
(866) 358-0285
Fax: (303) 733-3350
info@davisphinneyfoundation.org
www.davisphinneyfoundation.org

PARKINSON'S ORGANIZATIONS AROUND THE WORLD

Argentina

Grupo de Autoayuda Parkinson Argentina
Fundacion Alfredo Thomson
La Rioja 951
1221-Buenos Aires
Argentina
54 11 4932 4733
info@fund-thomson.com.ar
www.fund-thomson.com.ar/grupos.html

Acepar Asociacion Civil Enfermedad de Parkinson
Sarah Sidoti (Coordinadora)
Arroyo 980 P. 4°
Ciudad Autonoma e Buenos Aires
Capital Federala
1007

Argentina
54 11 4393 9422
Info@parkinsonargentina.org.ar
www.parkinsonargentina.org.ar

Australia

Parkinson's Australia Inc.
  Daryl Smeaton, CEO
  PO Box 717
  Mawson
  ACT 2607
  Australia
  61 407 703 328
  CEO@parkinsonaustralia.or.au
  www.parkisnosns.org.au

Parkinson's New South Wales
  PO Box 71
  North Ryde BC
  NSW 1670
  Australia
  61 2 8875 8900
  1800 644 189 (free phone, national)
  pnsw@parkinsonsnsw.org.au
  parkinsonsnsw.org.au

Parkinson's Queensland Inc.
  PO Box 1684
  Springwood
  QLD 4127
  Australia
  61 7 3209 1588
  1800 644 189
  pqi@parkinsons-qld.org.au
  www.parkinsons-qld.or.au

Parkinson's South Australia Inc.
  PO Box 466
  Unley
  SA 5061
  Australia
  61 8 8357 8909

info@parkinsonssa.org.au
www.parkinsonssa.org.au

Parkinson's Western Australia
   Centre for Neurological Support
   The Niche Suite B
   11 Aberdare Rd.
   Nedlands WA 6009
   Australia
   61 8 9346 7373
   pwaadmin@cnswa.com
   www.parkinsonswa.org.au

Brazil

Associação Brasil Parkinson
   Av. Bosque da Saúde
   1.155
   04142-092
   São Paulo—SP
   Brasil
   55 11 2578 8177
   parkinson@parkinson.org.br
   www.parkinson.org.br

APPP—Associação Paranaense dos Portadores de Parkinsonismo
   Av. Silva Jardim
   3180—Agua Verde
   80.240-021
   Curitiba—Paraná
   Brasil
   44 41 3014 5617
   www.appp.com.br

Canada

Parkinson Society Canada
   4211 Yonge St.
   Suite 316
   Toronto ON M2P 2A9
   Canada
   +1 416 227-9700
   (800) 565-3000 (regional)

general.info@parkinson.ca
www.parkinson.ca

Parkinson Society British Columbia
Suite 600, 890 W. Pender St.
Vancouver
BC V6C 1J9
Canada

Parkinson Society Canada
Maritime Region
7071 Bayers Rd.
Suite 150
Halifax
Nova Scotia
B3L 2C2
Canada
(902) 422-3656
(800) 663-2468
psmr@parkinsonmaritimes.ca
www.parkinsonmaritimes.ca

Parkinson Society Newfoundland & Labrador
136 Crosbie Rd.
Suite 305
St. John's
NL A1B 3K3
Canada
(709) 754-4428
(800) 567-7020
(709) 754-5868
parkinson@nf.aibn.com
www.parkinsonnl.ca

Parkinson Society Canada
Southwestern Ontario Region
4500 Blakie Rd.
Unit 117
London
Ontario
N6L 1G5
Canada
(519) 652-9437

(888) 851-7376
info@parkinsonsociety.ca
www.parkinsonsociety.ca

Parkinson Society Manitoba
  7, 414 Westmount Dr.
  Winnipeg
  MB R2J 1P2
  Canada
  (204) 786-2637
  (866) 999-5558
  howard.koks@parkinson.ca
  www.parkinson.ca

Parkinson Society Ottawa
  381 Kent St.
  Suite 300
  Ottawa
  Ontario
  K2P 2A8
  Canada
  (613) 722-9238
  (613) 722-3241
  psoc@toh.on.ca
  www.parkinson.ca

Parkinson Society Québec
  550 Sherbrooke West
  Suite 1080
  West Tour
  Montréal
  Québec
  H3A 1B9
  Canada
  (514) 861-4422
  (800) 720-1307
  infos@parkinsonquebec.ca
  www.parkinsonquebec.ca

Saskatchewan Parkinson's Disease Foundation
  PO Box 21010
  Gardiner Park RPO
  Regina

SK S4V 1J4
Canada
(306) 545-4400
(306) 790-9605
pss@sasktel.net
www.parkinson.ca

Parkinson Alberta Society
102, 5636 Burbank Crescent SE
Westech Building
Calgary
Alberta
T2H 1Z6
Canada
(403) 243-9901
(800) 561-1911
(403) 243-8283
info@parkinsonalberta.ca
www.parkinsonalberta.ca

Victoria Epilepsy and Parkinson's Centre
The Garth Homer Centre
813 Darwin Ave.
Victoria, BC
V8X 2X7
Canada
(250) 475-6677
(250) 475-6619
help@vepc.bc.ca
www.vepc.bc.ca

Chile

Liga Chilena contra el Mal Parkinson
Arturo Prat 1341
Barrio Av. Matta
Santiago
Chile
+56 2 555 7716
+56 2 554 5724
www.parkinson.cl

Czech Republic

Parkinson Slovácko o. s.
  Fr. Vlacha 1411
  696 03
  Dubňany
  Czech Republic
  420 511 119 420
  parkinson-slovacko@seznam.cz
  www.parkinson-slovacko.cz

Ethiopia

Parkinson Patients Association—Ethiopia
  PO Box 31
  Code 1032 Lafto
  Adddis Ababa
  Ethiopia
  + 251 1 09117 01362
  parkinsonassociation11@gmail.com

Germany

Deutsche Parkinson Vereinigung e.V.
  Moselstrasse 31
  41464 Neuss
  Germany
  +49 (0)2131/740 270
  +49 (0)2131/4 54 45
  info@parkinson-vereinigung.de
  www.parkinson-vereinigung.de

Kompetenznetz Parkinson
  Baldingerstrasse
  D-35043 Marburg
  Germany
  +49 (0)6421/5865 439
  +49 (0)6421/5865 308
  mahlae@med.uni-marburg.de
  www.kompetenznetz-parkinson.de

Hong Kong

Hong Kong Parkinson's Disease Association

Ground Floor
Wang Lai House
Wang Tau Hom Estate
Kowloon
Hong Kong
+852 2337 2292
+852 2337 2203
hkpda@netvigator.com
www.hkpda.org

Hong Kong Parkinson's Disease Foundation
Secretariat
Matilda Centre, Room A
Tung Chau Street
Kowloon
135-157
Hong Kong
+852 8100 5223
+852 2974 1171
info@hkpdf.org.hk
www.hkpdf.org.hk

India

Parkinson's Disease Society Gujarat
'Shaily' 9
Nehru Park Society
Opp. Loha Bhavan
Nr Gujarat High Court
Navrangpura
Ahmedabad 380 009
Gujarat
India
+91 7542371

Parkinson's Disease Foundation of India
604 Om chamber
Kemps Corner
August Kranti Maidan
Grant Road
Mumbai 400 036
India
+91 22 6664 0302

drmbhatt@gmail.com
www.parkinsonsdiseaseindia.com

Parkinson's Disease and Movement Disorder Society
6, Jasville, 1st Floor
Opp. Liberty Cinema
Marine Lines
Mumbai 400 020
India
+91 22 2200 7667
+91 99 6777 4944
mail@parkinsonssocietyindia.com
www.parkinsonssocietyindia.com

Indonesia

Yayasan Peduli Parkinson Indonesia
Perumahan Permata Puri blok F3 no 7
Cisalak
Cimanggis
Depok
Indonesia

Italy

L'associazione "Parkinsoniani Associati Mestre-Venezia e Provincia Onlus"
Via Brenta Vecchia
41 30172 Mestre Venezia
Italy
+39 041 983 108
+39 348 924 8317
info@parkinsonianiassociati.it
www.parkinsonianiassociati.it

Japan

Japanese Parkinson's Disease Association
3-1-11 Arai
Nakano-ku
Tokyo
165-0026
Japan
+81 (0)3 5318 3075
+81 (0)3 5318 3077

jpda@jpda-net.org
www.jpda-net.org

Malaysia

Negeri Sembilan Parkinson's Society (NSPS)
No 17, Bangunan Uda
70400 Seremban
Negeri Sembilan
Malaysia
+60 (0)3 606 763 6275/+60 (0)3 606 764 4177
+60 6 764 4179
Gharizah Hashim: gharizahh@gmail.com
Marchant Su: marchantsu@hotmail.com
www.nsmps-parkinson.org

Persatuan Parkinson Malaysia
Malaysian Parkinson's Disease Association
35 Jalan Nyaman 10
Happy Garden
58200 Kuala Lumpur
Malaysia
+60 (0)3 7980 6685
+60 (0)3 7982 6685
mpda1@streamyx.com
www.mpda.org.my

Mexico

Asociación Mexicana de Parkinson A.C.
Renato Leduc No. 113
04730
Mexico City
Mexico
52 43 94 36
contacto_ampac@yahoo.com.mx
www.parkinson.org.mx

Asociación Parkinson y Movimientos Anormales Mexico, A.C.
La Reyna 3616 Col. Chapalita
Zapopan
Jalisco
Mexico

CP 45040
+52 (33) 36 47 77 06
info@ParkinsonMexico.org
www.parkinsonmexico.org

Netherlands

Stichting Parkinson Plaza
    Postbus 67
    6680 AB
    Bemmel
    Netherlands
    info@parkinsonplaza.nl
    www.parkinsonplaza.nl

New Zealand

Parkinsons Auckland
    PO Box 16-238
    7a Taylors Road
    Sandringham
    Auckland
    New Zealand
    +64 (0)9 278 6918
    0800 000 408 (regional)
    +64 0(9) 845 2357
    aklparkinsons@xtra.co.nz
    www.parkinsonsauckland.org

Parkinson's New Zealand
    National Office
    Level 3, James Smith Buidling
    55 Cuba St.
    Wellington 6142
    New Zealand
    +64 (0)4 4722796
    +64 (0)4 4722162
    info@parkinsons.org.nz
    www.parkinsons.org.nz

Philippines

Parkinsons Support Group of the Philippines Foundation Inc.
    6,F Padilla Building

F. Ortigas Jr. Rd.
Ortigas Center
Pasig
Metro Manila
Philippines
+63 2 11531
+63 2 11546
parkinsons.ph@gmail.com

Saudi Arabia

King Faisal Specialist Hospital and Research Center
Movement Disorders Program
MBC#76
Department of Neurosciences
PO Box 3354
Riyadh 11211
Saudi Arabia
+966 (0)1 4647272 Ext.(32975)
+966 (0)1 4424763
mdp@kfshrc.edu.sa
www.movearabic.com

Singapore

Parkinson's Disease Society
c/o SNSA
26 Dunearn Rd.
Singapore 309423
+65 63535 338
+65 6358 4139
pdsspore@gmail.com
parkinsonsingapore.com

Spain

Apanet
Parkinson Internet Association
C/Collado de Mariches 3
3° A 28035
Madrid
Spain
+34 600 25 72 24
apanetmail@apanet.es

www.apanet.org.es

Párkinson Albacete
C/ Doctor Fleming, 12-2ª Planta
02003 Albacete
España
+34 96 755 89 08
parkinsonalbacete@hotmail.com
www.afepab.com

Párkinson Alcorcón
Centro de Asociaciones de la Salud
C/ Timanfaya, 15-23, local 2. Edificio Despachos
28924 Alcorcón
(Madrid)
España
+34 91 642 85 03
direccion@parkinsonalcorcon.org

Párkinson Alicante
C/ Lira, 5, Local A, entrada por C/Proción
17 bajo
03007 Alicante
España
+34 96 635 19 51
parkinsonalicante@hotmail.com

Párkinson Araba
C/ Pintor Vicente Abreu
7 bajo
01008 Vitoria-Gasteiz
(Álava)
España
+34 94 522 11 74
asopara@euskalnet.net

Párkinson Aragon
C/ Juslibol, 32-40
50015 Zaragoza
España
+34 97 613 45 08
asociacion@parkinsonaragon.com
www.parkinsonaragon.com

Párkinson Astorga
  C/ Juego de Cañas, 11 - 2° Dcha
  24700 Astorga
  (León)
  España
  +34 98 761 57 32
  parkinsonastorga@hotmail.com
  www.parkinsonastorgaycomarca.org

Párkinson Asturias
  C/ Ámsterdam
  733011 Oviedo
  (Asturias)
  +34 98 523 75 31
  aparkas@hotmail.com
  www.parkinsonasturias.org

Párkinson Ávila
  Centro Infantas Elena y Cristina
  Avda. Juan Pablo II, 20
  05003 Ávila
  España
  +34 92 025 20 69
  asociacionparkinsonavila@yahoo.es

Párkinson Bahia de Cadiz
  C/ Concha Perez Baturone, 9
  11100 San Fernando
  (Cádiz)
  España
  +34 95 659 19 28
  info@parkinsonbahiadecadiz.org
  www.parkinsonbahiadecadiz.org

Párkinson Bajo Deba
  C/ Ardanza, 1- bajo
  Apdo. 366 - 20600 Eibar
  (Guipúzcoa)
  España
  +34 94 320 26 53
  deparkel@deparke.org
  www.deparkel.org

Párkinson Balear
 C/ De la Rosa, 3 1º
 07003 Palma de Mallorca
 (Baleares)
 España
 +34 97 172 05 14
 info@parkinsonbalears.org
 www.parkinsonbalear.org

Parkinson Barakaldo
 C/ Murrieta, 13 bajo
 48901 Barakaldo
 Vizcaia
 España
 +34 654 692 879
 itziarzz@euskalnet.net

Párkinson Bizkaia
 C/ Erdikoetxe, 3 bajo
 48015 Bilbao
 (Vizcaya)
 España
 +34 94 448 32 70
 asparbi@euskalnet.net
 www.comunidades.kzgunea.net/ParkinsonBizkaia/ES/

Parkinson Blanes
 Avenida Juan Carlos I, 1
 17300 Blanes
 Girona
 España
 +34 972 35 00 35
 parkinsonblanes@telefonica.net
 www.parkinsonblanes.org

Párkinson Burgos
 Paseo de los Comendadores, s/n
 Centro socio-sanitario Graciliano Urbaneja
 09002 Burgos
 España
 +34 94 727 97 50
 asoparbur@gmail.com

www.parkinsonburgos.org

Párkinson Canarias
C/ Sor Brígida Castelló, 1
35001 Las Palmas de Gran Canaria
(Canarias)
España
+34 92 833 61 20
parkinsongrancanaria@hotmail.com

Párkinson Cartagena
C/ Carlos V, 3- bajo
30205 Cartagena
(Murcia)
España
+34 86 806 21 27
parkinsoncartagena@yahoo.es

Párkinson Castellón
C/ Cuadra Saboner, 1-bajo
12006 Castellón
España
+34 96 425 00 28
info@parkinsoncastellon.org
www.parkinsoncastellon.org

Párkinson Cataluña
C/ Concili de Trento, 16, Local 1
08018 Barcelona
España
+34 93 245 43 / +34 9693 246 16 33
associacio@catparkinson.org
www.catparkinson.org

Párkinson Ceuta
C/ Dr. Marañón, s/n (Junto a mercado)
51001 Ceuta
España
+34 95 652 12 82 /+34 95 650 99 50
asociacionparkinson@hotmail.com

Párkinson Comarques de tarragona
C/ Dr. Peyrí, 14–CAP de Sant Pere

43202–Reus
(Tarragona)
España
+34 66 649 23 03
parkinsonapct@terra.es

Párkinson Extremadura
C/ Baldomero Díaz de Entresoto, local 6
06800 Mérida
(Badajoz)
España
+34 92 430 32 24
parkinsonextremadura@hotmail.com
www.parkinsonextremadura.org

Párkinson Ferrol
Carretera de Castilla, 58-64 bajo A
15404 Ferrol
(A Coruña)
España
+34 98 135 95 93
parkinsonferrol@yahoo.es

Párkinson Galicia
Plaza Esteban Lareo, B1 17-sótano
Centro Gª Sabell
15008 A Coruña
España
+34 98 124 11 00
parkoru@telefonica.net

Párkinson Galicia-Bueu
Casa del mar de Bueu
C/ Montero Ríos, 18
36930 Bueu
(Pontevedra)
España
+34 98 632 45 77
parkinson.bueu@gmail.com

Párkinson Gandia-Safor
C/ Sant Pere, 54
46701 Gandia

(Valencia)
España
+34 96 295 09 54
safor@gmail.com

Párkinson Granada (Unidad de estancia diurna)
C/ Turina, 3 (Esquina C/Santa Clotilde)
18003 Granada
España
+34 95 852 25 47
parkinsongranada@hotmail.com
www.parkinsongranada.es

Párkinson Guipúzcoa
APaseo de Zarategui, 100. Edificio Txara
20015 San Sebastián
(Guipúzcoa)
España
+34 94 324 56 17
aspargui@aspargui.org
www.aspargui.org

Párkinson Hospitalet
C/ Josep Anselm Clavé, 24 Baixos
08902 L'Hospitalet de Llobregat
(Barcelona)
España
+34 93 332 48 83
Parkinson_lh_baix@hotmail.com

Párkinson Jovellanos
C/ Sta. Teresa, 11-bajo
33208 Gijón
(Asturias)
España
+34 98 515 09 76
asociacionparkinsonjovellanos@yahoo.es

Párkinson La Roda
Av. Juan García y González, 2
02630 La Roda
(Albacete)
España

+34 96 744 04 04
parkinson_laroda@castillalamancha.es

Párkinson Lorca
Avda. Alameda Cervantes, s/n
Local social "Paso a nivel"
30800 Lorca
(Murcia)
España
+34 96 847 87 02
aslep_2002@yahoo.es
www.parkinson.lorca.es

Párkinson Madrid
C/ Andrés Torrejó 18, Bajo
28014 Madrid
España
+34 91 434 04 06
parkinson@parkinsonmadrid.org
www.parkinsonmadrid.org

Párkinson Malaga
C/. Virgen de la Candelaria, s/n
Centro Social "Rafael González Luna"
29007 Málaga
España
+34 95 210 30 27
parkinsonmalaga@hotmail.com

Párkinson Móstoles
C/ Azorín, 32-34
Centro Social "Ramon Rubial"
28935 Móstoles
(Madrid)
España
+34 91 614 49 08
parkmostoles@telefonica.net

Párkinson Navarra
C/ Aralar, 17 bajo
31004 Pamplona
(Navarra)
España

+34 94 823 23 55
anapar2@hotmail.com
www.anapar.org

Párkinson Murcia
    C/ Clementes, 15 bajo
    30002 Murcia
    España
    +34 96 834 49 91
    parkinsonmurcia@regmurcia.com

Párkinson Segovia
    C/ Andrés Reguera Antón s/n
    Centro Integral de Servicios Sociales de la Albufera
    40004 Segovia
    España
    +34 92 144 34 00
    aparkinss@yahoo.es

Párkinson Sevilla
    C/ Fray Isidoro de Sevilla
    Hogar Virgen de los Reyes
    41009 Sevilla
    España
    +34 95 490 70 61
    parkinsonsevilla@arrakis.es
    www.parkinsonsevilla.org

Párkinson Soria
    C/ Diputación, 1
    Fundación Científica Caja Rural
    42002 Soria
    España
    +34 97 523 37 91
    parkinsonsoria@gmail.com

Párkinson Tenerife
    Avda. el Cordonal s/n-Pza. del Cordonal
    38108 Taco, La Laguna
    (Tenerife)
    España
    +34 92 262 53 90
    parkitfe@hotmail.com

Párkinson Valencia
C/ Chiva 10 bajo
46018 Valencia
España
+34 96 382 46 14
parkinsonvalencia@parkinsonvalencia.es
www.parkinson-valencia.com

Párkinson Valladolid
C/Aguilera s/n
47011 Valladolid
España
+34 98 329 23 84
aparval@hotmail.com
www.aparval.com

Párkinson Villarrobledo
C/ Luis de Góngora, 2A
02600 Villarrobledo
(Albacete)
España
+34 96 714 72 73
parkinsonvdo@telefonica.net

Párkinson Vigo
C/ Xilgaro, 17ª 4ºB
36205 Vigo
España
Att: José Fernández
+34 63 948 55 50
asociacionparkinsonvigo@gmail.com

South Africa

Parkinson's Disease & Related Movement Disorders Association of South
Africa
206 Barkston Dr.
Blairgowrie
Ranburg
Gauteng
2125
South Africa

+27 (0)11 787 8792
+27 (0)11 787 2047
karin.pasa@tiscali.co.za
www.parkindons.com.za

Taiwan

Taiwan Parkinson Association
c/o Department of Neurology
National Taiwan University Hospital
No. 7 Chung-shan South Rd.
Taipei
100
Taiwan
886 - 2 - 23123456 ext 5343

Appendix D

Parkinson's Disease Clinics

Columbia University Medical Center
   Neurological Institute
   710 West 168th St.
   3rd Floor
   New York, NY 10032
   (212) 305-5558

Comprehensive Parkinson Disease and Movement Disorders Clinic
   2000 6th Ave. S., 5th Floor
   Birmingham, AL 35233
   (205) 938-3847

Cox Health Parkinson's Clinic
   (417) 875-3681

Derby Parkinson's Disease Services
   London Road Community Hospital
   London Road
   Derby DE1 2QY England
   01332 254615

Florida National Parkinson Disease Center of Excellence
   3450 Hull Rd.
   Gainesville, FL 32607
   (352) 265-8408

Guy's and St. Thomas Parkinson's and Movement Disorders Clinic
Guy's Hospital Great Maze Pond
London SE1 9RT England
020 7188 7188

Maryland Parkinson's Disease and Movement Disorders
University of Maryland Medical Center
22. S. Greene St.
Baltimore, MD 21201
(800) 492-5538

Massachusetts General Hospital Parkinson's Disease and Movement Disorders Clinic
55 Fruit St.
Boston, MA 02114
(617) 726-2000

Mayfield Clinic
506 Oak St.
Cincinnati, OH 45219
(513) 221-1100
(800) 325-7787
comments@mayfieldclinic.com

Movement Disorders Clinic
University of Michigan Health System
1500 E. Medical Center Dr.
Ann Arbor, MI 48109
(734) 936-4000

Movement Disorders Clinic
Vanderbilt University Medical Center
1211 Medical Center Dr.
Nashville, TN 37232
(615) 936-0060

Muhammed Ali Parkinson Center
St. Joseph's Hospital and Medical Center
240 West Thomas Rd., Suite 301
Phoenix, AZ 85013
(602) 406-5266

Palliative Care Clinic for Parkinson's Disease at the Morton and Gloria Shulman Movement Disorders Center
Toronto Western Hospital
399 Bathurst Street, McLaughlin 7-421
Toronto, ON M5T 2S8 Canada
Fax: (416) 603 5004

Parkinson's Disease and Movement Disorders Clinic
Homerton University Hospital
Homerton Row, London, E9 6SR England
020 8510 5555
enquiries@homerton.nhs.uk

Parkinson's Disease Center and Movement Disorders Clinic
University of Kansas
Medical Center
3901 Rainbow Boulevard
Kansas City, KS 66160
(913) 588-5000

Parkinson's Disease and Movement Disorders Clinic at Beth Israel
330 Brookline Ave.
Boston, MA 02215
(617) 667-7000
(800) 439-0183

Parkinson's Disease Center at Kings Hospital Center
451 Clarkson Ave.
Brooklyn, NY 11203
(718) 245-3131

Parkinson's Disease Clinic
Royal Free Hospital
Pond Street
London NW3 2QG England
020 7794 0500
0844 8480700

Parkinson's Disease Clinic and Research Center
University of California, San Francisco
505 Parnassus Ave.
San Francisco, CA 94122

Parkinson's Disease Clinic at Bellevue Hospital Center
    462 First Ave.
    New York, NY 10016
    (212) 562-4141
    (212) 562-5555

Parkinson's Disease Research, Education and Clinical Center (PADRECC)
    (215) 823-5800
    (415) 221-4810

Houston PADRECC
    Interim Director: Aliya I. Sarwar, MD
    (713) 794-7841

Los Angeles (Southwest) PADRECC
    Director: Jeff Bronstein, MD, PhD
    (310) 478-3711

Philadelphia PADRECC
    Director: Matthew B. Stern, MD
    (888) 959-2323

Portland/Seattle (Northwest) PADRECC
    Director: Joseph Quinn, MD
    (503) 721-1091

Richmond (Southeast) PADRECC
    Director: Mark Baron, MD
    (804) 675-5931

San Francisco PADRECC
    Director: Graham Glass, MD
    (415) 379-5530

Penn Medicine Neuroscience Parkinson's Disease and Movement Disorders
Center
    Pennsylvania Hospital
    330 South 9th St.
    3rd Floor, Neurology
    Philadelphia, PA 19107
    (800) 789-PENN

St. John Providence Parkinson's Disease Clinic

St. John Hospital & Medical Center
Professional Building Two
22201 Moross Rd., Suite 360
Detroit, MI 48236
(313) 343-3073

University of Calgary Movement Disorders Clinic
Department of Clinical Neurosciences
Administration Office: Room 1195, Foothills Hospital
1403 29 St. NW
Calgary, Alberta T2N 2T9 Canada
(403) 944-1260
dcnsinfo@ucalgary.ca

University of North Carolina Interdisciplinary Parkinson Disease Clinic
University of North Carolina Department of Neurology
Physician's Office Building
170 Manning Dr.
Chapel Hill, NC 27599
(919) 843-1657

University of South Florida Parkinson's Disease and Movement Disorders
Center
Department of Neurology
12901 Bruce B. Downs Blvd., MDC 55
Tampa, FL 33612
(813) 974-3541
Fax: (813) 974-7138

Yale Parkinson's Disease and the Division of Movement Disorders
Yale Neurology Clinics
800 Howard Ave., Lower Level
New Haven, CT 06510
(203) 737-5259
Fax: (203) 785-4937

Appendix E

For Further Reading

Ahlskog, Eric. *Parkinson's Disease Treatment Guide for Physicians*. New York: Oxford University Press, 2009.

Belgum, David. *Living with Parkinson's Disease*. New York: Hamilton Books, 2008.

Biziere, Kathleen. *Living with Parkinson's Disease*. New York: Demos Vermande, 1997.

Bunting-Perry, Lisette. *Comprehensive Nursing Care for Parkinson's Disease*. New York: Springer, 2007.

Calne, Donald. *Advances in Neurology: Parkinson's Disease*. New York: Lippincott Williams & Wilkins, 2001.

Chaudhuri, Ray. *Non-Motor Symptoms of Parkinson's Disease*. New York: Oxford University Press, 2009.

Clough, Christopher. *Parkinson's Disease*. Albuquerque: Health Press, 2003.

Dawson, Ted Murray. *Parkinson's Disease: Genetics And Pathogenesis*. London: Informa Healthcare, 2007.

Duvoisin, Roger. *Parkinson's Disease: A Guide for Patient and Family*. Philadelphia: Lippincott Williams & Wilkins, 2001.

Edwards, Mark. *Parkinson's Disease and Other Movement Disorders*. New York: Oxford University Press, 2008.

Factor, Stewart. *Parkinson's Disease: Diagnosis and Clinical Management*. New York: Demos Medical Publishing, 2008.

Fernández, Hubert. *Ask the Doctor about Parkinson's Disease*. New York: Demos Medical Publishing, 2010.

Hunt Christensen, Jackie. *The First Year—Parkinson's Disease: An Essential Guide for the Newly Diagnosed*. Berkeley: Marlowe, 2005.

Jacob, Elliot. *Medifocus Guidebook On: Parkinson's Disease*. Silver Spring, MD: Medifocus, 2010.

Jankovic, Joseph. *Parkinson's Disease and Movement Disorders*. Philadelphia: Lippincott Williams & Wilkins, 2007.

Jenner, Peter. *A Molecular Biology Approach to Parkinson's Disease*. Amsterdam: IOS Press, 2000.

Koller, William. *Handbook of Parkinson's Disease*. Boca Raton: CRC Press, 2003.

Leader, Geoffrey. *Parkinson's Disease: Reducing Symptoms with Nutrition and Drugs*. London, Denor Press, 2006.

Lieberman, Abraham. *Shaking Up Parkinson Disease: Fighting Like a Tiger, Thinking Like a Fox*. Sudbury, MA: Jones and Bartlett, 2002.

Lieberman, Abraham. *100 Questions & Answers about Parkinson Disease*. Sudbury, MA: Jones and Bartlett, 2003.

Lyons, Kelly E. *Handbook of Parkinson's Disease*. New York: Taylor & Francis e-Library, 2005.

Marsden, David. *Parkinson's Disease: A Self-Help Guide*. New York: Demos Medical Publishing, 2000.

Meara, Jolyon. *Parkinson's Disease and Parkinsonism in the Elderly*. Cambridge, MA: Cambridge University Press, 2000.

Mittel, Charles. *Parkinson's Disease: Overview and Current Abstracts*. New York: Nova Science, 2003.

Müller, Thomas. *Diagnosis and Treatment of Parkinson's Disease: State of the Art*. New York: Springer, 1999, 210.

National Collaborating Centre for Chronic Conditions. *Parkinson's Disease, National Clinical Guideline for Diagnosis and Management*. London: Royal College of Physicians, 2006.

Pearce, John. *Parkinson's Disease and Its Management*. New York: Oxford University Press, 1992.

Pfeiffer, Ronald. *Parkinson's Disease*. Boca Raton: CRC Press, 2013.

Playfer, Jeremy. *Parkinson's Disease in the Older Patient*. London: Radcliffe, 2008.

Schapira, Anthony. *Parkinson's Disease*. New York: Oxford University Press, 2010.

Schapira, Anthony. *Principles of Treatment in Parkinson's Disease*. Philadelphia: Butterworth Heinemann Elsevier, 2005.

Schwarz, Shelley Peterman. *Parkinson's Disease: 300 Tips for Making Life Easier*. New York: Demos Medical Publishing, 2006.

Sharma, Nutan. *Parkinson's Disease and the Family: A New Guide*. Cambridge, MA: Harvard University Press, 2005.

Simuni, Tanya. *Parkinson's Disease*. New York: Oxford University Press, 2009.

Streifler, Max. *Parkinson's Disease: Anatomy, Pathology and Therapy*. Philadelphia: Lippincott Williams & Wilkins, 1990.

Tuite, Paul. *Parkinson's Disease: A Guide to Patient Care*. New York: Springer, 2009.

Weiner, William. *Parkinson's Disease: A Complete Guide for Patients and Families*. Baltimore: John Hopkins University Press, 2006.

Wellstead, Peter. *Systems Biology of Parkinson's Disease*. New York: Springer, 2012.

Wichman, Rosemary. *Navigating Life with Parkinson's Disease*. New York: Oxford University Press, 2013.

Willow, Marianne. *Focus on Parkinson's Disease Research*. New York: Nova Science, 2006.

Notes

PREFACE

1. "X-Plain Parkinson's Disease Reference Summary," US National Library of Medicine, National Institutes of Health, accessed November 24, 2012, www.nlm.nih.gov/medlineplus/tutorials/parkinsonsdisease.

2. L. I. Golbe, M. H. Mark, and J. I. Sage, *Parkinson's Disease Handbook* (New Brunswick: American Parkinson Disease Association, 2007).

3. W. Dauer and S. Przedborski, "Parkinson's Disease: Mechanisms and Models," *Neuron* 39, no. 6 (2003): 889–909.

4. Parkinson's Australia, "Mobility and Parkinson's Disease," Information Sheet 2.8, www.parkinsons.org.au/about-ps/pubs/InfoSheet_2.8.pdf.

5. Dauer and Przedborski, "Parkinson's Disease: Mechanisms and Models," 889–909.

6. P. Nausieda and G. Bock, *Parkinson's Disease: What You and Your Family Should Know* (New York: Parkinson's Disease Foundation, 2002).

7. Parkinson's Victoria, *Understanding Parkinson's Disease*, accessed January 12, 2013, http://www.parkinsonsvic.org.au/brochureenglish.pdf.pdf.

8. Parkinson's Disease Foundation, "Understanding Parkinson's: Parkinson's FAQ," 2010, accessed Febuary 2, 2013, www.pdf.org/pdf/fs_frequently_asked_questions_10.pdf.

9. Parkinson Society Canada, *Progression of Parkinson's Disease*, accessed November 22, 2012, www.parkinson.ca/atf/cf/%7B9EBD08A9-7886-4B2D-A1C4-A131E7096BF8%7D/progression%20of%20pd%20-%20en.pdf.

10. National Institute for Health and Clinical Excellence, "Parkinson's Disease: Diagnosis and Management in Primary and Secondary Care," June 2006, accessed December 13, 2012, http://publications.nice.org.uk/parkinsons-disease-cg35.

11. R. Hagestuen and M. S. Okun, *Parkinson Report* (Miami: National Parkinson Foundation, 2012).

12. Nausieda and Bock, *Parkinson's Disease: What You and Your Family Should Know*.

1. HISTORY OF PARKINSON'S

1. James Parkinson, "An Essay on the Shaking Palsy, 1817," *Journal of Neuropsychiatry and Clinical Neurosciences* 14, no. 2 (2002): 223–36.

2. "History of Parkinson's Disease," Viartis, accessed January 22, 2013, http://viartis.net/parkinsons.disease/history.htm.

3. Parkinson, "An Essay on the Shaking Palsy, 1817," 223–36.

4. Christopher Gardner-Thorpe, "James Parkinson (1755–1824)," *Journal of Neurology* 257 (2010): 493; Thomas C. Neylan, "Neurodegenerative Disorders: James Parkinson's Essay on the Shaking Palsy," *Journal of Neuropsychiatry and Clinical Neurosciences* 14, no. 2 (2002): 222.

5. Christopher Goetz, "The History of Parkinson's Disease: Early Clinical Descriptions and Neurological Therapies," *Cold Spring Harbor Perspectives in Medicine* 1, no. 1 (2011): 2; M. Parent and A. Parent, "Substantia Nigra and Parkinson's Disease: A Brief History of Their Long and Intimate Relationship," *Canadian Journal of Neurological Sciences* 37, no. 3 (2010): 316.

6. Anne Jeanjean and Genevieve Aubert, "Moving Pictures of Parkinson's Disease," *Lancet* 378, no. 9805 (2011): 1773.

7. Gardner-Thorpe, "James Parkinson," 493.

8. Goetz, "The History of Parkinson's Disease," 3.

9. D. Bereczki, "The Description of All Four Cardinal Signs of Parkinson's Disease in a Hungarian Medical Text Published in 1690," *Parkinsonism & Related Disorders* 16, no. 4 (2010): 290–93.

10. Bereczki, "Four Cardinal Signs," 290–93.

11. Parkinson, "An Essay on the Shaking Palsy, 1817," 223–36.

12. Marleide da Mota Gomes, "Neuronosology: Historical Remarks" [Neuronosologia: Observações históricas], Arquivos de Neuro-Psiquiatria 69, no. 3 (2011): 559–62.

13. Goetz, "The History of Parkinson's Disease."

14. Eric H. Chudler, "Milestones in Neuroscience Research," History of Neuroscience, accessed January 12, 2013, http://faculty.washington.edu/chudler/hist.html.

15. Da Mota Gomes, "Neuronosology: Historical Remarks," 559–62.

16. Da Mota Gomes, "Neuronosology: Historical Remarks," 559–62.

17. Da Mota Gomes, "Neuronosology: Historical Remarks," 559–62.

18. Da Mota Gomes, "Neuronosology: Historical Remarks," 559–62.

19. K. Tyler et al., "Part 2: History of 20th Century Neurology: Decade by Decade," in "History of the American Neurological Association in Celebration of the 125th Anniversary: *Tempus et Hora: Time and the Hour*," supplement, *Annals of Neurology* 53, no. S4 (2003): S27–S45.

20. Da Mota Gomes, "Neuronosology: Historical Remarks," 559–62.

21. Tyler et al., "History of 20th Century Neurology," S27–S45.

22. Tyler et al., "History of 20th Century Neurology," S27–S45.

23. Tyler et al., "History of 20th Century Neurology," S27–S45.

24. Tyler et al., "History of 20th Century Neurology," S27–S45.

25. Tyler et al., "History of 20th Century Neurology," S27–S45.

26. Goetz, "The History of Parkinson's Disease."

27. Tyler et al., "History of 20th Century Neurology," S27–S45.

28. Tyler et al., "History of 20th Century Neurology," S27–S45.

29. Tyler et al., "History of 20th Century Neurology," S27–S45.

30. Paul Unschuld, *Huang Di Nei Jing Su Wen: Nature, Knowledge, Imagery in an Ancient Chinese Medical Text* (Los Angeles: University of California Press, 2003).

31. Goetz, "The History of Parkinson's Disease."

32. Ecclesiastes 12:3.

33. Luke 13:11.

34. "Parkinson's Disease History," Parkinson's Disease Information, accessed November 14, 2012, www.parkinsons.org/parkinsons-history.html.

35. Parkinson, "An Essay on the Shaking Palsy, 1817," 223–36.

36. "History of Parkinson's Disease," Viartis, accessed January 22, 2013, http://viartis.net/parkinsons.disease/history.htm.

37. "History of Parkinson's Disease."

38. "History of Parkinson's Disease."

39. Bereczki, "Four Cardinal Signs," 290–93.

40. "History of Parkinson's Disease."

41. Goetz, "The History of Parkinson's Disease."

42. "History of Parkinson's Disease."

43. "History of Parkinson's Disease."

44. Goetz, "The History of Parkinson's Disease."

45. Tyler et al., "History of 20th Century Neurology," S27–S45.

46. J. W. Langston, "Accelerating Research on Genes and Environment in Parkinson's Disease," *Environmental Health Perspectives* 113, no. 2 (2005): 129.

47. Goetz, "The History of Parkinson's Disease," 2.

48. J. M. Pearce, "Aspects of the History of Parkinson's Disease," in "Special Supplement," supplement, *Journal of Neurology, Neurosurgery & Psychiatry* 52 (1989): S9.

49. Langston, "Accelerating Research," 129.

50. Langston, "Accelerating Research," 129.

51. Langston, "Accelerating Research," 129.

52. Langston, "Accelerating Research," 129; Richard Rosenbaum, *Understanding Parkinson's Disease: A Personal and Professional View* (Westport, CT: Greenwood, 2006), 72.

53. Langston, "Accelerating Research,"129.

54. Rosenbaum, *Understanding Parkinson's Disease*, 73.

55. Langston, "Accelerating Research,"129; Rosenbaum, *Understanding Parkinson's Disease*, 73.

56. Parent and Parent, "Substantia Nigra and Parkinson's Disease," 316.

57. Robert A. Hauser, "Levodopa: Past, Present, and Future," *European Neurology* 62 (2009): 2, accessed September 2, 2012, doi:10.1159/000215875.

58. Hauser, "Levodopa," 2.

59. Michael Balter, "Celebrating the Synapse," *Science*, October 2000, 424.

60. Parent and Parent, "Substantia Nigra and Parkinson's Disease," 318.

61. Hauser, "Levodopa," 2.

62. Hauser, "Levodopa," 2.

63. Hauser, "Levodopa," 3.

64. Jeanjean and Aubert, "Moving Pictures," 1173–74.

65. Pearce, "Aspects of the History," 10.

66. Pearce, "Aspects of the History," 9.

67. T. Foltynie and M. I. Hariz, "Surgical Management of Parkinson's Disease," *Expert Reviews of Neurotherapeutics* 10, no. 6 (2010): 903; Parent and Parent, "Substantia nigra and Parkinson's disease," 318.

68. Foltynie and Hariz, "Surgical Management of Parkinson's disease," 903.

69. J. G. Greenfield and F. D. Bosanquet, "The Brain-Stem Lesions in Parkinsonism," *Journal of Neurology, Neurosurgery & Psychiatry* 16, no. 4 (1953): 213.

70. Pearce, "Aspects of the History," 10.

71. Foltynie and Hariz, "Surgical Management of Parkinson's Disease," 903.

72. Parent and Parent, "Substantia Nigra and Parkinson's Disease," 318.

73. Foltynie and Hariz, "Surgical Management of Parkinson's Disease," 903.

74. Foltynie and Hariz, "Surgical Management of Parkinson's Disease," 903.

75. Foltynie and Hariz, "Surgical Management of Parkinson's Disease," 903.

76. Foltynie and Hariz, "Surgical Management of Parkinson's Disease," 904.

77. Pearce, "Aspects of the History," 10.

78. Niall Quinn, "David Marsden 1938–1998," *Advances in Clinical Neuroscience and Rehabilitation* 30, no. 2 (2010): 20.

79. David J. Brooks, "Professor C. David Marsden 1938–98," *Journal of Neurology, Neurosurgery, and Psychiatry* 66, no. 1 (1999): 2.

80. Quinn, "David Marsden 1938–1998," 20.

2. FAME AND PARKINSON'S

1. Christopher Gardner-Thorpe, "James Parkinson (1755–1824)," *Journal of Neurology* 257 (2010): 492.

2. John Pearn and Christopher Gardner-Thorpe, "James Parkinson (1755–1824): A Pioneer of Child Care," *Journal of Pediatrics and Child Health* 37, no. 1 (2001): 11.

3. J. M. Pearce, "Aspects of the History of Parkinson's Disease," in "Special Supplement," supplement, *Journal of Neurology, Neurosurgery & Psychiatry* 52 (1989): S6.

4. D. Burch and F. Sheerin, "Parkinson's Disease," *Lancet* 365 (2005): 623; Michael Jefferson, "James Parkinson 1755–1824," *British Medical Journal* 2, no. 5866 (1973): 601; Pearce, "Aspects of the History," S6.

5. Gardner-Thorpe, "James Parkinson," 492.

6. Burch and Sheerin, "Parkinson's Disease," 623.

7. Jefferson, "James Parkinson 1755–1824," 601.

8. Gardner-Thorpe, "James Parkinson," 493.

9. Gardner-Thorpe, "James Parkinson," 493; Jefferson, "James Parkinson 1755–1824," 602.

10. Burch and Sheerin, "Parkinson's Disease," 623.

11. Jefferson, "James Parkinson 1755–1824," 601.

12. Burch and Sheerin, "Parkinson's Disease," 623; Gardner-Thorpe, "James Parkinson," 492.

13. Gardner-Thorpe, "James Parkinson," 492.

14. Burch and Sheerin, "Parkinson's Disease," 625.

15. Gardner-Thorpe, "James Parkinson," 492.

16. James Parkinson, *Observations on the Nature and Cure of Gout; On Nodes of the Joints; and on the Influence of Certain Articles of Diet, in Gout, Rheumatism and Gravel* (London: Symonds, 1805), 16.

17. Gardner-Thorpe, "James Parkinson," 492.

18. Jefferson, "James Parkinson 1755–1824," 601.

19. Gardner-Thorpe, "James Parkinson," 493.

20. Gardner-Thorpe, "James Parkinson," 492.

21. Burch and Sheerin, "Parkinson's Disease," 625.

22. Parkinson, *Observations on the Nature and Cure of Gout*, 1–174.

23. Jefferson, "James Parkinson 1755–1824," 602.

24. Burch and Sheerin, "Parkinson's Disease," 625.

25. Parkinson, *Observations on the Nature and Cure of Gout*, 1–174.

26. Burch and Sheerin, "Parkinson's Disease," 626; Gardner-Thorpe, "James Parkinson," 493.

27. Pearn and Gardner-Thorpe, "James Parkinson (1755–1824)," 10.

28. James Parkinson, *An Essay on the Shaking Palsy* (London: Sherwood, Neely, and Jones, 1817).

29. Parkinson, *An Essay on the Shaking Palsy*, 29.

30. Burch and Sheerin, "Parkinson's Disease," 626; Thomas C. Neylan, "Neurodegenerative Disorders: James Parkinson's Essay on the Shaking Palsy," *Journal of Neuropsychiatry and Clinical Neurosciences* 14, no. 2 (2002): 222.

31. Parkinson, *An Essay on the Shaking Palsy*.

32. J. W. Langston, "Accelerating Research on Genes and Environment in Parkinson's Disease," *Environmental Health Perspectives* 113, no. 2 (2005): 129.

33. Gerald Stern, "Did Parkinsonism Occur before 1817?" in "Special Supplement," supplement, *Journal of Neurology, Neurosurgery, and Psychiatry* (1989): S12.

34. Parkinson, *An essay on the shaking palsy*, 1.

35. Christopher Goetz, "The History of Parkinson's Disease: Early Clinical Descriptions and Neurological Therapies," *Cold Spring Harbor Perspectives in Medicine* 1, no. 1 (2011): 3.

36. Goetz, "The History of Parkinson's Disease," 2.

37. Pearce, "Aspects of the History," 7.

38. Goetz, "The History of Parkinson's Disease," 2.

39. Pearce, "Aspects of the History," 7.

40. Pearce, "Aspects of the History," 8.

41. Pearce, "Aspects of the History," 7.

42. Pearce, "Aspects of the History," 9.

43. Goetz, "The History of Parkinson's Disease," 2.

44. Pearce, "Aspects of the History," 9.

45. Anne Jeanjean and Genevieve Aubert, "Moving Pictures of Parkinson's Disease," *Lancet* 378, no. 9805 (2011): 1773–74.

46. Goetz, "The History of Parkinson's Disease," 2.

47. Pearce, "Aspects of the History," 9.

48. Joseph Godwin Greenfield and Frances D. Bosanquet, "The Brain-Stem Lesions in Parkinsonism," *Journal of Neurology, Neurosurgery, and Psychiatry* 16 (1953): 213.

49. Pearce, "Aspects of the History," 9.

50. M. Parent and A. Parent, "Substantia Nigra and Parkinson's Disease: A Brief History of Their Long and Intimate Relationship," *Canadian Journal of Neurological Sciences* 37, no. 3 (2010): 317.

51. Parent and Parent, "Substantia Nigra and Parkinson's Disease," 316.

52. Graham McCann, "I Say! What a Bounder . . . All Dandy Comic Legend Terry-Thomas Really Liked was 'Jolly Eager Girls,'" *Mail Online*, September 5, 2008, accessed September 26, 2012, http://www.dailymail.co.uk/tvshowbiz/article-1052851/I-say-What-bounder--All-dandy-comic-legend-Terry-Thomas-really-liked-jolly-eager-girls.html.

53. Ronald Sullivan, "Ulysses Kay, Prolific Composer and Educator, Is Dead at 78," *New York Times*, May 23, 1995, accessed September 26, 2012, www.nytimes.com/1995/05/23/obituaries/ulysses-kay-prolific-composer-and-educator-is-dead-at-78.html.

54. Richard Goldstein, "Abe Lemons Is Dead at 79; Coached College Basketball," *New York Times*, September 6, 2002, accessed September 26, 2012, www.nytimes.com/2002/09/06/sports/abe-lemons-is-dead-at-79-coached-college-basketball.html.

55. "H R H Prince Claus of the Netherlands," *Telegraph*, October 8, 2002, accessed September 26, 2012, www.telegraph.co.uk/news/obituaries/1409427/H-R-H-Prince-Claus-of-the-Netherlands.html.

56. "Pope John Paul II Dies in Vatican," *BBC News*, April 3, 2005, accessed September 26, 2012, www.news.bbc.co.uk/2/hi/europe/4399715.stm.

57. Sarah Yang, "Donald Pederson, Pioneer in Integrated Circuit Design, Dies at 79," *UC Berkeley News*, January 5, 2005, accessed September 26, 2012, www.berkeley.edu/news/media/releases/2005/01/05_donpederson.shtml.

58. Eric Pace, "Theodore M. Edison; An Illustrious Father Guided Inventor, 94," *New York Times*, November 26, 1992, accessed September 26, 2012, www.nytimes.com/1992/11/26/obituaries/theodore-m-edison-an-illustrious-father-guided-inventor-94.html.

59. "'Sting' Director George Roy Hill Dies," *CBS News*, February 11, 2009, accessed September 26, 2012, www.cbsnews.com/2100-207_162-534537.html.

60. Bill Dwyre, "For Legendary Filmmaker Bud Greenspan, It Was All in the Games," *Los Angeles Times*, May 28, 2012, accessed September 26, 2012, www.articles.latimes.com/2012/may/28/sports/la-sp-oly-bud-greenspan-20120529.

3. ANATOMY AND PHYSIOLOGY OF PARKINSON'S

1. Jose A. Obeso et al., "Functional Organization of the Basal Ganglia: Therapeutic Implications for Parkinson's Disease," in "Levodopa Treatment and Motor Complications in Parkinson's Disease: Scientific Bases and Therapeutic Approaches," supplement, *Movement Disorders* 23, no. S3 (2008): 554.

2. Obeso et al., "Functional Organization of the Basal Ganglia," 550.

3. Niall Quinn, "Parkinsonism—Recognition and Differential Diagnosis," *British Medical Journal* 310, no. 6977 (1995): 449.

4. Charles Davie, "A Review of Parkinson's Disease," *British Medical Bulletin* 86 (2008): 120.

5. Davie, "A Review of Parkinson's Disease," 110.

6. C. Marsden, "Parkinson's Disease," *Journal of Neurology, Neurosurgery and Psychiatry* 57, no. 6 (1994): 674.

7. Ali Samii, John G. Nutt, and Bruce Ransom, "Parkinson's Disease," *Lancet* 363, no. 9423 (2004): 1785.

8. T. R. Guilarte et al., "Impairment of Nigrostriatal Dopamine Neurotransmission by Manganese Is Mediated by Pre-synaptic Mechanism(s): Implications to Manganese-Induced Parkinsonism," *Journal of Neurochemistry* 107, no. 5 (2008): 1236–47; M. Thiruchelvam et al., "Potentiated and Preferential Effects of Combined Paraquat and Maneb on Nigrostriatal Dopamine Systems: Environmental Risk Factors for Parkinson's Disease?" *Brain Research* 873, no. 2 (2000): 225–34.

4. CAUSES OF PARKINSON'S DISEASE

1. "Parkinson's Disease Statistics: An Overview," eMedTV, accessed October 15, 2012, http://parkinsons-disease.emedtv.com/parkinson%27s-disease/parkinson%27s-disease-statistics.html.

2. "Parkinson's Disease: Causes," Mayo Clinic, accessed October 14, 2012, www.mayoclinic.com/health/parkinsons-disease/DS00295/DSECTION=causes.

3. "Parkinson's Disease Statistics: An Overview."

4. "Genetic Causes of Parkinson's Disease," Viartis, accessed October 14, 2012, http://viartis.net/parkinsons.disease/genetic.causes.htm.

5. "Parkinson's Disease: Causes," Holistic Online, accessed October 14, 2012, http://www.holisticonline.com/Remedies/Parkinson/pd_causes.htm.

6. "Causes of Parkinson's Disease," University of Chicago Medical Center Department of Neurology, accessed October 20, 2012, http://parkinsons.bsd.uchicago.edu/causes.html.

7. Abraham Lieberman, "Parkinson Disease," *Microsoft Encarta 2009*, Microsoft Corporation, CD-ROM.

8. "Parkinson's Disease: Environmental Causes of PD," Movement Disorder Virtual University, accessed October 22, 2012, http://www.mdvu.org/library/disease/pd/par_ec.asp.

9. "Scientists Discover Genetic Mutation That Causes Parkinson's Disease," Mayo Clinic, accessed October 14, 2012, http://www.mayoclinic.org/news2011-jax/6431.html.

10. "A Possible Cause of Parkinson's Disease Discovered," ScienceDaily, accessed October 22, 2012, http://www.sciencedaily.com/releases/2011/02/110201122353.htm.

11. "Genetic Causes of Parkinson's Disease."

12. "Scientists Discover Genetic Mutation."

13. "Scientists Discover Genetic Mutation."

14. "Scientists Discover Genetic Mutation."

15. "Parkinson Disease," Genetics Home Reference, accessed December 3, 2012, http://ghr.nlm.nih.gov/condition/parkinson-disease.

16. Ted K. Koutouzis, "Parkinson's Disease," eMedicineHealth, accessed October 14, 2012, http://emedicinehealth.com/parkinson_disease/article_em.htm.

17. "Parkinson's Disease: Causes," Holistic Online.

18. "Differential Expression of Proteins in the Human Brain," Neuroscience Research Australia, accessed October 22, 2012, www.neura.edu.au/research/projects/differential-expression-proteins-human-brain.

19. Lieberman, "Parkinson Disease."

20. Lieberman, "Parkinson Disease."

21. "What Causes Parkinson's Disease?" WebMD, accessed October 22, 2012, www.webmd.com/parkinsons-disease/guide/parkinsons-causes.

22. Koutouzis, "Parkinson's Disease."

23. "Scientists Discover Genetic Mutation."

24. "What Causes Parkinson's Disease?"

25. "Parkinson's Disease: Causes," Holistic Online.

26. "Parkinson's Disease: Causes," Holistic Online.

27. "Parkinson's Disease: Causes," Holistic Online.

28. Koutouzis, "Parkinson's Disease."

29. "Parkinson's Disease: Causes," Holistic Online.

30. Lieberman, "Parkinson Disease."

31. Christian Nordqvist, "What Is Parkinson's Disease? What Causes Parkinson's Disease?" Medical News Today, accessed October 24, 2012, http://www.medicalnewstoday.com/info/parkinsons-disease/.

32. J. Stein et al., *Environmental Threats to Healthy Aging: With a Closer Look at Alzheimer's & Parkinson's Disease* (Boston: Greater Boston Physicians for Social Responsibility and Science and Environmental Health Network, 2008), 145–71.

33. "Parkinson's Disease," University of Pittsburgh Department of Human Genetics, accessed October 21, 2012, www.hgen.pitt.edu.

34. "Parkinson's Disease Risk Factors, Causes," Health Communities, accessed October 22, 2012, www.healthcommunities.com/parkinsons-disease/causes.shtml.

35. "Parkinson's Disease: Paralysis Agitans; Shaking Palsy," PubMed Health, accessed October 22, 2012, www.ncbi.nlm.nih.gov/pubmedhealth/PMH0001762/.

36. Stein et al., *Environmental Threats to Healthy Aging*, 145–71.

37. Nordqvist, "What Is Parkinson's Disease? What Causes Parkinson's Disease?"

38. Krisha McCoy, "The History of Parkinson's Disease," EverydayHealth, accessed October 25, 2012, www.everydayhealth.com/parkinsons-disease/history-of-parkinsons-disease.aspx.

39. Lieberman, "Parkinson Disease."

40. "Parkinson Disease."

41. "Genetic Causes of Parkinson's Disease."

42. Lieberman, "Parkinson Disease."

43. Lieberman, "Parkinson Disease."

44. Koutouzis, "Parkinson's Disease."

45. Parkinson's Disease: Causes," Holistic Online.

46. "What Causes Parkinson's Disease?"

47. "Genetic Causes of Parkinson's Disease."

48. "Genetic Causes of Parkinson's Disease."

49. McCoy, "The History of Parkinson's Disease."

50. McCoy, "The History of Parkinson's Disease."

51. McCoy, "The History of Parkinson's Disease."

52. McCoy, "The History of Parkinson's Disease."

5. SYMPTOMS IN GENERAL

1. Oksana Suchowersky and Gronseth Perlmutter, "Practice Parameter: Neuroprotective Strategies and Alternative Therapies for Parkinson Disease (An Evidence-Based Review): Report of the Quality Standards Subcommittee of the American Academy of Neurology," *Neurology* 66, no. 7 (2006): 976–82.

2. M. Barichella, E. Cereda, and G. Pezzoli, "Major Nutritional Issues in the Management of Parkinson's Disease," *Movement Disorders* 24, no. 13 (2009): 1881–92.

3. B. Crespi, P. Stead, and M. Elliot, "Comparative Genomics of Autism and Schizophrenia," in "Evolution in Health and Medicine Sackler Colloquium," supplement, *Proceedings of the National Academy of Science U.S.A.* 107, no. S1 (2010): S1736–41.

4. Crespi, Stead, and Elliot, "Comparative Genomics of Autism and Schizophrenia."

5. Blind Children Center, 4120 Marathon St., Los Angeles, CA 90029.

6. Lisa Kurtz, *Understanding Motor Skills in Children with Dyspraxia, ADHD, Autism, and Other Learning Disabilities: A Guide to Improving Coordination* (London: Jessica Kingsley, 2007).

7. Crespi, Stead, and Elliot, "Comparative Genomics of Autism and Schizophrenia."

8. Linda Harrison, Margaret J. Mayston, and Roland S. Johansson, "Reactive Control of Precision Grip Does Not Depend on Fast Transcortical Reflex Pathways in X-linked Kallmann Subjects," *Journal of Physiology* 527, no. 3 (2000): 641–52.

9. P. J. Koehler and A. Keyser, "Tremor in Latin Texts of Dutch Physicians: 16th–18th Centuries," *Movement Disorders* 12, no. 5 (1997): 798–806.

10. C. M. Burson and K. R. Markey, "Genetic Counseling Issues in Predictive Genetic Testing for Familial Adult-Onset Neurologic Diseases," *Seminars in Pediatric Neurology* 8, no. 3 (2001): 177–86.

11. Burson and Markey, "Genetic Counseling Issues."

12. E. D. Louis, "The Shaking Palsy, the First Forty-Five Years: A Journey through the British Literature," *Movement Disorders* 12, no. 6 (1997): 1068–72.

13. D. J. Brooks, "Imaging Approaches to Parkinson Disease," *Journal of Nuclear Medicine* 51, no. 4 (2010): 596–609.

14. M. Welsh, L. Hung, and C. H. Waters, "Sexuality in Women with Parkinson's Disease," *Movement Disorders* 12, no. 6 (1997): 923–27.

6. STAGE-BASED SYMPTOMS

1. R. Pahwa et al., "Practice Parameter: Treatment of Parkinson Disease with Motor Fluctuations and Dyskinesia (An Evidence-Based Review)—Report of the Quality Standards Subcommittee of the American Academy of Neurology," *Neurology* 66, no. 7 (2006): 983–95.

2. Paula Ford-Martin and Margaret Alic, "Parkinson's Disease Health Article," Yahoo! Health, accessed January 23, 2013, www.health.yahoo.net/galecontent/parkinsons-disease/.

3. C. G. Goetz et al., "Movement Disorder Society Task Force Report on the Hoehn and Yahr Staging Scale: Status and Recommendations," *Movement Disorders* 19, no. 9 (2004): 1020–28.

4. Ford-Martin and Alic, "Parkinson's Disease Health Article."

5. "10 Early Warning Signs of Parkinson's Disease," National Parkinson Foundation, accessed October 24, 2012, www.parkinson.org/Parkinson-s-Disease/PD-101/10-Early-Warning-Signs-of-Parkinson-s-Disease.aspx; "Parkinson's Disease: Hope through Research," National Institute of Neurological Disorders and Stroke, accessed January 22, 2013, www.ninds.nih.gov/disorders/parkinsons_disease/detail_parkinsons_disease.htm.

6. Ford-Martin and Alic, "Parkinson's Disease Health Article"; "Parkinson's Disease: Hope through Research."

7. Ford-Martin and Alic, "Parkinson's Disease Health Article."

8. Ford-Martin and Alic, "Parkinson's Disease Health Article"; Sietske N. Heyn, "Parkinson's Disease," MedicineNet, accessed December 2012, www.medicinenet.com/parkinsons_disease/article.htm#what_is_parkinsons_disease.

9. "Parkinson's Disease: Hope through Research."

10. "What Are the Symptoms of Parkinson's Disease?" National Parkinson Foundation, accessed December 4, 2012, www.parkinson.org/Parkinson-s-Disease/PD-101/How-do-you-know-if-you-have-PD-.

11. N. Hitzeman and F. Rafii, "Dopamine Agonists for Early Parkinson Disease," *American Family Physician* 80, no. 1 (2009): 28–30.

12. K. E. Anderson, "Dementia in Parkinson's Disease," *Current Treatment Options in Neurology* 6, no. 3 (2004): 201–7.

7. INPATIENT DIAGNOSTICS AND APPROACHES

1. "National Parkinson Foundation's Landmark Quality Improvement Initiative Enrolls 5,000 Parkinson's Patients," National Parkinson Foundation, April 23, 2012, accessed September 20, 2012, www.parkinson.org/About-Us/Press-Room/Press-Releases/2012/April/National-Parkinson-Foundation-s-Landmark-Quality-I.aspx.

2. Suzanne C. Smeltzer et al., *Textbook of Medical-Surgical Nursing*, vol. 2 (Philadelphia: Lippincott Williams & Wilkins, 2008), 2315.

3. Smeltzer et al., *Medical-Surgical Nursing*, 2315.

4. D. L. Bailey et al, eds., *Positron Emission Tomography: Basic Sciences* (Berlin: Springer-Verlag, 2003).

5. *Encyclopaedia Britannica*, 2011, s.v. "Single Photon Emission Computed Tomography (SPECT)."

6. National Collaborating Centre for Chronic Conditions, *Parkinson's Disease: National Clinical Guideline for Diagnosis and Management in Primary and Secondary Care* (London: Royal College of Physicians, 2006).

7. National Collaborating Centre for Chronic Conditions, *Parkinson's Disease*.

8. OUTPATIENT DIAGNOSTICS AND APPROACHES

1. Academy of Neurology, "Medical and Surgical Treatment for Parkinson Disease," Psych Central, 2012, accessed September 10, 2012, http://psychcentral.com/lib/2006/medical-and-surgical-treatment-for-parkinson-disease/.

2. "Speech and Swallow Therapy," UF Center for Movement Disorders & Neurorestoration, accessed September 15, 2012, http://mdc.mbi.ufl.edu/medicine/speech-and-swallow-therapy.

3. Patrick McNamara, "What Causes the Resting Tremor in Parkinson's Disease?," accessed September 15, 2012, http://parkinsons.about.com.

4. "Parkinson's Disease," Ohio State University Wexner Medical Center, accessed September 15, 2012, http://medicalcenter.osu.edu/patientcare/healthcare_services/parkinsons_disease/Pages/index.aspx.

5. Dan Bowman, "PET Scan Accurately Diagnoses, Differentiates Parkinson's Disease," FierceHealthIT, June 27, 2011, accessed September 13, 2012, www.fiercehealthit.com.

6. "DaTscan for Parkinson's: What Does It Mean?" Parkinson's Disease Foundation, accessed September 15, 2012, www.pdf.org/en/science_news/release/pr_1295578745.

7. Ravi Parikh, "Detecting Parkinson's with a Phone Call: TED Talk by Max Little," accessed September 15, 2012, http://medgadget.com.

8. "Max Little: A Test for Parkinson's with a Phone Call," TED video, 6:04, from a TED talk in June 2012, posted by TED (Technology, Entertainment, Design), August 2012, http://www.ted.com/talks/max_little_a_test_for_parkinson_s_with_a_phone_call.html.

9. DISORDERS ASSOCIATED WITH PARKINSON'S

1. Suzanne C. Smeltzer and Brenda G. Bare, *Brunner and Suddarth's Textbook of Medical-Surgical Nursing* (New York: Lippincott Williams & Wilkins, 2003), 1979–86.

2. "Parkinson's Disease: Hope through Research," National Institutes of Health, accessed December 4, 2012, www.ninds.nih.gov/disorders/parkinsons_disease/detail_parkinsons_disease.htm.

3. "Parkinson's Disease—Symptoms," NHS Choices, http://www.nhs.uk/Conditions/Parkinsons-disease/Pages/Symptoms.aspx.

4. D. J. Margolis, J. Knauss, W. Bilker, and M. Baumgarten, "Medical Conditions as Risk Factors for Pressure Ulcers in an Outpatient Setting," *Age and Ageing* 32, no. 3 (2003): 259–64.

5. "Secondary Motor Symptoms," Parkinson's Disease Foundation, accessed October 23, 2012, http://www.pdf.org/en/symptoms_secondary.

6. "Parkinson Disease," accessed January 3, 2013, http://emedicine.medscape.com/article/1831191-overview.

7. R. L. Doty, "Olfactory Dysfunction in Parkinson Disease," *Nature Reviews Neurology* 8, no. 6 (2012): 329–39.

8. Doty, "Olfactory Dysfunction."

9. "Orthostatic Hypotension (Postural Hypotension)," Mayo Clinic, accessed November 20, 2012, www.mayoclinic.com/health/orthostatic-hypotension/DS00997.

10. Tjalf Ziemssen and Heinz Reichmann, "Cardiovascular Autonomic Dysfunction in Parkinson's Disease," *Journal of Neurological Sciences* 289, nos. 1–2 (2010): 74–80.

11. C. Magerkurth, R. Schnitzer, and S. Braune, "Symptoms of Autonomic Failure in Parkinson's Disease: Prevalence and Impact on Daily Life," *Clinical Autonomic Research* 15, no. 2 (2005): 76–82.

12. Roberto Ceravolo, Carlo Rossi, Lorenzo Kiferle, and Ubaldo Bonuccelli, "Nonmotor Symptoms in Parkinson's Disease: The Dark Side of the Moon," Medscape, accessed October 14, 2012, http://www.medscape.com/viewarticle/734227_8.

13. "What Is Bruxism?" Bruxism Association, accessed October 23, 2012, http://www.bruxism.org.uk.

14. Ronald Pfeiffer, "Gastrointestinal and Urinary Dysfunction in PD," Parkinson's Disease Foundation, accessed October 22, 2012, www.pdf.org/en/spring07_gastrointestinal_and_urinary_dysfunction_in_pd.

15. Pfeiffer, "Gastrointestinal and Urinary Dysfunction."

16. Sharon Gillson, "Gastroparesis," About.com, accessed October 23, 2012, http://heartburn.about.com.

17. Z. S. Heetun and E. M. Quigley, "Gastroparesis and Parkinson's Disease: A Systematic Review," *Parkinsonism & Related Disorders* 18, no. 5 (2012): 433–40.

18. "Urination—Excessive at Night," last modified September 16, 2011, accessed February 4, 2013, www.nlm.nih.gov.

19. G. Schott, "Penfield's Homunculus: A Note on Cerebral Cartography," *Journal of Neurology, Neurosurgery, and Psychiatry* 56, no. 4 (1993): 329–33.

20. R. A. Armstrong, "Visual Signs and Symptoms of Parkinson's Disease," *Clinical and Experimental Optometry* 91, no. 2 (2008): 129–38.

21. G. Bronner, V. Royter, A. D. Korczyn, and N. Giladi, "Sexual Dysfunction in Parkinson's Disease," *Journal of Sex & Marital Therapy* 30, no. 2 (2004): 95–105.

22. Magerkurth, Schnitzer, and Braune, "Symptoms of Autonomic Failure."

23. Bronner, Royter, Korczyn, and Giladi, "Sexual Dysfunction."

24. Bronner, Royter, Korczyn, and Giladi, "Sexual Dysfunction."

25. Mitsuru Shiba et al., "Anxiety Disorders and Depressive Disorders Preceding Parkinson's Disease: A Case-Control Study," *Movement Disorders* 15, no. 4 (2000): 669–77.

26. C. Veazey et al., "Prevalence and Treatment of Depression in Parkinson's Disease," *Journal of Neuropsychiatry and Clinical Neuroscience* 17, no. 3 (2006): 310–23.

27. T. Foltynie, C. E. Brayne, T. W. Robbins, and R. A. Barker, "The Cognitive Ability of an Incident Cohort of Parkinson's Patients in the UK: The CamPaIGN Study," *Brain* 127, no. 3 (2004): 550–60.

28. "Mental Health Symptoms of Parkinson's," Parkinson's UK, accessed October 18, 2012, www.parkinsons.org.uk/default.aspx?page=10806.

29. Patrick McNamara, "Anxiety in Parkinson's Disease," About.com, August 28, 2009, accessed November 21, 2012, www.parkinsons.about.com/b/2009/08/28/anxiety-in-parkinsons-disease.htm.

30. E. Tandberg, J. P. Larsen, and K. Karlsen, "A Community-Based Study of Sleep Disorders in Patients with Parkinson's Disease," *Movement Disorders* 13, no. 6 (1998): 895–99.

31. Patrick McNamara, "Non-motor Symptoms of Parkinson's Disease," About.com, accessed December 16, 2012, www.parkinsons.about.com/od/signsandsymptomsofpd/a/Nonmotor.htm; J. P. Larsen and E. Tandberg, "Sleep Disorders in Patients with Parkinson's Disease: Epidemiology and Management," *CNS Drugs* 15, no. 4 (2001): 267–75.

32. Kevin J. Klos et al., "Pathological Hypersexuality Predominantly Linked to Adjuvant Dopamine Agonist Therapy in Parkinson's Disease and Multiple System Atrophy," *Parkinsonism Related Disorders* 11, no. 6 (2005): 381–86.

33. Daniel Weintraub et al., "Impulse Control Disorders in Parkinson Disease: A Cross-sectional Study of 3090 Patients," *Archives of Neurology* 67, no. 5 (2010): 589–95.

10. PAIN AND PARKINSON'S

1. L. Cleeves and L. J. Findley, "Frozen Shoulder and Other Shoulder Disturbances in Parkinson's Disease," *Journal of Neurology, Neurosurgery and Psychiatry* 52, no. 1 (1989): 813–14.

2. Marc E. Agronin and Gabe J. Maletta, *Principles and Practice of Geriatric Psychiatry* (New York: Lippincott Williams & Wilkins, 2011), 215.

3. B. Ford, "Pain in Parkinson's Disease," *Clinical Neuroscience* 5, no. 2 (1998): 63–72; J. I. Sage, "Pain in Parkinson's Disease," *Current Treatment Options in Neurology* 6, no. 3 (2004): 191–200.

4. B. Ford, "Pain in Parkinson's Disease," Parkinson's Disease Foundation, accessed December 22, 2012, www.pdf.org/en/winter04_05_Pain_in_Parkinsons_Disease.

5. K. Bayulkem and G. Lopez, "Clinical Approach to Nonmotor Sensory Fluctuations in Parkinson's Disease," *Journal of the Neurological Sciences* 310, nos. 1–2 (2011): 82–85.

6. Floyd E. Bloom, M. Flint Beal, and David J. Kupfer, *The Dana Guide to Brain Health: A Practical Family Reference from Medical Experts* (New York: Dana Press, 2006), 494.

7. Roger C. Duvoisin and Jacob Sage, *Parkinson's Disease: A Guide for Patient and Family* (Philadelphia: Lippincott Williams & Wilkins, 2001), 34.

8. Joseph Jankovic, *Dystonia: Seminars in Clinical Neurology* (New York: Demos Medical Publishing, 2005), 4.

9. Paul Tuite, Hubert Fernandez, Cathi Thomas, and Laura Ruekert, *Parkinson's Disease: A Guide to Patient Care* (New York: Springer, 2009), 40.

10. William G. Ondo, "Pain in Restless Legs Syndrome: A Guide to Help You Control and Manage Your RLS," *RLS Foundation Nightwalkers Archive* (Summer 2011): 1.

11. Elizabeth A. Coon and Ruple S. Laughlin, "Burning Mouth Syndrome in Parkinson's Disease: Dopamine as Cure or Cause?" *Journal of Headache and Pain* 13, no. 3 (2012): 255–57.

12. Bajaj Nin and K. Chaudhuri, *Pain in Parkinson's*, Parkinson's UK Publications (October 2011), 4.

13. Niall P. Quinn, "Classification of Fluctuations in Patients with Parkinson's Disease," *Neurology* 51, no. 2 (1998): S51.

14. Tuite, Fernandez, Thomas, and Ruekert, *Parkinson's Disease*, 38–40.

15. Laurie Mischley, *Natural Therapies for Parkinson's Disease* (Seattle: Coffeetown Press, 2009), 25.

16. Tuite, Fernandez, Thomas, and Ruekert, *Parkinson's Disease*, 42.

17. Karen Frei, Mayank Pathak, and Daniel Truong, *Living Well with Dystonia: A Patient Guide* (New York: Demos Medical Publishing, 2010), 77.

18. Mischley, *Natural Therapies for Parkinson's Disease*, 39.

19. K. Moriwaki, Y. Kanno, H. Nakamoto, H. Okada, and H. Suzuki, "Vitamin B6 Deficiency in Elderly Patients on Chronic Peritoneal Dialysis," *Advances in Peritoneal Dialysis* 16 (2000): 308–12.

20. Thomas C. Weiss, "Paresthesia—Facts and Information," Disabled World, April 15, 2010, accessed January 22, 2013, www.disabled-world.com/health/neurology/paresthesia.php.

21. Frei, Pathak, and Truong, *Living Well with Dystonia*, 55.

22. P. P. Ferry, M. Johnson, and P. Wallis, "Use of Complementary Therapies and Non-prescribed Medication in Patients with Parkinson's Disease," *Postgraduate Medical Journal* 78, no. 924 (2002): 612–14.

23. Ondo, "Pain in Restless Legs Syndrome."

24. J. M. Rabey, T. A. Treves, M. Y. Neufeld, E. Orlov, and A. D. Korczyn, "Low-Dose Clozapine in the Treatment of Levodopa-Induced Mental Disturbances in Parkinson's Disease," *Neurology* 45, no. 3 (1995): 432–34.

11. ALLOPATHIC TREATMENT

1. Rob Grant et al., *Parkinson's Disease: National Clinical Guidelines for Diagnosis and Management in Primary and Secondary Care* (Lavenham, UK: Lavenham Press, 2006), 3.

2. Norma Cuellar, *Conversations in Complementary and Alternative Medicine: Insights and Perspectives from Leading Practitioners* (Mississauga, Ontario: Jones and Bartlett, 2006), 4.

3. Rosanna Horton, *Will Collaboration or Affiliation between Allopathic Medical Schools and Complementary and Alternative Medicine Accredited School Better Incorporate CAM into Allopathic Medical School Curriculum?* (Miami: ProQuest, 2011), 132.

4. Leon Chaitow and Joseph Pizzorno Jr., *Naturopathic Physical Medicine Theory and Practice for Manual Therapists and Naturopaths* (New York: Elsevier, 2008), 4.

5. Rick Daniels, *Nursing Fundamentals: Caring and Decision Making* (New York: Delmar Learning, 2008), 812.

6. Richard Grossinger, *Planet Medicine: Modalities*, rev. ed. (Berkeley: North Atlantic Books, 1995), 484.

7. A. Lesage and A. Brice, "Parkinson's Disease: From Monogenic Forms to Genetic Susceptibility Factors," *Human Molecular Genetics* 18, R1 (2009): R48–59.

8. Anil Ananthaswamy, "The Parkinson's Fix," *New Scientist* 2457 (2004): 40.

9. M. Okun et al., "Mood Changes with Deep Brain Stimulation of STN and GPi: Results of a Pilot Study," *Journal of Neurology, Neurosurgery & Psychiatry* 74, no. 11, (2003): 1584–86.

10. Michele Tagliati and Selim Benbadis, "Stereotactic Surgery in Parkinson's Disease," Medscape, accessed November 23, 2012, http://emedicine.medscape.com/article/1153743-overview.

11. Stewart Factor and William Weiner, *Parkinson's Disease: Diagnosis and Clinical Management* (New York: Sheridan Press, 2008), 717.

12. "Thalamotomy for Parkinson's Disease," Norris Cotton Cancer Center Health Encyclopedia, accessed November 22, 2012, http://cancer.dartmouth.edu/pf/health_encyclopedia/aa140809.

13. Suzanne C. Smeltzer, Brenda G. Bare, Janice L. Hinckle, and Kerry H. Cheever, *Textbook of Medical-Surgical Nursing*, vol. 2 (Philadelphia: Lippincott Williams & Wilkins, 2008).

14. Stephen Dunnett, Lisa Kendall, Colin Watts and Eduardo Torres, "Neuronal Cell Transplantation for Parkinson's and Huntington's Disease," *British Medical Bulletin* 53 (no. 4) (1997): 756–776.

15. Andres Bjorklund et al., "Neural Transplantation for the Treatment of Parkinson's Disease," *Lancet Neurology* 2 (2003): 437–45.

16. S. B. Dunnett, A. C. Kendall, C. Watts, and E. M. Torres, "Neuronal Cell Transplantation for Parkinson's and Huntington's Diseases," *British Medical Bulletin* 53, no. 4 (1997): 761.

17. Bjorklund et al., "Neural Transplantation," 439.

18. "Surgery for Parkinson's Disease," WebMD, accessed September 10, 2012, www.webmd.com/parkinsons-disease/guide/parkinsons-surgical-treatments.

19. Rajesh Pahwa, Kelly Lyons, and William Koller, *Handbook of Parkinson's Disease* (New York: Mercel Dekker, 2009), 416.

20. "Parkinson's Disease—Treatment," Better Health Channel, accessed January 2, 2013, http://www.betterhealth.vic.gov.au/bhcv2/bhcarticles.nsf/pages/Parkinsons_disease_treatment.

21. Horst Przuntek, *Diagnosis and Treatment for Parkinson's Disease: State of the Art* (Berlin: Springer-Verlag, 1999), 75.

22. P. V. Rai, *Step by Step Treatment of Parkinson's Disease* (New Delhi: Jaypee Brothers Medical Publishers, 2010), 110.

23. Rai, "Step by Step Treatment of Parkinson's Disease."

24. "Long-Term Effects of Early Parkinson's Treatments Similar," Science Daily, March 9, 2009, accessed December 3, 2012, www.sciencedaily.com/releases/2009/03/090309162111.htm.

25. Warren Olanow, Fabrizio Stocchi, and Anthony Lang, *Parkinson's Disease: Non-motor and Non-dopaminergic Features* (London: Wiley, 2011).

26. Anthony Mosley, Deborah Romaine, and Ali Samii, *The Encyclopedia of Parkinson's Disease* (New York: Infobase, 2010), 20.

27. Marianne Willow, ed., *Focus on Parkinson's Disease Research* (New York: Nova Science Publishers, 2006), 45.

28. N. Borges, "Tolcapone in Parkinson's Disease: Liver Toxicity and Clinical Efficacy," *Expert Opinion on Drug Safety* 4, no. 1 (2005): 69–73.

29. Roger Duvoisin and Jacob Sage, *Parkinson's Disease: A Guide for Patient and Family* (Philadelphia: Lippincott Williams & Wilkins, 2001), 64.

30. "Is Treating Parkinson's Possible with New Neurotrophic Factor?" Science Daily, July 5, 2007, accessed September 13, 2012, www.sciencedaily.com/releases/2007/07/070704144646.htm.

31. R. B. Mythri and M. M. Bharath, "Curcumin: A Potential Neuroprotective Agent in Parkinson's Disease," *Current Pharmaceutical Design* 18, no. 1 (2012): 91–99.

12. OSTEOPATHIC TREATMENT

1. Glossary Review Committee of Educational Council on Osteopathic Principles (ECOP), *Glossary of Osteopathic Terminology* (Chevy Chase, MD: AACOM, 2011), 33.

2. Christopher T. Meyer and Albert Price, "Osteopathic Medicine: A Call for Reform," *Journal of the American Osteopathic Association* 93, no. 4 (1993): 473–85.

3. Walter Hartwig, *Med School Rx: Getting In, Getting Through, and Getting On with Doctoring* (New York: Kaplan, 2009), 28.

4. "Osteopathic Medicine," New York Institute of Technology College of Osteopathic Medicine, accessed January 22, 2013, www.nyit.edu/medicine/clinics/services_fhcc_CI/.

5. M. R. Wells et al., "Osteopathic Manipulation in the Management of Parkinson's Disease: Preliminary Findings," *Journal of the American Osteopathic Association* 100, no. 8 (2000): 521.

6. John C. Licciardone et al., "Osteopathic Manipulative Treatment of Somatic Dysfunction among Patients in the Family Practice Clinic Setting: A Retrospective Analysis," *Journal of the American Osteopathic Association* 105, no. 12 (2005): 537–44.

7. Kenneth E. Nelson and Thomas Glonek, *Somatic Dysfunction in Osteopathic Family Medicine* (Philadelphia: Lippincott Williams & Wilkins, 2007), 13.

8. Directory Review Committee of Osteopathic International Alliance, *Directories* (Chicago: Osteopathic International Alliance, 2012).

9. Larry A. Wickless, *The Osteopathic International Alliance: Unification of the Osteopathic Profession* (Chicago: Osteopathic International Alliance Steering Committee, 2006).

10. Mark E. Rosen, "The Philosophy of Osteopathy," Osteopathy: Art of Practice, accessed December 5, 2012, http://www.osteodoc.com/philosophy.htm.

11. Rosen, "Philosophy of Osteopathy."

12. "Doctor of Osteopathic Medicine," Penn State Hershey Medical Center, accessed November 13, 2012, http://pennstatehershey.adam.com/content.aspx?productId=117&pid=1& gid=002020.

13. Anthony G. Chila, *Foundations of Osteopathic Medicine* (Philadelpha: Lippincott Williams & Wilkins, 2009), 659.

14. Norman Gevitz, *The DOs: Osteopathic Medicine in America* (Baltimore, MD: Johns Hopkins University Press, 2004), 190.

15. S. T. Stoll, J. McCormick, B. F. Degenhardt, and M. B. Hahn, "The National Osteopathic Research Center at the University of North Texas Health Science Center: Inception, Growth, and Future," *Academic Medicine* 84, no. 6 (2009): 737–43.

16. Wells et al., "Osteopathic Manipulation," 521.

17. "Doctor of Osteopathic Medicine."

18. Tayson DeLengocky, "Osteopathic Medicine and the Growth of D.O. Graduates as Physicians," KevinMD.com, accessed December 16, 2012, www.kevinmd.com/blog/2011/03/osteopathic-medicine-growth-graduates-physicians.html.

19. Marc Jones, "How Safe is Osteopathy?" Osteopathic Vancouver, accessed January 4, 2013, www.osteopathyvancouver.com/may2006.html.

13. NATUROPATHIC TREATMENT

1. Jasnita Walia, *Naturopahy* (New Delhi: Fusion Books, 2003), 7.

2. Jerome Sarris and Jon Wardle, *Clinical Naturopathy: An Evidence-Based Guide to Practice* (Sydney: Elsevier, 2010), 32.

3. V. M. Kulkarni, *Healing through Naturopathy* (Lancaster, UK: Gazelle Book Services, 2002).

4. Kulkarni, *Healing through Naturopathy*.

5. Leah Hechtman, *Clinical Naturopathic Medicine* (London: Churchill Livingstone, 2012).

6. J. Vivas, P. Arias, and J. Cudeiro, "Aquatic Therapy [Hydrotherapy] versus Conventional Land-Based Therapy for Parkinson's Disease: An Open-Label Pilot Study," *Archives of Physical Medicine and Rehabilitation* 92, no. 8 (2011): 1202–10.

7. Karolyn A. Gazelle, "A Conversation with Bastyr University Researcher Leanna Standish about Naturopathic Research and Her Two NIH Funded Clinical Trials," interview, November 1, 2010, mp3 file, 30 min., *Natural Medicine Journal*, accessed September 16, 2012, www.naturalmedicinejournal.com/article_content.asp?article=70.

8. Richard Nelson-Jones, *Theory and Practice of Counseling & Therapy*, 3rd ed. (Thousand Oaks: Sage, 2003).

9. Sarris and Wardle, *Clinical Naturopathy*, 46–52.

10. P. Jenner, "Altered Mitochondrial Function, Iron Metabolism and Glutathione Levels in Parkinson's Disease," in supplement 2, *Acta Neurologica Scandinavica* 87, no. 146 (1993): 6–13.

11. R. N. Alcalay et al., "The Associations between Mediterranean Diet Adherence and Parkinson's Disease," *Movement Disorders* 27, no. 6 (2012): 771–74.

12. H. Tohgi et al., "Concentrations of Serotonin and Its Related Substances in the Cerebrospinal Fluid of Parkinsonian Patients and Their Relations to the Severity of Symptoms," *Neuroscience Letters* 150, no. 1 (1993):71–74.

13. K. C. Atwood, "Naturopathy: A Clinical Appraisal," *Medscape General Medicine* 5, no. 4 (2003): 39.

14. Atwood, "Naturopathy: A Clinical Appraisal," 39.

15. Christiaan M. Huidsen, "Modern-Day Naturopathic Medicine and Traditional Ayurveda in a Combined Attack against Parkinson's Disease," *Academic Journal of Suriname* 1 (2010): 53–58.

16. A. J. Lees, "Drugs for Parkinson's Disease," *Journal of Neurology, Neurosurgery and Psychiatry* 73 (2002): 607–10.

17. A. J. Lees, "Drugs for Parkinson's", 609–10.

18. O. Suchowersky et al., "Practice Parameter: Neuroprotective Strategies and Alternative Therapies for Parkinson Disease (An Evidence-Based Review)," *Neurology* 66, no. 7 (2006): 976–82.

19. G. Gorgone et al., "Coenzyme Q10, Hyperhomocysteinemia and MTHFR C677T Polymorphism in Levodopa-Treated Parkinson's Disease Patients," *Neuromolecular Medicine* 14, no. 1 (2012): 245–67.

20. Robert J. Ferrante et al., "Therapeutic Effects of Coenzyme Q10 and Remacemide in Transgenic Mouse Models of Huntington's Disease," *Journal of Neuroscience* 22, no. 5 (2002): 1592–99.

21. A. Lieu et al., "A Water Extract of Mucuna Pruriens Provides Long-Term Amelioration of Parkinsonism with Reduced Risk for Dyskinesias," *Parkinsonism & Related Disorders* 16, no. 7 (2010): 458–65.

22. Lieu et al., "A Water Extract of Mucuna Pruriens."

23. R. Katzenschlager et al., "Mucuna Pruriens in Parkinson's Disease: A Double Blind Clinical and Pharmacological Study," *Journal of Neurology, Neurosurgery and Psychiatry* 75, no. 12 (2004): 1672–77.

24. G. Lagalla et al., "Botulinum Toxin Type A for Drooling in Parkinson's Disease: A Double-Blind, Randomized, Placebo-Controlled Study," *Movement Disorders* 21, no. 5 (2007): 704–7.

25. Lagalla et al., "Botulinum Toxin," 705–6.

26. Kulkarni, *Healing through Naturopathy*, 59.

14. NONPRESCRIPTION TREATMENT

1. R. A. Armstrong, "Visual Signs and Symptoms of Parkinson's Disease," *Clinical and Experimental Optometry* 91, no. 2 (2008): 129–38.

2. P. Ferry, M. Johnson, and P. Wallis, "Use of Complementary Therapies and Non-prescribed Medication in Patients with Parkinson's Disease," *Postgraduate Medical Journal* 78, no. 924 (2002): 612–14.

3. Kelvin L. Chou, Robert A. Koeppe, and Nicolaas I. Bohnen, "Rhinorrhea: A Common Non-dopaminergic Feature of Parkinson Disease," *Movement Disorders* 26, no. 2 (2011): 320–23.

4. M. Barichella, E. Cereda, and G. Pezzoli, "Major Nutritional Issues in the Management of Parkinson's Disease," *Movement Disorders* 24, no. 13 (2009): 1881–92.

5. Barichella, Cereda, and Pezzoli, "Major Nutritional Issues," *Movement Disorders* 24, no. 13 (2009): 1881–92.

6. C. W. Shults et al., "Effects of Coenzyme Q10 in Early Parkinson Disease: Evidence of Slowing of the Functional Decline," *Archives of Neurology* 59, no. 10 (2002): 1541–50.

7. M. B. Youdim, D. Ben-Shachar, and P. Riederer, "Iron in Brain Function and Dysfunction with Emphasis on Parkinson's Disease," in supplement 1, *European Neurology* 31 (1991): 34–40.

8. M. Bousquet, "Beneficial Effects of Dietary Omega-3 Polyunsaturated Fatty Acid on Toxin-Induced Neuronal Degeneration in an Animal Model of Parkinson's Disease," *FASEB Journal* 22, no. 4 (2007): 1213–25.

9. M Anti et al., "Water Supplementation Enhances the Effect of High-Fiber Diet on Stool Frequency and Laxative Consumption in Adult Patients with Functional Constipation," *Hepatogastroenterology* 45, no. 21 (1998): 727–32.

10. Kelvin L. Chou, M. Evatt, V. Hinson, and K. Kompoliti, "Sialorrhea in Parkinson's Disease: A Review," *Movement Disorders* 22, no. 16 (2007): 2306–13.

11. Chou, Evatt, Hinson, and Kompoliti, "Sialorrhea in Parkinson's Disease."

12. L. Pérez-Macho and S. Borja-Andrés, "Digestive Disorders in Parkinson's Disease: Gastric Atony, Malabsorption and Constipation" [in Spanish], in supplement 2, *Revue Neurologique* 50 (2010): S55–58.

13. "Juicing: Your Key to Radiant Health," Mercola.com, November 13, 2011, accessed November 23, 2012, http://articles.mercola.com/sites/articles/archive/2011/11/13/benefits-of-juicing.aspx.

14. M. F. McCarty, "Does a Vegan Diet Reduce Risk for Parkinson's Disease?" *Medical Hypotheses* 57, no. 3 (2001): 318–23.

15. J. L. Barranco Quintana, M. F. Allam, A. S. Del Castillo, and R. F. Navajas, "Parkinson's Disease and Tea: A Quantitative Review," *Journal of the American College of Nutrition* 28, no. 1 (2009): 1–6.

16. X. Gao et al., "Habitual Intake of Dietary Flavonoids and Risk of Parkinson Disease," *Neurology* 78, no. 15 (2012): 1138–45.

17. R. B. Mounsey and P. Teismann, "Chelators in the Treatment of Iron Accumulation in Parkinson's Disease," *International Journal of Cell Biology* 2012 (2012): article ID 983245, doi:10.1155/2012/983245.

18. J. S. Lou, "Physical and Mental Fatigue in Parkinson's Disease: Epidemiology, Pathophysiology and Treatment," *Drugs & Aging* 26, no. 3 (2009): 195–208.

19. Ferry, Johnson, and Wallis, "Use of Complementary Therapies."

20. Claudio Pacchetti et al., "Active Music Therapy in Parkinson's Disease: An Integrative Method for Motor and Emotional Rehabilitation," *Psychosomatic Medicine* 62, no.3 (2000): 386–93.

21. Gammon M. Earhart, "Dance as Therapy for Individuals with Parkinson Disease," *European Journal of Physical Rehabilitative Medicine* 45, no. 2 (2009): 231–38.

22. M. S. Lee, B. C. Shin, J. C. Kong, and E. Ernst, "Effectiveness of Acupuncture for Parkinson's Disease: A Systematic Review," *Movement Disorders* 23, no. 11 (2008): 1505–15.

23. Suzanne C. Smeltzer, Brenda G. Bare, Janice L. Hinckle, and Kerry H Cheever, *Textbook of Medical-Surgical Nursing*, vol. 2 (Philadelphia: Lippincott Williams & Wilkins, 2008): 2315.

24. Ferry, Johnson, and Wallis, "Use of Complementary Therapies."

25. S. Polgar, "Ethics, Methodology and Use of Placebo Controls in Surgical Trials," *Brain Research Bulletin* 67, no. 4 (2005): 290–97.

26. Daniel E. Moerman, *Meaning, Medicine and the 'Placebo Effect'* (Cambridge: Cambridge University Press, 2002).

15. PREVENTION OF PARKINSON'S

1. E. Driver-Dunckley, J. Samanta, and M. Stacy, "Pathological Gambling Associated with Dopamine against Therapy in Parkinson's Disease," *Neurology* 61, no. 3 (2003): 422–23.

2. "Parkinson Disease," Genetics Home Reference, November 25, 2012, accessed November 27, 2012, http://ghr.nlm.nih.gov/condition/parkinson-disease.

3. G. W. Ross et al., "Association of Coffee and Caffeine Intake with the Risk of Parkinson Disease," *Journal of the American Medical Association* 283, no. 20 (2000): 2674–79.

4. A. Ascherio et al., "Prospective Study of Caffeine Consumption and Risk of Parkinson's Disease in Men and Women," *Annals of Neurology* 50, no. 1 (2001): 56–63.

5. Ascherio et al., "Prospective Study of Caffeine Consumption."

6. A. Ascherio et al., "Caffeine, Postmenopausal Estrogen, and Risk of Parkinson's Disease," *Neurology* 60, no. 5 (2003): 790–95.

7. K. P. Datla et al., "Short-Term Supplementation with Plant Extracts Rich in Flavonoids Protect Nigrostriatal Dopaminergic Neurons in a Rat Model of Parkinson's Disease," *Journal of the American College of Nutrition* 26, no. 4 (2007): 341–49.

8. X. Gao et al., "Diet, Urate, and Parkinson's Disease Risk in Men," *American Journal of Epidemiology* 167, no. 7 (2008): 831–38.

9. K. Murakami et al., "Dietary Intake of Folate, Vitamin B6, Vitamin B12 and Riboflavin and Risk of Parkinson's Disease: A Case-Control Study in Japan," *British Journal of Nutrition* 104, no. 5 (2010): 757–64.

10. Y. Moon et al., "Mitochondrial Membrane Depolarization and the Selective Death of Dopaminergic Neurons by Rotenone: Protective Effect of Coenzyme Q10," *Journal of Neurochemistry* 93, no. 5 (2005):1199–1208.

11. S. Zhang et al., "Intakes of Vitamins E and C, Carotenoids, Vitamin Supplements and PD Risk," *Neurology* 59, no. 8 (2002): 1161–69.

12. F. J. Jimenez-Jimenez et al., "Serum Levels of Beta-Carotene and Other Carotenoids in Parkinson's Disease," *Neuroscience Letters* 157, no. 1 (1993): 103–6.

13. X. Gao et al., "Habitual Intake of Dietary Flavonoids and Risk of Parkinson's Disease," *Neurology* 78, no. 15 (2012): 1112–13.

14. Alexandra Sifferlin, "Study: Flavonoids May Help Protect against Parkinson's," *Time*, April 5, 2012, accessed January 5, 2013, http://healthland.time.com/2012/04/05/study-flavonoids-may-help-protect-against-parkinsons/.

16. DIET AND PARKINSON'S

1. C. Anderson et al., "Dietary Factors in Parkinson's Disease: The Role of Food Groups and Specific Foods," *Movement Disorders* 14, no. 1 (1999): 21–27.

2. M. Etminan, S. S. Gill, and A. Samii, "Intake of Vitamin E, Vitamin C, and Carotenoids and the Risk of Parkinson's Disease: A Meta-Analysis," *Lancet Neurology* 4, no. 6 (2005): 362–65.

3. H. J. Powers, C. J. Bates and J. M. Duerden, "Effects of Riboflavin Deficiency in Rats on Some Aspects of Iron Metabolism," *International Journal for Vitamin and Nutrition Research* 53 (no. 4), (1983): 371–376.

4. K. Kashihara, "Weight Loss in Parkinson's Disease," in supplement 7, *Journal of Neurology* 253 (2006): VII38–41.

5. V. N. Kartha and S. Krishnamurthy, "Antioxidant Function of Vitamin A," *International Journal for Vitamin and Nutrition Research* 47, no. 4 (1977): 394–401.

6. M. Bousquet, F. Calon, and F. Cicchetti, "Impact of Omega-3 Fatty Acids in Parkinson's Disease," *Ageing Research Reviews* 10, no. 4 (2011): 453–63.

7. K. Murakami et al., "Dietary Intake of Folate, Vitamin B6, Vitamin B12 and Riboflavin and Risk of Parkinson's Disease: A Case-Control Study in Japan," *British Journal of Nutrition* 104, no. 5 (2010): 757–764.

8. P. Fernandez-Calle et al., "Serum Levels of Ascorbic Acid (Vitamin C) in Patients with Parkinson's Disease," *Journal of Neurological Sciences* 118, no. 1 (1993): 25–28.

9. L. M. de Lau and M. M. Breteler, "Epidemiology of Parkinson's Disease," *Lancet Neurology* 5, no. 6 (2006): 525–35.

10. M. G. Traber and H. Sies, "Vitamin E in Humans: Demand and Delivery," *Annual Review of Nutrition* 16 (1996): 321–47.

11. A. Tappel, "Vitamin E as the Biological Lipid Antioxidant," *Vitamins and Hormones* 20 (1962): 493–509.

12. M. L. Evatt et al., "High Prevalence of Hypovitaminosis D Status in Patients with Early Parkinson Disease," *Archives of Neurology* 68, no. 3 (2011): 314–19.

13. Y. Sato, M. Kikuyama, and K. Oizumi, "High Prevalence of Vitamin D Deficiency and Reduced Bone Mass in Parkinson's Disease," *Neurology* 49, no. 5 (1997): 1273–78.

14. C. S. Chan, T. S. Gertler, and D. J. Surmeier, "Calcium Homeostasis, Selective Vulnerability and Parkinson's Disease," *Trends in Neurosciences* 32, no. 5 (2009): 249–56.

15. S. Sirivech, J. Driskell, and E. Frieden, "NADH-FMN Oxidoreductase Activity and Iron Content of Organs from Riboflavin and Iron-Deficient Rats," *Journal of Nutrition* 107, no. 5 (1977): 739–45.

16. A. Wu, Z. Ying, and F. Gomez-Pinilla, "Dietary Omega-3 Fatty Acids Normalize BDNF Levels, Reduce Oxidative Damage, and Counteract Learning Disability after Traumatic Brain Injury in Rats," *Journal of Neurotrauma* 21, no. 10 (2004): 1457–67.

17. C. G. Coimbra and V. B. Junqueira, "High Doses of Riboflavin and the Elimination of Dietary Red Meat Promote the Recovery of Some Motor Functions in Parkinson's Disease Patients," *Brazilian Journal of Medical and Biological Research* 36, no. 10 (2003): 1409–17.

18. W. Duan et al., "Dietary Folate Deficiency and Elevated Homocysteine Levels Endanger Dopaminergic Neurons in Models of Parkinson's Disease," *Journal of Neurochemistry* 80, no. 1 (2002): 101–10.

17. PARKINSON'S AND EXERCISE

1. *New International Webster's Collegiate Dictionary of the English Language*, s.v. "exercise."

2. M. H. Mark and J. I. Sage, eds., *Young Parkinson's Handbook* (New York: American Parkinson Disease Association, Inc. 2000).

3. "Health Benefits of Exercise," NutriStrategy, accessed January 12, 2013, www.nutristrategy.com/health.htm.

4. "Parkinson's Disease and Exercise," Better Health Channel, accessed January 11, 2013, www.betterhealth.vic.gov.au/bhcv2/bhcarticles.nsf/pages/Parkinson%27s_disease_and_exercise?open.

5. "Parkinson's Disease and Exercise."

6. "Exercise: 7 Benefits of Regular Physical Activity," Mayo Clinic, accessed November 22, 2012, www.mayoclinic.com/health/exercise/HQ01676.

7. Noreen Kassem, "Exercises for Cognitive Skill Building," LiveStrong, May 8, 2010, accessed December 23, 2012, www.livestrong.com/article/118870-exercises-cognitive-skill-building/.

8. "Testing Your Mind, Strengthening Your Memory," *Washington Post*, accessed December 23, 2012, www.washingtonpost.com/wp-dyn/content/graphic/2007/01/03/GR2007010300535.html.

9. Kassem, "Exercises for Cognitive Skill Building."

10. Kassem, "Exercises for Cognitive Skill Building."

11. Melinda Smith and Lawrence Robinson, "How to Improve Your Memory," Helpguide, December 2012, accessed January 16, 2013, www.helpguide.org/life/improving_memory.htm.

12. *New International Webster's Collegiate Dictionary of the English Language*, s.v. "aerobics."

13. "Aerobic Exercise Improves Cognitive Functioning of Older Men and Women," Science Daily, January 17, 2001, accessed January 12, 2012, www.sciencedaily.com/releases/2001/01/010117074808.htm.

14. Catharine Paddock, "Fast Cycling Benefits Parkinson's Patients," Medical News Today, November 27, 2012, accessed December 28, 2012, www.medicalnewstoday.com/articles/253197.php.

15. Bastiaan R. Bloem, "Cycling is Less Affected Than Walking in Freezers of Gait," *Journal of Neurology, Neurosurgery & Psychiatry with Practical Neurology* 83, no. 5 (2011): 575–76.

16. *New International Webster's Collegiate Dictionary of the English Language*, s.v. "walk."

17. Jennifer Weuve et al., "Physical Activity, Including Walking, and Cognitive Function in Older Women," *Journal of American Medical Association* 292, no. 12 (2004): 1454–61.

18. "Exercises for the Parkinson Patient," Center of Neurologic Study, accessed January 20, 2012, http://www.cnsonline.org/www/archive/parkins/park-03.txt.

19. Fuzhong Li et al., "Tai Chi and Postural Stability in Patients with Parkinson's Disease," *New England Journal of Medicine* 366, no. 6 (2012): 511–19.

20. Marguerite Ogle, "What Is the Pilates Method of Exercise?" About.com, September 12, 2012, accessed January 2, 2012, http://pilates.about.com/od/whatispilates/a/WhatIsPilates.htm.

21. "Parkinson's Disease and Exercise."

22. "Parkinson's Disease and Exercise."

23. "Parkinson's Disease and Exercise."

24. "Parkinson's Disease and Exercise.".

25. "Parkinson's Disease and Exercise."

26. "Parkinson's Disease and Exercise."

27. "Parkinson's Disease and Exercise," National Center on Health, Physical Activity, and Disability, accessed January 19, 2013, www.ncpad.org/52/388/Parkinson~s~Disease~and~Exercise.

28. "Exercises For The Parkinson Patient," Center of Neurologic Study, accessed November 22, 2012, http://www.cnsonline.org/www/archive/parkins/park-03.txt.

29. Chelsea Hanson, "Exercise Safety Rules," LiveStrong, September 28, 2010, accessed November 14, 2012, www.livestrong.com/article/246453-exercise-safety-rules/.

30. "Exercise and Parkinson's Disease," WebMD, August 13, 2012, accessed December 4, 2012, www.webmd.com/parkinsons-disease/guide/parkinsons-exercise.

18. MOTIVATION IN PARKINSON'S

1. W. J. Weiner, *Parkinson's Disease: Diagnosis and Clinical Management* (New York: Demos Medical Publishing; 2002).

2. Robert S. Schwab and Lewis J. Doshay, "The Parkinson Patient at Home," The Center for Neurologic Studies, accessed October 20, 2012, http://www.cnsonline.org/www/archive/parkins/park-02.html.

3. Schwab and Doshay, "The Parkinson Patient at Home."

4. "The Importance of Motivation," About Balance & Control, accessed October 21, 2012, http://www.abc-stress.com/importance-of-motivation.html.

5. W. Huitt, "Motivation to Learn: An Overview," Educational Psychology Interactive, accessed November 5, 2012, www.edpsycinteractive.org/topics/motivation/motivate.html.

6. Linus Geisler, *Doctor and Patient—A Partnership through Dialogue*, Linus Geisler website, accessed October 21, 2012, www.linus-geisler.de/dp/dp00_contents.html.

7. "The Importance of Motivation."

8. Prasad R. Padala, William J. Burke, Subhash C. Bhatia, and Frederick Petty, "Treatment of Apathy with Methylphenidate," *Journal of Neuropsychiatry and Clinical Neurosciences* 19, no. 1 (2007): 81–83.

9. "Apathy and Negativity," Nelsons Natural World, accessed October 23, 2012, www.nelsonsnaturalworld.com/en-gb/uk/a-z-of-ailments/emotional-health/apathy-negativity/.

19. PARKINSON'S DISEASE AT HOME

1. Robert S. Schwab and Lewis J. Doshay, "The Parkinson Patient at Home," Center for Neurologic Study, accessed October 12, 2012, http://www.cnsonline.org/www/archive/parkins/park-02.txt.

2. C. W. Olanow, R. L. Watts, and W. C. Koller, "An Algorithm (Decision Tree) for the Management of Parkinson's Disease (2001): Treatment Guidelines," in supplement 5, *Neurology* 56, no. 11 (2001): S1–S88.

3. F.Taira, "Facilitating Self-Care in Clients with Parkinson's Disease," *Home Healthcare Nurse* 10, no. 4 (1992): 23–27.

4. Patrick McNamara, "The Emotional Challenges of Children Whose Parents Have Parkinson's Disease," About.com, accessed October 13, 2012, http://parkinsons.about.com/od/forcaregivers/a/children_of_pd.htm.

5. McNamara, "The Emotional Challenges."

6. Camille Peri, "Talking with Rasheda Ali-Walsh: Helping Children Cope with Parkinson'," Caring Incorporated, accessed October 13, 2012, www.caring.com/interviews/interview-with-rasheda-ali-walsh-about-helping-kids-cope-with-parkinson-s.

7. Rasheda Ali, *I'll Hold Your Hand So You Won't Fall: A Child's Guide to Parkinson's Disease* (West Palm Beach, FL: Merit Publishing, 2011).

8. McNamara, "The Emotional Challenges."

9. Schwab and Doshay, "The Parkinson Patient at Home."

10. Schwab and Doshay, "The Parkinson Patient at Home."

20. CONCLUSION

1. "Parkinson's Disease: Hope through Research," National Institute of Neurological Disorders and Stroke, accessed September 23, 2012, www.ninds.nih.gov/disorders/parkinsons_disease/detail_parkinsons_disease.htm.

2. "Parkinson's Disease: Hope through Research."

3. Bob Kuhn, "Parkinson's Disease and Hope," Insight for Living Canada, accessed September 25, 2012, www.insightforliving.ca/insights/parkinsons/parkinsons-disease-hope.html.

4. "Parkinson's Disease: Hope through Research."

5. "NINDS Mission," National Institute of Neurological Disorders and Stroke, accesssed September 12, 2012, www.ninds.nih.gov/about_ninds/mission.htm.

6. "About PDF," Parkinson's Disease Foundation, accessed September 23, 2012, www.pdf.org/en/about_pdf_sub.

7. "About Us," National Parkinson Foundation, accessed September 23, 2012, http://www.parkinson.org/about-us.aspx.

8. "Information & Referral Centers," American Parkinson Disease Association, accessed September 20, 2012, www.apdaparkinson.org/information-referral-centers/.

9. "Taking Care of You: Self-Care for Family Caregivers," Family Caregiver Alliance, accessed on September 12, 2012, www.caregiver.org/caregiver/jsp/content_node.jsp?nodeid=847.

10. Raymond B. Flannery Jr., "Disrupted Caring Attachments: Implications for Long-Term Care," *American Journal of Alzheimer's Disease and Other Dementias* 17, no. 4 (2002): 227–31.

11. M. Brod, G. A. Mendelsohn, and B. Roberts, "Patients' Experiences of Parkinson's Disease," *Journals of Gerontology: Psychological Sciences* 53, no. 4 (1998): 213–22.

12. Richard Shultz and Scott Beach, "Caregiving as a Risk for Mortality: The Caregiver Health Effects Study," *US National Library of Medicine* 282, no. 23 (1999): 2215–19.

Glossary

Acetylcholine. A neurotransmitter found in the peripheral nervous system and central nervous system and released to the synaptic clefts by process of exocytosis; it works by triggering muscle contraction.

Adrenaline. A hormone produced by the inner portion of the adrenaline glands, which react when there is elevated stress; also known as epinephrine.

Agraphia. A condition caused by damage in the language regions of the brain and thus affecting patients' writing ability.

Akinetic rigid syndrome. Symptoms where movement is too slow and stiffness of the muscle is felt; caused by increased dopaminergic denervation in the basal ganglia.

Amantadine. A drug prescribed to patients with Parkinson's disease that, when combined with levodopa, reduces the secretion of dopamine.

Aneurysm. A swelling condition of an artery caused by weakening of the artery walls.

Anhedonia. A symptom observed in patients with Parkinsonism characterized by the inability to feel happiness and enjoyment even when doing activities that give pleasure, such as sexual activities and social interactions.

Anticholergenic agent. A drug that inhibits transmission of nerve impulses by reducing and blocking the effects of acetylcholine receptors in the brain.

Aphasia. A disease observed in patients suffering from cerebrovascular accidents such as stroke wherein the patient loses the ability to speak.

Apoptosis. A type of cell death in which unneeded cells and dangerous cells, such as cancer cells, are eliminated via engulfment by the phagocytes.

311

Apraxia. A brain condition characterized by a patient's inability to synchronize muscle movement.

Arsenic. A natural element which, when combined with bromides and oxides, becomes a drug used to stimulate blood cell formation.

Basal ganglia. A portion of the brain made up of masses of gray matter that functions to receive input from the cerebral cortex and supply output to other parts of the cortex.

Belladonna alkaloids. A drug used to treat Parkinson's disease because of its ability to stop dopamine secretion.

Bradykinesia. A symptom of Parkinson's disease characterized by slowness of movement caused by impaired mobility.

Cannabis. A leaf used to treat Parkinson's disease because of its ability to activate dopamine.

Catechol-O-methyltransferase (COMT). An enzyme that works together with another enzyme, monoamine oxidase, to function in breaking down catecholamine chemicals.

Caudate nucleus. A type of basal ganglion that has a large head connected to a long, comma-shaped body. Together with the lentiform nucleus, it forms the corpus striatum.

Cerebellum. Second-largest part of the brain; controls balance and posture; considered to play a role in knowledge acquisition and language processing.

Cordotomy. A procedure of cutting certain pain fibers in the spinal cord that is performed on patients with extensive cancer or other incurable and painful conditions.

Dementia. A disease that affects a patient's mental coordination, causing a loss in the patient's ability to remember and judge, followed by changes in personality and leading to eventual insanity.

DOPA-decarboxylase inhibitor. A drug combined with levopoda that is used to treat the activity of dopaminergic systems in patients with Parkinson's disease, due to its reducing action in dopamine production.

Dopamine. One of the neurotransmitters included in the catecholamine family that help in transmission of nerve impulses for emotional responses, pleasurable experiences, and addictive behaviors.

Dopaminergic neuron. An iron-rich neuron found in the brain, particularly the substantia nigra, that synthesizes production of dopamine.

Dyscalculia. A learning difficulty characterized by inability to count or learn and comprehend arithmetic. Also known as numlexia.

Dystonia. A disorder exhibited by patients suffering from Parkinson's disease and characterized by abnormality in posture, muscle spasm, cramping, and pain.

Excitotoxicity. The destruction and death of neurons caused by elevated levels of a neurotransmitter called glutamate in the interstitial fluid of the central nervous system.

Extrapyramidal system. A network made up of somatic motor tracts that function for movement, involuntary reflexes, and coordination. This somatic motor tract includes rubrospinal, tectospinal, vestibulospinal, lateral reticulospinal, and medial reticulospinal.

Festination. A gait disorder exhibited by patients suffering from Parkinson's disease and caused by a lack of dopamine synthesized in the basal ganglion.

Free radical. An unstable and highly reactive atom or molecule that causes alteration or mutation of the genes and that damages the cell, particularly the DNA. This is considered to be one of the factors that cause Parkinson's disease.

Gag reflex. A reflex whose occurrence increases in Parkinson's disease patients; caused by elevated dopamine production in the central nervous system.

Gait disorder. A common symptom of Parkinson's disease characterized by abnormality in style of walking; caused by neuromuscular illness, aching, and changes in the body.

Gastroparesis. A condition characterized by a bloating sensation and discomfort of the stomach caused by damage to the nerves controlling the movement of food through the digestive system.

Globus pallidus. A part of the basal ganglion, particularly of the lentiform nucleus, that helps regulate movement on the subconscious level.

Glutamate. An amino acid produced by the mitochondria that acts as a neurotransmitter in the central nervous system. Together, gluatamate and aspartate have excitatory effects and cause damage to the nigrostriatal system.

Glutathione. An antioxidant that prevents damage of cells by neutralizing free radicals and compounds reactive to oxygen. Patients suffering from Parkinson's disease produce low amounts of antioxidants, particularly glutathione.

Hydrogen peroxide. A strong oxidizer that causes the increase of dopaminergic metabolism in the brain, which destroys the cell because of formation of free radicals.

Impulse control disorder. A type of behavioral disorder characterized by an inability to resist impulsive behavior that can harm the person who has the disorder or other people. This behavior is caused by drugs or medications used to treat Parkinson's disease.

Levodopa. A medication combined with carbidopa used in patients with Parkinson's disease. The drug is converted to dopamine, which helps relieve some symptoms.

Lewy bodies. Aggregates of proteins formed abnormally in the brain, particularly a-synuclein. Ages fifty and eighty-five are said to be the age range in which Lewy bodies develop.

Lipid peroxidation. A process by which lipids undergo oxidative breakdown; caused by actions of free radicals that damage the cell membrane, leading to cell death.

Meperidine. A narcotic used to relieve pain in patients suffering from Parkinson's disease because of its ability to destroy dopaminergic neurons.

Mesolimbic pathway. A type of dopaminergic pathway that is associated with reward and desire sensations. The pathway is affected when an individual suffers from Parkinson's disease.

Mitochondria. The part of the cell that functions to produce chemical energy known as adenosine triphosphate (ATP). In patients with Parkinson's disease, termination of dopamine secretion causes the mitochondria of particular brain cells to stop functioning.

Monoamine oxidase type B (MAO-B). An enzyme found in the outer layer of the mitochondria that breaks down dopamine secreted by the dopaminergic neurons.

Multiple sclerosis. A disease that affects the brain and spinal cord, mostly affecting women; symptoms are changes in speech, inability to walk, and partial paralysis.

Multiple system atrophy (MSA). A disease associated with Parkinson's because of a resemblance in symptoms; characterized by problems in movement, balance, and blood pressure regulation caused by the deterioration of nerve cells in some areas of the brain.

Necrosis. A type of premature cell death caused by external and internal factors, characterized by the breakdown of DNA, alteration of the cell plasma, and disappearance of the plasma membrane.

Neuromelanin. A dark pigment found in neurons of the substantia nigra, locus coereleus, and raphe nucleu produced by monoamine neurotransmitters.

Nigrostriatal dopaminergic pathway. A type of dopamine pathway that helps in production of movement.

NMDA receptor. A receptor of glutamate that plays a role in degradation of the brain's dopaminergic neurons.

Nocturia. An effect caused by hyperactivity of the detrusor muscle of the urinary bladder due to alteration of dopamine in the basal ganglion and causing the patient to wake up at night to urinate.

Norepinephrine. The main neurotransmitter of the nervous system and dopamine precursor that plays a role in dreaming, regulating mood, and awakening from deep sleep.

Pallidectomy. A treatment of Parkinson's disease by surgical excision of the ganglion cells in the thalamus of the brain.

Pallidofugal fibers. A fiber found in the globus pallidus of the basal ganglion that carries nerve impulses to the thalamus region and surrounding areas.

Paraplegia. A hereditary disease characterized by prolonged stiffness and contraction of the muscles. A disease caused by changes or mutations in the genetic material in precise genes of the chromosomes.

Paresthesias. A symptom observed in patients suffering from Parkinson's disease, characterized by burning, tingling, and prickling sensations as an effect of destruction of dopamine in the dopaminergic pathways.

Parkin. A protein produced by certain genes that causes destruction of dopamine by preventing protein buildup in the brain.

Phenobarbital. A drug used in calming nerves of patients suffering from shaking and contraction.

Phenytoin. Anticonvulsion drug that helps stabilize abnormal brain activities of patients suffering from seizure.

Plastic muscular hypertonicity. A symptom exhibited by patients with Parkinson's disease; characterized by stiffening of muscles, uncontrolled muscle spasms, and contraction of muscle groups.

Poliomyelitis. A disease obtained when a person is infected with a virus that affects the brain, causing partial or full paralysis. A patient with polio is treated with long-term rehabilitation and therapy.

Polyneuropathy. A neurological disease originating in damaged nerve cells caused by decreased blood flow, increased pressure on nerves, and inflammation of nerves.

Postencephalitic Parkinsonism. Weakening of nerve cells in the substantia nigra of individuals infected with the virus and causing Parkinsonism.

Presenile dementia. A disease exhibited by people of age sixty-five and younger. It is characterized by changes in personality or behavior, patients' experience of confusion of time and place, memory loss, and language problems.

Prolactin. A type of pituitary gland growth hormone that helps in production of milk and that plays an important role in maintaining structure of the ovary and hormones for pregnancy.

Putamen. A part of the dorsal striatum that functions in several motor skills, such as motor preparation, motor performance and task, motor learning, and movement. The development of Parkinson's disease affects the putamen, causing an uncontrolled production and or decrease of dopamine.

Pyrosis. A symptom characterized by feelings of burning sensations on the chest and abdomen experienced by patients suffering from Parkinsonism.

Serotonin. A neurotransmitter found in blood, the gastrointestinal tract, and the central nervous system and responsible for feelings of well-being and happiness.

Shaking palsy. A disease also known as paralysis agitans, characterized by shaking and trembling of hands, decreased muscular strength, and bending forward of the upper body.

Shell shock. A battle fatigue characterized by blindness, tremor, and paraplegia caused by damage to the spinal cord, cerebellum, and nervous system.

Shy-Drager syndrome. A disease caused by damage to regions of the self-governing nervous system; characterized by dizziness and fainting, momentary loss of consciousness, and problems in regulating body temperature.

Sleep apnea. A condition caused by Parkinsonism with the symptom of repeated abnormal pauses of breath during sleep for at least ten seconds due to loss of the pharyngeal muscle tone.

Striatal tyrosine hydroxylase. An enzyme synthesized by the striatum that helps neuron cells convert L-3,4-dihydroxyphenylalanine (L-dopa) to dopamine.

Striatum. A part of the brain located in the basal ganglion responsible for modulating movement, planning, and working memory. Increased and decreased activity of dopamine affects functions of the striatum, causing tremor and motor disabilities.

Substantia nigra. Part of the midbrain that controls eye movement and plays a role in learning, addiction, and motor planning. It is the part of the brain at risk of Parkinson's disease.

Supranuclear palsy. A disease that can be inherited from parents, affects the brain, and causes dementia, imbalance, fast walking, and fall.

Thalamic pain syndrome. A condition commonly observed in individuals who have suffered stroke; caused by damage in the thalamus portion of the brain. Characterized by pain and loss of sensation to parts of the body, specifically the arms, legs, and face.

Tissue plasminogen activator. A protein used to treat patients who have suffered from stroke; works by dissolving blood clot in nerves.

Tremor. A symptom observed in patients suffering from diseases in the nervous system, characterized by shaking or involuntary movement of the hands, eyes, legs, and head.

Vasomotor. Normal body mechanism that helps control the dilation and constriction of blood vessels in order to monitor continuous flow of impulses.

Wilson's disease. Genetic disorder that can be transmitted to patients' offspring, characterized by accumulation of copper in the kidney and brain, affecting the eyes.

Bibliography

PREFACE

Aragon, A., B. Ramaswamy, J. C. Ferguson, C. Jones, C. Tugwell, C. Taggart, F. Lindop, K. Durrant, K. Green, K. Hyland, S. Barter, and S. Gay. *The Professional's Guide to Parkinson's Disease*. London: Parkinson's Disease Society of the United Kingdom, 2007.

Fix, James D. "Basal Ganglia and the Striatal Motor System." In *Neuroanatomy*, 274–81. Board Review Series. Baltimore: Lippincott Williams & Wilkins, 2008.

Lang, A. E. "When and How Should Treatment Be Started in Parkinson Disease?." In "Supplement 2," supplement, *Neurology* 72, no. 7 (2009): S39–S43.

Parkinson's Australia. "Mobility and Parkinson's Disease." Information Sheet 2.8. www.parkinsons.org.au/about-ps/pubs/InfoSheet_2.8.pdf.

———. "Understanding Parkinson's Plus Syndromes and Atypical Parkinsonism." Fact sheet, Parkinson's Disease Foundation website. Accessed January 22, 2013. www.pdf.org/pdf/fs_parkinson_plus_atypical_08.pdf.

Weaver, F. M., K. Follett, M. Stern, K. Hur, C. Harris, W. J. Marks Jr., J. Rothlind, O. Sagher, D. Reda, C. S. Moy, R. Pahwa, K. Burchiel, P. Hogarth, E. C. Lai, J. E. Duda, K. Holloway, A. Samii, S. Horn, J. Bronstein, G. Stoner, J. Heemskerk, and G. D. Huang. "Bilateral Deep Brain Stimulation vs. Best Medical Therapy for Patients with Advanced Parkinson Disease: Randomized Controlled Trial." *Journal of the American Medical Association* 301, no. 1 (2009): 63–73.

CHAPTER 1

Ceravolo, R., D. Frosini, C. Rossi, and U. Bonuccelli. "Impulse Control Disorders in Parkinson's Disease: Definition, Epidemiology, Risk Factors, Neurobiology and Management." In "Proceedings of the LIMPE Seminar, 26–28 February, Pisa, Italy, 2009, 'Old and New Dopamine Agonists in Parkinson's Disease: A Reappraisal," supplement, *Parkinsonism & Related Disorders* 15, no. S4 (2009): S111–S115.

Charcot, J.-M. "On Parkinson's Disease." In *Lectures on Diseases of the Nervous System Delivered at the Salpêtrière*, translated by George Sigerson. London: New Sydenham Society, 1877, 129–56.

De Lacroix, F. B. *Nosologia Methodica*. Amsterdam: Sumptibus Fratrum de Tournes, 1763.

Factor, Stewart A., and William J. Weiner. *Parkinson's Disease Diagnosis and Clinical Management*. New York: Demos Medical Publishing, 2002.

García, Ruiz 2004. "Prehistoria de la Enfermedad de Parkinson" [Prehistory of Parkinson's disease]. *Neurologia* 19, no. 10 (2004): 735–37.
Gowers, W. R. "Paralysis Agitans." In *A System of Medicine*, edited by A. Allbutt and T. Rolleston, 156–78. London: Macmillan, 1899.
Hornykiewicz, O. "Dopamine Miracle: From Brain Homogenate to Dopamine Replacement." *Movement Disorders* 17, no. 3 (2002): 501–8.

CHAPTER 2

Barbeau, Andre. "L-Dopa Therapy in Parkinson's Disease: A Critical Review of Nine Years' Experience." *Canadian Medical Association Journal* 101 (1969): 59–68.
Lehmann, Helmar C., Hans-Peter Hartung, and Bernd C. Kieseier. "Leopold Ordenstein: On Paralysis Agitans and Multiple Sclerosis." *Multiple Sclerosis* 13 (2007): 1195–99.
Marsden, Charles A. "Dopamine: The Rewarding Years." *British Journal of Pharmacology* 147 (2006): 136–44.
Sourkes, Theodore L. "'Rational Hope' in the Early Treatment of Parkinson's Disease." *Canadian Journal of Physiology and Pharmacology* 77 (1999): 375–82.

CHAPTER 3

Davie, Charles Anthony. "A Review of Parkinson's Disease." *British Medical Bulletin* 86 (2008): 109–27.
Obeso, Jose A., Maria Rodríguez-Oroz, Beatriz Benitez-Temino, Francisco J. Blesa, Jorge Guridi, Concepció Marin, and Manuel Rodriguez. "Functional Organization of the Basal Ganglia: Therapeutic Implications for Parkinson's Disease." In "Levodopa Treatment and Motor Complications in Parkinson's Disease: Scientific Bases and Therapeutic Approaches," supplement, *Movement Disorders* 23, no. S3 (2008): S548–59.
Siegel, A., and H. N. Sapru. *Essential Neuroscience*. Rev. ed. Philadelphia: Lippincott, Williams & Wilkins, 2006.

CHAPTER 4

"Causes of Parkinson's Disease." University of Chicago Medical Center Department of Neurology. Accessed October 20, 2012. parkinsons.bsd.uchicago.edu/causes.html.
"Differential Expression of Proteins in the Human Brain." Neuroscience Research Australia. Accessed October 22, 2012. www.neura.edu.au/research/projects/differential-expression-proteins-human-brain.
"Parkinson's Disease." University of Pittsburgh Department of Human Genetics. Accessed October 21, 2012. http://www.hgen.pitt.edu/counseling/public_health/parkinsons.pdf.
"Parkinson's Disease: Causes." Holistic Online. Accessed October 14, 2012. http://www.holisticonline.com/remedies/parkinson/pd_causes.htm.
"Parkinson's Disease Risk Factors, Causes." Health Communities. Accessed October 22, 2012. http://www.healthcommunities.com/parkinsons-disease/causes.shtml.
"A Possible Cause of Parkinson's Disease Discovered." ScienceDaily. Accessed October 22, 2012. http://www.sciencedaily.com/releases/2011/02/110201122353.htm.

CHAPTER 5

Armstrong, R. A. "Visual Signs and Symptoms of Parkinson's Disease." *Clinical and Experimental Optometry* 91, no. 2 (2008):129–38.

Chaudhuri K. R., L. Yates, and P. Martinez-Martin. "The Non-motor Symptom Complex of Parkinson's Disease: A Comprehensive Assessment Is Essential." *Current Neurology and Neuroscience Report* 5, no. 4 (2005): 275–83.

McCoy, Krisha. "The History of Parkinson's Disease." Everyday Health. Accessed October 25, 2012. www.everydayhealth.com/parkinsons-disease/history-of-parkinsons-disease.aspx.

Mittel, Charles S., ed. *Parkinson's Disease Overview and Current Abstracts.* New York: Nova Science Publishers, 2003: 5–7.

Nordqvist, Christian. "What Is Parkinson's Disease? What Causes Parkinson's Disease?" Medical News Today. Accessed October 24, 2012. www.medicalnewstoday.com/info/parkinsons-disease/.

"Parkinson's Disease: Environmental Causes of PD." Movement Disorder Virtual University. Accessed October 22, 2012. www.mdvu.org/library/disease/pd/par_ec.asp.

"Parkinson's Disease: Paralysis Agitans; Shaking Palsy." PubMed Health. Accessed October 22, 2012. http://www.ncbi.nlm.nih.gov/pubmedhealth/PMH0001762/.

Politis, M., K. Wu, S. Molloy, P. Bain, K. R. Chaudhuri, and P. Piccini. "Parkinson's Disease Symptoms: The Patient's Perspective." *Movement Disorders* 25, no. 11 (2010): 1646–51.

Rieker, C., D. Engblom, G. Kreiner, A. Domanskyi, A. Schober, S. Stotz, M. Neumann, X. Yuan, I. Grummt, G. Schutz, and R. Parlato. "Nucleolar Disruption in Dopaminergic Neurons Leads to Oxidative Damage and Parkinsonism through Repression of Mammalian Target of Rapamycin Signaling." *Journal of Neuroscience* 31 (2011): 453.

"Scientists Discover Genetic Mutation That Causes Parkinson's Disease." Mayo Clinic. Accessed October 14, 2012. www.mayoclinic.org/news2011-jax/6431.html.

"What Causes Parkinson's Disease?" WebMD. Accessed October 22, 2012. www.webmd.com/parkinsons-disease/parkinsons-causes.

CHAPTER 6

Ford-Martin, Paula, and Margaret Alic. "Parkinson's Disease Health Article." Yahoo! Health. Accessed December 22, 2012. http://health.yahoo.net/galecontent/parkinsons-disease/.

Hitzeman, N., and F. Rafii. "Dopamine Agonists for Early Parkinson Disease." American Family Physician 80, no. 1 (2009): 28–30.

Pahwa, R., S. A. Factor, K. E. Lyons, W. G. Ondo, G. Gronseth, and H. Bronte-Stewart. "Practice Parameter: Treatment of Parkinson Disease with Motor Fluctuations and Dyskinesia (An Evidence-Based Review)—Report of the Quality Standards Subcommittee of the American Academy of Neurology." *Neurology* 66, no. 7 (2006): 983–95.

"Parkinson's Disease: Hope through Research." National Institute of Neurological Disorders and Stroke. Accessed January 22, 2013. http://www.ninds.nih.gov/disorders/parkinsons_disease/detail_parkinsons_disease.htm.

"10 Early Warning Signs of Parkinson's Disease." National Parkinson Foundation. Accessed November 23, 2012. www.parkinson.org/Parkinson-s-Disease/PD-101/10-Early-Warning-Signs-of-Parkinson-s-Disease.aspx.

CHAPTER 7

Bailey D. L., D. W. Townsend, P. E. Valk, and M. N. Maisey, eds. *Positron Emission Tomography: Basic Sciences.* New York: Springer-Verlag, 2003.

Biziere, Kathleen E., and Matthias C. Kurth. *Living with Parkinson's Disease.* New York: Demos Vermande, 1997.

Burneo, Jorge G., B. M. Demaerschalk, and M. E. Jenkins. *Neurology: An Evidence-Based Approach.* New York: Springer, 2011.

"Dopamine Agonists for Parkinson's Disease." WebMD. Accessed November 30, 2012. www.webmd.com/parkinsons-disease/dopamine-agonists-for-parkinsons-disease.

Factor, Stewart A., and William J. Weiner. *Parkinson's Disease*. 2nd ed. New York: Demos Medical Publishing, 2008.

Fuller, Geraint, and Mark Manford. *Neurology*. New York: Elsevier Health Sciences, 2000.

Okun, Michael S., and Hubert H. Fernandez. *Ask the Doctor about Parkinson's Disease*. New York: Demos Medical Publishing, 2012.

"Parkinson's Disease—Antidepressants." Medline Plus. Accessed September 13, 2012. www.nlm.nih.gov.

"Parkinson's Disease: Management." Clinical Knowledge Summaries, National Institute for Health and Care Excellence. Accessed November 18, 2012. http://cks.nice.org.uk/parkinsons-disease#azTab.

"Parkinson's Disease—Surgery." WebMD. Accessed October 3, 2012. www.webmd.com/parkinsons-disease/tc/parkinsons-disease-surgery.

"Poor Medication Management of Parkinson's Disease during Hospital Admissions: Patients and Families Can Improve Their Hospital-Based Management." Parkinson's Disease Foundation. Accessed November 5, 2012. www.parkinson.org/Patients/Patients---On-The-Blog/July-2010/Poor-Medication-Management-of-Parkinson-s-Disease-.

Schwarz, Shelley Peterman. *Parkinson's Disease: 300 Tips for Making Life Easier*. New York: Demos Medical Publishing, 2006.

CHAPTER 8

Ceballos-Baumann, Andres. "Parkinson's (Parkinson's Disease, Parkinson's Plus Syndrome). Diagnostics." Schön Klinik. Accessed September 10, 2012. http://www.schoen-kliniken.com/ptp/medizin/nerven/fortschreitend/parkinson/diagnostik/.

Murray, Peter. "Cutting Edge Gene Therapy Successfully Treats Parkinson's Symptoms." Singularity Hub. Accessed September 5, 2012. http://singularityhub.com/2011/04/13/cutting-edge-gene-therapy-successfully-treats-parkinsons-symptoms/.

Schoenstadt, Arthur. "Who Discovered Parkinson's Disease?" eMedTV. Accessed September 10, 2012. http://parkinsons-disease.emedtv.com/parkinson%27s-disease/who-discovered-parkinson%27s-disease.html.

Schrag, A., Y. Ben-Shlomo, and N. Quinn. "How Valid Is the Clinical Diagnosis of Parkinson's Disease in the Community?" *Journal of Neurology, Neurosurgery & Psychiatry with Practical Neurology* 73, no. 5: 529–34. Accessed September 10, 2012. http://jnnp.bmj.com/content/73/5/529.full.

The Inspiring Voices of People with Parkinson's. UCB Parkinson's Voices. Accessed September 15, 2012. http://www.parkinsons-voices.eu/_up/pv_eu/documents/The-inspiring-voices-of-people-with-parkinsons-07-2010.pdf.

Haomin Wang, Yanli Pan, Bing Xue, Xinhong Wang, Feng Zhao, Jun Jia, Xibin Liang, and Xiaomin Wang. "The Antioxidative Effect of Electro-Acupuncture in a Mouse Model of Parkinson's Disease." *PLOS One* 6, no. 5 (2011). Accessed September 10, 2012. http://www.ncbi.nlm.nih.gov/pmc/articles/PMC3100295/.

CHAPTER 9

Ceravolo, Roberto, Carlo Rossi, Lorenzo Kiferle, and Ubaldo Bonuccelli. "Nonmotor Symptoms in Parkinson's Disease: The Dark Side of the Moon." *Future Neurology* 5, no. 6 (2010): 851–71. Medscape. Accessed October 14, 2012. www.medscape.com/viewarticle/734227_8.

Weintraub D., J. Koester, M. N. Potenza, A. D. Siderowf, M. Stacy, V. Voon, J. Whetteckey, G. R. Wunderlich, and A. E. Lange. "Impulse Control Disorders in Parkinson Disease: A Cross-sectional Study of 3090 Patients." *Archives of Neurology* 67 (2010):589–95.

CHAPTER 10

Grimes, David A. *Parkinson's: Everything You Need to Know.* New York: Firefly Books, 2004.

Jankovic, Joseph. "Treatment of Dystonia." *Lancet Neurology* 5, no. 10 (2006): 864–72.

Jankovic, Joseph, and Ron Tintner. "Dystonia and Parkinsonism." *Parkinsonism and Related Disorders* 8, no. 2 (2001): 109–21.

Jankovic, Joseph, and Eduardo Tolosa. *Parkinson's Disease and Movement Disorders: Laboratory Management and Clinical Correlations.* Philadelphia: Lippincott Williams & Wilkins, 2007.

Ronken, Eric, and Guss Van Scharrenburg. *Parkinson's Disease.* Amsterdam, Netherlands: IOS Press, 2002.

Tugwell, Charles. *Parkinson's Disease in Focus.* Chicago: Pharmaceutical Press, 2008.

CHAPTER 11

Alzheimer's Association. "Alzheimer's Disease Facts and Figures," *Alzheimer's & Dementia* 8, no. 2: 2012.

Ascherio A., H. Chen, M. A. Schwarzschikd, S. M. Zhang, G. A. Colditz, and F. E. Speizer. "Caffeine, Postmenopausal Estrogen, and Risk of Parkinson's Disease." *Neurology* 60, no. 5 (2003): 790–95.

Carpenter, David O., Kathleen Arcaro, and David C. Spink. "Understanding the Human Health Effects of Chemical Mixtures." In "Reviews in Environmental Health 2002," supplement, *Environmental Health Perspectives* 110 (2002): S25–S42.

Chu, J., and J. Singh. "Deep Brain Stimulation in Parkinson's Disease." *American Journal of Nursing* 109 (2009): 6–31.

Datla, K. P., V. Zbarsky, D. Rai, S. Parkar, N. Osakabe, O. I. Aruoma, and D. T. Dexter. "Short-Term Supplementation with Plant Extracts Rich in Flavonoids Protect Nigrostriatal Dopaminergic Neurons in a Rat Model of Parkinson's Disease." *Journal of the American College of Nutrition* 26, no. 4 (2007): 341–49.

Gordon, B., and M. Stern. *Deep Brain Stimulation for Parkinson's Disease.* New York: Taylor & Francis, 2008.

Hauser, Robert A., Mark F. Lew, Howard I. Hurtig, William G. Ondo, Joanne Wojcieszek, and Cheryl J. Fitzer-Attas. "Long-Term Outcome of Early versus Delayed Rasagiline Treatment in Early Parkinson's Disease." *Movement Disorders* 24, no. 4 (2009): 564–73.

Jarrett, Doreen. *Explaining Parkinson's.* London: Emerald Publishing, 2011.

Lyotard, Jean-François. *The Postmodern Condition: A Report on Knowledge.* Minneapolis: University of Minnesota Press, 1984.

"Mediterranean Diet—Topic Overview." WebMD. Accessed November 29, 2012. www.webmd.com/heart-disease/tc/mediterranean-diet-topic-overview.

Mercola, J. "How to Diagnose Iron Overload." Mercola.com, December 18, 2002. Accessed November 29, 2012. http://articles.mercola.com/sites/articles/archive/2002/12/18/iron-diagnosis.aspx.

Moon Y., K. H. Lee, J. H. Park, D. Geum, and K. Kim. "Mitochondrial Membrane Depolarization and the Selective Death of Dopaminergic Neurons by Rotenone: Protective Effect of Coenzyme Q10." *Journal of Neurochemistry* 93, no. 5 (2005): 1199–1208.

Murakami, K., Y. Miyake, S. Sasaki, K. Tanaka, W. Fukushima, C. Kiyohara, Y. Tsuboi, T. Yamada, T. Oeda, T. Miki, N. Kawamura, N. Sakae, H. Fukuyama, Y. Hirota, and M. Nagai. "Dietary Intake of Folate, Vitamin B6, Vitamin B12 and Riboflavin and Risk of Parkinson's Disease: A Case-Control Study in Japan." *British Journal of Nutrition* 104, no. 5 (2010):757–64.

Pahwa, Rajesh, and Kelly E. Lyons. "Managing Essential Tremor Patients with Deep Brain Stimulation." In *Deep Brain Stimulation Management*, edited by William J. Marks Jr., 56–61. New York: Cambridge University Press, 2011.

Quintana, J. L., M. F. Allam, A. S. Del Castillo, and R. F. Navajas. "Parkinson's Disease and Tea: A Quantitative Review." *Journal of the American College of Nutrition* 28, no. 1 (2009): 1–6.

Rathlelot, J.-A., and P. L. Srick. "Subdivisions of Primary Motor Cortex Based on Cortico-motoneuronal Cells." *Proceedings of the National Academy of Sciences* 106, no. 3 (2009): 918–23.

Simuni, T., and P. Rajesh. *Parkinson's Disease.* New York: Oxford University Press, 2010.

Willow, M. *Parkinson's Disease: New Research.* New York: Nova Science Publishers, 2004.

CHAPTER 12

Channell, M. K., and Mason, David C. *The 5-Minute Osteopathic Manipulative Medicine Consult.* Baltimore: Lippincott Williams & Wilkins, 2009.

DiGiovanna, Eileen L., Stanley Schiowitz, and Dennis J. Dowling. *An Osteopathic Approach to Diagnosis and Treatment.* Philadelphia: Lippincott Williams & Wilkins, 2005.

DeLisa, Joel A., and Nicholas E. Walsh. *Physical Medicine and Rehabilitation: Principles and Practice, Volume 1.* Philadelphia: Lippincott Williams & Wilkins, 2005.

Hartman, Laurie. *Handbook of Osteopathic Technique.* London: Thomas Nelson, 2001.

Sammut, Emanuel A. *Osteopathic Diagnosis.* London: Nelson Thornes, 2008.

CHAPTER 13

Alcalay, R. N., H. Mejia-Santana, Y. Gu, L. Cote, K. S. Marder, and N. Scarmeas. "The Association between Mediterranean Diet Adherence and Parkinson's Disease." *Movement Disorders* 27, no 6 (2012): 771–74.

Atwood, K. C. "Naturopathy: A Clinical Appraisal." *Medscape General Medicine* 5 (2003): 39.

Ferrante, Robert J., Ole A. Andreassen, A. Dedeoglu, Kimberly L. Ferrante, Bruce G. Jenkins, Steven M. Hersch, and M. Flint Beal. "Therapeutic Effects of Coenzyme Q10 and Remace-mide in Transgenic Mouse Models of Huntington's Disease." *Journal of Neuroscience* 22, no. 5 (2002): 1592–99.

Gorgone, G., M. Currò, N. Ferlazzo, G. Parisi, L. Parnetti, V. Belcastro, N. Tambasco, A. Rossi, F. Pisani, and F. Calabresi. "Coenzyme Q10, Hyperhomocysteinemia and MTHFR C677T Polymorphism in Levodopa-Treated Parkinson's Disease Patients." Neuromolecular Medicine 14, no.1 (2012): 84–90.

Haygarth, John. *On the Imagination as a Cause and as a Cure of Disorders of the Body: Exemplified by Fictitious Tractors and Epidemical Convulsions.* London: Cadel and Davies, 1800.

Hetchman, Leah. *Clinical Naturopathic Medicine.* Sydney: Elsevier, 2012.

Huidsen, Christiaan M. "Modern-Day Naturopathic Medicine and Traditional Ayurveda in a Combined Attack against Parkinson's Disease." *Academic Journal of Suriname* 1 (2010): 53–58.

Lees, A. J. "Drugs for Parkinson's Disease." *Journal of Neurology, Neurosurgery & Psychiatry with Practical Neurology* 73 (2002): 607–10.

Moerman, Daniel E. *Meaning, Medicine and "Placebo Effect."* Cambridge: Cambridge University Press, 2002.

Polgar, S. "Ethics, Methodology and Use of Placebo Controls in Surgical Trials." *Brain Research Bulletin* 67, no. 4 (2005): 290–97.

Sarris, Jerome, and Jon Wardle. *Clinical Naturopathy: An Evidence-Based Guide to Practice.* New York: Elsevier Churchill Livingstone, 2010.

Suchowersky, O., G. Gronseth, J. Perlmutter, S. Reich, T. Zesiewicz, and W. J. Weiner. "Practice Parameter: Neuroprotective Strategies and Alternative Therapies for Parkinson Disease (An Evidence-Based Review): Report of the Quality Standards Subcommittee of the American Academy of Neurology." *Neurology* 66, no. 7 (2006): 976–82.

Walia, Jasnita. *Naturopathy.* New Delhi: Fusion Books, 2003.

CHAPTER 14

O'Sullivan, Susan B., and J. Thomas Schmitz. "Parkinson's Disease." In *Physical Rehabilitation*, 5th ed., 856–57. Philadephia: F. A. Davis, 2007.

Suchowersky, O., G. Gronseth, J. Perlmutter, S. Reich, T. Zesiewicz, and W. J. Weiner. "Practice Parameter: Neuroprotective Strategies and Alternative Therapies for Parkinson Disease (An Evidence-Based Review): Report of the Quality Standards Subcommittee of the American Academy of Neurology." *Neurology* 66 (2006): 976–82.

Tolosa, E., and J. Jankovic. *Parkinson's Disease and Movement Disorders.* 5th ed. Hagerstown, MD: Lippincott Williams & Wilkins, 2007.

CHAPTER 15

Calon, F., and F. Cicchetti. "Can We Prevent Parkinson's Disease with N-3 Polyunsaturated Fatty Acids?" *Future Lipidology* 3, no. 2 (2008): 133–37.

Kahle, P. J., J. Waak, and T. Gasser. "DJ-1 and Prevention of Oxidative Stress in Parkinson's Disease and Other Age-Related Disorders." *Free Radical Biology & Medicine* 47, no. 10 (2009): 1354–61.

Kedar, N. P. "Can We Prevent Parkinson's and Alzheimer's Disease?" *Journal of Postgraduate Medicine* 49, no. 3 (2003): 236–45.

CHAPTER 16

Christensen, Jackie Hunt. The First Year: Parkinson's Disease. New York: Marlowe and Company, 2005.

Robinson, Richard. "Parkinson's Disease." In *The Gale Encyclopedia of Neurological Disorders.* New York: Gale, 2005.

Seidl, S. E., and J. A. Potashkin. "The Promise of Neuroprotective Agents in Parkinson's Disease." *Frontiers in Neurology* 2 (2011): 68.

Weiner, William J., Lisa Shulman, and Anthony Lang. Parkinson's Disease: A Complete Guide for Patients and Families. Baltimore: Johns Hopkins University Press, 2001.

CHAPTER 17

McNall, Greg. "Exercises for Persons with Advanced Parkinson's Disease." LiveStrong, June 14, 2011. Accessed November 23, 2012. www.livestrong.com/article/306377-exercises-for-persons-with-advanced-parkinsons-disease/.

"Parkinson's Disease." Medline Plus. Accessed January 12, 2013. www.nlm.nih.gov/medlineplus/parkinsonsdisease.html.

Reinberg, Steven. "Exercise a Likely Tool for Parkinson's Patients." U.S. News & World Report, November 9, 2012. Accessed December 2, 2012. http://health.usnews.com/health-news/news/articles/2012/11/09/exercise-a-likely-tool-for-parkinsons-patients.

Rodrigues-de-Paula, Fátima, and Lidiane Oliveira Lima. "Physical Therapy—Exercise and Parkinsons Disease." International Encyclopedia of Rehabilitation. Accessed December 24, 2012. http://cirrie.buffalo.edu/encyclopedia/en/article/336/.

CHAPTER 18

Depue, R. A., and P. F. Collins. "Neurobiology of the Structure of Personality: Dopamine, Facilitation of Incentive Motivation, and Extraversion." *Behavioral and Brain Sciences* 22, no. 3 (1999): 491–517.

Habib, M. "Activity and Motivational Disorders in Neurology: Proposal for an Evaluation Scale [French]." *Encephale* 21, no. 5: 563–70.

———. "Athymhormia and Disorders of Motivation in Basal Ganglia Disease." *Journal of Neuropsychiatry and Clinical Neurosciences* 16, no. 4 (2004): 509–24.

Potvin, A. R., W. W. Tourtellotte, R. W. Pew, J. W. Albers, W. G. Henderson, and D. N. Snyder. "Motivation and Learning in the Quantitative Examination of Neurological Function." *Archives of Physical Medicine and Rehabilitation* 54, no. 9 (1973): 432–40.

CHAPTER 19

Duvoisin, Roger C., and Jacob Sage. *Parkinson's Disease: A Guide for Patient And Family.* New York: Lippincott Williams & Wilkins, 2001.

"Help for Patients and Caregivers : Parkinson's Disease." Santa Barbara Healthcare. Accessed October 14, 2012. www.santabarbarahealthcare.com/patientcaregivers.asp?issue=parkinsons_disease.

Hurwitz, A. "The Benefit of a Home Exercise Regimen for Ambulatory Parkinson's Disease Patients." *Journal of Neuroscience Nursing* 21, no. 3 (1989): 180–84.

Martinez-Martin, P., C. Rodriguez-Blazquez, and M. J. Forjaz. "Quality of Life and Burden in Caregivers for Patients with Parkinson's Disease: Concepts, Assessment and Related Factors." *Expert Review of Pharmacoeconomics & Outcomes Research* 12, no. 2 (2012): 221–30.

Peri, Camille. "Talking with Rasheda Ali-Walsh: Helping Children Cope with Parkinson's." Caring Incorporated. Accessed October 13, 2012. www.caring.com/interviews/interview-with-rasheda-ali-walsh-about-helping-kids-cope-with-parkinson-s.

Schwab, Robert S., and Lewis J. Doshay. "The Parkinson Patient at Home." Center for Neurologic Study. Accessed October 12, 2012. www.cnsonline.org.

Taylor, Glenda. "Parkinson's Symptoms in Children." eHow. Accessed October 14, 2012. www.ehow.com/about_5179785_parkinson_s-symptoms-children.html.

Vickers, L. F., and C. M. O'Neill. "An Interdisciplinary Home Healthcare Program for Patients with Parkinson's Disease. *Rehabilitation Nursing* 23, no. 6 (1998): 286–89.

CHAPTER 20

Aldren, Hayle T. "New Hope for Parkinson's." Natural Healing News, February 26, 2012. Accessed September 8, 2012. www.naturalhealingnews.com/new-hope-for-parkinsons/.

Brod, M., G. A. Mendelsohn, and B. Roberts. "Patients' Experiences of Parkinson's Disease." *Journals of Gerontology: Psychological Sciences* 53, no. 4 (1998): 213–22.

Flannery, R. B. "Disrupted Caring Attachments: Implications for Long-term Care." *American Journal of Alzheimer's Disease and Other Dementias* 17, no. 4 (2002): 227–31.

"Information & Referral Centers." American Parkinson's Disease Association. Accessed September 23, 2012. www.apdaparkinson.org/information-referral-centers.

Kuhn, Bob. "Parkinson's Disease and Hope." Insight for Living Canada, March 2010. Accessed September 28, 2012. www.insightforliving.ca/insights/parkinsons/parkinsons-disease-hope.html.

Snijders, A. H., M. van Kesteren, and B. R. Bloem. "Cycling Is Less Affected than Walking in Freezers of Gait." *Journal of Neurology, Neurosurgery & Psychiatry with Practical Neurology* 83, no. 5 (2011): 575–76.

United States Food and Drug Administration. *13th Meeting of the Neurological Devices Panel.* Rockville, MD: Neal R. Gross, 2000.

Index

About the Author

Naheed Ali, M.D., Ph.D., began writing professionally in 2005 and has written several books on medical topics and taught at colleges in the United States. Additional information is available at NaheedAli.com.